"ENLIGHTENING AND PROVOCATIVE."
—Publishers Weekly

"A MUST-READ FOR BASEBALL FANS and for anyone who would like to know how the very wealthy and the very ambitious manage the business of America's national pastime. . . Helyar takes us inside the most intimate meetings at some of the most crucial moments in baseball history."
—Kirkus Reviews

"A LUCID, COMPELLING ECONOMIC HISTORY OF THE GAME . . . A labyrinthine tale fueled by money and driven by a zany cast of characters that only baseball seems able to produce . . . Helyar not only covers a lot of ground, but, more important, he places all of the events and people into a coherent context."
—Booklist

"ONE OF THE MOST ENTERTAINING SPORTS BOOKS OF THE YEAR. [Helyar] deftly weaves the financial facts with in-depth and entrancing profiles of many major league owners. . . . [His] investigative skills make the book informative, while his sincere interest in the sport allows even the casual fan to read this work with great enjoyment. . . . Captivating and insightful . . . Highly recommended."
—Library Journal

Also by John Helyar:

BARBARIANS AT THE GATE (with Bryan Burrough)

LORDS OF THE REALM

The *Real* History of Baseball

John Helyar

BALLANTINE BOOKS • NEW YORK

To Betsy and Johnny
and in memory of Daisie Helyar

Copyright © 1994 by John Helyar

All rights reserved under International and Pan-American Copyright Conventions. Published in the United States by Ballantine Books, a division of Random House, Inc., New York, and simultaneously in Canada by Random House of Canada Limited, Toronto.

Library of Congress Catalog Card Number: 93-41944

ISBN 0-345-39261-2

This edition published by arrangement with Villard Books, a division of Random House, Inc. Villard Books is a registered trademark of Random House, Inc.

Manufactured in the United States of America

First Ballantine Books Edition: March 1995

10 9 8 7 6 5 4 3

"The magnate must be a strong man among strong men, else other club owners in the league will combine in their own interests against him and his interest, and by collusion force him out of the game."
—A. G. SPALDING,
Chicago National League owner, 1890

"The great trouble with baseball today is that most of the players are in the game for the money that's in it—not for the love of it, the excitement of it, the thrill of it."
—TY COBB, 1925

"Baseball was made for kids, and grown-ups only screw it up."
—BOB FELLER, pitcher

"You go through *The Sporting News* for the last one hundred years, and you will find two things are always true. You never have enough pitching, and nobody ever made money."
—DONALD FEHR, executive director,
Major League Baseball Players Association

"Gentlemen, we have the only legal monopoly in the country and we're fucking it up."
—TED TURNER, owner, Atlanta Braves

Acknowledgments

This book has its origins on a summer night in 1960, when my father took me to my first baseball game. It was at Fenway Park; Ted Williams got a double; I was hooked.

Baseball has since given me some of life's best moments (the Impossible Dream Red Sox of 1967) and its worst (the impossible agony of the ball going through Buckner's legs). As a college student, I minored in baseball, in the Fenway bleachers. As an adult, I've spent a glorious week at Grapefruit League exhibition games with the same set of friends every year since 1981.

As an adult, too, I sometimes wondered whether there was some strange law of compensation at work in baseball. Why was the grace of the game between the lines so precisely matched by the gracelessness of its off-field conduct?

The *Wall Street Journal* gave me the opportunity to find out. Norman Pearlstine lured me back to the newspaper in 1990 by offering me a beat covering the business of sports. I did several stories on baseball, and one in particular led to this book. I looked into what really happened during a three-year period when the owners froze the free-agent market.

What I found was less a price-fixing conspiracy than a fascinating group-dynamics study. It was a reaction to years of wrenching change in baseball and an effort by the owners to seize back control from the players. I found I couldn't examine the "collusion" era of 1985–1988 without understanding the events of the previous two decades. That was what provided the genesis of this book, a study of this quintessential American institution in transition.

I appreciate the support of Barney Calame, my boss, and Paul Steiger, the *Journal*'s managing editor and leading baseball savant. They allowed me to expend considerable time and column inches to tell a very old story, by daily-newspaper standards. My thanks as well to Norm Pearlstine, who hardly oversold the possibilities of the sports beat.

I give my agent, Andrew Wylie, a world of credit for being the first to see the possibilities of a baseball book, and his colleague Deborah Karl a large measure of gratitude for aid and comfort along the way. At Villard Books, my thanks go to Diane Reverand, who brought this book into the world, and Peter Gethers, whose belief in the project and baseball knowledge sustained and improved it.

This book is primarily based on interviews with more than two hundred people in the baseball business, many of whom I interviewed multiple times. Space permits me to acknowledge just a fraction of them, but my thanks go to all for sharing their memories and insights and especially to the following:

Buzzie Bavasi, Peter Bavasi, Bob Boone, Charles Bronfman, Jim Bronner, Bryan Burns, Ruly Carpenter, Bob Costello, Doug DeCinces, Don Fehr, Steve Fehr, Ed Fitzgerald, John Gaherin, Phil Garner, Bill Giles, Bob Gilhooley, Ray Grebey, Clark Griffith, Sandy Hadden, Randy Hendricks, Lou Hoynes, Bob Howsam, Larry Lucchino, Andy MacPhail, Lee MacPhail, Tim McCarver, Joe McIlvaine, John McMullen, Andy Messersmith, Ken Moffett, Dick Moss, Chuck O'Connor, Gene Orza, Dick Ravitch, Tom and Sam Reich, Jerry Reinsdorf, Lauren Rich, Robin Roberts, Barry Rona, Ken Schanzer, Bud Selig, Ted Simmons, Tal Smith, Jeff Smulyan, Joe Torre, Tom Villante, Dick Wagner, and Bill White.

In addition, Rich Levin and Jim Small of the commissioner's office kept extending me credentials and other courtesies despite my persistent failure to give them adequate notice.

A number of books were also essential resources for me, topped by Marvin Miller's *A Whole Different Ballgame* and Bowie Kuhn's *Hardball*. Despite their sharp difference and taken as complementary perspectives, they were useful primers on the baseball business. I am grateful to Marvin Miller in particular for elaborating at length on certain events, despite having only recently covered the territory in his memoirs.

I drew on the treasure trove of Dodgers literature to assist in my portrayals of Walter O'Malley, Branch Rickey, and Larry MacPhail. Of most note were *Bums* by Peter Golenbock; *The Lords of Baseball* by Harold Parrott; *Rickey & Robinson* by Harvey Frommer; *The Roaring Redhead* by Don Warfield; *The Dodgers Move West* by Neil J. Sullivan; and *The Boys of Summer* by Roger Kahn.

Some fine biographies aided other parts of the book, including *The Man to See* (Edward Bennett Williams) by Evan Thomas; *Collision at Home Plate* (Bart Giamatti) by James Reston, Jr.; and *Under the Influence* (Gussie Busch) by Peter Hernon and Terry Ganey. Three books were helpful in portraying the early Ted Turner: *Lead, Follow or Get Out of the Way* by Christian Williams; *Ted Turner: The Man Behind the Mouth* by Roger Vaughan; and *We Could've Finished Last Without You* by Bob Hope.

The memoirs of several players—Don Baylor, Curt Flood, Catfish Hunter, Reggie Jackson, and Dave Winfield—proved useful in presenting various events of the past twenty-five years. So did the trilogies of historians Harold Seymour and David Voigt in describing baseball's early days. Lee Lowenfish's *The Imperfect Diamond* provided a good historical perspective on baseball's labor relations.

Only a brave few baseball-beat writers have well chronicled the business side, and their contemporaneous accounts of events proved most helpful. Murray Chass of the *New York Times* did terrific blow-by-blow reportage of all the major labor confrontations described herein. Jerome Holtzman's year-in-review pieces in *The Sporting News Guides* of the 1960s and 1970s proved reliable and repeatedly useful. Tim Wendel of *USA Today's Baseball Weekly* gave me a wonderful eyewitness account of events at the Kohler, Wisconsin, revenue-sharing summit. And I would be remiss not to mention the late Dick Young, who coined the term The Lords of Baseball.

I was aided, along the way, by several good souls who read the manuscript while in progress and offered helpful suggestions: Bryan Burrough, my onetime collaborator and invaluable sounding board; John Huey, who *demanded* to look at new chapters and drove me on; Bill Gannett, my friend and longtime baseball companion; and Betsy Morris, my wife, my most demanding reader, and my dogged protector during the project's final harried months. Special thanks also to Deborah Hannula, who kept my son at bay and our house in order while I was holed up on this project.

The contributions of all of the above have shaped this book. Any of its deficiencies are mine alone.

—JOHN HELYAR
Atlanta
November 1993

$ 1 $

Before it was ever a business it was a game.

It came out of the 1840s, when teams from New York first crossed the Hudson River to Elysian Fields, laid out a diamond, agreed upon the rules, and played a game they called "base," later lengthened to "baseball."

It grew in the 1850s and 1860s, but it remained a gentleman's sport. Teams rode to their games in decorated carriages, singing their team songs. In country greens and city parks, thousands of young men played. It became too popular to remain amateur for long, in the young entrepreneurial nation.

In 1871, the first league was formed of teams who played for pay. It was called the National Association of Professional Baseball Players, and it was a slapdash thing. Over its five-year life, teams came and went with dizzying rapidity—twenty-five of them in all. So did players. The best ones, called "revolvers," jumped around between teams for the best offer.

But if it wasn't a stable business, it was well on its way to becoming the national pastime.

"Like everything else American it came with a rush," wrote John Montgomery Ward, a star player of the day. "The game is suited to the national temperament. It requires strength, courage and skill; it is full of dash and excitement and though a most difficult game in which to excel, it is yet extremely simple in its first principles and easily understood by everyone."

The changing landscape of the country had much to do with baseball's hold on America. As people moved from rural farms into urban tenements during the emerging Industrial Revolution, the game kept a nation in touch with its roots. Baseball was played on vast swatches of green in the middle of dreary, gray cities. Baseball celebrated the rugged individual within a team game. It came to be called the National Pastime, not just because it was played and watched by so many people but because it so resembled the national character.

Albert Goodwill Spalding tried to export baseball to other countries. The owner of a team and of a sporting-goods empire, he saw vast worldwide sales of bats and balls. In 1888, he even sponsored a globe-trotting tour of exhibition games that visited Hawaii, Australia, Ceylon, Egypt, Italy, France, England, and Ireland. In one far-flung locale after another, America's top players were watched with profound indifference. The game took root only in America.

Like the pioneering country still being settled, this game valued both brute strength and daring ingenuity. It also countenanced a certain amount of cheating. Baseball was beautiful but tough, a sport not unlike the Chicago of Nelson Algren: ". . . where the bulls and the foxes live well and the lambs wind up head-down from the hook."

So too would baseball mirror the period's epic struggles in commerce. Robber barons were coming to the fore and business was not polite. Disputes between labor and management were solved not by federal mediators but by Pinkerton thugs. Baseball would have its own early bare-knuckle fights for control of the game and business. Then the owners would seize it for a hundred years.

In the same spring when Sitting Bull swept Custer at the Little Big Horn, the National League of Professional Baseball Clubs was created. The year was 1876, and the enterprise was better known as the National League. It ushered in a new way of doing business in baseball: a central office in New York and an aim to curb the chaos that afflicted the previous league.

By 1879, its eight teams had developed a compact. At season's end, each would "reserve" five players, making them off-limits to any other team. The players were not told about this agreement. They'd simply discover that they couldn't catch on with any but their own team.

Thus the "reserve clause" was born, and the original was only a modest version. When another "major league," the American Association, began in the early 1880s, the compact was extended to them and the annual "reserve list" grew to eleven players. It was on its way to encompassing every player.

The first recorded owner's wail over salaries came in 1881. "Professional baseball is on the wane," declared Albert Spalding, owner of Chicago's National League team. "Salaries must come down or the interest of the public must be increased in some way. If one or the other does not happen, bankruptcy stares every team in the face."

The first recorded salary cap came in 1889. The owners set top pay at $2,500, with a tiered pay scale ranging downward from there. The lowest classified players would have to sweep up the ballpark or take tickets.

The Brotherhood of Professional Base Ball Players, a union formed in 1885, rebelled against the pay scale and the cap. It formed the Players National League, to begin play in 1890.

"There was a time when the League [that is, the original National League] stood for integrity and fair dealing; today it stands for dollars and cents," said John Montgomery Ward, the star player and union president. "Players have been bought, sold and exchanged as though they were sheep instead of American citizens."

Noble words, but the Players League lasted just one season. When the American Association went out of business too, the National League had the majors all to itself. It would until the turn of the century.

Then a man named Byron Bancroft Johnson, who was running a minor league in the Midwest, decided to capitalize on National League players' discontent with their $2,500 salary cap. He unleashed the owners in his Western League to sign the major-leaguers, and they attracted more than a hundred, including star second baseman Napoleon Lajoie. Then they moved the franchises into bigger cities and renamed themselves the American League.

They were soon outdrawing the National League. The new Boston Pilgrims, for instance, paid $4,000 to star third baseman Jimmy Collins to defect from the rival Boston Beaneaters. The Pilgrims picked up several other prominent National Leaguers, including Cy Young, from St. Louis. With the legendary pitcher winning thirty-three games, the new team attracted 527,000 fans in 1901, more than double the Beaneaters' draw.

At a "peace meeting" in 1903, the two leagues agreed on an end to raiding, a common reserve system, and a single ruling National Commission. It would consist of the president of each league, plus a third member to be agreed upon by them.

Baseball boomed in the early 1900s. From 1901 to 1909, the combined leagues more than doubled their attendance to 7.2 million. That growth closely tracked the rise of urban America. In 1900, 40 percent of the country's population lived in cities; by

1910, 46 percent. In 1920, it would reach 50 percent. Increasingly, the centerpiece of those cities was their major league ballparks. Filled by 30,000 and more cheering fans, they created a sense of community for the newcomers—whether from abroad or from the countryside. From 1909 to 1913 alone, six classics came on line: Philadelphia's Shibe Park, Pittsburgh's Forbes Field, Chicago's Comiskey Park, Boston's Fenway Park, and New York's Polo Grounds and Ebbets Field.

These great houses brought people together, in an age when cities had been splintered by industrialization and immigration. They created heroes for the waves of new immigrants, whose hopes and identities were wrapped up in players like Honus Wagner (for the Germans), Stan Coveleski (for the Poles), and Ping Bodie, born Francesco Stephano Pezzolo (for the Italians). Earlier, when Irish immigrants dominated baseball, stars like Mike "King" Kelly performed the same function.

As baseball grew into a bigger commercial enterprise, money dominated headlines and the public consciousness. When pitcher Rube Marquard was a dud for the Giants, after being bought for a princely sum, he became known as "the eleven-thousand-dollar lemon." A man named David Fultz, who had organized a new union called the Players Fraternity, spent much of his time disputing stories about overpaid players. Some of them didn't even make $1,000, he pointed out.

Baseball's growth and profitability ultimately drew backers for a new league in 1914. It was called the Federal League, and it was the best thing to happen to the players since the days of the "revolvers." The average salary, $3,800 in 1913, rose to $7,300 in 1915. Stars used the rival league's threat to ratchet up their pay. Ty Cobb nearly doubled his salary, to $20,000. Tris Speaker got an unheard-of two-year contract that totaled $36,000. The owner of the Philadelphia Athletics, Connie Mack, unwilling to meet such prices, sold off much of his pennant-winning 1914 team, including the famous "hundred-thousand-dollar infield" (for such was the sum his star infielders fetched).

The players finally had some leverage and the leagues grudgingly recognized the Players Fraternity. Fultz was able to win a few modest gains, like getting the teams to start paying for players' uniforms and giving ten-year veterans the right to an unconditional release. (Players were previously in the position of Mordecai "Three Finger" Brown, a top pitcher for the Cubs for years, whom they sold to a minor league team when they had no more use for him.)

Yet the Federal League, for all its vigorous bidding, still could land only a handful of established players. The Federal owners sued the established leagues in 1915, charging they'd blocked the newcomers from the player market, restraining free trade and violating antitrust laws. They endeavored to get the case before a Chicago judge they thought would lend a sympathetic ear.

Kenesaw Mountain Landis had been named for a promontory outside of Atlanta. His father, a Union Army surgeon, had been tending to wounded troops during Sherman's assault on that city when he himself was shot. For some reason, he wanted to remind himself of it through his son, who was born just after the war.

Young Landis grew up in Ohio and Indiana. After dropping out of high school, he drifted through a series of jobs, including one as a court reporter. He liked what he saw in that setting and went to a Chicago law school, despite his previous lack of education. Then he hung out his shingle in that prosperous city.

He was appointed a federal judge at age thirty-nine, thanks less to a brilliant legal career than to political connections—he had managed a failed congressional campaign. The unsuccessful candidate was offered a judgeship by President Teddy Roosevelt. He turned it down but recommended Landis in his stead. That was in 1905. By 1907, Landis had made a name for himself as a Rooseveltian trust-buster. He found Standard Oil guilty of violating the Sherman Antitrust Act and fined the company a whopping $29.2 million. Landis was overruled on appeal—a frequent occurrence in his judicial career—but he won renown.

He became even better known for a zealous brand of courtroom patriotism during World War I. Landis issued a summons for Kaiser Wilhelm II to answer for the sinking of the *Lusitania*. He found prominent socialist Victor Berger guilty of "impeding the war effort" and gave him the maximum punishment; and he would later observe: "It was my great disappointment to give Berger only twenty years in Leavenworth. I believe the law should have enabled me to have had him lined up against a wall and shot."

The Supreme Court reversed the decision, agreeing with Berger's lawyers that Landis's remarks about German-Americans ("their hearts are reeking with disloyalty") betrayed a prejudicial mind-set.

With his penchant for playing to the gallery, Landis was an utterly unpredictable jurist. The Federal League thought, however, that they had found in him an authentic trust-buster. What they got, rather, was a baseball devotee. Landis was that rare Chicagoan, a fan of both the Cubs and the White Sox. He interrupted the trial at one point to declare, "Both sides must understand that any blows at the thing called baseball would be regarded by this court as a blow to a national institution."

The trial concluded, but eleven months later Landis still hadn't made a ruling. He was hoping the parties would settle out of court, and he put the Federal League up against it. Unable to gain the sweeping court victory they needed, the Federal League settled for a modest cash settlement and quietly went out of business.

It had produced only three things of lasting importance. One was Wrigley Field, which was built for the Federal League's Chicago team. Another was the end of the Players Fraternity, spelling the end of any meaningful players' union for fifty years. The third was the coming of Kenesaw Mountain Landis.

In 1920, when baseball was under a dark shadow, the owners returned to their favorite judge. Eight White Sox players had played ball with gamblers out to fix the 1919 World Series. No matter that the players' reason was that they were embittered at owner Charles Comiskey, who, like other club operators, had screwed salaries back down after the folding of the Federal League. No matter, either, that the accused were actually acquitted in court of throwing the Series. The "Black Sox" scandal had raised serious doubts about baseball being on the level.

The worst part was that baseball had no leader to restore its good name. Its governing three-man National Commission was a warren of politics. The two leagues were at one another's throats again. It was decided that only an outsider of impeccable integrity could do the job.

A delegation of owners was appointed to approach Judge Landis. They were to meet him in his chambers one day but found, when they arrived, that he was still hearing a case. As they filed into the back of his courtroom, he scowled and intoned, "Unless that noise ceases, I shall have to clear the court."

Landis took the job, on the condition that he have absolute authority to act in "the best interests" of baseball. His first action was to banish all eight of the "Black Sox." "Baseball is something more than a game to an American boy; it is his training field for life work," he told one writer. "Destroy his faith in its squareness and honesty and you have destroyed something more; you have planted suspicion of all things in his heart."

Landis *looked* like God, or at least his cousin, with a jutting jaw, a high forehead, shaggy white hair, and a stern countenance. Operating out of a Chicago office with one word—BASEBALL—written on its door, he acted like God as well. In his first decade in office, Landis would banish eleven more players for gambling-related offenses and even go after the great Babe Ruth.

Landis forbade the Yankees star to go on any more postseason barnstorming tours. This was a lucrative venture for Ruth, who did it anyway and suggested that Landis could "go jump in a lake." Replied Landis: "It seems I'll have to show somebody who's running this game." He suspended Ruth for the first forty games of the 1922 season.

Under Landis, the morals of baseball were purified—and the business of baseball was ossified. The deeply conservative Landis had the same answer for anything new: no.

That's what he said when the Cincinnati Reds' president, Larry MacPhail, proposed installing lights at Crosley Field. "Not in my lifetime or yours will you ever see a baseball game played at night in the majors," thundered Landis.

That, again, is what he said when a beer company wanted to advertise on World Series radio broadcasts. Landis was slow even to secure revenues for baseball's broadcast rights—all the way into the mid-1930s—and when he did he was still more preoccupied with the moral than the financial implications. (Landis also had approval of World Series announcers and he turned down Dizzy Dean, citing his diction as "unfit for a national broadcaster.")

Landis said no frequently and vehemently to a man named Branch Rickey, when he came up with something called the "farm system." Rickey's St. Louis Cardinals came to own or control dozens of minor league teams and thereby avoided having to buy minor-leaguers' contracts. It was a brilliant idea, since a low-budget team like the Cardinals couldn't compete otherwise for minor league talent with a rich team like the Yankees. By developing and controlling their own players, they could.

Landis thought locally owned and operated minor league teams were an essential part of America's fabric. He railed against the farm system as "chain-store baseball" and threatened to punish Rickey vigorously if he caught him stepping over the line on the rules. This he did when he discovered that the Cardinals controlled entire leagues of minor league teams. Landis declared 163 Cardinals farmhands free agents in a two-year span.

Landis was no doubt right in his reading of Rickey, who had a remarkable ability to be at once pious and devious, but his frame of reference was askew. The minor league system he was trying to preserve was an anachronism in an urbanizing America. His actions did, however, enable him to portray himself as the champion of the players without actually ruffling anyone's feathers but the Cardinals'. On the subject of the reserve clause, he was at his most conservative. When a young Turk named Bill Veeck wrote him a letter saying that the reserve system was "morally and legally indefensible," Landis condescendingly replied, "Somebody once said a little knowledge is a dangerous thing, and your letter proves him to be a wizard."

The reserve system—and everything else about how baseball operated—had been upheld by the Supreme Court during Landis's second year in office. Justice Oliver Wendell Holmes wrote that baseball was exempt from antitrust laws on the grounds that "exhibitions of baseball are purely state affairs."

This was a piece of fiction, one that would grow sillier with each passing year. But it undergirded everything about the way baseball operated. The players were bound to one team for life—or at least for as long as it suited the team. The baseball owners answered to no one but Judge Landis. The business of baseball could operate just as archaically as it wanted. It was the only game in town.

It meant that Philadelphia Athletics slugger Jimmie Foxx could win the batting Triple Crown in 1933 and still have to fight a salary cut. (His owner, Connie Mack, wanted to reduce him from $16,670 to $12,000. He had, after all, slumped from fifty-eight homers to forty-eight.) Lou Gehrig, when he did the same in 1934, suffered similarly: he had to battle to stay at $23,000.

Baseball, in fairness, was struggling through the Great Depression like every other industry. Its attendance slipped back to levels of twenty-five years earlier. The St. Louis Browns drew only 81,000 fans all year in 1935. But even later, in better times, star players could get shafted. Ralph Kiner's salary was cut by 25 percent after he'd just led the National League in homers for a seventh straight season. "We finished last with you," Branch Rickey announced. "We could've finished last without you."

Interestingly, when it came to salary disputes, popular sympathy was almost always with the owners. Fans and writers saw it as a privilege for a man to play ball for a living. When Joe DiMaggio held out in 1938, after his first big season, for $40,000, the press scalded him for not accepting the proffered $25,000. The writers agreed with the Yankees' owner, Colonel Jacob Ruppert: "Why, $25,000 is enough to make him financially independent for the rest of his life."

Conditions were still ripe for an occasional run at organizing the players. In 1946, a Boston lawyer named Robert Murphy started a union he called the American Baseball Guild. He was appalled that even in the mid-forties some players made as little as $3,500. He thought it disgraceful that the great Jimmie Foxx was now penniless in retirement.

Murphy planned to make Pittsburgh his launching-off point. It was a good union town and the team seemed to be receptive to unionization. The guild had to be approved by two-thirds of the players to be certified as their bargaining agent. The vote was to be held before a mid-season game, and feelings ran high. Just beforehand, veteran pitcher Rip Sewell gave a fiery antiunion speech and owner William Benswanger reminded everyone that he'd "never hurt" them. (Taking no chances, however, he had a replacement team ready to take the field.)

The Guild drew twenty of thirty-six votes, just shy of two-thirds. The union never got back on track, and Murphy disappeared, but he did have an effect. Mindful that Murphy had come close with the Pirates, and fearful of raids from a new Mexican League, the owners handed the players a sop. They pledged to create a pension, set a minimum salary of $5,500 and a maximum pay cut of 25 percent, and pay spring training expenses of $25 a week. The stipend would forever be known as "Murphy money." (One player got a little something extra: Rip Sewell was presented with a gold watch by Commissioner Happy Chandler.)

Establishing a union beachhead wasn't hard only on account of management opposition. A lot of the players themselves resisted. As a group, they tended to think more like Judge Landis than John L. Lewis. They were heartland conservatives who chewed tobacco and hated Communists. They'd gotten to the majors on their individual initiative and talent. Such people didn't embrace group political action.

Mostly they wanted to play ball. It *was* a privilege to be there, and a precarious one. There were only sixteen teams and 400 major league jobs, with 8,000 minor-leaguers clamoring for them. The major league life was good, if not the pay: Pullman sleepers, Porterhouse steaks, clubhouse camaraderie, and a shot at glory.

The scale of the business and the preoccupations of the players were such that it still seemed an age of innocence. During the 1952 World Series, one inning ended with Jackie Robinson, the second baseman, catching a pop-up in front of Gil Hodges, the first baseman. General Manager Buzzie Bavasi glanced into the dugout between innings and saw Robinson and Hodges having a heated argument. He didn't like it and told Hodges so in his office the next day, when he made his daily stop in the office.

"This is the World Series," said Bavasi. "You shouldn't be carrying on like that. What was it about, anyway?"

"Well, I don't like to catch pop-ups," Hodges began. That was true; he was a converted catcher who never had gotten comfortable under a plummeting ball. "And I had a deal with Jackie. I paid him five dollars for any pop-up he caught in my territory. Well, he caught that ball and then he said the rate was ten dollars for the Series."

The dispute had been resolved, he assured Bavasi. "We settled on seven-fifty."

Forty years later, Bavasi laughed as hard as he did that day. "You didn't have the money then," he said. "That was the fun of the game."

In 1951, the average salary was $13,000, and even above-average players took second jobs. That winter, Robin Roberts, a twenty-one-game winner for the Phillies, sold cardboard boxes in the off-season. The Yankees' Yogi Berra and Phil Rizzuto sold men's clothing at a store in Newark. The Dodgers' Carl Furillo was a hardhat and teammate Jackie Robinson worked in an appliance store.

In the time-honored tradition, players groused about salaries, but nobody had outsized notions of what they should be. One season in the late forties, Bill Veeck left twenty-five blank contracts on his desk and told each of his Cleveland Indians to fill in an amount. He fought with a player over just one: Ken Keltner had *cut* his own pay by $5,000.

The top of the pay scale was $100,000 (first reached by Hank Greenberg in 1947), and players—as surely as owners—had to feel *worthy* of accepting it. "I don't deserve it," said Al Kaline, reminding Detroit general manager Jim Campbell he'd only hit .278. "Give me the same thing as last year, $93,000. Then I'll have a good year and make you really pay me."

Decades later, that story is still told with horror at the players' union. But it was a stance that reflected the values of the time and relationships with management. Many players had warm relationships with their owners, who, in the words of one baseball man, "would do anything for them but pay well."

When Phillies infielder Eddie Waitkus was shot by a deranged woman in 1949, owner Bob Carpenter paid for his winter-long rehabilitation in Florida, sending along the team's trainer. When Brooks Robinson lost a bundle in a sporting-goods business, Orioles owner Jerry Hoffberger bailed him out. General managers spent half their time getting players out of scrapes, though sometimes they wondered why. The Dodgers once provided counsel to a pitcher facing a paternity suit. When the plaintiff entered the courtroom, the player eyed her up and down and declared to his lawyer, "Boy, I'd like to bang her again."

The favors weren't all in one direction. Late in the 1947 season, Yankees players held a pregame ceremony to give team president Larry MacPhail a sterling silver set. All their names were inscribed on the tray with the message: "To Larry MacPhail, greatest executive in baseball, whose zealous efforts were a major factor in our nineteen-game streak and the winning of the American League pennant. From his Yankees, 1947."

MacPhail wept unashamedly.

Branch Rickey bought all the Dodgers players Studebakers after the 1946 season, when they improved vastly and only lost the pennant by a whisker. The players, in return, chipped in to buy Rickey a boat. They even made jokes about their futile trips into his office—known as "the cave of the winds"—from which they emerged, if they were lucky, with meager raises.

The players could take comfort in one thing: although they didn't make much money, neither did the owners. The Cubs, for instance, could meet their payroll out of concessions revenues ("I used to say the players were playing for peanuts," said Cubs business manager E. R. "Salty" Saltwell); but they also had the cheapest seats in baseball—one dollar for the bleachers until the mid-seventies—and held back 17,000 of them for walk-up sale each game.

"Mr. [Phil] Wrigley never took a penny out of the ball club, never took a dividend," said Saltwell. "He didn't care much about profits; he just didn't care to subsidize losses."

* * *

That fairly characterized the prevailing attitude in baseball. Some teams were operated as a family business—the Senators by the Griffiths, the Giants by the Stonehams, the Athletics by Connie Mack. But more were owned by wealthy individuals—self-styled "sportsmen." There was money involved, but it was a hobby, akin to horseracing. (Indeed, Pirates owner and real estate baron John Galbreath owned a horse named Roberto as well as a ballplayer of the same name, and the two meant about the same thing to him.) Phil Wrigley himself pretty much summed it up in the early fifties when he said, "Baseball is too much of a business to be a sport and too much of a sport to be a business."

That truism was so solace to aggrieved players so, around mid-century, two of them mounted challenges to the system. Danny Gardella, a Giants outfielder, had jumped to the short-lived Mexican League in 1946 and been blacklisted from U.S. baseball. He sued, challenged the reserve clause, and won a round in court, when a federal appeals panel ruled that his case merited trial. Baseball immediately settled out of court. Then George Toolson, a Yankees farmhand, sued baseball over the reserve system. It blocked his movement to another organization, he complained, where he might make the majors. The Supreme Court rejected his appeal in 1953, ruling it was up to Congress to overturn baseball's antitrust exemption.

Other players were frustrated over the pension, the initial funding of which was agreed to for only five years. Commissioner Happy Chandler had earmarked 80 percent of World Series radio and TV revenue for the pension during that period. But that generous formula was believed to have been an important cause of his firing and players feared the owners would pull the plug on retirement benefits altogether. When Allie Reynolds and Ralph Kiner, representing the players, tried to press the issue in a meeting at the 1953 All-Star Game, they were rudely rebuffed. They "got a luncheon from the magnates," as *The Sporting News* reported, but no satisfaction.

Reynolds, the Yankees pitcher, turned to a New York labor lawyer named J. Norman Lewis. He was an unthreatening sort, normally given to representing the management side, yet he was still anathema to the owners, who barred him from attending their meeting with Reynolds and Kiner that summer.

The owners did invite player representatives to attend their winter meetings in Atlanta that December, but with one caveat:

no Norman Lewis. Now the players were frosted. They set up their *own* meeting in Atlanta to discuss the pension issue. The Major League Baseball Players Association, as they called themselves, had existed previously but had been limited to such issues as the state of clubhouse bathrooms. This was clearly a new turn.

Yankees co-owner Del Webb called Reynolds on the carpet. "What are you attempting to do, start a union?" he demanded.

"That's the farthest thing from my mind," Reynolds explained. He made the point that the players just needed an organization so they could address the pension issue. That got the owners' attention. They set up a joint player-owner committee to decide on a funding formula, and in 1954 they came up with one. Sixty percent of the broadcast revenues from the World Series and All-Star Game would go to the pension.

"We were just infants, but we broke the ice," Kiner later recalled.

The fledgling players' group accomplished little else. Norman Lewis was eventually allowed at the table, and got the minimum salary nudged up to $6,000 in the mid-1950s. But his grander ideas—among them, getting the owners to commit 20 percent of their revenues to player salaries—got nowhere. And his lack of time for the players, compared to more lucrative clients, eventually led to discontent. In 1959, the players decided to nudge him aside and hire new counsel.

His name was Robert C. Cannon, and he was a municipal judge in Milwaukee. Perhaps key to his choice was the fact that he was the son of one Raymond J. Cannon, a militant players' advocate during the twenties and thirties. A Wisconsin congressman, Ray Cannon had tried to organize a players' union in the 1920s, attempted to mount a congressional investigation into the baseball business, and sought to win Shoeless Joe Jackson the back pay the Black Sox player claimed he was owed. Cannon struck out every time, but firmly established himself as a thorn in the side of organized baseball.

There would be no such militance from the son. His retainer was paid by the owners; he aspired to be commissioner; and the things he espoused the owners couldn't have said better themselves. "The thinking of the average major league ballplayer," he said at one congressional hearing, was: "we have it so good we don't know what to ask for next."

The player reps were often hand-picked by management. The general managers were invited to the annual meetings of the

Players Association, where Judge Cannon held forth on the Good of the Game. The players were more toothless than ever. The owners sat back, pleased. They were the masters of all they surveyed, the Lords of the Realm.

$ 2 $

WHEN PLAYERS MULLED the future of the Players Association in 1965, they weren't trying to start a revolution. They were merely coming to a belated conclusion. Without a permanent office and full-time director, the association would never amount to much. And they were coming to an important juncture.

The current pension plan was going to expire in March 1967. Some players—most notably pitcher Robin Roberts—were concerned. Since 1954 the plan had been funded by the 60–40 formula: 60 percent of the World Series and All-Star Game broadcast revenue. The players' share now amounted to $1.6 million a year.

Roberts sensed that TV revenues were about to expand dramatically. ("I can see a day when the pension contribution is *$15 million a year*," he told incredulous peers.) But he worried the players wouldn't get their fair share. ABC had paid $5.7 million to begin their *Game of the Week* coverage in 1965. The players hadn't gotten anything out of that. Their TV money was only tied to the All-Star Game and Series. Roberts was a respected figure, both as the longtime ace of the Phillies and the longtime player rep of the National League. He was neither, now—playing out his career elsewhere and relinquishing any formal role in the Players Association.

But he asked Bob Friend, his successor as NL player rep, if he could attend a meeting of the representatives in Houston in late 1965. There he presented his analysis on the TV-pension interplay and made the case for hiring a full-time director.

"Things are getting more complicated," said Roberts. "There's going to be a lot of money involved, and without a negotiator we won't get our share. I think we need someone full-time to do two things: work on the next pension contract and do more with group licensing."

15

(A man named Frank Scott did some work for the Association developing licensing programs. But he was also a commercial agent for several Yankees players and channeled most of his energies toward them. Roberts thought the players' merchandising outlets should be expanded beyond just baseball cards.)

He had a receptive audience. For one thing, the pension remained an enormously important issue. For another, the players were uneasy at changes they saw in baseball. They'd been comfortable enough in a stable environment, but by the mid-1960s, they'd seen the Braves move twice, the Yankees bought by CBS, and signs of more change to come. How could they keep relying on benign paternalism?

"The nature of ownership groups was changing dramatically," recalled Jim Bunning, the Phillies' pitcher and player rep. "We wanted to make sure we knew where we were going even if management didn't."

A search committee was formed to find a director: Bunning, Roberts, Bob Friend, and Harvey Kuenn. These were no rabble-rousers. Bunning would later become a Republican congressman. Roberts was a stout defender of the reserve clause, declaring at one congressional hearing, "I feel definitely that what is good for the owners is good enough for us players." Friend decried player militance, believing it would ruin the game for kids. As he once put it, "Stan Musial picketing a ballpark would look great, wouldn't it?"

The Pirates pitcher was close to Judge Cannon and to Pittsburgh owner John Galbreath. Galbreath lent the players a sympathetic ear. He was active in pension matters and saw merit in the players' having full-time professional representation. Of course, he saw that professional being Judge Cannon.

So, too, did the players at first. They'd worked with him for six years as legal counsel and they saw his cozy relations with the owners as a plus. Most of them bought his mind-set lock, stock, and barrel. Its principal assumption was that the owners' continuing benevolence was to be courted. "You were trained to think, 'Oh, you don't want to raise your voice about any issue; they might take the pension plan away,' " recalled Tim McCarver. "It was almost like the pension plan was a gift from the owners. If we stirred the waters too much the pension plan would go down the tubes."

The players' fealty to Cannon increased when he secured a generous $150,000-a-year commitment from the owners to fund a Players Association director and office. The search committee looked at other candidates, but the executive council's vote was overwhelming: Bob Cannon was their man.

The judge's hold on the job started slipping only when it came down to specific employment terms. The players wanted the office in New York; Cannon wanted to stay in Milwaukee. The players offered $50,000 a year; Cannon wanted them to also match his judge's pension. The players offered a compromise office site in Chicago and some compensation adjustment. Cannon refused. Peeved, the players withdrew the offer.

They would have to consider their second-choice candidate: someone named Marvin Miller.

Marvin Julian Miller grew up in Depression Brooklyn, the son of a struggling ladies-garment salesman and a schoolteacher. Like any son of Flatbush, he rooted for the Dodgers. And like many an ambitious son of immigrants, he worked his way through school.

Miller graduated from high school at age fifteen, and from New York University, with a B.A. in economics, at nineteen. The young Miller, newly married, took a succession of jobs. For a while he was a caseworker with the New York City Welfare Department. There he joined his first union—the State, County and Municipal Workers of America—and sat on his local's grievance committee.

World War II broke out, but Miller was disqualified from military service for medical reasons. (His shoulder had been irreparably damaged at birth. He couldn't raise his arm above his shoulder and he carried it at an awkward angle, away from his body.) Instead he joined the National War Labor Board. It was a federal agency created to arbitrate labor disputes and ensure vital factory production wasn't interrupted by strikes or lockouts.

Miller started out as an economist, became a hearings officer, and was soon adjudicating a wide variety of disputes. He was also soon enraptured. Some of America's top labor-relations men served on the board, including George Taylor, its chairman and a pioneer arbitrator. Miller found labor relations intellectually fascinating and morally compelling. He wanted to be a player in this arena—on the workingman's side, of course.

Yet when the War Labor Board dissolved in 1945, with the war's end, Miller was at loose ends. He bounced around for the next few years between unimportant jobs at the Labor Department's Conciliation Service, the International Association of Machinists, and the United Automobile Workers. By 1950, Marvin

Miller was thirty-two years old, had two small children, and had never held a job for more than three years. He was, by his own admission, "meandering."

Then came a call from a friend named Otis Brubaker. They had worked together at the War Labor Board; now Brubaker was research chief at the United Steelworkers of America. He had an opening for a staff economist. Was Miller interested?

Was he ever.

The Steelworkers' union was the apex of organized labor. Its size and importance mirrored postwar America's industrial might. It had 1.25 million members in 3,000 locals in forty-two states. Its settlements set the pace for wages and benefits throughout U.S. industry. Its strikes, which came with regularity, sent ripples throughout the domestic economy.

Marvin Miller was but a functionary in the big union bureaucracy—a mere "technician," in the parlance of the United Steelworkers. He had a sporty pencil mustache and a sharp pencil, and pored through government statistics, studying industry trends and learning his cost-of-living stats cold. Miller, dragging on cigarette after cigarette, stockpiled ammunition for bargaining. Quietly and industriously he made a minor name for himself. That would become important as the Steelworkers moved into the Age of the Technician.

That age was born with the ascension to union president of a man named David J. McDonald. He was big on wine, women, and limousines—all three at the same time, if possible. He had a flying wedge of bodyguards, a $21,000-a-year-suite in a Washington hotel, and an entourage of toadies.

But he had one saving virtue: an ensemble of brilliant technicians to whom he delegated virtually everything. Chief among them was Arthur Goldberg, the Steelworkers' brilliant general counsel. As McDonald shed progressively more leadership functions, Goldberg took them over. He was known as the union's "shadow president."

In the aftermath of what was history's longest steel strike, in 1959, Goldberg was restive. The 116-day siege had enabled customers to discover European competitors who had rebuilt their mills after the war. With their lower prices, they locked up some major customers with long-term contracts. U.S. steel output lagged behind prestrike levels. So did steel jobs.

Goldberg felt he had to find some vehicle for reconciliation: a means of studying and settling issues before contracts ended in deadline crises and strikes. He proposed setting up a joint study group, the innocuously named Human Relations Research Committee.

The logical choice to head up the union side was Otis Brubaker: this was a research committee and he was the research director. But Brubaker had a reputation for being abrasive and doctrinaire, so Goldberg looked elsewhere. It must be someone who could keep up with the economic arguments without getting into loud arguments. There was, he felt, just such a man toiling in obscurity. And so Goldberg reached past Brubaker into the backwaters of the research department and plucked out his choice: Marvin Miller.

With Miller at the helm, the Human Relations Committee promptly threw itself into a maze of thorny "work rules" issues: seniority, interplant transfers, crew sizes, and more. The committee soon evolved into more than a study group. It became an important off-peak negotiating force unto itself. "That," says Miller's friend and fellow technician Ben Fisher, "is what put Marvin in the big time."

Soon Goldberg tapped Miller to carry out another of his ideas. It was called the Kaiser Steel Long-Range Sharing Plan, a bold experiment in running that California steel producer. The plan was to be overseen by a tripartite committee composed of three top arbitrators, three Kaiser Steel members, and three Steelworkers members. But Miller was the primary architect. He huddled with company engineers to develop improvements in productivity. Then he developed a formula for sharing the increased profits with employees.

It worked. The plan went into effect in 1963, and Kaiser soon had the most productive steel mill in the country, and with the best-paid workforce. It was another feather in Miller's cap. As a result, when Goldberg left to become JFK's secretary of labor, Miller was named chief economist and assistant to the president. He was now in the front ranks of the technicians.

But McDonald's elite cadre of technicians was to become controversial. When the union's secretary-treasurer, I. W. Abel, challenged McDonald for president in 1964, he mounted not only the usual attack on the high-living president but went after his aides too. Decisions must be put "back in the hands of elected representatives of the membership," he declared. "We'll take it away from this palace guard that have surrounded the 'crown prince' and have been making decisions as to what's good, bad or indifferent."

Abel blamed Miller's Human Relations Committee for the

Steelworkers' slim wage increases of the early sixties. It had gained labor peace, he charged, at a stiff price for the workers. Abel also capitalized on grumblings about the Kaiser plan, charging that the company's chairman, Edgar Kaiser, backed McDonald's reelection as a means of continuing their "cozy little deals."

McDonald's years as a "tuxedo unionist," as his foes called him, and his reliance on Miller and the others had caught up with him. Regardless of the dubious merit of some of Abel's charges, they stuck. In April 1965, Abel was the new president of the United Steelworkers of America.

Abel's boosters jockeyed for top jobs; rumors raged about who was in and who was out. McDonald's general counsel was soon out, and Miller feared he was right behind him. Yes, Abel had told him his job was secure, but an Abel man named Larry Spitz was angling hard to become the ranking house intellectual. Others tried to talk Miller out of his funk. Ben Fisher, another top technician, had him over to his house and argued long into the night.

"This is premature, Marvin," he said. "Sure Spitz has a good relationship with Abel. But he can't hold a candle to you and Abe is going to see that. You're going to rule the roost."

But privately Fisher understood that Miller wasn't suited to these circumstances. "Marvin is not basically a politician," he reflected years later. "He's relatively orthodox and relatively absolute in his view of the world. His relationship with Abel was good, but you couldn't just think of Marvin and Abe. It was a palace-politics situation and you had to look at where you fit in."

Miller was so clearly in limbo, he started getting outside job offers. The Carnegie Endowment for International Peace made one approach. The think tank wanted him to head a study on how labor negotiating skills could be applied to diplomacy. He took a pass. John Dunlop, a fellow Kaiser Committee member and distinguished Harvard professor, approached him about a visiting professorship there. Miller, forty-eight years old and in midlife crisis, was tempted.

Then came another offer via another Kaiser Committee member. In December, Miller was at a Kaiser meeting in San Francisco. As he rode the hotel elevator down to the conference room, George Taylor got on. Miller knew him from way back at the War Labor Board. But Taylor had been much more since then: labor adviser to every president from Hoover to Johnson, author of a New York State law on public employees' strike rights, dean at the Wharton School of Business, and now a Kaiser Committee member.

For Miller, he was a giant in U.S. labor relations. Now, as they rode down together, he popped the most important question of Miller's life.

"Do you know Robin Roberts?" he asked.

Miller thought—the pitcher?

"Not personally," he said, "but I certainly know who he is."

Taylor barely knew him better. The pitcher had called him out of the blue the previous week, telling him he wanted to get someone to head the Players Association. Roberts said he knew of Taylor's reputation in labor and asked for recommendations.

"The first person I thought of was you," said Taylor. "Interested?"

"I don't know," said Miller, who really didn't. But he had to admit that it was at least mildly intriguing. "I'll certainly talk to him."

Within an hour, Taylor had arranged for Miller to meet with Roberts and the search committee. Miller had taken the first step leaving America's most powerful labor organization for its most impotent one.

Two weeks later, shortly before Christmas, Miller met in Cleveland with three of the four players on the search committee: Roberts, Bunning, and Kuenn. He'd had a chance to think it over and now he was genuinely interested. That wasn't reciprocated, for the most part, by the players. Kuenn was cool toward trade unions and their employees. Bunning was touting his own candidate, a lawyer who'd once represented him in a suit. The absent Bob Friend was, of course, for Cannon. Only Roberts was enthusiastic about Miller, growing more impressed with him as the interview went on.

At the players' Executive Council meeting, soon thereafter, Roberts championed Miller. "We need a negotiator," he emphasized, reiterating the importance of the pension. "This is the guy who can handle our negotiations."

It did no good, of course, and it was Roberts's duty to call Miller with the bad news: he'd lost. A few days later, however, he was delighted to call again. Cannon was suddenly out; would he stand for election again? Miller was not so delighted. He was miffed at the inside politics that had handed Cannon the job. He didn't care to go through anything like that again. But Roberts kept after him, calling him for several days. Friend, who had come around on Miller, even called to apologize and ask him to reconsider. Finally, Miller relented.

"If the players elect me," he told Friend, "I'll accept the job."

Even with the field down to a sole candidate—himself—Miller had a difficult path to the job. When the Executive Council met again, in Miami, some players wanted no part of an organized-labor operative. The most emphatic was Cubs pitcher Larry Jackson, who repeatedly hammered at the word "union," making it sound as tainted as an unearned run. There was no place in baseball for unions, said Jackson, who summed up his position concisely: "Let's consider anybody but Marvin Miller."

Miller ultimately won, since there was really nobody else to consider, but he still had to be ratified by all the players. The owners, belatedly sensing trouble, swung into action. A group of them held a threatening meeting with player leaders.

Roberts had tried to assure baseball's leaders that this wasn't a hostile action. He'd invited Commissioner Spike Eckert to the players' election meeting so that it would be understood, as he later explained, "this was on the up-and-up." (Eckert's aide, Lee MacPhail, did attend.)

But now the owners were sending a message: the players weren't ready for democracy. Certainly the Lords didn't like the results of this particular election. They wanted it rescinded or there could be trouble. "Maybe we should just cancel the pension and pay you that money up front," mused Walter O'Malley, the Dodgers owner.

M. Donald Grant of the Mets spoke up on behalf of his owner, the blue blood Joan Whitney Payson. She didn't want to get involved with any of these awful little union people. "We're sportsmen," he said. "We're not in this for the money."

"Like hell," growled Calvin Griffith, the Senators' owner. "This is my livelihood."

The long and the short of it was this, recalled Bunning: "Now we were convinced that we'd hired the right person."

They would have to contend with the owners' minions, however, who went forth through the clubhouses, whispering warnings against Miller: "Goons . . . strikes . . . labor boss."

There was no escaping it. Miller was, indeed, a Jewish, intellectual, left-leaning trade unionist. Moreover, he had a jarringly "outsider" appearance. A *Sports Illustrated* profile—a friendly one, at that—described the Miller look this way: suits of "shim-

mering blue" and slicked-back hair that "gives him the look of
the slippery 'mouthpiece,' so essential to 1930s gangster films."
The mustache made Robin Roberts so nervous, he suggested
Miller shave it. "It's probably not the best thing for your image," he said.

The ratification was to be held during spring training. Miller
would tour the Cactus and Grapefruit Leagues, meet with each
team's players, and then be subject to a vote. Miller knew he
was in trouble as soon as he walked into his first camp—the
California Angels'—and was renounced by the team's player
rep, catcher Buck Rodgers.

Rodgers, who had fallen under the influence of players still
loyal to Judge Cannon, was part of the stop-Miller effort. He
was behind a petition circulating among players that read: "Our
feeling is that [the players' association director] should have a
legal background that the owners can respect. . . . We have prog-
ressed a great deal in the past few years and we think this relationship between the owners and the players should continue."

Everywhere he went in the Cactus League, Miller was bush-
whacked. Team managers conducted the meetings, peppered him
with insinuating questions ("How can the players be sure you're
not a Communist?" asked the Indians' Birdie Tebbetts), and conducted the vote. Miller came out of the West with a 102–17 vote
against him.

Yet he was not doomed. Despite the disastrous Cactus League
swing and despite many players' deep conservative leanings, he
was speaking to a shared restiveness afoot.

This was the spring of the joint Sandy Koufax–Don Drysdale
holdout. The two were baseball's best pitchers in 1965: Koufax
at 26–8 with a 2.04 ERA and 382 strikeouts, Drysdale at 23–12,
with a 2.77 ERA. They were both Dodgers and they both felt
they deserved to make $100,000. (Koufax had earned $85,000 in
1965, Drysdale $80,000.) When the Dodgers steadfastly refused,
the two joined forces, hired a Hollywood agent, and shot the
moon: demanding a three-year $1 million package deal for the
two of them. Dodgertown opened for spring training and Koufax
and Drysdale stayed in California.

The Dodgers were outraged—both at the price and at the very
idea of a joint holdout. "Baseball is an old-fashioned game with
old-fashioned traditions," harrumphed owner Walter O'Malley.
"If we allowed this [joint] entry business to take hold, it would
lead to practices not possible to tolerate."

The agent, Bill Hayes, made noises about getting Drysdale a

movie contract. He lined up an exhibition tour in Japan for the two pitchers. He floated the notion they'd jointly shop their services to another big-league team. Drysdale and Koufax even called up O'Malley, asking whether he'd mind their talking to California Angels owner Gene Autry.

"You want to go see Gene?" O'Malley said. "Fine, go ahead. Of course, we have rules in baseball that prohibit you from doing such a thing."

That, of course, expressed perfectly the limit to their gambit. They had nowhere else to go. Koufax ultimately settled for $125,000, Drysdale for $115,000. It was only a fraction of what they'd first demanded, but it topped what they'd have gotten if they had bargained individually. The two stars had shown colleagues what was possible by exercising a little leverage. Marvin Miller was about to show them a whole lot more.

He would first have to survive more assaults by the owners' henchmen, who preceded him into each Florida camp. In the Yankees' Fort Lauderdale clubhouse, Joe Reichler of the commissioner's office sidled up to pitcher Jim Bouton to issue a solemn warning: "Be very, very, *very* careful about this guy Miller."

So when it came time for Miller's first meeting with the Yankees, recalls Bouton, "We were all expecting to see someone with a cigar out of the corner of his mouth, a real knuckle-dragging 'deze and doze' guy. Instead, in walks this quiet, mild, exceedingly understated man."

He told the Yankees, as he had the other nineteen teams, what *might* be possible with a strong union: a higher minimum salary, improved working conditions, and better benefits.

The owners are lying again, Bouton thought. *Marvin Miller's my guy.*

The tide had begun to turn. The player reps in Florida were a tougher lot and wouldn't roll over for the Lords. They, not management, would run the meetings. They wouldn't necessarily push Miller's candidacy, but neither would they collaborate in undermining it. Most of all, the difference was Miller himself, who'd gotten his sea legs and had started to gain players' confidence.

Robin Roberts was running wind sprints before the game at West Palm Beach one day, when Eddie Mathews trotted out to see him.

"I owe you an apology," said the Braves third baseman,

who'd uttered some pungent anti-Miller quotes. "Marvin Miller was just in our clubhouse, and he's certainly someone different than I thought."

"Don't apologize," said Roberts. "Just vote for him."

Mathews—and scores of other players—did so. Miller swept the late precincts in Florida to win ratification, 489–136. He was executive director. But of what? Miller headed a union with only a $5,400 bank account and a battered filing cabinet to its name. And yet the Major League Baseball Players Association had some things going for it. One was the very nature of the sport. Football players, Miller always figured, would have been tougher to organize. The players had shorter careers and lesser investment in the issues. The authority of the coach (read: management) was unquestioned. As Howard Slusher, a football player-agent, would later put it, "A football player believes in rules and regulations and order. From the day they put on pads, they listen to commands."

The players were also stratified by position. The elite ones—particularly the quarterbacks—were pampered by management. Thus, in any dispute, the marquee players were as likely to side with owners as fellow players. In 1974, when the NFL players staged a forty-two-day training-camp strike, rookies and free agents blithely crossed the picket lines. The strike was called off and it took three years to negotiate a labor contract.

Football players came into the pros as publicized All-Americans. Baseball players reached the majors after brutal minor league apprenticeships: long bus rides, rickety ballparks, scant pay, cramped apartments. As pitcher Mike Marshall put it, "We weren't BMOCs."

The experience drew players together and fostered, in many, a permanent cynicism about management. They didn't act on it, but they had a mind-set a union organizer could work with. They'd already shown some capacity for group-think. Baseball players had a pension plan before other pro athletes did. And they parceled out retirement benefits in an egalitarian spirit: not on the basis of career earnings but years played. The scrubeenies were worth as much as the stars.

There was all that, but most of all there was Marvin Miller. Long the Big Labor technician, the house intellectual, he could now roll up his sleeves, organize, negotiate, and make his mark in Small Labor. Long frustrated by the Steelworkers' bulk, he was now utterly free of bureaucracy. He commanded a powerless sloop, compared to the mighty battleship of the Steelworkers—but it was highly maneuverable and it was his. It was also a marvelous laboratory. Starting from scratch, and with such a small membership, he could test his ideas of how a union *should* be run. "I've always been aware of the criticisms about labor unions and bosses," Miller would later reflect. "I was trying to show that it wasn't necessarily so."

He set about making this a demonstration project: a union as democracy. Miller believed to his bones in an involved rank and file. If there was glory and romance to the labor movement, it was the uprising of the common man. The Steelworkers' brass didn't even know its membership. The union had 1.25 million members then in 3,000 locales, in forty-five states and assorted foreign nations. "If you wanted to meet with every member, it would have taken until the year 2000," says Miller.

The Major League Baseball Players Association had just 500 members. At the very least, Miller saw each of them during his annual spring training meetings with teams. He saw each team's player representative at least four times a year at the union's executive board meetings. He urged other players to attend those meetings. He also urged players to stop by the union office when their teams were in New York. "This is *your* office; this is *your* union," he told them repeatedly.

The Lords wouldn't make it easy. The first thing they did was withdraw the $150,000 they'd promised to fund the Players Association. The reality was: no Judge Cannon, no $150,000. The stated rationale was: My goodness, we've discovered it would be *illegal* for the owners to fund a union. Miller had to wheedle through a $344-a-year deduction from each player's salary to stake the organization.

Nor, at first, were the Lords even inclined to negotiate. Miller intercepted Commissioner William Eckert en route to a June 1966 press conference, where he planned to announce the amount of the owners' next pension contribution. Miller reminded him that was something that had to be bargained.

When the Lords did deign to negotiate, Miller was astounded at their stance in one early meeting: You talk, we listen. The owners' representatives—league presidents Joe Cronin, Warren Giles, and some others—set the ground rules at the start: they'd make no proposals, counterproposals, or even comments. While Miller and some player reps tried to carry the action, the Lords' minions sat across the table, tight-lipped. Finally, one of the players, pitcher Steve Hamilton, exploded.

"This has been insulting and inconsiderate to waste everyone's time this way," he said. "Since you had no intention of negotiating, or even of saying anything, you could have saved everybody's time by asking that we make a tape and send it to you."

It was typical of the owners' early tactics. It only put Miller on more solid ground and planted the germ of player militance. "I'll tell you what," said pitcher Jim Bouton, who observed the union's early workings. "If they'd have just said, 'We'll raise the minimum salary to $10,000, then raise it $1,000 a year for the next twenty years. Then we'll throw in an annual cost-of-living increase on the meal money.' If they'd have just done something like that, nobody would have looked to Marvin Miller. But with everything they did, they helped Marvin."

Miller and the owners did manage to talk enough, finally, to reach a new three-year pension agreement by year-end 1966. It increased the Lords' annual funding of retirement benefits from $1.5 million a year to $4.1 million. It also doubled the level of previous monthly pension payments and disability benefits. Yet it was not universally hailed. Bob Feller and Allie Reynolds, two early Players Association stalwarts, bitterly criticized Miller for de-linking the pension and TV revenues when he agreed to accept a flat sum rather than a percentage of World Series and All-Star Game broadcast rights.

Their brickbats didn't seriously threaten Miller, but they were a symptom of how shaky his status remained. Plenty of players still questioned what he was doing and what he stood for. Miller fielded one particular question almost as often as a shortstop takes ground balls: "Are we a union?"

It often had a nasty tone and, for the new man, it was definitely a tricky hop. Miller would answer carefully: "Any group of people working together to advance the interests of the group is, under the terms of labor law, a union."

He would hasten to move on to discussing those interests. And he would take pains to use the organization's proper and more neutral name, the Players *Association*. "He downplayed the word *union* when that was an alarming word," says Tim McCarver. But semantics wasn't the key to Miller's winning the players' hearts and minds. It was action. He listened to them. He educated them. And slowly he radicalized them.

The player reps had their first big meeting of the new era in the winter of 1967, in Mexico City. As they filed in, Miller handed a pad of paper and pen to each. "List every grievance you've got that you'd like to see addressed," he said. "We'll pile them up and go through them one by one."

Many gripes concerned working conditions: ballpark safety (take the Crosley Field scoreboard—treacherous to crashing outfielders); hotel accommodations (*fleabag* was too kind a term for some); clubhouse conditions (the wire that powered the Tiger Stadium whirlpool ran through water); and scheduling (doubleheaders after night games were killers).

Pitcher Milt Pappas even spoke up for the growing ranks of players abandoning crew cuts for the mod look. "There aren't enough outlets for hair dryers in the clubhouses," he complained.

His colleagues roared with laughter.

Miller himself chuckled, but said, "Now you laugh, but we're trying to straighten out everything from warning tracks to hair dryers. *Everything* counts."

But if the players were beginning to take their new union seriously, the owners were not. The players had met in Mexico City because the Lords were holding their winter meetings there. Miller was led to believe the two would hold a joint meeting at some point. But then the Lords sent word: Too busy.

"Let's go tell them to fuck themselves," declared Milt Pappas, leading a chorus of angry cries from the player reps. Miller, just as miffed but far more savvy, advised them to stay cool. Their time would come later, when they had more leverage.

That pattern would hold for a time. Miller wasn't so much vilified as ignored. The Lords hoped the players would settle back into passivity, and that Miller would settle for what crumbs they dispensed. American League president Joe Cronin even once approached him on a friendly Dutch uncle basis. "I've got some advice for you, young man," he said to Miller, then forty-nine years old. "The players come and go, but the owners stay on forever."

Marvin Miller would later come to be called by some the Great Emancipator. But the key was what he was at first: the Great Educator. He got the players talking, participating, arguing. He gave them a guided tour of the outmoded standard player contract, pointing out some of its more laughable features. There was, for instance, the provision that called for first-class travel but specified *trains*. It hadn't been changed since 1945, despite the fact that team train travel had disappeared in the 1950s.

He gave them a tutorial on pension law. Money contributed

for their benefit wasn't the Lords', it was *theirs*. It should be removed from an account that the clubs had commingled with their other funds. It was.

He got them to help in generating data he would need for his next negotiation: baseball's first collectively bargained Basic Agreement. It would cover working conditions, severance arrangements, minimum salary, the works. It was particularly for minimum-pay bargaining that he needed the players' assistance. The minimum in 1967 was $6,000, only $1,000 more than in 1947. (A player did have to be paid $7,000 if he was still on the roster thirty days into the season.) It was outrageous on the face of it.

Yet Miller needed to know more to intelligently negotiate its increase. How many players were at the minimum? How many just above? What was the average salary? To an economist like Miller, it was basic, necessary data. To the Lords it was a deep, dark secret—virtually a national security matter, if you asked them.

So Miller asked each player to write his salary on a slip of paper and give it to his team's player rep. The player reps would collect and send them to Miller. It would all be anonymous but quite accurate.

Miller quickly disseminated the data to the players. The average salary was $19,000. About 33 percent of all players were at $10,000 or less. More than 40 percent were paid $12,000 or less. Though only 7 percent of players were at the base $6,000, raising the minimum would lift many other players' salaries as well.

The information made some of them angry. Ron Fairly, the Dodgers' player rep, was livid when he turned his team's numbers in. He'd looked at them and discovered something.

"Buzzie Bavasi told me that after Koufax, Drysdale, and Wills, I was the highest-paid Dodger," Fairly told Miller. "He said if I got paid more, I would throw the team's salary scale out of whack. Do you know where I rank? Eighth!"

The education of a ballplayer was beginning.

"The most remarkable thing to me, looking back, is what a patient man Marvin Miller was," says Tim McCarver. "He realized how disparate his knowledge of negotiating and contracts was from ours. So he educated the player reps and they educated the rest. It was a very slow, methodical process. He never let the cart get before the horse. Everything was building from a base."

Yet even as Miller tried to start with small issues, those on the other side of the table felt there was no such thing. Accustomed to absolute control, they took nearly everything Miller wanted as an affront. When Miller brought up proposed scheduling changes, for instance—say, no doubleheaders after night games—American League president Joe Cronin was outraged. "The players have nothing to do with this," he stormed.

Cronin was typical of baseball's leaders: thoroughly rooted in the past and steeped in baseball's hoary traditions—a player in the thirties, a manager in the forties, and American League president since the fifties. Now at age sixty, he didn't comprehend how labor law could intrude upon baseball, so long a law unto itself. Even after years of go-arounds with Miller, he'd wail privately, "How do we get *into* these kinds of things? This isn't baseball."

The naïveté of baseball's leaders could also lead them, on occasion, to moments of surprising candor. When, in a meeting, Miller compared the meager raise in the minimum salary over the past twenty years to the inflation rate, National League president Warren Giles murmured, "Oh, my, that's awful." The owners' lawyers at the table silently groaned and, in turn, had to agree. This was awful. They needed a pro to counter the players' pro.

American League counsel Jim Garner had a man in mind. One of his other clients was the Scripps Howard newspaper chain. Garner's legal duties drew him into the New York newspaper wars, where he wound up in the trenches with a man named John Gaherin.

Gaherin (rhymes with barren) was president of the Publishers Association of New York, which jointly negotiated the newspapers' labor contracts. Gaherin had seen them through some of the brutal union battles of the 1960s and had a twenty-one-year-long labor-relations résumé. He'd been labor chief for several northeastern railroads and headed the Eastern Conference of Carriers, a joint bargaining association of railroads. He had also been a vice president for labor at American Airlines.

A street-smart New Yorker, he had a feel for the labor-relations trenches that transcended boardrooms and courtrooms. He liked to tell of when he was chairman of the New York Harbor Negotiating Committee in the midst of a bitter strike. He got a back-to-work court order, only to encounter a very unimpressed union chief. "Well, now, that's a pretty piece of paper," said the fellow, examining the order. "Will that fucking thing steer a tugboat?"

The owners could use a man of that ilk, thought Garner. He approached Gaherin one day. "Baseball is getting labor pains and we're looking for a labor expert," he said. "Can I put your name in the hat?"

Gaherin was ready to move on from the Publishers Association and, he thought, what the hell. He agreed to go to the ownership meetings in Chicago to talk about the position. Now, Gaherin *cared* nothing about the sport of baseball, and he *knew* nothing about the business of baseball; and by the time he had completed three days of interviews, he understood even less.

"The owners would have a committee of themselves," explained Lou Carroll, baseball's top outside lawyer. "You would be retained under an exclusive contract to consult concerning labor relations."

"So I don't work for anybody; I work for everybody," said Gaherin.

"Yes."

Gaherin wondered why he couldn't report to Commissioner Eckert.

"You can't work for the commissioner," said Carroll. "He wouldn't be involved in labor relations."

Gaherin was puzzled. The chief executive of a labor-intensive industry staying out of labor? The labor-relations structure being built by baseball was curious. Perhaps, he told himself, he just didn't understand this industry yet. Only after he'd taken the job, only after he'd come to understand the industry all too well, did the shape of the structure become clear. It was a scaffold, and he was standing on a trap door.

Marvin Miller gave Gaherin a curious gift of welcome: a *Sports Illustrated* piece on how Buzzie Bavasi negotiated contracts. It amounted to a primer by the L.A. Dodgers' chortling general manager on manipulating and swindling players. "I want you to see who you're working for," said Miller.

That was the other reason Miller wanted salary data. Players were totally in the dark about what other players made. (Well, not totally, according to Red Sox GM Dick O'Connell. "The wives knew and they would tell, adding a few thousand bucks," he recalls.) The players had precious little leverage to begin with. The lack of information only exacerbated it. GMs routinely lied about where the players stood in the salary structure.

After reliever Bob Locker had a terrific 1967, for instance, he went in to talk contract with White Sox GM Ed Short. Locker made his case: 20 saves, a 2.09 ERA, a league-leading 77 appearances. He deserved $18,000. Short countered with $16,000. That was a lot to ask, he argued, considering Phil Regan had just signed for $23,000. A year earlier, Regan had emerged as baseball's premier reliever: 14–1, 21 saves, and a 1.62 ERA.

"If Regan is making only $23,000, then I'm asking too much," Locker said. "You check that. If he signed for $23,000, I'll sign for $16,000."

The next day Short got back to him. "I called Buzzie Bavasi and he told me Regan was making $23,000 this year."

"All right," Locker said, "I'll take the $16,000."

He signed, but a nagging curiosity led him to drop a note to Regan. Would he mind, Locker wrote, telling him what he'd signed for? Regan wrote back with the figure: $36,500.

When the Lords rejected Miller's request for salary data, they stonewalled him. "That's confidential," sputtered Joe Cronin. No matter. The union simply filed a complaint with the National Labor Relations Board to get it. Miller had hired a bright young lawyer from the Steelworkers Union to take care of just such things. His name was Dick Moss.

One might have remarked, upon first glance, that he was playing Sancho Panza to Miller's Don Quixote. But that would have been to underestimate not only Miller but Richard M. Moss.

The thirty-five-year-old Moss was considered the sharpest arbitration lawyer in the Steelworkers' legal department. He went to the mat regularly—and often successfully—with Bethlehem Steel and American Can. He had only one known weakness. "If there was a conflict between watching a baseball game and negotiating a contract, you never knew which he was going to do," said Ben Fisher, his Steelworkers boss.

So Moss, the rabid Pirates fan, moved to New York to wed his avocation and his vocation. For the next ten years he would work in harness with Miller, though in some respects they were very different animals. To Miller, the working-class child of the Depression, labor was a life-and-death cause. The players were as exploited a class, he maintained, as the grapeworkers Cesar Chavez was organizing. ("I've never seen people more oppressed," he would tell friends.) To Moss, a rich-kid Harvard Law grad, it was a game. "Dick loves games, whether it's chess or arbitration, and he has to win," said Ken Moffett, a federal mediator who would come to know both men well.

Moss seemed the more aggressive, straining at Miller's leash. Miller—older by fifteen years, and softer of voice—came off as the more patient one. There was some truth to that. They had the same objectives—rearranging the game's balance of power—but Miller would settle for gains in smaller increments. There was also some gamesmanship to it. Miller and Moss had a good cop–bad cop act as smooth as in any precinct house around.

And yet Moss had the lighter touch, with a readier wit and a greater sense of fun than the ultraserious Miller. When the two of them huddled with Tim McCarver, prior to a 1967 meeting with the PRC (the Lords' player relations committee), they talked about how to handle the minimum-salary issue.

"What do I say when they make us an offer?" asked McCarver.

"If the offer is below twelve grand," Moss said, "it would be very helpful if you could throw up on the table."

Moss once drove to the Padres' spring training camp for a player meeting and, just for mischief, wheeled into Buzzie Bavasi's reserved parking space. Bavasi went off his gourd.

What Miller and Moss had in common was a sense of wonder at the uncharted territory that lay before them. The frontier might be settled in the rest of the labor world, but here was an industry that knew and cared nothing about the National Labor Relations Act. It was an assemblage of utter throwback capitalists. "It was incredible," Moss would later say. "This was a labor-relations scene from the thirties in the mid-sixties."

It was also a ripe opportunity. To Bruce Johnston, a U.S. Steel executive who would become Big Steel's chief negotiator, there was nothing exceptional about either man. Moss was a secondary player on a topflight legal team. And Miller he recalled as "certainly competent but you could have found two thousand guys like him." But they came out of a sophisticated, experienced, aggressive union.

"These were people trained in that system, then turned loose on an industry that was, in terms of labor relations, naïve and illiterate," said Johnston. "The owners were a loose amalgam of highly individualistic entrepreneurs, who are the worst people in the world to deal with labor. They're impatient, egocentric, and exasperating to represent. Most of them had never worked inside structures where cooperation with other strong personalities was required. They were thus very poor at cooperating in the face of unified opposition. The baseball industry presented open borders to a Panzer division."

* * *

Before they ever feared Marvin Miller, before they ever yielded anything to Marvin Miller, the Lords *hated* Marvin Miller. He had come crashing through the doors of their exclusive men's club, agitating the help and trying to rewrite the bylaws. He spouted obscure passages of labor law and cared nothing about the grand old game. He was a Jewish, trade-unionist rabble-rouser who oozed contempt for them, the Lords. Why not give him the bum's rush right out the door?

Indeed, why didn't they? Miller still had only a tenuous hold on the players—and his job. He hadn't even bargained a basic agreement.

And yet they didn't. For although the Lords profoundly despised Miller, they didn't profoundly fear him. Not at the beginning. The Lords might have been able to nip this union in the bud, but they were too conflicted about their vassals—the players—to unsheath their knives.

Frustrated owners occasionally asked Gaherin, "When are we going to tell these bastards to go to hell?"

"Anytime you want," he'd reply, "but you'd better mean it."

Much as they loathed Miller, however, the Lords were not prepared to stomp the union. The players were their product. The players were still, in some cases, their pets. And that gave them still another reason to hate Marvin Miller. He railed against "paternalism," and the Lords resented it mightily. What was wrong with taking care of the players? How dare he come between them and their boys? "Most of them saw the players as not real educated, naïve kids," says Gaherin. "They got paid for playing this great game, and they got laid on the road."

Buzzie Bavasi, the old trickster, performed a thousand kindnesses for his players. If one of them had just played a great game, Bavasi would whip out $100 and tell him to take his wife to dinner. If a player needed help with hospital bills, Bavasi was there. When bit player Dick Tracewski was pressed into service as a starter during the 1963 World Series and helped spark the sweep of the Yankees, Bavasi called him into his office afterward. He gave the infielder round-trip tickets to Hawaii for a vacation with his wife. For an $18,000-a-year ballplayer it was a big $900 thank-you.

Bavasi loaned Willie Davis so much money at Los Angeles that he had to sign him at San Diego after becoming president there, just so he could get repaid. The Padres paid Davis $70,000 in his last year, of which Bavasi garnisheed $35,000.

Bavasi was forever lending money to shortstop Zoilo

Versalles, primarily because Versalles was forever lending money to fellow Cuban emigrés. Anyone distantly related to Versalles hit up his "rich" ballplayer cousin for cash. "Everybody who comes in from Havana has two phone numbers," Dodgers farm director Fresco Thompson used to say. "The Immigration and Naturalization Service and Zoilo's home phone."

General managers routinely bailed their players out of scrapes. Boston GM Dick O'Connell forever came to the aid of Luis Tiant—with the Internal Revenue Service, various creditors, even home improvements. When Tiant's parents came to live with him, the pitcher asked O'Connell for money to add a room. "Sure," said the GM, "I'll give you seven or eight thousand." Tiant asked for $35,000. "What are you going to do," was O'Connell's incredulous retort, "put a *ballroom* in there?"

There was a baseball saying: "If you can hit the curveball, you can get away with murder." The flip side of that was not so attractive. If you weren't one of the favored, if you faltered on the diamond, you were dead meat.

"Miller understood, from a trade-union perspective, that you had to have a contract that applied to the least and the most," says Gaherin, adding slyly, "Of course, Marvin always wanted the most, plus a nickel."

As Marvin Miller struggled to establish a beachhead, he found help from an unexpected source: John Gaherin. Gaherin was a staunch management-side advocate, but, like Miller, a recent arrival from the real world. He knew labor law; he knew standard labor-relations practices of the sixties; and he knew that much of what Miller pressed for was perfectly reasonable. He was, moreover, attuned to working with unions, not busting them. Gaherin enjoyed the give-and-take of bargaining, enjoyed knocking back a drink and swapping lies with his foes when the deal was done.

"I grew up with union people, union procedure, the process of compromise," says Gaherin. If the Lords wanted a labor man who would kill the union in its crib, he reflected years later, "I was the worst possible selection."

Gaherin had one other thing in common with Marvin Miller. They had about the same reaction the first time they read Section 10A of the Uniform Players Contract. Miller had done a double take on first reading. The players believed that once they signed their first contract, they had no control over where they played. But the way this language read to Miller, a club had just a one-year option on a player's services:

On or before January 15 ... the Club may tender to the Player a contract for the term of that year by mailing the same to the Player. If prior to the March 1 next succeeding said January 15, the Player and the Club have not agreed upon the terms of such contract, then on or before 10 days after said March 1, the Club shall have the right ... to renew this contract for the period of one year.

Gaherin himself squinted and reread 10A. He'd heard about something called the "reserve clause." It gave clubs the rights to a player in perpetuity. The Lords believed it was enforceable by way of the clubs' one-year option right, enunciated here. Every time you renewed the contract you created a new link in the chain of a single contract: the option was extended; the player was captive. But to Gaherin, it didn't read that way at all.

He took it up one day with National League counsel Lou Carroll. "I've read it," he said, "and to me it means you can renew a player for one year and that's it."

Carroll was baseball's legal brain trust: a senior partner at Willkie, Farr and Gallagher (the National League's law firm since the mid-thirties), an adviser so estimable he was referred to less often by name than by the tag "The Wise Man." Baseball men would ask, "What's the Wise Man think?"

Lou Carroll looked at John Gaherin and nodded his agreement. "Don't ever let them try that renewal clause," he said.

Marvin Miller wasn't about to press hard on the reserve system his first time out. He had a building-block approach: go mainly for limited objectives and winnable fights at first. He would seek a minimum-salary raise. He would try to remedy the players' gripes about working conditions. Improvements in some basic areas would build the players' confidence in him and themselves, build some momentum, gain a foothold. Miller would hew closely to an old baseball maxim: "Swing for the singles. The home runs will come."

There was one exception: Miller did press hard for one structural change in his first Basic Agreement. It was called "grievance arbitration," and to Miller it was as basic as breathing. The Steelworkers Union of his era had pioneered its widespread use in labor relations.

The idea was simple: if an employee believed his rights were violated, if a union disputed a contract's meaning, the matters would be heard and decided by an independent arbitrator. The arbitrator was an institutionalized buffer who kept labor and management from each other's throats. It was no coincidence that the last great bloody labor battles had been fought in the 1930s, before such a mechanism existed. The War Labor Board, for which Miller had worked, was, in effect, the nation's first industrial arbitrator. It kept industry going by imposing settlements.

At the end of World War II, when the War Labor Board was dissolved, a major labor-management conference was called by the Truman White House to urge continuation of the wartime spirit of cooperation. It ended in acrimony, but the two sides did concur on one point: the merits of arbitration.

The steel industry took the postwar lead in its use. Steelworkers Union president Phil Murray, the man who hired Miller, joined with U.S. Steel to create the concept of a permanent independent arbitrator. Henceforth, all matters of dispute—employee firings, workplace conditions, contract interpretation—would go to arbitration. General Motors followed suit in an agreement with the United Auto Workers, and dozens of other companies did likewise.

The Steelworkers Union continued to take the lead in getting redress of labor grievances. It won the landmark Lincoln Mills case in 1957, which removed breach-of-labor-contract suits from state and local courts, often friendly to management interests, and established the federal courts' jurisdiction over these cases. Then, at a time when many companies still wouldn't submit disputes to arbitration or accept arbitration decisions (appealing them in court) the Steelworkers fought to establish arbitrators' sovereignty. The union yoked together three such cases, took them to the Supreme Court, and won. The so-called Steelworkers Trilogy decision held that arbitrators, not judges, had authority over labor-management disputes. The justices gave courts only narrow grounds for overruling arbitrators. And so arbitration was the law of the land and standard operating procedure in any number of industries.

But not in baseball. The commissioner remained the absolute authority—in disputes between leagues, between teams, and between players and teams. It mattered not that he reigned at the pleasure of the Lords and thus was less than neutral. The commissioner was still thought to be above the fray. He wouldn't even condescend to be in the same room when labor matters were discussed.

Thus it was that Commissioner Spike Eckert was absent when

John Gaherin presented to a roomful of skeptical Lords a brief-ing on the Basic Agreement talks. The "bucks issues," as he called them, were playing out fine. Some concessions that wouldn't sink the ship were being tossed the players' way: a small raise on "Murphy money," ditto the meal money. Yes, they would raise the minimum salary from $7,000 to $10,000.

Then he moved on to the "principle issues." Miller wanted changes in the reserve system. Fat chance, but he could be staved off with the creation of a committee to study the issue. Nothing in the world gathered dust like the report of a "blue rib-bon" panel.

The arbitration issue was another matter. "The union regards the commissioner as an extension of the multiemployer bar-gaining unit [the Lords] and a servant of that group," Gaherin said. They could deny it all they wanted, but that could be a problem. "There will come a time when there comes an issue that's so compelling for the players' side that the commissioner will be in a bad spot. If he sides with the clubs, it may look pat-ently unfair. If he sides with the players, he may be giving away the store."

There was room for compromise, Gaherin suggested. Sure, the commissioner should reserve the right to step in on big is-sues. But plenty of industries had learned to live with arbitration, and baseball could too. "My recommendation," he said, "is that we give them an arbitrator to handle the routine grievances."

A chorus of objections sang out. The Mets' M. Donald Grant scrambled to get the floor first. "Sure, other industries have had arbitrators," he said. "But baseball is different from other indus-tries."

"I've worked in the railroad business," Gaherin responded. "I've worked in the inland marine business. I've worked in the newspaper industry. And in each I've heard erudite presentations on how they're different. But since 1932 there hasn't been a la-bor union in this country who would go for a nonindependent arbitrator."

But that didn't slow the objections. Bob Carpenter of the Phillies invoked Judge Landis. He'd roll over in his grave, he said, if they rolled over for the union on this issue.

Gussie Busch of the Cardinals simply raged. "No," he said. "No, no, no. Did you hear me say no?"

"Sooner or later we'll have to do this, and we have to start in some form," Gaherin insisted. "You couldn't have the commis-sioner in this meeting to sully himself. Well, you can't have him in the middle of every grievance that comes along, either. You're dealing with a real union now, and they won't be shy about filing them."

But it was no use—the Lords were adamant. Baseball was a citadel, not a trade-union hall. Gaherin was given his instructions in no uncertain terms: table scraps, yes; independent arbitrator, no. After the meeting, Gaherin found himself exiting the conference room at the same time as Walter O'Malley. The Dodgers' owner took him by the elbow, guiding him out with the friendly but steel-gripped firmness of an Irish cop. "Tell that Jewish boy," he said, referring to Marvin Miller, "to go on back to Brooklyn."

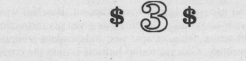

$ **3** $

WALTER O'MALLEY RAN baseball.

He was not born to it; he did not play it; and he was not devoted to it in any love-of-the-game sense. But he was the shrewdest operator in the business. He played every angle, at a time when most of the peers just played with their teams as a hobby. He played his fellow Lords like Koufax threw the curve—so deftly that nobody knew what had happened till it was by them.

Some men are born rich; some men earn riches; some men have riches thrust upon them. With Walter O'Malley it had been all three. He was born into comfort in 1903, the son of a New York dry-goods merchant turned Democratic politician. (O'Malley's father ultimately became the city's commissioner of public markets.) When O'Malley graduated first in his class at the University of Pennsylvania School of Engineering, his father gave him a cabin cruiser that slept eight. When he graduated from Fordham Law School, he became a corporate lawyer. The Great Depression, which ruined the father, helped make the son. Walter O'Malley astutely built up a practice in bankruptcy law.

One client was the Brooklyn Trust Company, an intriguing mélange of business and politics. Its president was George V. McLaughlin, a onetime New York police commissioner and a continuing power in the city. O'Malley would get steeped in the political arts there. He would also have plenty of work carrying out mortgage foreclosures on failing businesses.

And that's just what the thirties-era Brooklyn Dodgers were. They were the hapless "Daffiness Boys" on the field and deadbeats off. The club, owned primarily by heirs of Charles Ebbets, was $1.2 million in debt. Most of it was held by the Brooklyn Trust Company: a $500,000 mortgage on Ebbets Field plus $200,000 in operating loans. The bank didn't foreclose, but it did effectively control the franchise. McLaughlin put O'Malley in charge of its legal affairs.

The two had grown close. The ruddy-faced McLaughlin was a terror at the bank. He roared through the marble halls of Brooklyn Trust, where he was called, behind his back, George the Fifth. But O'Malley was a surrogate son and an eager protégé, studying at the knee and performing any service for the master. Not the least of them was getting McLaughlin safely home on the many nights he was in his cups.

But O'Malley was strictly a secondary figure at the Dodgers to the man McLaughlin hired in 1938 as its president. His name was Leland Stanford MacPhail, and he was fresh from resurrecting the Cincinnati Reds. In 1933, that club had finished last, having drawn a season attendance total of just 218,000. At year's dreary end, they hired Larry MacPhail as GM. This former minor league operator began improving the team immediately with astute trades and by installing baseball's first set of stadium lights.

MacPhail had the radical notion that this would make it easier for working people to attend games. Others considered it audacious. Clark Griffith of the Senators called night baseball "bush league stuff" and "just a step above dog racing." Said the Yankees' Ed Barrow: "It will never last once the novelty wears off."

But MacPhail convinced the one group he had to: the National League owners. It took him hours of talking at the 1934 winter meetings, but they agreed to give it a try. The next May, some 20,000 fans, a huge crowd for Cincinnati, watched the first night game. Before long, MacPhail was bringing in excursion trains from all over the Ohio River Valley to see baseball under the lights.

The Reds were revived, but the "Roaring Redhead," as MacPhail was known, was soon gone. He wore loud clothes and spoke in loud tones and drank altogether too much. And when he did, he often started brawling. One donnybrook with a Cincinnati cop landed all over the newspapers in late 1935.

"Boy, isn't that great publicity?" marveled MacPhail.

Owner Powell Crosley, a quiet, conservative industrialist, thought not. He fired him. MacPhail retreated to rural Michigan, where he ran a small bank with his father and brother.

Thus he was available when the Dodgers offered to make him their president in 1938. He accepted and proceeded to battle constantly with Brooklyn Trust over money. The first thing he did was put the Dodgers another $200,000 in hock to the bank by refurbishing crumbling Ebbets Field. The next thing he did was secure another $50,000 to buy first baseman Dolf Camilli. (For this he needed the personal dispensation of McLaughlin.)

MacPhail drove New York's other two teams into apoplexy. He installed lights at Ebbets, infuriating the day-ball partisans of the Yankees and Giants. He withdrew from a three-team compact that had kept games off the radio in New York. The other teams insisted it would hurt attendance. MacPhail showed it would only help. He hired away from Cincinnati an announcer named Red Barber, who brought the Dodgers alive with his lilting southern voice and attracted new fans to the ballpark.

Barber's hold was never more evident than on the day Brooklyn was playing a morning-afternoon doubleheader with the Cubs. The morning game was a makeup, and only a sparse crowd sprinkled Ebbets Field a half-hour before the ten o'clock start. Then Barber got going with his pregame show.

"It's a great day for a ball game," he said. "Come on out and we'll hold up the start until ten-fifteen." Suddenly, the streets leading to Ebbets were filled with people. The gate ultimately totaled 22,000.

(In addition to his radio exploits, MacPhail put the first big-league game on TV. It was broadcast in 1939, with one camera at ground level, another in the upper deck, and an awkward Red Barber doing between-innings commercials. Slicing a banana to put on a bowl of Wheaties, he declared, "That's a Breakfast of Champions.")

MacPhail was also quite capable of being a conventionally duplicitous baseball man. In 1938, Commissioner Landis declared more than a hundred Cardinals minor-leaguers free agents, as part of the long-running battle between the judge and Cardinals president Branch Rickey over his farm-system practices. Landis found that Rickey had been illegally shuffling players around between teams in which he had a hidden controlling interest.

Rickey couldn't abide losing one of those players, a young outfielder named Pete Reiser. He had personally scouted Reiser and thought he would become one of baseball's all-time greats. So he asked a favor of MacPhail, who owed him one. (He'd gotten MacPhail started in baseball at the Cards' Columbus, Ohio, farm club and subsequently recommended him for the Reds presidency.) MacPhail would sign Reiser, hide him in the minors for a couple of years, and then trade or sell him back to St. Louis. Agreed.

But Reiser lit up the Dodgers' spring training camp in 1940 with his brilliant play. In the course of three exhibition games, he reached base eleven straight times, with four home runs. Manager Leo Durocher bragged about his "find." The New York writers soon dubbed him "Pistol Pete." MacPhail had a fit. He fired off a telegram to Durocher: "DO NOT PLAY REISER AGAIN."

But Durocher kept playing Reiser anyway. So MacPhail flew to Florida to have it out. He met the manager in a hotel room, where he called him every name in the book and declared, "You're fired! You're through! Out of the organization! Pack your bags and get out!"

With one punch Durocher sent MacPhail flying over a bed. MacPhail thereupon rose, went over to Durocher, hugged him, and burst into tears. They walked out the door and off to the ballpark together. MacPhail ultimately convinced his manager that the kid needed more minor league seasoning, but Rickey never did get him back in St. Louis. Reiser was too good and had gone too high-profile for the scam to work.

The incident was vintage MacPhail. He was a walking keg of TNT. Throw him together with the fiery Durocher and you had explosions that regularly shook the franchise. MacPhail fired and rehired Durocher several times a season, often in the midst of a bender. There was a saying about MacPhail: "With no drinks he was brilliant, with one he was a genius, with two he was insane." He rarely stopped at one.

Yet by feverishly wheeling and dealing and spending Brooklyn Trust's money, he steadily improved the Dodgers. From seventh place in 1938, they rose to pennant-winners by 1941. The team totaled over a million in attendance for four straight years.

Still, MacPhail was living on borrowed time with the club's bank creditors. They cringed at his style, waiting for a slip, which ultimately he made. It came late in the 1942 season. The Dodgers were in first place but fading. MacPhail wanted to buy one Bobo Newsom for $25,000. Newsom was a world-class flake who not only referred to himself in the third person (announcing his arrival, for instance, by declaring, "Have no fear, ol' Bobo's here!") but called everyone else Bobo too. He was, however, a rubber-armed pitcher and a seasoned veteran. George McLaughlin forbade the deal, but MacPhail did it anyway. McLaughlin went bonkers: Newsom went only 2–2, and the Dodgers blew the pennant.

With the outbreak of World War II, MacPhail talked much about going back into the service. He was fifty-two years old but a fervent patriot and adventurer who'd taken part in a plot to kidnap Kaiser Wilhelm during World War I. (They made it into the Kaiser's lair but came away with only his ashtray.) George McLaughlin encouraged MacPhail's noble sentiments, but without promising to keep his job open. At the end of the 1942 season, MacPhail resigned as the Brooklyn Dodgers' president to become a colonel in the U.S. Army.

The players were sorry to see him go. He'd made them winners, made life interesting; he'd even walked, fully clothed, into the shower to console catcher Mickey Owen, after he'd blown the '41 Series with a passed ball. Dolf Camilli gave MacPhail a watch, on behalf of the gathered players, who wished him good luck "over there."

The writers were sorry to see him go too. He had installed baseball's first "press lounge" and started the tradition of free booze for scribes. "It is true I spent a lot of money around here," MacPhail told them at his final press conference. "I have spent about a million for ballplayers, and this year alone I spent $250,000 on repairs to the ballpark. But I leave the Brooklyn club with $300,000 in the bank, and in a position to pay off the mortgage."

MacPhail recited his accomplishments at some length before concluding, "I've talked enough. Let's have another drink."

He *had* put the Dodgers on firmer financial ground, making it the perfect time for Brooklyn Trust to attract new ownership. George McLaughlin soon engineered the sale of 75 percent of the Dodgers' stock to a triumvirate of partners. The moneyed one was John L. Smith, president of Pfizer Chemical Company, which made penicillin, and astonishing profits. The baseball man was Branch Rickey, the living legend who was hired away from St. Louis to become team president. The third was a lawyer, Walter O'Malley.

Nobody could fathom the role of this man, who said absolutely nothing at the introductory press conference. The best guess was that he was McLaughlin's inside man. Brooklyn Trust had loaned most of the $1,046,000 purchase price and wanted to be kept apprised. O'Malley was definitely McLaughlin's beneficiary. He paid only $82,000 out of pocket for his 25 percent stake in the Dodgers. The rest was to be funded by the club's future profits. There would be plenty of those.

From the start, Walter O'Malley and Branch Rickey didn't get along. They had a few things in common: silver tongues, constant cigars, ample girths, and love of money. They were also both brilliant originals, and therein lay most of the problem. Only one could be in charge, and the two had vastly different views and styles.

Rickey was a living, walking baseball legend: master judge of talent, master screwer of players, and an innovator of renown. By the time he arrived in Brooklyn, he had already pioneered the farm system, the use of scouts, and the modern spring training camp. He was referred to reverently as *Mister* Rickey. He had seeded baseball with his many protégés, each of whom proudly called himself a "Rickey man."

Rickey was sixty-two years old when he arrived in Brooklyn, but he wasn't ready to slow down or stop adding new wrinkles to the game. With the Dodgers, for instance, he went right to work *redefining* spring training. He set up the first system-wide camp, where every minor and major league player could be gathered together, centrally evaluated and uniformly instructed. He bought a former naval air base in Vero Beach, Florida, for this purpose and personally supervised the complex. Each day began with an 8:30 A.M. lecture to 500 players on the world according to Branch Rickey. In black suit and bow tie, with bushy eyebrows bobbing, he addressed such topics as "The Cure Is Sweat" and "Leisure Time Is the Anathema of Youth."

Then he would wander the grounds, watching players practice on the multiple diamonds of Dodgertown, and work at the very training devices he'd invented—pitching machines, sliding pits, even a hanging rectangle of string that gave pitchers a strike-zone target. The man had endless energy, and aides knew better than to let him take a break. They shook their heads knowingly. Give Mr. Rickey a fifteen-minute rest and he'd go all night.

The story was told in his Cardinals days of the time he spent all day watching 400 minor-leaguers work out in spring training. Then he spent all evening and on into the wee hours evaluating them with his scouts and managers. Finally, at 2:00 A.M., they were finished.

"It's been a great day, a fantastic day," Rickey said. "You've given me great insights on the players and I want to thank you. Now, does anybody have any questions?"

One of the managers, a man named Willie Duke, spoke up. "I've been reading about Russia," he said. "Can you tell us about communism?" So Rickey talked for an hour about the evils of communism.

Branch Rickey had that kind of godlike authority in baseball.

He also had a capacity for moralizing that was striking into a world with few choirboys.

He wouldn't attend Sunday games, though he would call in for attendance figures. He wouldn't swear, beyond frequent cries of "Judas Priest!" He wouldn't countenance beer advertising, which had led to a falling out with Cardinals owner Sam Breadon. He even had a choice moral dictum framed on his wall: "He that will not reason is a bigot. He that cannot reason is a fool. He that dares not reason is a slave." Rickey would soon put his convictions about bigotry into action, integrating the majors when he called up Jackie Robinson to be a Brooklyn Dodger.

Rickey spoke so fluently in parables and with such thundering moral conviction that it won him a nickname from New York baseball writers: "The Mahatma." (One of them had read John Gunther's description of Mahatma Gandhi: "a combination of God, your father and Tammany Hall." He thought that fit Rickey pretty well.)

Of course, the writers had another nickname for Rickey too: "El Cheapo." It was easier to get a camel through the eye of a needle than a raise out of Branch Rickey. Bill Veeck swore that Rickey had a gimmick in St. Louis—a special foot pedal under his desk. By stepping on it, he would activate a bell that sounded like a telephone's ring. Some player would come in hell-bent on a raise; the Mahatma's foot would pump; and the bell would ring.

Then Rickey would pretend to talk with one of his triple-A GMs who was all worked up over a hot new prospect. The prospect invariably played the same position as the player standing before him. Rickey would argue that the phenom needed another year's seasoning. He'd just barely talk the farm man out of promoting him. Then Rickey would hang up and start talking in apocalyptic terms about the Cardinals' financial plight. Between that and the player's pathetic gratitude at having a job—at least for another year—the raise request was abandoned.

The foot pedal may have been apocryphal, but Rickey's results weren't. Outfielder Gene Hermanski once sought a big raise after a big season for the Dodgers, and when he came out of Rickey's office, he was asked whether he got it. "No," he said, "but at least I didn't take a pay cut."

Rickey was a legendary cheapskate in other ways as well. When he ate at Schultz's, the restaurant below the Dodgers' office, he left the same tip every time: a nickel. When he went out for a haircut, he brought along a front-office aide, purportedly so they could keep working. When the barber was through, Rickey would open his little leather purse. "Oh, all I've got is a fifty-dollar bill," he said to the aide. "Can you pick this up?"

"He had the same fifty-dollar bill for thirty years," chuckled Buzzie Bavasi, a frequent victim.

As fervently as Rickey kept money from going out, that's how he gathered it in. In St. Louis, his contract called for him to keep 10 percent of the proceeds on player sales. With a base salary of $50,000 in the early forties, he cleared more than $80,000 a year. It was an enormous sum at a time when the average player made only $5,000. Rickey insisted on the same deal with Brooklyn, where his base salary was $65,000. He also got a bonus if attendance exceeded 600,000 in a season.

Rickey didn't care to see himself as a profiteer, of course. He preferred to see himself as an agent of Darwinism. Smoking his Antonio y Cleopatra cigar, crooking a hand to imitate a steam shovel, he would dip it down and explain: "If you scoop up enough talent, you can develop quality out of quantity." Or: "If you dig up enough rocks, a small percentage of them will become gems."

Rickey had inherited a decent farm system from MacPhail. Now he would quadruple the scouting budget to create even more quantity. And he would put his son, Branch Jr.—known as "Twig"—in charge of cultivating the minor league talent. The best of it would come up to the Dodgers. The excess talent would be sold for cash, although "talent" was sometimes an overstatement. The Mahatma was unmatched at putting a sheen on mediocre players and selling them as gems. If it came to talking trade, Bill Veeck, a pretty good talker himself, wouldn't even get in the same room with Rickey. He insisted on passing offers and counteroffers back and forth by note. Phillies owner Bob Carpenter marveled, "With that voice of his, and the way he used the language, he could absolutely *hypnotize* people."

Rickey once spent two hours with Carpenter, analyzing his team, position by position. He told him the Phillies were like the painting of a beautiful woman in which her beauty didn't really show because one of her eyes was sightly cocked. Just retouch that face a little, Rickey purred, and her true beauty will shine through. He said that touch was a slugging first baseman, and he happened to have one.

His name was Howie Schultz, called "Steeple" because of his six-foot-six height. Rickey, the consummate scout, observed that

Carpenter had a weakness for slow, strapping lunks—the hapless
Phillies were loaded with them. Anybody else could see that
Carpenter was overmatched by Rickey. The sixty-five-year-old
baseball demigod had won nine pennants and six world championships. The thirty-two-year-old Du Pont heir had won the Delaware State Badminton championship. He bought Steeple
Schultz for $75,000.

Steeple Schultz sparked the Phillies to a last-place finish in
1947, hitting .223 with six homers. The next year, he was traded
to the Reds, and at season's end he was released and out of
baseball.

John Galbreath, another new owner, was Rickey's favorite
mark. He sold the Pirates more than $2 million worth of mar-
ginal players in the 1940s. In one deal alone he shipped five
Brooklyn forgettables to Pittsburgh for $300,000 plus outfielder
Al Gionfriddo. Why the throw-in? "Rickey needed him,"
cracked one wag, "to carry all that gold back to the Dodgers."

The Dodgers prospered but O'Malley stewed. Rickey, that
psalm-singing phoney, was taking a huge salary. (O'Malley
maintained that Rickey had signed Jackie Robinson not so much
to integrate baseball as to pack Ebbets Field, thus enabling himself to collect his attendance bonus.) Rickey was a spendthrift.
(O'Malley blistered him for the heavy investment in Vero
Beach. This was before he came to understand the value of Florida real estate.) O'Malley also hated his wasting money on the
Beechcraft plane he used to hop cross-country on scouting expe-
ditions.

Rickey was also too good to the players, according to
O'Malley. This fault came as news to the players, though they
did have a certain affection for Rickey. They could even find
some humor in their yearly pay shaftings. The players had an
annual talent show at Vero Beach. Chuck Connors, a minor-
leaguer who would go on to become a TV actor, once did a hilarious impression of Rickey, concluding with this observation:
"There are two things Mr. Rickey loves. One is players, and the
other is money. But for some reason, he never lets them get together."

Rickey and O'Malley also clashed over the emerging medium
of TV. The Dodgers were in the first televised World Series in
1947, and this was clearly just the beginning. Rickey hated TV.
He thought televised games would keep people away from ballparks. He feared that as games were beamed into America's
backwaters, minor league baseball would suffer. Rickey had

ruthlessly exploited the minors, but he loved them, too, as baseball's training grounds and grass roots.

O'Malley, conversely, embraced TV. He saw baseball as metropolitan entertainment, not small-town sport. He saw TV as one more outlet for baseball to entertain and make money. (Before the final Dodgers–Giants playoff game of 1951, O'Malley spent all night dickering with the networks for TV rights. Bobby Thomson won the game for the Giants with his dramatic home run, "The Shot Heard 'Round the World," while O'Malley pocketed enormous fees for the first TV game seen 'round the country.)

The fight was, in essence, a conflict between baseball's past and its future. "To Rickey, baseball remained a civil religion which acted out public functions organized religion was unable to perform," wrote his biographer, Murray Polner. "O'Malley's faith rested on balance sheets and dividends."

Perhaps most of all, Rickey's country-parson style clashed with O'Malley's wheeler-dealer ways. Rickey worked all day at the Dodgers' offices on 215 Montague Street in Brooklyn Heights. His rival could often be found two blocks away at the Bossert Hotel, where he had converted room 40 into an invitation-only dining and drinking club. There, Walter O'Malley—raconteur, man-about-town, dispenser of box seats—swapped lies, did deals, and made barbed remarks about Rickey. The regulars included George McLaughlin, the politician and banker; Judge Henry Ughetta, another pol; Harry Hickey, an insurance man; and assorted other movers and shakers. Each spring, O'Malley would herd his gang onto a private railroad car for Vero Beach. "He understood what he had with the allure of baseball and he leveraged it," says Tom Villante, later to be the Dodgers' TV producer.

There was one other crucial difference between the two men. Rickey had only a five-year contract and no "in" with the Brooklyn Trust Company. He was more vulnerable to ouster. His contract was extended twice, each time by one year, but in 1950 O'Malley succeeded in squeezing him out. Each of the men owned 25 percent of the club, but in their bitter power struggle O'Malley was aided at precisely the right moment by the death, in July 1950, of John Smith, the Pfizer magnate who also held 25 percent of the Dodgers' stock. The Brooklyn Trust became coexecutor of Smith's estate, and guess which way the Smith block tilted? Rickey was out.

Not out of work, however, since his great trading partner, John

Galbreath, had asked him to be president of the Pirates. But to take that job, he'd have to sell his Dodgers stock. O'Malley offered him $346,667—exactly what he'd paid for it in 1943. Then he settled back comfortably to watch Rickey squirm.

Rickey was in a financial jam. He'd taken a big loss on some other stock he held and had borrowed to the limit on his life insurance. He needed the Pirates job, but to accept it meant selling his Dodgers stock at a rock-bottom price. Though the club's financial position and prospects were stronger than ever, he saw no chance of selling elsewhere. After all, who would want to be O'Malley's minority partner? A buyer, wrote one newspaperman, would have "about as much authority in the ball club as the head usher of Ebbets Field."

Suddenly, however, William Zeckendorf appeared. He was a New York real estate mogul and a friend of John Galbreath. He offered Rickey $1 million. A clause in Rickey's partnership agreement with O'Malley came into play. If either chose to sell his shares and had a genuine offer before him, the other had the option of buying the stock at the price offered.

O'Malley, with clenched jaw, paid the $1 million and, from that day forward, there was a rule in the Dodger front office: anyone who mentioned Branch Rickey's name was fined a dollar.

The Dodgers of the early fifties were America's team as well as Brooklyn's. The Yankees were baseball's dominant team, but, as noted sports columnist Red Smith once put it, "Rooting for the Yankees is like rooting for U.S. Steel."

The Brooklyn ball club took the national stage each October, in an elaborately staged morality play costarring the Yankees. They couldn't quite beat their Bronx rivals, except in 1955, yet they couldn't help but be more appealing. The Dodgers were magnificent but flawed, athletic but appealing, close but no cigar. Jackie Robinson, Gil Hodges, Roy Campanella, Pee Wee Reese, Don Newcombe, Duke Snider: even before they were immortalized in literature as "The Boys of Summer," they were emblazoned in America's consciousness.

In Brooklyn they were worshiped. A Giants fan arguing the merits of Mays versus Snider in Brooklyn was taking his life in his hands. A woman named Hilda Chester led cheers with a cowbell. A ragtag band called "The Sym-phoney" provided the music, along with a highly partisan organist named Gladys Gooding. (She was once ejected from a game for playing "Three

Blind Mice" after an umpire's disputed call.) The partisans regularly filled cozy Ebbets Field.

Long before Walter O'Malley would ever break their hearts, he would show himself as a hard-hearted businessman. In 1953, he decided to fire Red Barber, the announcer who had done so much to build the team's popularity. O'Malley had two problems with Barber. One, he was an open friend and admirer of Branch Rickey. Two, he made the huge sum of $50,000 a year. A talented young fellow named Vin Scully, who'd been the number-three man on the broadcast crew, and who made a modest $7,500, was elevated to replace Barber.

O'Malley explained it to some aides this way: Imagine a length of pipe that was full of peas, he said. If you squeeze another pea in at one end, a pea is forced out the other. He held the imaginary pipe up. "You put in Vin Scully at $7,500 here, and out there, at the other end, drops Barber at $50,000," he said. "That, gentlemen, is how you make money!"

The same year, Chuck Dressen managed the Dodgers to their second consecutive pennant. Soon after the 1953 season, his wife, Ruth, took it upon herself to write to O'Malley demanding a three-year contract for her husband.

O'Malley summoned Dressen to his office. He had two problems with the manager. One, he was another Rickey man. Two, he had been offended by Mrs. D.'s letter. Dodger employees actually had secure jobs, by baseball standards, but O'Malley didn't want to leave any doubt at whose pleasure they served.

"Is what Ruth says what you feel you've got to have?" asked O'Malley.

"Yeah," said Dressen.

"Then I think we should call a press conference for tomorrow morning. The policy here, as you know, Charlie, is one-year contracts. At the press conference we can announce together that you're leaving."

"Me and my wife got to have security," said Dressen.

"Of course," said O'Malley. "I wouldn't try to hold you."

O'Malley called a press conference the next day to announce they hadn't been able to come to terms. Dressen was moving on.

"I appreciate Charlie's views," he told the writers. "Many of his colleagues are getting long-term contracts. However, the Brooklyn club has paid more men not to manage than any other club. The one-year contract is our policy here, and if it weren't, I'd *make* it our policy."

The Dodgers thereupon hired Walter Alston, who, under a

succession of one-year contracts, served as manager for twenty-three years. Quiet and pliable, he never expressed any doubt about who was boss.

O'Malley was also moving fast toward "boss" status in another respect. For seven years he'd taken a back seat to Rickey at ownership meetings. But he was, at the same time, becoming influential in the business, partly because he was the rare owner who worked full-time at the business. "His colleagues were hobbyists; he was the CEO of the ball club," says Peter O'Malley, his son and successor. "People like the Carpenters and the Galbreaths recognized he had studied and researched the issues."

O'Malley studied and researched his fellow owners just as closely. He knew their net worths, their politics, their peccadillos. "Walter," Phil Wrigley once said at an ownership meeting, "what do I think?"

It is sometimes said there are only two emotions in business: greed and fear. By knowing each owner's hot-buttons, by using all the ward-politics savvy he'd picked up from the Bossert Hotel crowd, O'Malley knew how to play them. Irving Rudd, a Dodgers PR man, looked on in awe one day as O'Malley stroked Braves owner Lou Perini by phone. "Looouuuuuu, that's why you're so brave and brilliant," O'Malley cooed, reassuring him on the wisdom of moving from Boston to Milwaukee. "That is why you're a pioneer."

O'Malley quickly and skillfully accumulated friends and allies among his fellow owners. It was through them that he floated his ideas and accomplished his objectives. (The Carpenters and Galbreaths were often O'Malley's front men.) If a motion he instigated via someone else looked certain to pass, he might well vote against it. It gave him splendid deniability and fed his love for using indirect channels.

John Gaherin later would call him The Crocodile. O'Malley might sit in virtual silence for a whole meeting, just twirling his cigar holder, as discussion rambled on. Then, when someone finally advanced a position that approximated his own, he would snap at it like raw meat: "So moved."

O'Malley also drew people to him and dominated gatherings with humor. He had a vast repertoire of tales and bon mots, punctuated by a Cheshire cat grin. Informed at one meeting that his fly was down, O'Malley waved a hand dismissively. "This concerns me not," he said, "for a dead bird falleth not from the nest." (He'd copped the line from Winston Churchill, but was in no danger of being found out in this crowd.)

O'Malley's wit could also be acidly dead-on. When baseball's winter meetings were in New Orleans one year, the owners took a side excursion to Lake Pontchartrain. As a busload of them rode across the seemingly endless causeway that spanned the lake, O'Malley posed a question: "Did it ever occur to anybody how much better off baseball would be if we went off the road and right into the water?"

O'Malley only turned dour upon exposure to two things: American Leaguers, whom he thought an inferior breed, and any new owner impertinent enough to speak out. He called them "kooks." When baseball was expanding and creating divisions in the late sixties, the Mets' M. Donald Grant once prattled on about how it should work: divisional makeup, interleague play, and so forth. O'Malley regarded Grant as a mere arriviste from the last expansion and finally interrupted him.

"Why don't we settle it this way?" he said. "Let's put all the kooks in their own league."

Walter O'Malley was a man of influence in baseball for one other reason also. He was a winner. The Dodgers won the National League pennant four out of five times in the years 1952 through 1956. The responsible parties were the players signed by Branch Rickey, but it was O'Malley who hosted each Series and led the league in profits. Such a man was to be noticed and heeded.

The economics of the day were still pretty uncomplicated. The Dodgers had an average annual attendance of 1.2 million. With an average ticket price of two dollars, that worked out to a gross of $2.4 million. Add another $50,000 for radio rights. The team payroll in the early fifties was $550,000. (Duke Snider, at $40,000, was the top-paid player. Roy Campanella and Jackie Robinson each got about $36,000.) Even with farm-system, scouting, and other costs, that left a tidy little profit.

The key word here, however, is *little*. They played in tiny, decaying Ebbets Field, capacity 32,000. And, like much of the rest of middle-class urban America, their most loyal fans were moving in droves to the suburbs. The borough was turning poorer, browner, and blacker.

One day, O'Malley called Buzzie Bavasi into his office and pointed out the window. "Look down there," he said. "What do you see?"

Bavasi peered out at the welfare office across the street.

"I see a long, long line of poor Puerto Rican people getting their welfare checks," he replied.

Enough said, as far as Walter O'Malley was concerned. The changing face of Brooklyn made it harder and riskier for people to attend their games. There were only a few hundred parking spaces adjacent to the stadium. Otherwise, fans were on their own in the newly mean streets of Flatbush. Attendance had peaked at 1.8 million in 1948; all through the fifties it bounced between 1 million and 1.2 million.

O'Malley used TV aggressively to augment his gross. By the mid-fifties the Dodgers were broadcasting over a hundred games a year, yielding nearly $800,000 annually. The Dodgers pioneered televising road games, which was a novelty then due to the high cost of leasing long-distance phone lines. Dodgers TV producer Tom Villante had gotten an idea: get all the teams together, lease the lines on a pooled basis, then prorate the costs according to the number of games broadcast per team. Pooling made it economical to broadcast from afar, and nobody did it more than the Dodgers. "Walter believed road games were the best promotional tool you could have," Villante recalled. "It built up the interest for the next home stand."

O'Malley was also intrigued by pay TV. He'd met a fellow named Matty Fox, who was trying to make that embryonic technology a commercial reality. He and O'Malley hatched a plan: Fox's company, called Skiatron, would put Dodgers games on pay TV at a cost of one dollar a game for viewers. Skiatron would get two thirds of the gross, the Dodgers one third, and in this way the huge base of fans who couldn't squeeze into Ebbets Field would be harvested.

Of course, it never happened. The Dodgers were contractually committed to "free" TV through 1959, and the plentitude of televised baseball in the New York area worked against pay TV. (The Giants and Yankees each televised half their games.) The nascent medium also presented a variety of technical problems. But O'Malley shrewdly saw TV's possibilities at a time when most fellow owners wished it would disappear.

O'Malley, meanwhile, grew restive. He looked on in awe and envy at the Braves. They had a new 43,000-seat stadium, a sweetheart lease, and parking for 10,000 cars. Sad sacks in Boston in 1952 (attendance 281,000), they were monsters in Milwaukee. The Braves drew 1.8 million in 1953 and broke 2 million the next four years, the first National League team to reach that level.

A 2-million gate translated to financial muscle. O'Malley saw Milwaukee signing the top prospects, fielding the most farm teams, assembling a juggernaut. By 1956, the Braves had indeed come within a game of beating the Dodgers for the pennant. "If they take in twice as many dollars, they'll eventually be able to buy better talent," he groused. "Then they'll be the winners, not us."

O'Malley was, in a sense, crying all the way to the bank. The Dodgers were the most profitable club in the National League in the fifties. Their 1956 net profit was $487,000, compared to the Braves' $362,000. The truth was, however, that they had to make the Series to vault from marginally profitable to solidly so. They couldn't stay at that pinnacle forever. The Boys of Summer were graying. And O'Malley knew that his club's history was rife with boom-and-bust cycles. "The history of the Brooklyn club," he once said, "is that fiscally you're either first or bankrupt. There is no second place."

It was the summer of 1955. The Dodgers were on their way to a fourth pennant in five years. They would finally beat the hated Yankees in the Series, sending half of Brooklyn dancing in the streets. In the midst of all that, Walter O'Malley was setting events in motion that would take their beloved Bums away.

O'Malley said he needed a new stadium if he was going to make it work in Brooklyn and he had just the site. It was at the intersection of Atlantic and Flatbush Avenues, where the Long Island Railroad ended and two subway lines met. He made clear he wouldn't dream of involving the taxpayers in financing a municipal stadium. O'Malley was too shrewd for that. He wanted to finance and build it privately so he could privately reap the rewards. He had grand visions—of a domed stadium, before there ever was such a thing.

But he did need the government for one crucial element: the land. In August of 1955, O'Malley asked that the land be seized by right of eminent domain and turned over to him for the stadium. The request went to Robert Moses, New York's all-powerful czar of parks, highways, and urban renewal. Moses turned him down flat.

O'Malley immediately made an announcement: the Dodgers would play seven games in 1956 in a stadium in Jersey City, New Jersey. The Dodgers' owner was sending a message: he was feeling a little footloose. The city yawned. It had three base-ball teams. Mayor Robert Wagner did create a Brooklyn Sports Center Authority to study the stadium issue, but it accomplished nothing. O'Malley sold Ebbets Field to a developer and leased it back, but only for a three-year term. If that move was sup-posed to create a sense of urgency, it, too, yielded nothing.

Three thousand miles west was another big city, a big city with not even one major league ball club. As early as 1939, met-ropolitan Los Angeles was bigger than thirteen of the sixteen major league cities. By the mid-1950s, the city was en route to becoming the nation's number-two metropolis, gobbling up ev-ery orange grove in its path. And now L.A. was gone a-courtin'. That's how Kenneth Hahn, the Los Angeles county supervisor, happened to be attending the 1956 World Series. He was angling for Washington, which was, as the saying went, first in war, first in peace, and last in the American League. That went for attend-ance, too. Hahn assumed he would have to go bottom-fishing to attract a team.

He met with owner Calvin Griffith at Toots Shor's and ex-tolled the city's virtues: populous, sports-starved, and prepared to build a new stadium.

"Los Angeles Senators," mused Griffith. "Sounds pretty good to me."

They agreed he'd come out soon after the Series to meet with other local officials. He didn't like to fly, he said, so it would take a bit. But he'd be out there by train before October was out.

A buoyant Hahn was sitting in his Ebbets Field box, reflect-ing on the fine meeting, when an envelope was delivered to him. He opened it and saw the note was from Walter O'Malley. It consisted of three words: "Don't sign anything."

Walter O'Malley had spent his whole baseball life scrambling for baseball market-share in a three-team city. He knew lush, virgin territory when he saw it. He saw pay TV working in Los Angeles where it wouldn't in New York. Matty Fox was busily setting up Skiatron statewide. Most of all, he was unimpeded by rank sentiment. O'Malley operated like the old Tammany Hall pols, from whom he was spiritually descended. As one of them once said, in defending a colleague's greased-palm practices, "He seen his opportunities, and he took 'em."

While Calvin Griffith was packing to rumble across country by train, Walter O'Malley was jetting west to snatch Los An-geles. The Dodgers had reverted to form in the Series and lost to the Yankees. Afterward, they were to play a series of exhibition games in Japan. During a Columbus Day stopover in Los Angeles, O'Malley had his first meeting with Hahn. He quickly established that a big sales pitch would not be required.

"I'm coming," he said. "But I will deny it to the press, because I've got another season to play at Ebbets Field. You don't know the Brooklyn fans. They'll murder me, actually murder me if they know I'm coming."

"You've got to remember I'm a politician," said Hahn. "If I tell them and you deny it, they'll murder *me.*"

"Do you want me alive or dead?" O'Malley asked.

Hahn agreed to play it his way. O'Malley, for his part, dissembled beautifully to the Los Angeles press corps. He recited a whole list of reasons why the Dodgers wouldn't move there, including the biggest whopper of all: "Substantial progress is being made toward a new stadium in Brooklyn."

New York politicians were, in fact, working busily, at cross-purposes with each other. Robert Moses advanced his own proposal: a stadium at the 1939 World's Fair site in Flushing Meadows. Abe Stark, the New York City Council president, proposed both a new stadium for Brooklyn and an expanded Ebbets Field. The city's Board of Estimate kept the Atlantic-and-Flatbush site alive by including it in a redevelopment study.

O'Malley was unimpressed. In early 1957, he tightened the screws with an announcement: "Unless something is done within six months, I will have to make other arrangements."

Finally the alarm bells rang. Already the voices of moral outrage were being raised. Walter O'Malley simply didn't hear them. It was, as Don Corleone would say, just business. O'Malley was a son of the city and the protégé of one of its most powerful men. But he wouldn't even tell the Brooklyn Trust's president, George McLaughlin, what he was up to.

"It's great to have loyal friendships from the past," he explained to PR man Irving Rudd, "but sometimes you have to cut the cord to seek new horizons, and you can't be tied down by the past."

Walter O'Malley didn't need George McLaughlin anymore, but he did need his fellow owners. To make this radical move west, he'd need to win their approval. To even get into Los Angeles, he'd need to move one of the other owners out. Every professional baseball team enjoys exclusive territorial rights, and L.A. belonged to Phil Wrigley.

Wrigley was an odd duck, equal parts progressive and paleolithic. In the 1930s, he and Larry MacPhail pushed in vain to liberalize the reserve clause. He was one of the first owners to advertise, and in the off-season, yet: "Look ahead to sunshine . . . recreation . . . happy hours with the Cubs at Wrigley Field next summer." Wrigley was merely applying the principles of chewing-gum marketing and whetting fans' appetites to build advance sales.

Yet he stubbornly refused to install lights, sharing Judge Landis's prejudice against night ball. (He was preparing to illuminate Wrigley Field in the early 1940s, actually, but the Army desperately needed steel and he donated the towers. When the war was over, he decided to indulge his original prejudice.) Wrigley had also absorbed Judge Landis's lectures on the evils of the farm system and compliantly refused to develop one for the Cubs. Thus did he condemn them to decades of futility.

Wrigley did own a triple-A team in Los Angeles, however, due to its proximity to his real Southern California interest, a seventy-six-square-mile kingdom called Catalina Island. Whenever he journeyed there from Chicago, he stopped off to inspect his team, the Angels, and their ballpark, a second Wrigley Field. It all made for a splendid tax writeoff.

His father, William Wrigley, Jr., had bought the island in 1919 for $1 million and poured $7 million more into making it a luxury resort: one grand hotel, 1,000 cottages, and a twelve-story casino that included a 1,200-seat movie theater and a ballroom big enough for 3,000 couples. Oh yes, there was also a ballpark, where the Cubs trained until the early fifties.

Located just a ferry ride away from Los Angeles, Catalina was coveted by the city as a recreation spot. Rather than a playground for the rich, many thought, it should be available to the masses. In 1956, the L.A. County Board of Supervisors urged the state to buy the island for a park.

Phil Wrigley was furious. "They'll have to condemn it," he said, "I'm not selling." Privately, he called Los Angeles a "bush town."

Walter O'Malley knew all this. He made it his business to know every other owner's affairs. He also, of course, had excellent sources at the Board of Supervisors. So at the New York Baseball Writers Association in February, he made his move.

O'Malley passed a note to Phil Wrigley, who was up on the dais. "We'll trade you Fort Worth for Los Angeles."

He was referring to his triple-A minor league club in Texas.

Wrigley sent a note back: "My son-in-law will see you in the morning."

The son-in-law, Cubs president Bill Haganah, cut the deal the next day.

Consider: the Dodgers had paid $75,000 for the Fort Worth club ten years earlier and put $500,000 into a new stadium. Now, O'Malley had parlayed that, even up, into the territorial rights to Los Angeles. It was slicker than a Reese-to-Robinson-to-Hodges double play. It was along the lines of the Dutch buying Manhattan for twenty-four dollars.

O'Malley next turned to Horace Stoneham. The Stoneham family had owned the New York Giants since 1919. It was the storied franchise of Christy Mathewson, Carl Hubbell, and Willie Mays that had known glory as recently as 1954. The Giants swept the Indians in that year's Series, which was highlighted by Mays's legendary play in deep center known simply as "the catch."

But the Giants' problems in the mid-fifties were far worse than the Dodgers'. The Polo Grounds was a crumbling stadium in a deteriorating part of Manhattan. Like the Dodgers, the Giants suffered from a lack of parking and a fear of urban crime (there was a housing project nearby). Unlike the Dodgers, however, the Giants didn't have a borough identification to help sustain attendance through lean years.

The Giants drew 1.16 million in their Series year of 1954, but plummeted to 824,000 and 629,000 during the next two years, when they finished third and sixth, respectively. What kept them narrowly in the black was their comparatively big broadcast receipts (about $700,000) from the nation's largest TV market. They had lost the football Giants as tenants. And Horace Stoneham was thinking of leaving too.

But he was no O'Malley—no original thinker, no master manipulator, no revolutionary. He was simply an old-school baseball operator who could put away prodigious amounts of Scotch and who tried to put away a few bucks. Stoneham was thinking of Minneapolis, where he already owned a farm team, and thus the territory. He saw a comfortable fit in the Milwaukee-Chicago geographical axis, and he saw a new municipal stadium going up.

Then Stoneham got a call from O'Malley one day.

"Are you going to move?" he asked.

"I think so," said Stoneham. "I think the league will give me permission."

"Why don't we both move to the Far West together?"

Stoneham was floored. He hadn't a clue O'Malley was considering leaving. But he was highly receptive to the idea of transplanting their rivalry. He also liked San Francisco—which was a good thing since the Dodgers had already grabbed the much better market. "It was just more romantic to move to the Coast," said Chub Feeney, the Giants' GM and Stoneham's nephew.

O'Malley clinched it by bringing along Matty Fox for a meeting with Stoneham. Fox talked about Skiatron's big plans in San Francisco, and Stoneham heard the sweet sounds of money. Ka-*ching*.

O'Malley, the master of indirection, was on his way. With Stoneham in his sidecar, getting approved for the move was a cinch. Everybody loved Stoneham: baseball-steeped, besotted Horace. And everybody knew he was genuinely distressed. The National League owners authorized the dual move in May 1957, as long as the two clubs confirmed their intentions by October 1.

O'Malley turned his attention to nailing down the particulars with Los Angeles. The crucial issue was the stadium and the county supervisor, Ken Hahn, was again point man. He borrowed a Sheriff's Department helicopter one day and circled the city with O'Malley, explaining the city's layout and pointing out potential sites.

In time, they came to a 300-acre tract several miles from downtown. As they hovered over it, O'Malley squinted down at five freeways converging nearby. He gazed at the empty land. Visions of traffic flow, cash flow, and vast parking lots tumbled through his mind.

"Can I have that?" he asked Hahn, who was wedged between him and the pilot.

"Sure," said Hahn, immediately offering to build an access road at government expense.

The area was called Chavez Ravine, named after its original owner, an early Angeleno named Julian Chavez. It had been designated for public housing in 1949, but political wrangling kept it from ever being constructed. The helicopter settled down, and O'Malley walked the grounds like Columbus wading ashore in the New World.

Still, it was one thing for Ken Hahn to promise the site, quite another to deliver it. Political opposition began to well up over the sweet deal O'Malley insisted upon: 300 acres at Chavez Ravine in exchange for Wrigley Field. In addition, the city would have to commit $2 million for grading the stadium area and the county $2.7 million for access roads.

The Giants cruised into San Francisco with little difficulty, announcing completion of the deal in August. "I feel sorry for the kids," said Stoneham of the bereft tykes in New York, "but I haven't seen many of their fathers recently."

The Dodgers went down to the wire—and beyond. On the evening of September 30, the Los Angeles City Council was still debating the issue. Every opponent was taking the opportunity to address the council, thus dragging the process out. A final vote wouldn't even be possible for another week. Nonetheless, on that deadline eve, pro-Dodgers Mayor Norris Poulson sent a telegram to National League President Warren Giles saying he "had mustered the necessary ten votes."

It was a lie. The issue was still very much in doubt and even Poulson admitted, in a follow-up with Giles, that the final vote would be delayed. But his assurances won the Dodgers a two-week extension with the Lords. By then, all the requisite arms had been twisted and Chavez Ravine was O'Malley's, mineral rights and all.

In Brooklyn, where people are street-smart, they knew it was all over before then. The Dodgers played for the last time at Ebbets on September 24, 1957, in what was more of a wake than a game. Afterward, many of the 6,700 mourners came over the railing onto their beloved field. They dug up clumps of grass and dirt, while Gladys Gooding played "May the Good Lord Bless and Keep You."

Walter O'Malley had broken every heart in Brooklyn; he had also broken the mold in baseball by radically changing the major league map. In the mid-1950s, all sixteen major league clubs were in the Northeast and Midwest, clustered so closely that teams still commonly traveled by train. O'Malley took baseball where the population was migrating. By the end of the 1960s, there were six West Coast teams.

He'd also redefined baseball as a business. The Dodgers weren't the first team to move, but they were the first team that wasn't in distress to do so. The Brooklyn Dodgers had a supremely loyal following and a lofty place as cultural icon. This, however, was supremely irrelevant to their owner. He was scolded in Congress, vilified in editorials, and hanged in effigy.

It all made no difference to Walter O'Malley. The grass was simply greener in California.

"It had always been recognized that baseball was a business, but if you enjoyed the game you could also tell yourself that it was also a sport," columnist Red Smith once wrote. "O'Malley was the first to say out loud that it was all business—a business that he owned and could operate as he chose."

O'Malley had dictated terrific terms, and Los Angeles promised to be a strong market. Yet it was still a huge gamble, the success of which wasn't immediately certain. The Chavez Ravine deal was challenged in a referendum. It barely passed and survived. But Skiatron was also challenged in a statewide referendum, instigated by movie-theater owners, and it lost, which meant that the pay-TV plan was kaput. The stadium could be built, but could O'Malley now afford it?

He wasn't a Galbreath or a Carpenter with riches from other businesses. This *was* his business, and he'd already generated as much cash from it as he could. He'd sold Ebbets Field for $3 million and his Montreal farm club for $1 million. But that still left $11 million to go to make the nut on the new stadium.

Buzzie Bavasi walked into O'Malley's office one day and found him sitting at his desk, head in hands. "I'm strapped," he said. His voice cracking, he told Bavasi he didn't know where the next installment for preliminary stadium work would come from.

It was only when Union Oil chairman Reese Taylor stepped forward that O'Malley stepped back from the precipice. For $11 million, Union Oil got the first ten years' broadcast rights and the only sign on the scoreboard. This put Walter O'Malley over the top.

When he moved from the makeshift confines of the L.A. Coliseum into the new Dodgers Stadium in 1962, he was a made man. While other teams were lucky to draw 1 million, the Dodgers were averaging 2.5 million in their first five years there. Beyond that were the benefits of owning the stadium. O'Malley had total control over functions like concessions. He made sure they translated into both pluses for the fans and profits for himself. The Dodgers had the best hot dogs, the coldest beer—and the fewest water fountains—of any team. The stadium had squeaky-clean stands, gleaming restrooms, ample parking, and beautifully landscaped grounds.

At a time when most clubs just opened the gates and counted

on a winning record to draw fans, O'Malley was far more sophisticated. He recognized he was competing for the entertainment dollar. He could see that Angelenos didn't eat, sleep, and
breathe baseball the way New Yorkers did. They had more
choices for their leisure time, jumping into cars to head for the
beaches, the malls, or, gulp, Disneyland. O'Malley first visited
the theme park soon after moving west, and he came home raving: "You just have to see that place—the presentation of it, the
restrooms, the food." Recalls son Peter, "He realized the standard had been set by Disneyland."

O'Malley tried to ape Disney with his stadium ambience and
he ran promotions the way Maury Wills ran the base paths—
constantly. There was the Straight-A program, which gave four
free tickets to top students; there was a steady stream of community nights; there were plenty of giveaways. The Dodgers had a
speakers bureau, staffed by former players, and a fan club,
which, for a five-dollar membership fee, brought all manner of
goodies.

O'Malley had a two-pronged approach to filling the stadium.
First, he drew station wagons full of families by keeping ticket
prices low (box seats stayed at $3.50 for eighteen straight years)
and starting games early. Dads could afford it; kids could stay
awake through it; and cash registers rang steadily at the concession stands as they filled up on Dodger Dogs. "We once figured
out," said Buzzie Bavasi, "that if we let everybody in for nothing we'd still make a profit."

The second prong was season tickets. That was $3 to $4 million the Dodgers got up front and invested. It was money they
took in whether the team won or stunk. Most clubs sold few season tickets. The Dodgers started out with a base of 12,500 and
built from there. Reds executive Dick Wagner once asked ticket
manager Walter Nash how he did it. "We kiss the ass of our season ticketholder," he was told.

Having lost out on pay TV, O'Malley put few Dodgers games
on "free" TV. He didn't particularly need it, with the popular
Vin Scully "creating the appetite" on radio and the Dodger Stadium turnstiles spinning merrily. The live crowds shed so much
cash that he had little incentive to risk losing them for incremen-
tal gains in TV revenue.

The Dodgers of the 1960s cleared annual profits of about $4
million. It was a huge sum for the time, although O'Malley, in
the best poor-mouthing tradition of baseball, would never admit

to it. Buzzie Bavasi and Walter Alston were in his office one day when the owner moaned about having lost $2 million.

Bavasi just smiled. After they left, Alston turned to him and said, "He says he's lost $2 million and you practically laugh. How can you do that?"

"Walt, what he meant was, he only made $4 million, not $6 million."

Yet despite his abundant self-interest, O'Malley necessarily also had a broader view of the industry good. A degree of parity was necessary, because nobody came out to see patsies play. O'Malley also knew, as a wily politician, that power accrued not to the hoarder of goodies but to their distributor. "It was like carving up a chicken," recalls Montreal Expos owner Charles Bronfman. "A breast to you, a drumstick to you. And maybe he'd save the best for himself, but everyone got something."

In the mid-sixties, for instance, clubs were shelling out huge bonuses to sign up the brightest prospects. At a time when major-leaguers averaged $19,000 a year, "bonus babies" were pocketing upward of $100,000 just for scribbling their names on a contract. The apogee came in 1964, when the Angels signed a collegiate star named Rick Reichardt for $205,000.

Finally, in the hope of ending the bonus madness, talk turned to following the lead of the NFL and NBA and having an annual player draft. The proponents were mostly the poorer franchises. The Dodgers' baseball men were firmly opposed. They had the most scouts and they benefited the most from wide-open signing opportunities.

"We argued with Walter about it," recalls GM Buzzie Bavasi. "We had the greatest scouting system; we'd be hurt by being restrained on who we could sign. But he said, 'No, it's good for the game.' "

It was good, indeed, for the owners' cost structure. Outfielder Rick Monday, the top choice in 1965's first amateur draft, got just a $100,000 bonus. Signing bonuses never reached Reichardtian heights again until 1980, when the Mets signed Darryl Strawberry for $210,000. O'Malley benefited from the savings as well, of course. And it had been a magnanimous sop to throw to the peasants.

The Dodgers' scouting *was* the best in baseball. So was their huge farm system. The Dodgers owned their minor league affiliates outright, enabling them to control all operations and instruct all players in the Dodger Way.

O'Malley's key operatives on the baseball end of things were holdover "Rickey men" who were discreet enough not to mention the man's name. Bavasi, the GM, admitted that Rickey had taught him "everything [he] knew about negotiating and trading." Al Campanis, the scouting director, was entrusted by Rickey to school Jackie Robinson in playing second base. Fresco Thompson, whom Rickey had made farm-system chief, remained long in that capacity for O'Malley.

They kept alive the Dodgers' player-development tradition by appealing to O'Malley's business sensibility. "I had a deal with Walter," Bavasi said. "He wouldn't cut down on the farm system as long as I could sell enough players each year to pay for Dodgertown."

The differences between O'Malley and Rickey couldn't have been summed up better. Rickey had built Dodgertown; O'Malley tolerated it. The farm system was Rickey's pride and joy; O'Malley saw it as a costly but necessary source of raw product. It was astounding, really, how little interest baseball's most powerful man had in the on-field game.

After the Dodgers won the last game of the 1965 World Series, Buzzie Bavasi mingled with the glitterati at the postgame party. "You know," he said to a group, "if it hadn't been for Yom Kippur we might actually have swept this thing."

He explained: Sandy Koufax couldn't pitch the first game because of the religious holiday. Don Drysdale pitched instead with too little rest. He lost. Koufax pitched the second game with too *much* rest. He was wild and lost, too. The Dodgers came back to win four of the next five games and the Series. Of course, Bavasi noted, by going to seven games the Series had netted O'Malley an extra million bucks.

Bavasi turned to Cary Grant. "Here's a question for Walter," he said. "Why don't you ask him if he'd rather win in four straight or lose in seven."

He was pretty sure he knew the answer.

$ 4 $

THE DODGERS REPRESENTED the future and the best of the baseball business in the sixties. But the game as a whole was hurting. The problem had its roots in the 1950s. Paeans would later be sung to this period as a golden age of baseball—the game—but it was one long recession for the business of baseball. Attendance plunged from a postwar peak of 20 million in 1948 to 14.4 million in 1953. Not until 1960 did the gate struggle back to the 20 million level.

The malaise was most acute in the American League, where the Yankees won every year and the fans in every other city dozed. From 1950 to 1958, league attendance declined from 9.1 to 7.3 million. In 1959, Orioles GM Paul Richards felt obliged to write an article for *Look* magazine entitled "The American League is Dying."

But the Lords only acknowledged their problems by fleeing them. Two AL teams moved in the fifties—St. Louis to Baltimore, and Philadelphia to Kansas City—and three NL teams—the aforementioned Braves, Giants, and Dodgers.

Stagnation continued in the sixties. The American League spiked up to 10.2 million in 1961, the first expansion year. But by 1965 it had slid back to 8.9 million. The National League had the embarrassment of seeing the Braves move for the second time in thirteen years. The thrill was gone in Milwaukee; attendance sagged to 730,000, and in 1966 the club left for Atlanta.

What had been a quiet slump in the fifties grew to a full-blown crisis in the sixties. The National Football League's skyrocketing popularity put baseball's problems in bold relief. People were saying it right out loud: baseball was no longer the national pastime. *Forbes* magazine put a battered baseball on its cover with the headline: BASEBALL: THE BEAT-UP NATIONAL SPORT.

Football, of course, had been an American passion for nearly as long as baseball. But as a professional sport it was a poor relation. The early NFL's second-rate status was reflected in its second-tier cities: Canton, Ohio (the Bulldogs); Racine, Wisconsin (the Cardinals); Decatur, Illinois (the Staleys); and Marion, Ohio (the Oorang Indians—an all-Indian team featuring Jim Thorpe and sponsored by the Oorang dog kennels). Broke teams were as common as broken tackles. Franchises shuttled in and out of the league like players in and out of the game. Pro football for long was eclipsed by college football; in the late fifties its twelve teams were still largely concentrated in frost-belt cities.

Then, in 1960, Alvin Ray "Pete" Rozelle became its leader. He was a PR man who had fallen into the position of GM at the Los Angeles Rams. When NFL commissioner Bert Bell died suddenly in 1959, the thirty-three-year-old Rozelle won the job as a compromise choice.

Nobody knew Pete Rozelle from a goalpost, but Pete Rozelle sure knew something: marketing and media. His first priority was to overhaul the NFL's approach to TV. The 1958 New York Giants–Baltimore Colts championship game, decided in sudden-death overtime, had captured the nation's imagination. Televised by CBS, the game climaxed in Alan Ameche's dramatic touchdown run for the Colts, which was the talk of the nation for weeks. Knowing that TV's reach and power were growing every year, Rozelle moved brilliantly to harness the NFL's TV appeal.

At that time, each NFL team sold its own TV rights. The champion Colts got top dollar in 1959, at $600,000 a year. From there it scaled all the way down to the Green Bay Packers at $80,000. "I wanted to try to package up the TV [rights] as a league," Rozelle recalled. "I thought it would give us better leverage."

He had to wait until existing TV contracts expired, and until Congress passed a special bill allowing the league to do this. (The NFL wasn't blessed with an antitrust exemption.) But in 1964 it all paid off when CBS bid $28.2 million for two years of NFL broadcast rights. That was ten times the pre-Rozelle TV receipts and vaulted the NFL way past baseball in network TV revenues. (The rival American Football League soon followed suit with a five-year $35 million contract with NBC.)

Rozelle's move not only profited his league but beautifully marketed it. National TV enabled—coerced—fans to follow the total game, not just their local team. It built up interest in the championship game, no matter who was in it. It also provided two games per Sunday at standardized times—a steady, predictable diet for the nation's growing ranks of couch potatoes. Football, by its very nature, was well suited for TV. Rozelle took it a step further, and made sure it *revolved* around TV.

Yet despite its emphasis on television, the NFL played to sellout crowds, in stark contrast with baseball's yawning expanses of empty seats. Total attendance nearly doubled during the sixties, to 6.1 million by 1969. That was also due, in part, to more teams and an expanded schedule, but average attendance per football game, a good constant measure, rose 36 percent, to 54,430.

Rozelle, the marketeer, was also furiously cranking out NFL merchandise. In 1963 he created a company, NFL Properties, to license goods bearing NFL teams' logos. A lot of it was strictly schlock (NFL Properties' first big hit was a bobble-headed doll, bedecked in logoed helmets), but it got the NFL into stores and onto kids' T-shirts all across the country.

Later, Rozelle launched NFL Films, to distribute the league's artful highlights movies. With its dramatic music, stentorian voices, and clear narrative lines, NFL Films vividly presented and promoted the guts and glory of pro football. "It was up to us to create the 'Gods of Autumn,' " recalled Steve Sabol, who with his father produced the reels. "We made it a larger-than-life contest, with the fate of the universe at stake."

The key to it all was what some NFLers called "league-think." Rozelle preached constantly that owners were to think of what was best for the NFL, not just their own franchise. With the exception of some stray mavericks—later, most notably, the Raiders' Al Davis—they did.

League-think wasn't all Rozelle's doing. It was rooted back in the bad old days, when owners had to hang together or hang separately. It was then that they'd begun the 60–40 gate split between host team and visitors. It was a far more even split than in baseball, and it resulted in greater economic parity. (The American League was 80–20; the National League gave visitors forty-seven cents per ticket.)

Rozelle's TV plan wouldn't have flown but for the assent of owners like Wellington Mara of the New York Giants and George Halas of the Chicago Bears. They willingly gave up the advantages of their big-city markets. "There was a recognition by the right people that the league was no stronger than the weakest link," recalled Jim Finks, then the Minnesota Vikings GM.

Even the NFL's costly war with the upstart American Football League boosted football's profile and popularity. When the New York Jets signed Joe Namath for $400,000 in 1964, the deal's astonishing proportions brought attention to the young league and instant stardom to the rookie quarterback.

Baseball, meanwhile, prided itself on keeping salaries low—Willie Mays topped the scale at $105,000—and keeping TV out. The Lords had only one measure of success: the gate. They hadn't yet embraced TV as a moneymaking and marketing tool. They dreaded it as a threat to attendance. So at a time when that medium was growing fast—the number of American homes with TVs grew from 9 to 54 percent between 1950 and 1954—baseball was trying to keep it at bay.

In 1953 ABC approached baseball about doing a *Game of the Week*. The Lords agreed, but with draconian restrictions. The network couldn't broadcast the game in major league cities. In the interest of protecting their home turfs, they'd banned ABC from showcasing baseball—their *product*—in the best markets. The network had to settle for the hinterlands.

The Lords weren't practicing league-think in their TV dealings when it came to money, either. Money from the *Game of the Week*, which eventually moved to CBS, was divvied up according to how many times a club played on it. The Yankees were on CBS nearly as often as Lucille Ball. In 1964, the Bronx Bombers got two thirds of the $895,000 the network paid for the weekly choice game. Network TV money helped sustain their economic superiority, their dynasty—and baseball's malaise. (In August 1964, CBS's relationship with the Yankees grew even closer. It bought the team.)

Not until 1965 did baseball start dividing *Game of the Week* loot equally. It shot up to $5.7 million that year, because the Lords finally allowed ABC to beam the *Game* into big-league cities. After years of careful conditioning, however, fans' interest was purely local. Ratings were abysmal and ABC dropped it in 1966. NBC struck a three-year deal that year: packaging the *Game of the Week*, the All-Star Game, and the World Series for $11.8 million per annum.

It was a pitiful total compared to the NFL, which by now reaped $18.8 million a year. (This wasn't even counting the four-year $9.5 million TV deal for Rozelle's latest brainchild: something called the Super Bowl.) But baseball had gotten what it deserved. The Lords had hoped TV would just go away. They had put local prerogatives over group action. If the motto of the NFL owner was "All for one and one for all," the motto of the Lords was: "I've got mine."

The marketing of baseball also paled beside that of football. To be sure, it was almost nonexistent. Typical was the Cincinnati Reds' idea of promotion: a three-foot-square sign on the front of Crosley Field that said: GAME TODAY. The only thing that changed was the time.

Baseball people believed, essentially, that real men didn't market. "The old-line guys didn't want anything they didn't understand," recalls Clark Griffith, scion of the family that owned the Senators (later the Twins). "The law was, you had to win, and if you did you'd get people to come out."

George Weiss was once approached about having a Cap Day at Yankee Stadium. He was horrified. To him it was like licensing the pope's vestments. "Do you think I want every kid in this city walking around with a Yankee cap?" he asked.

Later, as the Mets' president, he continued grimly to fight the radical idea of fun at the old ballpark. During the team's awful first year, its hearty, rabid fans took to unfurling banners: LET'S GO METS, and WE DON'T WANT TO SET THE WORLD ON FIRE—WE JUST WANT TO FINISH NINTH, and, simply, PRAY.

Weiss at first ordered security guards to confiscate the banners. The official reason was that they obstructed other fans' view. The real reason was that they offended George Weiss. Banners were a desecration, a disgrace. The confiscations stopped only when New York's baseball writers started writing about the Mets' anti-banner storm troopers.

Eventually, other Mets officials even saw their way clear to make the banners an *institution*. The team started an annual Banner Day, with an on-field parade and contest. But as long as George Weiss was around, he still looked on frowning. "These people . . . these noisy people with their bedsheets," he was once heard to mutter. "Where do they come from? . . . Why don't they keep quiet?"

Weiss was a prototype of the GM, just a bit more Prussian than most. He ran the business without being a businessman. He was a baseball man. He didn't know from marketing; he knew players. His job was to produce as many of them as possible and pay them as little as possible. He was in trouble when the job involved anything else. So, in the 1960s, was baseball. Teams weren't losing money—their low payrolls protected them from that—but they were losing an awful lot of fans.

Like crocuses blooming on barren tundra, however, there were a couple of owners who showed some promotional flair. At first they would be reviled as crackpots, but later revealed as visionaries.

One was Ray Hofheinz. He didn't look like a baseball man. He wore black suits and smoked twenty-four cigars a day. He was six feet tall and looked, in the words of one associate, "like he'd swallowed nine bowling balls." He lasted for less than a decade as a force in baseball—a bright flame that burned out quickly. He didn't even care very much for baseball as entertainment, much preferring the circus.

Yet Roy Hofheinz would prove a revolutionary figure. He was a true boy wonder: a lawyer at nineteen, a state legislator at twenty-two, a county judge at twenty-four, and Houston's mayor at forty. Along the way, Hofheinz built a business empire in real estate (advance knowledge of the path of Houston's new roads helped a lot), radio stations (the first FM station in Texas among them), and the glamorous business of slag (steel-mill waste).

Hofheinz's forte was getting wealthier parties to provide most of the cash for his ventures. One of these investors was a prominent Houston oilman named R. E. "Bob" Smith. When a group of Houstonians approached Smith in 1960 about trying to get a baseball team for their city, he told them to talk to Hofheinz—he was the big thinker.

The Judge, as everyone called him, was already working on a big concept: a huge enclosed shopping mall. He'd gotten the idea from a picture of the Roman Colosseum's velarium, a space covered by a curtain that was supported by slaves. Hofheinz wanted to create a structure very much like that—minus the slaves, of course. He ran the idea past Buckminster Fuller, the inventor of the geodesic dome, who told Hofheinz it was possible to cover a space of any size "if you didn't run out of money."

So far, the shopping-mall capital hadn't come together and the project was languishing. When the baseball group approached Hofheinz, he jumped at their proposal. He and Bob Smith organized the Houston Sports Association, whose purpose was to get a team and whose stock was to be held by a group of wealthy boosters. Its largest shareholders were Hofheinz and Bob Smith.

One day Hofheinz was talking about it with a friend and financial adviser named Ben McGuire.

"You know," Hofheinz said, "people in Houston aren't going to sit in big numbers in the hot sun and high humidity in the daytime or fight mosquitoes at night to see baseball. We've got to have a covered, air-conditioned playing field."

"You've lost your marbles," said McGuire.

Nonetheless, Hofheinz began lining up architects to work on it. By October 1960, he had a scale model to show the NL owners, on the basis of which they awarded Houston one of the two expansion franchises—called the Colt .45s—to begin play in 1962.

Hofheinz had to rebuild a temporary stadium in the meantime and survive three bond-referendum votes on the domed one. Its construction was publicly financed and its cost kept climbing, from an initial estimate of $15 million to a final $35.5 million. The dome just squeaked by in two of the votes, and only Hofheinz's political know-how carried the day. He sent cars through the streets of Houston's black areas, mounted with loudspeakers and carrying the voices of Hank Aaron and Ernie Banks urging pro-dome votes. He also lined up people to "volunteer" to distribute opposition pamphlets—then dump them in the nearest landfill.

In the meantime, Hofheinz spent all of his considerable energies planning the stadium. He wanted it to have a futuristic, space-age motif, befitting a city that was home to NASA headquarters. The team name would be changed to the Astros, and the stadium would be called the Astrodome.

Planning a stadium without precedent was a mammoth exercise, which Hofheinz undertook largely through rambling brainstorming sessions with his staff. These happened at odd hours and odd places: at the end of Colts games and on into the wee hours at the Judge's country retreat on Galveston Bay, called Huckster House.

Hofheinz's fertile mind pounced on any remotely promising remark. Weary of trying to dream up stadium-club names, and having heard the forty-eighth bad idea for a space-theme moniker, Tal Smith said, "Yeah, and why don't we call the grounds crew the Earthmen."

"Great!" said Hofheinz, and the Earthmen they were.

There wasn't just one club, mind you, but three. The Skydome Club was a Japanese steakhouse replica with a spectacular view of downtown Houston. The Astrodome Club included a hundred-foot-long bar made of African mahogany and touted as the world's longest. The Trailblazer was a little less exclusive, but it still had ambitious decor: "a historical theme," as publicity materials put it, "depicting man's struggle for a better life down through the ages."

This wasn't counting the two restaurants for the general public, the Countdown Cafeteria and the Domeskeller. At a time when ballpark cuisine elsewhere consisted of hot dogs and peanuts, the Astrodome was in a culinary league of its own. Hofheinz wanted to get more women as fans and, a prodigious eater and skilled cook himself, he thought this would help draw them. Over and over he asked his brainstormers the question: "What's the patron interested in?"

When someone mentioned how so many fans liked to sit behind the dugouts, Hofheinz lit up. "Great!" he said. "Let's make a longer dugout!" The Astrodome's 120-foot-long dugouts dwarfed all others.

When the group got into plans for Hofheinz's private stadium box, someone mused, "Wouldn't it be great if businesses could have VIP suites, like owners?"

Bingo. Suddenly the plans were ripped apart to allow for fifty-three suites way up on the ninth level of the dome. Exhausted architects would work until all hours, sustained only by the spicy chili and eggs ranchero Hofheinz cooked himself and kept shoveling to them.

Wealthy Texans snapped up five-year $15,000 leases on every last Skybox, as they were called, before a game was ever played. Each was decorated differently, reflecting Hofheinz's eclectic, eccentric taste, and each had its own name—Imperial Orient, Las Vegas, Roman Holiday, Old Mexico, Grecian Delight, and Venetian Holiday, to name just a few.

As the Astrodome came together, no detail was too small for Hofheinz's attention. He selected the silver and china for the AstroClub. He picked the tile for the corridor, the furniture for the suites, the colors of the stadium seats. The day before the first game, Hofheinz went into every restroom to make sure the toilet paper was installed.

When players and fans saw it for the first time, for an Astros–Yankees exhibition game on April 6, 1965, they were stunned. They were used to standard-issue green ballpark seats, and the Astrodome was a riot of Hofheinz-inspired color: from lipstick red to burnt orange to royal blue and every stop on the rainbow in between. They squinted up at the 4,600 Lucite panels of the dome; they gaped at the 474-foot-long, four-story-high score-board. "It reminds me," said Mickey Mantle, leaning against the batting cage, "of what I imagine my first ride would be like in a flying saucer."

It wasn't just the Astrodome's appearance but its gimmicks that changed the whole ball-game experience. The $2 million scoreboard contained 1,200 miles of wiring, allowing elaborate animation. When an Astros player hit a homer, a cartoon depiction of the Astrodome's top blowing up in a huge explosion appeared, while lights flashed and thunder crashed. A huge baseball appeared, bearing the words HOME RUN and touching off more explosions. Next cowboys came riding onto the score-board, firing guns. Then came two giant steers, each sprouting an American flag and a Texas state flag from their horn tips. The cowboys chased the steers off, twirling lariats, and the show concluded with a multicolored skyrocket display.

It all took forty-five seconds and made the previous tradition of hearty cheering wholly inadequate.

The Astros' scoreboard was also baseball's first to exhort and extort cheers from fans. They were prompted to chant "Go! Go! Go!" And they repeatedly heard a six-note trumpet call followed by the command to holler "Charge!"

The fans heard it so often because Hofheinz loved it, and also because he loved to drink. After a few belts of Scotch, he would commence calling Bill Giles, the Astros PR chief who ran the board.

"Put up 'Charge!' Put up 'Charge!' " he would order.

Along about the sixth inning, Giles had to start resisting.

"But, Judge, we've put it up eighteen times," Giles would reply. "I think we ought to ease up."

The Astrodome was an immediate smash with fans. Even people who cared little about baseball wanted to see this "Eighth Wonder of the World," as Hofheinz, with typical Texas reserve, called it. By the end of June, Astros attendance broke 1 million. The Houston club had never reached that level in an entire season outdoors.

While the business end of things was a triumph, the aesthetics of the game suffered tremendously. As a playing field, for example, the Astrodome was impossible. The first exhibition game established that every fly ball would be an adventure. Outfielders, looking up against the cream-colored dome surface, had a devil of a time following the ball. Routine plays became extra-base hits.

Hofheinz painted over the Lucite, and the problem abated. But he created another: the grass started dying. By September, it was wiped out. The last two weeks of the season, the Astros had to spray-paint the field green.

Hofheinz called Tal Smith, the Astros' assistant GM, into his office one day. "You've got to find a solution to the grass problem," he said. "You've got unlimited resources; just do it."

Every day, Smith would get proposals—from big companies, concerned fans, wacky inventors, the works. Every day, he would sink deeper into despair over what to do. Finally, something intriguing came over the transom. A division of Monsanto, the giant chemicals maker, was trying to develop a synthetic grass. Smith was invited to take a look at the one place it was being tested, a school in Providence, Rhode Island.

He came back impressed. Monsanto sent samples of the experimental grass to Houston, where Smith tried it out at the old Colt Stadium. He got the University of Houston football team to scrimmage on it, cars to run over it, sheriff's horses to ride on it, circus elephants to urinate on it.

Smith was finally convinced it would work. It only remained for Hofheinz to work out a deal.

"We're thinking of $375,000," said the man from Monsanto.

"That's interesting," said Hofheinz. "Coincidentally, that's exactly what I was going to charge you for promoting the product."

And that is why the synthetic grass was called AstroTurf, and why the Astros had the first field full of it gratis.

By the end of the sixties, Roy Hofheinz would be in trouble. He fell out with his partner Bob Smith and had to borrow heavily to buy out Smith's stake. Then Hofheinz borrowed even more heavily to expand the Astrodome complex. He built Astroworld, an amusement park; Astrohall, a convention center; and the Astroworld Hotel. For good measure, he also bought a controlling interest in the Ringling Bros. and Barnum & Bailey Circus.

He was, said one associate, "the dumbest genius I ever met. He was like a Napoleon. He'd never cover his flanks or rear. He just kept stretching his financial burdens."

In 1970, they snapped. Bank lenders forced Hofheinz to fold all his holdings into one company, called Astrodomain Corporation, to be controlled by a creditor-dominated board. That year

Hofheinz also suffered a stroke that put him in a wheelchair for the rest of his life. He would never recapture his old vigor and vision.

But his legacy was secure. By the 1990s, five big-league teams played in domed stadiums, and nine had artificial turf. (There were countless other domed and AstroTurfed stadiums in other sports as well, of course.) Artificial turf changed the way the game was played, putting a heavy premium on speed and, so many athletes charged, causing numerous injuries. The Astrodome also changed the way the game was presented. By the 1990s, nearly every big-league stadium had scoreboards that showed animated pictures and led cheers. The Astrodome's Skyboxes and fancy restaurants were also forerunners of the stadium of the future. In the nineties, Baltimore's Camden Yards and Chicago's Comiskey Park would take ballparks still further upscale—and without the kitsch. But they owed an undeniable debt to the Astrodome of the sixties.

Said Tal Smith, later the Astros' president: "Hofheinz took baseball out of its drab surroundings and completely revolutionized it with comfort and color."

Charles Oscar Finley was a born salesman. As a boy in Birmingham, Alabama, he bought discolored, rejected eggs for five cents a dozen and sold them in downtown office buildings for fifteen cents a dozen. He later won a medal and a bicycle for selling 12,500 subscriptions for the *Saturday Evening Post*.

Finley was also a born maverick, whose picture in the high school yearbook bore the caption: "He who mischief hatcheth, mischief catcheth." He graduated from high school in Gary, Indiana, where his steelworker father had been transferred by U.S. Steel. Finley followed his father into the mills, but sold health insurance on the side. By the mid-1940s, he'd switched to insurance full-time, setting a company record for policy sales in his first year.

Finley also drove himself to exhaustion, contracted TB, and wound up in a sanitarium, both his physical and financial healths ruined. He'd neglected to sell an insurance policy to himself. While he recovered, however, Finley had plenty of time to think about where he might locate whole classes of underinsured professionals. A lightbulb clicked on. They were all around him: doctors!

A recovered Finley developed an insurance plan for physicians and sold group policies based on it to the American College of Surgeons, the American Medical Association, and other medical societies. By the early fifties, he was a multimillionaire and ready to conquer new worlds.

He fixed his sights on baseball. Finley loved the game. He'd been a batboy for the minor league Birmingham Barons. He'd also played a lot of semipro ball as a youth. At age nineteen he had "owned" his first team, the Gary Merchants. Finley got retailers to contribute twenty-five dollars in return for putting a store's name on a player's back. He bought sweatshirts for just ninety-eight cents apiece, cheaply stenciled on the names, and turned a nifty profit. Now he wanted to try his hand at the big leagues.

Finley tried to buy the Philadelphia Athletics in 1954, but lost out to another bidder, a man named Arnold Johnson. Johnson was a business associate of Yankees co-owner Dan Topping, and thus had connections with deeper pockets. Finley then unsuccessfully bid for the White Sox. Then he went after the expansion Angels franchise, even trying to get Roy Rogers into his syndicate to counter Gene Autry's group. But he lost that one too.

Finally, the Athletics came around again. Arnold Johnson dropped dead in 1960 and Finley was the first to get to his widow, paying her $2 million for Johnson's 52 percent stake. Joe Iglehart, the Orioles' chairman, was assigned by the Lords to check out this guy who'd haunted ownership meetings for years but about whom little was known. "Under no conditions," he reported back, "should this person be allowed into our league."

But who else would buy the Athletics? Johnson had moved the club to Kansas City, where it became a colony for his friend Dan Topping's team. From 1955 to 1960, the Yankees and Athletics exchanged twenty-nine players in trades, with the A's supplying up-and-comers like Roger Maris, Hector Lopez, Art Ditmar, and Ralph Terry and getting over-the-hill coots in return.

The Athletics jockeyed with the Senators for last place in the standings and in attendance. After reaching 1.4 million in 1955, their first Kansas City year, the A's headed straight downward to 775,000 by 1960. Since nobody else wanted the sad-sack franchise, Finley's purchase from the Widow Johnson was approved. "I wanted to get into baseball in the worst way, and that's what I did," he later joked.

Baseball in Kansas City was awful as ever, but it sure looked different. Finley painted the box seats citrus yellow, the reserved and bleacher seats desert turquoise, and the foul poles fluorescent pink. Finley railed against the "eggshell white" and "prison gray" of baseball uniforms. He outfitted his team in kelly green and "Fort Knox gold" uniforms and white "albino kangaroo" shoes.

The players had to endure cruel bench-jockeying for their slow-pitch softball-team look. (They were particularly vulnerable to it because of their record.) But Finley had a standard response. "I used to see nothing but black cars," he'd say. "Today, you look down in the parking lot from the stadium and you see every color in the rainbow. Well, you want to put some color in the game, too."

Finley also brought livestock into the stadium. He set up a zoo beyond the right-field fence that included sheep, monkeys, pheasant, and rabbits. He made a mule the team mascot and named it Charlie O. It was sometimes paraded through town in the company of pretty girls who passed out ballpoint pens, caps, and other green-and-gold novelties. Finley himself once rode Charlie O. through Times Square in New York.

Kansas City's Municipal Stadium was laced with gimmicks. A mechanical rabbit rose every so often out of the ground near home plate to supply the umpire with balls, while the organist played "Here Comes Peter Cottontail." A compressed-air device blew dirt off the plate, saving the umpire the trouble. It was called "Little Blowhard." An electronic grid on the scoreboard dispensed informational tidbits, called "Fan-a-Grams."

Finley had theme days for just about every special-interest group going: Shriners, bald-headed men, you name it. On Farmers Day in 1963, starting pitcher Diego Segui was delivered to the mound on a hay wagon. That was just one of Finley's efforts to play to his rural market, which also included pregame pig chases, cow-milking contests, and players trying to ride Charlie O.

None of this, it should be noted, helped attendance a whit. It dropped into the 600,000's during Finley's first two years. For the Athletics, the American League expansion in 1961 simply meant that they could now finish *lower* than eighth. Finley, meanwhile, was more or less openly exploring the possibility of moving to other cities: Atlanta, Dallas, Oakland, Louisville— anywhere but what he privately called "this horseshit town."

That was Finley—prophetic and profane, dynamic and devious. He had no use for either the conventions of the game or the pecking order of the Lords. New owners were supposed to be seen and not heard. Finley, his gravelly voice rumbling, his bushy eyebrows bobbing, put himself at the center of every ownership meeting.

He harangued them about speeding up the game. For a time in Kansas City, he enforced the rule that allowed no more than twenty seconds between pitches, installing a special clock on the board for the purpose. He pushed for orange baseballs—a more interesting and easier-to-follow color, he maintained. He argued that they should play World Series games at night.

"Today's children are tomorrow's fans," Finley preached. "The kids can't see the game in the afternoon. Neither can the working man in the steel mills or coal mines."

Finley got on the soapbox most of all for rules changes that would stress the offense side of the game. "Look, the average fan comes to the park to see action, home runs," he said. "He doesn't come to see a one-, two-, three-, or four-hit game. I can't think of anything more boring than to see a pitcher come up [to bat], when the average pitcher couldn't hit my grandmother. Let's have a permanent pinch hitter for the pitcher."

Finley was mostly ignored. He had the capacity to be charming, but mostly he was impatient and abrasive. His contempt for his fellow owners—particularly at their failure to recognize his genius—was raw and naked. Even his wardrobe was an affront to the blue-suit types in the old guard. Finley was typically clad in kelly-green blazer, white linen pants, yellow tie, and white shirt, with "Charlie O." monogrammed on French cuffs.

Finley also offended his fellow owners by rolling up those sleeves and immersing himself in the nitty-gritty of the business. He not only promoted his team like a carnival barker but scouted, signed, and traded players. By the old guard's lights, an owner was supposed to watch the games and write the checks. Detroit's John Fetzer, the consummate old-guarder, once approached Finley and gently suggested he hire a GM.

"When the day comes that I find a GM who can do a better job than Charlie O., I'll hire the son-of-a-gun," he retorted.

"He had some wonderful ideas," said Ewing Kauffman, who would eventually succeed him as an owner in Kansas City, "but he rankled the owners so much that anything he proposed didn't have a chance of being approved."

Only years later, when circumstances absolutely demanded change, were Finley's ideas embraced. The permanent pinch hitter came into being in the American League as the designated hitter in 1973. The World Series started being played at night in 1971. Other teams began appearing in colorful uniforms.

But for now, in the sixties, baseball remained mostly unchanged. Finley and Hofheinz were the exceptions to the rule—

and the rule was, unfortunately, never more rigid than in the selection in 1965 of baseball's new commissioner.

His name was William D. Eckert. A retired one-star general who had once been the Army's chief procurement officer, he was obscure even within the Pentagon. Legend has it that the owners, when they hired him, had Eckert confused with General Eugene Zuckert, a former secretary of the Air Force. When Eckert was appointed, one sportswriter gasped, "My God, they've hired the Unknown Soldier." Spike Eckert, as he was known, never shook that tag.

Ineffectual and low-profile, he came to symbolize the game's personality disorder in the sixties. At a time when Pete Rozelle was powering the NFL forward with TV, he had zero sense of marketing. He had no clue about labor relations—this at a time when Marvin Miller was bringing it to the fore. He didn't even know baseball. And he was so ignorant and easily intimidated that he had administrative assistant Lee MacPhail listen in on his phone calls, as a security blanket.

Eckert was disastrous as baseball's leading spokesman, delivering speeches in a mumbling monotone. Speech coaches advised him to use notecards instead of wading through text, and soon he was famous for shuffling the cards out of order and delivering spectacularly disjointed talks. He was also apt to deliver the wrong address at the wrong time. Eckert once addressed a group of baseball men with a speech intended for the Retired Airline Pilots Association.

Baseball was, in a sense, only getting what it wanted. There hadn't been a strong commissioner since Judge Landis, and many owners liked it just fine that way. They weakened the office after Landis died in 1944 and commenced electing commissioners they thought they could control.

Landis had been succeeded by Kentucky senator A. B. "Happy" Chandler. He was hired as more of a political fixer than anything else, as baseball saw its greatest potential dangers being mostly political. Beginning in the 1940s, the Lords would have to repel repeated challenges to their antitrust exemption.

Chandler's appeal quickly wore thin. First of all, he was subject, without notice, to bursting into choruses of "My Old Kentucky Home." He was also suspiciously sympathetic to the interests of the players. And then he totally botched baseball's first big TV deal. In 1949, Chandler sold World Series TV rights to Gillette for six years at $1 million per annum. Gillette turned around and resold the rights to NBC for $4 million a year. Fred Saigh, the Cardinals' owner, took to calling Chandler "the bluegrass jackass." Saigh, together with Yankees co-owners Topping and Webb, engineered his ouster in 1950.

Chandler was succeeded by Ford Frick. A onetime sportswriter, whose résumé included ghostwriting for Babe Ruth, he'd been NL president since 1934. Frick would come to be derided by many for ducking hard decisions as commissioner, repeatedly invoking the excuse: "That's a league affair."

But Frick was very much a product of baseball's traditional governance system, which did, in fact, reserve most decision-making power for the leagues. Judge Landis's dramatic Black Sox entry and his autocratic bearing had created the myth of the all-powerful commissioner; and the commissioner did, indeed, have sweeping authority to take actions in the "best interests of the game"; but in practice, that authority applied mainly to disciplinary matters. In business matters, the commissioner existed only as a tie-breaker between the two leagues.

The leagues held joint meetings just twice a year—though they were not especially joint. They met in different rooms, with different agendas, dispatching junior lawyers to ferry questions back and forth. When the two circuits finally did assemble in one room, the meetings were perfunctory—purely to exchange voting results.

"Gentlemen, I want to congratulate you," said Frick at the conclusion of one. "This has been our finest meeting. We finished everything in seven minutes."

Frick busied himself with enforcing rules, taking care of administrative details, and giving little offense. Of the first eight commissioners, he would be the only one to leave office voluntarily. He retired in 1964 after two terms, saving his only blasts for the end. He strongly recommended that the Lords put the teeth back in the office (which they did). And he frankly admitted problems, admonishing the Lords about them in his final address:

"So long as the owners and operators refuse to look beyond the day and the hour; so long as clubs and individuals persist in gaining personal headlines through public criticism of their associates; so long as baseball people are unwilling to abide by the rules they themselves make; so long as expediency is permitted to replace sound judgment, there can be no satisfactory solution. . . ."

In the annals of wise parting words, it ranked somewhere up there with Eisenhower's warning against the military-industrial complex. It was paid about the same heed, too. Frick was saying that the Lords needed seriously to reevaluate themselves and their business. Instead, they hired Spike Eckert.

Eckert was particularly done in by the dreadful year 1968. The season confirmed everything critics had been saying about baseball vis-à-vis football: boring. Batters in the National League hit a collective .243; in the American League, .230. There were only six .300 hitters in all of baseball. Carl Yastrzemski won the AL batting championship by hitting a mere .301. The year saw 1,000 fewer home runs than 1962. Ten teams didn't hit a total of 100 homers. There were 339 shutouts—21 percent of all games—and of them, 82 were 1–0 games. Games averaged a combined 6.8 runs, the lowest such figure since the turn-of-the-century deadball era.

This last statistic seemed appropriate. While America was exploding, politically and psychedelically, baseball was contracting into some horse-and-buggy relic. Baseball's 23.1 million gate in 1968 was 1.2 million off the total for 1967 and 2 million off for 1966. Attendance-hungry baseball kept on playing through the King and Kennedy assassinations and caught hell for that, too. The game's profound slump was underscored by the retirement of one of its greatest legends and box-office draws, Mickey Mantle.

The 1968 season was Mantle's last, and it was also Spike Eckert's. Walter O'Malley had seen enough after three years; at the winter meetings, in December, he had the skids greased for Eckert's "retirement." Ewing Kauffman, the expansion Royals' new owner, pitied Eckert when he saw him sitting by himself at lunch. He was being ritualistically shunned before being fired. Kauffman joined him.

Eckert went quietly, like the good soldier he was. Just a few years later, in 1971, he died and was buried in Arlington National Cemetery. A number of baseball officials walked behind his horse-drawn casket as it made its way through the grounds. The horses stopped at one point, and during that brief pause, National League president Chub Feeney looked off to the side. There was the grave of Abner Doubleday, baseball's purported founder. Feeney tugged at Phillies owner Bob Carpenter.

"Bob, Bob, look at that," he said, pointing to the grave.

Carpenter looked and quickly absorbed the rich irony.

"I don't know whether to laugh or cry," he said.

$ 5 $

WHILE THE LORDS were foundering through the 1960s, Marvin Miller was quietly, efficiently building. First, he was winning the players' confidence through modest, practical gains. In the 1968 Basic Agreement, he got the minimum salary raised to $10,000 and the maximum pay cut reduced to 20 percent. He got spring training "Murphy money" raised from $25 a week, where it had been stuck since 1947, to $40. The players' life on the road would get better too: mandatory first-class travel and hotel accommodations, and increased meal money.

Miller had failed to get an independent arbitrator, but he had, at least, installed a grievance arbitration procedure. Players who felt they had been wronged had access to a systematic appeals process, even if the final arbiter was the commissioner.

Miller was also slowly but surely politicizing his players and developing a cadre of player leadership. It was called "consciousness-raising" in the parlance of the day, and it would give him the confidence to mount his first major challenge to the Lords.

The Lords had tried to tar Miller as a labor boss. But, in fact, he was nothing of the sort. His genius wasn't in dictating to the players but in involving them. The quarterly executive board sessions of the union were lively town meetings. Miller wasn't a czar but a professor, teaching by the Socratic method. Miller could take a player's rambling soliloquy, separate the rhetorical wheat from the chaff, and concisely focus the speaker's main points. "Now, is this what you mean?" he'd say. "If it is, this is what's likely to happen."

Recalled catcher Bob Boone, "He was a master at never telling anybody how to do anything. He would just ask questions until you could see the answer for yourself. Marvin was a master at leading you down the right road."

It was an excruciating process. Some players were such extremists that others tuned them out. Reliever Mike Marshall, for instance, was either so far to the left he was right, or so far to the right he was left. Nobody was ever quite sure which. Here, for instance, is Marshall on salaries: "We're a union. Let's take the total pot available and *we'll* decide how to divide it up, not the clubs."

The meetings would grind on for hours on end.

"The repetition was, from time to time, unbearable," recalls Ted Simmons, star catcher and GM for the Pittsburgh Pirates. "But Miller and Moss would patiently wait for everybody to have their say. Because it was through the repetition process that everybody came to see the issue and develop a focus. Now, Marvin and Dick could have very early on stood up and said, 'This is how simple this is. Now, why don't you guys go out to lunch and think about it?'

"But then the ones on the low end of the learning curve might not get it and feel like they'd been dragged along into something. Then they might say something back home that would do us irreparable harm. Everybody had to feel he'd made a contribution, however inane. Everybody had to be on board. If there was a loose cannon, it was a huge danger."

That was the understanding. The players could hash everything over seven ways to sundown. They could insult and interrupt and scream. There was just one understanding: at the end of the day, they had to leave the room unified.

Miller pounded the unity theme like Hank Aaron pounded fastballs. Over and over, he said it: they must take positions that *all* players could support. "Anything less than 100 percent is unacceptable," was his unshakable motto.

The pattern was repeated time and again. A firebrand—a Reggie Jackson or a Mike Marshall—would stand up and make a storm-the-barricades speech. Then, Miller, stroking his chin, speaking softly, would respond. "I don't know what kind of support we could have for that position," he'd say. "We can't have 85 or 90 percent. We need 100 percent."

Recalls Jim Bouton: "Marvin was always the least gung-ho of anyone in the room. It was basically Marvin versus the firebrands."

Miller's message was simple. If there were divisions in the union, the owners would find them, exploit them, and destroy the Players Association. If they were united, there was nothing they could not do. He used the same words over and over: "Together you are irreplaceable."

And there is something else he said repeatedly, to break them of their old mind-set of subservience to the Lords: "*You* are the game," he told the players. "Without you there is no game."

Mark Belanger recalls listening as a young Orioles shortstop: "He brought out the pride we had that maybe we hadn't even known was there."

Slowly, patiently, Miller was making something happen. To all outward appearances, the baseball business still looked and worked pretty much the same in the late sixties. But behind closed doors in the Players Association, two amazing metamorphoses were taking place: that of Marvin Miller, from functionary technician to dynamic leader; and the players, from compliant peons to budding rebels. Their views and loyalties were being reshaped by this understated intellectual, the very antithesis of the baseball man.

"Every time he spoke you could hear a pin drop," said catcher Joe Torre.

There were approximately 600 major league baseball players in the late 1960s. Like any group that size, it encompassed a wide range of abilities and behaviors: smart and dumb, active and passive, straight and wild. And like any subculture, it had its own stratification of status: veterans and rookies, pitchers and hitters, stars and scrubeenies.

One of the keys to Marvin Miller's success was his ability to single out from that spectrum the best, the brightest, and the stars. To look down the roster of the early player leaders was to see just that. Joe Torre was an MVP and a future manager. Ditto Don Baylor. Mike Marshall was a Cy Young Award winner (and a Ph.D.). Brooks Robinson, Tom Seaver, and Reggie Jackson were future Hall of Famers. Ted Simmons was a star catcher and future general manager. Jim Bunning was a future congressman. Tim McCarver would become baseball's premier TV analyst.

Miller wasn't charismatic in the conventional sense. But his powers of logic and communication drew such players to him. Bob Boone, a young catcher and Stanford psychology graduate, attended his first union meeting and thought, "Wow, this guy has a way of taking a totally boring subject and making it interesting."

He became a Miller acolyte and union leader for much of his

twenty-year career, during which he set a major league record for games caught.

Miller recruited stars for several reasons. Being a union activist was inherently hazardous to a player's career. One needed look no further than the players who'd championed Miller's hiring in 1966. Robin Roberts was released by the Cubs after that season and was out of baseball. Jim Bunning was traded by Philadelphia in 1967, though he'd led the National League in strikeouts that year and won seventy-four games over the past four seasons.

But stars were less vulnerable to retribution. The Orioles had eight player reps in eight years from 1960 to 1968. When Brooks Robinson took the job, *mirabile dictu*, the turnover stopped. "To the extent the player rep job was always pushed on to a rookie or a relief pitcher, the union wasn't going to work," Miller would later say.

Stars were also looked up to by fellow players. They were the people others turned to when a job action loomed and it was gut-check time. "When you have a rookie worrying about his salary and he sees Reggie Jackson or Dave Winfield or Tom Seaver stand up and say we've got to take a stand, it makes all the difference," said Doug DeCinces, a long-time union leader.

Finally, who could offer better testimony than the stars about how players got screwed? Mickey Mantle hit .365 one year and Yankees GM George Weiss tried to cut his salary by $5,000. (Mantle ultimately eked out a small raise.) One winter, Brooks Robinson was presented with his contract at a sports banquet where his GM tried to publicly pressure him into signing. (He refused.) "The marquee players had lived this," says Ted Simmons. "They'd have an outstanding season and have absolutely no leverage—sixty thousand, eighty thousand, whatever the club wanted to give them."

The more time went by, the more Miller drew his players into the negotiating arena. Leaders like Joe Torre and Brooks Robinson would take prominent roles at the bargaining table, with Miller sitting off to one side. Miller also encouraged other players to attend sessions as spectators. It unnerved the members of the PRC (the owners' player relations committee) to meet with glowering players close up. (Miller was tickled to see the whole Pirates team show up at a meeting once in Bradenton, Florida, where they trained.)

A strong showing of players also gave Miller a hell of a gallery to play to. Sometimes he reacted to Gaherin's latest proposal by heaving a long sigh and slowly shaking his head. Other times it was a mirthless chuckle and a shrug of the shoulders. In any case, it was decidedly an expression of scorn, and it cued the players' reactions while infuriating the Lords' negotiators. (It was almost as infuriating to them as when Miller referred to players occasionally as "workers.")

Sometimes the players would sit silently, then explode upon leaving the room. "That son of a bitch, how could he say that?" a player would ask Miller. "Speak up!" urged Miller.

Increasingly they did. If Miller left in disgust, as he sometimes did, a player was likely to step in and deliver an even stronger message. Bob Boone did it more than once. "Marvin's not here now," he'd begin, "and we want you to understand something. You're fighting us, not him. We're telling Marvin what to do."

If the occasion called for it, a player could also dramatically stomp out. Mike Marshall once did so by prearrangement with Miller. "I had a plane to catch," he explained years later.

Rank-and-file participation did carry with it some hazards for Miller. Into a negotiating session, one day, marched Mrs. Elston Howard. She took her place beside Miller. "Mrs. Howard," he said, introducing the catcher's wife, "is going to make our presentation."

Joe Cronin immediately called for a caucus of his PRC colleagues.

"What's she doing in there?" he asked, once they were closeted.

"Under the law, the union can select any representative they want," said Gaherin.

Cronin grumbled, then rumbled back into the other room.

Mrs. Howard got right to it. Blacks had a terrible time in Florida, where remnants of Jim Crow remained. During spring training, black players often had to find housing far from the camps. They had to drive long distances to find restaurants and Laundromats that would serve them. It was thus only fair, she concluded, that blacks get a higher spring training allowance—"Murphy money"—than whites.

Gaherin squinted. He looked at Miller. "That's your position?"

Miller cleared his throat. "That's *a* position."

"What's *the* position?" asked Gaherin.

"We'll come back to that as we go along."

The session did move along from there, and Cronin contained himself until it was over. Once in private, again, he exploded.

"Jesus, we can't give them more than the white guys!" he said. "We'll have a revolution! They'll tar and feather us!"

Gaherin laid a reassuring hand on him.

"Don't worry, they'll tar and feather Marvin. We'll never hear from them on this one again."

Despite the occasional awkward moment, these sessions were superb field trips in the Great Educator's Labor Relations 101 course. It further illuminated the issues and dynamics for the players. And, having seen the enemy up close, they would never again be intimidated. They could tell, with the visceral instinct of athletes, that it was the other side that was scared. "You could just feel the attitude from the other side of the table," recalled Joe Torre. " 'We're afraid to open the door a crack because it may just crash in on us.' "

Miller's slow building-block process would pay off as the first open challenge to the Lords began to build in 1968. It revolved around the one issue that had long been the players' rallying point: the pension.

The first pension agreement Miller had negotiated was to expire in March 1969. The Lords' current contribution was $4.1 million annually, and he wanted a big increase. Baseball's network TV money had risen another 40 percent, to $16.5 million a year. Baseball's addition of four expansion teams in 1969 would add one hundred more players who would have to be covered. The nation's inflation rate had climbed steadily, and a COLA maven like Miller would always expect to match it.

By mid-1968, Miller had his proposals ready:

- A $5.9 million annual contribution to the pension (an increase of 44 percent).
- A reduction in the waiting period to qualify for the pension, from five years to four. (Miller, ever the assiduous researcher, had found that the five-year threshold excluded 59 percent of all players who made the majors. A four-year rule would cover over half of those previously excluded.)
- A retroactive application of the increased benefits and lower vesting requirement. Anyone who'd played in the last ten years would share with current players in the improvements.

Miller went to Baltimore to meet Orioles owner Jerry Hoffberger and try to get talks going at least informally.

Hoffberger was the American League's representative on pension matters. He was, as Miller later recalled, "friendly, polite, and not particularly sympathetic."

It only got worse. The Lords announced that they didn't want to bargain during the season: something about it being "harmful to the players and taking their minds off the game."

Miller suspected an ulterior motive, though he was sufficiently offended by the condescension of the stated one. He thought the Lords were going to play hardball. In September, he met with every team to tell them so. He wanted the players to know what they might have to do if the Lords refused to budge on the pension: refuse to sign 1969 contracts.

The players had already gotten their first taste of the power of group action. That spring they had done the once unthinkable: refused to sign their baseball-card contracts.

The Topps Company was as much a baseball-business icon as Hillerich and Bradsby, the maker of the Louisville Slugger. Its baseball cards were religiously collected, traded, flipped, and installed in bicycle spokes. Their arrival in grocery stores was a rite of spring for American boys. They tore open the waxed packs, inhaled the sweet smell of bubble gum, and thumbed through the cards, hoping against hope for a Mays or Mantle.

Topps seemed more a piece of Americana than a business—unless you were a player. They signed contracts with Topps that were astonishingly one-sided. The company got to every raw kid in the minors and gave him five dollars for exclusive rights to the use of his picture on a card. A player, flattered to death, would scribble his name on the contract and hope to God he was eventually worthy of a card.

If a player made it to the bigs, he signed a five-year contract for $125 a year. That wasn't quite all. Every spring, Topps's Sy Berger would make an eagerly awaited visit to each team. Berger's corporate title was "player liaison," but his function was a cross between Santa Claus and a mobile S&H Green Stamp redemption center. Berger bore a catalog full of merchandise: everything from radios to refrigerators, luggage to lawn furniture. The players picked their gift; Topps shipped the goodies to their homes; and players figured they'd gotten something for nothing—sort of like being Bulova Star of the Game. They were also, of course, heroes with their wives.

Sy Berger, haunting big-league clubhouses and bush-league locker rooms alike, was such an ingrained part of the scene he was once crowned "King of Baseball." The title was bestowed at each year's winter meetings on a wizened baseball lifer. Nobody was exactly sure what it signified, but it was a hoary tradition that called for the king to wear a crown and robe at the meetings' big banquet.

Berger's most important function for Topps was to keep every player under contract. Topps signed everybody to five-year contracts. Two years into each, it was renewed for another five years for a "bonus" of seventy-five dollars. In baseball's best tradition, Topps thereby reserved every player in perpetuity. No competitor could ever take away a player—or any piece of the baseball-card business.

The players didn't mind. Topps wasn't about money; it was about status. Al Ferrara, when asked once whey he wanted to be a ballplayer, answered, "I always wanted to see my picture on a bubble-gum card."

But Marvin Miller saw it as another blatant screwing of the players. He also saw opportunity. If he could bargain a group contract with Topps, the players could get a better deal and the union might get a cut, too. The union needed the operating funds and Miller had already seen the possibilities of licensing. A two-year $120,000 licensing deal with Coca-Cola—to put players' pictures on bottle caps—had kept the union afloat in the early days.

Miller set up a meeting with Topps's president, Joel Shorin. There he launched into the inequities of the system and his proposals for change, going on at some length with his usual impeccable logic. Shorin's reply was briefer: "There will be no changes, because, honestly, I don't see any muscle in your position. Topps has the players signed to contracts, and I don't see what you can do about it."

Miller *did* do something about it. As he met with players during spring training of 1968, he brought up Topps. He told them how unfair a contract they had, how unresponsive Shorin had been, and concluded: "The only leverage you have is not to sign renewals. Eventually Topps will have contracts with no one."

Sensing trouble, Sy Berger scrambled around the Grapefruit League trying to get to the players before Miller. But it was too late. Players, in droves, were refusing to sign on anymore. The next meeting, at midseason 1968, came at Topps's request. "I see your muscle," said Joel Shorin. "Let's sit down and talk."

The new deal doubled the players' yearly fee to $250 from $125. More important, it paid the union 8 percent on sales up to

$4 million a year and 10 percent on sales over that. The first year of the arrangement would yield the union about $320,000. It was only a trickle in the torrent of baseball-card royalties to come, but it was like found money and it reinforced the players' confidence in Miller.

Having shown it to Topps, now he would show the Lords his muscle.

The Lords' silence on the pension remained absolute into December. When baseball's winter meetings convened in San Francisco early that month, Miller gathered his executive board there, too. He hoped to get a joint meeting and get the talks off the ground. But once there, the players got the word: forget it. The Lords were too busy.

They *were* very busy, in fact, firing Spike Eckert and trying to decide what to do next. But with the memory of the Mexico City snub still fresh, and with frustration over the pension mounting, Miller and the players weren't in an understanding mood. They would never again convene the union's annual meeting in the shadow of the Lords'. Nor would they delay any longer. It was time, urged Miller, to take the fight to them.

His idea was to use an old tactic—the holdout—but with a new twist. Instead of a single player refusing to report until satisfied with his contract, *hundreds* of players would hold out. The board bought it. That day, it voted to recommend that no player sign a 1969 contract until there was a pension agreement. The player reps then recessed for a phone-a-thon, in which they called every teammate reachable that day, asking if he'd publicly support the board's position. In five hours they'd reached 450 players, and gotten 450 endorsements.

Miller held a press conference the next day—at the winter meetings site, the Palace Hotel, to be sure the Lords noticed. There he announced the mass holdout and called the roll of players on board: Willie Mays, Hank Aaron, Roberto Clemente, Pete Rose, Frank Robinson, Willie Stargell, Willie McCovey, Don Drysdale, Ernie Banks, Tommy John, Rod Carew, Harmon Killebrew, Frank Howard, Eddie Matthews, and on and on.

It was Miller's first public-relations masterstroke. There were scores of writers covering the winter meetings, and they ate it up. They may not have understood the National Labor Relations Act but they understood an all-star lineup of holdouts.

It was also the first indication of Miller's fine sense of tactics and timing. In 1966, 1967, maybe even 1968, it would have been too early to put the players in this spot. It still would have been too early to call for an outright strike—too many players were still chary of even *being* in a union. But a holdout: that was something everybody understood and many of them had done individually.

In mid-December, the Lords finally formulated an offer: $5.1 million. The two sides were $800,000 apart on the annual pension contribution and worlds apart on the other issues. The Lords wanted to keep the number of years to vest at five. They wanted to confine benefits increased to current players. They utterly rejected Miller's contention that the contribution keep pace with the TV money. The two had been de-linked in the 1966 negotiations, John Gaherin argued, and they would stay that way.

Miller, outraged, did some math, which he shared with the players. The current pension deal required each of the twenty clubs to contribute $205,000 per year. The new offer only increased the per-club contribution to $212,500. (There were now four more clubs to help divide the costs.) That was just $125 more per player. Running in place like that was really sliding backward. It was just as Robin Roberts had feared in the mid-sixties: the Lords were trying to cut the players out of the TV growth.

Miller put it to a vote. Having been informed they'd been insulted, the players could vote just one way: thumbs down, 491-7. They were ready to hold out.

Now it was the Lords' turn to be insulted. *Nobody* defied them like that. It particularly galled the players' immediate superiors, the GMs, who were accustomed to absolute control. The stories were legion.

Pitcher John O'Donoghue had once agreed to contract terms by phone with Kansas City A's GM Eddie Lopat. The actual contract didn't arrive until spring training, and the salary figures in it were considerably less than discussed.

"But you agreed to a different figure on the phone," O'Donoghue said.

"Prove it," Lopat sneered.

Of course, Lopat had learned at the feet of the master: George Weiss, GM of the Yankees' dynasty teams of the 1950s. More precisely, he'd been kicked by the feet of the master. As a Yankee pitcher, Lopat went 15–10 one year and got no raise because, according to Weiss, "You didn't pitch against contending clubs."

The next year Lopat went 18-8, and this time he kept close track of the opponents. Twelve of his wins were against contenders. "You can't tell me nothing now about contending clubs," he told Weiss. Lopat won a hard-fought $2,000 raise.

That was Weiss, a man who countered Mickey Mantle's bid to double his 1957 salary with a detective's report. Mantle wanted $65,000 after his Triple Crown season of 1956 (52 homers, 130 RBIs, and a .353 batting average). Weiss wanted him to know that his off-field exploits—also eye-popping—had been documented. "It can hurt your image, Mickey," he said. It was unnecessary for Weiss to add the words "to say nothing of your marriage," but the implications were clear.

Not all GMs were as tight-fisted and mean-spirited as Weiss. The Dodgers' Buzzie Bavasi whipped hundred-dollar bills out of his coat pocket to stake his boys' nights on the town. He fined them for their hijinks but never collected. He also made their contract negotiations a game, albeit one that heavily favored the house.

There was, for instance, the dummy-contract ruse. Ron Fairly once came into Bavasi's office looking for a big raise. The GM made sure to leave Tommy Davis's contract out on his desk, then made an excuse to leave the room. Fairly couldn't resist looking, as Bavasi knew he would. The figure was $18,500. This changed Fairly's thinking. He'd planned to ask for much more, but, hey, Davis was the NL batting champion. Fairly signed for $18,500, not knowing it was a fake contract. Tommy Davis made $50,000.

But Bavasi also had a game for players whom he thought asked for *less* than they should. Gil Hodges once came in seeking $25,000. This was under what Bavasi had in mind, but he couldn't tell Hodges that. Word would get around that the old man was getting soft.

"Gil, you're a horseplayer," he said. "You want twenty-five, and I'll let you play the odds. I'm going to put five slips of paper in his hat—twenty-three, twenty-four, twenty-five, twenty-six, and twenty-seven. You've got three chances out of five at getting at least twenty-five thousand. You game?"

"Let's do it," said Hodges.

Bavasi scribbled on five slips, mixed them up in the hat and let Hodges draw. It was twenty-seven. The first baseman was delighted. He didn't know that every slip in there said twenty-seven.

But whether GMs took the fascist or friendlier approach, the dynamic was the same. They were all-powerful. "If owners were the kings," said the Twins' Clark Griffith, "the GMs were the princes."

Players occasionally tried to use an agent, but the GMs consistently sent them packing. (Players had no right to representation until the 1970 Basic Agreement.) When pitcher Earl Wilson brought one in for contract talks with Jim Campbell, the Tigers' GM wouldn't hear of it. The agent, Bob Woolf, sat out in their car while Wilson kept taking bathroom breaks and scooting out for consultations. That was Woolf's introduction to baseball.

(Football can "boast" an even better agent-rebuff story. It seems that a Green Bay Packers player once brought an agent into Vince Lombardi's office, announcing that he'd be negotiating the contract for him. The legendary coach and GM excused himself, then returned a few moments later. "Your agent will be negotiating with the Cleveland Browns," said Lombardi.)

The GMs were united in their commitment to the existing order, and their own tight fraternity. They sent each other telegrams on Opening Day wishing best of luck. They generally conducted their affairs—whether trading or just swapping information—over cocktails. "Drinking was an integral part of this business, and poor drinkers were in trouble," said Red Sox GM Dick O'Connell.

(The Lords, for that matter, wouldn't think of meeting without libations. The National League only ended the practice when it came to cause too much confusion. Horace Stoneham would case his vote one way in the morning and then, three sheets to the wind by afternoon, demand to change it. The NL's new teetotaling policy didn't stop Stoneham. He'd just pop over to the bar at the American League meeting.)

The GMs even consulted one another on salary decisions. Brooks Robinson and Al Kaline both had great seasons one year in the sixties. Baltimore GM Lee MacPhail and Detroit GM Jim Campbell put their heads together and agreed they each deserved a healthy raise: $7,500. Thus did the GMs ensure that baseball's pay scale remained in order.

Nevertheless, the GMs weren't above hornswoggling each other. Much of Branch Rickey's legend was built on just that. But, hell, that was as much a part of the game as loading up a spitter. Everybody got over it and got a good laugh out of it. Veteran baseball men Chub Feeney and Lee MacPhail had a running joke for years about the Bill Monbouquette trade. When Feeney was the Giants' GM, he'd obtained the veteran pitcher from the Yankees, only to find he couldn't lift his arm above his shoulder. MacPhail, then the Yankees' GM, was shocked, *shocked* to learn of it.

Mostly, however, the GMs governed themselves by gentlemen's agreements that worked to everyone's mutual benefit—everyone except the players, of course. Take the so-called Rule 5 draft, which enabled clubs to draft other clubs' minorleaguers. If a player had been in the minors three years and wasn't on the forty-man major league roster, he was eligible to be drafted. A GM who didn't want to lose a prospect but didn't have room on his roster worked a "parking" deal with a GM buddy. The player would be drafted by the buddy team. Then, for some small consideration, he'd be quietly returned to his original team the next spring. It was everyday business to the GMs and a cruel hoax on the player.

Years later, when the Lords stopped signing free agents and the union accused them of collusion, a veteran baseball man was discussing the situation. He sighed nostalgically: "There was no collusion like old-style collusion."

The GMs were ferocious in their attack on Miller and on this union that would dare challenge the existing order. The most vehement was the Braves' Paul Richards. A tall, gaunt westerner, out of Waxahachie, Texas, he had the leathery face and piercing eyes of the classic "baseball man," which he was—a 1930s-vintage catcher who'd been in the game ever since. The press, whom he cultivated, dubbed him "The Wizard of Waxahachie." As Hoyt Wilhelm's manager on the 1950s Orioles, he'd invented the oversized catcher's mitt, widely used for handling knuckleballers. As a GM in Baltimore, Houston, and Atlanta, he was an expert conniver. He'd tried to keep outfielder Chuck Hinton out of the 1961 expansion draft by faking an injury. He'd tried to hide a prospect in the Orioles' farm system by not reporting his signing bonus. (At the time, "bonus babies" had to go on the major league roster.) Richards was definitely of the George Weiss hardball school.

Paul Richards hated the union even more than he hated a tengame losing streak. He called Marvin Miller everything from a Communist to a "mustachioed four-flusher"—fighting words in Waxahachie. "Miller speaks mainly for a few rabble-rousers and greedy ballplayers," he insisted.

As the players' mass holdout movement picked up steam, so did Richards's vitriol. In the Lords' private councils he urged opening the season with minor-leaguers if need be. In frequent public comments, he blasted away.

"Let 'em strike," Richards barked in mid-January. "Maybe if they do, it will get the guys who don't want to play out of the game and let the fellows who appreciate the major leagues play." Of course, he noted a bit later, "I don't think the players have enough guts to strike."

Richards did intimidate some Braves into breaking ranks and signing contracts. But overall he only succeeded in stiffening the players' resolve. Frank Lane called up to tell his lodge brother so. "Paul, for God's sake, stop talking," he said. "All you're doing is aiding the enemy."

Miller worked feverishly to maintain the players' unity. Early February was a crucial juncture. It had been a long two months since the San Francisco no-sign vows, and it was a few short weeks before spring training camps opened. He had to ensure that the resolve didn't crumble. So Miller summoned a half-dozen or so players from each team to a meeting in New York. Then he held his breath. This was the dead of winter and the bulk of players lived far away. How many would come?

About 130 players crowded into a ballroom at the Biltmore Hotel on February 3, the largest nonsporting gathering of players in baseball history. It was an astonishing session—part pep rally, part revival meeting. Player after player stood up to testify.

Dick Allen, in flowing dashiki, made a quiet, eloquent speech.

Joe Torre, his voice cracking from a cold, spoke passionately about the importance of sticking together.

Players' activism would keep the Spirit of Biltmore alive long after the meeting broke up. The players set up regional phone networks to keep information flowing and spirits up. Miller kept in steady contact with about two dozen players in different parts of the country. They, in turn, would disseminate the latest. Gary Peters, for instance, lived in Sarasota. The White Sox pitcher would phone a set list of other Florida residents, who would, in turn, call other players. It was thus possible for virtually every player to get daily progress reports, instead of relying on newspaper stories.

That was important, for press coverage was heavily antiunion. Most sportswriters, dependent on management sources, and indignant that business had intruded on sport, toed the Lords' party line. *The Sporting News*, baseball's bible, which then received a small subsidy from the commissioner's office, was vitriolically anti-Miller. Some teams sent packets of columns blasting the "privileged, pampered players" out to players.

Press coverage also dwelt heavily on players who had splintered off and signed contracts. Miller came out of the Biltmore meeting with over 400 holdout commitments, but there were, in fact, defectors: Jim Palmer and Pete Richert of Baltimore, Clay Carroll of Cincinnati, Jerry Grote of the Mets, and a handful more.

In addition, some stars, although they didn't sign, were seriously waffling. The Cubs' Ron Santo said he'd report to spring training March 1, the official reporting date, whether or not the pension dispute was settled. "Mr. Wrigley has been good to me, and I'm going to be good to him," he said. Carl Yastrzemski declared his fealty to Red Sox owner Tom Yawkey, and said he too might report if the dispute went on too long.

The Lords didn't budge. With the opening of spring training, they were sure the trickle of signing players would turn into a flood. There was a chance they were right. The 400 declared holdouts comprised 80 percent of the players, but that number was surely subject to erosion. Miller, only in his third full year, didn't command overwhelming loyalty.

On a mid-February Friday, John Gaherin finally gave Miller a new proposal. It had barely budged from that of mid-December. But it was all he was going to get, Gaherin told him.

"That's the last, final, best offer," he said. "Take it out and see what you can do with it. Get it voted up or down."

Miller hung up, discouraged. The siege would continue. But there was something he did not know. Nor did Gaherin, for that matter. The Lords were not nearly as unified as they appeared. Their internal politics was about to stumble over the pension standoff. Not for the last time would an ultimatum from the Lords wither.

Getting Spike Eckert cashiered at the winter meetings was no problem. Neither was finding a remedy to baseball's collective batting slump. (At the meetings, the Lords voted to lower the pitching mound and shrink the strike zone.) Electing a new commissioner, however, turned out to be a huge problem.

Three weeks after the winter meetings, the Lords flew to Chicago to meet at an airport hotel and elect a commissioner. They settled around a long U-shaped table—and into a long stalemate. The National League was lined up behind Chub Feeney, vice president of the Giants. The American League solidly backed Mike Burke, the Yankees' president.

The differences between the two reflected the two leagues. Feeney was still a relatively young man of forty-seven, but, as Horace Stoneham's nephew, he moved comfortably in old-boy circles. Burke had been in baseball only since 1964, when CBS bought the Yankees. He had long hair and a long, colorful résumé: the OSS, CIA, Ringling Brothers, and CBS. The National League disdainfully called him "the circus guy."

The meeting began at 4:15 P.M. and went through round after round of deadlocked vote. A commissioner needed 75 percent support from both leagues and it seemed hopeless. There was also a brief swell for John McHale, GM of the new Montreal Expos, minor support for Supreme Court Justice Byron R. "Whizzer" White, and even some mention of the players' old advocate, Judge Cannon. Calvin Griffith of the Twins voted for Joe Cronin, his brother-in-law, round after round. By 3:00 A.M., things were so desperate that Yankees GM Lee MacPhail was called to see if he'd be interested. No, he mumbled. He drew thirteen votes anyway.

At 4:55 A.M., after nineteen ballots, they gave up.

In early February 1969, the Lords reconvened in Bal Harbour, Florida. The Feeney-Burke stalemate quickly set in again, and there was nothing to do but recess and regroup. Walter O'Malley called a caucus of seven of baseball's elders, his fertile mind again at work. A blank neutral choice would be the perfect stuff of compromise. A short tether would help: maybe a probationary commissioner, just to make certain they had no Eckert replay. A National Leaguer would be ideal, for O'Malley's control purposes, and he had just the man in mind.

"There's somebody we know," the Dodgers owner said when the meeting began again. "There's somebody who did very well with the Milwaukee case . . . and that's Bowie Kuhn." Bowie Kent Kuhn was the forty-two-year-old assistant counsel of the National League.

In the mid-sixties, the good burghers of Milwaukee had been sore about the Braves' plan to leave for Atlanta in 1966. Milwaukee County and the state of Wisconsin sued to keep the club there, claiming that Major League Baseball had violated state antitrust laws in approving the Braves' move. Bowie Kuhn was pressed into service as the Lords' lead counsel.

He lost in Milwaukee County Court, where the judge enjoined

the Braves from leaving. But Kuhn was successful when he argued the appeal before the Wisconsin Supreme Court. Now, Bowie Kuhn wasn't brilliant, as would be seen in later years. But he was swinging at the law's equivalent of a hanging curveball. Baseball's federal antitrust exemption, he argued, undercut any claim made under state antitrust law. Baseball won the appeal and Kuhn won some favor with the Lords.

Kuhn did have the regal bearing of commissioner material. He was an imposing six feet five inches tall and spoke in the measured, patrician tones of the Princeton-educated, white-shoed lawyer he was. (Like "Wise Man" Lou Carroll, he was a partner at Willkie, Farr and Gallagher.) Kuhn also did genuinely love baseball. He'd been a scoreboard boy at Griffith Stadium in his native Washington, D.C., and could rattle off the starting lineup of the 1944 St. Louis Browns, among other feats of trivia. Kuhn had one other vital trait: he was a consummate servant of the establishment.

Kuhn's nomination finally broke the logjam. He was elected commissioner pro tem, for a one-year term, and quickly accepted.

There was one thing Bowie Kuhn couldn't abide in his first month as baseball commissioner: no baseball. That was just what he was facing in mid-February, as spring training opened for pitchers and catchers. Minor-leaguers and rookies who weren't union members reported. So did some fringe veterans and boycott-breakers like Jim Palmer. But overall, players were holding the line. The White Sox canceled a series of early exhibition games that had been scheduled in Mexico City. Kuhn stewed.

He jawboned owners. He kept lines open to Miller. He urged both sides to talk seriously and often. And on the very day Gaherin made his "last, best offer," Kuhn called the Cardinals' Dick Meyer, the PRC chairman.

"This is no way for a commissioner to start out," said Kuhn.

Meyer was the president of Anheuser-Busch and, among the owners, the most intelligent voice on labor. He'd overseen it for years at the brewery. Meyer was foursquare behind the hardline position, not because he was a throwback to the days of antiunion goons but because he knew, from experience, that if you gave an aggressive trade-unionist like Marvin Miller an inch, he'd take a mile. Miller wasn't that strong yet, and Meyer wanted to keep him that way.

But Meyer knew something else. Baseball had been through a bad winter of deadlocks and setbacks. Kuhn wanted to hit the ground running. He couldn't do it with quicksand under him. And baseball didn't need another black eye after its awful 1968. The two men talked for a while. Kuhn urged some more bargaining and some more "give." Meyer, with some misgivings, said he'd do what he could.

Before doing anything else, he called Chub Feeney in Scottsdale, Arizona, where the Giants were training. Meyer had backed Feeney for commissioner, liked him personally, and wanted him to know what was going on.

"Bowie's got us back at the bargaining table," Meyer said. "He doesn't want to start off his regime with a strike."

Feeney was shocked and dismayed. He knew there were Giants holdouts holed up in motels within five miles of camp. He'd heard that even the team's player reps were wavering. All the owners had to do was hold out a little while longer. "The players are dying to come back," he told Meyer.

But Meyer went ahead and called John Gaherin the next morning at home, where he was spending a Saturday relaxing. All was right with the world. Feeney's words were still ringing in his ears from when they'd wrapped up the talks: "We've got him [Miller] by the balls. You did good."

Meyer's call immediately shattered Gaherin's feeling of well-being.

"Bowie called me," said Meyer. "Let me tell you where I stand on this, because I have a little different perspective than you. I wear two caps. I'm chairman of the PRC. I'm also president of the St. Louis Cardinals. I just voted for Bowie for commissioner, and I'm not willing to see him begin his tenure with a strike. Can you recontact Miller?"

"I can always contact him, but hear this," said Gaherin. "You're a labor man; you know what that means. If I call and ask if we can meet again next week, Marvin knows goddamned well I have orders to shift. The balance of power will have shifted from management to union henceforth. He's going to know from now on that 'no' is not 'no.'"

"You're right," conceded Meyer, "but I don't want to see a strike. Offer them another $200,000."

"Have a nice weekend, Dick," Gaherin sighed.

Gaherin assuredly did *not* have a nice weekend.

* * *

He made the new offer to Miller: they could go to $5.3 million.
Miller rejected it with a show of scorn—and with secret delight.

One week later they reached an agreement that tilted a long
way toward the players. It included:

- A $5.45 million pension contribution.
- A lowering of the vesting requirement to four years.
- A $10-a-month increase in benefits for each year a player
  spent in the majors. (A player could now collect $60 a month
  at age fifty for each year he'd played.)
- A ten-year retroactive application of benefits and vesting requirements.

It was a disheartening juncture for Gaherin and a magnificent
win for Miller. Not because of the money, which, as Gaherin
later reflected, "was peanuts." But he'd discovered the players
could hold their ground. He'd gained still more of the players'
confidence, and was greeted by their applause at all his training-
camp meetings that spring. Yes, he had discovered that the
mighty Lords weren't invulnerable after all.

The Lords would get their little revenges on players, however.
Spring training was right on top of them, and the dispute had
left little time to negotiate contracts. Players weren't allowed to
suit up without one, and to miss much spring training was
dangerous—you could lose your job, or lag in conditioning. The
players, left with no time to negotiate contracts, were vulnerable
to take-it-or-leave-it offers. Some GMs squeezed the player ring-
leaders particularly hard.

Paul Richards busily revenged himself on Joe Torre. The
Braves catcher had suffered through a sub-par 1968: 10 homers,
55 RBIs, a .271 average. Now the Waxahachie Wizard wanted to
cut his salary the maximum 20 percent. Torre refused to sign.

Now, Torre was a lifetime .294 hitter in eight years with the
Braves. He'd had a 36-homer, 101-RBI, .315 season in 1966. He
was a heady catcher, destined to become a manager. He'd had
the relatively bad year because of injuries. But nothing got a
player on Paul Richards's master shit list like being a union activist. "For as much good as he's done this club," Richards told
the writers, "I don't care if he holds out until Thanksgiving."

After spring training was under way, Braves chairman Bill
Bartholomay offered to fly Torre to Florida to meet with Richards. He thought a face-to-face meeting might help. So did Torre

until he walked into Richards's office. The GM quickly and frostily made clear he wasn't budging from his 20 percent cut position.

Torre, who'd been working for a Wall Street municipal-bonds firm in the off-season, put his business card on the GM's desk. "If you need me, here's where you can reach me," he said.

Richards picked up the card gingerly, as though disposing of some noxious waste, and dropped it in the wastebasket. Two weeks later, Torre was traded to St. Louis.

Gussie Busch was also furious. The pension dispute had ended, but his rage at the players went on and on. The impertinence. The ingrates. They didn't know how good they had it. Well, he was going to give them a piece of his mind.

The St. Louis Cardinals' owner *was* good to his players. St. Louis had baseball's first $1 million payroll in 1968. (A *Sports Illustrated* cover showed the starting nine and listed their outlandish salaries on an overleaf.) On the road, the players had private rooms in the best hotels. When they came home, they each got a free case of beer. Busch hosted picnics for players' families. When teams still traveled by rail, Busch's luxurious private Pullman, the *Adolphus*, was often hitched to the back of the Cardinals' train for the players' use. Now they flew in roomy chartered jets. (To be sure, if a player ate on the plane it cost him four dollars of his eight-dollar-a-day meal allowance.)

But this had all been granted by the beneficent hand of Augustus A. Busch, Jr. No damned union was going to tell him what to do. He wasn't a Lord of baseball only, he was corporate royalty. His grandfather, a German immigrant named Adolphus Busch, brewed the first beer sold nationwide and ruthlessly conquered new markets with price wars. His father, Augustus A. Busch, Sr., had artfully nursed Anheuser-Busch through prohibition by selling ingredients for home brew. Gussie took over the company in the forties. He managed it like he did everything else, said one aide: "by the seat of his pants."

Gussie Busch was a visceral, not an intellectual, being who dropped out of school after ninth grade. He was a brawler who once installed a boxing ring at his mansion; a boozer who tossed back three martinis and six beers with dinner; a womanizer who went through three wives; and a relentlessly domineering tyrant.

God should live as well as Gussie Busch. His country estate was called Grant's Farm, because it had been tilled by Ulysses S. Grant before he went on to military and political pursuits. The house was a French Renaissance–style chateau, where the servants were summoned by a bell rope. The sprawling grounds, which Busch toured by horse-drawn carriage, were stocked with bison, deer, elephants, cattle, camels, zebras, llamas, yaks, and various other animals.

"He lived in a feudal style—the castle, the animals, the horse and carriages—and he had the attitude of an old feudal lord," Ewing Kauffman, the Kansas City Royals owner, later recalled. "He could be generous but his attitude was, 'I'll pay you what *I* say.' "

His positions—reactionary and emotional as they were—did much to shape baseball's official line. Busch could stampede opinion at ownership meetings through his sheer vehemence. It also happened that he headed a company that sponsored many teams' broadcasts. "He was very inattentive; his attention span was moments," recalled Sandy Hadden, the commissioner's aide. "But the thing that gave him a platform was Anheuser-Busch."

Thus did the richest of the Lords move them, on union matters, toward the lowest common denominator.

Baseball had been very, very good to Gussie Busch. His 1953 purchase of the Cardinals for $3.75 million was integral to bringing his brewing company back from the doldrums. Publicly he maintained at the time that he was just acting as a civic angel. Fred Saigh had to sell and the city feared the team would move.

Privately, it was another matter. The first thing he did was move to rename Sportsman's Park "Budweiser Stadium." (Aides talked him out of it.) The second thing he did was make an announcement to his board. "Development of the Cardinals will have untold value for our company," said Busch. "This is one of the finest moves in the history of Anheuser-Busch."

He was right.

Beer is an image product, and suddenly Budweiser was synonymous with the sport Joe Sixpack loved. Gussie Busch was Budweiser's leading salesman, and suddenly, as a baseball owner, he was a celebrity. This raised his profile and made him one hell of a salesman: Gussie Busch on the cover of *Time* magazine; Gussie Busch at a brewery opening; Gussie Busch crisscrossing the nation in his *Adolphus* railcar, delivering pep talks to distributors. When the pre-Cardinals Gussie Busch came to town, his PR people had to beg for coverage. Now he was a media event.

Cardinals games blanketed the Midwest via a fourteen-state radio network. They were filled not only with play-by-play action but with nonstop Budweiser plugs from announcer Harry Caray. The stadium itself featured a huge neon Anheuser-Busch eagle, echoed with the sounds of the Budweiser theme song, and occasionally featured the corporate Clydesdales.

It was the beginning of a sports-marketing blitz that carried Anheuser-Busch from a weak second in the American brewing industry to, truly, the king of beers. Four years after its acquisition of the Cardinals, in 1957, the company passed Schlitz and never looked back. Anheuser-Busch, which brewed 6 million barrels of beer in 1953, had nearly quadrupled production by the early seventies.

The difference between the owners' and the players' positions on pension funding was the equivalent of a few drops of spillage from a brewing vat. It amounted to $800,000 for baseball collectively, just $33,000 for the Cardinals.

Yet Gussie Busch was mortally offended. It went to the heart of his need to bestow rather than be dictated to. It wasn't that he'd never encountered a union. His company had dealt with them since the 1880s, when Adolphus Busch had reluctantly negotiated with his brewery workers on a reduced workweek: six twelve-hour days. But Gussie was accustomed to co-opting and controlling labor leaders. Teamsters president David Beck was downright reasonable after his son got the Anheuser-Busch distributorship for the states of Washington and Alaska. But you couldn't do business like that with this Marvin Miller character.

Moreover, he viewed ballplayers differently from the brewery masses. Baseball was a matter of patronage, not collective bargaining. Busch set up Stan Musial in the restaurant business in St. Louis. He awarded Roger Maris an Anheuser-Busch distributorship in Florida. He gave Lou Brock a yacht when he retired.

On March 22, 1969, he walked into the Cardinals' spring training clubhouse at St. Petersburg. His boys needed to be straightened out. He even brought in Anheuser-Busch's directors and the Cardinals' beat writers to witness the dressing-down.

"Gentlemen," he began, "I don't think there is any secret about the fact that I am not a very good loser. One thing is for sure. I don't like to lose in baseball, and I don't like to lose in the beer business. For that reason, you can well understand that there have been a number of times in the past seventeen years when I felt like giving the club away."

Busch recited the selfless sacrifices he had made: pouring millions into sprucing up old Sportsman's Park; investing $5 million in the new Busch Stadium, while absorbing a 500 percent increase in rent and forgoing all sources of stadium revenue except for the gate. He told them they should also appreciate all the "civic-minded" people who put up the money for Busch Stadium never expecting to see any return.

They had to build that stadium, he continued, because people were demanding modern conveniences at the ballpark. Baseball had to compete hard for the entertainment dollar now with basketball, hockey, and football. The fans had a lot of choices.

"But I wonder if we are putting them all in focus these days," he said. "If you don't already know it, I can tell you now—from the letters, phone calls, and conversations we've had recently— that fans are no longer as sure as they were before about their high regard for the game and the players.

"Let's take a good look at the past winter ourselves. What do we see? We almost didn't have a season at all. Some of our players who ought to be in top condition reported late for spring training. Baseball's union representatives made all kinds of derogatory statements about the owners. We suddenly seem to be your greatest enemies. Your representatives threw down all kinds of challenges, threats, and ultimatums.

"Believe me, it wasn't easy for most owners to agree not to answer back on some of the allegations, charges, ultimatums, and challenges thrown down to us during the past months. But, in the main, we didn't engage in this kind of inter-quarreling because we didn't think it would help baseball or the players.

"In any case, you now have the most liberal pension plan to be found anywere, in any business, in any profession or in any sport in the whole world. As a group, your salaries are higher than they have ever been at any time. . . . True, you deserve to be well paid in accordance with your playing ability. But I must call your attention to the fact that you take few, if any, of the great risks involved.

"I know you may think I am lecturing to you. And some of you will be very cynical about what I have said. I must tell you that it's all right with me. I do believe, however, that as the president of a major league baseball team with the highest salary total in all the history of baseball, I have a right to talk to you and to talk to you as men . . . frankly and straight from the shoulder.

"I do believe I have an obligation to remind you that this year, instead of talking baseball all during the off-season, most fans have had a steady diet of strike talk and dollar signs. I hope that is all behind us now. It has to be behind us. Too many fans are saying our players are getting fat ... that they now only think of money ... and less of the game itself. And it's the game they love and have enjoyed and paid for all these years.

"I hope that many millions of fans will retain their loyalty to baseball. We are going to do everything we can do to make sure they do. But you can bet on one thing ... the fans will be looking at you this year more critically than ever before, to see how you perform, and to see whether or not you are really giving everything you have.

"I am not asking you to do anything for me. I am not going to talk about such corny things as 'hustle.' That's supposed to be old-fashioned. But if we don't have the right attitudes, if we don't give everything we have to those who pay their way into the park, then you can be sure they'll know it and we'll know it.

"Personally, I don't react well to ultimatums. I don't mind negotiations—that's how we get together—but ultimatums rub me the wrong way, and I think ultimatums rub the fans the wrong way. This is no pep talk. I have not tried to bawl you out. But I have tried to point out that baseball is at a serious point in its history.

"I don't know what the future will bring. I do believe we can shape and influence that future. If you are counting on security at age fifty—or sixty-five—then you have an obligation to help make the people who love the game—who pay to see it played, who listen to it day after day—enjoy watching and listening to it."

Busch asked if the players had any questions. Dead silence. The meeting broke up and the writers circulated among the players. Any comments? No one said a word. One of the players stood there in a particularly raging silence. His name was Curt Flood.

By 1968, CURT FLOOD was baseball's finest center fielder. Willie Mays partisans would have given you an argument, but a *Sports Illustrated* cover that year proclaimed him such. The record spoke for itself. Flood had set a major league fielding record for most consecutive games without an error: 223. In all, he went 568 chances without an error, another record for outfielders. Flood had also made himself into a fine hitter over his twelve years with the Cardinals. His career average was .293. He hit .335 and .301 in 1967 and 1968, to finish fourth and fifth in the league, respectively.

Flood was a vital link in the great Cardinals teams of the sixties, if overshadowed by more colorful characters, such as Bob Gibson, the imposing fireballer; Lou Brock, the stolen-base king; Orlando Cepeda, the slugger and spiritual leader. They were an animated, outspoken bunch, and the 1965 roster alone included eleven future broadcasters.

Flood was a quiet man, a deep thinker, and an independent cuss. He told friends on the club that he'd refuse to go if the Cardinals ever traded him. He'd quit before he left St. Louis. He had strong ties to the city, after playing for the Cardinals since 1958, and had begun a photographic and art business on the side. Flood was an outstanding portrait painter, whose rendering of Gussie Busch hung in the saloon of the owner's yacht.

Busch looked with rather more favor on that than on Flood's 1969 salary demand. The Cardinals offered $77,500; the player firmly rejected it. He'd slowly, steadily climbed the salary scale through the 1960s: $16,000 in 1962, to $23,000 in 1964, to $45,000 in 1966, to $72,500 in 1968. Now, at age thirty-one, he wanted to reach closer to the magical $100,000 while still in his prime.

"If you people want a .300 hitter who also happens to be the best center fielder in baseball it will cost you ninety thousand dollars," said Flood, "which is not seventy-seven five and is not eighty-nine thousand, nine hundred, and ninety-nine."

Flood got his $90,000, after a brief holdout. But he never did get over Gussie Busch's clubhouse speech. "Busch had been talking to us in code," Flood later wrote. "He had been telling us to behave or get out. I no longer felt like a ninety-thousand-dollar ballplayer but like a green recruit. . . . I was sick with shame and so was everyone else on the Cardinals except Busch and his claque."

Flood slogged through a sub-par year, hitting .285. The Cardinals slumped to fourth place. After the season, in early October, Flood was sitting in his apartment reflecting on it when the phone rang.

"Hello, Curt?"

"Yes."

"Jim Toomey, Curt."

It was GM Bing Devine's assistant.

"Curt, you've been traded to Philadelphia."

Flood was silent, stunned.

"You, McCarver, Horner, and Byron Browne. For Richie Allen, Cookie Rojas, and Jerry Johnson."

Still Flood said nothing.

"Good luck, Curt."

It was only later in the day that Flood spoke his first and true reaction. "There ain't no way I'm going to pack up and move twelve years of my life away from here," he told a friend. "No way at all."

Things started moving fast—as fast as Curt Flood tracking down a gapper. In November, Flood called Marvin Miller to tell him he wanted to file a suit against Major League Baseball, challenging the reserve system. In December, the union committed to paying Flood's legal expenses, and to handle the case, Miller lined up his old Steelworkers mentor Arthur Goldberg. But first there was the formality of pleading for freedom with Bowie Kuhn. Flood dropped a letter in the mail to him on Christmas Eve.

Dear Mr. Kuhn,

After 12 years in the major leagues, I do not feel that I am a piece of property to be bought and sold irrespective of my wishes. I believe that any system that produces that result violates my basic rights as a citizen and is inconsistent with the laws of the United States and the several states.

It is my desire to play baseball in 1970 and I am capable of playing. I have received a contract from the Philadelphia club, but I believe I have the right to consider offers from other clubs before making any decisions. I, therefore, request that you make known to all the major league clubs my feelings in this matter, and advise them of my availability for the 1970 season.

Curt Flood

Before New Year's Day, Flood had his reply: no way.

By January, Flood's suit against Kuhn had been filed. It was the first assault by a player on baseball's antitrust exemption since 1953, when the Supreme Court ruled against Yankee farmhand George Toolson.

In May, the case went to trial in New York before a U.S. District Court judge named Irving Ben Cooper. The plaintiff's witnesses hacked away at the reserve clause: Jackie Robinson, Bill Veeck, slugger-turned-GM Hank Greenberg, and reliever-turned-author Jim Brosnan testified. Baseball's witnesses swore to the system's sanctity: Joe Cronin, Chub Feeney, John McHale, Kuhn himself—at length—and, for comic relief, Joe Garagiola.

"You sign a contract and are with them [the club] until they get rid of you, and they got rid of me several times," said the catcher-turned-announcer. "But to me it's the best system. If you changed the name, everybody probably would be happy."

In the time-honored tradition of judges losing their judicial bearing under the influence of baseball, Judge Cooper pronounced: "Now you have thrown the ball to me, and I hope I don't muff it."

In August he ruled against Flood, but this was just a preliminary skirmish. *Flood* v. *Kuhn* was going to the Supreme Court. Flood, meanwhile, went off to Denmark, while Miller moved his artillery into position to fight on another front. He was going to step up the pressure for an independent arbitrator. It was a less flashy issue than Flood, but, to Miller, just as important. He needed to attack via labor law as well as antitrust law. He'd failed in 1968. But as he negotiated a new Basic Agreement in 1970, he now had an important lawsuit for leverage. How could baseball argue that Curt Flood was wrong and the industry was eminently fair to players if their only appeal on grievances was to the commissioner? "We were going to make hay on how ridiculous this was," says Miller.

He said as much to Gaherin, who promptly stepped up his own campaign among the Lords for an arbitrator. "Sooner or later we've got to do this and we've got to start in some fashion," he told them. "Marvin wouldn't accept Christ Almighty as an arbitrator if he didn't think he was a neutral."

Gaherin's biggest problem now was Bowie Kuhn. It turned out he *liked* being commissioner, with all the trappings and powers of office. Kuhn was only two months on the job before he invoked his "best interests" power. The Astros had traded Rusty Staub and some throw-ins to the Montreal Expos for Donn Clendenon and some throw-ins. When Clendenon announced he'd retire rather than go to Houston, Kuhn ordered the trade restructured and consummated. The fledgling Expos, he decreed, would benefit from a young star like Staub.

It was extraordinary for a commissioner—to say nothing of a commissioner pro tem—to inject himself into a trade. But that was Kuhn. He even made an early grab for the power to name and control the league presidents. He also proposed other reorganizations to boost the commissioner's power. All of this was rebuffed, but the tone had been set.

Kuhn wasn't brilliant. He leaned heavily on advisers, most notably a Willkie, Farr partner named Lou Hoynes. As Lou Carroll, the "Wise Man," faded with cancer, this crackerjack young lawyer was emerging as a force in baseball. Hoynes, a Harvard Law grad, came to be called, variously, "the shadow commissioner" and "Bowie Kuhn's brains." Kuhn's details man was Alexander "Sandy" Hadden, a Cleveland lawyer who'd been American League counsel and was now Kuhn's all-purpose factotum. If Kuhn was at a meeting, so was Hadden, scribbling down every word said. If follow-up was required, Hadden would take care of it.

To complicate matters, however, Kuhn was a czar with a master: Walter O'Malley. When Lou Hoynes was tapped to handle the Curt Flood case, for instance, he had first to make a pilgrimage to Dodger Stadium, where he was received, queried, and found worthy. "It sounds like a good idea, and I'm in favor of it," O'Malley told Hoynes. "But don't embarrass me."

It was the late sixties, and the time had come for Walter O'Malley to move his son, Peter, into the upper ranks of management. Peter had been schooled at Wharton, seasoned at the

Dodgers' Spokane minor league team, then put in charge of Dodger Stadium operations. With O'Malley *père* now sixty-five and O'Malley *fils* thirty, it was time to acquaint the young successor with the throne. But to make way, Buzzie Bavasi had to be moved out.

O'Malley found a graceful way. The National League was to add two expansion teams in 1969. Montreal got the inside track for one club, and Dallas was the top choice for the other. But Roy Hofheinz screamed bloody murder about putting a team just up the road from Houston. As an alternative, O'Malley pushed for San Diego—successfully, naturally. The new owner, C. Arnholt Smith, was so grateful, he hired the man O'Malley recommended as president—Buzzie Bavasi.

San Diego was in a hopelessly disadvantaged geographic position as a franchise. It had Mexico to the south, the Pacific to the west, the desert to the east, and Los Angeles to the north. It had a minuscule drawing area and minuscule early attendance.

Bavasi was once shooting the breeze in his office with Padres trainer Doc Mattei when he got a message. A former Dodger player was on the way over to hit him up for money. Bavasi groaned and asked Mattei where he might hide. "You might try down by the ticket windows," he said. "Nobody's ever there. Or maybe the upper deck. Nobody's ever there, either. Just be careful not to fall. They'd never find you until football season."

But the San Diego Padres suited Walter O'Malley's purposes, and he sold Bavasi on their presidency as a career move. He'd own 37 percent of the club as part of the deal, and it would be good to have something that, as O'Malley put it, "sticks to your ribs." Unfortunately, when C. Arnholt Smith later went bust, Bavasi's stock was worthless.

It worked out about as well as the last time O'Malley had fixed up Bavasi with something to "stick to his ribs." When the Dodgers moved west, he told Bavasi he was giving him the land under the old Ebbets Field parking lot. Bavasi never got a deed, but every so often he calculated how much the plot had appreciated. Only after Walter O'Malley died did he learn that O'Malley had sold the land years before.

When Padres ownership foundered, Kuhn, as a Washington boy, pushed to have the franchise moved to that city. He was motivated partly by sentiment and partly by politics, knowing that an endless supply of free tickets to D.C. VIPs would only help the game's antitrust exemption. But O'Malley wanted the Padres to stay in San Diego.

Even though he knew of O'Malley's feelings, Kuhn assembled a Washington group to buy and move the Padres. It wasn't, however, a particularly strong collection of investors, and when the Lords went over their financial statements in an ownership meeting, O'Malley immediately attacked. He was the lead inquisitor, focusing on the group's leader, a minor supermarket magnate named Joe Danzansky. Each time he mentioned the man's name, he pronounced it differently.

"Now, this Mr. Danzanewsky, what do we know about his bank lines?"

"What are the liquid assets of Mr. Danzanowicz?"

"How does Mr. Danzansitz propose to do this?"

"What percentage would Mr. Danzanzin's partners take?"

O'Malley's questions were studiously neutral, but his delivery was deadly. The Lords sat transfixed, wondering how the poor fellow's name would come out next. The point was subtle but effective. Was such an eminently forgettable fellow worthy of admission to the club?

No. The Lords rejected Danzansky, the Padres stayed in San Diego, and the capital never did get a team. And Kuhn learned it was not wise to cross O'Malley. None of this stopped Kuhn from taking himself terribly seriously, however. He continued to refer to himself in the third person—"The commissioner feels . . ."

He bridled when the Astrodome scoreboard defamed him during the Clendenon flap. It posted a multiple-choice quiz on "Who's the most unpopular man in the world?: (A) Frankenstein, (B) Pete Rozelle [who'd just denied Houston's bid to host the Super Bowl], or (C) Bowie Kuhn." The answer was given in code, one character for each letter of the name: "xxxxx xxxx." The crowd roared; Kuhn harrumphed—and called scoreboard operator Bill Giles onto the carpet.

Kuhn also took seriously the traditional concept of the office: protector of integrity; overseer of the owners', the players', and the fans' interests alike. As one associate later put it, "Bowie saw himself as a benevolent monarch."

Monarchs do not surrender power, especially to little men called arbitrators. Moreover, Kuhn didn't *have* to do so. A commissioner's powers can't be diminished without his assent, under the terms of the Major League Agreement that created the office. Gaherin had only one hope. Kuhn had to be jollied into it.

In the spring of 1970, Basic Agreement talks were otherwise moving along well. On the "bucks issues," as Gaherin put it, the Lords continued to concede modest ground: increasing the minimum salary from $10,000 to $12,000; setting a 30 percent limit on the maximum pay cut over two years; and increasing severance pay for released players, to sixty days from thirty.

But on the arbitrator issue they remained stalemated, and the talks were adjourned to Arizona. Miller and his associate, Dick Moss, were touring the Cactus League, meeting with players on different teams each morning and with the PRC negotiators each afternoon.

Late one afternoon, as the day's negotiations were winding down, they all moved outside to sit on Miller's hotel-room balcony: Miller and Moss along with Gaherin, Hoynes, and Barry Rona, another PRC lawyer. Gaherin decided it was time to make his move.

"Marvin, you've got to make up your mind on something," he said. "I think we can sell everything we've agreed on to the owners. And on changing the grievance system, I think that with Lou's help I can deliver Bowie. But you've got to be willing to do one thing: leave the commissioner in there somewhere."

"What do you mean 'somewhere'?" Miller asked.

"The nuts and bolts go to the arbitrator," said Gaherin. "But the son of God would still get the last word in some areas."

"What are nuts and bolts?" asked Moss.

"Anything that isn't very vital."

There was a long silence.

"I don't think we can do anymore today," said Moss.

The PRC Three left. As they walked out of the building, Hoynes said to Gaherin, "You reached Dick. Not Marvin, but Dick. Now we reach Bowie."

The next morning they met for breakfast with Kuhn, who was touring the Cactus League. All Gaherin had to say was "arbitrator" and he turned prickly as the desert flora.

"I'll accept no diminution of the power of the commissioner," he said, launching from there into a monologue on his solemn responsibilities. The others busied themselves with their toast and coffee, as he invoked familiar terms: *integrity, fairness, Judge Landis,* and so forth.

Finally, Hoynes broke in. "John's not taking anything away from you," he said. "You're going to give Marvin the nickels and dimes. You'll get the dollars."

"We'd let the arbitrator handle the nuts-and-bolts matters," said Gaherin. "You'd still rule where legitimate 'best interests' matters were at stake."

Kuhn frowned and echoed Moss's question. "What do you mean by nuts and bolts?"

"Let's say, for example, we get into an argument over whether a hotel is first-class," said Gaherin. "It's a legitimate thing to grieve but it's a tedious exercise."

(He knew from experience. When the union had protested the Senators' accommodations in Minneapolis, he was dragooned into handling the matter. It was hard to say which was worse: flying all the way there to inspect the hotel with Dick Moss or having to tell Bob Short, who owned the hotel, that he agreed with the union—*fleabag* was too kind a word.)

"The arbitrator wouldn't touch anything fundamental, like determining the number of games played or disciplining a gambler," Gaherin continued. "You'd only be getting rid of cases you're best rid of."

"Hmmm," said Kuhn. "I want to talk with Lou."

Gaherin and Rona left. Hoynes and Gaherin met later.

"So are you Bowie's negotiator now?" Gaherin teased.

"No, but I know what he wants: what he has now and no subtractions."

"I don't care what he wants," Gaherin said. "It's going to be less."

So Hoynes drafted language that would weave a careful line and support the contradictory interests. What Kuhn wouldn't give up, he told Miller, was authority over cases that involved alleged corruption. After all, that was why the commissioner's position was first created. So it was agreed: the commissioner would continue to adjudicate any cases that reflected on "the integrity of the game" and "public confidence" in it. An arbitrator would handle everything else.

Kuhn had gotten enough to hold his head high. Miller had gotten the rest—and it would turn out to be plenty.

Before long, the union was peppering the owners with grievances. The initial ones *were* for nickels and dimes. One filed against the San Diego Padres, for instance, centered on the difference between what the club paid for lodging at its spring training hotel—$6.75 per player per day—and the lodging allowance it gave players who stayed elsewhere—$6 a day. The Basic Agreement required that off-campus players get an allowance equal to the hotel rate. "It was a bullshit case," Dick Moss later admitted, noting that the mammoth total of $200 was at stake. "But you had to show the players had rights."

The arbitrator ruled for the union. Then, contending the Padres still weren't paying up fully, the union grieved and won again. Padres president Buzzie Bavasi was furious. It wasn't the money; it was this insidious new process of turning players against management and turning everything into litigation.

"For years there was this paternalistic relationship between players and management," recalled Peter Bavasi, Buzzie's son, then the Padres' farm director. "There was no way Miller could amass any influence unless he destroyed that. So he stepped in and drove a wedge between them."

Buzzie Bavasi began revenging himself on Miller through his players. A pitcher named Mike Corkins claimed he was owed $334.68 in travel expenses, incurred when he was optioned to the Padres' Hawaii triple-A team. Bavasi wouldn't pay. Miller took the matter to the PRC, the first step in the grievance process. Gaherin agreed Corkins should be paid. Under the rules, the Padres had ten days to do so. Bavasi dawdled. Finally, belatedly, he cut a check and backdated the postage meter to appear to be within the grace period.

Miller didn't buy it. He filed a grievance and tried to win Corkins his free agency for want of the $334.68. The arbitrator chided Bavasi for "unbusinesslike practices" and added an interest penalty to the Padres' payment—but Corkins remained a Padre.

Bavasi fumed some more. He knew what Miller was doing. "This was his way of telling the players who was the boss, that he was on their side," he later recalled. And he hated it. Miller once laughed at something Bavasi said, and the GM snapped, "Do that again and I'll knock you on your fanny."

Miller would elicit even stronger reactions. Everywhere the owners turned now, he seemed to be on the attack: in court, in arbitration, in bargaining. He was cool and calculating and contemptuous of their great institution. The Lords were beginning to take this personally.

They often referred to him not by name but as "that gimpy-armed Jew bastard." Bob Carpenter, who had more breeding, preferred "that plebian socialist." Leo Durocher, an old-schooler of the first rank, disrupted one of Miller's spring training meetings by fungoing fly balls into the outfield, where he was clustered with the Astros players.

"It was vitriolic," recalled Tim McCarver. "You talk about thick skin—this guy [Miller] was a rhinoceros."

It was against this backdrop that the pension issue came rumbling around again.

The agreement reached in 1969 expired on March 31, 1972. As that date approached, Miller made his requirements known: a 17 percent increase in the owners' annual contribution, to match the past three years' inflation. This would bring the owners' annual tab to $6.5 million, but Miller had a proposal to ease their out-of-pocket costs. The pension plan had accrued a surplus of $800,000. If that were applied to the benefits increase, he suggested, it would cost the clubs hardly anything.

To his surprise, Miller was turned down cold. Moreover, during simultaneous negotiations on health-insurance benefits, Gaherin suddenly pulled an offer of a $500,000 increase off the table. On the order of the Lords, he reduced it to $400,000. Now the union was being stonewalled by the Lords on two fronts, and Miller was alarmed.

"The perception on our side was that the union was still weak," John Gaherin recalled years later. "This was the time to take it on. People like Gussie Busch were screaming about Marvin. He wasn't a very welcome sight in anybody's parlor."

Since 1969, Gussie had become only more irate about the uppity players. The Cardinals were one of the teams to be hauled into arbitration on one of Miller's typically nettlesome, nit-picking cases. It was over a plane ticket. At the end of 1971 spring training, the Cards commissioned a charter flight to shuttle players and wives back to St. Louis. Pitcher Jerry Reuss's wife took a commercial flight instead. The Cards bought her ticket, but deducted the cost from Reuss's paycheck. He protested. The arbitrator sided with Reuss, saying clubs couldn't dock players without prior notice.

Gussie Busch was furious. He didn't have to offer any damned charter flight for the wives to begin with. To him, it seemed that Reuss was asking for change from a free lunch.

Quite apart from the union, Busch was also frustrated with the new-breed ballplayer. Stan Musial and Red Schoendienst used to go duck hunting with Busch and glad-hand with his cronies. They weren't terribly pushy on pay, aware that lifetime employment awaited "good boys."

But more of today's players went their own way and wanted their rewards *now*, and in cash. Six players had reached the heights of $125,000 a year: Frank Robinson, Carl Yastrzemski, Frank Howard, Willie Mays, Hank Aaron, and Bob Gibson. Other top players were pressing to move up the scale. The early 1970s saw a growing number of acrimonious contract battles.

Two involved the Cardinals' Steve Carlton. He held out through most of 1970 spring training, after his third straight fine season in '69. The left-hander went 17–11 with a 2.17 ERA and, in one game, tied a major league record with 19 strikeouts. Carlton wanted his salary doubled to $50,000, but Busch wouldn't hear of it. "I don't care if he ever pitches another damn ball for us," he growled.

They finally found a middle ground and Carlton signed. But when Carlton went 20–9 in 1971 and demanded $55,000, Busch hit the roof.

"Give him fifty," he told GM Bing Devine, "and if he won't play for that, get rid of him!"

Carlton wouldn't accept $50,000 and by the start of 1972 spring training, the future Hall of Famer was exiled to the hapless Phillies. In a fit of pique, Busch had ordered up the Cardinals' all-time worst trade. Carlton went 27–10 in 1972, winning the Cy Young award. He racked up four more twenty-win seasons and three more Cy Youngs for the Phillies and had a career total of 329 wins, second, among lefties, only to Warren Spahn.

But Gussie Busch sure showed him who was boss. In the same spirit, he ordered Jerry Reuss traded a month later, after he too refused to close a $5,000 negotiating gap. Reuss went on to win 198 games for other teams. Busch sometimes growled about how this player-rebellion stuff must have something to do with all the damned protestors out there these days. About that he was right.

"I can't understand it," he once said. "The player contracts are at their best, the pension plan is the finest, and the fringe benefits are better than ever. Yet the players think that we [the owners] are a bunch of stupid asses."

Miller traveled through Florida and Arizona in March, meeting with his players, explaining the situation, and collecting strike authorization votes. The players voted for it 663–10. Four of the ten dissenters were on the Red Sox, where owner Tom Yawkey had handsomely looked after not only Yastrzemski but several other favorites.

John Gaherin pooh-poohed the vote to the owners. This was strictly pro forma, a public rattling of the sabers. It didn't necessarily portend a strike at all. "Any labor leader who can't get a strike vote might as well quit and go home," he said.

Miller actually felt much the same. "They're giving me a vote of confidence," he thought. But that wasn't the same as undertaking—or even understanding—a strike. The players were the world's best at baseball, but they'd never played labor hardball. There had never been a strike of baseball players—or any other pro athletes, for that matter. Miller didn't think they were ready for one.

But Gaherin, a compromiser by nature, didn't want a confrontation either. He tried to suppress the Lords' appetite for battle. "We're just talking about money here," he told the Lords. "Money is not the maiden's virtue, it's the currency of whores."

But anti-Miller feeling was running so high that his arguments fell mainly on deaf ears. The Braves' Paul Richards, as usual, was among those to put it best and bluntest. The players had better acquiesce, he warned, or "there isn't going to be any baseball for a long, long time. The owners simply aren't going to let Marvin Miller run over them anymore."

Gaherin, trying to make rational discourse prevail, started lining up a mid-March PRC meeting. He was making phone calls from his hotel room in Scottsdale, where he'd been huddling with NL president Chub Feeney. They agreed it would be important to have the Cardinals' Dick Meyer, a wise labor head, at the meeting.

Gaherin placed a call to Meyer, while Feeney got on the room's extension line.

Meyer begged off, reciting a hopelessly crowded schedule. It was a crunch time of year at Anheuser-Busch, where he was president.

"I've got a business to run," he said. "I'll send Gussie."

"Oh Jesus, Dick," said Feeney, breaking in. "Don't send *him* down there."

Gussie Busch's voice came blasting onto the line from the extension *he* was on.

"You son of a bitch, Feeney, I'll go where I want to go!" he shouted. "You work for me; I don't work for you!"

And so to the labor summit Gussie Busch went.

The meeting, held on March 22, produced a consensus: the strike deadline was March 31, the pension plan's expiration date. The owners would hold firm and not sweeten their offer now. In another week they'd make a judgment. They'd gauge just how brave Miller and the players still were with a strike staring them in the face.

As the meeting came to a close, they agreed on one other thing. They would say nothing to the press, who were camped outside. As the owners emerged, a chorus of shouted questions confronted them:

"Did you come to any agreement?"

"What are you going to do?"

"What was the vote?"

Every owner shouldered his way silently past the writers— everyone except Gussie Busch.

"We voted unanimously to take a stand," he snapped. "We're not going to give them another goddamn cent. If they want to strike—let 'em."

The quote was tacked up on clubhouse bulletin boards throughout the Grapefruit and Cactus Leagues. It was passed from mouth to mouth and embellished. The players were coming to a boil.

They didn't expect to get rich from baseball, but they did expect some old-age security from their short, young careers. It was no windfall: $2,092 a year for a four-year major-leaguer if he started drawing the pension at forty-five, $7,416 at sixty-five. But it was *something*, and it was the very *raison d'être* for the Players Association. It was all they had asked of owners: not freedom of movement, not higher salaries, but decent pensions. Now they were being told, succinctly, "Drop dead."

Still, Miller cast about for milder solutions. Just two days before the deadline, he proposed submitting the dispute to arbitration. He'd even let the owners pick the arbitrator: President Nixon, former president Johnson, or former chief justice Earl Warren—whomever they liked.

No dice, said the Lords.

Miller kept meeting with Gaherin and the league presidents, Feeney and Cronin. He kept arguing that they use the $800,000 in earnings generated by the fund. "Imprudent," they replied. That $800,000 was to be kept in reserve, to be drawn on for benefits. That was the prudent approach and the Lords were prudent men.

Miller even made a personal appeal to Walter O'Malley, paying a visit to Vero Beach. That accomplished nothing, either. Finally, he was out of time. On March 31, he and Dick Moss met with the forty-eight player reps and alternates in Dallas to decide what to do.

The two had concluded their Cactus League swing the day be-fore and met that night in Miller's hotel room in Phoenix. The situation was, they agreed, hopeless. "How do we get out of this pickle?" asked Moss.

They went over the problems for the hundredth time. The pension was a vexing matter but not a *central* one, like the re-serve system. How long could the players stay fired up over a cost-of-living pension provision? And then there was the play-ers' inexperience in these matters: they hadn't a clue about a strike's harsh realities—hostile fans, owner retributions, and more. The players needed more education and the union more maturity before launching a job action. That was to say nothing of the mismatch of resources. The Lords had tons of money, le-gions of lawyers, and most of the newspapermen on their side.

The players had Marvin Miller, Dick Moss, and a secretary back in New York.

On top of that, the timing was all wrong. Players weren't paid during the off-season. Many were now tapped out, waiting anx-iously for their first paycheck, trying to scrape together rent money. The union had no strike fund to sustain them. The own-ers were perfectly set up to starve them out. The union had learned to walk, but it wasn't yet ready to walk *into battle*.

There was only one solution, they agreed: to fold as grace-fully as possible. Moss grabbed a legal pad, and began writing what they called, with black humor, their Sacco and Vanzetti speech. (The reference was to the defiant farewell statement of two 1920s leftist radicals, convicted and executed for murder.)

It would be worded in the form of a resolution, to be voted upon by the players and released to the press. The statement, as scrawled by Moss, conceded the impossibility of the players tackling a conglomerate of twenty-four multimillionaires. The players weren't yet a match for them. There would be no strike. The players would keep playing, and negotiations would con-tinue throughout the 1972 season. If the pension couldn't be re-solved then, it would become part of the bargaining for the next Basic Agreement, in 1973. If it couldn't be resolved then, the players would take their case to Congress. Justice would prevail, et cetera. Miller and Moss hoped some heavy rhetorical fire would mask an abject retreat.

The next morning, Miller and his wife, Terry, boarded the flight to Dallas. They slipped into their seats and saw familiar faces in the next row back. "Good morning," said Reggie Jackson, the

Oakland Athletics' alternate player rep. He was sitting with pitcher Chuck Dobson, the A's player rep.

Inwardly Miller groaned. He was exhausted and dispirited and needed the time to prepare further for the meeting. But Jackson kept popping over the back of the seat, peppering him with questions and observations. From what he'd read, said Jackson, the owners figured the players were afraid to strike. Well, he and Chuck weren't afraid. The A's weren't afraid. What did Miller think?

As always, Miller answered cautiously, circumspectly. He was concerned about the "lack of experience" of the players. This wasn't necessarily the right issue to make a stand on.

The conversation began to assume a pattern—Miller, in veiled language, suggesting strategic retreat; Jackson, in vehement tones, trumpeting a call to arms. "No, no, no," Jackson protested, as Miller demurred again. "We can't do that."

"In retrospect," Miller would recall, "it's clear the two Oakland players were closer to the tenor of the players than I was."

They landed in Dallas and went to a motel near the airport. Terry went off to type up the resolution and make copies on the motel's mimeograph. Miller and Moss went into the conference room, which was filling up with players. Outside, reporters were beginning to gather by the swimming pool.

Miller started off by recounting the bargaining-table events of the past ten days. He was, as always, low-key, factual, even dry. But it had been at least two weeks since he'd seen many of the player reps, and he wanted them all to have the same information.

Then Miller walked the players down the path of logic he and Moss had traversed: why this wasn't the time to strike, how they should keep their powder dry for a more propitious time. "There are just some times," he said, "when you tuck your tail between your legs and accept what they have to offer."

Tim McCarver, now the Phillies' player rep, had an instant, visceral reaction. "Well, screw that," he thought. And he could see eyebrows going up all around the room.

Miller opened the floor to a bombardment of militance.

Reggie Jackson was in the lead. "Goddammit, there are just times when you've got to stand up for your rights," he shouted.

Ray Sadecki, the Mets pitcher, was every bit as vehement.

Other player reps joined in, reminding everyone of Gussie Busch's "Not another goddamn cent" insult.

Miller played the devil's advocate, countering the players'

passion with cold reason: they had no strike fund, no field offices, no legal team, no PR machine.

"I hear you. I understand that. You have justifiable resentment," Miller said quietly. "But it's important that you know what you'd be getting into with a strike."

"'How long would a strike last?" he was asked.

"I don't know," said Miller. "But it would be a terrible mistake to start something you're not prepared to finish. That would be a disaster. It's especially hard to calculate if you don't understand the provocation. If their aim is to break the union, this strike will never be over. They will maintain their unity until you crawl back like whipped dogs."

But increasingly, talk turned from *whether* to strike to *when*. Brooks Robinson said the Orioles would want to honor an April 1st charity exhibition game in Birmingham, Alabama. Jim Merritt of the Reds suggested April 8, when the first nationally televised TV game was scheduled. Others suggested that striking before the All-Star Game would hit the owners hardest.

"I don't know about that," Miller cautioned. "By then you'll have four players on every club who are having career years and won't want to go out."

Every player in the room had his say. Of all of them, only the Dodgers' Wes Parker was for caving. "Look, guys, I can't do this," he pleaded. "I just bought a new house."

He was hooted down.

Finally, with the meeting more than three hours old, it was time for a vote. All in favor of a strike, stand up. Forty-seven players stood up. Wes Parker abstained.

The first players' strike in U.S. sports history was on. The "Sacco and Vanzetti resolution" was scrapped. The wording of a new one was immediately drafted: "We will not permit the owners to breach our union. Accordingly, as of March 31, the Major League Baseball Players Association is on strike."

Terry Miller bustled off to crank out copies on the mimeograph machine. Marvin Miller left the conference room to find a pay phone. He had promised to call Gaherin with the meeting's results.

"John, we've had a long, thoughtful meeting," Miller began. "I've never been at a meeting like this before. Everybody spoke, some of them five or more times. There will be no spring training games tomorrow. There will be no games until this is resolved."

"You're not pulling my leg," said Gaherin.

"No."

There was a long silence before Gaherin finally spoke again. "What are your travel plans?" he asked.

"I'm long past my flight. Hopefully I can be in New York in the morning."

"We ought to meet at once."

"I'll call in the morning and let you know," Miller said.

"We should meet in an office other than yours or mine, because there's going to be a lot of press."

Miller went back into the room for one last word with the players.

"I'm impressed with the courage you've shown against overwhelming odds and opponents," he said. "You've shown that you refuse to be browbeaten any longer."

Only later would Miller reflect on how badly the labor "pros" on both sides had miscalculated. In an old-line union, authorizing a strike was a mere symbolic act. Management knew it; members knew it; the sabers were rattled but still safely sheathed. But to the members of the fledgling Major League Baseball Players Association, it was *very* significant. They had never taken such a vote before. They had never risen up to defy the Lords like this. To them, it was a bold new step, not a tired old gesture.

Miller had also done more than he knew to educate and motivate players. He'd always told them to think not only of themselves but of what they could do for future generations of players. Now they were prepared to do something dramatic.

"He did an excellent job of convincing veteran players, who'd made low salaries and little pensions," recalled Tom Grieve, then a rookie outfielder on the Texas Rangers. "People like Frank Howard, Don Mincher, and Jim Hannon on our club were outspoken. This was my first chance to make a major league team, and I had no money in the bank. But when it came time to vote, I listened to the veterans and voted for the strike."

The owners' hardline stance—punctuated by Busch's "not another goddamn cent"—had also gotten the players' competitive juices flowing. It was those juices that fueled the major league ballplayer. More than hair-trigger reflexes, more than fastball movement, more than bat-speed whip, that's what got them to the bigs and kept them there. They battled long bus rides and rocky infields to get there. The lesser players battled each spring to stay there. The big dogs battled each other for bragging rights. The pitchers battled the hitters. The catchers battled the base runners. In their spare time, they all tried to beat each others' brains out in card games.

"A professional baseball player, from the time he's nine years old in Little League, is accustomed to success," said Ted Simmons, a young catcher then. "His attitude is: 'I don't care how big a truck you have; I'm going to stand in the middle of the road and survive this.' "

The players would now see if they could survive a strike.

The Lords were stunned and angered. In Lakeland, Florida, the next morning, workers at the Tigers' spring training camp were loading gear into a truck to be hauled north. There were the bats and uniforms and other miscellaneous equipment. There were also mounds of personal gear of players and their families. The Tigers had long invited players to use the truck's leftover space to save them the trouble and expense of shipping. Despite the strike, players were coming by in a steady stream to drop off their goods.

Jim Campbell, the Tigers GM, saw them from his office—and he saw red. He came storming out, shouting at the workers, "These guys are on strike. Get every goddamned thing of theirs off this truck."

He faced the players there at the moment. "If you're not going to play, we're not going to take your goods to Detroit," he said. "We've been good to you all this time. Now, goddammit, Santa Claus is fucking dead."

At the Padres' spring training camp in Yuma, Arizona, Buzzie Bavasi steamed, too. He went public with the favors he'd done players: salary advances to fourteen of them since the first of the year. "If Mr. Miller resents paternalism, then we'll go strictly by the book from now on," he said.

In Clearwater, Florida, the Phillies' Bob Carpenter belatedly tried to turn back the clock. In a series of meetings, player reps Tim McCarver and Terry Harmon tried to explain the union's position to him and GM John Quinn, who resolutely didn't get it.

"If you get rid of Marvin, we could work this out ourselves," Carpenter told them. "Let's go back to the way it was."

The talks summarily ended when Miller learned of them.

"You're doing more damage by trying to negotiate individually with your owner than if you'd just leave," he said. McCarver left immediately.

Jerry Hoffberger, the Orioles owner, met with his players in a multi-hour anti-Miller session. He called Miller's pension proposal "ridiculous" and urged the players to take another team strike vote. "Take the leadership. Change your votes and accept the [owners'] proposal," he said.

The Orioles took the new vote. The result stayed the same.

Other owners delivered their attacks through the press. Gussie Busch, of course, led the league in inflammatory quotes. "How can I pay a guy $150,000 and have him in the middle of orchestrating a strike?" he asked, referring to union stalwart Joe Torre.

Players across baseball hung together. The Twins' Jim Perry lined up housing for strapped younger players with better-fixed veterans. He arranged for a place for the team to work out and a bus to transport players there. The Braves practiced on a high school field until they ran out of balls. Hank Aaron had hit them all into a grove of trees. Chris Cannizzaro of the Dodgers worked out with the Padres in San Diego, where he lived. Vada Pinson of the Angels worked out with the Athletics in Oakland, where he lived.

Miller hustled around keeping up players' spirits between negotiating sessions. He talked to the Twins players by phone, over a gymnasium public address system. He met with Orioles players at Brooks Robinson's home. Then he met with Reds and Pirates players as well.

Miller also gathered his player reps again, in a back room of the Four Seasons restaurant in New York. One was Willie Mays, pressed into service to represent the Giants after both that team's player rep and his alternate had been traded. (Of the twenty-four player reps at the start of 1971, sixteen were traded or released by the spring of 1972.) As a favored pet of the Stonehams, Mays had never been much of a union participant. But in the twilight of his career, in the midst of the strike, he was a standup guy for Marvin Miller.

"I know it's hard being away from the game and our paychecks and our normal life," he said. "I love this game. It's been my whole life. But we made a decision in Dallas to stick together, and until we're satisfied, we *have* to stay together. This could be my last year in baseball, and if the strike lasts the entire season and I've played my last game, well, it will be painful. But if we don't hang together, everything we've worked for will be lost."

For the most part, the players faced withering press and public criticism. It was as though they had stolen America's inalienable right to Opening Day. The strikers did find *some* support, however. On what was to have been Opening Day at Boston's Fenway Park, a group of Wesleyan University students picketed with signs reading SUPPORT OUR BOYS IN UNIFORM. But most sentiment was squarely with the owners. When Reds pitcher Gary Nolan walked into a Cincinnati restaurant, one patron screamed, "Get out of here, Nolan!"

They were taking their cues from the writers, who, as they had in 1969, lambasted the "privileged, pampered players" (average salary: $34,000) and their "labor boss." *Baltimore Sun* columnist Bob Maisel called Marvin Miller an "Edgar Bergen with 600 Charlie McCarthies." *The Sporting News* called the strike's April Fools Day start "the darkest day in sports history." Edwin Pope of the *Miami Herald* reported that twenty-four players now made $100,000. The message was clear: *What more do they want? Where will it all end?*

The salary figures were true, but baseball's pay scale actually still ran below other major sports. One good measure was the top of the pay scale. Hank Aaron, at $200,000, had baseball's top salary. Joe Namath had football's, at $250,000; Bobby Hull had hockey's, at $275,000. The top-paid *rookie* in the NBA, Bob McAdoo, made $333,000.

Yet, when it came to the National Pastime, people found something uniquely immoral about money. Baseball players were supposed to be folk heroes, not union members. They were supposed to consider themselves lucky to play this great game for a living. They were certainly ingrates to grouse about the terms. Even former players joined in that chorus.

"I think playing baseball is a privilege," said Jackie Jensen, a 1950s-era outfielder. "I enjoyed it and it was a game to me. It doesn't look like it is anymore. And if it isn't, it isn't going to be much fun from here on in—either to the fans or the players. And I think that's a tragedy."

One notable ex-player directly contacted Marvin Miller, ripping into him for leading a strike. It was a body blow to the game, he said. Even after Miller had explained in detail why it came to pass, even after he'd emphasized it was the players' decision, this critic could not be satisfied.

"No matter what the reason," Robin Roberts insisted, "a strike is bad."

Years later, he would explain his dismay. He'd pushed for candidate Miller as a negotiator, and the man had, indeed, achieved solid gains for the players. But in Roberts's eyes a good negotiator should be able to work things out short of war.

He remembered Miller once absolutely *promising* him there would be no strikes (Miller denies it).

"As far as I was concerned, there was plenty of money out there; it was all in how you were going to share it," said Roberts. "I never anticipated both sides would be so thick-headed it would threaten the game."

John Gaherin went way back with a top partner at the Philadelphia firm of Towers, Perrin, Forster and Crosby. The man was John Able, and the firm specialized in employee benefits. It consulted with companies about structuring compensation and funding employee benefits plans. Now, with the strike on, Gaherin retained Able to help find a way out of it.

Able pored over the structure and the finances of the pension plan and reported back to Gaherin. He personally didn't see anything so "imprudent" about using the $800,000 surplus to fund the benefits increase.

"Look, the use of the reserve is a matter of fiduciary judgment," he said. "If the plans' actuary doesn't say this is detrimental, you can certainly go ahead and do it."

Gaherin knew more groundwork was required before he informed the Lords that his consultant agreed with Marvin Miller. He sent Able around to meet and educate some of the owners. Then, when the strike was four days old, he set up an ownership meeting in Chicago.

There they were still of a mind to strut and roar. Said Gene Autry to Gaherin, "Tell Miller I can still saddle up my horse and make a living that way."

Gussie Busch offered to put up $1 million to help any teams needing assistance. He saw it as a grand gesture. Walter O'Malley saw it as a sign that Busch had no understanding of baseball's economics.

"The Dodgers alone lose one million dollars each weekend the strike goes on," he told him.

And there, Gaherin saw, was the problem. Interests were beginning to splinter. "Some guys wanted to give the players nothing and make it retroactive," said Gaherin. "But the big guys, in particular, were pragmatic. To take a strike would hurt business."

Ewing Kauffman saw it, too. The Royals owner was on the Executive Council, and as he went into meetings, the same owners who rattled sabers publicly tugged at his coat privately. "They would wait in the lobby and stand there begging to get this settled," he said. "They said they could go broke."

* * *

John Able finished his round of owner briefings and met with Gaherin. He was totally discouraged. Their eyes had glazed over at what he was trying to explain; their reactions to Miller's proposal were purely visceral. "*These* are the money people of this country?" Able asked.

But, as it turned out, he had gotten through to some. The Braves' Bill Bartholomay, an insurance executive, understood pension mechanics. So did Charlie Finley, the old insurance hustler. "Very few owners actually knew there was any surplus in the pension fund," Finley told reporters. "The owners didn't understand what this was all about."

The statement drove the other owners crazy, of course, but Able had provided Finley—and the rest of the owners—with an excuse to cave. One week into the strike, a growing number of owners were ready to do so. In terms of finances and firepower, they had it all going for them. But they had put something in motion that they had no experience handling. In each of their cities, the pressure to let the games begin was mounting fast.

The Twins' Calvin Griffith was in the midst of his usual anti-Miller rantings when Gaherin interrupted.

"If you want to beat him, keep 'em out till May first," he replied. "Make 'em hungry."

"But what will the press do to me?" Griffith bleated.

"Do you want to break the union or not?"

Calvin Griffith was reduced to mumbles, and the situation, to Gaherin, was reduced to its essence. "Marvin had it all going for him," he later reflected. "Everybody wanted to shoot him but nobody wanted to pull the trigger."

By April 11, Gaherin and Miller had the outlines of a compromise settlement. They would take $500,000 out of the surplus to increase the owners' pension contribution. It took two more days' wrangling, however, to determine whether a total of eighty-six lost games would be rescheduled (they weren't), and if players would be paid for their time out (they weren't). The strike ended April 13.

"John," said John Able to Gaherin, as he wrapped up his consulting assignment, "don't ever call me again."

The delayed Opening Day, April 15, was dreary. In St. Louis, only 7,808 people came out for the Cardinals-Expos opener. Not even Gussie Busch showed, although he did weigh in with an announcement. His players would no longer have the luxury of private rooms on the road. They would double up to save the club $10,000.

As Bob Gibson struggled through the first inning, a fan yelled, "Hurry up, I've got to go to a union meeting!" When outfielder Jose Cruz misplayed a single, another spectator shouted, "Put a dollar sign on it!" When Joe Torre, National League MVP and union stalwart, came to bat, he was booed.

It was that way across America that day. Fans would never again view baseball in quite the same light. Neither would the players. For the second time in four years, the Lords had refused to give them peanuts. Instead, they had ultimately handed them a great victory. Santa Claus *was* dead. But then the players didn't need him now. Marvin Miller's union had come of age.

$ 7 $

A TWENTY-ONE-YEAR-OLD catcher with a ponytail promptly threw a new challenge in the Lords' face. His name was Ted Simmons, and he refused to sign his 1972 contract. Nobody had ever done that before. It was against the rules: Major League Rule 3C, to be exact. It forbade players to suit up if they hadn't signed a contract.

It was, in effect, the enforcer of the reserve clause. With a signed contract, a player was always two years away from freedom: one year for the length of the standard contract, one year for the club's option on it. It was like a tablet handed down from Judge Landis. And nobody had ever challenged it—until Marvin Miller.

Even he didn't do so right away. In 1969, Yankees pitcher Al Downing was a holdout into spring training. Finally the Yankees unilaterally renewed his contract. That was their right, under baseball's rules. A player had until March 1 to come to terms. After that, the GM could fill in whatever figure he liked, up to the maximum cut.

The Yankees' Lee MacPhail had done so, but the miffed lefty still wouldn't sign. Downing had been one of New York's best pitchers through the sixties, going 14–10 with a 2.63 ERA as recently as 1967. But injuries had limited him to 15 games and a 3–3 record in '68. The Yankees wanted him to take a pay cut. Downing resisted. No sign, no play, said MacPhail. Downing called Miller. Was that right? Was there anything he could do about it?

Miller's answer: no and no. Downing had been renewed and thus was under contract. In Miller's opinion, that meant he didn't have to sign it. On the other hand, if he fought it, he could only appeal to the commissioner. Guess who Bowie Kuhn would side with. "The club has the whip hand," said Miller.

130

Given that bleak analysis, and the fact that he needed to get in shape, Downing signed and reported.

An independent arbitrator changed everything. Miller got that in the 1970 Basic Agreement. Now he could hope that a neutral outsider would read 3C or 10A the way he did. Now he was emboldened to challenge these baseball canons. The commissioner no longer had the final say.

Miller began planting the seeds of challenge in March 1971. At each spring training meeting he read Section 10A word for word, then gave his interpretation:

"We read the language of the contract to mean what it says," he said. "If you're not in agreement on salary by March first, the club can, in the next ten days, renew your contract for one year. That means you're under contract again and you're not required to sign anything. By signing last year's contract, you've given the club the option to unilaterally renew it.

"In my view, the contract is clear. At the end of that season there's no further contractual tie between the player and his club. He can become a free agent."

A recent basketball case supported his view, Miller continued. In 1967, Rick Barry had jumped from the NBA's San Francisco Warriors to the ABA's Oakland Oaks. The Warriors sued to keep their star forward. A court did bar him from joining the Oaks until the expiration of the option year in his Warriors contract. But the point was this, said Miller: the NBA's player-contract language was, word for word, the same as baseball's. A federal judge ruled the Warriors only had Barry for one year, not forever.

"Now this is a matter that shouldn't be undertaken lightly," said Miller. "There will be all kinds of pressures on any player who doesn't sign. The clubs disagree with me. They think they have perpetual renewal rights. This would probably wind up before an arbitrator. It would be an ordeal. But I'm confident that I'm right, and it's something to keep in mind."

Ted Simmons, sitting in the St. Petersburg clubhouse of the Cardinals, did just that. He was a stocky six-footer, just three years removed from being an all-state high school fullback in Michigan. He went to the University of Michigan on a football scholarship. But when St. Louis drafted him number-one in 1967 and offered a $50,000 signing bonus, he left the gridiron for baseball.

Simmons advanced rapidly through the minors, hitting less

than .317 only in his first professional year. But in the off-season he continued to attend the University of Michigan, which proved a profound counterbalance to minor league baseball. The Ann Arbor campus was one of America's most radical. The leftist Students for a Democratic Society was founded there. Protests against the war in Vietnam erupted regularly.

Simmons was no bomb-thrower; he was a jock from suburban Detroit. But he was significantly influenced by his time at Ann Arbor. He had shoulder-length hair, just to show which side he was on. He rode a motorcycle, just to flaunt his individuality further. He was a rebel in shinguards.

By 1970, Simmons was in the bigs. By 1971, he was the Cardinals' full-time catcher, playing 133 games. Simba, as he was called, was a curiosity to his teammates—"a flower child," Joe Torre said with a smile years later. But he was already a heady receiver and a demon hitter. Simmons batted .304 in 1971 and he would eventually set a National League record for career home runs by a switch-hitter (182).

But Simmons was still making so little—$14,000—that he had to move in with his in-laws during the strike. He couldn't afford to do anything else. Simmons was "horrified" at his precarious position, though perfectly ready to follow Marvin Miller into battle. To him, it was another just cause against the establishment.

Simmons had begun an individual battle, too, that would only come into focus after the strike. He refused to sign a contract with the Cardinals. As an emerging premier catcher, he thought he was worth $30,000. That wasn't even up to the major league average of $34,000, he argued. But Cardinals GM Bing Devine said it was too much too fast. He was only willing to go as far as the low twenties.

The 1972 season belatedly opened, with Simmons, sans contract, behind the plate for the Cardinals. For the first time, a big-leaguer was playing a season without one. It was the baseball equivalent of a draft-card burning. Simmons later recalled: "When someone representing the establishment said, 'This is what you'll do,' I was just bulletproof enough, naïve enough, and political enough to say, 'I'm not going to.' "

The Lords wouldn't respond with brute force. GMs no longer dared pull the kind of stunt the Yankees' Ralph Houk once had: threatening Jim Bouton with $100-a-day fines as long as he remained unsigned. Marvin Miller would haul them before an arbitrator in a New York minute.

But there were other ways to pressure the player, and that's what John Gaherin counseled. "Get a hold of this. We don't want to test it," he told Bing Devine. "Sign him. Don't let him go through this year without a contract."

The Cardinals put on the pressure. Gussie Busch cornered Simmons in manager Red Schoendienst's office before a game and harangued him. The first pitch had to be delayed until Busch was through. Bing Devine crept up his offer into the higher twenties. When Simmons wouldn't bite, Devine did. He reminded him he could always cut him back to the minimum $12,000. It was tough stuff for a player who'd already lost 5 percent of the year's salary to the strike. But Simmons wouldn't budge. *The number is $30,000.*

Marvin Miller looked on. At one level, he loved the prospect of a test case. At another, he feared for the kid. He counseled Simmons, reminding him of the realities. He could have a good case yet still lose. Curt Flood did. (His suit was pending at the time before the Supreme Court.) He could be a talented player yet lose his career to this challenge. Curt Flood did.

"Teddy, we don't know what's out there," said Miller. "You'll just have to decide what's best for you."

Simmons responded to the pressure with torrid hitting. By mid-season he was at .340. *Bam.* Another line drive. "I'll show you," Simmons thought. *Bam.* "I'll show you."

The weight of pressure began to shift to the Cardinals. Ted Simmons, the no-contract, low-salary star, was getting attention and sympathy. He'd only gain more in the All-Star Game, which he'd made as the National League's backup catcher.

Simmons was in his Atlanta hotel room the morning of the All-Star Game when the phone rang. It was Bing Devine. "Why don't you come up to my room?" he said. "I'd like to talk about your contract."

Simmons went up and so did his eyebrows. The Cardinals were offering $30,000 for 1972 and $45,000 for 1973. Simmons couldn't believe it. *A two-year contract. More money than he'd ever dreamed of.*

He went back down to his room and called his wife. "Maryanne, Jesus Christ, here's what's happened," he said. He laid out the terms. "I've got to do this."

Miller didn't have a test case but he had an insight. The Lords had betrayed how they really felt. They didn't want to see this tested. They'd rather give a kid catcher $75,000 than hand Section 10A over to an arbitrator. Another player, another time, thought Miller.

The Curt Flood case came down that summer. The Supreme Court, by a vote of 5–3, rejected his appeal. It wasn't a ringing endorsement of baseball's antitrust exemption: the majority opinion called it "an anomaly" and "an aberration." It recognized that baseball was interstate commerce, which the original 1922 opinion had not. But when it came to overturning the exemption, the justices ran the other way. "If there is an inconsistency and illogic in all this," the opinion said, "it is an inconsistency and illogic of long standing that is to be remedied by the Congress and not by this Court."

If the Supremes weren't embarrassed by their twisted logic, they should have been by Justice Harry Blackmun's writing in the majority opinion. It paused to recite the names of eighty-eight legendary players, from Goose Goslin to Wahoo Sam Crawford to Rube Waddell. It was the only Supreme Court opinion in history to include an ode to the double play, written by Franklin Pierce Adams:

> These are the saddest of possible words,
> "Tinker to Evers to Chance."
> Trio of bear cubs, and fleeter than birds,
> "Tinker to Evers to Chance."
> Ruthlessly pricking our gonfalon bubble,
> Making a Giant hit into a double—
> Words that are weighty with nothing but trouble:
> "Tinker to Evers to Chance."

But as in baseball, all that counted was the final score. The owners cared not that this was the judicial version of "Winning Ugly." Marvin Miller had been put back in his place. Their status as all-powerful Lords was affirmed. All was right with the world again.

As the champagne corks popped, John Gaherin still cautioned: Flood's defeat hadn't brought an end to the forces of change; it had only bought them some time.

"Read that decision more closely," he said. "The justices said you're not covered by the Sherman Antitrust Act. But if you were, you'd get your pants taken off. And they invited Congress to do something about it."

A man named Lou Susman, who was Gussie Busch's attorney

and all-purpose consigliere, was incensed. "Where'd you get your law degree, P.S. 109?"

Gaherin held his ground. "Fellas, this is the twentieth century," he said. "You can't get anybody, drunk or sober, to agree that once a fella goes to work for the A&P, he has to work for the A&P the rest of his life."

Miller would find another route of attack, Gaherin warned. He would find other test cases. He would win congressmen to his side. If the owners didn't make changes, somebody else would impose them. "Marvin's going to be pouring gas all over the floor and lighting matches," he said.

He was right. In 1973, five more players took the field without contracts: pitcher Stan Bahnsen, catcher Dick Billings, infielders Mike Andrews and Jerry Kenney, and outfielder Rick Reichardt. But four of them signed during the season, and Kenney was released.

The next year brought seven more. All but two had signed, however, as the 1974 season wound down. One of the no-signers was reliever Sparky Lyle. He kept the pressure on the Yankees with a fine season: 9–3, with a 1.66 ERA. Finally, with two weeks to go, they tumbled to a two-year contract: $87,500 for 1974 (a $7,500 raise) and $92,500 for 1975.

Bobby Tolan went the distance. He was a speedy center fielder who'd stolen as many as fifty-seven bases in a season and once led NL outfielders in total chances. He came to San Diego in an off-season trade and was at loggerheads with the low-budget Padres from the start. He wanted a $25,000 raise, to the $100,000 neighborhood, and he wouldn't sign his 1974 contract without it.

By September, John Gaherin saw Tolan as trouble. Tolan had been traded by Cincinnati after a series of conflicts with management in which he'd been saved from disciplinary action only by union intercession. Tolan had a chip on his shoulder the size of a Louisville slugger. He also had reason to be grateful and helpful to Marvin Miller.

"I'm concerned," Gaherin told Chub Feeney. "Marvin's looking for a test case, and as sure as God made little green apples, if he doesn't sign, Marvin will test 10A."

The two of them agreed: Buzzie Bavasi had to be pressed into action. They met with the Padres' GM for a long liquid lunch. They implored him to do whatever it took to sign Tolan—"for the good of the industry."

"What do you want?" Bavasi asked. "You want my soul?"

"No," said Gaherin, "just sign the SOB."

But the season ended with Tolan still unsigned. A couple of perfunctory meetings that fall got them no closer: "Me refusing to sign and them refusing to budge," as Tolan later put it.

Marvin Miller filed a grievance, seeking to declare Tolan a free agent. But in December, just days before the scheduled hearing, the Padres caved. Tolan signed a contract that paid him close to the desired $100,000 for 1974 and a like sum for 1975.

Gaherin had dodged the bullet again. But he still couldn't convince the Lords they were under siege and needed to change. In part, he was seen as too prone to compromise. Some owners told a running joke: "Gaherin said we won another great victory. We only had to give them ninety percent of what they asked for."

In part, he wasn't backed by baseball's top attorneys. They weren't labor lawyers, with Gaherin's feel for the ebb and flow of labor relations. In the wake of the Flood case, they were a bit cocky, certain they could prevail again. And, like most lawyers, they were only taking their client's lead. "Lou Hoynes was a brilliant lawyer," said a contemporary, "but with a streak of 'My client, right or wrong, but my client.' "

Partly, too, there was the feeling that a Lord needn't listen to a mere hired hand. "John was very good at what he did," said Ed Fitzgerald, the Milwaukee Brewers' chairman who was to become PRC chief. "But baseball owners looked down on him. They weren't about to entrust their lives in John Gaherin's hands."

They were instead listening to Gussie Busch, roaring, "If any club *mentions* making changes in the reserve system, they should be fined." And they listened perhaps most of all to Robert L. Howsam, whose approach was once humorously summed up this way: "Make no change and make it retroactive."

Bob Howsam was president of the Cincinnati Reds and architect of the Big Red Machine—that river city's great teams of the seventies. He had transformed the Reds from a shoestring operation to one of baseball's most sophisticated and profitable franchises. "Howsam wasn't articulate, but he was well-respected," said Sandy Hadden, the commissioner's aide. "He had a lot of friends who were led by what he thought."

Howsam thought baseball would collapse if the reserve system were ever modified and free agency allowed. Team spirit

would break down. Fan loyalty would suffer. Clubs that had
scouted and developed the best players—like his, say—would be
raided. Chaos would reign. And a man he despised would triumph: Marvin Miller.

Howsam was a Rickey man. He'd gotten to know the Mahatma in the fifties as owner and operator of the triple-A Denver
Bears—the club had a working arrangement with Rickey's Pittsburgh Pirates. The young Howsam had to overcome a disastrous
first encounter with Rickey and his son, Branch Jr. "Hi,
Branch," Howsam had said. "Hi, Twig." *Nobody* called the old
man anything but *Mister* Rickey. And nobody called his son
"Twig" to his face.

But Howsam went on to become yet another Rickey disciple
and protégé. In 1964, when Rickey was seeing out his days as
a Cardinals consultant, he got Gussie Busch to hire Howsam as
GM. In 1967, after three years in St. Louis, Howsam moved
over to Cincinnati.

There, using Rickey principles, he built the Big Red Machine.
He refused to join the Major League Scouting Bureau, believing
a club should find its own prospects the old-fashioned way:
scouring the bushes. He put a Rickey man named Rex Bowen in
charge of doing just that. He doubled the number of farm teams
and demanded players be taught the Reds Way. Howsam
dropped in on his farm teams unannounced to see that they
were. "The only way you could put together a team that had
Bench, Rose, Perez, and Concepcion was with great scouting
and player development," said Barry Rona, the PRC lawyer.
"Howsam found it abhorrent that someone on his team could be
taken away with *money.*"

He further resented the union's intrusion into his prerogatives.
Howsam's Teutonic lover of order and discipline pervaded the
organization. His chief enforcer was the Reds' number-two man,
Dick Wagner, known behind his back as "the Führer." Riverfront
Stadium was immaculate—tidied throughout games so as to be
as spotless in the ninth inning as in the first. Reds players had
to be clean-shaven and wear polished black spikes. They had to
eat their meals at spring training at the club's complex in Tampa,
signing in at the cafeteria like schoolchildren. Howsam believed
it built team cohesion and ensured good nutrition. Said John
Gaherin: "Bob looked on the players as overgrown kids whom
he had an obligation to protect."

Marvin Miller, of course, looked on the players as oppressed
workers whom *he* had an obligation to protect. He clashed with

Howsam repeatedly. The union filed grievances against the Reds' suspension of Bobby Tolan (for his "divisive attitude"), air-travel practices (for bumping players out of first-class to make room for club officials), and spring training practices (for not paying players their meal money when they ate at the complex). The union won all three and Howsam seethed.

Howsam was in his mid-fifties and had fixed ideas about what baseball was supposed to be. It was not supposed to be about nit-picking over the fine points of labor law. The spring training case particularly vexed him. "You could talk baseball, build friendships and fellowship the way we had it," he later explained. "Now they'd be off to the beaches, off fishing. They weren't talking baseball, which was part of getting them ready to play."

Howsam wasn't a skinflint, like a lot of the conservatives. (The joke in baseball was that swimming was invented when Calvin Griffith first came to a toll bridge.) The Reds were the first team with four $100,000 players: Pete Rose, Johnny Bench, Tony Perez, and Joe Morgan. And, unlike most of the conservatives, Howsam was as good a businessman as a baseball man. Minor league operators had to be sharp promoters, and that's what he was. One year, his Denver Bears outdrew two big-league clubs, with 463,000.

Howsam put Bears ads on the back of taxicabs, changing them for each series. He set up a speakers bureau, a radio network, and a charter-bus service to run fans in from outlying areas. He ran special nights for dozens of Colorado towns, whose citizens turned out en masse at Bears Stadium. Of Yuma's 1,400 souls, for instance, 1,200 turned out for Yuma Night. It featured Yuma's most noted commodity: wild jackrabbits. Dozens were released on the field before the game, each with a tag that said "$5" or "$10." Players dove to catch them and claim the money while the crowd went wild.

Howsam didn't do anything that flamboyant in Cincinnati, a conservative midwestern burg. But together with Dick Wagner, he sold the hell out of the Reds. They used the most sophisticated marketing in baseball this side of the Dodgers. With in-stadium questionnaires and phone surveys, the Reds learned more about their audience. Then they went after it hard, amassing the names of 80,000 eager fans on a computer and bombarding them with mailings.

For the first time in the club's history, the Reds aggressively sold season tickets, building from a base of about 1,200 up to

17,000. They opened a Reds retail store in downtown Cincinnati. They drew kids with a "Straight-A" program, which provided three pairs of tickets to high school and junior high students with top grades. Howsam and Wagner made the Reds into a regional franchise. Players and coaches went on midwinter "Red Caravans" through the Ohio River Valley. A hundred-station Reds radio network saturated Ohio, Kentucky, and Indiana.

The Reds, who'd drawn 1 million only four times in their pre-Howsam history, became the first club other than Los Angeles to draw 2 million in consecutive years. Of course, it had something to do with moving out of little Crosley Field (29,600) into roomy Riverfront Stadium (53,000) in 1970. But mostly it had to do with Howsam's aggressive marketing and his juggernaut team. The Reds won the NL pennant in 1970 and 1972 and the NL West in 1973. They would be world champs in 1975 and 1976.

It was ironic. The same Bob Howsam who was on the cutting edge of the baseball *business*, nevertheless represented—and would tolerate—*only* the best of baseball's old-time values. His inflexibility greatly influenced others. And so, as Howsam raged and Gussie Busch brayed, the Lords steadfastly refused to change.

As talks began for the 1973 Basic Agreement, Miller pressed anew for some negotiated form of free agency. His line to Gaherin was the same as it always had been.

"I know the clubs invest money to sign and bring along players, and they're entitled to have their services," he said. "But not forever, John. At one time in his career, a player should have the opportunity to test the market."

He made a reasonable suggestion. Players with three years in the bigs and making less than the average salary qualified to be free agents. Likewise a five-year veteran making less than one and a half times the average salary. Ditto a seven-year man who wasn't making twice the average.

The union also proposed unrestricted free agency for players who'd put in seven, twelve, and seventeen years. At each of these junctures a player could test the market. But it imposed a stiff requirement on the signing team: paying the player's former team a sum equal to half his most recent annual salary.

Miller was turned down cold. He'd done much for the union in six years, but he still hadn't gotten to first base on free agency. He didn't know where to turn next. Would any player

ever really play out his option and test 10A? Or would the owners always find a way to stave off free agency?

Then, on a silver platter, he was handed a momentous case to
help the cause.

HERTFORD, NORTH CAROLINA, is approximately fifty miles from nowhere. Tucked away on the state's northeast corner, near the Virginia line, it's far from the nearest interstate highway. This is peanut and soybean country: miles and miles of farms and not much else.

James Augustus Hunter grew up on one of them. It was the late 1950s and early sixties, but he was a throwback to a turn-of-the-century archetype: the farmboy who threw potatoes when he ran out of baseballs, who grew up playing country hardball. Hunter was the youngest of a tenant farmer's ten children. He and four brothers formed the nucleus of a local baseball team that challenged kids in nearby towns. But young Jim Hunter was clearly the best of them. By the time he was playing American Legion ball, he'd found his position: pitcher. One season he threw two no-hitters and struck out 138 hitters in 87 innings. Even in this backwater, that'll attract scouts.

The one who came most often was Clyde Kluttz. He'd been a second-string big-league catcher back in the forties. Now a man in his fifties, he was a Kansas City Athletics bird dog. He lived in Salisbury, North Carolina, 300 miles away—just a whoop and a holler in these parts. Kluttz had the weathered face, crew cut, and soft drawl that marked him as a native. He did some farming himself. He and Hunter were simpatico, though neither knew the word.

Kluttz was a combination coach and Dutch uncle. He taught Hunter how to throw two kinds of fastballs. And, settled into a chair on Hunter's porch, he advised him about handling money and the fast-lane life of major league baseball. It was coming, he assured him.

At the end of Hunter's final Legion year, in 1964, Charles O. Finley himself came to Hertford. Kluttz had passed on rave reports and Finley wanted to see Hunter firsthand. He passed out A's warm-up jackets, green bats, and gold baseballs all over town, trying to convey the impression to competitors that Hunter was all wrapped up. But he also had to satisfy himself that a hunting accident that left sixty pellets in Hunter's foot hadn't diminished his potential. As Hunter pitched in the state Legion finals, Finley watched from the stands.

That was the Charlie O. personal touch. He was fresh from Macon, Georgia, where he'd signed a kid named Johnny Lee Odom. This phenom had gone 42–2 with eight no-hitters in high school. As his graduation approached, the Red Sox had the inside track. A Boston scout was literally camped out at the Odoms' house, paying fifteen bucks a night for lodging. It was a lot of money for this dirt-poor family. But then Finley came along.

"He's not doing you right; he should be paying you more," he told Mrs. Odom. "I'll give you thirty dollars for a room."

Sold. Finley moved in, then went to a produce store and bought mounds of groceries: watermelons, peanuts, chicken, and every vegetable under the sun. It took a half-ton pickup to deliver it all to the Odoms. That night, Finley rustled up a wondrous feast. Drawing on his southern roots and prodigious cooking skills, he whipped up fried chicken, corn on the cob, black-eyed peas, collard greens, the works.

Finley stayed at the Odoms just one night. By the time he checked out, he'd signed the boy for $75,000. It was something Walter O'Malley would have never done, but that was Finley. Partly he was a closer; partly he fancied himself a keen talent judge; partly he was cheap. "If it became necessary to offer a player more than twenty-five thousand, I wanted to go see that player myself," he said.

Now, in Hertford, he offered Jim Hunter $75,000 too. It was a mind-boggling sum for the tenant farmer's son. But he'd promised the Phillies, Orioles, and Mets that he'd listen to their offers. He said he needed another day or two.

"I'm gonna sign you today, kid, or never talk to you again," said Finley, in full insurance-salesman mode.

Hunter looked at his father. The father looked back.

"I'll sign," he said.

There was just one more thing. Finley, ever the showman, wanted his top prospects to have colorful nicknames. He thought it added to their gate appeal. If they didn't already have one, he'd assign one. Johnny Lee Odom had already become Blue Moon Odom.

"Do you have a nickname?" he asked Hunter.

"No, sir."

"Well, to play baseball you've got to have a nickname. What do you like to do?"

"Hunt and fish."

"Fine," said Finley. "When you were six years old you ran away from home and went fishing. Your mom and dad had been looking for you all day. When they finally found you about, ah, four o'clock in the afternoon, you'd caught two big fish . . . ahh . . . catfish . . . and were reeling in the third. And that's how you got your nickname. Okay?"

"Yes, sir, Mr. Finley."

"Good, now repeat it back to me."

His mother was appalled. No son of hers had ever run away; no one had ever called him "Catfish"; and wasn't Jim a perfectly nice name? But to a nation's baseball fans, Catfish Hunter it was. They knew him by the next year, because he was pitching in the majors at age nineteen. The last-place A's presented instant opportunity.

Hunter's maturation and improvement tracked the club's. In 1968, he pitched a perfect game and, for the second straight year, won 13 games. By the early seventies, after the A's had moved to Oakland, Hunter had developed pinpoint control and a beautiful feel for pitching. He didn't have the best stuff in the game, but he had no peer when it came to keeping hitters off-stride or throwing the right, paralyzing pitch at the right time. As the A's piled up championships, Hunter racked up twenty-win seasons: four in a row, 1971 to 1974.

As he learned all about pitching, Jim Hunter also learned all about Charlie Finley. The man had a generous side. He gave Hunter a $5,000 bonus after his perfect game. He offered to invest players' money in the stock market, personally guaranteeing they'd lose no money. Hunter once gave him $50,000 to do that. Six months later, when he asked to cash out, Finley handed him $100,000. When Hunter mentioned he wanted to buy 300 acres of the most fertile farmland in North Carolina, Finley quickly advanced the needed $150,000.

But Hunter saw the other side of the owner too. They'd agreed in early 1969 he would repay $20,000 a year plus 6 percent interest on the loan. Just a few months later, however, Finley told him he wanted the whole $150,000 back. Hunter had by now bought the property; he didn't have the money. But Finley, who'd overextended himself buying NHL and ABA franchises, demanded it. Before Hunter's every scheduled start, he got a call.

"Cat," said the raspy voice, "do you know who this is?"

"Yes, sir, Mr. Finley."

"You know you owe me a hundred and fifty thousand dollars?"

"Yes, sir. Let me go home and I'll make arrangements to get the money."

Finley wouldn't let him. He'd just keep repeating: "I . . . need . . . my . . . money." Rattled, Hunter slumped to a 12–15 season. He finally sold all but thirty acres to raise the money for Finley. Hunter built a house on the remaining plot, giving him a close-up view of what might have been: a cornucopia of soybeans, peanuts, and corn. (The man who bought it won awards for the crops he raised there.) To a man with farming blood and farming aspirations like Hunter, it was a bitter pill.

Hunter wasn't the only player to cross swords with Finley. Reggie Jackson had epic contract battles with him. After his first big season in 1969 (47 homers, 118 RBIs), Jackson went for his first big raise (from $20,000 to $75,000). Finley wouldn't budge above $40,000. Only a week before Opening Day did he finally inch up to $45,000 and a rent-free apartment.

Jackson signed, but, having missed spring training and still upset by the negotiations, he had a miserable season. He was benched repeatedly and his production was halved. Finally, one game, he broke out of it long enough to hit a grand-slam homer. Jackson paused to admire the drive, slowly trotted toward first, looked up at Finley's box, and mouthed the words "Fuck you." Charlie O. later forced a public apology out of him, but it was a magnificent gesture at the time.

Vida Blue wanted a mega-raise after he burst into stardom, too. As a twenty-three-year-old rookie in 1971, he was 24–8 with a 1.82 ERA, 8 shutouts, and 301 strikeouts. Blue got an agent and got the notion that he should be making $100,000. Finley wouldn't budge above $50,000. That's what he was paying Catfish Hunter. He summed up his position to Blue pretty bluntly one day:

"Well, I *know* you won twenty-four games. I *know* you led the league in earned run average. I *know* you had three hundred strikeouts. I *know* you made the All-Star Team. I *know* you were the youngest to win the Cy Young Award and the MVP. I *know* all that. And if I was you, I would ask for the same thing. And you *deserve* it. But I ain't gonna give it to you."

Blue announced his retirement in favor of a public-relations job with a plumbing-fixtures company. He stuck to his guns all the way through April, when Bowie Kuhn stepped in as peacemaker. Blue wound up with $63,000. He also wound up with a 6–10 record for 1972 and permanent scars. He went on to win 209 games in his career but was never quite the same. He was never as powerful as before, failing to even reach the 200-strikeout plateau again. Nor was he ever again the happy-go-lucky kid America had embraced. He was bitter and withdrawn, eventually developing a drug problem that landed him in court.

Jim Hunter finally hit the $100,000 plateau in 1974: a two-year contract to pay that sum both years. The contract had one wrinkle: he wanted $50,000 of his 1974 pay deferred, put into an annuity collectible in ten years. It was Hunter's country conservatism. He wanted the money down the line, when he no longer drew a major league salary. His contract stipulated the $50,000 be paid to a North Carolina insurance company over the course of the season.

Finley never did. He discovered belatedly that the $50,000 wasn't tax-deductible, like current salaries. He could only take the deduction years later, when Hunter collected. He also wouldn't have the use of the funds, as he did with the $40,000 Reggie Jackson deferred in his 1973 contract.

Hunter's lawyer began pressing for the $50,000 annuity payment in August. Finley began dissembling. He couldn't catch up with his tax consultant. He couldn't get his estranged wife, the A's corporate secretary, to sign off on the deal. He feared other players would want this kind of provision. And so on.

September came. Hunter was having his greatest season yet: 25–12 with a league-leading 2.49 ERA. The A's were en route to their third straight World Series. Yet he was deeply unhappy. Charlie Finley was out to screw him again. He began talking about it openly with teammates and writers.

Marvin Miller read about it and contacted Hunter. Did he want the union to get involved? Damn straight. In mid-September, Dick Moss sent a contract-violation notice to Finley. He had ten days to square accounts with Hunter—those were the rules of the Basic Agreement. The ten days passed. On October 4, the eve of the Oakland–Baltimore divisional playoffs, Moss sent another notice to Finley, invoking Section 7A of the Uniform Players Contract: "The Player may terminate this contract, upon written notice to the Club, if the Club shall default in the payments to the Player provided for."

Finley was sitting in his Oakland Coliseum office holding the telegram when Jim Hunter walked in that day. The owner had summoned him for a meeting. Sitting there, too, was a witness: American League president Lee MacPhail.

"Cat, I've always been willing to pay you, and I'll give you a check right now," growled Finley. "But I will not sign that application with the insurance company."

He held out a check for $50,000.

"No, I don't want that money paid to me," said Hunter. "I want it paid just like the contract calls for, deferred payments to an insurance company or whoever I designate." And he walked out.

Somehow Hunter was his usual impeccable self in the postseason. He won the final playoff game against Baltimore 2–1. He pitched a five-hitter to beat Los Angeles in game three of the Series. Oakland won the championship in five games, their third straight. The champagne spray had hardly dried when the union drew up its claim that Catfish Hunter was a free agent.

Dick Moss first made a courtesy call to Gaherin, at home on a Saturday morning. "We're going to declare the Hunter contract in default," he said. "I just wanted to give you a chance to get your ducks in a row."

Gaherin tracked down Finley at his farm in La Porte, Indiana. "This is serious," he said. "I think we're going to have to arbitrate it."

Then he called up the other key labor-relations figures: Lou Hoynes, Barry Rona, Ed Fitzgerald, and American League counsel Jim Garner. They all agreed they'd have to get cracking. They would meet in Chicago the next day to see Finley and figure out what kind of a defense they could mount.

It was an uncomfortable position for the baseball establishment, which, by and large, considered Charlie Finley indefensible. The men at the Chicago meeting had been repeated combatants with Finley and were more comfortable as such. Only the dreaded words *free agent* could possibly put them on the same side.

Finley caused such wrangles in his repeated efforts to leave Kansas City that the American League's longtime lawyer quit in disgust. Ben Fiery, league counsel since the 1930s, didn't know what disgusted him more: Finley's antics or his fellow owners' toleration of them. One day he called a junior partner, Sandy Hadden, into his office.

"I'm sick and tired of trying to lead the troops up the mountain, only to find that not only are they not following me but they're shooting at me," he said. "Screw it. You take over."

Thus did Finley become Sandy Hadden's cross to bear, one that Hadden was admirably quick to shoulder. Immediately upon hanging up from talking to Finley, he wrote a memo. It was the only way of keeping straight Finley's constantly shifting version of things. Recalled Hadden, "He couldn't remember for half an hour what he'd said." (Put another way, by Boston GM Dick O'Connell: "Charlie has such a high regard for the truth that he uses it sparingly.") Hadden needed the documentation for the constant suits, arbitrations, and disciplinary proceedings that Finley spawned. He was the equivalent of a Lawyers' Full-Employment Act. He was also a lawyer's nightmare.

Finley once begged off flying to New York for a deposition, citing his bad heart (he did have two major bypass operations), requiring a squadron of lawyers to come to Chicago instead.

It was like a deathbed scene in Finley's office. He lay on his couch, reaching over to an oxygen tank every few sentences to take a hit. The court reporter and the lawyers leaned forward to hear his raspy, weak words. Then his secretary stuck her head in the door.

"The La Porte High School marching band is here," she said.

Finley jumped up and bounded out of the room. Everybody else sat looking at each other.

Bleary-eyed from Sunday-morning flights, Gaherin, Hoynes, Rona, Garner, and Fitzgerald met in a conference room at the O'Hare Hilton. Finley kept them waiting an hour, before entering with his son, Paul. Then he launched into his version of the Hunter contract story, the lawyers scribbling notes as the room filled with Finley's rhetorical flourishes. Suddenly he stopped.

"How's that sound to you?" he said.

"There are some spots you're vulnerable," said Gaherin, "but on the whole it sounds defensible."

"Well, it's bullshit," Finley said. "Now I'll tell you what happened."

"Charlie, you son of a bitch," said Ed Fitzgerald, drawing himself up to his full, bulky six feet three inches. "One of these days I'm going to forget who you are and who I am and I'm going to throw you through the window." (Fitzgerald doesn't remember making this remark.)

On the flight back to New York, Lou Hoynes turned to Gaherin. "What do you think?" he said.

"It's a tough one to prepare for," Gaherin replied. "We'll never know when he's telling the truth."

The arbitrator, Peter Seitz, had the same problem. Finley denied ever receiving documents that Hunter's lawyer had mailed in February and June. Those documents laid out the mechanics of making the annuity payment. He claimed to have been surprised in August when the lawyer started pressing for the $50,000. He said his understanding was that this was another "Reggie Jackson deal."

Baseball's lawyers tried to make much of the fact that Finley had, in MacPhail's presence, offered Hunter the $50,000 on the spot. They argued that even if there was a breach of contract, it was effective only upon the arbitrator's ruling. Finley should still have ten days to make good. Privately, John Gaherin doubted they could pull it off.

As a member of the arbitration panel hearing the case, he was privy to Seitz's thinking. The panel was composed of three members: Gaherin, Miller, and Seitz. The votes of the first two canceled each other out, of course, which left the decision in Seitz's hands. The panel discussed the case after the hearing and Seitz had been blunt.

"John," he said to Gaherin, "you know your client's a liar."

"What else is new?"

"I don't believe him."

"You've got to make those judgments. That's why you're in the job you're in."

Gaherin reported back to his camp. Seitz was leaning strongly toward Hunter. The best they could hope for was that he'd let Finley off lightly.

When Seitz gave the other two panel members a draft of his decision, Gaherin's heart leapt with hope. Seitz had ordered Finley to make the $50,000 payment and had terminated Hunter's contract. But it didn't say anything about him being a free agent.

Miller instantly saw it, too, and he saw in the ambiguity a protracted battle with the Lords. He turned to Seitz.

"If you don't make his status clear," he said, "you're leaving the way open for them to claim that Finley has to pay the $50,000, but Hunter has to go back to Oakland."

"Hmm," said Seitz. "I want a recess. I'm going off by myself to think about this."

When Seitz came back in, he'd changed the wording: "Mr. Hunter's contract for service to be performed during the 1975 season no longer binds him and he is a free agent."

The decision came down on December 13. Kuhn immediately forbade any bidding on Hunter. He wanted to review the decision and allow Finley time to appeal, if he wished. (Finley did go to court, but was unsuccessful.) Marvin Miller snarled. He'd sue if Kuhn abrogated an arbitrator's ruling. The commissioner backed off, and on December 19, the Catfish Hunter Derby opened. The race to Ahoskie, North Carolina, was on.

It was the next town over from Hertford, but pretty much the same place: a sleepy town of 5,500 souls. Downtown Ahoskie was an eight-block stretch, bisected by railroad tracks. It had three traffic lights, two restaurants, a few stores, and the offices of Hunter's attorney, J. Carlton Cherry.

Cherry was a sixty-eight-year-old country lawyer whose clientele consisted largely of peanut and soybean farmers. He came to represent Hunter because he used to drive his American Legion team to their games. "If you ever need a lawyer, don't forget where Ahoskie's at," he told the young pitcher.

But Cherry was no pushover. He'd already survived hand-to-hand combat with Charles O. Finley. He set up his firm's tiny conference room to do business with the baseball people and waited for them to come.

How they came. Every owner in baseball at least inquired about Hunter, except for Horace Stoneham, who was in dire straits, and Charlie Finley, who was in a state of apoplexy. They all hated the *concept* of free agency, mind you, and pledged allegiance to the reserve clause. But still, they all salivated at the idea of having Catfish Hunter in their rotation. It was like, "Baby, I love my wife, but oh, you kid."

Corporate jets whisked into nearby Tri-County Airport. Rental cars tore down U.S. 13, coming south from the Norfolk, Virginia, airport. Carlton Cherry's calendar filled up with appointments, and the forty-eight-room Tomahawk Motel filled up with owners, GMs, and assorted aides. Ahoskie's citizens gawked as each new wave of baseball men arrived.

Phillies owner Ruly Carpenter got out of his rental car and

walked toward Cherry's office, trying to jump mud puddles with dignity. He noticed five barber-shop patrons across the street, their noses pressed to the window, and almost thought he could hear them: "Look at those damned Yankees. Carlton's gonna skin their asses."

The firm of Cherry, Cherry and Flythe was located in a former bank, a Greek Revival structure fronted by two-story columns. Hunter himself would emerge every so often to feed another penny into the parking meter out front, where his muddy gray pickup truck was parked.

Inside they talked of millions—sums such as had been paid in other sports but never in baseball. The average basketball player's salary had risen to $90,000, courtesy of the ABA–NBA war. Kareem Abdul-Jabbar had a five-year, $2 million contract. The war between the NHL and World Hockey Association had done wonders for hockey pay. Bobby Hull had a ten-year, $2.75 million contract; Gordie Howe was lured out of retirement for $1 million. The NFL and AFL had merged, but players still reaped the benefits of wartime bidding. Their average salary was $40,000. In baseball, with an ironclad reserve clause and no war, the average salary was $35,000. The top salary was $250,000; the long-term contract was unheard-of.

But here was Jim Hunter: a Cy Young winner, in the prime of his career, at age twenty-eight, on the open market. Baseball was in uncharted waters. There was no benchmark to go by—only Hunter's one firm contract demand: five years, guaranteed.

"How much do you think it will take to sign him?" Indians owner Ted Bonda asked his GM, Phil Seghi.

"At least a million," he said.

"You're crazy!"

"I'm not crazy. It could be two million."

The bidding *started* at $2 million, phoned in by the Mets the first morning, December 19. That afternoon, Red Sox executives Dick O'Connell, Haywood Sullivan, and John Harrington plunked a $3 million offer on Carlton Cherry's conference-room table.

Next morning came the San Diego delegation: GM Peter Bavasi, manager John McNamara, and pitching coach Bill Posedel. The latter two brought no negotiating acumen but, the Padres hoped, much goodwill. McNamara had once been Hunter's manager, Posedel his pitching coach. He particularly liked Posedel—even named a hunting dog after him.

"What's this going to cost?" asked Padres owner Ray Kroc before the party left.

"Oh," said Bavasi, "one hundred thousand a year for four years."

Kroc gave his blessing. It was loose change to the founder of McDonald's Corporation, worth an estimated $500 million. He'd just bought the Padres earlier that year and was one of a new breed of owners. He sought and enjoyed the limelight. Watching his first Padres game as owner—a typically pathetic performance by the team—he grabbed the PA mike and bellowed: "This is Ray Kroc. We are putting on a lousy show for you. I apologize for it. I'm disgusted with it. This is the most stupid baseball playing I've ever seen." Kroc was suddenly more famous for his baseball team (revenues: $20 million a year) than for his hamburger chain (revenues: $1 billion a year), and he loved it. If he landed Hunter, he'd be all over the papers with him. Kroc was also an impatient man. He wanted a contender as quickly as he demanded a Big Mac: he wanted a right-hander to go.

Peter Bavasi knew this as he settled into the conference room and tried to stay clear of a stream of tobacco juice. Hunter was slowly filling a Styrofoam cup, with less control than he showed on the mound.

"Young man, we represent farmers," Cherry said. "We deal right on top of the table, and we get right to the point. Would four million dollars scare you off?"

"No, sir," said Bavasi, "our owner told us to come down and sign Hunter. If that's what it takes, that's what it takes."

Actually, it petrified Bavasi and stunned Posedel, who nearly fell off his chair. Cherry started scrawling the proposed terms on a legal pad: five years' guaranteed salary, deferred money, farmland, and assorted odds and ends. The total: $3.8 million.

"One more thing," he said. "Jim wants a $25,000 annuity for each of his two children for college."

"Shit," said Bavasi, "for three-point-eight million he could buy a small university!" But what the hell, it was only another $50,000. He agreed to it. Then Bavasi threw another card on the table he'd been prepared to play. Kroc wanted to offer Hunter a McDonald's franchise. The company was scouting the area for new locations, and they'd be glad to throw in a store.

Hunter looked vastly disinterested and Cherry took his cue.

"We don't want it," he said. "It's only a complication."

Bavasi said he'd get back to them later, and the delegation returned to the Tomahawk.

"Jesus-fucking-Christ," Posedel moaned. "We came here talking about four hundred thousand and you're talking about four million. You're going to get us all fired. Let's have a drink."

The night before they'd driven clear to the next county to find a liquor store—Hertford County was dry—but they all agreed as they drew on the bottle of Wild Turkey that it had been worth the trouble.

Bavasi decided he'd better check in with Kroc that afternoon. His secretary said he was out sailing in the Caribbean and wouldn't be back for three days. Bavasi used ship-to-shore to reach him aboard his yacht, the *Joni Ray*. On account of the static on the line, they could barely hear each other.

"What's the deal?" asked Kroc.

"Four million," said Bavasi.

"Outstanding, young man. You brought him in for four hundred thousand?"

"No, sir. Four million."

"I heard you the first time. Four hundred thousand."

The line suddenly cleared up, and Bavasi gave the figure again.

"Four *million*?" said Kroc. "Four damned *million*?"

"Yes, sir."

Bavasi heard the sharp voice of Joni, Kroc's wife, in the background. She never had understood baseball. (When Kroc first told her he'd bought the San Diego Padres, she said, "Oh, Ray, you have all the comforts you could want in life. What would you want with a monastery full of priests?")

"Shut up," said Kroc, directing his voice toward his hectoring wife. "I told you to shut up. If I want to spend four million on a ballplayer, I will. If I want to spend twelve million, I will. Joni, it's my goddamn money and I'll do what I want."

Kroc got back on the ship-to-shore: "You take that four million or whatever else it takes and sign him."

Bavasi got off the line and looked into the anxious faces of Posedel and McNamara.

"Did we get fired?" they asked, as one.

"No, we got a deal."

Bavasi went right back to Cherry's law office. He reported he'd checked with Mr. Kroc and the terms were fine.

"Do we have a deal?" asked Bavasi.

Cherry shook his hand.

"Now it's up to Mr. Kroc's lawyers to draft this," said Bavasi. He decided to hang around Ahoskie and make sure nobody snatched Hunter away. He enlisted a couple of teenagers who hung around Cherry's office as spies. Each morning, Bavasi tore a ten-dollar bill in two and gave them one half. At day's end they brought a report and got the other half. They couldn't get close enough to eavesdrop, but Bavasi could at least track the movements of the other teams.

"There were three men in there," said one of the boys, describing that afternoon's entourage. "One of them walked on his toes and had slick, black black hair."

Aha. Al Campanis of the Dodgers.

Everybody had a gimmick. Gaylord Perry, ace Indians pitcher and fellow North Carolina farmer, preceded owner Bonda and GM Seghi into town. Mike Hegan, a former Oakland teammate and now Milwaukee's catcher, accompanied Ed Fitzgerald and Bud Selig. Ruly Carpenter figured he had an ace in the hole: the offer of hunting privileges on the Carpenters' South Carolina spread.

Some cozied up to the locals, believing this somehow curried favor with Hunter. Gene Autry stood on a street corner, passing out 45's of his Christmas classic "Rudolph the Red-Nosed Reindeer." Bavasi himself bought rounds of beer in the pool hall—until he figured out nobody there knew Hunter.

Some clubs concentrated on the financial wrinkles. The Pirates offered $750,000 over five years, with $1 million in insurance and annuities, $400,000 in deferred money (in stocks or T-bills), and limited partnerships in five new Wal-Mart stores. The Royals offered a six-year contract worth $825,000 in salary, a farm-equipment purchase option, $5,000 per year per child for college, and $50,000 a year for life, up to age seventy. Cherry put the value at $3.5 million.

But Hunter had a question: What if he died before age seventy?

"Well," said GM Joe Burke, "that's the end of the contract."

"How about my wife?"

"Well . . . we won't have to worry about that, will we? You'll be dead."

Hunter mentally crossed Kansas City off his list. What a heady feeling it was: swallowing Charlie Finley's guff for all those years and now waving away the Lords who displeased him.

One by one, clubs dropped out. The Mets and Cardinals resigned at $2 million. So did the Twins and Angels. The Indians bowed out at $2.4 million; the Braves and Expos at $2.5 million;

the Phillies at $2.6 million. The Pirates gasped and exited at $2.8 million. The Red Sox stopped at $3 million. The Royals were hanging in at $3.8 million, but in Hunter's mind were out of it. San Diego, the leader in the clubhouse, was looking like a winner.

Bavasi checked back with Cherry three days after the first meeting. It was two days before Christmas.

"I'm going to stay right here until we get this done," he said.

"Now, you don't have to do that," said Cherry. "A young man like yourself should be getting home to his family."

Bavasi believed him. He figured you had to believe a man who said he "dealt off the top of the table." He caught the last flight out for San Diego on Christmas Eve.

What Peter Bavasi never saw, hanging around the fringes, was the New York Yankees. In the ten years since their dynasty's end, they'd drifted into irrelevance. The Mets now owned New York. In the past six years, they'd won two pennants and one world championship. The Yankees were a drab .500 club of Horace Clarkes and Gene Michaels. The Mets' 1969 miracle season launched a run of four straight years with 2 million attendance. The Yankees hadn't drawn two million since 1950. Worse yet, they had to share Shea Stadium with the Mets in 1975 while Yankee Stadium was refurbished.

The Yankees had been bought for $10 million in 1973 by a group headed by shipbuilder George Steinbrenner. The new owner took a low profile at first. "We plan absentee ownership," he told an introductory press conference. "We're not going to pretend we're something we aren't. I'll stick to building ships." The new owner was also tight with a dollar at first. He blanched when he learned Bobby Murcer had been signed for $100,000.

But Steinbrenner quickly developed a taste for the celebrity of ownership. Especially in New York, with its blaring tabloids, myriad radio and TV stations, and baseball-mad populace. It was intoxicating. One minute he was a nobody from Cleveland, the next he was an important personage. Only one thing could make it better for Steinbrenner: the adulation that would come of winning and reclaiming the town from the Mets.

But Steinbrenner couldn't directly lead the assault on Catfish Hunter. In November, he was suspended as the Yankees' general partner. He'd been caught up in the Watergate dragnet, convicted of making illegal contributions to Richard Nixon's 1972 reelection campaign. That, ruled Bowie Kuhn, disqualified him as a baseball owner for two years.

His suspension, however, had no effect on the executive he left in charge. This was veteran baseball man Gabe Paul, who had cut his teeth in the business in the 1920s at Branch Rickey's Rochester, New York, farm club. Paul wasn't a legendary GM like Rickey and, indeed, had never won a pennant. But then, in his thirty-two years as GM of Cincinnati and Cleveland, he'd always run clubs on a shoestring.

Baseball insiders respected Paul as a hard worker. ("Only whores make money in bed," he growled at underlings who tried to sneak out before midnight.) He was also a savvy and relentlessly persistent trader, called by some "the smiling cobra."

Lee MacPhail once took a day off, while Yankees GM, to attend his son's college graduation. There the strains of "Pomp and Circumstance" were interrupted by an announcement: "Will Lee MacPhail please report to the college office for an emergency phone call?"

MacPhail hustled to the office, wondering what kind of disaster had occurred in his life. His wife was beside herself. The voice on the phone was Gabe Paul's: "Lee, would you have any interest in Gary Bell?" Cleveland had been trying to unload the pitcher all over the league. MacPhail had already passed on him three times. But that was the indefatigable Mr. Paul.

The most important deal he'd ever cut was the one that landed George Steinbrenner the Yankees. Paul knew CBS was trying to unload them and also that the Cleveland shipbuilder was eager to buy any baseball team he could. He'd recently taken an unsuccessful run at the Indians. Paul put Steinbrenner together with CBS's Mike Burke, and the rest was history. Paul's reward was to succeed Burke as Yankees president.

At long last, he'd landed in a big market with a rich owner. Being a shrewd judge of talent, he was itching to get Catfish Hunter. The Yankees had inched up to second place in 1974, just two games behind the Orioles. Paul had already made an off-season trade for outfield dynamo Bobby Bonds. The addition of Hunter just might push this team over the top.

But Gabe Paul, penurious by habit, didn't make a blockbuster bid right off. In fact, for some time he didn't show up in Ahoskie at all. On the first day of bidding, he sent an emissary to Carlton Cherry with no offer at all, just an expression of interest. The emissary was Clyde Kluttz.

The man who'd snagged Jim Hunter a decade earlier for the

A's was now the Yankees' scouting director. He'd left the A's in a typical Finley falling-out. Kluttz had asked for a brief stint as a coach. It would qualify him as a ten-year man in his pension plan and get him higher benefits. Finley refused.

Though now with another club, Kluttz remained close to Hunter. He'd come over to Hertford in the off-season to hunt and talk baseball. He was still Hunter's baseball guru. He was, in short, the Yankees' secret weapon.

Kluttz skirted the baseball crowd in Ahoskie and checked into a motel in another town, Elizabeth City. There he whiled away the days watching TV and reading newspapers. By night, he went around Hertford, telling Hunter's friends and family that Jim belonged in New York. He was enlisting their support for decision time.

Then he'd either call or drop in on Hunter himself—tell him New York wasn't such a bad place. It had some nice suburbs; even a country boy like him had gotten used to it. Sure San Diego was a fine place: "But how many players from San Diego ever made it to the Hall of Fame?" As for New York's pressure, how could it be any worse than playing for Finley? Hunter knew he was getting a major league sales job, but, then, there was no denying it: Clyde Kluttz had never lied to him.

Gabe Paul twice popped down to Ahoskie in person: once to weigh in at five years for $1.5 million, a second time, when he found how pitifully inadequate that was, to go higher. Kluttz would meet Paul's private jet at the Suffolk, Virginia, airport, drive him to and from Ahoskie, and update him on his courtship of Hunter.

The Yankees weren't at the front of the pack in bidding. They hadn't even gotten much press, compared to the attention given some clubs' entourages. But that was just the lay-in-the-weeds style of both Kluttz and Paul. They just wanted to be sure they were around at the end.

The end came suddenly. On the morning of New Year's Eve, Jim Hunter woke up and told his wife, "I'm gonna sign with someone today." After two weeks of meetings in Cherry's office, the prize of the Catfish Hunter Derby was getting antsy. Deer season was almost over and he'd barely set foot in the woods. He met Clyde Kluttz for breakfast and told him the same: he had to make a decision before he went out of his mind.

"Jimmy, what would it take for you to come and play for the Yankees?" Kluttz asked.

Hunter recited his list of requirements: five years' salary, guaranteed; fifteen years' deferred money; and the annuities for his kids' college education. Could the Yankees do that, he asked, and at what kind of dollars could they do it?

Kluttz picked up a paper napkin, took out a pen, and wrote down the terms:

- $1 million as a bonus
- $1 million in life insurance
- $750,000 over five years
- $500,000 in deferred money
- $200,000 for attorneys' fees
- $50,000 each for the college-education annuities

The total was $3.5 million.

"Is that your offer?" asked Hunter.

"Yes, Jimmy, that's it," said Kluttz. "And it's our final offer."

"Don't leave town. I'll get with you in an hour."

Kluttz, of course, wasn't about to go anywhere. He waited while Hunter showed Cherry and his partners the napkin and gave them the word: he wanted the Yankees. The lawyers were mystified. For this they'd conducted a two-week auction? So Hunter could take the third-best offer?

They pointed out the Padres' and Royals' superior offers. Hunter said he didn't care, as long as the Yankees' offer was close. Cherry conceded it was in the ballpark. He also conceded Hunter was the client. Whatever he wanted.

Kluttz was summoned in. Cherry waved the napkin.

"I don't agree with all this, but Jimmy insists on picking his own club," he said. "Is this the offer, then?"

"Yes," Kluttz said.

"Then he's a Yankee."

Kluttz's eyes brimmed with tears. Hunter smiled broadly.

Peter Bavasi was the last to know, but the first to suspect. He'd tried to keep things going from afar: a barrage of we-love-ya letters to Hunter, a flurry of contract-drafting calls to Cherry. But the lawyer was sounding cooler, and he wasn't returning all of Bavasi's calls. Bavasi hinted that the Padres, already at $4 million, could go higher if need be. But he had a bad feeling Hunter wasn't wrapped up.

A conference call had been scheduled for that morning between Peter Bavasi in San Diego, Ray Kroc's lawyers in Chicago, and Carlton Cherry. It was to work out some further contract details, and one of Kroc's lawyers got it started.

"Mr. Kroc makes one request of Catfish, because of the size of the deal," he said. "He'd like McDonald's to have some of the value here as well as the club. He'd like Mr. Hunter to do some TV and radio commercials for McDonald's."

"Gentlemen, my client would never consider endorsing a product," Cherry said coldly. "He only plays ball. He does not smoke, drink, or dissipate, and he will not do ads for McDonald's. Discussions of this deal are over. Good day."

He hung up. In San Diego and Chicago, mouths hung open. Bavasi tried to ring him back, but Cherry's secretary said he was too busy. He was—preparing to fly to New York.

The Yankees wanted the deal done that day for tax purposes. They scheduled a press conference that evening and sent a private jet, bearing Ed Greenwald, a Yankees investor and lawyer. Hunter, Kluttz, and the lawyers boarded at the Suffolk, Virginia, airport. They were whisked to New York, Greenwald scrawling out the contract on a legal pad, a blinding snowstorm whirling around them.

In New York, at the Yankees' offices, Greenwald and Cherry jousted over the final details for three hours. The press conference's scheduled 8:15 P.M. start slipped by. It wasn't until 8:32 that a strange collection of people filed before the writers: Yankees officials, country lawyers, and, hair flowing out wildly from a $6.25 Yankee cap, Catfish Hunter.

"Happy New Year, fellas," said Gabe Paul.

By the time the ball had dropped in Times Square, Hunter was back in North Carolina, his greatest wish fulfilled. He could get out in the woods in the morning, the last day of hunting season. The Lords who'd received word of the signing were drinking hard at parties, trying to keep from thinking too hard about the Hunter Derby. But when New Year's Day dawned, so would the awful truth: Marvin Miller had all the more motive to attack the reserve clause. Said Lee MacPhail, now the American League president: "This had shown everybody exactly what free agency could amount to."

Gabe Paul, however, was unconflicted. He was elated. But, it might be asked, was this not mixed with some anxiety? Was this not a huge decision to make without consulting George Steinbrenner? Under the terms imposed by Bowie Kuhn, the suspended owner couldn't be involved. And here Gabe Paul had just committed $3.5 million to one player, when the whole franchise had been bought in 1973 for $10 million.

But no, Gabe Paul revealed years later, he was not anxious in the least. "I had breakfast with George, and we talked about it," he said.

The "smiling cobra" smiled.

$ ⑨ $

CATFISH HUNTER GOT the sirloin; Marvin Miller got the scraps. It was called salary arbitration. The procedure had been used for some time with municipal unions. To avert disruptive strikes and end bargaining standoffs, labor and management submitted their proposed terms to an arbitrator, who'd choose one or the other. It was called "final offer arbitration."

John Gaherin had been suggesting it since the late sixties. Now Ed Fitzgerald, the new PRC chairman, embraced it. Since entering baseball as head of the Milwaukee Brewers' ownership group, he'd heard Miller's mantra about the players: "peonage . . . pieces of property . . . powerless."

"Let's take Marvin's argument away from him," said Fitzgerald. No, players still couldn't go free-agent. But they could go to an outside party for salary justice. Gaherin fleshed out the details. Players with two years or more in the bigs qualified for arbitration. If they couldn't agree with their GM on a contract, each side would file a proposed salary with an arbitrator. Then they'd have two hours apiece to make their cases, which were to be based on certain criteria: the player's performance in the past season, his career overall, and how his pay stacked up against similar players. The arbitrator then chose one figure or the other.

Fitzgerald argued the benefits to his fellow owners. Arbitration would end holdouts, an increasingly vexing problem. It would neutralize Miller's efforts to end the antitrust exemption. (At a recent congressional hearing he'd illustrated the long reach of the reserve system. When Lefty O'Doul died at seventy-two, Miller said, he was still the property of the Giants; he'd never been released and was still reserved by the club.) And, Fitzgerald concluded, it shouldn't be terribly costly. Yes, the players would win some cases and some more money, but not a lot more.

It was okay with most owners. Bowie Kuhn backed it. So did Walter O'Malley. Some knew in their heart of hearts that the system needed change. "I was very much in favor of arbitration," recalled John McHale, the Expos' president and a forties-era first baseman. "I remembered as a player walking into a GM's office and having no court of appeal."

Charlie Finley, to no one's surprise, screamed bloody murder. "We'll be the nation's biggest assholes if we do this," he declared. "You can't win. You'll have guys with no baseball background setting salaries. You'll have a system that drives up the average salary every year. Give them anything they want, but don't give them arbitration."

Finley had one vocal ally: Dick Meyer of the Cardinals. Meyer, as Anheuser-Busch's labor chief, was experienced in arbitration, and he didn't like it either. "This will be baseball's ruin," he said darkly.

But it was Finley who carried the opposition, who "fought it tooth and toenail," as he put it. He harangued in meetings and worked the phones as only Finley could: nonstop, all hours. In the end, he was sure he had fifteen votes against salary arbitration. "They thanked me for taking the time and showing them the light," he recalled.

They lied.

The vote was 22–2, for it. Only the A's and the Cardinals were opposed. The Lords made a habit of ignoring Charlie Finley, no matter what they might say to get him off the phone. His warnings were ignored.

Finley's stance, what's more, betrayed a powerful element of self-interest. He had baseball's best team (World Series winners, 1972–74) yet baseball's second-lowest payroll. When baseball's first salary-arbitration season came, in February 1974, the A's accounted for nine of the twenty-nine cases.

Finley growled about the process that winter, as did fellow tightwad Calvin Griffith. (When an arbitrator awarded pitcher Dick Woodson a $30,000 salary, over the Twins' proffered $23,000, Griffith groaned, "This is going to kill us.") But overall, Fitzgerald was proved right. The clubs weren't out that much—Finley's combined arbitration "losses" totaled $87,000—and holdouts subsided. Said the Lords' virtual house organ, *The Sporting News*: "All in all, arbitration seemed palatable to both sides."

The economic problems of salary arbitration wouldn't become evident until years later. The more immediate problem was that it failed to slow Marvin Miller. The Catfish Hunter case had freed just one player, but it had shown everyone the power of free agency. He would redouble his efforts to find a wider-reaching test case.

"Marvin had already decided to dynamite the reserve clause," said John Gaherin. "If we'd started salary arbitration earlier, we might have forestalled him. But I got no interest in our camp for years."

By 1975, a genie was coming out of the bottle, and it had a name: Andy Messersmith.

John Alexander Messersmith had grown up in Anaheim, California, and become an All-American pitcher at the University of California, Berkeley. In 1966, the twenty-one-year-old signed with the hometown Angels and by 1969 he was pitching in the big leagues. Messersmith was the essence of Southern California: curly golden locks, happy-go-lucky, slightly flaky. He was also an outstanding pitcher: a six-foot-one, 200-pound right-hander, with a live fastball and a changeup to die for. In his first four seasons with the Angels, pitching for lousy teams, he went 59–47 with a 2.77 ERA. In 1971 he was a twenty-game winner and All-Star.

Traded to the Dodgers in November 1972, Messersmith was just as good in the National League. He was 14–10 with a 2.70 ERA in 1973, the fifth-best earned-run average in the league. In 1974, at the age of twenty-nine, he went 20–6 with a 2.59 ERA—one of just two twenty-game winners in the NL and the league leader in winning percentage. He was a vital element on L.A.'s pennant-winning club.

But as the 1975 season approached, he was at loggerheads with the Dodgers on his contract. He reported to spring training without one, and it was there that he fell out with GM Al Campanis. As they sat in his Vero Beach office, discussing what kind of raise Messersmith was due over 1974's $90,000 salary, Campanis infuriated the pitcher. Quite apart from how well the pitcher had performed, quite apart from how much the Dodgers could allegedly afford, he injected a deeply "personal issue." (Even eighteen years later, the matter cut so deep with Messersmith he wouldn't elaborate on it.)

Two things happened. One, Messersmith severed talks with the GM. "This is way out of the boundaries of negotiations; this is something else," he told Campanis. "I'm not going to deal with you anymore." He insisted on shifting the talks to Peter

O'Malley, the club's president. The other thing to emerge was a new non-monetary demand. No way, Messersmith decided, would he let Al Campanis be in a position to dictate his career. He'd already had to change teams once when he crossed his first GM, the Angels' Dick Walsh. Now he wanted a no-trade clause in his contract. "I'm going to have some control of my destiny," declared Messersmith.

Peter O'Malley was more pleasant than Campanis but no more pliant. "We've never given one [a no-trade] and we aren't going to start now," he said.

So Messersmith simply refused to sign.

"I never went into this for the glory and betterment of the Players Association," he would later say. "At the start it was all personal. Al Campanis had stirred my anger, and it became a pride issue. When I get stubborn, I get *very* stubborn."

He took out his anger on National League batters that year. In 1975, Messersmith was a tireless pitching machine. He led the league in games started, with 40; complete games, with 19; and innings pitched, with 322. He was second in ERA, with 2.29; third in wins, with 19; tops in shutouts, with 7. On a Dodgers team that slumped to a distant second, 20 games behind the pennant-winning Reds, he was the brightest spot.

Yet it was an excruciating season, as Messersmith endured the uncertainties of being unsigned. He carried the weight of constant scrutiny from the writers ("So, how 'bout that contract, Andy?") and carried the hopes of every player who understood the stakes. "Every time he took the ball, everybody in management wanted him to fail and everybody from the players wanted him to succeed," said Ted Simmons, who fully understood the pressures. "He was doing it for us all."

One day, Messersmith was talking with Bobby Tolan, who also understood this ordeal. The outfielder commiserated, but also explained why he'd finally signed: not just for the sweetened contract the Padres finally offered but because of the fear he'd never again play ball. It only underscored what Messersmith had already been feeling. Most of all about that season, he would later recall, "I remember being very alone."

In August, he finally became a little less so. Marvin Miller called. Six players had begun the season without a contract and now, as nearly as he could tell, only a single active one remained: Messersmith. They talked about his contract status and agreed: if he was still unsigned at season's end he would file a grievance seeking free agency.

They would continue to talk through the remainder of the season—Messersmith updating Miller on the Dodgers' latest proposal, Miller schooling Messersmith on Section 10A of the Uniform Players Contract. Finally, the issue at the center of Messersmith's embattled season began to evolve. As he turned it over and over in his mind, it was being transformed from a private battle with the Dodgers into a broader cause for the players.

The Dodgers held firm. They were willing to move up on the money. In fact, the better Messersmith pitched and the later the season got, the sweeter the pot. By September, they were talking about a three-year deal in the vicinity of $150,000 for 1975, $170,000 for 1976, and $220,000 for 1977. But the no-trade clause remained a sticking point.

No team had ever agreed to one, and the Lords didn't want the Dodgers to start now. Chub Feeney, PRC member and National League president, strongly urged Peter O'Malley to hold the line. O'Malley did so, insisting in negotiations that the guarantee simply wasn't necessary. The good old Dodgers would do right by him.

"We had no intention of trading Andy Messersmith," he later recalled. "He was a quality individual, a quality performer, and a delight to have on the team."

Messersmith wasn't buying. For one thing, Al Campanis still lurked in the front office. For another, Marvin Miller's talks on player empowerment had firmly taken hold.

"When Peter came up with the dough, I was adamant," the pitcher said. "The money was incredible, but they wouldn't bring the no-trade to the table. I'd gotten stimulated by Marvin and Dick [Moss]. Now I understood the significance of what this was all about. I was tired of players having no power and no rights."

Andy Messersmith pitched on with a vengeance and without a contract.

John Gaherin was worried. Some twenty players had now gone into a season unsigned since '72. Whether it was Messersmith or someone else, it was just a matter of time. Miller would get his test case and, Gaherin feared, that would be the end of the reserve clause.

"You don't test the crown jewels," he told the owners, urging them to negotiate changes before an arbitrator imposed them. "The deal you make for yourself, no matter how onerous and unpleasant, is better than the deal someone makes for you."

Finally he had a like-minded PRC chief: Ed Fitzgerald. The Milwaukee Brewers' chairman came from one of that city's first families. His father, chairman of Northwestern Mutual Life Insurance Company, was prominent enough to have had a Great Lakes ship named after him. Its sad fate was immortalized in a song, "The Wreck of the Edmund Fitzgerald."

The son was called "Young Ed," but was an impressive figure in his own right. Fitzgerald was six-foot-three, 250 pounds, and had led a Marine detachment in Korea. Now he was the CEO of Cutler-Hammer, an electronics firm, and was a tireless contributor to Milwaukee civic causes. Said an admiring John McHale: "Ed's the hardest-working rich man I ever saw."

Indeed, it was civic duty that originally drew him into baseball. In 1962, he was approached by the Milwaukee Braves' ownership syndicate to join their board. They were mostly Chicago businessmen who said they wanted more local representation. Fitzgerald agreed to do it. "Little did I know," he said, "they were looking to get out."

The Braves left for Atlanta in 1966, and Fitzgerald was left to catch the slings and arrows of the outraged locals. When an organization was formed to seek a new franchise, he joined it "to try to clear my good name." In 1970, Milwaukee landed the Brewers, and Fitzgerald became chairman.

He came to chair the PRC the same way people come to run a winter charity ball: by default. From his work at Cutler-Hammer Fitzgerald knew labor relations—a subject about which Major League Baseball was obviously in the dark. He looked on, appalled, during the 1972 strike. "It was a stupid argument which baseball finally lost," he said. "The players walked out; the owners caved in; and I wondered how we could have gotten caught in such a bad decision to force the issue."

When Dick Meyer no longer wanted to head the PRC, Fitzgerald agreed to do it. He would soon learn exactly how bad decisions got made.

Baseball was preparing for a new round of collective bargaining, to begin at year end 1975, and Ed Fitzgerald was coming to a conclusion. This was the time to negotiate some changes, to allow some form of free agency. He consulted with John Gaherin, learned all the facts and options, and finally, one ownership meeting, put it straight to his peers.

"The reserve system is doomed in the long haul," said Fitzgerald. "We'd like permission to begin negotiating a revised reserve system beginning this fall."

He gave them the facts of life. Marvin Miller was committed to getting a test case. So far, they'd staved him off, but he would eventually get his desired grievance and that would leave the whole industry at the mercy of an arbitrator.

"Maybe the reserve system can stand the test, and if it does, fine," he said. "But if it doesn't it fails in a catastrophic mode. Baseball cannot afford that catastrophe. Marvin can afford to lose a hundred times as long as he wins once.

"If we begin to negotiate, we could work out changes in the reserve system that would allow us to gradually adjust over a period of time. The clubs could get used to working with it. We could be comfortable with it. But if we lose in arbitration, we're going to be in trouble from day one. We need to negotiate while we're in a power position."

Fitzgerald explained how a compromise system might work. Clubs could still reserve a player for, say, eight years. They might even be able to get ten.

As he went on, a rapt Clark Griffith took it all in. The Twins' executive vice president was a conservative, but a bright, Dartmouth-educated one. He'd been troubled by Section 10A—the reserve clause—from the moment he'd first read it. "I thought it would appear in some illuminated documents handed down by Moses," he recalled. When he read the actual words, he murmured, "So this is it?" Griffith was delighted to hear Fitzgerald's concise, logical presentation. It made sense: moderate changes to prevent radical ones.

Griffith was appalled by what followed. Fitzgerald was lambasted by owner after owner: Gussie Busch, Bob Howsam, Horace Stoneham—all stepped up for a whack: "We can't give in to the players. . . . It's been tested by time. . . . Ridiculous. . . . Goddammit, Marvin Miller can't tell us what to do."

"What the hell are they doing?" Griffith asked himself. "This is knowledge and vision being laid down. The moment is ripe and this has been perfectly stated."

It made no difference. The first and loudest voices stampeded opinion, as always. The Brewers' chairman might be PRC chief but he was still a baseball newcomer: a "civilian," as some GMs sneered. What did he know?

Ed Fitzgerald, chastened and shell-shocked, didn't even remember if there was a vote. "Maybe 100–0?" he guessed, years later. He did remember one thing: he never tried that again.

"The biggest event [of this period] was the lack of events," said John McHale, the Expos' president and a PRC member. "It was becoming obvious to some of us that some relaxation of the reserve clause was needed. But ownership, leadership refused to do that. They wanted the pleasant, paternal relations with players before Miller came along. They'd been brought up to think of baseball as a privileged business. This was an accident waiting to happen. Somebody was going to do a number on us."

Still, Marvin Miller wasn't at all sure the "accident" would be Andy Messersmith. He still harbored doubts the pitcher would go the distance. The Dodgers certainly had the means and motivation to sign their staff ace. And Walter O'Malley, who would ultimately call the shots, was much too smart to risk the whole reserve system over a no-trade clause. Wasn't he?

Miller sat down with Dick Moss. What could they do? As they talked, Miller remembered something: Dave McNally. The pitcher had quit the Expos, but he was still technically an unsigned player. Miller looked up his home phone and began dialing.

McNally had been a terrific pitcher. He'd won 181 games for his previous team, the Orioles, once racking up four straight 20-win seasons. In tandem with Jim Palmer, he anchored the staff of the Orioles' excellent teams of the late sixties and early seventies. When Baltimore sought to make over its team, following the 1974 season, McNally was packaged up in a major trade with Montreal.

He was miserable there, feeling he'd been misled. The trade had required McNally's approval, as a 10–5 man (ten years in the majors, the last five with the same team). He told the Expos he wanted a two-year contract at $125,000 per. The answer: "no problem." But once the deal was done, Montreal offered something quite different: one year for $115,000, the same he'd made in 1974. McNally refused to sign.

His misery was compounded that spring by a sore arm. McNally was a pro. He tried to pitch through it. But two months into the season—his record 3–6, his ERA 5.26—he'd had it. After losing the first game of a doubleheader June 8 he quit. McNally went back to his Billings, Montana, hometown and his Ford dealership there.

"Are you coming back to play?" asked Marvin Miller.

"No, never," said McNally.

"I'd like to add your name to the grievance as insurance if Andy decides to sign a new Dodger contract."

McNally, with the bad taste from Montreal still in his mouth, had a quick reply. "If you need me," he said, "I'm willing to help."

Word reached Walter O'Malley quickly, as always. If Miller had McNally, it changed all his thinking about Messersmith. He'd been willing to give him the moon to thwart a union test case. Now Miller had one anyway. There was now no reason to capitulate to Messersmith.

It was Gaherin's turn to be frantic. He called up Expos president John McHale. "Go out to Montana," he said. "For Christ's sake, get the bastard drunk and sign him."

McNally was stunned to pick up the phone one day and hear McHale's voice.

"I happened to be passing through Billings," he said. "Can we sit down and talk about your situation?"

McNally met him the next day at a hotel restaurant and took in an amazing pitch. McHale offered $125,000 to sign for 1976—more than McNally had ever made in his career. He'd give him another $25,000 as a signing bonus.

"Gee, I don't know," said McNally. "I'm not sure I can even pitch at the major league level anymore."

"Don't worry about it," said McHale. "I'll give you the $25,000 just to sign and come to spring training."

(McHale would later maintain he was simply trying to salvage something from the Orioles deal. Not only had McNally left but outfielder Rich Coggins, the other principal in the deal, had developed a thyroid condition, finishing him as a player. The players Montreal traded—Ken Singleton and Mike Torrez—were meanwhile starring in Baltimore.)

McNally called Miller the next morning. They had a good laugh about how McHale "just happened to be passing through Billings." Then the conversation turned serious.

"What are you going to do?" asked Miller. It was a lot of money to dangle, especially when every recently retired player entertained comeback fantasies.

McNally said he wouldn't sign.

"McHale wasn't honest with me last year, and I'm not going to trust him again," he said. "It's tempting to show up in spring training for twenty-five grand, but I have no intention of playing, and it wouldn't be right to take the money."

Marvin Miller breathed again.

* * *

The union filed the Messersmith and McNally grievances in early October. Baseball was on edge. On the field, as each autumn before, the championship was at stake. Off the field, as never before, the old order hung in the balance. Everyone knew it.

When Oakland lost the divisional playoffs to Boston, its players didn't mourn their dynasty's end. They crowded into Boston manager Darrell Johnson's office. There, following the last game, Rollie Fingers, Joe Rudi, Reggie Jackson, and Sal Bando talked with Red Sox owner Tom Yawkey, GM Dick O'Connell, and Johnson. They wanted them to know how much they yearned to leave the A's and join the Red Sox. They finally dared hope they had the chance.

The Lords counterattacked. Baseball's lawyers filed for an injunction, trying to keep Messersmith-McNally out of arbitration. In a federal court in Kansas City, they argued that reserve-system matters were outside an arbitrator's authority. The judge disagreed and ordered the hearings to proceed.

But before whom? Baseball's arbitrator was still Peter Seitz. Debate raged among the Lords. Should they let him hear the case or let him go? He'd freed Catfish Hunter, but most felt that meant little. Some disagreed with his free-agency order, but few quibbled with his findings. Finley had been guilty as sin.

After almost two years as its arbitrator, Seitz still had a slight record in baseball. But, at age seventy, he was a veteran arbitrator in industries ranging from steel to pro basketball. Seitz had a lawyer's training but an English professor's bearing, reveling in classical literature and poetry.

PRC members began checking on him. Bruce Johnston, the steel industry's chief negotiator, warned against him. Seitz had so badly mangled a case involving a U.S. Steel cement-making subsidiary that it led to a strike. "He's not an analyst, he's a poet," said Johnston. One steel company dismissed Seitz not because his decisions were always for labor but because they were always baffling. Said the company's negotiator: "We lost the grievances we should have won and won the ones we should have lost."

Some came down for bouncing him. Lou Hoynes thought the Hunter case bared Seitz's bias toward granting free agency. Bowie Kuhn counseled against Seitz. John McHale said they should heed the warning of his friend Walter Kennedy, the NBA commissioner: "He's really a players' man."

But more argued for giving Seitz a try. He didn't look the part of baseball's assassin. He was a pipe-smoking grandfather who wore dark blue suits and lived in a lovely apartment overlooking the Central Park reservoir. "Any arbitrator is a compromise," said Gaherin. "Better to go with the devil you know."

By a vote of 6–1, with only McHale dissenting, the PRC voted to keep Seitz.

The greatest World Series of recent memory had ended less than a month earlier. It was the year of Luis Tiant's twirls and Dwight Evans's catch and Carlton Fisk's wee-hours homer. Only on the visitors' last at-bat in the last possible game was it decided: Cincinnati in seven.

Now, a few days before Thanksgiving, a contest of even greater moment would play out. In a dreary conference room of the Barbizon Plaza Hotel, hearings began on the case of *John A. Messersmith* v. *Los Angeles Dodgers*.

"Mr. Seitz," began Dick Moss, "you have before you today a simple question of interpreting a phrase which is part of the collective-bargaining agreement between the parties and is also part of the individual contract between Mr. Messersmith and the Los Angeles club, and we believe your task will be an easy one.

"Now, sitting across the table from me are my friends Lou Hoynes and Jim Garner and Barry Rona [the owners' lawyers]. They are all experienced lawyers familiar with the arbitration process."

"Are they your only friends?" Seitz asked.

"No. Their job here today is to try their best to confuse you and to make this matter sound much more complicated than it really is. You are going to hear from them all about the hundred-year-old inviolate reserve system, old congressional hearings, the Flood case, and statements made by various people, all of which is totally irrelevant to the issue in this case.

"This case involves one thing and only one thing, the interpretation of the phrase in Paragraph 10A of the Uniform Players Contract which says, 'The Club shall have the right to renew this contract for the period of one year on the same terms.'

"The issue is whether that phrase means that the club can renew the contract for one year, at the end of which there is no longer any contractual relationship between the club and the player and he is a free agent, as we submit it means, or whether it means that the clubs can continue to renew the renewed contract year after year into perpetuity, as the clubs submit."

Moss also offered Seitz a helpful guide to his opponents'

strategy. They were splitting the case into two issues—one on jurisdiction, one on the merits—to tempt the arbitrator into splitting his decision: "part of the case in favor of one party and part in favor of the other."

"That regards arbitrators as being very naïve," Seitz interjected. "It is strange that you concur in that theory."

"My next point, Mr. Seitz, is that I would never do such a thing with you because I do not regard you as that naïve," said Moss, recovering smartly.

Lou Hoynes, as advertised, did present a more complicated picture. The reserve system wasn't just the renewal language being challenged by Messersmith. It was an interwoven set of statutes: Major League Rule 4A, defining the reserve list; Major League Rule 3G, forbidding tampering with another club's players; and, of course, Paragraph 10A of the Uniform Players Contract. Pull out one thread and the whole industry would unravel.

"We have to reach back something like a hundred years in order to be able to give you the full flavor of what's happened, and so I am going to start back in the nineteenth century," he said.

"Fortunately, your chairman was around at that time and may remember a large portion of it," said Seitz.

Hoynes went over the Tripartite Agreement of 1883, in which the three major leagues of the time agreed to reserve eleven players per club. He introduced an affidavit by the leader of the Brotherhood of Professional Baseball Players, saying this early union "had no desire whatever to in any way change or affect the question of salary or the reserve rule." Hoynes presented Cy Young's 1891 contract renewal language and Edd Roush's "reserve card" from 1930, a year when he refused to sign with the Giants but was nonetheless still their property. It was a historical tour de force and a defense that, when reduced to its essence, cried out: "But we've *always* done it this way."

Back and forth the two sides went. Moss made a straightforward case: the 10A language meant what it said. In the NBA, with the same renewal language, six players had played out their option years and left for the ABA. Hoynes, for his part, produced ornate, precedent-laden arguments. He described practices in other pro sports. He turned Miller's bargaining-table words against him. He even introduced purloined union memos, which, he contended, belied its current arguments.

The introduction of these documents irked Moss, who repeatedly asked where Hoynes had obtained them. But he never received a satisfactory answer.

It was 7:30 P.M., at the end of the second grueling day, when Bowie Kuhn swept in. With all but a flourish of trumpets, he was introduced by Lou Hoynes: "The commissioner has indicated to us that he has views he would like to express to the arbitration panel."

Kuhn took the stand to talk of the horrors free agency would unleash.

"If you go back into the history of baseball, before there was a reserve system, the problems of integrity in the form of outright dishonesty by clubs and players alike was flagrant, and there was no public confidence in the game.

"The reserve system is the cornerstone of baseball. It gave baseball the stability, economic stability, to develop a system where you were able to eliminate the problems of integrity that had been flagrant in the game."

If it were eliminated, he went on, "What I see is the loss of clubs—some of our clubs would not be able to survive it. You'd have the loss of employment opportunities for our players and our other personnel, the elimination of any possibility that in the near term we could expand into cities that have much wanted baseball, the loss of minor leagues—if not all of them, most of them, and, not inconceivably, the loss of a major league. I say that very carefully and very thoughtfully to the chairman. I think the loss of a major league is quite possible.

"Now, I think there is another solution, and I think that the other solution is the one that I have fought for as long as we have had a collective-bargaining relationship in this industry. That is to solve problems of this kind through collective bargaining. I think the record shows that there has been very substantial movement in collective bargaining, not only with respect to the overall reserve system, but in all other areas where demands have been put on the table by the Players Association."

Dick Moss carved up Kuhn on cross-examination.

"Are you seriously suggesting that if Mr. Messersmith wins this case that the game will become dishonest, games will be thrown, players will gamble?" he asked.

"I don't think there has been anybody more vocal than I have with respect to the basic honesty of the players in the game of baseball," said Kuhn. "The problem, however, arises in the area of public suspicion. You have a player who performs in a key game at the end of the season, let's say, against a team that wins that game. The player commits an error, strikes out, pitches badly, or what have you. What can happen is that the public, when they see him move on to the team he performed against, is apt to become suspicious of his performance against that team."

"Now let's try to analyze what you have said in terms of this case," said Moss. "Start with the proposition that you do not believe the players are intrinsically dishonest—is that correct?"

"Yes, that's correct."

"So a player for the Los Angeles Dodgers, playing under a renewed contract, is not going to commit an error against the San Diego Padres so he can sign with the San Diego Padres next year, is that right?"

"In my judgment, that is right."

"In fact, it would sort of be a silly thing to do. I don't really understand why the San Diego Padres would consider him more attractive for the following year if he made an error on their behalf this year."

"I would agree with you."

"Then you are talking about if that player made an error against the San Diego Padres and then, when he became a free agent and negotiated with the twenty-four clubs and signed with the San Diego Padres that would create some public suspicion. What do you think the odds of that are mathematically?"

"Odds of what?"

"That he signed with the team that he made an error against that was somehow crucial enough and publicized enough that the public was suspicious."

"I think you underestimate the press," said Kuhn.

Seitz pressed Kuhn on his collective-bargaining remarks.

"It is a little late in the game, I realize, to ask whether collective bargaining can determine this issue rather than the panel," he said. "But I don't know where your statement leaves us. I don't know whether I am to take your statement as encouraging me to persuade the parties to try some more, or whether you are merely deploring the fact that both of them, or one of them, has not done all that it might have done in collective bargaining to avoid this conflict. Perhaps you can enlighten me on that."

"When I said that I felt collective bargaining can solve the problems that exist, I said that very seriously," said Kuhn. "But I must say to you that I cannot sit here and tell the panel or you,

Mr. Chairman, that the commissioner of baseball has the power to require the clubs to take any particular position. The power resides in the clubs. The bargaining power resides in the Player Relations Committee. Where I have been effective in the past is to use the not inconsiderable powers of persuasion of the commissioner in one direction or the other. But I can't seriously tell you that I have the power to require them to go anywhere."

"I wouldn't expect that," said Seitz. "But do you have any advice for the panel as to what its procedure is to be? Shall we just go ahead as the contract requires us to—a resolution by decision, by award? Or is there some other procedure that perhaps would be more desirable in the interest of all?"

"I think it is a very important question," said Kuhn. "I just wonder. It is one I frankly would like to reflect on before I would try to give you an answer."

"Arbitration is a procedure, just as procedures of the courts," said Seitz. "It is not perfect, and it is desirable because it is better than anything else that seems to be available at the time. If anything else is available, if you reflect on it and have any idea, I will be very glad to know what they are."

"I would be very happy to give them to you," said Kuhn.

"Call me collect," said Seitz.

Dick Moss finished his case with a newspaper clipping:

"An overall theme of the clubs' entire presentation was that everybody has always understood that baseball clubs can control players for life despite the language of 10A and that somehow we conjured up this outrageous argument which is contrary to what everyone knows."

He picked up the clip. "Well, let me demonstrate just how wrong that premise is."

He began talking about Calvin Griffith. He'd been in baseball since 1928, when he was a batboy for his adoptive father's team, the Senators. He'd been majority owner of the Senators and later the Twins since 1955. If anyone knew the business, said Moss, it was Calvin Griffith.

He introduced Players' Exhibit 13—a *Minneapolis Star* story dated March 5, 1974—and began reading:

In one corner of the paneled office behind a desk sat Calvin Griffith. In another corner of the small room sat Tony Oliva. It was said by one Twin official to be a Mexican standoff. The two men, one the Club's president who has been in baseball over fifty years, the other the Cuban-born star who has been a holdout most of his major league life, argued for 45 minutes yesterday. When the smoke had cleared, Oliva remained unsigned and Minnesota's only holdout.

Griffith refused to increase his salary offer of $84,000, while Oliva continued to ask for the $91,000 he received last year when as a designated hitter he batted .291 with 16 home runs and a team-leading 92 runs batted in.

It is also clear this is not a typical spring training contract squabble. This is a battle between strong-willed men and involve principle more than money, and it contains bitterness and irony.

For example, as Oliva left Tinker Field carrying his equipment bag so that he could start practicing alone, he said, "I should have gone to arbitration. I felt he, Griffith, would be happy if I didn't do that. I thought he would be more reasonable. Now I see that meant nothing to him. If I knew what I know now, I would have applied for arbitration. I would have won, too, just like the other guys." Dick Woodson, Steve Braun and Larry Hisle were the only Twins to submit to arbitration and each won additional money.

Griffith said he was mad that the three defeats cost $15,000 and that he would get them back "even if I have to trade them."

Later, after an inquiry from Commissioner Bowie Kuhn, he denied making the statement. Ironically, Marvin Miller, executive director of Major League Baseball Players Association, said one reason the Association demanded binding arbitration was Griffith's salary and negotiating policies. At the time Oliva could have applied for arbitration, he was the only player considering the move who was being asked to take a cut. Woodson, Braun and Hisle were being offered raises they felt were too small, while Oliva was being offered the full 20 percent slash permitted by the basic agreement. In short, he had nothing to lose by submitting to arbitration.

"But just before the deadline, the offer was raised to $84,000," Oliva said. "I thought if I pleased him and didn't apply, I could talk him into giving me what I made last year. That's all I wanted. Other designated hitters, Orlando Cepeda of Boston, Deron Johnson of Oakland and Tom Davis of Baltimore, got raises but I only want the same."

In his office, Griffith indicated Oliva might end up playing for $73,000 or a full 20 percent cut. "If he doesn't sign by

March 10, Sunday, I can invoke the option clause," the president said.

"If I do that, I can cut him as much as I want up to 20 percent. Of course he would then be playing out his option. At the end of the season he would become a free agent. . . ."

"Now," said Lou Hoynes, "what do the clubs want here today?" He had risen to make his final arguments to Seitz.

"Well, we want to maintain the basic system as it existed for years, as the Association found it, and as we believe the rules clearly provide.

"We recognize that this system will be subject to changes in collective bargaining, with safeguards for clubs' rights that we may negotiate as we make those changes, but we ask this panel to maintain the status quo. We ask the panel not to adopt a sudden abandonment of what now is on a willy-nilly basis. That would simply be wrong and, we believe, beyond the panel's power.

"The Association has absolutely nothing to lose here by testing its theory out with this panel. If it loses, it is right back where it started. It tested a theory out in the Flood case and when it lost we were right back at the bargaining table where we were before trying to shape some compromise on a modification to the reserve system and when . . . it loses this grievance, as it did the Flood case, it will again have lost nothing of substance. We will be right back at the bargaining table trying to figure out how we can, together, reshape the reserve system for the future.

"On the other hand, if the clubs lose, the baseball world, we feel, will be turned upside down and the fondest dreams of the leadership of the Association will be substituted for the reality of what always has been within the baseball community."

The two sides had consumed three days, filled 842 pages of transcript, and filed ninety-seven exhibits, leading Seitz finally to refuse more. "Whole hillsides are being decimated of standing timber for the exhibits in this case," he said, cutting off further exhibits on "environmental grounds."

Finally the arguing was over, and the Seitz watch was on. Which way was he ruling?

The truth was, he didn't want to make a ruling. That was clear from the moment Marvin Miller and John Gaherin sat down with Seitz in his magnificent apartment at the Dakota. It was the first week of December. A few days had passed since the hearings. The view of Central Park was terrific, the coffee served by Mrs. Seitz was bracing, and the look on Seitz's face was pensive. On the threshold issue, he told Miller and Gaherin, he had arrived at a decision: the matter was within his jurisdiction.

"Now the fat's in the fire," he said. "We're dealing with issues that are very important to both sides. This may be the most serious grievance I've ever been asked to deal with. If I decide this, somebody's going to get hurt."

He turned to Gaherin.

"Your boss said this should be negotiated, not arbitrated," he said.

"Bowie's not my boss."

Seitz ignored that and plowed ahead.

"I notice the timing is most propitious for you to come to a negotiated settlement," he said, referring to the coming Basic Agreement talks. "What are the possibilities, given enough time, for resolving this problem among yourselves? I'm prepared to be of whatever service the parties want of me."

"We've always wanted to negotiate this," said Miller. "We've been trying to negotiate this since 1967."

"I'm perfectly willing to negotiate," said Gaherin. "I don't want you to do this if we can make some accommodation. But I'll have to consult with my people."

Miller asked only for a time limit.

"I'll have to have a resolution of this by February, because of spring training," he said.

Seitz nodded.

"If the two of you bargain I'll mediate, if that's acceptable to you," he said.

Both men nodded concurrence and the meeting broke up, with only a final word from the arbitrator to the PRC chief on his way out.

"Look, take this case out of my hands," said Seitz. "Negotiate with the players and settle your differences."

Gaherin headed off for baseball's winter meetings at the Diplomat Hotel in Hollywood, Florida. Seitz had followed up his meeting with a letter, putting in writing his plea to negotiate and offer to mediate.

"He doesn't want to decide this case," Gaherin told the PRC

board. "He says there's too much at stake for both sides and both sides should try to resolve this."

What to do? The PRC members pored over the letter, analyzing its every word and comma. Bob Howsam and the Orioles' Frank Cashen, ever the hawks, wouldn't hear of negotiating. Why fight the case only to cave? Ed Fitzgerald, the moderate, listened closely to Gaherin, who strongly favored negotiating.

"If Seitz wrote the letter, doesn't it behoove us to try?" he said. "What have we got to lose by finding out the other side's position?"

Sitting in on the meeting, conspicuously silent, was Bowie Kuhn. The great advocate of bargaining—at least in Seitz's presence—wouldn't back up Gaherin before the PRC. He fell back on his legal brain trust.

"What do the lawyers think?" asked Kuhn.

"I'd say we've got a fifty percent chance of winning the case," said Hoynes, who came out against bargaining.

"I'd say fifty percent," Garner concurred.

"John?" asked Kuhn.

"I say 'shit,' " was Gaherin's response. "If you read this the way I do here's what Seitz is saying: 'Let this chalice pass from me, Father, but if I have to drink it I'm going to spit it all over you.' "

The PRC courageously sidestepped the decision, opting to put the matter before the rest of the Lords. Then they joined them at the elite Indian River Club, an escape venue from the rest of the baseball rabble at the Diplomat.

Kuhn interrupted the hum of conversation to make an announcement: "John has a report for you."

Gaherin repeated his assessment. They were likely to lose the Messersmith case. They'd been invited by Seitz to negotiate, and, in his judgment, their best chance was to offer the union some limited form of free agency.

The howling commenced promptly.

"How much have *you* got invested in baseball?" shouted Charlie Finley.

"I don't have enough to pay for my carfare," said Gaherin.

"You want to give away this industry!" roared Gussie Busch. "Bullshit! Bullshit!"

"What makes you think we're going to lose?" asked Lou Susman, his lawyer.

Well, Gaherin replied, his reading of Seitz and his own reading of the contract.

"Well, then, you're not the one to represent our interests," Susman shot back.

Fitzgerald jumped to Gaherin's defense.

"John, in my judgment, is right," he said. "We're not giving anything away by talking to them."

But he was the only one to counter the howlers, Kuhn having again fallen mute. Susman interrogated Gaherin further, the braying ran its course, and the PRC chief finally turned to his assistant, Barry Rona. "Let's get this thing over," he said.

Gaherin called Miller, who was holding meetings of his own (with the union's executive council) in nearby Bal Harbour. They arranged to meet at his hotel, where they settled onto the balcony of Dick Moss's room with coffee.

"There's no change in our position," said Gaherin, before the refreshments had even begun to cool. "The clubs feel they have a vested right in the player."

Miller heaved one of his deep sighs.

"If that's it then you should call Seitz," he said.

There was some brief desultory talk, then Gaherin left to do just that.

"The answer is: there's no change in our position," he told the arbitrator. "So turn the crank."

It was two weeks later, just two days before Christmas, when Seitz summoned Miller and Gaherin again. He had a decision. It was sixty-four pages long, elaborately reasoned and laden with footnotes. But both men skipped all that and flipped right to the back for the result: *The grievances of Messersmith and McNally are sustained. There is no contractual bond between these players and the Los Angeles and the Montreal clubs, respectively.*

Miller, glowing, signed the line that said "Assent." Gaherin scribbled his signature on the "Dissent" line, then looked up at Seitz.

"That's that and this is for you," he said, handing him a letter that said he was fired as baseball's arbitrator. "Peter, I'm sorry. I love you dearly, but you're out."

The news swept through baseball like the first reports of Pearl Harbor.

Clark Griffith was at a Christmas party when he heard it on the radio. "Oh, shit," was all he could say.

People stared. Griffith tried to explain about the apocalypse being at hand. But everyone drifted back to their revelry. He was left muttering darkly to himself.

John McHale spread the word to the Expos' investors.

"This is a disaster," he said, "but not nearly as much a disaster for other cities as Montreal. We've got so many negatives in drawing and keeping players here."

Plenty of baseball men weren't satisfied with merely firing Seitz. They wanted him to face a firing squad. As Seitz himself later put it, the owners' wails "sounded like the last five minutes of the *Götterdämmerung*, or The Twilight of Baseball."

Ted Simmons was choked up. Messersmith had done it. Everything was changed. "Curt Flood stood up for us; Jim Hunter showed us what was out there; Andy showed us the way," he said. "Andy made it happen for us all. It's what showed a new life."

Messersmith himself was more happy for others than for himself. It had been a brutal experience, and he didn't know where the road went for him now.

"I did it for the guys sitting on the bench," he said, "the utility men who couldn't crack the lineup with [the Dodgers] but who could make it elsewhere. These guys should have an opportunity to make a move and go to another club.

"I didn't do it necessarily for myself because I'm making a lot of money. I don't want everyone to think, 'Well, here's a guy in involuntary servitude at $115,000 a year.' That's a lot of bull and I know it."

Little did Andy Messersmith yet know what "a lot of money" really was. He and many other players were about to find out.

$ 10 $

MARVIN MILLER WAS like the dog that caught the bus. *Now* what did he do?

He could demand what Seitz had given him: total free agency. Every player had the right to play out his contract and walk. But Miller wasn't one to swagger and plunder. In his new position of power, he was the same low-key, wily operator he had been when he was powerless. It was time to negotiate smart terms for the long run, not terms of surrender that would yield only short-term satisfaction.

Miller didn't want to bleed the owners dry, no matter what they thought. It was a first tenet of the Steelworkers: healthy employers paid better wages and benefits than bankrupt ones. Miller thought some parts of the old structure needed to be preserved, even as others were destroyed. "Marvin wasn't an anarchist," said Gaherin. "He could see that the clubs spent a lot of money on farm teams and scouts. They had a right to players they'd developed for a certain period of time."

Miller was, rather, an economist. He could also see that flooding the market with players would only depress salaries. It was the simple law of supply and demand. It was why Catfish Hunter had soared to $3.5 million: one player, twenty-four bidders.

Before he ever bargained with the owners, Miller would have to educate the players. He began leading discussions to determine what they wanted from the New Order. Some wanted Full Seitz, most notably Mike Marshall.

"I want what we've got," he declared, "one and one [that is, the contract year plus the renewal year]."

The Socratic master jumped in.

"But are we talking about flooded markets here?" asked Miller. "That's something we should talk about."

They did, endlessly. Bob Boone finally reduced the issue to its essence at an executive board meeting.

"What do you think the players want more," he asked, "the ability to move—total freedom of movement—or the ability to maximize their earning potential? Let's try to answer that question in this room."

They went around the table.

"Maximize movement," said Mike Marshall. "You've got to have the ability to make your choices of where you want to go."

He picked up support from Jerry Reuss and a few others. But the great majority came down on the other side: earnings, baby.

Marshall would hear none of it. "If you guys give up one-and-one I'm suing you all," declared the dead-serious pitcher.

Miller, siding with the majority, tried to calm Marshall. "What looks like a move in their direction will work to our benefit in the future," he said.

He and the player leaders started tinkering with different models. Their aim was to make free agency a vehicle that would drive the whole pay scale. "In any industry, if you took your most talented people and let them set the salary structure it would make everybody higher," said Phil Garner of the A's. "We wanted to let the very best players establish the scale."

The trick was setting the free-agency threshold: high enough so it took a top player to reach it, low enough so he wasn't washed up by the time he got there. They knew the owners would propose something like ten years—way too high. But how to counter? They were starting to feel more like actuaries than ballplayers—figuring average career lengths, percentages of players that made it to each successive year of service, and so on. But slowly a magic number began to emerge.

"The odds of a player getting to six years weren't very good," said Garner. "Somewhere around three years people began to drop off. If you made it to six, the odds were very high you'd make it to ten. Your very best players were the only ones who made it to six."

Another nice thing about that number: "There was a chance a player could be eligible for free agency twice in his career—six years and twelve," said Ted Simmons, now a staunch union activist.

"What we did was artificially limit the supply of free agents," said Bob Boone. "If you came in behind it with salary arbitration, then everybody was artificially high."

Salary arbitration, that pre-*Messersmith* sop, had an important post-*Messersmith* use. As Miller envisioned the system, players with two to five years' experience would qualify for salary arbitration. They couldn't be free agents, but they could compare themselves to free agents. The rising tide of salaries in the open market would lift all boats.

The Lords had crafted no such well-reasoned proposal. Their Cro-Magnon response was to lock the players out of spring training. The camps wouldn't open, they announced, until there was a new labor contract. They would try to relieve the pressure on them by pressuring the players.

Some owners remained in severe denial. *Messersmith* had now gone up the line to a federal appeals court; maybe they'd win there. Some believed the *Messersmith* ruling applied only to Messersmith. They *still* shouldn't allow free agency for others. "You guys make good money," said Howsam at a meeting with players. "Why are you trying to do something that will ruin baseball?"

Charlie Finley argued the opposite. "Make 'em *all* free agents!" he declared. An owner had finally spoken out loud about the players' most dreaded scenario. "Finley understood the market," said Phil Garner, who played for him. "The other owners only understood monopolistic power."

Marvin Miller heard of Finley's proposal and held his breath. "My main worry was that somebody would listen to him," he later recalled. "It would have been an impossible box. You could not have said you were opposed to freedom."

But since it was Finley, nobody paid any attention.

Gaherin finally proposed just what Miller had expected: a ten-year free-agency threshold. It would also limit free agents to negotiating with eight teams. The players scoffed. Some negotiating sessions turned fiery. At one point Johnny Bench exploded: "How can you say a player must play ten years to be a free agent? Only four percent of all major-leaguers ever play that long!"

The two sides dug in. Ed Fitzgerald called his friend Ralph Evinrude. "Could you do me a favor?" he asked the outboard-motor magnate. "Could you take Gussie Busch out on your yacht for the duration?"

In bargaining sessions, Miller insisted that *he* was the one in the impossible position. He didn't know whether he could give the clubs a hold on players for *any* number of years. He said that the players would haul him into court, claiming their rights had been bargained away. Miller even got Bob Boone, Tom Seaver, and Mike Marshall to threaten such suits, but by now even Marshall didn't mean it.

Miller was throwing a fastball up and in to a set up a curveball low and away. He was priming the Lords to agree to a lesser number of years—that magic number six—by swearing he wasn't sure he could give them any at all. He made a proposal. If the owners would assume full liability for any suits, maybe—just maybe—he would consider a limited reserve system.

Then he waited. It was one of the things Marvin Miller did best. He'd learned it in the '69 pension holdout and the '72 strike; now he imparted that lesson to the players. "Wait," he said. "They will crack."

Miller saw some cracks in his own position as well. Players were restless to play. Their seasonal migratory instincts had brought hundreds to Florida and Arizona. Willie Stargell and Tom Seaver organized workouts at a college field in St. Petersburg, where players from four teams gathered. Phillies players worked out at a high school field in Dunedin. A dozen Reds worked out at a Little League complex in Tampa.

This gave aid and comfort to the owners, who imagined that raring-to-go players must be ready to cave. The press also flocked to the workouts and picked up their share of "let's play ball" quotes. "I think the players should stop crying about slavery and worry about baseball," declared George Scott, the Brewers first baseman. "If they played as hard as they complain, they'd all be superstars."

That was just The Boomer, straight out of the Ayn Rand school. As he once put it to the Brewers' chairman, "You know, Mr. Fitzgerald, if we're gonna win, the players gotta play better, the coaches gotta coach better, the manager gotta manage better, and the owners gotta own better."

But Marvin Miller didn't want rugged individualists at this moment. He wanted unity. Scott and the rest of the quotees got a trip to the woodshed with him. "Obviously you have the right to say anything you want to," he told them. "But you're hurting the rest of the players, because these 'let's play ball' statements are misinterpreted. If five players are quoted that way, some of the owners will take that to mean there must be hundreds more saying the same thing and the union can't long stay united. That's only going to drag this out further."

It was a tougher, more subtle issue than the union's earlier

battles. The pension issue had gotten everybody's dander up.
The shape of the new reserve system was a far more technical
argument, and outside the union's inner circle, the stakes weren't
well understood. "The players didn't realize the full ramifica-
tions of being a free agent," said Tim McCarver.

The strains among the players increased as the lockout lengthened into mid-March. It was the very scenario the owners had
hoped for. "Most of the players were broke by spring training,"
said Ed Fitzgerald. "They weren't getting paid, and the IRS had
to be paid soon. The ownership leverage was at its highest."

It even strained the union's inner circle. At one player-rep
meeting, debate raged over offering the owners free-agent compensation. It would allow clubs losing a free agent to get a
player back from the signing club. Proponents said it would win
the peace and, besides, it was only fair. "I felt because of all the
money the owners had invested they should get something
back," said Joe Coleman, the Tigers' player rep.

"Free agency with compensation is not free agency," said
Miller, and most of the players agreed. The motion lost, 21–4.

The players were also divided when they received the owners'
"best and final offer" on March 15. It permitted players to become free agents after eight years. It gave every player who
hadn't yet signed a contract for 1976 a chance to play out his
option. It also gave every player with at least seven years' experience the right to demand a trade between the end of the season
and November 1. If he wasn't moved by the following March,
he could be a free agent.

There was enough in it to tempt a fair number of players. Two
days later, the player reps met in Tampa to review the proposal.
The vote was 17–5 against, with two clubs unrepresented. But
that was more of a split decision than usual. The usual practice
of the executive board was to emerge with total unity. "Our information was that the power on the players' side was eroding,"
said Barry Rona.

(Both sides gleaned intelligence, though Miller's was usually
superior. Some owners were compulsive leakers to the press.
Some blabbed to players, hoping to win points with them. Some
occasionally spoke directly with Miller. He once had the results
of an owners' meeting so quickly that Gaherin wondered if
someone had called immediately afterward. "No," replied Miller,
"during the recess.")

Miller would forever deny he was on the ropes, but that's
what most owners believed. They were content to continue the

lockout and tighten the screws. They weren't losing dates and money, as during the 1972 strike. Spring training *cost* them money. With Opening Day still three weeks away and so much at stake, they wanted to play this out.

Then, on March 18, Bowie Kuhn called John Gaherin. It was a Thursday afternoon. The negotiator was back in New York, preparing for a Sunday ownership summit there.

"I've been talking to O'Malley," he said. "You know, there's no sense in keeping these camps closed. I'm going to open the gates. Is there any difference between doing it now and doing it Sunday?"

"None, if you've made up your mind," said Gaherin. "But I'd consult with the PRC first. Have you talked to Fitz?"

Kuhn said he hadn't.

Gaherin suspected he wouldn't. Fitzgerald was a moderate by inclination but a hawk on the lockout. He'd raise hell. Gaherin himself was upset. If they went into the season locked up, he felt, the players would force Miller to moderate his position. ("Cut off their water," he'd urged the PRC.) But he didn't argue with Kuhn. He knew from experience it was fruitless. He did try to make one point: a lot of owners would be upset.

"You're the leader," said Gaherin. "But remember what Lou Carroll used to to say: 'When you're charging up the hill, always make sure the troops are behind you.' "

Gaherin hung up.

Ed Fitzgerald had to learn of the lockout's end from his mother. She'd heard it on the news and mentioned it to Young Ed when he happened to call. "I understand the lockout's over," she said.

"What?" he yelled at the startled Mrs. Fitzgerald.

His serious shouting was reserved for Bowie Kuhn. He was a close friend, but this was business, and it was a betrayal.

"Goddammit," he shouted at Kuhn, "why does my *mother* have to tell me you opened the spring-training camps? I think you owed it to me."

Lee MacPhail called the Twins' Clark Griffith with the news.

"Bowie's opening the camps," he said.

"What?" screamed Griffith. "But we've got 'em!"

Later, Griffith and others would reconstruct what had happened. O'Malley had surely played on Kuhn's self-image as the fans' commissioner and the game's great protector. One student of O'Malley scripted just how it had gone: "Bowie, this isn't in our interests. People could get used to not going to ball games.

We may be shooting ourselves in the foot trying to gain a slight bargaining advantage."

O'Malley was, of course, the great protector of his own interests. He knew the Dodgers would prosper under any system. What he couldn't abide was the prospect of missing a single lucrative date. Said John McHale, another upset PRC member, "Walter's approach was to keep the game going, keep the schedule moving."

(Though it was a universally held belief in baseball that O'Malley had ordered the lockout's end, Kuhn would forever deny it. "People like O'Malley and Steinbrenner were troubled by the lockout, but the principally troubled person was me," he said. "Ultimately I did what I did for my own reasons.")

The Sunday owners' meeting went ahead anyway. Gussie Busch screamed about the camps' opening. The Orioles' Jerry Hoffberger decried the precedent. The players would never seriously negotiate with the PRC, he said, as long as they thought the commissioner would step in. And it was true, as PRC lawyer Barry Rona privately admitted: "Whatever shred of credibility we had for being able to engage in hardball negotiations was gone."

Walter O'Malley had something to say about free agents, too. The Lords had just exhausted their last appeal on the Seitz decision. It was now open season on Andy Messersmith. O'Malley wanted to state the Dodgers' policy on signing free agents: never. He made it sound like an act of moral turpitude to even touch one. To many in the room, baseball's most powerful man was sending a powerful, if veiled, message. They shouldn't pursue Messersmith either.

They didn't. Messersmith was greeted by a deafening silence, except some insulting feelers on whether he'd sign for $50,000. He and his agent were reduced to seeing whether he could pitch in Japan or Mexico. "It was a nightmare," recalled Messersmith, whose seeming blackball from baseball was augmented by hate mail from fans.

Then a new owner stepped forward. He didn't know Walter O'Malley from Walter Brennan, and he was determined to buy a star. He offered Messersmith $1 million for three years—*and* a no-trade guarantee. The pitcher signed. The Lords were getting their first taste of an independent fellow named Ted Turner.

From boyhood, Robert Edward Turner III was part crackpot, part genius. He was so sharp, he was the Tennessee high school debating champion. He was so high-strung, his military-academy classmates called him "Terrible Ted." Turner was an incurable romantic, studying Greek classics and naval history at Brown University. He was an incorrigible carouser, suspended as a sophomore for his part in a drunken fracas. "I think you are rapidly becoming a jackass," Turner's father wrote to him.

It was the father who fueled young Ted's manic drive and erratic behavior. Ed Turner was a stern, self-made man who'd amassed a modest fortune in the billboard business in Georgia. Nothing his son did was good enough for him. He beat him with a coat hanger as a youngster and punished him if he didn't read one book every two days. When Ted Turner was kicked out of Brown for good, for entertaining a woman in his room, he joined Turner Advertising Company, determined to prove himself to his father.

Then Ed Turner blew his brains out. The son soon discovered that his father had just sold the company's biggest division. He put his manic energy to work undoing the deal. It wasn't quite closed so he set to work scuttling it. Turner shifted around contracts between divisions, threatened to destroy financial records, vowed to build billboards in front of the buyer's. Finally, worn down, the buyers sold back the business. Ted Turner set about proving himself to his dead father.

He went on to push the company to greater profits and growth than Ed Turner ever had. In a few years, however, he was bored with billboards. In 1970, looking for new fields to conquer, he decided to buy a UHF TV station in Atlanta. It was a sorry business. Channel 17 ranked fifth out of the city's five TV stations and was losing $600,000 a year. Turner's accountants begged him not to buy it. He was gambling everything he'd made in billboards for this loser. Turner bought it anyway, and gave it the call letters WTCG: Watch This Channel Grow.

Turner, still in his mid-thirties, was like a hyperactive child. He talked loud and nonstop. ("His thoughts arrive just in time to be spoken," a writer later marveled.) Each new Turner idea was punctuated with a deafening cry of "Awright!" He literally couldn't sit still. Turner paced nonstop—seventy-four consecutive circles around his office once, by an aide's count.

Turner was his own chief salesman. ("Do you know why you should advertise with us?" he asked prospects. "You will reach that person of higher intelligence and higher income who knows how to tune in a UHF channel.") He was also his own programming director. He had a gut feel for what people wanted to watch and a strategy called "counter-programming." Whatever the network affiliates broadcast, WTCG offered the opposite. During the news hour, it carried *My Little Margie* and *The Rifleman*. Against the Sunday-morning devotional shows were old movies: *Academy Award Theater* with your host, Ted Turner. Against the networks' prime-time series, sports was a natural.

Turner knew nothing about sports—except for sailing. His father had been a yachtsman, and even on the sea did Ted compete against the ghost of Ed Turner. After working eighteen-hour days all week, he would sail all weekend. Turner, a boor among blue bloods, soon began competing in top yacht races. In 1974, he took his first try at the America's Cup.

Turner knew he needed something a little more plebian for TV than yachting. The answer was baseball. The Atlanta Braves' TV contract was up after the 1973 season. The incumbent was WSB-TV, Atlanta's biggest TV station, owned by the Atlanta-based media giant, Cox Enterprises. It was seemingly absurd for WTCG to compete. Turner Communications, as the company was now called, had stopped losing money, but it employed just sixty people and was grossing only $5 million.

Naturally, Turner won the contract. He bid $600,000 a year, three times more than WSB had been paying. WTCG would also televise three times the number of games WSB had—about sixty. Turner bought the Braves' TV broadcast rights for five years and his accountants again had a fit. It was an audacious move.

At about the same time, Turner was buying a Hollywood film library that gave him eternal reruns of *Andy Griffith*, *Gomer Pyle*, *Leave It to Beaver*, and *The Beverly Hillbillies*. The public-TV crowd could snidely chuckle if they wished, but these shows were a fair step up from *My Little Margie*, and they could be made into a nice one-two punch. Turner ran *Andy Griffith* and the *Hillbillies* back-to-back at news time and carried a good-sized audience into the Braves game.

Turner was leveraged to the hilt at this point. He even had to host a telethon at his Charlotte, North Carolina, UHF station to keep the wolf from the door there. But he'd put in place the elements of a TV lineup people would actually watch. "Ted saw the value of programming," said Gerry Hogan, his ad sales chief.

Turner also saw the world as a place where there were still possibilities for bold, heroic action. He couldn't replicate the feats of Lord Nelson or Odysseus, who'd captured his imagination in college. But he could explore and conquer the vast new frontiers of technology.

His conquests began with a simple experiment. Turner found that he could relay WTCG's signal by microwave dishes throughout the Southeast. It broke the station loose from its Atlanta boundaries and into Alabama, northern Florida, and the Carolinas. Since he now had the Braves and *The Beverly Hillbillies*, cable systems carried them.

But he had something far grander in mind. In 1975, an RCA satellite had been launched into space. It was reserved for broadcasters, but its only regular user so far was something called Home Box Office. It bounced eighty-two hours a week of movies and special events off the satellite to cable systems around the country. Cable subscribers paid an extra ten dollars a month for HBO.

Turner took one look and immediately wanted access. With enough Braves, *Beaver*, and B movies, he thought he could sell humble Channel 17 nationally just as he did regionally: as an alternative to the networks.

There were just a few hitches. First, the FCC hadn't yet made it legal for over-the-air broadcasters to do this. Second, the Braves were in danger of moving, which meant, of course, that the core of WTCG's sports programming would go with them. The mid-seventies Braves were stocked with forgettables like Larvell Blanks, Rowland Office, and Marty Perez. They sunk to forty games out of first in 1975. Attendance plummeted to 534,000, and rumor had it they were leaving for Toronto.

Turner was at a sparsely attended late-season game and drifted up to the box of Dan Donahue, the club's president.

"Hey, Dan," he said, "what are we going to do to get these Braves going?"

"I don't know what you're going to do, but we're bailing," Donahue said.

"Oh, my God. Who're you going to sell it to? I got a five-year contract and this is only year two."

"To you."

"To me? For how much?"

"Oh, about ten million."

"Yeah, well, how much is it losing this year?"

"Oh, about a million bucks this year."

"What, I'm going to pay you that much so I can lose a million a year too?" said Turner. Then a headline flashed through his mind: BRAVES MOVE TO TORONTO. His sports programming would be gone with it. So, too, might his dreams of going national. He softened his tone with Donahue. Maybe, just maybe he could swing it at $1 million down and the rest to be paid over seven or eight years.

Donahue and his syndicate did even better. The Braves had $1 million sitting in the bank. They let Turner use that as the down payment for the club. The rest could be paid in time, from future earnings. That's how eager they were to get out. Turner jumped at it.

Baseball, however, did not. The other National League owners had to approve the sale, and they knew the franchise was listing. Who *was* this thirty-eight-year-old seat-of-the-pants entrepreneur? They insisted that Donahue and Bill Bartholomay, the Braves' chairman, remain involved with the club. And they were to stay on the hook to assume ownership again if Turner bombed out.

They also had questions about Turner's broadcast plans. He was already bouncing WTCG's signal around the Southeast. That was fine; that was the Braves' TV territory. But he betrayed certain ambitious tendencies that made them uneasy. What if he tried to expand beyond that? The Lords didn't want to admit to their number someone who might beam Braves games into *their* markets. Bartholomay was asked to get a letter of intent from Turner on the subject.

He promptly wrote one: "It is Turner Communications' and my personal intention to comply with the best interest of baseball in all matters, including baseball's collective posting on cable television."

Turner was admitted to the club, and appropriately so. He'd shown his aptitude for dissembling.

When Turner attended his first National League owners' meeting, he was asked to say a few words. "I'm glad to be here because I love competition," he said. "There's nothing like being on the ocean, with the strong winds blowing and the wind in your face and not knowing your destiny."

"Son," said Walter O'Malley, "you came to the right place."

By the time Turner had been in baseball six months, the Lords were no longer sure he was in the right place. His "sins" were numerous:

- He broke ranks, signing Messersmith for $1 million. He then assigned him number 17, and on his back, in place of his name, was the word *Channel*, making Andy Messersmith a walking billboard for Channel 17.

- He entertained his Opening Day crowd by leading a pregame chorus of "Take Me Out to the Ballgame" and later jumping onto the field in the first inning to congratulate the Braves' Ken Henderson after a homer.
- After the Braves had blown a ninth-inning lead, he once grabbed the PA mike and barked, "Nobody is going to leave here a loser. If the Braves don't win tonight, I want you all here as my guests tomorrow." (Since the gate that night was only 3,000, Turner wasn't in any danger of straining capacity. The 1,100 fans who accepted the offer swelled the next night's crowd to 2,109.)
- He brought in a minister to lead the crowd in prayer during a losing streak. It didn't work. Then he tried to raise spirits by having the ballgirls sweep off the bases. During the Braves' twelfth straight loss, Turner himself lay on top of the dugout, hands folded on chest as though mortally wounded.
- He buddied up to his players. He learned their lingo ("Not too shabby" became a Turner catchphrase), took up their vices (Red Man chewing tobacco), and played poker with them in the clubhouse.
- He set up an incentive pay system. For every win above .500 in the final record he'd give each player a $500 bonus; for every 100,000 in attendance over 900,000 they'd get an additional 5 percent over their base salary.
- He led the league in promotions, often participating personally. Turner competed in a pregame ostrich race. He was runner-up in a motorized bathtub race. He edged out Phillies pitcher Tug McGraw in the Baseball Nose Push, touted as the Braves' answer to the Olympics. (Turner scraped his nose bloody inching a ball around the infield.) He did *not* participate in Wedlock and Headlock Day, a bizarre combination of wedding ceremonies and wrestling matches.
- He made himself an overnight celebrity, which was great for both his TV station and his ego. He strutted around his office singing "Rhinestone Cowboy," bellowing the line about "receiving cards and letters from people I don't even know."

The fans loved him. Turner's baseball people did not. He knew nothing about baseball or doing things in big-league style. Turner employees, who were used to running on a shoestring, flew coach and stayed in the cheapest motels. The Braves, meanwhile, traveled first-class and stayed in four-star hotels. GM Eddie Robinson, whose perks included a Cadillac, was ordered by Turner to cut back.

"The trouble with you," said Robinson, "is that you don't have any class."

Turner, who was particularly proud of his yachting contacts, replied, "I know four kings on a first-name basis and I've eaten with Queen Elizabeth. Now get outta here!"

Robinson was demoted to a scout and consultant.

Turner ordered traveling secretary Donald Davidson to stop staying in hotel suites on the road.

"I want you to get a regular room," he said.

"I've *always* had a suite," huffed Davidson.

"You could sleep in a closet!" Turner screamed at Davidson, who, in fact, stood about four feet tall. "You're going to have a *room*."

Davidson was soon fired, after nearly forty years with the Braves.

And that was nothing compared to Turner's clashes with the baseball establishment. Before the 1976 season was just two months old, he was called on the carpet by Chub Feeney. The National League's president lectured him about the grand traditions of baseball and the expected standards of owner comportment. He ordered him to take "Channel" off Messersmith's uniform, scrap the incentive pay system (it violated the Basic Agreement), and stop playing poker with the players.

"It wouldn't look good if they wound up owing you a lot of money," he said.

"So what?" said Turner. "They can afford it."

Turner did promise to try to behave. But he was so excited at being instrumental in simultaneous revolutions in TV and baseball that he couldn't long contain his true stripes. There clearly would be some kind of free-agent market next winter and Turner could hardly wait. When he spied top reliever and potential free agent Al Hrabosky before a Braves-Cardinals game, he yelled to him, "Don't sign!"

Back on the carpet went Ted, while the rest of the Lords rolled their eyeballs. If Turner ever tried going on the field in Cincinnati, growled Bob Howsam, he'd have him arrested. Who was this nut case? Turner *was* crazy, but crazy like a fox. In a more lucid moment, he blared out his plan to Bill Giles: "I'm gonna conquer the world with television."

Baseball would help give him his start. He saw its value as

programming. It filled countless summer nights and, if he went national, put him on scores of cable systems. Compared to buying a film library, buying a ballplayer was nothing. Ted Turner had seen the future, while the rest of the Lords raged at the dying of the light.

Charlie Finley had seen the future, too, and he feared he wouldn't be a part of it. Salary arbitration had been the first assault on his ability to operate Finley-style. He needed low costs and high finishes to eke out a profit. It was a precarious formula, and it was finished by free agency.

He'd seen it from the moment of the *Messersmith* decision. His stars wouldn't sign for anything less than multiyear guaranteed contracts. Joe Rudi, who'd been making $84,000, now wanted a three-year, $375,000 contract, with no-cut and no-trade provisions. Rollie Fingers, who'd been making $93,000, wanted $435,000 for three years, also guaranteed. Finley made the same counteroffer to each: $100,000 for *one* year. Eventually, he moved up to multiyear offers, but with no guarantees.

It was a different world, and Finley's mind-set and money were better suited to the old one. He could come on with all the bluster and blarney he wanted, but no longer could he overwhelm players with it. Most of them now had agents—skilled advocates who could thrust and parry right along with Finley. Rudi, Fingers, and three other unsigned A's were represented by the same lawyer, a young fellow named Jerry Kapstein.

First Finley revenged himself on his unsigned players by renewing their contracts at the maximum 20 percent cut. Then, starting in early 1976, he tried dealing them off. Finley aimed to get *something* for his stars before he lost them to free agency. He hoped to pick up players who'd be easier to sign.

Just before Opening Day, he traded Reggie Jackson, Ken Holtzman, and a minor-leaguer to Baltimore for Don Baylor, Mike Torrez, and Paul Mitchell.

Then Finley started burning up the phone lines with the Red Sox on a blockbuster trade: Rudi, Fingers, Vida Blue, Gene Tenace, and Sal Bando for Lynn, Fisk, and a couple of throw-ins. At the same time, he was dangling Blue before the Yankees for catcher Thurman Munson and one of their starting outfielders— Roy White or Elliott Maddox. Then it was Rudi for Munson, straight-up. Finley was also talking with Milwaukee about Rudi for Darrell Porter. Say what you like about Charlie Finley, but he was an equal-opportunity wheeler-dealer. He would eventually talk trade with every American League club but Kansas City.

Finley hadn't quite given up on signing his stars, either. Shortly before the trading deadline, with his A's playing in Chicago, he gathered them in the manager's office at Comiskey Park. He wanted to sign them all, he said. He loved them like sons. But he couldn't go for these no-cut-no-trade deals they all wanted.

"You have those kinds of contracts on your ball club, you have handcuffs on your hands; you can't maneuver," he said. "You could have the entire club signed but not be able to trade a single player. One of you gentlemen could have a motorcycle accident and lose a leg and I'd still have to pay your salary. That I don't approve."

As for their damned agent, Kapstein: "You know, it is awfully hard for me to make a deal when I have continuously requested your agent to come to Chicago and sit down and talk to me. He has yet to come in. I don't know where the hell I am at."

He begged and he wheedled. He talked about all those World Series rings and World Series checks, at $20,000 a championship. Would they be able to get those at another club? If they left, would they ever know the glories of the A's? Old Charlie wasn't a cheapskate. He could only pay what he could afford. He wasn't drawing 2.5 million like the Dodgers. He was lucky to get 1 million. He didn't have big broadcast money like some of the others. He *paid* a radio station $300,000 to put on the games. The master salesman gave it his best, but it was a hard sell. For one thing, he'd cut all their salaries by 20 percent. For another, they knew him far too well.

And those few who didn't were advised. "Anytime you hear him clearing his throat he's lying," Joe Rudi told the newly acquired Don Baylor. "If you hear him say 'a-hem,' watch out."

Charlie Finley was one day away from the June 15 trading deadline, his stars still unsigned. He had to make a move. Dick O'Connell of the Red Sox was antsy too. Whatever Finley was cooking up, he wanted to be in on it. He and another Boston executive, Gene Kirby, hopped a plane on Sunday, June 14, and flew to Oakland. He wanted to be near both Finley and Boston's manager, Darrell Johnson, who was starting a series there with the team Monday.

They landed in San Francisco, rented a car, and went to DiMaggio's restaurant. O'Connell called Finley from a pay phone there. But, as it turned out, he'd left Oakland and was in Chicago. O'Connell tracked him down at Eli's restaurant there.

"I'm with Gabe," he said, setting off alarm bells in O'Connell's head. Yankees president Gabe Paul had obviously done a better job of getting close to Finley. And Finley had abruptly changed his tune. Instead of talking players, he was now talking money.

"I'm offering Rudi, Blue, Fingers, or Tenace for a million apiece and Bando for half a million," he said. "Are you interested?"

O'Connell was stunned, but came back with a quip.

"Don't you like dagos?"

"I don't like *him*."

O'Connell reviewed the smorgasbord, calculated owner Tom Yawkey's net worth, and made his choices.

"We'll take Fingers and Blue for a million," he said. "But I think I ought to talk with my manager first."

He said he'd get back to him ASAP.

O'Connell made two calls: one to the team's banker to line up $2 million, the other to Darrell Johnson in Minnesota. The Red Sox had a game against the Twins that afternoon before flying west. He reached Johnson in the visitors' clubhouse.

"Darrell, if you could have two players on the Oakland ball club, which two would you take?" he asked.

"Rudi and Fingers," he said.

O'Connell was surprised about Rudi. The Red Sox were loaded with outfielders. On the other hand, Rudi was a hunting buddy of Johnson's.

"Rudi's a great player," he said, "but where the hell's he going to play?"

They kicked that one back and forth a while, as Johnson made the case for the changes he'd make to accommodate Rudi. Then O'Connell rejoined Kirby, and they talked it over. The more they discussed and drank, the more O'Connell was confirmed in his thinking: Vida Blue made more sense. Boston had no left-handed pitching and had no strong need of another bat. The two decided to meet the team's flight and huddle with Johnson.

"We'll change Darrell's mind," O'Connell said.

O'Connell slipped behind the wheel of their rental car and turned the ignition key. Nothing. The car was dead. By the time they reached the airport, the flight was in and Johnson gone. O'Connell and Kirby tried for hours to track him down, to no avail.

The call was up to them alone. The choice, they finally decided, was this: better to take Rudi and Fingers—hang the expense and duplication of talent—than cross the manager. If they didn't take action, they might get nothing at all. O'Connell called Finley back.

"Are Rudi and Fingers still available at a million dollars apiece?"

"Yes, they are."

"Well, we just bought both of them."

Finley's bushy eyebrows shot up. He hadn't expected this. He asked O'Connell if he was aware that they were both unsigned.

"Don't be concerned about that. That's my responsibility," replied O'Connell. "How do you want your money?"

"What do you mean?"

"Send you the cash immediately or paid to you over a period of time?"

"Well, you take me by surprise," said Finley. "Do you mind giving me a few hours to think it over?"

"No problem."

When O'Connell called back that night, Finley was still with Gabe Paul.

"Gabe's going to talk with Steinbrenner about Blue," he said. "The meat on the hoof is worth a million."

O'Connell worked out payment terms on Rudi and Fingers, exchanged some chitchat, and hung up. His calm demeanor with Finley masked alarm. The Yankees were the team to beat in the American League East. If Gabe Paul landed Vida Blue, this was just a zero-sum game. The Red Sox ratcheted up a notch; the Yankees ratcheted up a notch; and he'd just dropped $2 million to no advantage—or even worse. Blue could mean more to the Yankees than Rudi and Fingers to Boston.

And one other thing, he thought. The Yankees buying Vida Blue was like waving a red flag in front of Bowie Kuhn. He'd already suspended Steinbrenner once and didn't appear to like him a bit. He might find an excuse to void both sales if the Yankees were in the middle of this.

O'Connell looked up the home number of Tigers GM Jim Campbell. He knew the Tigers were interested in Blue, and he had to get them back in the hunt. It was the wee hours by Eastern time, and Campbell was fast asleep. He woke up quickly, however, on hearing O'Connell's words.

"Get a million bills and buy Vida Blue," he said. "Get the son of a bitch away from the Yankees."

Campbell snapped right into action. He called Finley and matched New York's offer. O'Connell went to sleep happy. He would learn the sad truth only the next day. All he'd really done was force the Yankees to pay more.

"The meat has aged today," Finley chortled to Gabe Paul. "It's better meat."

The Yankees countered the Tigers' offer with $1.5 million and got Blue.

Gabe Paul had cut a better deal than O'Connell in one sense, however. The Yankees' purchase was contingent on Finley getting Blue signed. He had just one day to do it. On Monday morning, Finley called up Blue's agent, Chris Daniel.

"Can we talk contract?" he asked.

"I can't talk contract until I get in touch with Vida."

"See if you can find him."

Early that afternoon, Daniel called back with Blue. They made a proposal: $200,000 a year for three years. Finley growled a response: "Astronomical."

"Well, you're going in on figures so low we might as well make our going-in figures just as high," said Daniel. "Maybe we could negotiate this thing out."

They began dickering. Finley countered at $100,000 for 1976, $125,000 for 1977, and $150,000 for 1978. That was good money, he argued, for a man who'd made $80,000 in 1975. Finley wasn't even playing with his own chips, of course. But he was so cheap by nature he still drove a hard bargain. The Yankees had themselves a superb negotiating agent.

Next he offered Blue three years at $112,500/$137,500/ $162,500. Then, groaning and moaning, he went to $125,000/ $150,000/$175,000. Finally, after three hours, they came to terms: $135,000 for 1976, $145,000 for 1977, and $205,000 for 1978.

Later that day, Blue and Daniel would learn they'd been snookered. The Yankees announced the $1.5 million purchase, and the math told quite a story. Finley stood to profit more from Blue's value to New York than Blue himself.

Finley called the A's clubhouse to tell manager Chuck Tanner about the sales. A *Chicago Tribune* writer took down the owner's end of the conversation:

"We'll rebuild, Chuck. I'm sorry we had to do this today. The big thing, Chuck, as I'm telling the press here, was the agent,

Jerry Kapstein. He kept me in the dark continuously, right up to the last minute. Never made one trip to come talk to me.

"Is Vida there? I couldn't find him. The damn Yankees released the story on me, and it makes me look bad because I didn't tell him. Joe Rudi said he cried for half an hour. I know he feels bad. Let me talk to them, Chuck. All of them. One at a time.

"Vida? This is Charlie Finley. I know how you feel. The damn Yanks jumped the time on me. They promised they wouldn't make an announcement and then we all heard it on the news. . . . What do you mean, what announcement? I traded you to the Yankees . . . just you. For money.

"Vida, this will mean an awful lot to you. I've appreciated all you've done to help me and all the contributions you've made. . . . Well, I appreciate your acceptance of this in a professional manner. I hate to see you go. We couldn't have won three straight world titles without you. I love you, buddy, and believe me when I tell you that."

By now, word of Finley's fire sale was circulating throughout the baseball world.

Brad Corbett of the Rangers called to find out if he could get in on it. He flung down an offer to Finley: $1 million for Don Baylor. Bill Veeck called to find out the asking price on Sal Bando.

Finley confirmed the sales to a writer, who asked whether there would be more.

"The night is young," chortled Finley.

Bowie Kuhn got the news at Comiskey Park, where he was watching the White Sox play the Orioles. Chicago GM Roland Hemond brought him the story off the AP wire: *$3.5 million* for Rudi, Fingers, and Blue. Kuhn was dismayed but not surprised.

He'd taken a call from American League president Lee MacPhail a day ago. He said he'd heard Finley was thinking about selling a player for a million dollars.

"Charlie is cannibalizing his ball club," said Kuhn. "You better talk him out of this."

"There's no use," said MacPhail. "I've tried and he hung up on me."

Now it had happened. So much for the pitchers' duel he'd been enjoying between Baltimore's Jim Palmer and Chicago's Goose Gossage. Kuhn saw a duel ahead between him and Charlie O.; and it was not their first. He picked up a phone in the box and called across town to Finley's insurance office. It was already after 9:00 P.M., but the familiar raspy voice answered.

Kuhn coolly told him he was at Comiskey. He'd just heard about the sales and thought they were a "disaster." He planned to look into them.

"Commissioner, it's none of your damn business," said Finley, who was supported by history in that assertion. A previous owner of Finley's franchise, two cities and many decades ago, had done the same. Connie Mack broke up great Philadelphia Athletics teams in 1914 and again in the thirties, selling off stars because he needed the money. Kuhn had plenty to do without meddling in player transactions, Finley said. Then he assumed a hurt tone: "It's sort of funny you're here in town and don't even talk to me about it directly."

Kuhn explained that he'd been in Chicago for a PRC meeting and made an offer: "I'd be happy to talk to you about it directly."

"No," Finley came back. "I don't think that would serve any purpose."

They sparred back and forth a while longer, reiterating their positions. Then Kuhn said, "I want to come back to your first suggestion. I really think we ought to get together and talk. I think you had a good suggestion."

"Oh, okay," Finley grumbled. They agreed to meet downtown in an hour at the Pick-Congress Hotel, a block from his office.

They were natural enemies. Kuhn was the epitome of the establishment, Finley the consummate maverick. Kuhn was the guardian of tradition, Finley the champion of change. Kuhn was starchy and proper, Finley crude and profane.

He once took some baseball men on a pub crawl through Chicago that wound up at the Billy Goat Tavern. It was a beer-and-a-shot dive near Finley's office. His companions couldn't believe their eyes. There, behind the bar, was the World Series trophy, on loan from Charlie O. Wow, said one, what if Kuhn ever saw *this*?

"Fuck 'im," growled Finley. "Did Bowie ever get a hit?"

The two fought for years. In 1970, Kuhn reprimanded Finley for trying to punish holdout Reggie Jackson with a demotion to the minors. In 1972, he infuriated Finley by stepping into the Vida Blue salary dispute. Kuhn endured being told to "go to hell," and much worse, for just so long; then he fined Finley $500. It galled Kuhn to present those championship trophies in

1972–74, particularly since no Series involving Finley could be properly dignified. There was, for instance, the time the A's owner let Charlie O., the mule, graze through the buffet at a VIP reception.

Kuhn also slapped Finley with fines for his Series gamesmanship. In 1972, it was $5,000 for giving illegal bonuses to players during the Series. In 1973, it was $7,000 for an assortment of infractions, the most serious of which was dropping second baseman Mike Andrews after he'd committed two damaging errors. Finley falsely declared him disabled, a ruse to get a replacement player on the roster.

At the disciplinary hearing regarding the '73 incidents, Finley showed his customary respect for Kuhn, whose name he always gave the exaggerated pronunciation "Coooon."

"Did you get a telegram from the commissioner to be here?" asked the baseball lawyer handling the inquiry.

"I must have," replied Finley. "I'm here."

"Did you have a conversation with Mr. Kuhn pursuant to receiving that telegram?"

"I did."

"Isn't it a fact that you told him he could shove that telegram up his ass?"

A pause.

"No," said Finley. "It is my recollection I said he could shove it right up his big, fat ass."

In 1975, when Kuhn was up for reelection, Finley led an insurrection. A 75 percent majority in each league was required to win a new seven-year term for the commissioner. Finley would need three other nay votes—besides his own—in the American League to stop Kuhn, and he wooed and won them: Baltimore's Jerry Hoffberger, Texas's Brad Corbett, and New York's George Steinbrenner. (Steinbrenner was still suspended but eligible to vote on such matters.)

The "Dump Bowie Club," as the group called itself, wasn't just fueled by Finley's hatred of Kuhn. It was a more general rising up of the "outs" versus the "ins," of American League "new money" versus National League "old money."

Kuhn's inner circle of owners was the executive council. Its two permanent members were the Tigers' John Fetzer and Walter O'Malley. (O'Malley had been on it for twenty-five years.) Other owners—Kuhn allies all—rotated through. Ed Fitzgerald and the Expos' John McHale were the other current members. They were privy to information the others never saw, and they often simply presented decisions as faits accomplis. Kuhn frequently stood before general ownership meetings and pronounced, "The council has decided . . ."

"A lot of owners felt they were on the outside," recalled the Reds' Dick Wagner. "It wasn't unusual to get the minutes of the executive council meeting after you'd already left for a general ownership meeting. That was so you didn't have a chance to see in advance what they'd done."

The "Dump Bowie Club" saw Kuhn as a willing captive of National League interests. They seethed at the senior circuit's contempt for them, and they'd just received a fresh taste. The American League was to expand into Seattle in 1977, to settle that city's lawsuit over the Pilots' desertion. AL owners were thinking of adding just one team, which would create ideal circumstances for interleague play. (In place of a fourteenth team, each AL team could play each NL team once.) The American League owners approved it unanimously. The National League owners wouldn't hear of it.

"Much of this was colored by the presence of Veeck and Finley," recalled Kuhn. "It was like, 'Why should we get involved with *those* people?' You went from the extremes of Carpenter to Finley, Wrigley to Veeck. One was royalty, the other riffraff."

Walter O'Malley's contempt was quite open. He once interrupted Jerry Hoffberger, the chairman of National Brewery, who owned the Orioles: "Hey, leave it alone, Jerry. I haven't got time for beer salesmen today." He once stopped Bob Short, well, short. "When you can buy the chips, you play," O'Malley told the perennially strapped Rangers owner. "When you can't, don't."

It was O'Malley who saved Kuhn's job. Finley made his run at the 1975 All-Star Game, in Milwaukee. At a joint ownership meeting, he stood up to say he had four firm anti-Kuhn votes. The Lords broke up into separate league meetings and Kuhn retreated to his suite at the Pfister Hotel.

O'Malley went to work. First he succeeded in postponing a vote with a parliamentary maneuver. Then he went to work on changing the vote. But which one? Not Finley, obviously. Not Hoffberger, who hated Kuhn's pomposity nearly as much as Finley. Probably not Steinbrenner, who'd been suspended by Kuhn.

That left Brad Corbett. He'd owned the Rangers less than a year, having bought the team from Bob Short. He was still under the sway of Short, who remained as a minority owner, and who was a confirmed Kuhn-hater. The commissioner had tried to thwart Short's moving the Rangers from Washington to Texas. But Corbett had no deep-seated hatred of his own for Kuhn. So O'Malley went after him.

First he had to find him. Corbett wasn't in Milwaukee. He'd left his proxy with a club attorney. But O'Malley, his resourcefulness undiminished at age seventy-two, tracked him down in the wee hours at a Florida hotel, and proceeded to work on him long and hard, long-distance. Finally, O'Malley rejoined a roomful of Kuhn allies and handlers. The atmosphere was funereal. Heads were down; hands clasped. With a twinkle in his eye and a Cheshire cat grin, Walter O'Malley changed all that. "I got his vote," he announced.

The next day, the American League owners voted 10–2 to re-elect Kuhn. (When Steinbrenner learned of Corbett's switch, he switched too.) The National League vote was 12–0.

The crisis and the meetings were over. A press conference soon followed. As Kuhn was about to start taking questions, he noticed Finley in the back of the room, surrounded by a gaggle of writers who were taking down his version of events.

"Charlie," Kuhn said, for all to hear, "you may leave my room."

"Thank you, Commissioner," Finley barked. "That just shows more class."

He left, the gaggle of writers trailing behind.

Now the two eyed each other across a table in the Pick-Congress Hotel coffeeshop. It was just after 10:00 P.M. Kuhn's second was Hadden; Finley's, his son, Paul. The owner tried to break the tension with a suggestion: How about a round of Black Russians?

Kuhn was normally a martini man. A Black Russian, Finley explained, was a mixture of vodka and Kahlúa. It sounded pretty horrible, but, in the best interests of baseball, Kuhn agreed. It was Black Russians all around.

"Don't butt into this," Finley began. "There are other things the commissioner should be doing. Don't butt into this."

He showed Kuhn his sale agreement with the Yankees on Blue, laid it on the table, and launched into a monologue. He'd built up the A's from scratch before, and he could do it again. He recited the legend of Charlie O.: how he'd personally signed top prospects, how he'd wheeled and dealed and assembled the

team that won five straight AL West titles and three straight
World Series. He could do that again, he told Kuhn.

Kuhn finally found an opening to say, "I doubt it."

Finley, undeterred, gulped his Black Russian and rambled on.
"Commissioner, I can't sign these guys. They don't want to
play for ol' Charlie. They want to chase those big bucks in New
York. If I sell them now, I can at least get something back. If I
can't, they walk out on me at the end of the season and I've got
nothing, nothing at all. Now, if I get the money for them, I can
sign amateurs and build the team again, just the way I did to
create three straight World Series winners. I know how to do it.
You know I do. You've seen me do it. And you shouldn't be
thinking about getting into this. Hell, owners have been selling
players forever and no commissioner ever said they couldn't.
Not Landis, not anybody. This free-agency thing is terrible. The
only way to beat it is with young players. That's where I'll put
the money."

He described the sad state of his finances. He could only draw
a million in attendance in Oakland by selling 380,000 half-price
tickets for family nights. He projected a loss of $700,000 for this
year. He was faced with another team across the Bay, and he
played in a damned icebox. Yes, he'd tried to trade Rudi, Fingers, and Blue for other players. He recounted his efforts. But finally he'd decided on cash instead. Charlie O. was a damned
good salesman at getting players to sign with the A's. With $3.5
million, he could attract some and start building great teams
again.

By the time Finley's cascade of words finally slowed, it was
midnight. The coffeeshop had closed down and they had to exit
through the back door. Before they did, Kuhn let Finley know he
was unpersuaded. As commissioner, he reminded him, he could
step in wherever he saw an issue involving "baseball's best interests." He had to consider the competitive balance of the game,
the public's confidence in it, and the Oakland fans.

"I'm still very troubled by this situation," he said. "I'd like to
think about it overnight and get back in touch with you."

Kuhn returned to it in his Rockefeller Center office the next day.
He ordered the Red Sox and Yankees not to play their newly acquired players, and he set up a conference call with the executive council. He told them he was considering voiding the sales,
and he wanted to get their thoughts.

They all agreed Finley's deals were just terrible for baseball:

awful, awful, awful. No one moaned louder than John Fetzer, whose Tigers had bid for Blue less than forty hours earlier. But they disagreed about Kuhn's course.

"If you get into this, Finley is surely going to start a fight," said Lee MacPhail, who as AL president was a PRC member. "We're going to have the unpleasantness of court proceedings. I doubt that's very good for the game."

He also doubted it would help the contract bargaining, still grinding along. It would feed Miller's suspicion that Kuhn was out to undermine free agency. Chub Feeney agreed with him. Even Fetzer, for all his moaning, was persuaded that Kuhn ought not to intervene.

On the other side, Ed Fitzgerald urged Kuhn to have at it. "It seems to me we have an integrity question here very clearly," he said. "All we can do is tell the commissioner what we think, and he is going to have to make up his mind what he wants to do."

Then there was the one voice that truly mattered: Walter O'Malley's. He'd scribbled some notes to himself: *The absence of reserve clause. This makes a travesty of the integrity of baseball. Pennants are not to be bought.*

Now he expounded on those themes. If Finley did this, it would be clear to everybody in baseball that anything goes. That was a bad message at a time when the business needed to be stabilized. If a player auction in June decided pennant races, who'd go to ball games? If the talent all went to rich clubs, what kind of competition would they ever have?

"You must not allow this to happen," he said. "You have to turn it down."

(Kuhn doesn't remember O'Malley making such a directive. The quote was unearthed by the impeccably sourced Milton Richman of UPI.)

Kuhn knew he must. It was the right policy—Walter O'Malley had told him so—and it was a satisfying feeling: whacking a vulnerable Charlie Finley. All that was required was a show of due process. Kuhn held a hearing the next day and issued his ruling the following day: the sales were off; the players were remanded to the A's. It was all couched in lofty language, culminated by this passage:

> Nor can I persuade myself that the spectacle of the Yankees and Red Sox buying contracts of star players in the prime of their careers for cash sums totaling $3,500,000 is anything but

devastating to baseball's reputation for integrity and to public confidence in the game, even though I can well understand that their motive is a good-faith effort to strengthen their clubs. If such transactions now and in the future were permitted, the door would be opened wide to the buying success of the more affluent clubs, public suspicion would be aroused, traditional and sound methods of player development and acquisition would be undermined and our efforts to preserve the competitive balance would be gravely impaired.

For sheer hysteria, the reaction to Kuhn's decision rivaled what followed Seitz's.

He was "the village idiot," Finley screamed. He followed up with "the nation's idiot" and "his honor, the idiot in charge." Then he sued Kuhn for $10 million.

Yankees manager Billy Martin, bitter at losing Blue, called the decision as great a scandal as Watergate. Chuck Tanner, the A's manager, called it "the biggest I-don't-know-what-you-call-it in the history of baseball."

"The whole game has gone completely crazy," said Rico Petrocelli, the Red Sox third baseman.

"We're not in a pennant race," said Orioles owner Jerry Hoffberger. "What we are in is a lawyers' full-employment program."

It was a dual irony. Bowie Kuhn, who hailed from that most Republican of law firms—it bore the name of Wendell Willkie, after all—had come down against the free market. He was less commissioner than King Canute, the medieval monarch who futilely ordered the tides to roll back.

Charlie Finley, who squeezed a penny until it screamed, had already established the stars' huge market values—sometimes to the players' own amazement. "Hey, I'm worth a million dollars," said Rollie Fingers. "Somehow that just doesn't sound right."

It sounded just great to Jerry Kapstein. He was part of a formidable new breed in baseball: the player agent. He was, in fact, the top one. He had sixty clients, including some of the game's best names: Fingers, Rudi, Gene Tenace, Don Baylor, and Bert Campaneris on the A's alone. Of Kapstein's stable, eighteen were still unsigned in June. He was itching to wade into the postseason market. He only needed to know the ground rules.

* * *

Baseball finally set them in early July. Gaherin had made a suggestion to Miller, when the post-lockout negotiations resumed.

"Let's get the goddamned lawyers out of the room," he said. "We've fucked things up enough with legalisms."

Miller readily agreed, though he insisted on keeping Dick Moss inside. The stripped-down talks went forward: John Gaherin, Lee MacPhail, and Chub Feeney for the owners; Miller and Moss for the union. Every day they met at the Biltmore Hotel, where they slowly, arduously reinvented the baseball business.

They were still far apart on the free-agency threshold, but there were myriad other issues to work out. Gaherin wanted the new reserve system, in whatever form, to be retroactive. Miller wanted the sixty or so presently unsigned players to be eligible for free agency. There was much more. How would the free-agent market be set up? How often could a player be a free agent? And—Marvin Miller's pet cause—how could the commissioner's powers be further trimmed? "The big political nut," as Gaherin later put it, "was Bowie's nuts."

In his dislike of Bowie Kuhn, Miller took a back seat only to Charlie Finley. He hated Kuhn's air of self-importance, which was doubly galling since he was, in reality, Walter O'Malley's messenger boy. And he hated Kuhn's acting as if he were czar over them all when, in Miller's view, he represented only the owners' interests.

Ed Fitzgerald explained Kuhn's view of his role as reflecting the origins of the office: "He knew Landis was brought in not to be the head man of the owners, but to protect the institution of baseball against those who would do something bad against it. That was his vision of commissioner too. He saw himself as the owners' commissioner, the players' commissioner, and, most important, the fans' commissioner. Bowie felt very strongly he wasn't just there to protect the interests of the ownership. It was his role to protect the national jewel of baseball.

"Miller resented Bowie acting as though he had the players' interests at heart. He went out of his way to embarrass him on that point. He was telling the players, 'Bowie Kuhn isn't here to protect you. I am.' He didn't like the commissioner acting as though he were the God of baseball and all the disciples were watched over by him."

Miller and Moss feared what Kuhn might do, during this unsettled period, in the name of "integrity of the game." They'd been scared to death he would snatch the *Messersmith* case from

Seitz on those grounds. (Indeed, Kuhn seriously considered doing so.) Now they wanted the Basic Agreement to explicitly bar the commissioner from getting involved in matters subject to bargaining. It would further curtail his power to scandal-related issues.

Recalled Miller: "I just kept thinking, 'What if we negotiate all this and the commissioner stepped in and said, "I rule that free agency involves the integrity of the game"?' "

It was a replay of 1970: Gaherin trying to yield enough ground to satisfy Miller, then trying to soft-sell the package to Kuhn. This time, Kuhn resisted even more stubbornly. He'd been in office longer, and he'd seen what came of tossing Miller a bone. That independent arbitrator who "wouldn't handle anything vital"? Right—he only gutted the reserve system.

"No. No, no, no," Kuhn told one meeting of the PRC board. "This is a diminution of the commissioner's power."

Bob Howsam spoke up. "Bowie, we've already compromised on the meal money. What's so sacrosanct about your powers?"

Kuhn seethed. That day's business was effectively over. Later, Fitzgerald approached Gaherin.

"Can you make a deal without this?" he asked.

"No," said Gaherin. "If Bowie screws around on this, Marvin will be one hundred percent convinced he wants to screw around with free agency."

"Well, I think if you can get the rest of it, Bowie will buy it."

It was a few weeks later when the two sides finally got down to the short strokes. The player leaders, who had left the bargaining table to play ball, were reassembled. The last cards were laid on the table. Clubs had until August 9 to sign any unsigned players; if they weren't signed by then, they moved on to free agency. Bowie Kuhn's powers were, indeed, being whittled away. As a threshold for free agency, the owners proposed six years.

Phil Garner, the A's infielder, would always remember the moment he heard that number: "You're trying not to grin and you're trying to say, 'Aw, Christ, this is going to kill us.' Meanwhile, inside, you're going, 'Yes! Yes! Yes!' "

The morning after the All-Star Game, the Lords assembled at the Bellevue-Stratford Hotel in Philadelphia to review the proposed settlement. Many were in foul temper. Kuhn was still being pilloried for ending the lockout. Some owners were sure they could have gotten better free-agency terms had the lockout continued—eight years, probably, or at least seven. Others were after Gaherin's scalp.

"If anyone does not believe that we had our ass kicked in this labor matter, they are dead wrong," Gussie Busch declared. "We have lost the war, and the only question is, can we live with the surrender terms."

Ed Fitzgerald defended it. Seitz had denuded the old reserve system; Gaherin had done a hell of a job to negotiate a new limited one. Baseball would at least be reclothed in some manner. These last few months had shown how important that was. He urged them to ratify the deal and end the chaos.

"Any deal is better than no deal," he said.

"Gentlemen, I never heard of anything so damned asinine in all my life," barked Charlie Finley. "You've got to be crazy to believe that."

He offered his solution yet again: "Make 'em *all* free agents!" Again he was ignored.

The ratification vote was an unusually divided 17–7; the contract got through "by the skin of our teeth," as Gaherin put it. It portended much more acrimony to come.

$ 11 $

THE WORLD SERIES that fall was a mismatch. The Big Red Machine had never run so powerfully, rolling over the Yankees in four straight. Johnny Bench batted .533 and was named Series MVP. Sportswriters compared the 1976 Reds to the legendary 1927 Yankees.

Bob Howsam was happy with the rout-in-progress, and yet subdued. It was his greatest triumph in baseball, but he knew it was the end of an era. His empire would begin to be dismantled in two weeks, when the first free-agent market opened. He'd lose Don Gullett. Others would surely follow.

"This is the last of the great teams," he told an interviewer.

Ted Turner saw to it there would be off-field excitement to counteract the on-field yawns. Game four in New York was washed out by rain, driving baseball men into the hospitality suite at the Americana Hotel. Into the room, that evening, reeled Turner. He'd just flown in from Chicago, downing six drinks en route.

Turner spied Bob Lurie, the Giants' new owner, and made his way toward him. He coveted Giants outfielder Gary Matthews, who'd hit .279 with 20 homers and 84 RBIs that year—totals far exceeding the combined efforts of Turner's motley outfield. Turner's GM, John Alevezos, had even twice approached Matthews's agent during the season, telling him Atlanta was hot for the unsigned Matthews. That landed the Braves in hot water. They were fined $10,000 by Bowie Kuhn for violating baseball's antitampering rules. Now the free-agent draft was just ahead, and Turner wanted to personally gibe Lurie.

Three sheets to the wind, he first razzed him about dreadful Candlestick Park. Why didn't he move the team to a less windy place, like Phoenix? Then he ragged on him for making a federal case of Alevezos's approaches.

"Now you've made me really mad," said Turner, in his usual hundred-decibel voice. "I'll do everything I can to get Gary Matthews." He told Lurie just how he planned to wow him in Atlanta Saturday. Matthews would be flown there and see a billboard just outside the airport: WELCOME, GARY MATTHEWS. Then he'd be whisked to a party in his honor at the Stadium Club.

Writers stepped out of the shrimp line and over to the ruckus Turner was stirring up. A growing crowd gathered around the laughing Braves owner and the tight-lipped Lurie.

"There's gonna be a gala celebration," Turner continued. "The major celebrities from Atlanta are gonna be present. So is the mayor and the governor. Whatever you offer him, Lurie, I plan to pay him double. In fact, I have offered him twice as much as your attendance was last year. Let's see, that was about 630,000 or so. Well, he can count on that much to play for us."

The next morning's newspapers reported Turner's harangue. The Giants' owner was no match for Turner in repartee. Lurie wasn't a mad genius like Turner but the mild-mannered heir to a real estate fortune. He'd put a small portion of it into buying and saving the Giants earlier that year.

"It's tampering," complained Lurie to baseball's general counsel, Sandy Hadden. Under the labor contract, the Giants still had exclusive negotiating rights to Matthews until November 1. But the player wouldn't even bother talking to him after reading Turner's statements.

It wasn't the first such complaint heard by Hadden. Some owners had been, as they say, "pitching on the black" on tampering all year. Early on, Jerry Hoffberger complained bitterly about owners sending messages through the press to his eleven unsigned players. An owner would be quoted on how they'd love to have this or that Oriole. The player would become that much more impossible to sign. There were accusations of certain GMs playing footsie with certain agents, though only the Alevezos charge stuck.

Kuhn felt compelled to send out a stern antitampering directive in late August: "While I have tried to view such conduct with a certain amount of tolerance in the past, that is no longer possible under the radically changed circumstances of the present time."

But still it happened. In mid-September, a writer reached Gussie Busch at home and tried to draw him out on his free-agent wish list. The fellow ran down some names, and got the same response for Rollie Fingers and Joe Rudi: "You're coming awfully close."

It made a good little story for the writer and a $5,000 fine for Busch. He and Lou Susman met with Kuhn to appeal. When they got nowhere on the facts, Susman asked for pity. Busch was seventy-five, an old man now. Kuhn was unyielding.

Countless other secret dealings never surfaced. The A's played their last series of the year in New York, and Yankees first base coach Elston Howard spent the whole three games lobbying Oakland first baseman Don Baylor. Great city, great team. Finally, he handed him a note: "If you are interested in coming to the Yankees, tell Elston yes or no." It was unsigned, but Baylor guessed the author was a somewhat higher authority than Howard.

Turner's public harangue was something altogether different. If Lurie wanted to pursue it, said Hadden, he should write up what happened and file a complaint. Lurie, fuming, said he would.

On a clear, brisk November morning, baseball's owners and GMs assembled at the Plaza Hotel in New York for the first "reentry draft." That's what everybody called it, anyway, though the term was a misnomer. Teams were really just there to declare their *interest* in particular players and to stake out negotiating rights with them. The teams, picking in reverse order of finish, were limited to "drafting" a maximum of twelve free agents apiece and signing a maximum of two. The Lords had pressed for this format, believing it might bring a modicum of order to the brave new world.

Marvin Miller was there, watching like a hawk. It was the moment he'd awaited for ten years. Yet, as always, deeply suspicious of the owners, and mindful of O'Malley's influence, he was still worried that the owners might collude and not make a single bid.

He relaxed only when Charles Bronfman bounced to his feet to make the first pick. "The Montreal Expos," he said, voice aquiver, "are proud to draft Reggie Jackson."

The room was lit by bright chandeliers, the sound muted by thick carpet, the atmosphere that of an elegant art auction. The twenty-two players on the block ranged from Rembrandts (Rudi, Fingers, Jackson) to remainders (Tito Fuentes, Paul Dade, Billy Smith). Most teams would participate with gusto, since drafting cost nothing.

But not all. Bob Howsam made the same dour statement each time it was the Reds' turn to draft: "In fairness to the players who have won the world championship for us two years in a row, and considering the way our organization is structured, we do not think it would be right for the Cincinnati club to get into bidding contests that must come out of this draft."

In short: "We pass."

By noon, it was over. The clubs had completed seventeen rounds, drafting fast and hard. A total of thirteen players were picked by the maximum twelve clubs.

By midafternoon, Bowie Kuhn had convened a hearing on the Gary Matthews affair. Turner and Lurie gave their versions. Kuhn gave Atlanta the go-ahead to negotiate with Matthews but he reserved the right to revoke his signing. He all but promised disciplinary action against Turner.

By nightfall, the first free agent was signed. It was Bill Campbell, the American League's top reliever, who'd refused to re-up with the Twins after Calvin Griffith refused to meet his salary demand of $27,000. In 1976, Campbell merely tied a league record for most wins by a reliever (17) and set a record for innings pitched by a reliever (168).

After the draft, Campbell and his agent went upstairs at the Plaza with Red Sox assistant GM John Claiborne. At 10:00 P.M. they came down to make an announcement. Campbell had signed a five-year, $1 million contract. The pitcher, whose income had just multiplied tenfold, was so dazed as to be totally frank.

"Honestly, I couldn't believe what was happening," he said. "A million dollars? No one's worth that, but if they want to pay me, I'm certainly not going to turn it down."

The first newspaper story ever to mention Jerry Kapstein is illuminating: "Young Jeremy Kapstein and a friend, both 14-year-old ninth-graders, bicycled 62 miles to Otis Air Force Base in Falmouth, Mass., to get a firsthand look at the state of U.S. national defense."

The *Providence Journal-Bulletin* story went on to tell how Jeremy talked his way past the guard at the front gate and got a guided tour of the base, lunch at the Officers Club, an audience with the base commander, and a ride back home in a helicopter.

Clearly, this boy would have a future as a player's agent. Kapstein didn't know this yet, since it was 1958 and there was no such thing. But from age nine, when he began poring over box scores, he was headed that way. He loved sports; he reveled in statistics; and, as a teenager, he talked his way into keeping stats for the Providence College basketball broadcasters for five dollars a game.

Kapstein was also a straight-A student and went on to Harvard. There, one Saturday, he met announcer Keith Jackson, who was calling the Harvard–Dartmouth football game. Kapstein talked his way into doing some work for ABC Sports, where he developed all kinds of new wrinkles in football stats. The world has Kapstein—whose nickname at Harvard was "Statstein"—to thank for time-of-possession comparisons.

Kapstein even did radio play-by-play for a semipro football team named the Providence Steamrollers. He called one game while sitting in the stands amid supporters of the opposition. Upon describing one Providence touchdown a little too enthusiastically, Kapstein was beaten up. Few of his preppier Harvard classmates could claim such an experience.

In the early seventies, after law school and the Navy, Kapstein settled in Washington and turned to agentry. His first brush with it was when his brother, Dan, got a tryout as a punter with the New England Patriots. He was cut, but Kapstein was intrigued by pro-sports contracts. He picked up a smattering of baseball, football, and hockey players as clients. But he kept his "day jobs": doing stats work for ABC and as color man on Washington Bullets TV games.

Kapstein even managed to schedule baseball contract negotiations to coincide with Bullets road trips. One time he came in to see Padres GM Peter Bavasi, carrying his road duffel bag. Bavasi, wary of all agents, suspected it contained a tape recorder.

"Hold it," he said. "I'm not going to talk with you until I see what's in that duffel bag."

Kapstein unzipped it and threw two handfuls of dirty laundry at Bavasi. Such incidents, together with his propensity for doing business out of phone booths, branded him as a flake. But hey, this was baseball. There was always room for one more. He was at least an intriguing one: part Sammy Glick, part Marty Glickman.

With the advent of salary arbitration, Jerry Kapstein got his break. It was made for Kapstein, since it was all about statistics. What numbers put a player in the best light? How did players compare in performance and pay? It was an arena swirling with

Mark Twain's three kinds of untruths: lies, damned lies, and statistics. A wizard like Kapstein could transform a utility infielder
into Babe Ruth reincarnated.

Kapstein was preparing Ken Holtzman's first salary arbitration
case in the winter of 1974 when two Oakland teammates, Rollie
Fingers and Darold Knowles, approached him about handling
theirs. Kapstein took on Charlie Finley, *mano a mano*. Finley
tried his usual bluster and blarney. In Holtzman's case, he said
he won twenty-one games only because of great relief pitching.
In Fingers's case, he said he'd only been third in the league in
saves because those great A's starters handed him so many leads.
But he was no match for Kapstein's blizzard of stats.

Kapstein produced thirty exhibits between the three cases, was
successful in all three, and was immediately the toast of the A's
clubhouse. Anybody who could beat Finley out of $26,000—the
total spread in the three cases—was okay. Joe Rudi, Bert
Campaneris, Gene Tenace, and Don Baylor signed on as clients
too. Kapstein rapidly built his baseball clientele from there; and
finally he dropped his day jobs.

Yet with the reserve clause in full force, there still wasn't
much money in it. Agents had no leverage and players still averaged $44,000 a year. It was a rare bird who tried to make a go
of full time agentry.

"How can you make a living at this?" Barry Rona once
asked.

"Well, I have twenty-five players and that's five thousand
here and ten thousand there," Kapstein replied.

And so, by default, Jerry Kapstein had a big stable of
players—about sixty of them—come 1976 and was always hus-
tling for more. Outfielder Tom Grieve once took a phone call in
the Rangers' dugout ten minutes before game time.

"This is Jerry Kapstein," said the caller. "Do you need an
agent?"

Grieve, taken aback, mumbled thanks but no thanks.

A lot of players didn't have agents then, nor were they sure
they wanted one. Richie Bry, a St. Louis stockbroker-turned-
agent, handed out brochures headlined: WHY YOU NEED AN AGENT.

Most players had no idea, in this brave new world, what kind
of money a skilled negotiator might get them. "Why should I
give somebody ten percent when I do all the work?" asked
pitcher Mark Fidrych. But they had a very good idea what their
GMs thought of agents. "[Players] were still afraid to have one,"

recalled Bry. "They'd ask, 'But if I have one, what's going to happen to me?' "

Had there been more players with agents, there would have been more players going through the 1976 season unsigned. Hundreds came to terms on the cheap, unaware of the riches ahead, or unwilling to endure the wait.

Kapstein himself didn't know exactly what was out there just over the horizon, but he urged his players to wait and see. It was no coincidence, then, that the only three unsigned Red Sox players were Kapstein clients. Of the sixty or so unsigned players at midseason, eighteen were Kapstein's.

Suddenly this thirty-two-year-old operator was one of the most powerful men in baseball. He wasn't flashy, like the Gucci-clad Bry. He constantly wore the same corduroy jacket and drove a sensible 1973 Grand Prix. He worked out of his suburban-Washington townhouse, assisted only by his brother, Dan. But he put in eighteen-hour days, ran up $500-a-week phone bills, and logged 100,000 air miles a year. He lost his wife in the process, but he developed tight relationships with his clients.

Kapstein tried to take care of their every need and worry, telling them, "You have me seven days a week, twenty-four hours a day." He was not only baseball's first "superagent" but also the first to see that handholding was as important as negotiating. Steve Garvey called him "my closest friend apart from my mom and dad." Said Rick Burleson: "Jerry has done more for me than any man on this earth. He doesn't only negotiate my contract; I turn to him for everything I need."

GMs resented Kapstein's referring to clients as "my players." They still thought of them as *their* players. Some so disliked Kapstein that they got rid of his clients just to get rid of *him*. "He almost hypnotized his players," said the Reds' GM, Dick Wagner, who disposed of several Kapstein players.

Wagner once had pitcher Will McEnaney and Kapstein in to talk contract and made a proposal.

"Will, that's three times the salary you're getting now," Wagner said. "That's a good offer."

"Three times?" blurted McEnaney. "I'll take it."

Kapstein jumped up and dragged his client out the door to talk sense into him. It was an *insulting* offer. So McEnaney didn't sign.

In late 1976, the Reds traded McEnaney and another Kapstein client, Tony Perez, to Montreal. Reds president Bob Howsam later admitted it was the worst trade he ever made. McEnaney was a washout in Montreal, but Perez was a productive hitter for another ten years—and a huge loss to the Reds as a clubhouse leader.

Most GMs didn't react to Kapstein so violently, however. He may have had the bad habit of calling them at all hours, since he worked all hours, but he was unfailingly pleasant, chitchatting about the GM's wife and kids before getting down to business. "Courteous and costly" was how Rangers GM Dan O'Brien described him.

The GMs' big complaint wasn't just the high cost of Kapstein's clients but the huge toll on their time. Kapstein so loved the art of the deal he dragged out every negotiation. "The whole process was so elongated," groaned John Schuerholz, then with the Royals. "It was like a play, and it had to go through three acts before it could end."

Roland Hemond of the White Sox finally reached an agreement in principle with Kapstein, after three weeks of dickering on a contract. The agent said he'd fax the final contract as he drafted it. Two days passed. On a hunch, Hemond called the Padres and asked to see the latest contract of pitcher Randy Jones, a Kapstein client.

The first page of the Chicago player's contract finally came in. Hemond laid it beside the Jones contract. Except for the name, it was identical. The next day another page came. It took about four days in all and not a word had been changed. That was just Kapstein.

He had some other quirks too. He wouldn't take calls, only return them. He wouldn't put anything in writing, even bragging he'd never sent a letter. And he still didn't have an office. That's why baseball's first great free-agent mart was conducted on the fourth floor of a bank building in Providence.

They were the two strangest datelines in America that November: Plains, Georgia, and Providence, Rhode Island. At one, President-elect Carter received the political world; at the other, Jerry Kapstein the baseball world.

He rented room 4B of the downtown Hospital Trust Bank Building. There, at a big rosewood table, Jerry Kapstein did business. He was auctioning off ten of the twenty-two available free agents—most of his stars. He had set up the auction block nearly as far from the beaten path as Ahoskie, North Carolina. Kapstein said he was trying to avoid the "circus atmosphere" of a place like Washington or New York. Others believed the local-boy-made-good was sending his hometown a message: "SEE ME! SEE ME!"

The scene in room 4B rivaled anything ever seen in Carlton Cherry's office. Kapstein's mother, Gladys, screened phone calls and made hotel arrangements for players and owners. Brother Dan shuttled to the airport to pick up players and owners alike. Two boyhood pals stood by to go out at all hours for the cheeseburgers, milk shakes, and coffee that kept Kapstein going.

Owners and GMs took a number and got in line. Players killed time trying the specials at nearby Haven Brothers Diner. They usually didn't have to wait long. The signings came fast and furious.

WEDNESDAY, NOVEMBER 17—

Kapstein had an afternoon doubleheader of deals, and that day's events established a ritual. The two sides would come to terms, catch an elevator to the twenty-fourth floor, and there meet the press in the bank's boardroom. The player would wear his new team's hat, and everybody would say how delighted they were.

The first players signed had leapt quickly to get off Charlie Finley's farm: Gene Tenace to the Padres for $1.8 million over five years, and Don Baylor to the Angels for $1.6 million over six years.

THURSDAY, NOVEMBER 18—

At 6:00 P.M. Kapstein announced Montreal's signing of second baseman Dave Cash for $1.5 million over five years.

At midnight, a second Angels signing in twenty-four hours: Joe Rudi, for $2.09 million over five years. Rudi got as much in a signing bonus—$1 million—as Finley had tried to sell him for in June.

Still, said Rudi, "Money isn't everything. Being treated as a human being is as much as anything else."

At 3:30 A.M. Kapstein roused the writers for yet another announcement: Bert Campaneris to the Rangers for $950,000 over five years.

"Bert is going to the Rangers and will play shortstop," he said. "I've already talked to Toby Harrah, and he has agreed to move to third base. Toby is also my client. And I'm hoping that the Rangers bring up Bump Wills from the minors and give him a chance at second base. Bump is *also* my client."

Texas owner Brad Corbett and GM Dan O'Brien looked on without objection. Who could do anything but nod dumbly at that hour?

FRIDAY, NOVEMBER 19—

Early that morning, Cardinals GM Bing Devine and Busch attorney Lou Susman flew out of St. Louis for an appointment with Kapstein. They hoped to sign pitcher Don Gullett. He'd gone 91–44 with a 3.03 ERA in his seven-year career with Cincinnati. He was still only twenty-five, and he was a lefty.

In the Boston airport, as they awaited their connection for Providence, the two were paged. It was a message from Kapstein's office. Forget it. The meeting was off. They would learn why only later: Kapstein was in the process of finalizing a six-year, $2 million deal for Gullett with the Yankees.

"I consider him a modern-day Whitey Ford," purred Gabe Paul at the press conference.

Lou Susman took the episode as a personal insult—to be stood up by Kapstein and aced out on Gullett, and on the same day. He muttered darkly that he'd never deal with Kapstein again. Any last illusions the Lords had about maintaining control were being quickly shattered.

They were all "kind of embarrassed," said Montreal's John McHale, but they were all helpless.

"I think Kapstein had made up his mind in advance where everybody was going," said McHale. "He just kind of parceled them out."

SATURDAY, NOVEMBER 20—

Wayne Garland, who'd earned $23,000 with Baltimore that year, signed with Cleveland for $2.3 million over ten years. Cleveland owner Ted Bonda and GM Phil Seghi expressed appropriate delight at landing the crop's single twenty-game winner.

And then the Jerry Kapstein Show went dark for a few days. He had no new announcements. There was still plenty of activity, however, in room 4B of the Hospital Trust Building. The initial flurry had depleted his stock of players. Teams that hadn't signed anyone were in a white heat to get what remained. Providence was crawling with owners and GMs awaiting their appointment with Rollie Fingers, while on two coasts, a contest was being played out for Bobby Grich.

* * *

Grich was perhaps baseball's finest second baseman. As an Oriole, he set one-season records for that position for highest fielding average (.995) and most putouts (484) and tied another: fewest errors (5). He could also hit, averaging .262, 14 homers, and 61 RBIs over his five-year career. At age twenty-seven, Grich was in his prime.

He was also the prime target of George Steinbrenner. Having bagged Don Gullett, he could sign just one more free agent, and he wanted it to be Grich.

"We are not going to win a championship with Fred Stanley at shortstop," said Steinbrenner, opening a post-Series meeting with his baseball brain trust. He couldn't forgive Stanley for a throwing error that cost New York game two of the Series. Quite apart from that, Stanley was just a middling shortstop and a nonhitter, with a lifetime .225 average.

Gabe Paul had an idea. He hadn't much use for the only true shortstop among the free agents, Bert Campaneris. He'd been a fine player for the A's but, at age thirty-four, was already in decline. Paul knew that Grich had been a shortstop in the minors—why not convert him back to one?

The Yankees were one of twelve teams to pick Grich in the draft, but they considered themselves the one with the inside track. Steinbrenner made a proposition to Kapstein. If he were allowed to be the last person to talk with Grich, he'd guarantee to top all other offers. Kapstein agreed.

Bobby Grich was in the midst of a leisurely cross-country drive, from Baltimore to his Long Beach, California, home. He was stopping to see various landmarks along the way and unwinding from the season. He checked in with Kapstein from some Indian ruins in New Mexico. What really intrigued him was Baylor's signing with the Angels.

Don Baylor was Grich's best friend in baseball. They came up together through the Orioles' minor league system and remained close in Baltimore. Now he'd be playing in Anaheim, where Grich had grown up and near where he now lived. For the first time, Grich was mildly interested in the Angels. They'd drafted him and Grich had briefly spoken to Angels GM Harry Dalton, formerly Baltimore's head man. Grich liked him, but he wanted to play with a contender. California was a perennial tail-ender.

He was approaching Las Vegas when the news came over his radio: the Angels had called a press conference to announce Joe Rudi's signing. Now Grich was excited. California could really be something, and he wanted to be part of it. He called Kapstein and told him so. The agent tried to get word to Harry Dalton, but he'd already flown west.

Kapstein did succeed in reaching George Steinbrenner. He told him that Grich was leaning toward the Angels now. Pursuant to their agreement, he wanted to give the Yankees their last at-bat. They set up a meeting. Steinbrenner and Gabe Paul whisked into Providence from New York, and Grich flew east from California.

George Steinbrenner, though a shipbuilder by trade, was every bit Charlie Finley's equal as salesman. It was why he wanted last crack. Between his blarney and his money, he always thought he would prevail.

Steinbrenner laid it on thick for Grich. He wanted to be with a contender? The Yankees were already the American League's top team, and he was determined to win a world championship. Grich's addition would guarantee that championship. He also considered him the kind of class guy he wanted on his club. Steinbrenner implied Grich could pretty much write his own ticket.

"In my opinion, Bobby, you're just one heck of a ballplayer," Gabe Paul chimed in. "I want nothing more than for you to play for us." He explained how they wanted to make Grich a short-stop and how confident he was that would work.

Grich said he was flattered but reminded Steinbrenner he was a California boy. The revamped Angels made the West Coast an attractive situation for him. Besides, he didn't think he cared for living in New York.

"My hopes are leaning strongly toward California," he said. "But my mind isn't completely made up. I'll think very seriously about what you have said."

Steinbrenner knew a polite no when he heard one. He saw a future of Mickey Klutts at shortstop. He resorted to threats. Grich had better think carefully before signing with the Angels, he warned. Dalton had played fast and loose with the rules that allowed him to sign a third free agent. (In general, only two were allowed per club. But if a team lost more than two players to free agency, it could sign more. Dalton had traded in September for an unsigned utility infielder named Tim Nordbrook. When he became a free agent, Steinbrenner charged that Dalton had just "rented" him for a month.) Steinbrenner would demand an investigation if Grich signed. The contract would probably be voided.

Dalton denied Steinbrenner's allegations when he met Grich the next day, and denounced the Yankees owner. He'd turned around and returned to Providence just six hours after landing in California. He was taking seriously the mandate of the Angels owner, spoken in his distinctive Texas drawl: "Get me some bawlplayers."

Gene Autry loved baseball. He made the 200-mile round-trip from Palm Springs every day his team played. He enjoyed the company of baseball men, who could match him drink for drink—no mean feat. He was generous to players—as he could well afford to be. Autry was famous as a singing cowboy, but he was rich from his ownership of TV and radio stations. He'd gone to the 1960 winter meetings looking for baseball broadcast deals and wound up buying the expansion Angels.

From the start, they were the Dodgers' poor relations. They were, in fact, the Dodgers' tenants for four years, before Anaheim Stadium's construction—a singularly unpleasant period for the new club. Angels GM Fred Haney stormed in to see Buzzie Bavasi at the Dodgers' offices one day waving an invoice. "We've been charged $258 for window-washing," he said. "We don't *have* any windows."

Walter O'Malley was nothing less than the Landlord from Hell. The Angels were charged for half the stadium's toilet-paper and paper-towel costs, though their meager crowds used far less than half the tissues.

Even in their own park, the Angels never escaped the Dodgers' shadow. The Dodgers were identified with Frank Sinatra, a frequent patron. The Angels, in Anaheim, just down the road from Disneyland, were identified with Mickey Mouse. The Dodgers were drawing nearly 3 million; the Angels were lucky to break a million. The Dodgers won the 1974 pennant; the Angels finished last—and to show it was no fluke, they did it again in 1975. California did manage a fourth-place tie in 1976, but finished last in the league in hits, runs, RBIs, homers, and batting average. Said Boston pitcher Bill Lee: "The Angels could take batting practice in the lobby of the [Anaheim] Grand Hotel and not chip a chandelier."

Gene Autry loved baseball, but he'd grown to hate losing. Someone once recited the famous Grantland Rice line, "It's not whether you win or lose, it's how you play the game." Said

Autry: "Well, Grantland Rice can go to hell as far as I'm concerned."

With free agency, he suddenly had the chance to buy what he couldn't build: a winner. He did harbor reservations about taking the plunge. He'd been faithfully reciting the party line, after all, about how awful this was for baseball. But Harry Dalton helped Autry see his way clear. "Gene, if I felt our staying out would prevent anything, I would," he said. "But it will not."

After committing $3.7 million to Baylor and Rudi, Autry declared, "I've hocked the horse; I've got a saddle left; and that's about it." But when Dalton told him Grich was theirs for the taking, Autry took: "Any bawlplayer who wants to play for us that bad, let's go get him."

Grich signed for $1.55 million over five years. In one week, Autry had committed $5.2 million to three players. It was more than twice what he'd paid for the franchise in 1960. It was also a close call on who was more overwhelmed, the players or the Providence bank that handled their money. Kapstein instructed his nouveau riche clients to take their signing bonuses and immediately buy treasury bills. One by one, they walked into a Bank of Boston branch to do so: Baylor with $580,000, Rudi with $1 million, Grich with $600,000. The bank officers were hard-pressed to handle the transactions with their mouths closed.

The baseball world was astounded too by the time Kapstein closed out his auction the day after Thanksgiving. Rollie Fingers signed with the Padres for $1.6 million over six years, and the final totals were in. Jerry Kapstein's ten clients had cleared more than $16 million. The agent's own cut was a cool million.

It was left to George Steinbrenner, however, to top off the market. Jilted by Bobby Grich—whose Angels contract was cleared, over Yankee protests—he now went hard after Reggie Jackson. Steinbrenner would later, characteristically, make a virtue of necessity. "Reggie was meant to be a Yankee," he declared.

The truth was, Steinbrenner was determined to sign two star free agents. It meant the difference between winning a pennant and taking a Series. It was the difference between being ignored until next Opening Day and being splashed across every New York tabloid during the off-season. On draft day, Steinbrenner openly identified Gullett, Grich, Baylor, and Jackson as the Yankees' top choices. He'd signed Gullett, but the other two had slipped away. He was left, by default, with Reggie Jackson.

The slugger was not without other ardent suitors. Charles

Bronfman flew Jackson to Montreal for a lavish dinner at his mansion and an even more lavish offer: nearly $5 million over five years. Ray Kroc of the Padres was, as always, willing to spend: $3.4 million for a five-year deal. The Orioles weighed in at $3 million for five years.

But the moment Steinbrenner set his sights on Jackson, it was clear to some how this would play out. As soon as one Expos investor saw the news of Grich's Angels signing crawl across his TV screen, he picked up the phone to call Bronfman. "We just lost Jackson," he said.

George Steinbrenner swept Reggie Jackson off his feet. During Thanksgiving week, he did Manhattan with the slugger: a lunch at 21, a tour of the town in the owner's limo, with its "NYY" license plate. As they trolled Midtown, he painted a glorious picture of the lifestyle Jackson would lead in New York: here the finest high-rise, there the best haberdasher. It was all for the taking. The two got out to walk the streets, where New Yorkers recognized both men and called out to Jackson, "Sign!"

Steinbrenner's contract offer topped out at $3 million for five years, below both the Expos and Padres. But this wasn't Montreal or San Diego, he noted. It was New York, where Jackson's outside earnings could dwarf his baseball pay. That played beautifully with a man who'd never felt properly celebrated in Oakland. "If I played in New York," he once humbly said, "they'd name a candy bar after me."

Steinbrenner kept after Jackson over the next few days, deluging him with flower sprays and "We want you" telegrams even when they were apart. He talked to him as though he were a peer and a pal. It was just so much malarkey, as Jackson would eventually discover. But it was so different from Charlie Finley that he couldn't help but be taken in. Finally, like many other ardent suitors, Steinbrenner followed Jackson to another city to be close to him.

It was Chicago, where Jackson was taking final bids at the O'Hare Hyatt. Steinbrenner cooled his heels while other teams made their presentations. Finally Jackson summoned him to his suite. Throw in another $63,000 for a Rolls-Royce Corniche, he said, and he was a Yankee. Done.

It wasn't the $3 million or the Rolls that had carried the day, though. It was Steinbrenner's sheer, relentless persistence. Gasped Jackson later: "He hustled me like a broad."

* * *

Baseball's 1976 winter meetings convened two weeks later in Los Angeles. What a difference a year made for the Lords. Last December, in Hollywood, Florida, they'd told Seitz to get lost. This year, near Hollywood, California, they'd lost their own way. New powers, new forces ruled. The Lords still hadn't recovered their footing in a baseball world ripped loose from its moorings. They might never.

The losers groused bitterly. "We've seen a handful of clubs that have been unsuccessful at building teams go out and use checkbooks to achieve things they couldn't accomplish through organizational efforts," said Baltimore's Hank Peters, who'd lost Grich, Jackson, and Garland and signed nobody. "It's very clear that to some players loyalty means nothing."

Agents prowled the lobby of the Los Angeles Hilton, with closeout sales on lesser free agents like Eric Soderholm, Steve Stone, and Richie Hebner.

Also in the lobby was Ted Turner, making all his previous antics look mild. One minute he was on his hands and knees, barking like a dog. The next he was shouting that the commissioner was going to kill him. Two aides—GM Bill Lucas and PR director Bob Hope—finally dragged him into the hotel bar.

"Ted, there's a fine line between being outrageous and being absolutely out of your mind," said Hope. "You've gone over that line."

"Do you think I should get on a plane and fly back to Atlanta?" asked Turner.

"Yes, if you can't get your mind together and act right."

"Do you think I've convinced him I'm crazy?"

"Yes."

The truth, Hope learned, was that Turner *wanted* to be suspended from baseball for the Gary Matthews incident. Last summer he'd become an Atlanta icon: the Braves' wacky, populist owner. Next summer he planned to be away competing for the America's Cup. How would he explain that he cared more about a yacht race than a pennant race? Where would his "man of the people" image be then? He needed Bowie Kuhn to solve his problem.

Kuhn received him the next morning in his suite. It was 7:00 A.M. but Turner was already going full-bore. The commissioner sat in a chair and took it in—Turner pacing intently, addressing him as "Principal." (At other times, he called him "Super Chief." Chub Feeney, in Turnerspeak, was "Chief.")

"C'mon, Principal," said Turner, "you can't take me seriously when I've had a few drinks. But no matter what, you can't take Gary away from me."

The Braves had signed Matthews, who had been suitably impressed by Turner's Stadium Club party with 300 VIPs and his five-year, $1.2 million offer. But the contract was subject to Kuhn's approval.

"I know you're the boss of baseball; suspend me if you must," cried Turner. "Suspend me for a year if you must, but don't take away the Matthews contract."

Turner carried on for forty-five minutes, darting through the suite—dining room, bedroom, bathroom, atrium—appearing, vanishing, reappearing.

"I've tried," said Turner. "This was my first year in baseball, and I didn't know very much about it when I came into it. I've been trying to learn and I've been trying to be a good citizen. I needed the help of you and the other leaders to tell me what it is you want me to do. It's like a kid who joins the Boy Scouts and doesn't know much about it, because there are really no written books of proprieties and improprieties.

"Now you've held up Gary Matthews's contract; you've kept us in mental anguish this whole month; and I get the feeling that I'm persona non grata with you and Sandy Hadden.

"Yeah, suspend me for a year. Let the punishment fit the crime. I know I was wrong in saying this. You're always wrong when you get drunk and open your big mouth, and I committed an impropriety. It's not a gentlemanly thing to do to get drunk and even jokingly threaten somebody who, it turns out, doesn't have the same kind of sense of humor I do.

"Take it out on me! Fine me, suspend me, do anything, but don't take away Gary!"

Kuhn was happy to comply. He suspended Turner for a year and allowed Matthews's signing to stand. To complete his martyr's pose, Turner appealed the suspension. An Atlanta federal judge upheld it, just as a Chicago judge upheld Kuhn in Charlie Finley's damages suit. Turner was free to pursue the America's Cup in 1977, which he won aboard his yacht *Courageous*.

Kuhn was free to take a broad view of his "best interests" powers. He would use them most aggressively in bringing to heel unpopular mavericks like Turner and Finley. But for broader purposes, he was more than ever King Canute. The first tide of free agents had engulfed baseball, tumbling over every club and, in one way or another, changing them all. There wasn't a thing Bowie Kuhn could do about it.

John Gaherin had once hired a man named Leo Brown as a consultant. Brown was a rare combination: an arbitrator, a business school professor, and a Jesuit priest. He gave some GMs and owners a day's tutorial on how to handle salary arbitration, and afterward had a drink with Gaherin.

"There's one thing you need to learn to survive with these kinds of people," said Father Brown, who was a quick study. "You've got to be able to distinguish the words from the noises."

Their words about the New World were the same as ever. It was just awful: awful, awful, awful. Even Gene Autry moaned with the best: "I don't believe all of this is good for baseball."

But their noises were like a herd of moose in full rut: braying and panting. They wanted to win pennants more than they wanted to hoard cash. Each wanted to be the toast of his town for producing a winner. Most wanted to keep up with the Joneses in this tight little fraternity. They weren't, by God, going to let Steinbrenner or Autry or Kroc corner the market in talent. Those three had led the assault on Providence, and the rest followed in waves.

Baseball men knew there was nothing more fragile than a pitcher's arm. Yet every one of them in Kapstein's stable got at least a six-year contract. Wayne Garland blew out his arm two years into his ten-year Indians deal. The 20-game winner of 1976 won 28 games the rest of his career. Don Gullett won 14 games for the Yankees in 1977, but blew out his arm in 1978. Two years into his six-year contract, he was through.

Baseball men had little use for some of the players they signed. Ray Kroc was strangely attracted to Gene Tenace, a so-so catcher who'd be thirty-six by the end of his contract. Buzzie Bavasi unenthusiastically lavished $1.8 million on him. Jerry Kapstein convinced the Texan Brad Corbett that Bert Campaneris was a "young" thirty-four. Ranger GM Dan O'Brien knew better and said so. But Corbett signed him anyway for $950,000 over five years. Campaneris lasted only two of them.

By the time of the Los Angeles meetings, the impact of this wild year 1976 on the economics of 1977 was clear. The average salary would rise 41 percent, from $52,300 to $74,000. Some twenty players had climbed over the $300,000 level. Baseball's total payroll would shoot up from $31.3 million to $48.1 million. Catfish Hunter, once the only player with a long-term contract, was now joined by dozens of others.

It was no immediate disaster, despite doomsday pronouncements from the Lords and their commissioner. Baseball had underpaid its players ever since the Federal League folded. Salaries amounted to a scant 25 percent of revenues in the early seventies. There was plenty of room for players to catch up and owners to continue to prosper.

It was, rather, the behavior displayed and the precedents set that bothered the more thoughtful people in management. The framers of the 1976 Basic Agreement were appalled. This wasn't what they'd had in mind at all.

"It should have worked. The structure seemed reasonable," Lee MacPhail later reflected. "The owners themselves were responsible for it working so badly. What happened was that baseball wasn't governed by supply and demand. The owners wanted to win so badly they didn't care about breaking even. They always thought, 'We're just one player away.'"

They could rant at Marvin Miller. They could rail at Jerry Kapstein. But they were easy meat for the rules Miller created and the market Kapstein orchestrated. No agent would ever dominate a free-agent market as he did in November 1976. Other high-powered player's agents would rush in, drawn to baseball like Willie Sutton to bank vaults: because it was where the money was. (Dick Moss was one of them, leaving the union in 1977 to become an agent.) They would exploit every loopy deal and find every weak link among the Lords.

Yet what lay ahead was still off in the mist, beyond the imagination of either owners or players. Reggie Jackson, at $580,000 a year now, was discussing the possibilities one day. "Do you think," he asked dreamily, "there will ever be a million-dollar player?"

The answer to that was still unclear. One thing, however, was *very* clear: the owners had met the enemy and it was themselves.

$ 12 $

THE LORDS HADN'T listened to Ed Fitzgerald; they hadn't listened to Barry Rona; most of all, they hadn't listened to John Gaherin. But when blame is to be assessed, one thing about the Lords is for sure. As one of their longtime advisers puts it: "These guys will do anything but look in a mirror."

Naturally, they turned on Gaherin, whom they had long criticized as a compromiser. Now it got vitriolic. Gussie Busch and Lou Susman made their who-lost-China speeches. Fitzgerald, who had been a stout ally, turned cool. Kuhn started edging away. So did Kuhn's consigliere, Lou Hoynes, who liked Gaherin but realized he'd have to go. "We'd had a disaster," he later explained, "and now we were going to have to fight our way back inch by inch. To do that, we knew we had to go in a different direction on a negotiator."

And so, with Gaherin's employment agreement nearing its end, Fitzgerald summoned Gaherin to Milwaukee. "You know, John," he said, "they're not going to renew your contract."

Gaherin wasn't stunned. But he was sixty-four, and he thought he'd given a decade's good service. He didn't want to just slink out.

"I thought I could get another year," he said. "What can you do for me?"

The answer, in essence, was: not much. Now Gaherin was getting a taste of how players felt at the end of the line. The Lords had used him up, handed him his unconditional release, and suggested he not let the door hit him in the ass on the way out.

At a farewell dinner in 1978, he did get a clock (whose engraved plaque eventually fell off), a gold pass to every major league ballpark (which he would never use), and many glowing testimonials, from Bowie Kuhn on down.

Finally, it was Gaherin's turn to speak.

"Gentlemen," he said, "this night recalls for me an Irish wake that was held in South Boston for a politician whom, in life, no person in his constituency had a good word for. As the praises droned on, his widow said to her oldest son, 'For the love of God, Dinny, look in the casket and be sure it's your father they're talking about.' "

The Lords turned to picking a replacement, hiring the executive recruiting firm of Heidrick and Struggles to find a new PRC director. The headhunters came back with three top candidates.

The first was Arthur Brennan, a veteran of the rough-and-tumble of airline labor relations. He had served on both sides of the battle, having represented management, at Hughes Air, as well as labor, as chief negotiator of the Air Line Pilots Association. He also had a feel for baseball, as a onetime pitching prospect courted by his hometown Red Sox.

The second candidate, Jack Donlan, also came out of aviation. He was labor chief for National Airlines, where he'd recently slugged his way through a fourteen-month strike by the Machinists Union. He was the most-likely-to-bust-the-union candidate. " 'You want muscle, I'm muscle'—that was the gist of it," recalls one person involved in the hiring.

The third was C. Raymond Grebey, Jr. He was number two in labor relations at General Electric, which had also knocked around a few unions in its time. Indeed, in labor lingo there was a term called Boulwarism, stemming from a onetime GE labor-relations chief named Lemuel Boulware. Boulwarism, essentially, was bargaining with a snarl: "Take it or leave it."

Boulwarism was ancient history at GE, Grebey told the Lords. The company now took an enlightened win-win approach to negotiating. (He mentioned the pending settlement of an affirmative-action case with the Equal Employment Opportunity Commission, of which he was proud.) Grebey certainly didn't *look* like a management goon. He looked like a professor, forever puffing on a pipe and favoring tweeds.

Grebey was also a big baseball fan. He'd grown up in the same Northside Chicago neighborhood as some of the thirties-era Cubs: Gabby Hartnett, Billy Jurges, Stan Hack, Phil Cavaretta, and others. As a child, his family had season tickets at Wrigley Field. As an adult, his auto license plate read: "Cubs Go."

But it wasn't his love of the game that counted with the owners. It was his ability to talk a good game on labor relations. "He was intelligent, subtle, and sophisticated," recalls Lou Hoynes. "We thought he'd be a good match for Marvin."

When the six screening-committee members ranked the candidates, Grebey was the top choice of four. He was hired.

(Donlan would go on to prove his hard-liner mettle in another sport. As the NFL's labor-relations chief from 1980 to 1991, he twice took on the players' union in long strikes. The owners crushed the players both times. The second effectively broke the union for years. During Donlan's tenure with the NFL, no meaningful free agency ever came to pro football.)

Grebey was introduced to the owners at a dinner meeting of the Lords in a private upstairs room at the 21 Club. The booze flowed; the bonhomie oozed; and there was much brave talk of putting Marvin Miller to rout.

As the Lords wound their way down the stairs at evening's end, they exchanged positive murmurings about the new man. There was uttered, however, one jolly remark a participant would remember with chilling clarity: "Let's see," said someone, "how long the poor bastard lasts."

"You're going to enjoy working with Marvin," a man named Bill Caples told Grebey. "He always does his homework, he's a straight shooter, and he's a gentleman."

Caples was once Inland Steel's chief negotiator and was Grebey's first boss, so he listened closely. It was thus with the best of hopes and the friendliest of intentions that Grebey met his foil. They exchanged pleasantries, talked of people they knew in common, and prepared to be off.

"My door is always open," said Grebey, in supremely friendly fashion.

Miller took it otherwise. To him it sounded condescending, like something an old-school industrialist would say to an employee. He smiled thinly. "That's good, because my door is always open too," he said. "We'll talk to each other with our doors open."

Ray Grebey quickly discovered how much love of baseball counted for in the business of baseball. At his first meeting with the press, he was asked about his rooting interests. He'd been a Cubs fan from boyhood, Grebey replied, which had helped prepare him for being a labor negotiator. "In both situations, you suffer immensely," he said.

It was supposed to be a playful bon mot, but Cubs GM Bob Kennedy took umbrage. Suffer, eh? He fired off a communiqué to Grebey: "I hope you don't ever come to this park, and I hope you're not in this job any longer than it takes to read this letter." (Grebey moved quickly to make amends.)

The newcomer soon made the pilgrimage all newcomers made: to Dodger Stadium and Walter O'Malley's office, down the left-field line. O'Malley now was somewhat weakened by a bout with throat cancer, but he was still the nonpareil mind of baseball.

"I heard you're a cigar smoker," O'Malley said, in greeting. "Yes."

"You see that globe down at the end of the office? If you open it up, and if you don't tell anybody, will you sneak a smoke with me?"

They lit up and he pulled a black binder from his desk drawer. "Now, I'm going to tell you about every owner and you're not going to tell anybody a word," he said. He went through them one by one, and it was all there: what kind of person, what kind of money, what kind of tendencies. Grebey would only marvel at it more as time went by and O'Malley's dossier was borne out. "He was one hundred percent right one hundred percent of the time," he later observed.

The problem—for Grebey, and for all of baseball—was that O'Malley would be dead within two years, and his like would not be seen again. Already, the center, the force of consensus he represented, was cracking. George Steinbrenner and the other New Boys never hung on O'Malley's every word the way the old guard did. And once he was gone, the center could not hold. Reflected one baseball man: "O'Malley got sick and so did the industry, at the sane time."

Grebey would tour the baseball world widely in his early days and in the process discover something: that he'd walked through the looking glass and into a very different land when he departed the buttoned-down Fortune 500. Where he came from, people arrived for their appointments on the dot. In Cincinnati, his first stop on a nationwide tour of clubs, he waited two hours for Bob Howsam. Couldn't be helped, the Reds' chairman apologized. He'd been called in to referee a nasty altercation between a player's wife and mistress.

Howsam was the first and loudest voice Grebey heard clamoring for an antidote to the poisonous free-agent process. The Big Red Machine, a mid-seventies dynasty, had been systematically stripped in the wake of the *Messersmith* decision. Pete Rose, Joe Morgan, and Don Gullett went free-agent. George Foster and Ken Griffey were traded to avoid losing them to free agency. Howsam signed no free agents. He hated the very concept more than ever, and he hated the man who had forced it on baseball.

Marvin Miller, fumed Howsam, "cared nothing about the institution of baseball." Howsam had little more use for his own side's "compromisers," a word he bit off so bitterly it might as well have been "Communists." He wanted to make a stand: force clubs that signed a free agent to make reparations to his former club. In private talks with Grebey and in meetings of the PRC, on which he served, Howsam was a broken record: "When am I going to get meaningful compensation?" he said, in his flat Colorado accent. "When am I going to get meaningful compensation?"

This was code language for a return of control, or at least some measure of it. The sixty-two-year-old Howsam remained influential because he'd been so successful. He spoke for other old-line baseball men: people like Jim Campbell of the Tigers, Calvin Griffith of the Twins, and Haywood Sullivan of the Red Sox. They weren't necessarily the smartest guys, but they were the loudest, and they stampeded opinion to the conservative side at every ownership meeting. "I was the moderate right," recalled fellow PRC member Clark Griffith. "I called Howsam the radical right."

Howsam's other great ally was Gussie Busch. He was in his eighties now, but he could still rage at the players, like King Lear on the moor. And he still exercised clout because of the power of Anheuser-Busch and the maneuvering of his personal attorney, Lou Susman.

Susman was a smooth St. Louis corporate lawyer: a "rainmaker" for his firm and an operator in Democratic Party circles. He became particularly important to Busch in 1975, when, in a boardroom coup, August Busch III ousted his father as chief executive. Susman was retained by the stunned elder Busch to look after his interests. He did win his client a consolation prize: continued control of the Cardinals.

In Busch's dotage, Susman became his all-purpose operative. He provided translation services, following up Busch's ramblings by interjecting, "What the Colonel meant to say is . . ." (Busch liked to be called "the Colonel"—a reference to the rank he'd earned as a desk-warrior at the Pentagon during World War

II.) Susman also steadied Busch as he entered and left ownership meetings, which he frequently did for trips to the men's room. On a more substantive level, he was to Busch what Dick Meyer once was: his details guy. (Meyer had fallen out with Busch and left both ball club and brewery.) Gussie ranted in meetings; Susman followed up with arm-twisting. John Gaherin used to call him "Gussie's Rottweiler."

In the Lords' inner circles the tone was being set. It was payback time.

In public the issue was framed quite differently. Baseball invoked the principle of competitive balance: without free-agent compensation, the rich clubs would get the stars and the poor clubs the dregs. Why, just look at the free-spending Yankees, winners of two of three American League pennants post-*Messersmith*.

This argument was a canard. Tight-fisted Baltimore, which had been raided for free agents and which ranked eighteenth of twenty-six clubs in payroll, had won just as many games as New York. The Orioles had a fine farm system, acute talent judgment, and, in Earl Weaver, a great manager. Small-market, low-spending Kansas City had won two of the last three American League West titles.

The existing system, moreover, had gotten out of hand. The average player's salary had nearly tripled, from $52,300 in 1976 to $143,756 by 1980. It was driven by wide-open free agency, and it was driving baseball to ruin. Bowie Kuhn outdid himself rhetorically in each of his State of the Game addresses. Free agency was a "time bomb." Collapse was imminent, "barring the discovery of oil wells under second base."

This too was a canard. Total attendance was up 39 percent in the three post-*Messersmith* years, and total revenues were up 66 percent. Fans *loved* the free-agency era. They were also much less forgiving of players now, demanding perfection in exchange for these princely salaries, while blaming those high-salaried players for ticket-price increases. San Diego fans derisively chanted "Two-eight-five" at Oscar Gamble, referring to his $2.85 million contract. Bill Campbell, Boston's first free-agent signee, was greeted at Fenway Park with a sign: SELL CAMPBELL, BRING BACK $1.50 BLEACHERS.

Yet free agency gave fans grist for constant speculation, second-guessing, and hope. It sold tickets, as new stars arrived in new cities. It increased competitive balance, in contrast to the predictions of the Cassandra commissioner. It appealed to a very visceral interest. As Arthur Kaminsky, an agent, put it: "Americans are fascinated by money. They love to see and hear the figures these guys sign for, then try to translate those figures into dollars per hit and things like that. Reggie Jackson was always a star, but if he hadn't been the highest-paid star in New York he'd never have been the name he became."

Yes, owners' profits were a little "softer" than before. But most teams were fine, and most indicators showed baseball embarking on a golden age.

No, the real issue was control. The rules of the baseball business had changed radically, but mind-sets hadn't. Players were no longer chattel, but owners still thought of them as such. When young Ozzie Smith held out in the late seventies and his agent said he might seek other lines of work, Joan Kroc, the San Diego owner's wife, had a suggestion: he could be her yard man, she said. "It was an affront for a player to declare free agency," said Don Fehr, then the union's lawyer. "There were some owners who still thought, 'We won *Flood*, so how could all this be happening?' "

Grebey himself was amazed at some of baseball's practices and attitudes. The ownership meetings were overrun by lawyers. Every owner brought one; both leagues brought them; the commissioner's office had them by the gross. What was worse, Grebey thought, hardly any of them were labor lawyers. "A labor lawyer is proactive and these lawyers were reactive," he said years later. "There was a legalistic approach, not a studied strategy."

Grebey saw the owners' labor-relations stance as a three-legged stool. One leg was power; one was money; and one was winning. "It was 'Fuck you, because I'm stronger, because I'm richer, and because I can beat you,' " he said.

Grebey insisted *he* didn't think that way. But he did think he had to start doing what Miller had once done so brilliantly: look a few negotiations out, decide where he wanted to go, and try to get there a bit at a time. He probably couldn't get as much "meaningful compensation" as Howsam craved. But if Miller would concede the owners a player *somewhere* off the twenty-five-man major league roster, that would be a start.

Marvin Miller needed only to hear the very word *compensation* to get his back up. He first heard it in the fall of 1979, at the 21 Club, where Bowie Kuhn had invited him for a drink. The cocktails had barely arrived when Kuhn got to the point. "Marvin," he said, "the owners need a victory."

He recounted how salaries had exploded since the advent of free agency. He rambled on about how this was an experimental system and everybody'd known it in '76. Now it was time to make adjustments. The owners wanted some form of compensation for free agents lost.

Miller's reply was more succinct.

"Bowie," he said, "they'll get compensation over my dead body."

By early 1980, the proposal was on the table. Grebey presented it as the very essence of moderation and reason. A team losing a top player to free agency would get a player in return. Not an equal player, necessarily, but at least a certified big-league player. (That was a far shot removed from an amateur draft choice.) The "premium" free agents, to be called Type A, would be established by an assortment of stats. (For example, they would be ones drafted by eight or more teams.) The signing team could choose fifteen players to protect; all others were vulnerable as compensation picks.

This was no Rozelle Rule, Grebey insisted. In the NFL, Commissioner Pete Rozelle replenished teams losing a free agent with one or more players of equal value from the signing team. That had stopped football free agency dead in its tracks. But according to Grebey, under his plan only a few baseball players would be classified as Type A (that is, liable for compensation). If it had been implemented in 1980, for instance, there would have only been three, he claimed.

"Trust me," said Grebey, "I'm not out to dry up the free-agent market."

The players weren't buying it. Their union leader had done too good a job of teaching them economics. It didn't matter *how* few free agents required compensation; it was *who* they were—the best. Miller had drummed in the lesson in '76: the stars set the pay scale. Tamp down the salaries at the top and everyone else's moved down too. "To me," said Phil Garner, "it became a trade instead of a free-agent signing."

Not that every player was chomping at the bit to *be* a free agent. "You try to move an old tree to California and you just might damage the roots," said Willie Stargell, happy to stay in Pittsburgh.

But the bad old days were still fresh memories to everyone.

Having proudly thrown off their giant shackles, the players felt, why put even tiny ones back on? And if they needed any more reinforcement for their resolve, Miller was happy to provide it. "The owners," he said, "are out to control themselves through you."

Marvin Miller, at sixty-three, was facing his last battle before retirement. It was not one he intended to lose. After all the Jew-baiting, after all the union-bashing, after the wars of '69 and '72 and '76, he was determined to keep his union's gains intact, to retire as the undefeated champion of the players.

He was, further, keenly aware of the general labor climate. A deep recession had the economy—and the nation's major unions—reeling. "Give-backs" were the order of the day. The United Auto Workers had made the biggest: $642 million in wage and benefit concessions to Chrysler to assist the company's federal bailout. Miller wanted the players' union to stand out as the exception. He wanted to affirm his every labor belief. "I was never a give-backer," he says.

Miller took a different approach. He was, by background and nature, a tenacious researcher, and he began researching Ray Grebey. He found him to be loathed by the unions that dealt with GE. They'd felt him to be inflexible and abrupt and had complained bitterly about him to others at the company. In 1973, Grebey was supplanted as chief negotiator in the midst of major contract negotiations. He was subsequently diverted from the bargaining front lines and into other labor matters. Miller relayed his findings to the players: they couldn't trust this guy.

One player-leader needed no briefing. Mark Belanger's mother had worked in a GE plant in Pittsfield, Massachusetts, for more than thirty years and in 1969 had gone through a 102-day strike there. When her son mentioned that an ex–GE negotiator named Grebey had been hired to represent the owners, she blanched.

"Oh, that's the guy who handled the one at GE," she said.

Recalls Belanger: "I knew we were in for a battle."

Ken Moffett was ready to pull his shaggy hair out. The deputy director of the Federal Mediation and Conciliation Service had been called into baseball in late March. The union had set a May 22 strike deadline, and the talks were going nowhere. The owners had asked for a mediator.

Moffett was one of the best in a job requiring the endurance of a long-distance runner (which he was, logging seventy miles a week) and the nerves of a relief pitcher (which he'd once hoped to be, though he admits to a "fastball that should have been arrested for loitering"). But in twenty years' experience, he'd never seen an industry in which so little actual negotiating took place. Yes, meetings were scheduled. He'd set them up in a conference room at the Doral Inn in New York. But here's how a typical day went in room 1706:

- A morning meeting to swap proposals and dissect the day's newspaper accounts of the talks. The two sides argue about who said what to the *New York Times* and the *Washington Post*.
- Break for lunch and press briefings. Spin doctors on each side tell the writers what happened and how outrageous the other side has been.
- Back to the bargaining table for a couple of fruitless hours. Then out.
- Begin fresh the next morning by sniping about what was in the papers. Everything is grandstanding and posturing.

Moffett had originally scheduled seven meetings for the first three weeks of April. By mid-month, however, he gave up. He called a recess until May 6.

The routine remained much the same: petty squabbling over the minor issues, such as the pension and the minimum salary; total stalemate over the 800-pound gorilla of free-agent compensation. They couldn't even talk civilly about how to define a "premium" free agent. The Lords' latest statistical measures would have put half the players in that category. "They started out giving us Rod Carew and Vida Blue as examples of what they meant by premier free agents," fumed Miller. "Now their eleventh-hour proposal includes hitters with .222 averages and pitchers with earned-run averages above six."

"Trust me," Ray Grebey kept saying, "we don't want to take away free agency."

The players *didn't* trust Grebey. He seemed ill at ease with them, and they were likewise with him. "Trust me" got to be a running joke, in fact—playerspeak for a whopper. "Anybody know a good restaurant around here?" someone would ask. Back would come a recommendation and the reassuring words: "Trust me." It never failed to get a howl.

* * *

The days grew short and the players rattled their sabers fiercely. "Any time Marvin Miller whispers 'Strike,' every major league player is going to scream it at the top of his voice," said Rudy May, the Yankees' player rep. "Man, don't the owners know that there's going to be a whole generation of ballplayers' sons who grow up with the middle name Marvin? After all that this man has done for us, who's going to be ungrateful enough not to lose some paychecks if we have to?"

And even if a player happened to be somewhat less than devoted to Miller, he would still have to consider the price of deviation. Asked whether any players might agree with the Lords, George Brett spat: "Anybody who does that is going to spend the rest of his career in the dirt, ducking pitches thrown at his head."

But how strong was the resolve really?

As of mid-May, Red Sox shortstop Rick Burleson figured thirteen of twenty-five Boston players would vote against the strike if they had the chance now. In the Boston clubhouse, he and Dwight Evans openly argued about it. "What it boils down to," Burleson told the outfielder, "is that you've got the big contract and don't want a strike and I don't have the big contract and want the strike."

By now there was a whole generation of players who hadn't been around for the last big strike in 1972. And there were plenty who hadn't lived through the 1976 lockout. There was an increasing stratification of players' salaries and interests. Kansas City catcher Jamie Quirk gave voice to it in one player meeting. "If there are going to be million-dollar players," he asked, "is there any room for hundred-thousand-dollar players?"

Could the center hold? Even Miller wasn't sure.

"Do you think the players can pull off a midseason strike?" he asked Don Fehr.

Fehr frowned and thought and finally said yes.

"We'd better be right," said Miller.

Across America, fans braced for a strike.

In Cincinnati, newspaper columnist Mark Purdy suggested that fans boycott a Reds-Mets game that week and mail their unused tickets to either Miller or Grebey to show their disgust. At least a hundred people did so. In Chicago, after the Cubs finished their last home game before the deadline, the crowd remained in the stands, chanting, "No strike! No strike!"

Edward Bennett Williams was roaming around the ownership

camp chanting the same. The Baltimore Orioles' owner normally loved a good scrap. He was a Washington powerbroker par excellence and America's most famous trial attorney, having fought court battles for infamous clients the likes of Joe McCarthy, Jimmy Hoffa—and George Steinbrenner. But this was one fight he couldn't afford.

Williams didn't own a brewery like Busch, or a drug company like Kauffman. He wasn't a real estate tycoon like Galbreath or a broadcast baron like Autry. He was a lawyer who had leveraged himself to the hilt to get into baseball. He'd paid $11.8 million for the Orioles: $500,000 cash and the rest paper. He'd borrowed against his D.C. real estate holdings and his ownership interest in the Washington Redskins. The games had to keep going, the revenue keep flowing, or he'd be ruined.

Williams had taken this kind of chance because he was taken with the notion of being an owner. He'd been a regular at Toots Shor's, the famous New York sportsman's saloon. He loved rubbing shoulders there with his idol, Joe DiMaggio, and other stars who wandered in. (Toots himself once broke off a conversation with Sir Alexander Fleming, the discoverer of penicillin, upon spying Mel Ott, the great Giants player. " 'Scuse me," he said. "Somebody important just came in.") Sports yielded Williams's even more primal male status and satisfactions than the law. "If you want to have power, own a team," he once advised a fellow lawyer.

He warmed up for baseball by buying 5 percent of the Redskins in the sixties. Despite the slim stake, he effectively controlled the team and thus its tickets, Washington's most valuable social currency. On any given home-game Sunday, Williams's twenty-seat box was loaded with Kennedys, Supreme Court justices, and influential friends like Ben Bradlee.

But Williams far preferred baseball as a game. When Orioles owner Jerry Hoffberger decided to get out, Williams knew he wanted in. What he didn't know when he closed the purchase in October 1979 was how close baseball was to labor war.

He found out at his first ownership meeting—a full-fledged council of war. As a strapped new owner, he wanted no part of it. As a veteran of the NFL's labor battles, he wanted everyone to know he brought some wisdom to the table. But when he tried to question Grebey about strategy, the negotiator cut him off.

"Wait around a little, Mr. Williams, and you'll see how this works," he said.

By May he knew only too well. He thought Grebey was second-rate. He thought the owners' testosterone was getting in the way of their logic. He began putting his silver tongue to work. "This is the wrong issue," he lectured other owners. "The reserve system is Marvin Miller's monument. There's no way he's going to give up what he's gotten."

To anyone who would listen, Williams preached settlement over strike. "This is like nuclear war," he said. "It will only cause permanent damage to both sides."

And he absolutely hounded Bowie Kuhn. "Bowie, we're getting no leadership in this," he said in call after call. "Lead, Bowie. Take charge, Bowie. We are desperate for it. It's going to be on your tombstone: 'Bowie Kuhn, the Commissioner When Baseball Died.' Forget the rest. Just remember one thing. What you do now will be your epitaph."

The spiel finally took. With just two days to go, Kuhn started appearing at negotiating meetings. George Steinbrenner and Astros owner John McMullen started helping Williams talk up strike-averting solutions. But was it already too late?

Deadline day got off to a terrible start. Federal mediator Ken Moffett scheduled a 10:00 A.M. start. Grebey & Co. didn't show up until eleven.

Miller wanted to start off with a batting-practice fastball. Players were concerned that umpires weren't calling games quickly enough in bad weather, he said. They didn't like the increased injury risk. Could the Joint Health and Safety Committee study "appropriate field conditions"?

The Lords' men asked for a recess. They returned twenty-five minutes later. Their answer was no.

Across America, big-league players weren't boarding their scheduled flights for their next games. Word was passed in to Chub Feeney.

"Do you know what's happening in San Francisco?" he blurted. "The Dodgers are scheduled to play the Pirates in Pittsburgh tomorrow—and they *won't get on the plane*."

"I certainly hope they won't," said Miller. "Those are our recommendations."

"There's a *game* tomorrow!" Feeney shouted.

"Not without a settlement," Miller responded.

He turned to Don Fehr and heaved one of his sighs. "They never believe it," he said.

* * *

That afternoon, things suddenly began to happen. Miller, Grebey, Kuhn, and Moffett gave the slip to reporters, going down the freight elevator and over to the Barclay Hotel to meet privately in Grebey's room.

Nothing came of it immediately. Indeed, there was an inordinate amount of chatter about Kuhn's tennis elbow. But by the time the official bargaining was reconvened at five o'clock, the atmosphere had changed. "It was just something you smelled, almost animal-like," recalls Lou Hoynes. "There was some greater willingness to compromise."

Everybody finally agreed on one thing: a roomful of people was no good. Miller and Grebey retreated to the bedroom of Ken Moffett's suite. No lawyers, no notes. Just talk.

Everybody else idly munched on the Goldfish crackers and oatmeal cookies in the suite's living room and settled in to see what would happen. Moffett played blackjack and gin rummy with Fehr and Dick Moss, who'd returned to lend a hand in the crisis. But the real poker was being played in the bedroom, where Miller and Grebey stayed closeted for hours.

At last they emerged. Grebey looked tired but buoyant. Miller looked awful—gray and haggard. Grebey wasn't openly gloating, but he was, as one onlooker put it, "quietly triumphant."

He'd staved off the strike on terms he thought favored the owners. Under the bedroom accord, the two sides would reach agreement that night on every issue but one. That issue—free-agent compensation—would be referred to a player-management study committee.

The committee would issue a report by next January 1. Then the two sides would begin bargaining anew. By February 15, if the matter were still unsettled, the owners could impose their last proposal (namely: allowing signing teams to protect fifteen players and allowing the team losing the free agent to pick any other). The players, in turn, had the right to strike on the issue by June 1. What we had here, in short, was an elaborate process leading right back to square one.

But in Grebey's mind it gave the owners strategic advantage. It was like getting the PLO to recognize Israel's right to exist. The players had signed on to a document that contained the Lords' compensation proposal. Sure it left the union an out for rejecting it next year—but in the meantime the concept was embedded in the agreement and it was the players' burden to remove it. "It established some form of compensation," he later said. "It was finally recognized as legitimate."

In everyone's mind, it was a huge relief. The 1980 season was saved, although it took all night to draft the details. Finally, at about 5:00 A.M., everyone entered the press room to announce the settlement. Bowie Kuhn went from there to the *Today* show to take credit for the unexpected reprieve. The people who'd done all the excruciating drafting work staggered off to sleep.

One of them, Grebey aide Barry Rona, awoke at noon and went groggily into the office. There was Grebey still: he had never gone home. He had, in fact, been very busy.

He'd already sent out a memo to the Lords and a press release to the media. He handed a copy to Rona, who started scanning it, first casually, and then with a mounting sense of alarm. Grebey had, in effect, declared victory.

In 1981, the Clubs' proposal for compensation becomes a part of the Basic Agreement and it cannot be removed without agreement of the two sides.

The AP had already put out a story based on the release. It said the Lords' compensation proposal, based on a formula of freezing fifteen players in exchange for a premium free agent, would be in effect next season.

Rona was sick. Marvin would surely go crazy.

Miller found out about it when the AP called him for comment. He immediately punched the PRC's number and asked Grebey whether he'd seen that blather on the wire.

He waited for Grebey's reply. It was a chuckle.

"What can you do about those people?" he asked, putting the onus on the wire-service reporter.

It was only later, when he saw Grebey's press release, that Miller went truly ballistic. It hadn't been thick-headed writers after all. It was that pig-headed Grebey. In the name of one-upmanship, he'd poisoned the bargaining well. The Lords would think they had the upper hand. The players would think they'd been sold out. Everybody would have to be reeducated.

With public comments and private vitriol, Miller blasted back. "The press release is so horribly inaccurate that I don't know where to begin," he told one writer. "I can only ascribe it to fatigue. They've turned purple into green and night into day."

Grebey was nonplussed. Yes, he'd rushed the memo and release out. But it was only because he didn't want Miller to get his usual jump on spin-control. He was a master at declaring victory and shaping press opinion. "Marvin just couldn't take someone getting a better quote," said Grebey. "It's like a guy who's hit thirty straight home runs and you strike him out."

But Miller's howls had an effect. Suddenly the owners weren't so sure about their man Grebey. Yes, they detested Marvin Miller. But they had never heard him attack Gaherin this way. There might be something to it.

Rona was barraged by calls from owners: "Who's telling the truth here, anyway?"

The young attorney could only do a fast soft-shoe. He was trying to avoid an answer, and hoping desperately the Study Committee would come up with one.

But to some, this was clearly only a lull until the next battle. Ed Williams, wanting access and influence when it came, began cultivating Ken Moffett. In September, when Moffett's Mediation Service colleagues threw him a surprise fiftieth-birthday party at an Orioles game, Williams entertained him royally in his private box.

He was at the top of his form.

"How could an owner be so lucky?" he asked. "I've got Samuel Gompers at third base and John L. Lewis at shortstop." (He was referring to Doug DeCinces and Mark Belanger, two union leaders.)

"How can I make any money?" he groaned, complaining of the discount seats for that night's promotion. "We give away all these tickets to the Little Sisters of the Poor."

Williams also commiserated with Moffett about the idiots in baseball. ("Couldn't run a two-car funeral.") Grebey was a louse and Moffett a saint for putting up with him. "He really knew how to work the crowd, and he was working Ken Moffett," the mediator later recalled. "He could see what was coming in 1981, and he wanted a pipeline."

It was a lovely evening, climaxed by DeCinces and the Orioles players presenting Moffett with a birthday cake and a gift: a black T-shirt emblazoned with the words TRUST ME.

$ 13 $

THE LAST DAYS of Charlie Finley were desperate, even by the standards of this seat-of-the-pants impresario. Denied the $3.5 million from the Rudi-Fingers-Blue sales, and stripped of his dynasty-team talent, he ran his club through the late seventies on pure guile and gall. He had only one scout, having fired the rest in 1978. But he still had his legendary phone.

"Whaddaya hear? Whaddaya hear?"

When those words came through the phone, at all hours, in gravelly, growly tones, baseball men knew exactly who was calling and what was coming. Charlie Finley was about to pick their brains. Amazingly, almost everyone let him. He had the supersalesman's knack of getting his foot in the door, wisecracking his way into their confidence.

"Hey, I can't be on long," Finley might start. "There's a girl pounding on my apartment door." Pause. "She's been trying to get out for two weeks."

Primed and laughing, GMs would tell him whatever he wanted to know: the best prospects in double-A, the lowdown on that left-hander in Cleveland's bull pen, you name it. They thought of Finley more as one of *them* than as part of the ownership class. They were also no match for his cunning.

Once, as a trading deadline approached, Finley repeatedly pestered Cubs GM Salty Saltwell about his outfielder (and a former Oakland hand) Rick Monday. "Charlie wanted Rick back but had nothing no offer," says Saltwell, who was talking about a Monday deal with several other clubs too.

Saltwell was in his hotel room at eleven-thirty, a half-hour from the trading deadline, when Finley called. He prattled on and on, with a medley of small talk and with no mention of Monday. Finally, he asked Saltwell the time.

He looked at the clock. "It's 12:05," he said.

"I gotta go," said Finley.

"Charlie," said a puzzled Saltwell, "why did you call me?"

"If I had you on the phone," chuckled Finley, "I knew nobody else could get to you."

Finley's liquidation sales continued. He sold Vida Blue to Cincinnati for $1.75 million, trying to disguise it as a trade by taking a minor-leaguer named Dave Revering in return. Kuhn voided it (he'd set a $400,000 limit on cash transactions). But the sales of lesser lights for lesser sums continued.

Finley would even try peddling players he didn't have. He once called up Toronto's Peter Bavasi to talk up a veteran shortstop—"great in the clubhouse . . . stabilize that young infield . . . wonderful fella named Dal Maxvill . . ."

"Charlie," said Bavasi, "you released him last week."

"What? What?" Finley stammered. "Must have been something those people in the office did."

"Charlie, you don't have anybody in the office."

He didn't. The A's front-office staff was down to six people. One was a fourteen-year-old gofer named Stanley Burrell, listed on Oakland's organizational chart as a vice president. He was black with a moon face that made him slightly resemble a young Hank Aaron. His nickname became "Hammer." Years later, he would use it for his stage name, when he became rapper MC Hammer.

A teenage vice president was just the way Finley continued to thumb his nose at the establishment. He made Curt Flood one of his broadcasters. Not that anyone could hear him on the A's rinky-dink radio station.

For these reasons and many more, the A's had come to be called the Triple-A's. They were paid like minor-leaguers: a $49,000 average salary in 1978, as compared to the major league average of $121,000. They played like minor-leaguers too, going 54–108 in 1979 to finish a distant last. Total attendance that year was 306,853, or 3,788 lonely souls per game. The scorecards were run off on a mimeograph machine. The vendors sold stubby little pencils for five cents. The press lounge was catered by Kentucky Fried Chicken.

The only thing Finley would spring for was a first-class toupee for himself. A baseball executive called for Finley one day and his secretary said he was out getting a haircut.

"Oh," said the caller, "he doesn't send it out?"

When told about the crack, Finley went ballistic.

All of baseball watched and rooted as Finley tried to unload his sorry franchise. In the late seventies it seemed certain the A's would be sold to Denver oilman Marvin Davis and move to Denver. The big hang-up was Finley's Oakland Coliseum lease. The Coliseum Authority wasn't about to let him break it and skip town scot-free. It would take about $4 million to pay off Finley's obligations.

In the spirit of anything-to-get-rid-of-Finley, baseball took up a collection. Each club would kick in $50,000, for a total of about $1 million. Bob Lurie of the Giants would kick in another $1 million. Marvin Davis would add another $1 million. Finley would contribute the final $1 million. But Finley began welshing on his commitment, the Coliseum Authority began haggling over terms, and the Coliseum's other major tenant got a case of wanderlust too.

In January 1980, Al Davis announced he was moving the NFL Raiders to Los Angeles. Oakland wasn't about to let its one other major league team go. The Marvin Davis deal was kaput. So, it seemed, was baseball's hope of being free of Finley.

Then, suddenly, a miracle! Walter A. Haas, Jr., the sixty-four-year-old Levi Strauss blue-jeans magnate, appeared that summer. He had a warm place in his heart for baseball, as well as for Oakland. He thought it would be a nice romp for his son-in-law, Roy Eisenhardt, and for Haas's son, Wally, who became president and vice president, respectively. Most important, from Finley's perspective, he had hard cash in hand: $12.75 million. Charlie O. took the money and ran.

"During the time we were winning championships, survival was a battle of wits," he said at a valedictory press conference. "We did all right then. But it is no longer a battle of wits but how much can you have on the hip. I can no longer compete."

Bill Veeck was the master showman, the consummate gadfly, and a hilarious writer. In one area, however, he was terrible: timing. Though ahead of his time in the fifties, he reentered baseball at precisely the wrong moment.

On December 5, 1975, Veeck was voted in as the new owner of the Chicago White Sox. On December 23, he was decorating his Christmas tree when word arrived: Peter Seitz had made Andy Messersmith a free agent and turned baseball on its head.

"A flagrant case of life being unfair," Veeck would later write. "For twenty years, I had been telling baseball people that they were doing something illicit with the Constitution and urging them to moderate the reserve clause while they still had the power to shape whatever form and structure the new agreements would take."

Veeck had, of course, been ignored, a pariah in baseball for years, even though he came from good baseball stock. His father, Bill Veeck, Sr., had been president of the Chicago Cubs and a fine operator. The elder Veeck invented Ladies Day and fielded the first club to draw one million. But the younger Veeck, who had been raised in the business, loved mostly to raise eyebrows in the business. "Bill started out on the right side of the tracks and spent his whole life trying to get over to the other side," said his wife, Mary Frances.

The other owners hated him. They hated his constant, zany promotions, which desecrated their game. Veeck made his first splash at age thirty-two, buying the sad-sack Cleveland Indians in 1946 and producing a gimmick a day. One time he stuck S&H green stamps—thousands of them—under certain stadium seats. Then, at a given signal, everyone jumped up and closed their seats to see if they'd won. The crashing of the seats was an exclamation point on the moment's excitement. For his version of Ladies Day, the younger Veeck didn't just offer women the usual discount tickets, he gave each one a gorgeous orchid— "Flown directly from Hawaii!" When a night watchman named Joe Early wrote to complain about special nights for big shots who hardly needed the attention or gifts, Veeck threw a Good Old Joe Early night. Joe got a car, a boat, and more while the throngs cheered.

Veeck thought games should be fun for the non-hardcore fans. He had pregame circus acts and postgame fireworks. He would later develop the "exploding scoreboard," which belched smoke and rockets each time the home team hit a homer. "The other owners looked down their noses at him," recalled Bill Giles, son of Warren Giles and later the Phillies' president. "They thought baseball was too pure for all that."

They also hated him because he wasn't a millionaire country-clubber like them. Veeck was a carney and a hustler, always operating on a shoestring. He had an open-collared shirt and an open door for writers, both of which went against the code of the Lords. It also irked them to see Veeck written up just like he wanted: as the champion of the little guy. He was, in truth, fully as much a business sharpie in his own way as Walter O'Malley.

Veeck was the first to develop the idea of depreciating players for tax purposes. He was the first to put together ownership syndicates, devising a tax-advantaged stock-and-debenture structure that gave investors a dandy capital-gains play. It was one reason he jumped in and out of baseball throughout his adult life. "You don't make money *operating* a baseball club," he sometimes said. "You make money *selling* it."

Indeed. When Veeck sold the Indians in 1949, three years after purchase, he and his investors reaped twenty dollars for every one they invested. Of course, it helped that he'd taken a club that drew 558,000 in 1945 to a major league attendance record of 2.6 million in 1948.

In 1951, he set out to reap the same windfall in St. Louis. The Browns and Cardinals shared the town, a town that wasn't big enough for the both of them. Veeck thought he could make over the hapless Browns, his new club, and drive the Cardinals out of town. It was here that he staged some of his most outrageous stunts: for example, sending midget (three-foot-seven) pinchhitter Eddie Gaedel up to bat, and staging Grandstand Managers Day, when fans decided strategy by waving placards—HIT AWAY, BUNT, and so on. Pointedly, his crosstown rivals even felt compelled to change their motto: "The Cardinals, A Dignified St. Louis Institution."

Then something terrible happened. Fred Saigh, the Cardinals' owner, was convicted of tax evasion. That wasn't the terrible part. The terrible part was that he had to sell the club, and Gussie Busch bought it. The Anheuser-Busch chief was at once Mister St. Louis and Mister Moneybags. The Cardinals were soon revived and Veeck was soon in trouble.

By 1953, Veeck was in such dire straits that he came up with his ultimate promotional idea: Creditors Day. Everybody owed money would be admitted to the park free and allowed to cut up the day's receipts.

Veeck never did it, but he did get busy plotting his escape to a new city. His best shot was Baltimore, but his prickly relations with the Lords would come back to haunt him. In particular, Veeck had been feuding with the Yankees, the most powerful club in the American League. Partly it was because he thought good feuding was good business. Fans responded to rivalries and bought tickets; partly he genuinely couldn't stomach Yankee owners Dan Topping and Del Webb—or their GM, George Weiss.

"Bill, you've got to stop needling these guys," warned Frank Lane, then the White Sox GM. "They'll find a way to get even with you."

They did. The American League allowed the Browns to move to Baltimore, but on one condition: that Veeck sell them. He did.

One thing about Bill Veeck, though: he was as much a pain out of baseball as in it. After a brief return to run the White Sox (1959–61), he wrote a book called *Veeck as in Wreck*. It told all the Lords' secrets and punctured all their pretensions. A few years later, when Marvin Miller needed witnesses for Curt Flood, there was Bill Veeck, testifying against the reserve system. The Lords wanted him never to darken their door again. He took up the life of a country squire on Maryland's Eastern Shore, raising his nine children. When he got bored, he ran Boston's Suffolk Downs racetrack in the late sixties, dreaming up events like the Ben Hur Handicap (a chariot race) and the Lady Godiva Handicap (an all-female-jockey race, or, as Veeck advertised it, "Eight Fillies on Eight Fillies").

But in the fall of '75, he was back knocking at the Lords' door once more. White Sox owner John Allyn was in desperate straits, hardly able to meet his payroll late in that season. Veeck put together a group to buy 80 percent of the White Sox from him for $8 million—Veeck's usual mulligan stew of stocks and debentures, intended to maximize his investors' tax advantages.

There were three problems with his bid. First, the Lords preferred to see the White Sox go to Seattle and thus resolve a thorny legal problem—Seattle was still suing baseball for allowing its Pilots to leave. Second, they didn't understand the stock-debenture structure. Third, they didn't like Bill Veeck any more in the 1970s than they did in the 1960s. Perhaps even less, due to his testimony at the Flood trial. "He knocked the game and now he wants to reenter it," growled Gene Autry. "I can't bring myself to vote for a man like that."

In late November, the American League owners voted to reject Veeck: 8–3, with one abstention. When Veeck threatened to sue, the Lords made him a proposition: if he changed the debentures to preferred stock and raised another $1.2 million in capital, they'd reconsider at the winter meetings in Florida the following week.

Veeck went right to work. He began canvassing Chicago for more money. He assigned a team of lawyers to frantically redraw the investors' agreements. He was backed by a televised Save-the-Sox pep-talk from Mayor Daley. Veeck finally pushed it over the top by sacrificing himself. He gave up his own 15 percent stake—his interest for putting the deal together—in order to boost the other investors' equity. Then he told his wife,

Mary Frances, what he'd done. "What you're telling me," she said to him, "is that it isn't an investment anymore, it's a vendetta."

To the Lords' amazement, Veeck entered the winter meetings with everything they'd asked. He was still turned down. He'd turned around the vote to 8–3 in favor (again with one abstention), but the bid needed three-quarters approval, or nine votes.

Then an unlikely ally came to Veeck's defense. It was John Fetzer, the Tigers' owner and the very epitome of the baseball establishment. A young UPI reporter named Bill Madden was listening through the wall from an adjacent room and took down his words:

"I've been in the league for twenty years, and over that time I've seen one slipshod thing after another. We rush in here to vote and then rush out to get drinks. We've done more soul-searching on this deal than at any time before, and now that it has been set, we have left these people over a barrel. We told them to go do it and they did it. We've got to be men about this. Look, I don't like it any more than you do that we're allowing a guy in here who has called me an SOB over and over. But, gentlemen, we're just going to have to take another vote."

They did, and Veeck was approved, 10–2.

He descended to a raucous press conference, entering with a triumphant kick of his wooden leg and a broad smile. "I hope it's as much fun as I expect it to be," said Veeck. "It's not often a one-legged sixty-one-year-old man gets started again in a new go-around doing something he loves."

Veeck patched together a staff of old warhorses and young kids. There was Rudie Schaffer, his sidekick of forty years, to handle the business-end nuts and bolts. There was Paul Richards, the wizened Wizard of Waxahachie, to manage. On the other extreme was his twenty-five-year-old son, Mike Veeck, a shaggy-haired rock musician, and David Dombrowsky, who'd come to Hemond researching his college thesis and hired on for $8,000 a year. He did everything from running the scoreboard to signing prospects. About the latter, the old owner had just one piece of advice for the kid: "Sign 'em for as little as you can. Remember, we don't have any money."

They really didn't. The 1976 White Sox lost a lot of money—$670,000 on revenues of only $6 million—and a lot of games—a league-high ninety-seven. "By the fifth inning," recalled Chicago pitcher Ken Brett, "we were selling hot dogs to go."

Before the 1977 season, Hemond had to trade shortstop Bucky Dent to the Yankees for three players and $400,000. The key was the 400 grand. Without it, the gates at Comiskey couldn't have opened for the season.

The Dent deal did, however, mark the first appearance of what Veeck called his "rent-a-player" strategy. The White Sox were willing to trade for a player with one year to go until free agency. It was short-term thinking, but such is the way of the hustler. "What the heck," Veeck told Hemond. "We'll provide our fans with an entertaining club for that long, anyway."

So the White Sox got slugger Oscar Gamble for Dent. At about the same time, they got slugger Richie Zisk from Pittsburgh for Goose Gossage and Terry Forster. Gossage, in particular, would go on to become a world-class reliever. But, Veeck reasoned, nobody bought tickets to watch relievers.

It looked like the 1977 White Sox had a ticket to nowhere. This was baseball's first year A.M. (after *Messersmith*). While the players' average salary had jumped 41 percent, to $74,000, the strapped White Sox players only averaged $65,000. The rich teams had gobbled up the star free agents—Reggie Jackson and Don Gullett to the Yankees; Joe Rudi, Don Baylor, and Bobby Grich to the Angels—and their annual payrolls now topped $3 million. The White Sox had to settle for discards like Steve Stone and Eric Soderholm. Their payroll was $1.6 million. In short, the Yankees were supposed to clean up and the White Sox were supposed to give up.

Instead, the rent-a-player Sox were a wonder. Some one hundred games into the 1977 season, they led the Western Division by six and a half games and had a better record than the Yankees. They were called the South Side Hit Men, and would eventually hit a team-record 192 home runs. The biggest bopper, Richie Zisk, was the AL's consensus first-half MVP and the darling of Chicago's huge Polish community.

The Poles, and many more, jammed Comiskey to the rafters that summer. The fans' noise was deafening. They wouldn't stop cheering a particularly heroic home run until the hitter reappeared to wave. (The dugout curtain call was to become a staple all around the bigs.) They would sing fortissimo to opponents' departing pitchers: "Nah-nah-nah-nah, nah-nah-nah-nah, hey, hey, goodbye." (It gave the rock group Steam a whole new outlet for its one hit, "Kiss Him Goodbye.")

The White Sox eventually faded to third, but their record was still a respectable 90–72. They drew a club-record 1.7 million fans, and Veeck was named baseball's Executive of the Year. It would turn out to be his last hurrah.

The name players moved on that winter. Zisk took a ten-year, $3 million deal with Texas. Gamble, however, actually seemed signable for a while. Soon after the season, Veeck offered $300,000. A month later, Gamble had gotten no better offers—nor should he have. He'd enjoyed a great season, hitting 31 homers and batting .297. But he'd had only a mediocre career before '77 as a part-timer with a .256 lifetime batting average. Gamble's agent called Chicago to see if the offer was still good. Veeck said he'd make it even better: three years at $350,000 per.

Gamble was all set to sign when his agent put the brakes on. The Padres had called and they should at least hear them out, he said. When Gamble and the agent met with owner Ray Kroc, they couldn't belive their ears.

"I'm offering you $2.85 million over six years," said Kroc. "But you've got to take it or leave it right now. I'm not going to let you guys get me into a bidding war."

Gamble and his agent retreated to another room, purportedly to mull it over. In actuality, they exploded with glee. Their laughter could be heard throughout the Padres' front office. The sound that echoed throughout baseball was more like an A-bomb blast. *Three million dollars for Oscar Gamble?* That was Reggie Jackson money. That was Goose Gossage money (he was that year's top free agent). The price of even so-so outfielders had just gone out of the ballpark—at least Bill Veeck's low-budget one.

The White Sox slipped back to 71–90 in '78. The cupboard was bare of tradeable talent to procure a rent-a-player. The White Sox could only afford four farm teams, and the owner occasionally slipped into black moods. "We are doomed," Veeck told the Twins' Calvin Griffith, another old-style shoestring operator. "We are the last dinosaurs in a forest where there are no more trees to feed on."

It wasn't that Veeck resisted change. As an iconoclast, he'd urged it for years. As a hustler, he rather enjoyed a wide-open market. He even got along splendidly with players' agents, the bane of other veteran baseball men.

Jim Bronner and Bob Gilhooley, two Chicago-based agents, would show for a 10:00 A.M. meeting with Veeck. The three would talk about everything under the sun for hours, while Veeck chain-smoked Salems and knocked back beers. (You had to start early to put away a case a day, as he did.) Invariably, the afternoon shadows had grown long before Veeck finally said, "Now, what was it you guys were here for?"

It was usually to talk up some marginal player, the kind Veeck could afford. Also, he was a sucker for comebacks. "If you were trying to recover from something, he'd always give you a chance," said Bronner.

(One Bronner-Gilhooley reclamation case turned out to be a star of that magical '77 team. Third baseman Eric Soderholm recovered from a severe knee injury to hit twenty-five homers and win AL Comeback of the Year honors.)

But it was wearying to be in a hopelessly disadvantaged position. The ragtag front-office staff of twenty were always flying by the seat of their pants. ("Don't worry about doing a budget," Veeck told Roland Hemond. "We don't have any money.") And they were always working, except when they were in their oak-paneled lounge on the press-box level. It was called the Bard's Room and it was the perk for pulling this kind of duty.

Bill Veeck held court there every night, running an open house and open tap for every scout, writer, and broken-down baseball man in town. He would lead rambling discussions on everything under the sun, though he had everyone overmatched on any subject but baseball. Veeck read four or five books a week while soaking his stump and knew something about almost everything.

But mostly the Bard's Room crowd talked baseball. Argued baseball, actually, because Veeck loved a good argument. He would posit that Buddy Bell was better than George Brett just to get one going. Old friends knew how to sidestep him. ("Bill, you may be right," Paul Richards would demur.) But young Turks always took the bait. Tony LaRussa, who got his first big-league coaching and managing job from Veeck, argued until he was blue in the face.

As the wee hours turned into the not-so-wee hours, Roland Hemond would try to sneak out to go home. "I tell people I worked for Bill Veeck five years, but it was really ten, because I never slept," he says.

Out of those Bard's Room nights were born ideas: trades, schemes, and, above all, *promotions*. Veeck never stopped trying to promote his way out of the hole. He brought in circus acts, as always. He staged Shakespeare Night, featuring a couple of scenes from the Bard. He had ethnic nights for just about every group in polyglot Chicago. All were impeccably politically correct, of course. Take, for instance, Mexico Fiesta Night, for which coach and ex-player Minnie Minoso dressed up as a matador and took on a fellow in a bull costume.

To Veeck, music was always a natural. It was his idea to have Harry Caray sing "Take Me Out to the Ballgame" during the seventh-inning stretch. He once built a whole promotion around that stretch anthem. On Music Night at Comiskey, anyone with an instrument got a half-price ticket; anyone without got a complimentary kazoo. In the middle of the seventh, the Chicago Symphony Orchestra's associate conductor mounted a podium at home plate in white tie and tails and led the crowd in "Take Me Out to the Ballgame."

Mike Veeck was always pushing for postgame rock concerts. Veeck *père* hated the music, but Veeck *fils* could usually talk his cash-starved dad into it with a promise. "I can give you $300,000 with three rock-and-roll shows."

He delivered, though it was offensive to baseball purists and hell on the playing field. David Dombrowsky was once trying to sign a prospect and brought him to Comiskey, hoping an intimate look at the majestic park would clinch the deal. They walked out of the dugout and saw—sand. All of right field was covered with it. The grounds crew was trying desperately to undo the effects of a concert trampling. Chicago once had to forfeit a game, on a perfectly fine day, due to its unplayable field.

Perhaps the worst music-related abuse of the Comiskey turf occurred on July 12, 1979: the legendary Anti-Disco Night. Admission was ninety-eight cents (a nod to the promotion's cosponsor, WLUP FM-98) *and* a disco record. The records would be collected and blown up on the field between games of a twi-night doubleheader. "It was my mistake," Mike Veeck later admitted. "It simply worked too well."

Some 50,000 paid customers filled Comiskey to the rafters. About 5,000 more rushed the gates and entered unpaid. Another 15,000 were outside, clamoring to get in, and yet another 20,000 were stuck in a hopeless traffic jam on the Dan Ryan Expressway, trying to reach the park.

The first game went fine, though the pervasive smell of marijuana suggested that this was not a traditional baseball crowd. The problem came at the climactic moment, when the WLUP disc jockey blew up thousands of records. Imbued with anti-disco fervor and pot, the youthful crowd began pouring over the railings and onto the field in waves. They slid into bases, ran randomly around the outfield, pulled the batting cage from behind the center-field wall and destroyed it.

Chicago's mounted police were ready to storm the park and restore order. Bill Veeck, fearing their horses and billy clubs would only make things worse, refused to help. But his own puny security force of seventeen was no match for the mob. He stood at home plate with a microphone, pleading over and over: "Please get off the field. . . . Please get off the field."

Suddenly, he looked every bit an old, irrelevant man. The bedlam continued around him, the kids ignoring the owner until they finally ran themselves out. The field was strewn with shards of disco records. An occasional record sailed down from the stands. The umpires declared the second game a forfeit to the Tigers.

Veeck *was* getting old. He'd put in four hard years since buying the Sox and was now sixty-five. The game hadn't necessarily passed him by. He still had the most fertile mind around for game-day promotions. But at a time when other clubs had begun to market season tickets hard—and tap a new revenue stream—the White Sox did little. Veeck was firmly committed to the good old Joe Earlys of the world. He couldn't abide wooing the corporate crowd that bought the season tickets. (Veeck even balked at son Mike's idea of converting an old press box into a "party suite," which they could make available to companies for $1,000 a game. He relented when Mike projected the revenues for a season. "This is an extra $70,000," he said. "We can pay Chet Lemon with that!")

At a time, moreover, when some clubs were starting to rake in big money for their TV rights, Veeck had no idea—no interest in, really—how to exploit the nation's number-two TV market. "Bill wasn't familiar with what a club should get from TV revenue," says Jack Gould, one of his investors and later a White Sox executive. "He had WGN and he was getting peanuts."

Indeed, Veeck spent less time on local TV matters than he did complaining to Bowie Kuhn's office about national TV. Veeck constantly badgered Kuhn's broadcast aide, Tom Villante, about how network games hurt his gate. To him, the turnstile count was still the thing.

It was only one way Veeck reestablished himself in baseball as a royal pain. When the Lords locked the players out of spring training camps in 1976, Veeck opened Chicago's to minor-leaguers and free agents. When Anti-Disco Night exploded, everyone rolled their eyeballs. Ray Grebey, who'd befriended this fellow Kenyon College man, once asked for a moment of silence for Veeck at an ownership meeting. Veeck was undergoing surgery that day and Grebey thought it would be a nice gesture. He then discovered the extent of anti-Veeck feeling. After the meeting, one of the owners approached him. "If you ever pay a public compliment to that guy again, you're fired," Grebey was told.

Veeck's health *was* failing. He had chronic emphysema, resulting from his four-pack-a-day cigarette habit. He had chronic infections in his leg stub, requiring annual operations. He was going deaf and his hearing aid sometimes whistled. "The good news is that with a little deft fingerwork on the adjustment, I can play a fair approximation of 'Yankee Doodle Dandy,'" Veeck said. "The bad news is that I can no longer creep up on mine enemies, unawares."

He was troubled by worsening health and deepening gloom. As Chicago's losses widened, he could have gone back to the well for more capital from his partners: deep-pocket types like industrialist Lester Crown. But it was a point of pride with him: he'd never turned to them for a bailout and he'd always turned them a profit. "He simply wouldn't go back to his investors for more money," says Andy McKenna, who was one of them.

So Veeck started looking to sell. He put out feelers to Denver, but that was still Finley country. He dickered with Edward DeBartolo, the big shopping-center developer. In August 1980, Veeck agreed to sell him the club for $20 million, but American League owners, encouraged by Kuhn, refused to approve the transaction. They voted down DeBartolo twice, for two stated reasons: he wasn't local and he owned racetracks. The real reason was that he was reputed to have some unsavory associates—Italian-American, don't you know. As Bowie Kuhn put it over cocktails while lobbying a baseball executive, "He's not RP." Come again? "Right people."

DeBartolo and his people screamed bloody murder about anti-Italian prejudice. But what's the use of an antitrust exemption if you can't use it to control membership in the club?

Veeck wasn't just disgusted, he was discouraged. As Dave Winfield prepared for his walk down the runway as 1980's top free agent, he sent out a form letter to seventeen clubs. Reduced to its essence, it said: *Forget it. I want to play with a winner in a big market. You are a loser and/or a small market. Don't bother drafting me.* One of these letters went to the White Sox.

"It had a profound impact on Dad; it was deeply disturbing to him," says Mike Veeck. "It said, 'You're off the track before you could ever get on.' It didn't even give you a chance to structure a deal."

If Bill Veeck couldn't deal his way out of a corner, he didn't want to be in baseball. One month after the final rejection of DeBartolo, Veeck gladly accepted the next offer that came along. It was from two young men named Jerry Reinsdorf and Eddie Einhorn.

Reinsdorf, forty-four, was the Brooklyn-born son of a peddler of used sewing machines. As an IRS lawyer in the sixties, he'd learned all about tax shelters. As cofounder of Balcor Company in the early seventies, he constructed them. Balcor would raise $650 million from investors for real estate partnerships. If Reinsdorf played a little fast and loose—and what syndicator didn't?—he was also a forerunner of the 1980s man. When one baseball executive asked Reinsdorf his business, he replied, "OPM." Pardon? "Other people's money," he smiled.

Einhorn, also forty-four, was a law-school classmate of Reinsdorf and a syndicator of another kind. In the 1960s, he bought the TV rights to the basketball games of several Midwest colleges—Notre Dame, Marquette, and some others—and packaged them up to sell to local TV stations. "Fast Eddie," as the hyperactive Einhorn was known, went national in 1968, when he landed the big UCLA–Houston game. Hoops fans remember it as the game when Houston broke UCLA's forty-seven-game winning streak. TV people remember it as the game when Fast Eddie was screaming into the phone at halftime: "We've got avails [commercial time available] in the second half! We've got avails in the second half!"

Both men loved baseball. Reinsdorf's office resembled a Brooklyn Dodgers memorabilia museum. Einhorn, according to his partner, "would drive two hundred miles to see two high school teams play." But both were primarily business creatures. Reinsdorf put together an OPM deal to buy the club. He wanted to make a baseball syndicate pay off as surely as a real estate one. He just thought it would be more fun. Einhorn saw the White Sox as ripe for pay TV. He would pull most of their games off free TV and put them on a subscription service, to be called SportsVision.

They were sharpies in a wholly different way than Veeck,

who instantly recognized this fact. In ceremonies to close the sale, he handed over the keys to Comiskey Park.

"Now Calvin is the last of the dinosaurs," he said.

Change swept Comiskey instantly. The old seat-of-the-pants operation was now harnessed by accounting and budgeting systems. The exploding scoreboard was replaced by a Diamond-Vision screen. The Bard's Room was converted into office space, and the old owner was treated rather shabbily. "We're going to make this a first-class operation," announced Eddie Einhorn.

Bill Veeck would never again set foot in Comiskey Park. He would see out his days across the city, in the bleachers of Wrigley Field. The Cubs had changed hands too—bought from Bill Wrigley in 1981 by the Tribune Company, whose superstation, WGN, carried the Cubs. Like Ted Turner, this media conglomerate saw the value of baseball as programming. Owning the Cubs would make this a nice, vertically integrated operation. But Wrigley Field was as much a throwback as ever, the place where, as a boy, Veeck had planted the outfield walls' vines. It gave some comfort to Veeck, who'd spent a lifetime jousting with the old-line Lords but left more bitter at the new boys.

By 1981, more than one third of the clubs had owners with less than five years in baseball. They had very different means and markets. But they had common traits: ego, involvement, and ignorance.

First of all: *ego*. They wanted to win and they wanted to preen. They were creatures of the dawning eighties. For decades, baseball had been an old-money business. Owners held their teams partly as a hobby, partly as a civic trust. Now new money was coursing in, with a "see me" mentality. Seagram's heir Charles Bronfman, the Expos' owner, figured he heard it summed up perfectly once. He ran into a fellow who mentioned he was trying to buy a pro sports team. Bronfman, himself struggling to make a go of the Expos, asked him why. Said he, "I'm rich but nobody knows it."

Then there was the question of *involvement*. The old-line Lords let the GMs run their clubs. But, drawn by the spotlight, the new boys waded right in. They were entrepreneurs, used to hands-on action. They were also quite inexperienced.

Which brings us to *ignorance*. Baseball men knew success was built on good scouting, good drafting, good farm systems.

It took time and cultivation. The new boys didn't know it and didn't want to know it. "Patience is for losers," said George Argyros, the Mariners' new boy.

Seattle, Texas, and Houston—new boys' clubs all—formed a "combine" to pool scouting information. They also leaned heavily on the Major League Scouting Bureau, created in baseball by 1974 to augment individual clubs' scouts. All this enabled them to slash their own scouting staffs.

It also made the new boys pigeons for sharp players' agents. Preferring instant gratification to player development, they made loopy deal after loopy deal. If Ray Kroc wasn't signing Oscar Gamble for $2.85 million, Brad Corbett was matching the sum with Richie Zisk. If Ted Turner wasn't signing Al Hrabosky for $2.2 million, John McMullen was signing Nolan Ryan for $4.5 million.

It was the Ryan contract, signed with the Astros in late 1979, that broke the $1 million barrier and finally broke Bill Veeck's spirit. Nolan Ryan wouldn't attain national monument status until years later. At the time he was considered just a hard-throwing underachiever. Said Mike Veeck: "It was the high price of mediocrity that bothered Dad."

Price was no object to John J. McMullen. He'd entered baseball under George Steinbrenner, the dean of the new boys and a fellow player in the maritime business. McMullen had parlayed a Ph.D. in engineering—he preferred to be called *Doctor* McMullen—into a thriving mini-conglomerate that included naval architecture, real estate, cable TV, and more. When Steinbrenner bought the Yankees, McMullen was a limited partner, an experience he once summed up famously: "There's nothing quite so limited as being a limited partner of George Steinbrenner's."

But he'd gotten a whiff of what majority ownership brought: fame, status, and, if your team won, acclaim. John McMullen was a household name only in the McMullen household, and he was determined to change that. He bought the Astros in 1979 from the Ford Credit Company, which had seized them from the physically and fiscally ailing Judge Roy Hofheinz.

McMullen had known little about baseball before becoming an owner. "What's an RBI?" he asked, early on. On another occasion, he was leafing through *The Sporting News* and observed, "Hey, this has a lot of good baseball stories."

But in a short while he came to consider himself a world-class expert. Ace reliever Dave Smith gave up just one home run in 1980, but it came in a game at Shea Stadium, with McMullen watching. "Get rid of that guy," the owner barked.

The Astros were an aggressive, running club, its players schooled in taking the extra base. But when one of them was thrown out, McMullen would "go ballistic," recalls Tal Smith, then Houston's GM. At one point, McMullen demanded that third base coach Bob Lillis be fired. Smith quietly transferred Lillis to first base coaching rather than fire him.

Smith had been with the Astros from the start, except for a brief stint with the Yankees. He had been president and GM since 1975, and he ran a tight ship. He believed in keeping base salaries low and loading up contracts with motivating incentives. The Astros had Jose Cruz at a base of just $250,000, Cesar Cedeno at $220,000, and J.R. Richard at $200,000. They ran a strong second to Cincinnati in the NL West in 1979 with the league's lowest payroll.

The J. R. Richard contract was a good display of Smith's handiwork. By 1979, James Rodney Richard had blossomed into one of the game's elite pitchers. He was six feet eight inches of pure heat who had struck out fifteen men in his first big-league game and gone on from there. In 1978, he'd led the league with 303 strikeouts and racked up his third straight season with 18 or more wins. At the conclusion of the 1979 season, he qualified to become a free agent.

If Richard was baseball's top power pitcher, Tom Reich (pronounced: *rich*) was its top power agent. He was a brassy, bearded Pittsburgh lawyer who was very good at what he did. He would eventually represent one of every six major-leaguers, with a heavy emphasis on black and Latino players. Reich had been an agent for ten years—starting out before there was a whiff of money in it—and he knew all the tricks. In the case of a star client who was nearing free agency and enjoying a great year, Reich's gambit was to stall for time and make a GM sweat.

This is precisely what Reich was doing for Richard. J. R. was on a pace to lead the league in strikeouts (he again broke 300) and ERA (he wound up at 2.71) and would again reach 18 wins (18–13). Reich and Tal Smith huddled all over the country throughout that season, meeting to argue the merits of J. R. Richard wherever the Astros happened to be playing.

They finally settled it in Reich's backyard—in Pittsburgh, during the Pirates-Orioles World Series. Smith had to give ground on the contract length: five years, which was longer than he liked. But he'd managed to keep the base salary at $200,000, with the Astros' usual Christmas tree of incentives: bonuses for innings pitched, Cy Young Awards, and more. If J. R. Richard shot the moon, the package could max out at $800,000 a year.

Two weeks later, the Astros signed Nolan Ryan for $1 million a year. No incentives, no contingencies, just seven big figures a year for three years, guaranteed. Tal Smith, of course, had nothing to do with it. Dick Moss, Ryan's agent, had dealt directly with Astros owner McMullen, who gave Ryan the store and in return got the attention he craved. It was baseball's first million-per-year contract, making headlines not just in Houston but nationwide.

The attention from baseball men was less than adoring. GMs were queued up on Tal Smith's phone line to ask *what the fuck the Astros were thinking.* Yes, Ryan had led baseball in strikeouts with the Angels but he'd also led it in walks. Yes, he'd pitched four no-hitters but he'd pitched only .500 ball for his career. Asked how he'd replace Ryan, who'd gone 16–14 in '79, a nonplussed Buzzie Bavasi said, "I guess I'll have to sign two 8–7 pitchers."

Smith too was mortified. He figured four teams would bid on Ryan, tops, and he figured him for $650,000, tops. The top-paid players in baseball were Pete Rose, at $805,000; Rod Carew, $800,000; and Dave Parker, $775,000. Ryan wasn't the equal of any of them. Nevertheless, with no other offers on the table and the Astros bidding against themselves, he'd landed the first $1 million contract. Others would soon follow. "It broke an enormous psychological barrier," said Don Fehr of the players' union.

It also broke Tal Smith's eardrum when Tom Reich got him on the phone. The moment Reich heard about the Ryan deal, he called Smith, began screaming at him, and didn't stop until the GM agreed to renegotiate J. R. Richard. A few weeks later, the two met with McMullen and drew up a new contract: a guaranteed $800,000 a year for four years. (The guarantee turned out to be important. In July 1980, Richard suffered a stroke and never pitched again.)

The Astros' salary structure, constructed so carefully by Smith, was left in shambles, as if a fierce hurricane had blown in off the Gulf. "Ryan completely destroyed all the parameters we'd established with J. R., Cruz, and all these other people," Smith recalled.

The 1980 Astros were not only richer but better. They won

the National League West and very nearly the pennant. (The Phillies took a riveting five-game playoff series, winning the last game in extra innings.) They drew a record 2.3 million fans. And they provided all the instant gratification a new boy could want—except for the credit.

That went to Tal Smith, who was lauded by the Houston press and the baseball world in general. McMullen seethed. They clashed. When the GM got into a crossfire between McMullen and his investor partners, who were feuding, he was gone. He was fired in October, shortly before being named *The Sporting News*'s Executive of the Year.

That winter McMullen paid big for another free-agent pitcher, Don Sutton: four years, $3.5 million. Sutton, who'd spent his first fifteen years in the bigs with L.A., was asked what had become of his loyalty to Dodger blue. "Loyal?" said Sutton. "I'm the most loyal player money can buy."

Up the road, in suburban Dallas, Brad Corbett was the first of the new boys to flame out. He'd started out behind the eight ball and never operated from any other position.

Corbett bought the Texas Rangers from Bob Short in 1974 for $9 million, but he hadn't bought much. His club had no TV revenue. Short, in a typically desperate move, had sold the first ten years' broadcast rights to the city of Arlington, Texas, for $7.5 million. His club had few premium-priced tickets to sell. Of the 35,000 capacity, 19,000 seats were bleachers. Corbett's own resources were limited. He was thirty-six years old, and sufficiently full of himself to be a self-described "Fort Worth industrialist," but he was rich only in relation to Bob Short.

Nonetheless, Corbett spent the late seventies signing big-name players and spending himself into oblivion. He operated, as Bill Veeck put it, "in the desperate hope of coming up with a winner before the train hit him." Corbett's GM, Dan O'Brien, put it another way: "We spent money like we had it."

The Rangers' Hall of Shame included:

- A five-year, $950,000 contract for the thirty-five-year-old shortstop, Bert Campaneris (signed in '76).
- A ten-year, $3 million contract for one-dimensional slugger Richie Zisk (signed in '77).
- A four-year, $1 million deal (signed in '77) for Doc Medich, certainly a better doctor than a pitcher. The Rangers got a sec-

ond four years from this M.D., at $50,000 per, as the team's "medical adviser."

- A $5.1 million contract (signed in '80) for catcher Jim Sundberg, stunning terms for a middling backstop ($500,000 per season as a player for six years, to be followed by ten years as a broadcaster and promotions man).

Sundberg readily—eagerly—accepted the deal laid before him, but Corbett's own executive board overruled it. Sundberg had to settle for a straight six-year contract as a player for a total of $3 million. Still, a pretty handsome arrangement.

And the trades. Oh, the trades. Corbett's baseball men tried to save him from folly. ("I was Brad's no-man," said Dan O'Brien. " 'No, don't do that! No, not him!' ") It did no good. Wily executives on other clubs employed the same tactic as wily agents: go around the GM and get right to the owner.

Early in the 1977 season, for instance, the Toronto Blue Jays wanted to trade for Rangers third baseman Roy Howell. He was a promising young player, and Eddie Robinson, another Corbett-era GM, insisted on value in return: say, pitcher Jim Clancy and some prospects. Toronto GM Pat Gillick balked and the talks foundered until Gillick mentioned something to his club's president, Peter Bavasi.

"You know," said Gillick. "Brad Corbett loves Jim Mason."

Mason was a shortstop of such modest talent he couldn't crack Toronto's lineup. And this was a club that would lose 108 games that year. But, Gillick explained to Bavasi, Mason *did* play one thing regularly: golf, with Corbett, in the off-season.

Bavasi chuckled evilly. He checked the Rangers' schedule. They should be en route to Detroit. He called Eddie Robinson's office. Was he in? No, said his secretary, he was traveling with the team. He'd be out of contact for six hours or so. The coast was clear. Bavasi called Corbett in Fort Worth.

"Hey, Brad, we're trying to conclude the Roy Howell deal with Eddie," he said.

"Oh."

"You know we're damned close, but he wants this player that I don't want to give up."

"Doesn't he want some of your farm prospects?"

"No, he wants Jim Mason."

"Oh, I like Mason. He's a real good friend."

"Well, he's quite a player, too: real competitive, great leadership skills, I'd hate to give him up," Bavasi lied. "But I'd like to conclude this deal. Owner to owner, now, if I give you Mason can we do this deal?"

"Oh, I'd better not. It sounds good to me, but I've got to talk to Eddie."

"Brad, I can't wait, and frankly I'm surprised. Back in the old days the top guys used to make these decisions themselves. Aren't you the owner? Isn't Eddie your employee? Look, I'll throw in Steve Hargan [a broken-down pitcher] and two hundred thousand dollars with Mason."

"Oh, son of a bitch—I'll make the deal."

Bavasi quickly announced it so Robinson wouldn't have a chance to reverse it. Howell hit .316 that year for the Jays, leading the team in batting average. He went on to a fine major league career. Mason hit .218 and played 36 games for the Rangers that year. He was out of baseball by 1979.

Corbett himself was out of baseball by 1980. He sold the Rangers for a mere $4 million—but then, the buyer was also taking on $21 million in deferred salary obligations.

A man named Eddie Chiles led the buying group. He was a Fort Worth oilman who had also gained some regional renown as a conservative radio commentator. His broadcasts always started with the words, "I'm mad."

Before long, he would be mad at baseball.

Al Hrabosky was the made-for-TV relief pitcher. He wore a menacing Fu Manchu mustache. He stood behind the mound between hitters, facing the center-field camera and visibly psyching himself up for his next opponent. Then he'd whirl and purposefully stalk back up the mound. He was a great act and an okay reliever, and he was known as "The Mad Hungarian."

Naturally, Ted Turner had to have him. He'd coveted Hrabosky for some time. In 1976, it will be recalled, he'd gotten in trouble for exhorting Hrabosky, "Don't sign!" Turner was eventually suspended as a repeated tampering offender and Hrabosky ended up staying with the Cardinals in 1976. He was traded to Kansas City in 1977, and came up for free agency again after the 1979 season. Along the way, he'd also lost a yard off his fastball. Turner didn't care. Hrabosky was great TV, and Turner was less in the baseball than the TV business.

As a team, the Braves were terrible. In Turner's first three years, they finished last in the National League West each time. But as programming, they were hot. The SuperStation, launched in early 1977, was soon adding 200,000 cable subscribers a month. It spread like wildfire across the vast rural areas of the country with no local TV stations or home baseball teams. Starved for alternatives to network shows, Turner proved people would watch *Beverly Hillbillies* reruns. He also proved that, starved for baseball beyond the *Game of the Week*, people would watch bad baseball.

At one point, an *Atlanta Constitution* columnist wrote that he doubted anybody was watching the wretched Braves on the SuperStation. Play-by-play announcer Skip Caray mentioned this on the air and invited viewers to call the newspaper. Their calls swamped the *Constitution's* switchboard.

A lot of calls were coming into Bowie Kuhn's office too, but not from devoted viewers. "What the hell is this?" yowled George Steinbrenner from Tampa. "I'm getting Braves games here!"

"I'll tell you what I'm going to do," growled Dick Wagner of the Reds, as the Braves came into Cincinnati for a series. "I'm not going to let him plug in his equipment here."

Lou Hoynes and Sandy Hadden had to talk him out of it. Yes, he was right to be offended at Braves games being beamed into Reds territory night after night. Yes, the SuperStation was a burr under everyone's saddle. But this wasn't the way to solve it. They had to thwart Turner in Washington.

They tried. Time after time, baseball got bills into the hopper to amend broadcast laws and, in effect, scrap "Super-stations." Time after time, Bowie Kuhn and Ted Turner would square off in congressional hearings. Kuhn talked about how WTBS, as it was now called, usurped and devalued clubs' local broadcast rights. Turner talked about how he stood for viewer choice and against the networks' monopolistic power.

Forget the merits. The starchy Kuhn was no match for the colorful Turner. He was a self-styled populist hero. "I break the monopoly," he told the congressmen. "I give people a way out of the school bus attacked by truck drivers wearing bikinis. You give people a choice between watching garbage or maybe a fine classic movie, and many people will watch the movie. With the superstation, and the other cable channels you can get with the satellite, everybody can watch different things if they want. Free choice! That scares the networks to death, let me tell you."

Baseball's amendments never got to first base and the SuperStation rolled on. When it began reaping national advertising in 1978, it became a money machine. By the early eighties, it had 20 million subscribers. Much of the credit went to the

Braves, now audaciously called by Turner "America's team." They filled hundreds of hours of TV time through the summer and drew viewers from as far away as Valdez, Alaska, where a local bar was renamed "The Braves Lounge," and Storm Lake, Iowa, where a billboard read: THE ATLANTA BRAVES: IOWA'S TEAM.

For Turner, signing a few marquee players was just a modest programming investment. Thus did Al Hrabosky, his made-for-TV reliever, get a $2.2 million contract in 1979: a signing bonus of $250,000, a salary of $390,000 per annum for five years, and deferred payments through the year 2009. It was pretty good money for a guy whose eleven saves were one third the total of league leader Mike Marshall. Still, Hrabosky insisted on one other clause as the clincher: a post-career shot at broadcasting.

Turner's hot temper and big mouth did make some negotiations an adventure. In 1979, he wanted to cut Bob Horner's contract the maximum 20 percent. The ensuing battle with his agent, Bucky Woy, got so ugly that an arbitrator had to settle the matter. In the midst of hostilities, Braves GM Bill Lucas died of a stroke. Turner accused Woy of killing him.

Turner also bristled at the ubiquitous Jerry Kapstein. "I'll tell you the way Kapstein conducts his business and the reason I don't like him," he once said. "After all, you should have some reason to dislike a guy besides the fact that he wears a full-length fur coat and is a Jew."

Since Turner said this at a sportswriters' banquet, word got out rather fast. Turner hastily apologized to howling Jewish groups. He also apologized to Kapstein, sort of. Turner signed his letter to the agent, "Yours in Christ."

But Turner was generally easy pickings for agents because, as a negotiator, he was never one to sweat the details. He was once finishing up a contract with Rick Camp when the reliever's agent, Dick Moss, threw in one final request.

Camp was a farmer on the side, in his native Trion, Georgia. In addition to a guaranteed three years' worth of salary, Moss said, his client would like a tractor.

Turner waved his hand at this trifle.

"Whatever he wants," he said casually.

Moss was a bit more careful. He made the contract specify not just any old tractor but a 1983 Ford TW20 tractor. It was equipped with electric windows, air-conditioning, and a six-speaker stereo, making Rich Camp the envy of Trion and sending Ted Turner into sticker shock. It cost $83,000.

With each crazy contract, with each new SuperStation incursion, the Lords screamed bloody murder. Yet Turner was tolerated by most of them. He was the entertainment at otherwise boring ownership meetings. "They'd watch in fascination and some affection," recalls Bowie Kuhn. "He was sort of an enchanting kid."

Sometimes Turner offered stream-of-consciousness monologues, concluding with, "A strong letter will follow." Sometimes Turner cut right to the heart of the matter. "Gentlemen," he once said, "we have the only legal monopoly in the country and we're fucking it up."

And then sometimes he brought proceedings to a dead halt. An ownership meeting was once getting started and the Braves' seats were conspiciously empty. Suddenly the door swung open and Turner walked in, a trench coat slung over his shoulder and a woman in spiked heels and a leopardskin dress on his arm. "Hi, everybody," he grinned. "I just got in from Paris and this is my friend Fifi LaVoom."

That wasn't really her name, but then nobody could really remember it. The meeting never did quite recover.

Jaws also dropped on November 15, 1980, but for a different reason. On that date—less than twenty-four hours after the reentry draft—Turner signed Claudell Washington to a five-year contract. This was the same Claudell Washington who'd averaged ten homers and fifty-nine RBIs in his six full big-league seasons. It was the same guy whose indifferent outfield play caused fans near his Comiskey Park station to hang a banner: WASHINGTON SLEPT HERE. He'd bounced around between four teams the past five years, most recently traded even-up for a minor-leaguer.

Turner's contract with Claudell Washington amounted to an astonishing $3.5 million.

Ruly Carpenter nearly gagged on his Saturday-morning coffee when he saw the headline. It was as if a hand grenade had been tossed into his sports section. *Seven hundred thousand a year for Claudell Washington?* He wouldn't believe it until he called up Chub Feeney in San Francisco—woke him up, actually—and got a mumbled confirmation. The baseball world had gone quite mad.

Carpenter's family had owned the Phillies since 1943, when Ruly's grandfather bought the club as a present for Ruly's father, Bob. The Carpenters enjoyed the camaraderie of the Lords. They reveled in bringing Philadelphia its first-ever championship in 1980. They loved the game itself, and none more than Ruly.

Ruly Carpenter could have turned out a rich-kid dilettante. He was Du Pont money, heir to a family fortune estimated at $330 million. But in 1964, at age twenty-four, he rolled up his sleeves and went to work in the guts of the Phillies organization. He spent a year in the treasurer's department, then moved over to the farm system.

That was Ruly Carpenter's true love: player development. He came to feel almost a religious fervor for it. When he became president of the Phillies in 1973, he elevated scouting director Paul Owens to general manager. They hired more minor league coaches. They hired away top scouts from other clubs. They put more scouts in Latin America.

The Phillies, doormats through most of the sixties and early seventies, perked up. Players who had come through their revamped development system reached the majors: Mike Schmidt, Bob Boone, Greg Luzinski, Garry Maddox, and others. They took the National League East in 1976, the year Andy Messersmith won free agency.

Ruly Carpenter hated the *Messersmith* decision. He didn't just like developing players; he liked palling around with them, nurturing a family feeling. "He was one of the boys," says Tim McCarver, a Phillies catcher then. "He would sit by your locker and have a good time. He was the closest owner there was to the players."

Messersmith smashed all notions of family. "Free agency was like a dagger in his heart," says Steve Mann, a Philadelphian and baseball-business consultant. "It was a betrayal of everything Ruly loved about baseball. Money was the name of the game."

The worst part, thought Carpenter, was what happened with owners. As the money grew, the sense of fraternity shrunk. Money splintered interests. Money spawned duplicity. Money replaced the concept of "What's best for baseball?" with "What's in it for me?"

He was hardly the only old-liner to be appalled at the new ways. Bowie Kuhn once asked a gathering of baseball men what they saw as the biggest changes of recent years. Veteran GM Gabe Paul spoke up: "To me, it's that someone's word is no longer any good. You'd better get it in writing."

There had always been a certain amount of swindling and sleight-of-hand in the business. It was as accepted as stealing signs from the dugout. But there was also a certain code of honor. A handshake sealed a deal. Duplicity only went so far. That didn't apply with those growing numbers of people who, as Gabe Paul put it, "weren't brought up in the game."

There was one other thing about money that offended an old-guard scouting-and-development man like Ruly Carpenter. The new boys thought it would buy pennants. What's worse, they were right, at least initially. Steinbrenner's Yankees won it all in 1977 and 1978, the first two post-*Messersmith* years. "He bought instant success," Carpenter would reflect years later. "If he'd failed, I don't think you'd see what you do today."

As it was, however, Steinbrenner only encouraged the other new boys to binge too. And the only thing worse than their duplicity was their stupidity. Ruly Carpenter was horrified as he watched the Turners and Corbetts operate. He blanched at the thought of a future with business partners like them.

Still, Carpenter had the competitive drive and the cash on hand to play the new money game. He signed Mike Schmidt to one of the first mega-contracts in 1977: $560,000 a year for six years, a total of $3.36 million.

The following year he took the plunge on his first major free agent. The Phillies were so close to a pennant Carpenter could taste it. They'd won the NL East three straight years, 1976–78, but lost each LCS to the West champ. One more player—just the *right sort* of player—might put them over the top. That was Pete Rose.

"Charlie Hustle" played the off-field game the same as between the lines: hard, harder, and hardest. As a young player with the Reds, his goal was to be the first singles hitter to make $100,000. He made it in 1970. When the Reds balked at giving him a $5,000 raise the next year, he held out through two weeks of spring training. As the self-proclaimed "most famous white athlete in America," Rose aggressively sought endorsements and got a $600,000 deal with Mizuno, the Japanese sporting-goods company.

And, as the post-*Messersmith* era dawned and salaries took off, Rose was fiercely competitive about pay. He wanted to be far-and-away the top salary stud on the Big Red Machine. He openly blasted teammates like Dave Concepcion, who simply wanted to ride his coattails. Said Rose of Concepcion's three-year, $1 million contract demand: "That's a lot of money for a shortstop."

Rose got a two-year contract averaging an annual $365,000.

But he also got his nose permanently out of joint with Reds president Dick Wagner. When the term was up at the end of 1978, he spurned Wagner's $470,000-a-year offer, turned free agent, and took his show on the road.

Agent Reuben Katz put together a twenty-five-minute highlights video, a five-city itinerary, and declared the Pete Rose auction open. He and Rose were off to:

Atlanta. Ever the eager stalking-horse, Ted Turner opened bidding by offering $1 million a year for five years and $100,000 a year for life after that. Or whatever the hell Rose wanted. "Join me for two years at a million a year," Turner told Rose. "By then, Dick Wagner will be fired and you can go back to your hometown."

Kansas City. The Royals had never gone after big-name free agents, but after losing the LCS to New York three straight years, Kauffman felt like Carpenter. "My buddy over in New York wins the pennant every year in the free-agent draft," he told Rose. "I gotta try to do the same thing." Kauffman's offer not only matched Turner's $1 million per annum but included pharmaceutical and oil investments.

St. Louis. Rose and Katz visited Gussie Busch in the hospital, where he was preparing for hernia surgery. "I probably would have had a hernia too," cracked Rose when he left, "if I had to carry all the money he was offering me." Besides salary, Busch was offering a lifetime's largesse from Anheuser-Busch. Would Rose care to be Bud's spokesman? How about a distributorship? Rose didn't drink beer, but that didn't bother Gussie Busch.

Pittsburgh. The Pirates' owners, John and Dan Galbreath, owned something else that intrigued Rose: thoroughbreds. The Galbreaths knew this. (Who, then, would have guessed that his compulsive betting on horses—and other sports—would eventually bring him down?) They tailored their offer to that interest: a top salary, of course, but also a top-notch broodmare. With its championship bloodlines, it could produce great horses and great income. Rose was goggle-eyed. "I know people with millions who can't get into a syndicate of a Triple Crown winner," he'd later say, "but I could have."

* * *

Philadelphia. The road show's last stop was the Carpenter estate in Delaware. Ruly Carpenter and Bill Giles greeted Rose and Katz warmly, but they had hardly settled into the hunting-box living room when signing prospects vanished.

"What kind of money would it take to get Pete to the Phillies?" asked Carpenter.

"Well, we already have an offer in seven figures, guaranteed for three years," Katz said.

"My God," said Carpenter. "Let's have lunch. It's all over."

The Welsh rarebit and bacon were wonderful. The talk was stilted. Carpenter mentioned the modest numbers he'd had in mind: $2.1 million for three years. Rose said he'd probably go with the Royals, where he liked both the money ($3 million for three years) and the ballpark (AstroTurfed).

Giles wasn't quite ready to give up. He sensed that down deep Rose preferred the Phillies. Larry Bowa and Greg Luzinski were good friends of Rose. Giles himself was a fellow Cincinnatian and racetrack devotee. The team was a contender, and it was, finally, in the National League.

Giles would play up the last point hard. While driving Rose and Katz to the airport, he produced a copy of the National League Green Book, which lists all league record-holders. Giles, appealing to Rose's vanity, began reciting all the categories in which he ranked high.

"You're going to be able to set all sorts of records," he said. "You've got to stay in the National League."

Giles invoked his father, whom Rose had liked. Giles invoked Rose's unborn grandchildren, who'd be so proud of a record-holding grandpa. Giles just kept jawing all the way to the airport. But he had no idea that it had any effect until he heard from Reuben Katz the next day.

"Why don't you see if you can get creative with a package?" he said.

Giles went right to work. He called WPHL, the Philadelphia television station that broadcast the teams games. The Phillies had just signed a three-year contract extension at $1.35 million a year. The club also got a fifty-fifty split of advertising revenues above a certain level. Giles said they had a chance to sign Pete Rose but he didn't work cheap and, frankly, they needed some help.

"Now, if we sign him, the ratings are going to go up and you can charge more for your advertising," he said. "So why don't you pay us an extra $600,000 a year?"

If WPHL could guarantee the Phillies that much more for the

ad-revenue split, he explained, the club could see its way clear to boosting its bid for Rose. WPHL went for it—not just for the one year Giles had asked but for all three years.

Giles hustled back to Katz with a new offer: $800,000 for four years. It was still short of Kansas City, but because it was longer-term the total dollars were higher. It would also still be a record-breaking contract, thus satisfying Rose's ego requirements.

All they had to sweeten it, as it happened, was another $5,000. Rose wanted to exceed the $800,000 being paid David Thompson by the NBA Denver Nuggets. That would make him the highest paid athlete in team sports.

Rose signed. Within sixty days, the Phillies sold $2.5 million more in season tickets than they ever had, and they would draw a club-record 2.8 million in attendance in 1979. Within two years, the Rose-inspired Phillies won the Series. He sealed the final victory, in game six, by catching a foul pop-up deflected off Bob Boone's glove.

In the annals of Philadelphia history, the celebration parade ranked just behind the Declaration of Independence signing. The players stood on flatbed trucks and waved to 500,000 joy-crazed fans as the parade crawled down Broad Street to Kennedy Stadium. There, 80,000 people listened to their heroes' speeches. Ruly Carpenter sat there glowing that sunny afternoon, bathing in the sounds of the love fest.

Not one month later, he sat numbly over his coffee and sports section. *Claudell Washington?*

It was the final straw, for it told Carpenter two sure things:

One: he'd always thought of his fellow owners as partners, but with partners like Ted Turner, who needed enemies?

And two: the owners couldn't possibly win on free-agent compensation. The madness would continue. Claudell Washington was a message big as skywriting to the union: DISREGARD POSTURING. BUSINESS AS USUAL.

The Carpenters, father and son, had a talk that day about their future in baseball. That began a dialogue that lasted several months, and in the end, they quite agreed: they would hang the FOR SALE sign on the Phillies.

Ruly Carpenter's eyes were moist a few weeks later, when he told Ray Grebey. "Ray, I've got to leave," he said. "You can't work with people you can't trust." Grebey murmured his condolences to a man he considered a class act. It was like being told of a death in the family. Grebey didn't realize the funeral was also his own.

$ 14 $

THE FINAL SCORE of the free-agent compensation study committee: eight meetings, zero progress.

They were four reasonable people: Sal Bando and Bob Boone for the players, Frank Cashen and Harry Dalton for the owners. They had an entirely unreasonable burden: conducting rational discourse while Marvin Miller and Ray Grebey glared at each other. Miller tried to get Grebey to admit he'd misrepresented their 1980 agreement. Grebey hissed he'd done nothing of the sort.

"Now, we don't want to rehash that," said Cashen, the Mets GM. "Let's focus on the compensation proposal."

But they couldn't.

"The four of us felt we had a good early rapport," recalled Dalton, the Brewers GM. "But every time we seemed to be making progress, either Grebey or Miller would confuse the issue. It was like the red flag and the bull." By the end, the two sides were so dug in that they issued separate reports.

"The clubs' argument is based on logic," wrote Cashen and Dalton, "stating that when a club loses a ranking player in the Reentry Draft, that it is losing an asset; that it frequently has a ten-year investment in that asset (four minor league seasons plus six seasons at the major league level); and that the player is all too frequently leaving just as he is coming into his peak years."

The Bando-Boone report, actually written by the union's Don Fehr, blasted the players-as-assets notion: "Major league baseball players ought to have the same rights as other Americans, who, after an employment contract expires, are free to seek work elsewhere, on the best terms they can negotiate, without any new employer being required to pay 'compensation' to the former employer. . . . Ownership of property is consistent with the principles of our society; ownership of people is not."

And there, deeply dug into their positions and trenches, the two sides remained. In February 1981, the PRC invoked its compensation proposal of the previous May. The players' union set a May 29 strike deadline. Ken Moffett returned to mediate. Everybody prepared to do it all over again.

Grebey hated it. Dozens of players would pack into the conference room for negotiations. Imagine: players in on the players'-union negotiations! It offended his professional sensibilities.

It began with the dress. He wore his tweedy professor outfits—Moffett wore blue blazer, button-down shirt, and gray slacks. But the players wore . . . blue jeans, sweat suits, or worse. They would drift in and out, jump right in with comments, react to Marvin's sighs. It drove Grebey wild. "These guys would just show up!" he declared years later. "Sometimes thirty, forty, fifty guys!"

Reggie Jackson was great for cameo appearances. You never knew when he'd show up—although a session well covered by writers and cameras was a good bet—and you never knew what he'd say.

One time Miller had just made a new proposal and Grebey was repeating it back, point by point. He often did this, feeling it kept Miller from fudging about his meaning later on.

In the middle of this restatement, Jackson walked in. He listened until the end, then turned on Grebey. "Ray, we've taken enough of that shit," he said. "There's no way we're going to agree to that."

"Reggie," said Grebey. "I'm reciting what I just heard from Marvin."

"Well," said Jackson, clearing his throat, "I'd better find out what's going on."

If Grebey was uneasy with the players, they were even less comfortable with him. He struck them as devious, arrogant, and condescending. He peered over his half-glasses and, literally, looked down on them. He openly doubted their commitment. One day he turned to Ted Simmons, who had recently signed a $640,000-a-year deal with the Brewers.

"Teddy, you just signed a long-term contract," he said. "You mean you're willing to throw it away for *this*?"

"Mr. Grebey, that contract I signed I feel I earned," Simmons bristled. "What you're telling me to do with my contract is to turn it into a noose and hang myself with it. I have no intention of doing it. That kind of money doesn't spend very well."

With each acid exchange, the players' resolve was only stiffened. "It was like a fastball up and in," Doug DeCinces would recall years later. "The players are going to respond to that."

Grebey and Miller's relationship continued to deteriorate. They were the mongoose and the cobra, continually circling and hissing. Grebey called Miller "Marv," just to get his goat. Miller wasn't normally given to histrionics, but more than once he stomped out on Grebey.

"Until you start directing yourself to the true issues, this deal isn't going to come close to being settled," he once said, furiously gathering up his things. "You're playing with the futures and the economics of people who depend on baseball."

Some thought Grebey's hostility owed as much to jealousy as ideology. Miller was the George Washington of his organization, Grebey a high-paid messenger-boy in his. Miller got back-channels help from the owners. Grebey got second-guessing and interference from the owners.

Miller had, in fact, also become a more difficult, less reserved person with age. The scales of power now tipped in his favor, of course, so he could afford to be. But Miller also seemed to be revenging himself on the owners for all their past slights. Yes, he *had* gotten more rigid and dogmatic with age. "Marvin viewed the world as flawed, and he was going to correct it," said Clark Griffith.

At about this time, the NBA players' union was in negotiations that would eventually produce pro basketball's salary cap. It guaranteed the players 53 percent of league revenues in return for a limit on each team's payroll. The cap would pull the NBA back from the brink of ruin and begin a spectacular rise through the eighties, benefitting both owners and players. Yet Marvin Miller was privately contemptuous of NBA Players Association chief Larry Fleisher, believing no union should limit members' earning power.

His stance spoke volumes not only about the two men but also about the leagues' respective dynamics. Fleisher, a lawyer who doubled as a player agent, had a deal-maker's mentality, not a trade unionist's. ("My job," he once told an NBA owner, "is to take you right up to the brink of bankruptcy, but no more.") He was a good match for NBA executive vice president (and later commissioner) David Stern, also a lawyer and a deal-maker. They were capable of drafting a win-win labor contract, while baseball—its throwback labor leader on one side, its feudal Lords on the other—was capable only of fighting.

"Marvin couldn't make a deal," said Lou Hoynes. "Everything was just a truce on a battlefield."

Ken Moffett was back in the mediator's chair, but he was stumped. It was a one-issue negotiation. There were no chips to swap. There was no more middle ground than in the average Middle East peace conference. For Moffett, there wasn't much to mediate.

The Lords moved little from their 1980 offer. A "ranking" free agent, requiring compensation, was in the top 50 percent of players. Whoever signed him could protect fifteen players if the free agent rated in the top 33 percent of players or eighteen if rated from 34 to 50 percent. Anybody else on the twenty-five-man major league roster could be taken for compensation.

Grebey spent less time on new proposals than preparing for war. He lined up $50 million in strike insurance from Lloyd's of London. He set up a $15 million "mutual protection fund" by getting the clubs to set aside 2 percent of their revenues in 1979 and 1980. He also imposed a code of silence, punishable by a fine of up to $500,000, to avert the usual ruinous leaks and loose-cannon comments.

Harry Dalton promptly ran afoul of it. "I hope that we are not about to witness another macho test of wills," he told *Washington Post* writer Tom Boswell, thinking he was off the record. "From what I hear, the Players Association is genuinely looking for a compromise if we'll just offer them something that they can accept without losing too much face."

(Dalton was fined $50,000, though he never paid it. After hostilities were over, clemency was offered to gag-order violators.) But there was one owner who didn't intimidate easily and who, now more than ever, couldn't handle a strike. He was a man being eaten alive by interest rates. With big loans at two points over prime (and the prime rate had soared to 18 percent), debt payments were killing Edward Bennett Williams.

A leading criminal defense lawyer, William's mind was unsurpassed when it came to finding avenues of escape. Now he had to find one for the gathering labor war. He began by applying his charm and preaching peace daily on the phone with Bowie Kuhn. He made use of his pipeline into the union—Orioles players DeCinces and Belanger—and argued by the hour with the PRC's counsel, Barry Rona.

Williams was a superb judge of opponents, and he thought Marvin Miller too good a fighter, and too heavily identified with the current system, to ever yield. "If you think you're going to change what he's already written on his tombstone, you're crazy," he told Rona. "There's no way he's going to give ground on it. Marvin would commit suicide before he'd agree to that. In fact, the only way to achieve anything is to wait for him to die."

"It's not that simple, Ed," Rona said. "We're trying to establish a labor-relations situation where there can be give and take, meaningful compromise on both sides. That's not going to come without a cost."

"But the reserve system is the wrong issue," Williams insisted. "You've got to fight this on something other than Marvin's monument."

Williams used flattery. ("You're the brightest person in baseball," he told Rona.) He used threats. ("You'll be remembered for burying baseball," he thundered to Kuhn.) He used connections. (He got DeCinces's parents tickets for the Reagan inauguration.)

Some put up with Williams because he was a silver-tongued devil and powerful man. Ray Grebey was one who couldn't stand him. Grebey saw Williams as the Neville Chamberlain of baseball: ready to bargain away the industry for an illusion of peace. At a time when Grebey desperately needed a united front, Williams was an eloquent symbol of disunity.

PRC chairman Ed Fitzgerald had much the same view as Grebey. As Williams was holding forth at one meeting, Fitzgerald finally blew up: "We've had enough of your shit. Now sit down and shut up."

Indeed, for all his eloquence and machinations, Williams barely slowed the rush to war. "Gentlemen, let me tell you something," said Bob Howsam. "This is your only chance to achieve something. If you capitulate this time, you'll never achieve anything again. It's now or never."

Howsam restated this thought several times, and in several different ways. It was a direct challenge to the Lords' manhood, a challenge to which they could respond in only one way. Damn right they'd draw a line in the sand.

"That gimpy-armed bastard," exclaimed Ted Turner. "We'll run him out of town once and for all."

* * *

Marvin Miller knew that talk was cheap. He also felt that the Lords' talk could be turned back against them. Now, as the May 29 deadline drew near, he would try to do just that.

It was the law in labor relations: if an employer made an issue of his economic condition, he had to open up his books. And this, Miller contended, the Lords had done. Ever the researcher, he assembled all the clips of all their gloom-and-doom statements and threw them in their faces.

Bowie Kuhn's latest, from the 1980 winter meetings: "The prospect of staggering losses for our clubs is an emphatically real prospect."

Charles Bronfman, on why the clubs needed free-agent compensation: "As an industry, baseball is not healthy."

Calvin Griffith: "Some teams are going to go broke. It's bound to happen."

Bob Lurie: "Just wait until one or two teams go under."

And so on.

Okay, said Miller, let's see the proof. He demanded to see each club's operating statement for 1978 through 1980. No way, said Grebey, so Miller immediately filed a "failure to bargain" complaint with the National Labor Relations Board. He was angling for an injunction as a means to avert a strike.

On May 28, just twenty-four hours before the strike deadline, the NLRB found for the union. That threw the matter into Federal Court and staved off the players' walkout. Miller didn't fare so well, however, with a federal judge named Werker.

On June 10, after two days of hearings, Judge Werker made his decision. He found the owners hadn't made an issue of their economic condition, contrary to Miller's assertion. He also found Miller's eleventh-hour request for financial data a mere "bargaining tactic by the Association to prevent the implementation of the PRC's proposal." The injunction was denied. The last line of Judge Werker's opinion read: "PLAY BALL!!! SO ORDERED."

The effect, of course, was the opposite. The strike-postponing agreement of May 29 had given the players twenty-four to forty-eight hours after Werker's decision to walk.

It was an agony of an interval. Baseball on the field was having a banner season. Total attendance was running 1.2 million ahead of 1980. Los Angeles was gripped by Fernandomania, a stadium-packing phenomenon that occurred every time sensational rookie Fernando Valenzuela pitched. Billy Martin was reviving the moribund Oakland A's with his scrappy "Billyball."

Pete Rose was set to pass Stan Musial as the National League's all-time hits leader, with 3,631.

In Philadelphia, 3,631 balloons were ready for release the moment it happened. Rose was at 3,629 and could tie the record with a two-hit game. That Thursday night Rose got one single, but was retired by Nolan Ryan his other three times at the plate.

At 12:30 A.M., the 3,631 balloons filled the sky over Veterans Stadium. Few saw them and none cheered. They recognized not Rose's accomplishment but reality. The balloons would be deflated long before Musial's record was broken.

The strike began Friday, June 12.

It was four days old when Bowie Kuhn took a call from Edward Bennett Williams. As a gadfly new boy, he was something of a thorn in Kuhn's side, but their personal relationship remained warm. Williams knew Kuhn had been helpful in his landing the Orioles. And Kuhn enjoyed the insights and company of the smoothest operator in Washington, a town where he had to operate plenty himself.

Williams got right to the point: Was Kuhn free for dinner that night? He'd be glad to fly up to New York to meet him. Sure, said Kuhn, and they arranged a time and place. A few minutes later, Kuhn got on the phone to Lee MacPhail: Would he join them? The AL president was a good listener, a wise old hand, and a good addition to almost any meeting.

But not this one. The dinner, at a Midtown restaurant called Christ Cella, went badly. Conversation was strained. Williams was sulking. When MacPhail finally left, just before dessert, Williams let Kuhn have it.

"This is the end of our friendship," he began.

Bringing MacPhail along meant one thing, Williams charged. Kuhn didn't trust Williams and wanted a witness. Kuhn protested that that wasn't the case, but Williams remained offended and adamant.

"I feel deep sorrow that this is necessary," he said. "I deplore it, I really deplore it. I'm so sorry that circumstances have brought our friendship to an end."

Williams stalked out of Christ Cella.

He appeared in Kuhn's office the next morning at nine-thirty. Eddie Chiles of the Rangers had a previously scheduled meeting then and had brought Williams and George Steinbrenner along as seconds. Kuhn's was, once again, Lee MacPhail.

It was Chiles's first visit to the commissioner's Rockefeller Center office. He made a show of admiring the view of St. Patrick's Cathedral and of inspecting the adjoining conference room and executive bathroom. "Pretty fancy digs," Chiles drawled.

Then he attacked.

"You're sitting here in your fancy office doing nothing," he growled. "If you can't figure out anything else to do, you could at least put your desk out on the sidewalk and talk to the fans. It's up to you to do something! But as far as I can see, you're not doing a damned thing. I won't tolerate that! You and Lee MacPhail work for me! I pay your salaries! You're just like any other employees I've got. I tell you what to do, and you're supposed to do it."

Chiles finally stopped. A silent tension gripped the room.

"Are you through?" asked Kuhn.

More silence.

"Eddie, you're nothing but a lamebrained old fool," Kuhn said. "I'm embarrassed for you and I suspect everyone in this room is as embarrassed as I am. You have no appreciation of the distinguished office I am proud to hold or of the traditions which lie behind the major league baseball structure. If you did, you would know that the commissioner exists to tell the owners what to do and not the other way around. As to the labor situation, I find your remarks nothing short of insulting, and as far as I'm concerned you can get the hell out of here!"

Kuhn turned to Williams and Steinbrenner and challenged them: Did they subscribe to what Chiles was saying? Um, no, not altogether, they said. But they did agree that something had to be done. That was why they had come.

Williams blasted Grebey and the PRC members. He put forth more of his pet ideas for a settlement. He told Kuhn he was disappointed in his leadership. Would he ever get around to acting if he thought the game was "self-destructing"?

Of course, said Kuhn. But that moment hadn't arrived only five days into the strike. The meeting was over.

Later that day, the first poststrike bargaining session convened with one conspicuous absentee: Marvin Miller.

He had removed himself from the negotiations. It was as though George Washington was a no-show for the Constitution's drafting, as though Churchill had skipped the Yalta Conference. Everyone was stunned. But Miller had his reasons.

The stated one was that he feared *he* had become the issue,

He was being vilified by the owners. He was at daggers drawn with Grebey—to whom he would no longer talk without a witness. He said he wanted to make a point: the players' union was not Marvin Miller, it was the players. So he would turn the negotiating over to them.

The players themselves were dismayed. What was Miller doing, going off in a purple snit when they needed him most? Don Fehr, the union's young lawyer, would sit in, but he wasn't the patriarch. "I thought it was horseshit ·of Marvin to step aside," recalls Orioles shortstop Mark Belanger.

Nonetheless, the burden and spotlight shifted to Belanger and the other members of the players' negotiating committee—Doug DeCinces, Bob Boone, Phil Garner, and Steve Rogers.

Doug DeCinces had been drawn into the Players Association as a young Orioles player in the mid-seventies, when staunch union men like Ken Holtzman, Reggie Jackson, Brooks Robinson, and Belanger were on the club. They saw this bright young fellow as a comer and made him the Orioles' alternate player rep.

DeCinces succeeded not only in the huge task of replacing Robinson at third base but in advancing in the union's leadership. By 1980 he was American League player rep.

DeCinces and Miller weren't ideological soulmates. Miller was the New York liberal, DeCinces an Orange County conservative. Miller's every breath was devoted to the trade-union movement. DeCinces was uncomfortable even calling the Players Association a union. It was the subject of a running argument.

"We're an association of professionals," DeCinces insisted. "We band together for certain purposes. But we're not a union."

Miller would just laugh and say, "You don't know what you're talking about."

DeCinces did, however, do most of the talking at the bargaining table. He had great command of the finer points of the contract and could go toe-to-toe with Grebey on any of them.

Bob Boone was the players' other leading voice. The National League player rep was an intriguing pastiche. He had a psychology degree from Stanford, yet chewed tobacco like an oldtime ballplayer. (He slowly filled two plastic cups with tobacco juice at each bargaining session.)

He was, in fact, the son of an oldtime ballplayer named Ray Boone, a third baseman for the Indians and Tigers in the fifties.

Boone had grown up playing catch in major league ballparks. But he'd also grown up knowing that this beautiful game was also a tough business. That knowledge had drawn him to the union early in his career, along with his admiration for Miller. He'd been a player rep since his second year as the Phillies' catcher.

Now he was in its front ranks, but in the same low-key style that made him the cool handler of pitchers. He made his points more quietly, sat more patiently than DeCinces. Grebey had glommed on to Boone as "the reasonable one." At the bargaining table, Grebey often addressed him directly as he tried to make points. Outside, he tried to cultivate a personal relationship. At the end, he would pull Boone aside to say, "I'm sorry you and I had to be on opposite sides of the negotiation."

Grebey didn't know a "good cop" act when he saw one. In the union's private councils, Boone was no conciliator. "Bob was more passive in front of them, but behind the scenes stronger," DeCinces recalled.

Phil Garner was the son of a Baptist minister and had a B.A. in business administration from the University of Tennessee. He didn't have an ounce of union spirit in his wiry infielder's body. But he was, in his own words, "a bit of an Ayn Rand character," believing fervently in individual choice and destiny.

Garner bridled at a baseball system that utterly quashed individuality. "The system can trade me; the system can sell me; none of it was really based on my ability to make a choice," Garner would later say. "I could have gone with IBM or anybody out of college. I had my choices in front of me. But the thing that irked me was that I was drafted by a team and had to sign with that team."

He vowed if he ever made the majors he'd be active in the players' union and try to change the system. Like DeCinces, he'd never wanted for mentors. He was a rookie on the last of the A's championship teams, in 1975, and Charlie Finley had made raving radicals of them all.

Garner didn't actually agree with every union tenet. He debated Miller about the minimum salary (he opposed it) and the maximum 20 percent pay cut (ditto). As a free-marketeer, he thought those shouldn't be regulated. He never won those arguments—nor did he ever win over any fellow executive board members. But he left those differences behind when he sat at the negotiating table. There he was as intense as when playing third base for the Pirates.

Steve Rogers was the Montreal Expos' ace pitcher, winner of sixteen games in 1980 and league leader in complete games with fourteen. He was quiet, almost bookish, a collector of Indian artifacts and a holder of a petroleum engineering degree from Tulsa University. But when the union was looking for a new generation of leaders in the mid-seventies, as stalwarts like Joe Torre were retiring, he stepped up to it.

"I got very interested because it was an interesting time," he later recalled. "The Messersmith-McNally decision had just come. Absolutely nobody I was around really understood what it meant, but it clearly suggested change."

Rogers became part of baseball's greatest change agent, the union, in 1976. He was elected National League pension rep then, and in 1980 became part of the negotiating committee. He was a calm, analytical voice in the committee's caucuses, if a seldom-heard one in the bargaining sessions.

Occasionally, however, he exploded in frustration. Chub Feeney set him off once by remarking, "You know, we really don't want to be here. We're really trying to settle this."

It was a seemingly innocuous statement, but it hit Rogers the wrong way. He was sick of dealing with a group that couldn't make any decisions, couldn't even make any spontaneous reactions. They had to go running back to the owners to see what they thought. He was sick of getting the same tired old proposals and rhetoric—"a puff of smoke and 'Trust me,'" as he later put it. And so he lashed out at Feeney.

"That's bullshit," Rogers screamed. "You're here to stonewall. If you weren't this would be settled!"

His outburst solved nothing, but it did give him quite a bit of pleasure to see Feeney's veins bulge.

Mark Belanger's seminal moment in the union was the 1972 strike meeting in Dallas. He was still a kid then, and the Orioles' alternate player rep. He looked on in silent awe at the fiery discussion about the strike. When it came time to vote, he finally spoke to the Orioles' lead rep, the legendary Brooks Robinson.

"What do I do?" he asked.

"Follow me, kid," said Robinson.

When Robinson stood up to support the strike, so did Belanger. In a sense, he had never sat down. Hooked on the cause, he became Miller's worker bee, sitting on both the Pension Committee and the executive board. If there was a meeting, count on Belanger to be there. If there was a task, count on Belanger to do it. If there was a hard-line position to be staked out, count on Belanger to take it.

At the bargaining table, he said little. His grace with language didn't match his grace at shortstop. But every so often he would explode, thoroughly getting the other side's attention.

"This isn't going anywhere!" he would snap. Or: "That's horseshit! That's wrong!"

In the strike's first week, the two sides met face-to-face for only two hours and ten minutes.

The ten minutes was on Friday, June 19, when they sat down within the familiar four walls of the Doral Inn's room 1706 in New York. DeCinces asked Grebey whether the PRC had given any more thought to the pooled-compensation proposal.

No, Grebey replied.

Did they have any questions for the players, DeCinces wondered.

No, Grebey replied.

"When you're ready to talk, let us know," said DeCinces. The players began packing up their papers, snapping shut briefcases.

"You mean you're calling off negotiations?" said Grebey.

"Have you got anything new?"

Grebey didn't. So the room emptied out and Moffett headed back to Washington to occupy himself with something easier: stopping a nationwide strike of air-traffic controllers.

Later, someone found a doily left behind on the bargaining table with four words scrawled on it: "No runs, no hits."

The players took just one satisfaction: Miller could get Grebey's goat without even being there. Freed from the bargaining table, Miller would hold court with reporters, exercise spin-control on events, and communicate with his players through the press.

Grebey hated reporters. He hated the massive attention and complications their stories brought to negotiations. He was stiff and defensive with them, sometimes confining himself to reading from prepared statements. He resented Miller's ease with them and his ability to give good quotes. Once, while Miller held forth at a post-briefing press conference, Grebey spun away, growling, "There's no news here."

After one early session, as Grebey plowed his way through

the cameras and microphones, a reporter provoked him with one shouted question.

"Was Marvin there?" he asked.

"Marvin who?" said Grebey, tight-lipped, striding on.

Despite Miller's superior PR skills, most fans disapproved of the players' actions. When NBC conducted a call-in survey of people watching its sports shows the weekend of June 13, 53 percent sided with the owners. Other measures were even more lopsided. Polls by the New York *Daily News* and the Cleveland *Plain Dealer* each ran two-to-one in favor of the Lords.

With players averaging $196,000 a year, many felt the athletes had no right to gripe. "A lot of people work harder and make a lot less money," one Tigers fan told *U.S. News & World Report*. "I go with the owners."

Some fans took refuge in minor league ball. In Denver, the triple-A Zephyrs drew 59,000 fans for one game. A California League game played in San Diego's Jack Murphy Stadium drew 37,000 fans. Another at Anaheim Stadium drew 9,000. The minors would enjoy a resurgence in the eighties, and some team operators believed it began with the strike.

Newspaper sports sections tried desperately to fill the void. The *Washington Star* ran game stories from the Senators' season of ten years earlier, which was pretty desperate indeed. The *Philadelphia Inquirer* ran *fictional* Phillies game stories. Thus did Pete Rose finally break Musial's hits record. TV stations scrambled too. New York's WPIX carried the Yankees' triple-A Columbus Clippers games, complete with Phil Rizzuto and Bill White. Other stations rebroadcast classic games.

But there was no substitute for the real thing. Fans grew restive, occasionally showing up at the Doral Inn to express themselves. Two of them picketed outside one day, carrying signs that read: NO MORE STALL, LET'S PLAY BALL.

On the scheduled day of the All-Star Game in Cleveland, 15,000 people gathered downtown. At what was to have been game time, they let loose a collective boo. It registered 130 decibels, loud as a thunderclap.

Bud Selig, the Brewers' president, was at his regular lunch spot—a drive-in hot-dog stand—when another patron recognized him.

"I agree with you guys, Bud," he said.

"Well, thank you," said Selig. "I sure hope it all works out."

"Yeah, I'm with you. I'll never pay a nickel to see those SOBs play again."

"*Great,*" thought Selig. "Where does that leave *me*?"

There was only one notable development in the strike's second week. The Lloyd's of London insurance policy kicked in. After a total of 161 games were canceled, each club collected $100,000 per lost game. That would last up to 500 lost games, or August 8.

It meant one thing: most owners suddenly had far less incentive to settle than they did before. If talks had produced negligible progress before, they now yielded none. The players suspected their proposals were going off into a black hole, courtesy of C. Raymond Grebey.

Phil Garner was sure of it after a meeting he had with Pirates owner Dan Galbreath and GM Pete Peterson. The two Pittsburgh execs had asked Garner if he would assemble the players who were still in the Pittsburgh area. They wanted some face-to-face talk. Garner got about ten players together at a Holiday Inn for the session.

Galbreath, a PRC member, faithfully recited the party line about how unnecessary this strike was. Very few players would be affected by compensation, and the formula was so reasonable. Peterson urged the players to moderate their position, mentioning several specific points he thought would be reasonable compromises.

"Pete," said Garner, "you'd better look at what's on the table, because that's precisely where we are. That's our proposal."

Peterson swiveled to look at Galbreath; Galbreath shot a look back. The meeting was suddenly over.

"It was an embarrassment for them," recalls Garner, "because they didn't know."

He held Ray Grebey responsible for that. The players felt Grebey distorted his progress reports on bargaining in order to keep the owners behind him. Doug DeCinces sometimes spent half the night on the phone with Edward Bennett Williams straightening him out on what had gone on during the day. Williams would get his telex from Grebey and call up, hurling angry questions at DeCinces: "Why are you doing this? Why are you doing that?"

"No, no, Mr. Williams," DeCinces would politely interject. "That's not what happened." Then he would give his version.

One day, as Grebey was chanting "Trust me" for the 129th time, Doug DeCinces lost it.

"Let's get something straight here," he shouted. "I *don't* trust you. I don't *intend* to trust you. I know what you're doing, and what I think you're doing to baseball is an atrocity."

Rusty Staub, who attended every meeting, though not formally a negotiating-committee member, brought in fifteen copies of the *New York Times* crossword puzzle one day. He started handing them out around the table, snarling at Grebey, "If we're going to continue with these word games, let's at least do something that's constructive."

Ken Moffett's most valuable moment during the strike may have come one day when the players were particularly frustrated with Grebey. The mediator sat in on a meeting of the union negotiating committee, watching them work themselves into a lather over the PRC chief. They decided the time had come to deal with things clubhouse-style. "The next time we heard the same blatant lie we'd heard for the last three or four days," recalled Steve Rogers, "we were going to stand up, turn over the table, and walk out."

Moffett ambled over to the PRC's caucus.

"Uh, fellows," he said, "I don't think that session this afternoon would be such a good idea."

He waited to schedule the next one until after the players had cooled down a bit.

To Moffett, the players' disgust for Grebey reflected as much their inexperience as his alleged sins. "This was a lot of players' first negotiation, and there were nuances they didn't pick up on," he later said. "If they submitted a substantive proposal and got flimflam back, they got angry and mistrustful. They didn't realize that might just be an initial response or a coded reply."

Years later, Phil Garner came around to believe Grebey hadn't been so much lying as scrambling. "I think at the time he was trying to get something done," he said. "He was working with a fractious bunch and he had to tell different interests different things to keep it all together."

That was for sure.

"The internal disparity [of the owners] was much more difficult to deal with than the union," Grebey later recalled. "You can't go forward as crown prince of the Balkan states."

On the one hand, there was what Grebey called "the war at any price" faction. These hawks were led by Bob Howsam, still a broken record on "meaningful compensation." It included such helpful sorts as the unnamed owner who gave Grebey this advice: "Get a Jewish labor guy and buy Miller off."

It also included Lou Susman, doing everything he could to discourage any deviant thinking about moderation. Gussie Busch's henchman constantly got second opinions on the PRC's actions from Anheuser-Busch's labor lawyers. Those attorneys, at the Morgan, Lewis and Bockius firm, constantly disagreed with the PRC's counsel, Willkie, Farr and Gallagher. Morgan Lewis, after all, hoped to win the baseball account from Willkie Farr one day. The effect was just what Susman intended. The PRC had to think about how everything would play with Busch's people.

On the other end of the spectrum, Grebey was being undermined by the peacenik owners. George Steinbrenner fiddled with a pooled-compensation formula of his own and passed messages back and forth to Miller through umpires' union lawyer Richie Phillips. The Boss even had one secret tête-à-tête with Miller at the Hyatt Regency Hotel.

Edward Bennett Williams, facing financial ruin, was working every back channel he could find. The interest rate on his debt was at 20 percent, and the strike insurance only partly stanched the bleeding. At Williams's sixty-first birthday party, guest Art Buchwald cracked, "This is the last time we'll ever eat meat in this house."

Williams was on the phone with Doug DeCinces or Mark Belanger every day, gauging the mood in the players' camp and making suggestions for breaking the stalemate. (The players, meanwhile, got a valuable backstage peek at the owners from Williams.) Ed Williams was also burning up the lines with Ken Moffett. Every day, like clockwork, a call came into the mediator's office from Williams. Sometimes he brought a piece of intelligence, sometimes an idea. And sometimes he was totally full of it.

One day he called to say, "I've come up with a formula I want to share with you."

Moffett, trying to juggle the baseball crisis with the air-traffic controllers' crisis, said he'd send over his assistant, Nancy Broff. Upon returning, she reported, "He didn't have anything. He just wanted to find out what *we* knew."

Williams was also working the phones hard with other owners. He played on their worst fears like a Horowitz on the Steinway. "We are going to ruin this game, maybe forever," he thundered. "If this goes on much longer, we'll lose this season and you might as well forget about next too. See what that does for your investment."

He'd given up on Bowie Kuhn. The commissioner was invisible to the public and unavailable to Williams ever since the stormy meeting with Steinbrenner and Chiles. Williams roared with laughter when one wag opined: "If Bowie Kuhn were alive this never would have happened." He raged with hurt at Kuhn's shunning of the dissidents. "Here was a guy who sat with presidents, who knew everybody, who was this powerful lawyer," said White Sox owner Jerry Reinsdorf of Ed Williams. "He had a wall covered with plaques—award after award after award. But he was against the strike and he couldn't get an appointment with Bowie Kuhn. It just drove him crazy."

In early July, Marvin Miller finally came back to the bargaining table. He'd made his point, he asserted. He wasn't the problem; the owners' compensation proposal was. He was already in full rhetorical stride his first day back, calling Grebey's latest proposal "an outrage—the gap between us is so wide it defies my vocabulary to describe it." (The owners had offered to reduce slightly the maximum number of free agents subject to compensation each year.)

Reggie Jackson chose the day of Miller's return to make his cameo appearance for the strike. He wanted, he said, to address the concerns of the "senior player." Jackson proposed that "senior" free agents, which he, as a thirty-five-year-old, would be at season's end, be exempt from compensation. There'd be no market for them if a signing club had to give up a young stud.

It was a stunning piece of pure special-interest lobbying, but everybody listened because Reggie was Reggie—a future Hall of Famer and a good show. (Jackson was once embroiled in a heated argument with Grebey before dramatically breaking it off with a challenge: "You get a .45 and we'll meet at 3:00 A.M. Whoever wins gets the contract." Even Grebey had to laugh.)

Even Jackson could see around his ego well enough to discern that "senior players" were the least of the problems in Doral room 1706.

"I didn't come the first two weeks because I didn't think anything would happen," he said. "But we're so far apart, maybe we should all take a break and enjoy the Fourth of July."

Miller quietly sighed. Jackson was a wild card. As a fiery, articulate speaker, he had lighted up many players' meetings. But as a bargaining participant, who knew when he'd show up or what would pop out? This time he was out of sync with his own side.

"I disagree," said Miller. "I think we should stay at the table."

The two sides did, in fact, keep at it through the holiday weekend. But they'd seen the last of Reggie Jackson for a while, though he did log some quality time in the press room on the way out. Asked if there would be baseball on the Fourth of July, he said, "Have a nice barbecue."

The total number of games canceled reached 251 that day.

Edward Bennett Williams was also busy that weekend. He was busy collecting signatures: eight of them. They were from owners requesting a joint meeting of the leagues. They weren't necessarily doves, but they weren't necessarily thrilled with how the strike was going, either. Williams had convinced them of his inalienable right to make Ray Grebey squirm.

It was Bowie Kuhn's call. He was contemptuous of most of the eight—new boys all. But a meeting might help clear the air. It might even put this minority to rout. He called a meeting for Thursday, July 9, in New York.

Ed Williams's little band of peaceniks met at the Carlyle Hotel three hours before the 5:00 P.M. joint meeting. It was no coincidence that most of them were American Leaguers. The junior circuit's owners were, well, more junior and less well-fixed than the National League's. They were feeling the pinch and they weren't wedded to the past.

The senior circuit was inhabited by the staunchest of the old guard. Even the NL newcomers quickly adopted the coloration of old guarders and looked down their noses at the American Leaguers. Said the Mets' Fred Wilpon of White Sox co-owners Reinsdorf and Einhorn, "I have more money in my pocket for lunch than those guys have together."

(The Chicago duo at least provided occasional comic relief. They sometimes voted different ways on the same question, causing great confusion about where the franchise stood. Einhorn enlivened one midstrike meeting by making a confession. "Geez, I told the writers on my way in we'd have a settlement," he said, as the meeting lurched toward an inconclusive end. "What do I say now?" One owner offered a suggestion: "You could always plead insanity.")

The National Leaguers didn't care for Ed Williams. He'd been an owner for less than two years and didn't know his place, which was to be seen and not heard. He wasn't motivated by baseball's best interest but by naked self-interest. But Williams was persuasive, and that made him dangerous. So the National Leaguers sent one of their own as a spy into the Carlyle meeting.

It was Buzzie Bavasi, now the Angels' GM but for twenty-six years a senior-circuit operative. There was just one problem after two hours' exposure to Williams: Bavasi came out a convert. But that would be Ed Williams's only victory of the day.

The joint meeting began at 5:00 P.M. at the Citicorp Club, high atop the Citicorp Building in midtown Manhattan. The partitions had been removed between several small dining rooms, making the space into one long, skinny room.

Bowie Kuhn chaired the meeting, flanked by members of the PRC. Grebey gave a brief status report. Then Ed Williams took the floor. He recited his curriculum vitae: defender of union leaders and mafia dons, counsel to mighty corporations. "And now here I am, reduced to slavery," he said, "walking around with a broom up my rear end saying, 'Yassa, Mister Grebey; yassa Mister Grebey.' "

Everybody roared—including Grebey—and then Williams got down to business. He poked holes in the PRC's approach. He questioned its proposals. He repeatedly raised the specter of permanent damage being done to the game. He grilled Grebey and PRC counsel Barry Rona as if he were cross-examining witnesses.

Kuhn then asked for other opinions. Eddie Chiles produced a long, rambling "Amen" to Williams's attack, but many more lashed out in frustration at the players and Miller. The group dynamics dictated that they flaunt their manhood. The tide was soon moving against Williams until the meeting turned into little more than a PRC pep rally.

The most poignant moment belonged to Ruly Carpenter. He'd reached an agreement a month earlier to sell out to a group led by Bill Giles. He understood he might never again be with this group he both loved and hated. What Carpenter delivered was not just another unity stem-winder but, really, his farewell speech.

"We are getting out because we can't trust our partners," he said, looking squarely at Turner. "I have some things I'd like to say before we leave.

"I know you all want to win, but you've got to be realistic.

Listen to your general managers, listen to your field people, and let's get some common sense back in the game. Try to develop your players from your own farm system and do it the right way.

"Think of your partners. We have institutional responsibilities, and the players don't."

PRC chairman Ed Fitzgerald had the last word.

"We aren't playing hardball; we're being flexible," he insisted. "We want a settlement, but a fair one. We have to stand together or they're going to run all over us for years to come."

As the meeting broke up, the Lords did seem to be standing together. Williams's assault had been repulsed, and owners took turns issuing unity statements to the writers downstairs.

"There are no dissidents," said Ed Fitzgerald.

"We feel very strongly that the games are over," said Ruly Carpenter. "Here's our offer, let's go."

Only one forlorn figure tried to skirt the microphones and slip out a side door. Some reporters caught up with him anyway.

"I have spent my whole life in contest living, and one lesson has become embedded very deeply," said Ed Williams. "I have learned to win with humility and to lose with grace. I have nothing more to say."

Williams walked out into the steamy Manhattan night.

For days, nothing happened. No meetings, no movement, no prospects. When a photographer asked Doug DeCinces to pose in a T-shirt bearing the words "I Survived the 1981 Baseball Strike," DeCinces refused. He wasn't sure he would.

Ed Williams was beside himself. More dissidents were slowly joining him. For example, Ballard Smith of the Padres was down on Grebey, not because he was a dove but because he felt Grebey wasn't passing along the straight dope. Lou Hoynes had to plug that hole by calling Smith with daily updates. Williams also had the pleasure of reading anonymous quotes from owners sniping at Grebey. (The PRC felt obliged to debunk speculation he'd be replaced, dismissing the stories with "disgust and revulsion.") But Williams couldn't content himself with a slow accretion of allies now. It was mid-July. He saw the season—and his net worth—slipping away.

So the ultimate Washington insider pulled a classic Washington gambit. He called a cabinet member. How about getting involved, he asked Secretary of Labor Ray Donovan. The secretary, who desperately needed *something* to divert attention from other problems, said yes. Donovan was off to a terrible start in office. He faced allegations of illegal payoffs to ensure labor peace at his construction company. He had filled top Labor posts with inexperienced campaign aides and stumbled over every issue in his path. He desperately needed to look good by ending the baseball strike, not that he had a clue how to do it. He also had absolutely no support within the White House.

Moffett was having his first meeting with Donovan at the Labor Department when a secretary interrupted. There was a call for Mr. Moffett from Craig Fuller, Vice President Bush's chief of staff. Moffett picked up the phone.

"Can I talk?" asked Fuller.

"Um, yes," said Moffett, looking at Donovan three feet away.

"If that guy gives you any trouble, let us know."

"Okay."

Moffett hung up.

"What did that son of a bitch want?" Donovan asked.

Said Moffett to the secretary: "Oh, he just wanted to know what was going on." Said Moffett to himself: *Holy shit. If this guy is in that kind of trouble, what can he do?*

The next day, the two flew to New York, where Rusty Staub ominously greeted Donovan at the Doral. "Watch your step, Mr. Secretary," he said. "You're walking into a lion's den."

It was, Donovan later recalled, more like "walking into a butcher's cold freezer." He moved negotiations to Washington on July 20, imposed a news blackout, and restarted talks at the Federal Mediation Service's building. They would take over the same ninth-floor negotiating room Moffett had used for the air-traffic-controller talks.

But within two days, Donovan was totally discouraged. The metaphor for the whole bloody thing was the building elevator. Moffett had run out during a lunch break. He was taking the elevator back up to his office for a quick shower when it got stuck. Moffett was eventually freed, but Donovan knew the same helpless between-floors feeling.

The antipathy between the two sides was so strong that he hardly knew where to begin. He was like the poor sap who'd made the mistake of inviting the Hatfields and McCoys to the same dinner party. Now all he could do was sit quietly at the head of the table, hoping there would be no gunplay. Nobody walking into this cold could possibly understand the jumble of issues, motives, pasts, and personalities—to say nothing of straightening them out.

All Donovan could do was earnestly implore everyone to think of the national pastime. Baseball was important to this great nation. Each side must be prepared to give some ground in the interests of a settlement. He intended to keep everyone there until they reached one.

At the end of one such spiel Phil Garner spoke up.

"Mr. Secretary, I personally admire your stated goal of staying here until we have a settlement," he said. "But I and many of us in this room feel like the owners have an agenda that's shooting for a specific date, when their strike insurance runs out. We feel like we have legitimate and workable solutions on the table, yet they refuse to reply or discuss them in any detail. I go home at night with a clear conscience that we're doing everything to achieve what you said."

"Conscience has nothing to do with it," snapped Donovan. "It's business."

Garner was at once stunned by the blunt reply (Donovan doesn't remember it) and visited by a sudden insight: *the owners couldn't win*. To them, this was business. To the players, it was a cause.

"Free agency was a right," said Garner years later. "We had it. We'd fought to get it. We'd fight to keep it. They could not win that fight."

Indeed, the only immediate result of Donovan's intervention was to cause Marvin Miller a big problem. His news blackout presented his worst problem since the strike's start. The press briefings had served, in effect, as his player briefings. Murray Chass of the *Times* was Miller's East Coast outlet, Jerome Holtzman of the *Chicago Tribune* the Midwest, and the West Coast players made do with the wire services. Miller spoke to writers and The Word went forth to all the players.

With the blackouts, they were in the dark. It was one of the Lords' few wartime advantages. There were only 26 of them and there were 650 players. Ray Grebey could communicate with his whole group via one telex. Marvin Miller had 650 players, and the news blackout put the burden on player reps to contact them all. Some teams used a relay system to keep players informed. The player rep related the day's events to four players, who in turn relayed it to four players and so on down the line. But facts and shadings could get lost as word went along the grapevine. Or, in these primitive days before answering machines, players might just be out and never get the call. "You might have the phone to your ear all day and get seventeen guys," recalls Ted Simmons. "But that still left eight guys loose."

In one mid-strike meeting, Miller went around the room asking each player rep how he saw support on his team. The Dodgers' Jerry Reuss admitted he'd had trouble staying in touch with his whole team. "I can't get ahold of some of my players," he said. "But we have fourteen housekeepers who are right behind us."

Now, with the strike in its sixth week, many players were getting restive. Some had found temporary work. Rangers pitcher and medical doctor Doc Medich logged time on his residency at a Fort Worth hospital. Tigers first baseman Richie Hebner dug graves in suburban Boston. Reds second baseman Ron Oester helped his wife run her day-care center. Brewers second baseman Jim Gantner worked as a plumber. Dodgers pitcher Dave Stewart worked in a hardware store for six dollars an hour. Orioles pitcher Steve Stone ran his restaurant in Arizona. Teammate Ken Singleton tried his hand at reporting for a Baltimore TV station.

But it wasn't like drawing a big-league paycheck. And it wasn't like the rhythms of the summers they were used to. A player who was running out of money, and now also deprived of information about what was happening in Washington, was a dangerous union member. He might start popping off publicly. One quote could blow a big hole in the players' perceived unity. Mark Belanger had a rule of thumb: "They hear one guy and multiply it by ten," he said.

As always, Miller would move to hush and educate the offenders. But now brushfires were starting to break out quicker than he could stamp them out. Champ Summers of the Tigers: "I wish I could afford this, but I don't want anyone playing chess with my money. I won't be a martyr and give up $200,000 so [teammate] Steve Kemp can become a free agent." Dennis Eckersley of the Red Sox: "Screw the strike. Let's play ball."

The news blackout *was* taking a toll. So was the specter of dwindling bank accounts. The union had no strike fund, and many of its members were really feeling the pitch.

"This was when the money was really starting to get big, and a lot of players had leveraged themselves too highly," recalls one, naming tax-shelter investments and fancy houses as the prime culprits. "I personally had a huge house note I couldn't make. I believe ownership didn't know how close they were to causing huge cracks."

On Wednesday, July 22, talks droned on through the first part of the day. At 2:00 P.M. Moffett announced a three-hour lunch break to reporters.

Miller, Fehr, and the five-player bargaining committee walked across the street to a burger joint. The PRC negotiators slipped out the back entrance of the Mediation Service building. Donovan, Moffett, and Nancy Broff headed for a nearby health-food eatery. The press corps watched everybody leave, then dispersed to take a break themselves.

That left all negotiating parties free to reconvene at a secret meeting site six blocks away at the federal Office of Personnel Management. There, waiting in a fifth-floor conference room, was the six-man PRC board: Ed Fitzgerald, Joe Burke, Clark Griffith, Bob Howsam, Dan Galbreath, and John McHale.

They had been waiting in the wings in the capital, along with Bowie Kuhn and his executive council. The Lords had been dividing their time between the Washington office of Baker and Hostetler and the Hay Adams Hotel. (The baseball establishment was definitely *not* about to patronize Ed Williams's hotel, the Jefferson.)

They'd had two days of nothing more interesting than listening to John Fetzer's predictions of an imminent settlement. (The Tigers' owner, for all his conventional conservatism, had beliefs in mystical powers and occult forces. He felt higher powers were moving things toward a conclusion.) Now they wanted in, and Ray Donovan was more than happy to have them.

The Lords wanted to show their faces primarily to shut up Marvin Miller. He maintained this was dragging on because Grebey was keeping them in the dark. Miller had sent a telegram to all twenty-six clubs that week outlining his latest pooled-compensation proposal. (The players were willing to drop the protected list for compensation to twenty-four from thirty-six.) The inference was clear: Miller didn't trust Grebey to tell them.

Nothing substantive happened that afternoon: speechifying and handing back and forth taped pieces of paper—the latest proposals, literally stitched together. But at least they had twenty-two people in one room, eyeball to eyeball.

The expanded group met again Thursday morning, and the players sensed something was afoot. They were hearing a lot more from Lee MacPhail, the American League president, and a lot less from Ray Grebey. They were hearing fewer statements and, for the first time, more questions: "Would a club have to contribute to the compensation pool if they didn't draft any free agents?"

The players straightened up in their chairs, silently excited. Could a deal finally be coming on? The meeting went on for hours, the most substantive one since the strike's beginning.

Then a PRC staffer hurried in, thrusting a piece of paper before Grebey. He peered at it through his half-glasses, then looked across the table. "Could we have a caucus?" he said.

After a few minutes, the PRC delegation filed back in. Discussion continued but the owners' ranks had rehardened. The two sides had been moving toward each other rapidly; now suddenly they could go no further. It was like a ninth-inning rally that fell a run short. The day ended; dispirited, the players left.

Only later did they learn what had happened. That morning's *Los Angeles Times* had carried a story headlined LOPES TAKES SOME SHOTS AT DECINCES. It had been picked up by the wires and brought to the PRC's attention.

Dodger second baseman Davey Lopes had called the negotiations "a circus," and that was just the beginning:

"Each side has handled it poorly," he declared. "What the hell is the players' executive board doing in negotiations? I don't think they have credentials to be in a labor meeting. Do Doug DeCinces and Bob Boone have legal backgrounds? . . . I didn't see any postal clerks going into their negotiations. As an entity, we have become the laughingstock of the United States. Everybody's laughing at us. We are not to be respected as a union. . . .

"The last thing I want to do is pick up a paper and read Doug DeCinces' synopsis about the players' feelings because he is not qualified and he doesn't know what he's talking about. The forget-the-season attitude really eats at me. Before we do that, brother, we better stop and take a vote.

"We all better stop and think about that before we get so deep in this strike that we can't dig ourselves out. We've got to get back to the field. It's my life, it's my livelihood."

The players grimly read it for themselves. Clearly, the Lords saw the players' resolve crumbling. If Davey Lopes was popping off, how many other players must be set to throw in the towel? It was the old multiply-by-ten rule.

DeCinces turned to Miller.

"Marvin, that's it," he said. "We're going to hear our constituents. Let's get going and set up some meetings."

Miller was exhausted. He was sixty-four, a weary old fighter hanging on in the late rounds. He didn't want to jet around the country. He didn't want to recess the talks. It might only compound the impression that the union was in disarray.

"No," he said, "let's just go back to New York."

DeCinces was drained too. He'd wrenched his back just before the strike. Had the season continued he'd have been on the disabled list, taking therapy. Instead, he'd been sitting in hard chairs, staying up all hours, jousting with Ray Grebey. He was having trouble walking, sitting, and sleeping. Last weekend he'd had a spinal tap at a Baltimore hospital. But DeCinces was adamant.

"This ball could start rolling downhill in a hurry," he said. "We've got to get out there."

Miller nodded his head wearily. He would go along.

Leland Stanford MacPhail, Jr., was as different from Leland Stanford MacPhail, Sr., as a double was from a double play. The father was called Larry MacPhail, the "Roaring Redhead." He'd left his mark on the Reds, Dodgers, and Yankees in ten short years, then flamed out. The son was called Lee MacPhail. Though he hadn't an ounce of flash, he had been a loyal servant of baseball for forty years: a GM at Baltimore and New York, an assistant to Spike Eckert, and, since 1973, president of the American League.

MacPhail had taught at Deerfield Academy before entering baseball, and retained the polished air of the prep-school master. He had a placid oval face, listened to classical music, and had a bland demeanor. They were unusual qualities in a baseball man, but they would come in quite handy now.

MacPhail had been around the battlefront all summer. He was a member of the PRC, if only the supporting cast. He constantly took soundings among the American League owners. MacPhail was also a steady producer of thoughtful ideas. At age sixty-three, he was old-line but not hardline. He'd been trying to figure out a form of pooled compensation that might satisfy both Miller and the Lords. "Lee was drafting and noodling all the time," says Barry Rona.

MacPhail was about to be pushed to the fore. As the strike crept past its fortieth day, in late July, the Lords' attitudes were shifting. The strike insurance was going to run out soon. The season was going to be lost if games didn't start again soon. The fire in their belly on free-agent compensation was dying. "More people started thinking, 'This isn't worth fighting over,'" said Jerry Reinsdorf. "The American League was in open rebellion."

Grebey had been fine when the Lords wanted someone to stick it to Miller. But now they needed someone who could talk to Miller. They were ready to deal. "Relations between Grebey and Miller were so acrimonious, it was time to put a new face in there," recalled Chub Feeney, the National League president. "Lee is a super person and was much more malleable to compromise."

MacPhail resisted. He knew he was no labor negotiator, and he didn't want to undercut Grebey. But Bowie Kuhn, Lou Hoynes, Chub Feeney, and other old-guard stalwarts pressed him. Ed Williams, the new boy, clinched it. He had petitioned for another ownership meeting and gotten it: next Wednesday, July 29. To MacPhail, his choice was finally clear: either take action or let Ed Williams seize it. "Okay," he finally told his old-guard friends, "I'll do it."

Marvin Miller was preparing to leave for the first player meeting, in Chicago, when the call came from MacPhail. Would he be willing to meet alone? Miller, intrigued, quickly agreed.

They met at the Helmsley Palace Hotel in Manhattan on Monday morning. MacPhail put it to him straight out: What would it take, bottom line, to get a settlement? Miller once again went over pooled compensation. He insisted players get service time for the strike. (This was important, since players needed full seasons to qualify for free agency and salary arbitration.) MacPhail listened quietly and said he'd get back to him.

Miller left and flew to Chicago. He wondered what was going on with the owners. He wondered, too, what was going on with the players.

Bob Boone took a deep breath, as though relaxing himself for a 3–2 pitch. He was looking out at nearly sixty players in this O'Hare Hilton conference room: twenty-six player reps, comprising the executive board, and about thirty others who lived in the Chicago area.

"Okay, here's what's before us," said Boone.

For five and a half hours they would hash it all out. Boone and DeCinces recounted the history of the negotiations. Miller explained how the Lords' notion of compensation was designed to punish clubs signing free agents. He outlined his own pooled-compensation idea, which he felt answered the clubs' purported needs for "competitive balance" without killing free-agent demand.

"If you had to take a team vote today," Miller asked the player reps, "do you think the clubs' proposal would get majority support?"

Two of the reps saw it as "iffy." The other twenty-four had no doubt: no way.

At 11:00 P.M., when the players emerged to a phalanx of cameras and microphones, they were true believers, to a man.

"I came here in communications limbo," said Mike Krukow, the Cubs pitcher. "I was getting impatient. I was ready to shout fire and brimstone, but all my questions were answered by Marvin before I could ask any of them."

Echoed teammate Bill Buckner: "I'm behind the negotiating team one hundred percent. I was feeling uncomfortable when I came here tonight. I don't like sitting around. Now I can sit out the season and not feel quite as bad."

He and Krukow left together, saying they weren't going to work out anymore. They were going to look for jobs.

In Los Angeles, about seventy players filed into the ballroom of the Marriott Hotel near L.A. International Airport. Doug DeCinces looked out at them anxiously. The Chicago meeting had gone fine but this was Lopes country.

"Okay," he began, "some of you have been dissenting. We want to hear from you now."

Jerry Reuss, the Dodgers' player rep, echoed that sentiment, declaring, "If someone has an objection, damn it, say something."

Reggie Smith, the Dodgers outfielder, verbally leveled Lopes. Other players piled on. Hadn't they all learned about the need for unity?

Then Lopes stood up. Yes, he'd spoken out, he said, but his remarks had been taken out of context. What really irked him was the players who were getting paid through this whole thing. Some players had negotiated contracts that guaranteed their salary: Steve Carlton, Larry Hisle, Bill Madlock, John Montefusco, Gene Garber, and Lopes's own teammate Steve Garvey.

"When there are all these guys out here who are striking and suffering, I think anybody taking money from the owners is just a joke," said Lopes. "I didn't think any players were going to get paid, and if there ever was another strike I'd want to know that in advance."

Bobby Grich disagreed. "I think anybody in this room would have gotten the same deal if he could have," he said. "More power to them. At least we're whacking them for a few more dollars."

There was little other disagreement. DeCinces had feared a donnybrook. Instead he got a love fest. After two and a half hours, Rod Carew called for a voice vote. All in favor of continuing the strike: seventy voices bellowed "Aye." All against: silence.

Afterward, Lopes made his way over to DeCinces and stuck out his hand. "I'm sorry," he said.

DeCinces shook it. "I appreciate that," he said. "Thanks for coming to the meeting."

It was supremely ironic. The players had halted bargaining to tighten their ship. They hadn't realized they'd also be tightening the screws on the owners. The longer they had no foil on the other side of the table, the more the Lords turned on one another. They were collapsing faster than a spent pitcher.

It was midday on Wednesday, July 29, day forty-nine of the strike, when the American League owners met in the league's Park Avenue offices. Ed Williams was gloating. He had eight solid votes in his pocket to force binding arbitration. With that AL bloc, he planned to force the issue at the later joint meeting. "Here we are," he said, delighted with his coalition, "arrayed politically from Genghis Khan [gesturing to Clark Griffith] to Mahatma Gandhi [himself]."

Lee MacPhail wasn't amused. He coolly made two requests of Williams. One: stop mouthing off to every baseball writer in America. Two: stop acting like he was running the American League. He, not Williams, would decide when league meetings would be held.

But overall, the hour belonged to the dissidents. "This [standoff] is insane and asinine," said Jerry Reinsdorf. "We should call it off."

After they'd gone around the table, Roy Eisenhardt of the A's spoke up. "I move that it hereby be resolved the strike issue be submitted to arbitration," he said.

Gabe Paul of the Indians seconded it. Eight of the fourteen owners were prepared to vote for it when MacPhail stepped in with a plea. "This isn't the time to break ranks and throw out the whole bargaining process," he said. "I believe things are moving again in negotiations."

He described briefly his own emerging role and his diplomatic initiative with Miller. The union chief was heading back from L.A. and they would resume talks tomorrow.

"Let's give this a little longer," he said. "Trust me."

Since this was Lee MacPhail and not Ray Grebey speaking, they did.

What a difference three weeks made. The Lords who gathered at Citicorp Center for the joint meeting that afternoon were not the same bellicose bunch of earlier in July. They would deliver no tub-thumping speeches on solidarity. They held no illusions about seizing back control. Only Ted Turner could still manage to fire off a few stray parting shots of rhetoric.

"I say we do what God did," he thundered. "Put two players on a boat and drown the rest of the fuckers."

He paused.

"A strong letter will follow."

Only weak laughter followed in this room, for everyone knew the truth. They were embarking on the dreary endgame of this strike, in which they'd once again been drubbed by Marvin Miller. All that was left to discuss, really, was how best to restart the season.

"Every strike is a war of attrition," Barry Rona later reflected. "This one had been a tremendous battle of strengths—who's going to blink first?"

After standing eyeball-to-eyeball for seven weeks, it was the Lords.

That night, Lee MacPhail called Marvin Miller again. Could they meet at the National League office in the morning?

MacPhail brought Grebey; Miller brought Fehr; the tone was quickly set. "We're here to make a settlement," said MacPhail.

It was clear who was in charge. When Grebey tried to interject points, MacPhail cut him off. When MacPhail suggested amendments to Miller's proposals, the union chief cut *him* off.

"This is it," Miller said. If he made any substantive changes, he told MacPhail, he'd have to reassemble his executive board. It would take time and they both knew the season hung in the balance. Unspoken was another important reality. Miller finally had the Lords by the short hairs and he knew it. They'd have to swallow it all: free-agent compensation his way, player service credit for the strike's fifty days, the works. He coldly refused to cut any slack. "I wanted nothing less," he later wrote, "than complete and unconditional surrender."

It took until 5:00 A.M. the next day to dot all the *i*'s and cross all the *t*'s. The twenty-two-page settlement had more provisions than the recent Camp David peace treaty, but the major points told the story:

- Clubs signing free agents could protect twenty-four players: nonsigners twenty-six. All remaining players went into the compensation pool. Clubs that lost a free agent got the pick of the pool. Clubs that lost a player in the pool got $150,000, drawn from an industry fund to which everyone contributed.
- A maximum of nine free agents per year were subject to compensation. They had to rank among baseball's top 20 percent of players, as determined by a formula. Lesser free agents would be compensated by amateur draft picks.
- Players who had at least twelve years in the bigs or were going through free agency a second time weren't subject to compensation. (Reggie Jackson got his "senior player" provision.)
- Miller agreed to drop the NLRB complaint and extend the new Basic Agreement an extra year, to 1984. Nobody wanted to do this again anytime soon.

Barry Rona found himself using one phrase over and over as he explained the provisions to owners: "better than nothing."

The two sides staggered into a 6:00 A.M. press conference at the Doral. As everyone assembled on the podium, Mark Belanger turned to Lee MacPhail. "Lee," he said, "we can never let this happen again."

Terms were announced; questions answered; and the briefing wound down. Photographers clamored for the traditional handshake by the negotiators.

DeCinces leaned toward Miller. "I don't think you should pose with him," he said. Miller agreed and turned away from Grebey.

Grebey, trying to find *some* hand to shake, approached Rusty Staub. The player pivoted and walked away. Grebey followed him. Staub walked around a table, trying to put distance between them. Grebey pursued. "You're a liar," Staub screamed at him, still circling the table. "You're always going to be a liar, and you're not going to be my friend."

Finally, Grebey gave up. The writers turned to their stories; the sun came up over Manhattan; the strike was over. It had lasted fifty days and taken away 712 games from the season.

Ray Kroc threw open the doors gratis for the Padres' first poststrike game. It was a sweet gesture, and it drew 52,600 fans. The same evening, 60,500 fans paid their way into Veterans Stadium to see Pete Rose resume his assault on Stan Musial. He got his record-breaking hit in the eighth inning, and 3,631 balloons were released (again).

But otherwise, the aftertaste was sour all around.

Bowie Kuhn attended Hall of Fame induction ceremonies two days after the strike's end. Bob Gibson and Johnny Mize were being enshrined, and Cooperstown in August was always aglow with the myths and mystique of baseball. Kuhn was thunderously booed.

He was also privately blasted by some owners for baseball's jerry-rigged second half. Cincinnati wound up with baseball's best overall record (66–42) yet didn't make the playoffs. St. Louis had the National League East's best record (59–43) and was left out, too. The Howsam–Susman axis had new reason to be furious. (The Reds and Cardinals were also the only clubs to vote against the new labor contract's ratification.)

Susman, the hawk, and Ed Williams, the dove, would soon join forces to launch an anti-Kuhn putsch. Williams first had to endure an inquisition into his own actions during the strike. Some owners wanted him brought up on sedition charges. An independent attorney was retained to investigate, but after some time had passed and tempers cooled, the matter was quietly dropped.

By December 1981, nine owners joined under the Williams–Susman banner and signed a Bowie-must-go letter. It was the beginning of more than two years of bloody infighting, during the course of which Williams switched sides. But in the mood of poststrike discontent, Kuhn's demise was set in motion. He ultimately resigned in 1983.

Indeed, the stature of the entire old guard was severely eroded. "We used to take new owners aside and take them to the woodshed, if necessary, to make sure they stayed with the program," said Lou Hoynes. "We'd lost our authority. The center wouldn't hold."

Peter O'Malley's influence also went into eclipse with Kuhn's demise. After thirty years' hegemony over baseball, the House of O'Malley was toppled. The Dodgers' president was just another owner.

Ed Fitzgerald, who became a scapegoat for the failed strike, resigned as PRC chairman and got out of baseball altogether. He would eventually become chairman of Northern Telecom, the telecommunications giant. Ray Grebey was gone by 1983 as well.

Lee MacPhail and Chub Feeney saw their league-presidency powers wane, as a restructuring committee weakened the leagues' autonomy and centralized more power with the commissioner. MacPhail left as American League president and succeeded Grebey at the PRC.

New owners came to the fore. The Brewers' Bud Selig, until now Ed Fitzgerald's second banana, headed the search for a new commissioner. Jerry Reinsdorf went on the executive council. Oakland's Roy Eisenhardt cochaired the restructuring committee.

But there was a danger in the old guard's passing, a vacuum that couldn't readily be filled. Paul Porter, the legendary Washington lawyer and counselor to commissioners, used to joke that the sport should be called "disorganized baseball." After 1981, it was no joke.

The immediate battle toll was staggering on both sides: $72 million in losses for the owners, offset by $44 million of strike insurance proceeds; and for the players, $28 million in lost salaries. But just as stats alone do not win a pennant race, the dollars don't tell the whole story.

The point was that the owners had failed to grab back control. The union hadn't been broken but strengthened, its free-agency rights intact and its battle-worthiness forever established. "Our strength was our naïveté," Phil Garner recalled. "There was a right and there was a wrong. Free agency was a right, and it was wrong not to have it, and we weren't going to give it up. That was a strength, and it carried over for a number of years."

It was Marvin Miller's finest hour, especially to one who viewed his union in a broader labor context. The American landscape was littered, that summer, with other tattered unions. PATCO, the air-traffic controllers' union, was broken, its striking members fired. The United Mine Workers splintered into factions, carrying out wildcat strikes to little effect. But the reputation of the Major League Baseball Players Association was made. In the age of Reagan, with the labor movement in rout, it would be held up as a notable exception. Some would come to call it America's most successful union.

That didn't mitigate the players' mistrust and anger, which carried over in negotiations for years to come. "The strike left such a foul taste with me; it permanently colored the way I viewed people and their motives," said Don Fehr. "It left significant scars that were still there five years later."

By then, he and the players would be dealing with a new commissioner, a man who would usher in a new age of baseball-as-business; a man who symbolized the breakdown of the cumbersome old-guard conventions; a man to whom the Lords would give themselves over.

"That's what happens when you become desperate," Lou Hoynes later reflected. "You look for a man on a horse, a superpower to do the job for you. You say, 'Here you are, our emperor, take us to the promised land.' "

The man on the horse was Peter Ueberroth.

$ 15 $

Pitcher Mike Norris, on losing at salary arbitration:
"No problem. I was either going to wake up rich or
richer."

THE JOKE WAS on the Lords. They'd fought the wrong war. Obsessed with getting free-agent compensation, they didn't see the real enemy: salary arbitration.

A harmless mechanism when created in 1973, it was to become a monster in the post-*Messersmith* world. In salary arbitration, players linked their demands in salary arbitration to what free agents commanded in the open market. Linking those two, said Ray Grebey, "was like putting a gun in your mouth and a saber in your side."

It would become a matter of legend, in the Lords' inner councils. They'd been snookered by Marvin Miller and failed by their own negotiators. They hadn't foreseen, in 1976, how free agents' riches would rain onto other players.

Not true, said Ed Fitzgerald, who chaired the PRC then. It wasn't lack of wisdom but lack of leverage. "Marvin had us with nothing," he said. "The only way he would agree to a six-year wait for free agency was if that group of three-to-five-year players was able to do something about their salary."

In salary arbitration, players with that level of service had a court of appeals. If they couldn't come to terms with their teams by mid-January, the two sides each filed a proposed pay figure. Then, in February, an arbitrator heard each case. At the end, he picked either the player's or the team's figure.

The truth, Fitzgerald later maintained, was that the mechanism of salary arbitration wasn't the problem. It was the handling of it. GMs caved in to players' salary demands to avoid it. GMs made crazy deals, which set benchmarks for other players to use in arbitration. Many old-line GMs were uncomfortable and unskilled—and sometimes outraged—in this forum.

"You'd say, 'Sure this player might have hit .278, but he can't inside-out the ball,' and the arbitrator would look at you kind of funny," said Dodgers GM Al Campanis, referring to the ability to hit behind the runner. "We knew the players' real contributions to the team, but arbitrators went solely by statistics."

Angels GM Buzzie Bavasi couldn't believe the nerve of a .211 hitter trying to get an 83 percent raise. But that's just what outfielder Bobby Clark went for in salary arbitration. When the arbitrator interrupted the presentation to ask what an RBI was, Bavasi stomped out. By his lights, baseball had gone mad. Clark won his case and a $145,000 salary.

By contrast, top agents reveled in salary arbitration. Most of them were lawyers, and this was a quasi-judicial proceeding. They were skilled at putting together arguments; GMs were skilled at putting together baseball teams. It was, in many cases, a mismatch.

"There's a great deal of strategy and gamesmanship in reaching your filing number and negotiating [for a settlement]," said veteran baseball man Tal Smith. "For an agent, this is all he has to do. A GM has *lots* of things to do."

In the late seventies, when he was Houston's GM, Smith suggested a way around this. Each November the GMs had an annual meeting. At one, Smith proposed they hire outsiders to do their contract negotiations.

"It's the same reason players have agents," he reasoned. "We don't have the expertise, and it's very time-consuming."

The idea was met with hoots: "Boy, you do that and the next thing you know that guy's going to have your job."

The GMs, in other words, would rather do the job badly than allow any encroachment on their responsibilities. They were thus easy meat for the sharper agents. It didn't make that much difference when the stakes were low. Through the 1970s, the highest salary ever awarded by an arbitrator was $140,000—to Reggie Jackson. In a whole winter's worth of salary arbitration, no more than $275,000 was at stake. (That is, the total amount in dispute between all clubs and all players did not exceed that amount. The average spread was less than $20,000.)

But as the price of free agents climbed, so did the ante for salary arbitration. Skillful player agents figured out how to ride the coattails of the free agents.

Among the more skillful was a team of brothers: Randy and Alan Hendricks. Back in the early seventies, when they were in their early thirties, they were immersed in Houston's galloping real estate development, Randy as a lawyer, and Alan as an investor.

On the side, almost as a hobby, they did some agenting. They both liked sports and they'd met Elmo Wright, a University of Houston receiver. When he was drafted by the Kansas City Chiefs, they represented him. That led to their handling of a few more Texas football players.

In the mid-1970s, two things happened to change their lives. The Houston real estate market bottomed out, and the pro-sports business changed. Tight end John Mackey sued the NFL over its restrictive free-agency system and won. The "Rozelle rule," requiring compensation for a free-agent signing, was overturned. A more open market for pro football players lay ahead—along with greater incentives for representing them. At about the same time, baseball's *Messersmith* decision came down. The brothers Hendricks looked at each other, looked at the vacancy rates in Houston, and jumped into agentry full-time.

By 1978, they had seventy-five NFL clients and were making solid inroads into baseball as well. They got their start in Cleveland, where the Hendrickses met Indians pitcher Fritz Peterson at a real estate investment seminar. Before long they represented fifteen of that team's twenty-five players. GM Phil Seghi would see them coming and start crooning an old song: "No, no, a thousand times no."

It was a more lighthearted response than they got from some GMs. The Royals' John Schuerholtz actively despised agents as a breed, calling them "the Darth Vaders of baseball." Sputtered the Mets' Frank Cashen: "They're unregulated, unqualified, and unprincipled."

The Tigers' Jim Campbell never did get over footing the bill for one agent's training. He was once all set to release a first baseman named George Kalifatis from Detroit's triple-A farm team, when Kalifatis made a plea. He was going to law school and if the Tigers would keep him just one more season it would finance his last year. Campbell agreed.

Kalifatis got the law degree, got out of baseball, and got a job with International Management Group, the multi-sport representation giant. When Campbell next saw Kalifatis, he was sauntering into the Tigers' spring training camp carrying a briefcase and wearing a natty suit.

"Jim, I want to thank you for what you did for me," Kalifatis said. "If there's anything I can ever do for you, let me know."

"Well, there is something you can do," said Campbell. "Stay the fuck away from our clubhouse and our kids."

But even inveterate agent-haters could stomach the Hendricks brothers. They had the good-old-boy manner, even though they were actually Kansas City transplants. And they played off each other well—Alan, the owlish nice guy; Randy, the shaggy-haired, tart-tongued one. They drove a hard bargain, but they didn't make it unpleasant. As one GM put it, "I would enjoy having dinner with Alan while he was picking my pocket."

Hendricks Sports Management grew as their original Indians players were traded. By this means their clients were seeded throughout the majors, leading to referrals on other teams. By the late seventies, they represented more than sixty baseball players.

It was then that they decided to concentrate on baseball. Football was like a fraternity rush. The top college players expected to be wooed, entertained, and pampered by prospective agents then they'd choose one. Baseball players were less apt to be spoiled brats.

There was also a huge difference between the two sports' unions. Marvin Miller saw agents, when correctly deployed, as union allies—even lieutenants. They helped to remind players of their best economic interests. And they were a great source of intelligence from the owners' camp. But he certainly didn't like all agents equally. For example, he despised Jerry Kapstein, feeling he'd poorly represented some players and reaped unconscionable fees. (Kapstein, of course, was also something of a rival to Miller for influence with players.)

"He was very respectful and regarded agents as a key element in the equation," recalled Randy Hendricks. "Ed Garvey, with the NFL Players Association, was antagonistic."

The baseball union's positions came out of endless discussions among the players, moderated, of course, by Miller. The football union's positions came straight out of Garvey's mind, finished products he then tried to sell to the players. One approach built a strong foundation for player unity; the other was prone to cracking under stress.

Miller tied all of his players' interests together, using the top players' pay to lift all players' pay. Garvey separated his players, saying, "This union is for the guards and tackles. The quarterbacks can take care of themselves."

The final difference was that Ed Garvey fumbled away free agency. In return for a number of considerations, the union in

1977 allowed the NFL to return to the Rozelle rule. The considerations yielded short-term gains: a five-year, $107 million benefits package, a payment of $13.65 million in damages on the Mackey suit, and a system for deducting dues from players' paychecks that shored up the union's shaky finances. But it cost players their newly won mobility.

"The baseball system was just far better," said Randy Hendricks.

He and his brother became masters at pulling the system's levers. When the Astros granted the first million-dollar-a-year contract to Nolan Ryan in 1979, the Hendricks brothers quickly turned it to the advantage of their client Joe Sambito.

Sambito was Houston's ace reliever. In 1979, he was 8–7 with a 1.78 ERA. He made the All-Star Team and had twenty-two saves, the fourth most in the league. He made $71,500 and the Astros offered to double his salary for 1980, to $143,000. The Hendrickses wanted it tripled. They filed for salary arbitration at $213,000.

Randy Hendricks gave the arbitrator a tutorial on relievers. They weren't second-string pitchers; they were vital cogs. He recited the salaries of every other player on the All-Star Team, all dramatically higher than Sambito's. Then he trained his guns on Nolan Ryan.

"Now, the Astros are paying this man one million dollars in anticipation of his being a big attendance draw," he said. "But let's look at the record."

Hendricks had charted Ryan's value as a gate attraction with the Angels. It showed California averaged fewer fans when Ryan pitched (31,000) than in other games (34,000).

"Mr. Arbitrator," he said, "can you believe the Astros would take all this money and give it to a player like that while trying to get away with offering $143,000 to my client?"

Sambito won. At the time, the $213,000 award was the highest ever in salary arbitration. It wouldn't be for long. Two sharp Chicago agents were about to go to bat for one sharp Chicago pitcher.

Jim Bronner and Bob Gilhooley rode the commuter train into the Loop each morning from the north suburbs. While other commuters buried themselves in the morning papers, they talked baseball. Bronner was a trial lawyer who also dabbled in real estate. Gilhooley was a former Detroit Tigers farmhand, now in marketing.

One morning in early 1977, they passed a newspaper story back and forth. Marvin Miller had announced the union was taking steps "to control abuses by player agents." He blasted the high fees reaped by Jerry Kapstein and representatives of other first-time free agents. "It represented nothing less than gouging," he said. Miller also charged that the agents' ranks were rife with "conflicts of interest" and "quick-buck artists."

They shook their heads. Bronner wondered aloud, "Wouldn't it be interesting to get involved and provide a different level of service?"

Gilhooley was intrigued. "Let's see if we can do the job," he said.

They got their start from Steve Stone's mother, a cousin of Gilhooley. She put him on to Stone, and Stone put him on to Cubs teammate Rick Reuschel. The pitcher was having problems with an investment he'd made in a downstate Illinois farm. After Bronner and Gilhooley helped work out his problems there, Reuschel asked them to negotiate his next contract with the Cubs.

His letter to them, laying out his objectives, is still framed in their office. His goal was to make at least $100,000. The agents' goal, recalled Gilhooley, was "to approach Rick's contract as though he were a businessman. No executive in the fifty percent tax bracket would take that whole tax hit. We didn't think Rick should, either."

They drew up a forty-three-page contract that was their pride and joy and GM Bob Kennedy's despair. It bagged Reuschel his $100,000 but also got him valuable deferrals and myriad other goodies. That contract became the fledgling agents' ticket to representing more Cubs.

One of them was Bruce Sutter. After his first two years in the bigs ('76 and '77), the pitcher was negotiating his next contract with the Cubs. He and Kennedy agreed on the basic terms—three years at $150,000 per—but then Rick Reuschel offered a suggestion. Why not let Bronner and Gilhooley help him structure the payments?

They agreed to do the job, though they wondered if he hadn't already sold himself short. Sutter had established himself as a promising reliever. "What if you do great?" Bronner asked. "You've locked yourself in."

Sutter, who'd already shaken hands on the terms, didn't want to renege. He did, however, authorize the agents to send out a feeler. "Would you be interested in leaving the third year open to renegotiation?" Bronner asked Kennedy.

The GM was cool.

"This would give you the right to renegotiate down as well as up," Bronner reminded him.

Now, *that* had some appeal. The Cubs always expected the worst of their players.

"You'd give me the right to go *down* as well as up?" asked Kennedy. "Nobody's ever done that."

They struck a bargain that was sufficiently unusual that it required the blessing of both union and PRC: two years, guaranteed, at $150,000, with the third year subject to renegotiation. If the two sides were at an impasse at that time, it would go to salary arbitration.

Sutter proceeded to become baseball's finest reliever. He'd perfected a split-finger fastball that batters were helpless against. In 1979 he led the National League in saves with thirty-seven and won the Cy Young Award.

It was a banner season and it came in his contract's second year. Naturally, Sutter wanted to renegotiate the third. Bronner and Gilhooley proposed a new three-year contract, at $550,000 per. Bob Kennedy countered with $400,000. Back and forth they went until they finally struck a compromise: five years at $475,000 per. Sutter was happy to trade off some bucks to stay in Chicago and to enjoy the security of a long-term contract. Done, said Kennedy.

But when the two sides took the proposed contract to Cubs owner Bill Wrigley, he turned it down flat. Sutter recalled the tone of one meeting in a corner office of the ornate Wrigley Building: "Mr. Wrigley didn't think a player should get that much."

The two sides filed for salary arbitration, the Cubs at $350,000, Sutter at . . . *$700,000.* The baseball world gasped. Only a few veteran players made that kind of money: Pete Rose, at $805,000; Rod Carew, $800,000; Dave Parker, $775,000. Only one pitcher made more: the recently signed Nolan Ryan, at $1 million. Now Sutter was trying to zoom up there with the elite.

Nobody ever tried doing that in salary arbitration. The convention was that players were compared with players of similar experience. Sutter, with only three-plus years in the majors, was saying he was in the same salary league with graybeards like Rose, Carew, and Ryan.

In truth, Sutter never expected such a salary and never expected to go before an arbitrator. Talks continued toward a multiyear deal Wrigley could live with. The pitcher was still more interested in security than the stratosphere of $700,000. "We filed beyond what we wanted," recalled Bronner, "but that number gave us negotiating room."

At least 80 percent of all salary arbitration cases are, indeed, settled by negotiation between the time parties file for salary arbitration in December and cases are heard in February. Sutter and the Cubs still hadn't closed the gap, however, when their scheduled arbitration day came. Walking into the hearing room, Bronner saw Kennedy. They made small talk, and the agent sensed the GM really had no stomach for the proceedings.

"Are you sure you want to go ahead with this?" he asked. "We could probably come to terms right now."

Kennedy hesitated.

"Let me check," he said.

He called Ray Grebey in New York. No, the labor chief advised, go ahead with the case. The Cubs had a winner, he assured the GM.

The Cubs' case was presented by Andy MacPhail, Kennedy's assistant. He was twenty-seven years old and looked five years younger. But he had excellent baseball bloodlines—son of Lee MacPhail, grandson of Larry MacPhail—and he'd prepared assiduously. "I felt the weight of the baseball world on my shoulders," he recalled.

The young MacPhail waded right in. He pointed out that Goose Gossage, the American League's premier reliever, was only paid $330,000 a year. Joe Sambito of the Astros, who had come up the same year as Sutter and who was also a quality reliever, had just won his arbitration case for $213,000. The $350,000 the Cubs would pay Sutter exceeded anything ever paid a three-year man. Even Bronner would later concede: "MacPhail did a wonderful job."

Nonetheless, he effectively counterattacked. Sutter had tied a National League record for saves in 1979. He'd been among the NL's top four relievers in saves every full year he'd pitched. Bronner pointed out how few other relievers had ever won the Cy Young (only two). He argued that Sutter's value to the Cubs transcended his pitching stats. On an otherwise blah fifth-place team, he was a prime attraction. Bronner entered in evidence the Cubs' ticket brochure, with Sutter's picture on the front.

He emphasized Sutter's accomplishments versus the game's other top-paid players and minimized MacPhail's comparisons with other relievers. Bronner hammered home a repeated theme: "A star is a star is a star." He reminded the arbitrator, "You don't have to find that Bruce Sutter is worth $700,000. You only have to find he's worth one dollar more than $525,000 [the midpoint between the two sides' numbers]." He even tried to frame it as a moral, as opposed to a mere fiscal, issue: "You have the power to put an end to this artificial constraint on salaries."

The arbitrator, an NYU law professor named Tom Christensen, mused, "I could be pretty popular with the players if I go for Mr. Sutter. And I could be pretty popular with the owners if I go for the Cubs."

The next day he went for Sutter. Christensen was indeed a popular fellow with the players, though they didn't get to know him personally. It was years before he ever got another salary-arbitration case. Andy MacPhail was devastated. He was unconsoled when the Wrigley Company lawyers complimented his performance, when Gilhooley offered him a job, when Dick Moss called it "the best management presentation of a case I ever saw."

MacPhail knew only that the case would have huge repercussions. The old convention that players were compared with players of like seniority was out. The sky was the limit, and from that sky free agents' riches could now rain even on junior players.

The case jumped not only Sutter's pay but his agents' stock. Hitherto, they'd been so obscure that Reds executive Dick Wagner, who met with them soon after the landmark case, didn't know they were its masterminds.

"What did you think of those buttholes who won the Sutter case?" asked Wagner.

Bronner and Gilhooley beamed. "*We're* the buttholes," they said, as one.

The team remained undefeated in salary arbitration for six years, which didn't hurt their reputation, or their practice. Out of a modest suburban-Chicago office, Bronner-Gilhooley had assembled, by the end of the eighties, one of baseball's biggest client stables. They also underscored another factor that drove up the stakes of salary arbitration. It provided a great forum for an agent to make a big score and a big name.

* * *

Three years after Sutter, a young player would go for the next big salary-arbitration milestone when Fernando Valenzuela shot for $1 million. Though the Dodgers pitcher was only twenty-three years old and a two-year veteran, his agent made the case, again persuasively, that "a star is a star is a star."

The agent was Dick Moss, who had parlayed his longtime union post into superagent status. Moss's clients included Andre Dawson, Gary Carter, Nolan Ryan, Jack Morris, and, perhaps the most appealing of all the early-eighties stars, Valenzuela.

He came out of nowhere in 1981. Pressed into service as an emergency Opening Day starter, Valenzuela pitched a shutout and just kept going. He threw seven more shutouts that year, tying a big-league record despite the strike-shortened season.

It wasn't just that he won games—thirteen his first year and nineteen his second, both times second-best in the league. It wasn't just that he struck out batters—a league-high 180 his first year, a fourth-best 199 the next. It wasn't just that he pitched more complete games—twenty-nine—than anyone in the league those two years.

It was how he did it. He was a roly-poly figure who rolled his eyes skyward with each windup. He baffled batters with a killer screwball and a pitching savvy that belied his age. He was only two years removed from the Mexican League and he attracted throngs of proud, roaring Mexican-Americans to each Dodgers game, a phenomenon that came to be known as "Fernandomania."

After his second year, Valenzuela was eligible for salary arbitration. As Dick Moss saw it, a man for whom a whole mania had been named was worth $1 million. Even he would later concede that it was a tough sell. The Dodgers' $750,000 offer was 40 percent more than the most ever paid a two-year veteran—namely, Rickey Henderson's $535,000. It would more than double his $350,000 salary of 1982. Nonetheless, he went for the million.

Moss harkened back to the last pitcher to explode on the scene like Valenzuela: Mark "The Bird" Fidrych. In 1976 he won nineteen games and the hearts of millions of fans. He talked to baseballs before pitching them, groomed the mound on his hands and knees, and displayed a general radical innocence. Like Valenzuela, The Bird was arguably his league's top pitcher as a rookie, compiling the best ERA (2.34) and throwing the most complete games (24).

Then, midway through his second season, Fidrych blew out his arm and his career was essentially over. "He never got paid what he should have," Moss argued. "You have to pay special players like Mark Fidrych and Fernando Valenzuela what they're worth *today*. You can't assume they're going to be able to keep going on into the future."

Moss produced charts to show what Valenzuela was worth to the Dodgers right now. He'd analyzed attendance for each of the pitcher's starts, factoring in days of the week, promotions, and the opposition. The finding: Valenzuela was worth 6,000 to 7,000 extra fans per game. He'd helped propel the Dodgers to a major league record gate of 3.6 million. What's more, he'd gained the Dodgers a vast new Hispanic market.

Moss presented a video montage of "Fernandomania," capped off by a clip from an interview with Dodgers GM Al Campanis: "All through the years, Mr. O'Malley used to talk about how wonderful it would be if we had a Mexican player. I know that Walter O'Malley is looking down on us and smiling now, because his dreams have come true."

Fernando Valenzuela won his $1 million. When Orel Hershiser had a huge second season two years later, going 19–3, he used the precedent to get his own $1 million. And the money ball bounced on.

Tom Reich was another master of the game. He'd been at it longer than almost any other agent—going back to 1969, when agents could still be thrown out of a GM's office. He lived in Pittsburgh, where he was a corporate lawyer. He was a self-confessed baseball fanatic, with Pirates season tickets, and, in his own words, "a cause-oriented guy."

When he met Dock Ellis at a party one night, the two interests merged. Ellis was a Pirates pitcher and an original. He wore an earring decades before it was fashionable. He once pitched a no-hitter on LSD. He was a black man who wore hair curlers to get his "do" just right. He was complaining, at the party, about being shafted by Joe Brown, the Pirates' GM.

"I'll go in and do your contract for free," said Tom Reich.

Reich proceeded to knock heads with Brown over Ellis and a succession of other Pirates: Dave Parker, Manny Sanguillen, Al Oliver, John Candelaria, and more. Then, through a Cincinnati business contact, he began representing Joe Morgan, George Foster, Ken Griffey, and Dan Driessen of the Reds.

The makeup of those teams meant Reich's early client base was predominantly black and Latino. That led to referrals to other blacks and Latinos: Jose Cruz, Bob Watson, Omar Moreno, J. R. Richard, Enos Cabell.

"He relished the idea he was the defender of the poor minorities," said Chuck Berry, one of a team of assistants he assembled. "He became the Black Knight, in a sense."

Reich's clients didn't stay poor after the *Messersmith* decision, of course, and Reich's baseball practice wasn't perpetually pro bono. Like Jerry Kapstein, he was perfectly positioned for the dawn of free agency. He soon abandoned the rest of his practice and plunged full-time into the baseball scene.

He loved it. He'd close down a bar with players at 2:00 A.M. and huddle with a GM over breakfast at eight. Or vice versa. "I had my best time with it in the seventies," he recalled, "when you could still do deals with general managers on bar napkins."

By the eighties he was baseball's biggest agent. While Jerry Kapstein was scaling back, Reich's stable just kept growing. He eventually had more than eighty players and a staff of lawyers to handle all the details.

Reich was bearded and boisterous and loved the sound of his own voice. Every meeting with an owner or GM had to open with a soliloquy on The World According to Tom Reich. Still, he had more good relationships with management than the likes of Dick Moss.

"Moss hates owners and anytime he can get more somewhere else, it's *adios*," said one GM. "Tom will build a bridge between clubs and players."

It was a toll bridge, however, and Reich aimed to collect top dollar. He was at his most aggressive in salary arbitration. When players and teams exchanged their filings in mid-January, Reich's numbers often left his own staff gasping. This time, they said, he'd surely overreached himself.

Usually not. Reich had a riverboat gambler's feel for how the cards would fall. The trick was to gauge in mid-January where the market would be by the time a player's case was heard in February. Bellwether cases would be won or lost. Cases would often settle by negotiation, each redefining the market. It was more art than science, but Tom Reich's faith in the inflationary push of the market was rarely disappointed. His brother, Sam, took care of the rest.

Sam Reich was a top trial attorney in Pittsburgh. Each winter he took time out from his regular practice for the salary arbitration season. When Sam Reich's courtroom polish was combined with Bill James's statistical wizardry, the other side was really in trouble. James was best known for his bestselling books that analyzed baseball's numbers in new and unique ways. He also hired out for the arbitration season.

When Mario Soto went 14–13 for the last-place Reds of 1982, James dredged up historical records that showed that winning records for starters on last-place teams were rarer than hens' teeth. Phil Niekro, for instance, who would win 318 games in his career, was a twenty-game *loser* on the 1977 Braves. He also documented how much better Soto's record could have been with some support. He won every game in which the Reds scored three or more runs; he lost every one in which they didn't.

"It was a pretty one-sided case," recalled Sam Reich, and Soto pocketed $625,000. (The Reds had filed for $450,000.)

For an arbitration on behalf of Tim Raines, James compiled what they called "the Hall of Fame exhibit." James listed every leadoff hitter in Cooperstown—Lou Brock, Lloyd Waner, Max Carey, and numerous others—and listed their four best consecutive seasons. Then he compared them with the Montreal outfielder's first four seasons. Raines's numbers sparkled beside those of the immortals.

Sam Reich moved in for the summary.

"You know, Mr. Arbitrator, Tim Raines is worth exactly what the club says he's worth" . . . dramatic pause . . . "if you cut off his legs. But if you consider what he's done with his legs—his stolen bases, his runs scored—then he's worth what we've asked for."

He got it.

Certainly not all agents were brilliant and bold.

The agent representing Alan Trammell and Lou Whitaker presented his case in all of about eight minutes, summing it up thus: "You can see these guys are great. Just look it up."

Nick Buoniconti, the linebacker-turned-agent, scrawled out his case for reliever Ron Davis on a legal pad en route to the hearing. It looked pitiful against the Twins' binderized, offset-printed presentation, but that amateurish quality only turned out to be a help.

"One thing I don't consider is the quality of the presentation," said the arbitrator during a recess. "The clubs can afford to pay whatever they need to do it, and the players can't."

He helped Ron Davis escape poverty by awarding him $475,000.

Bob Woolf tried to make his case for Toronto pitcher Dave Lemanczyk by giving the arbitrator copies of news stories and profiles about himself as a sports attorney and expert.

With the weaker agents, the union took an active hand in coming up with the filing number and preparing the argument. Its leaders appreciated the fact that each case contributed to setting the salary scale. Its lawyers would even sometimes step in and take over cases in midstream.

Wade Boggs was trying to become the first non-pitcher to win $1 million in arbitration, and union lawyer Gene Orza didn't like how the hearing was going. When it came time for the final argument, he pinch-hit for Boggs's agent.

"In salary arbitration, people say a lot of silly things," he began. "You have guys trying to prove Chico Carrasquel is better than Ted Williams. But I'll tell you something that is true." He picked up a copy of *The Baseball Encyclopedia.* "There are thirteen thousand players in this book—everyone who's played major league baseball since 1871. You'll only find two people with higher lifetime averages than Wade Boggs: Ty Cobb and Rogers Hornsby. So go home tonight and decide this case. Rule whichever way you want. But remember to call your grandchildren and tell them you spent an afternoon with the third-greatest batter in history." (Orza's claim was true, but it was a comparison of Boggs's first three and a half seasons with the *entire careers* of Cobb and Hornsby.)

Wade Boggs got his million dollars.

Orza also once displayed his rhetorical flair on behalf of pitcher Zane Smith, who was going for a huge raise after finishing 15–10 and being named to *The Sporting News*'s All-Star Team as the NL's best left-hander. But the Braves, pointing out that this was his first good season, seemed to be winning their argument that he was worth $450,000 and not $550,000.

Then Orza jumped in.

"Let me tell you how little $550,000 is in the major league pay structure today," he said. "The Braves pay Ted Simmons $550,000. Ted Simmons can't catch, he can't run, he can't hit much. He is paid $550,000 solely for his brain. [Indeed, Simmons was serving out the twilight of his career in Atlanta.] So surely you can feel comfortable giving $550,000 to the National League Left-Handed Pitcher of the Year."

The arbitrator *wasn't* comfortable with that, and the Braves won, but even Orza's opponents had to admit it was a bravura performance. It also pointed up the difference between the players and the owners: the union sent activist advocates; the PRC sent quiet functionaries.

The Lords did retain one serious countervailing force as salary arbitration moved into megabucks. It went by the name of Talbot M. Smith.

Tal Smith was a wiry, intense man who never wanted to do anything but work in baseball. He spent his boyhood haunting Shibe Park and his college springs doing baseball play-by-play at Duke, during the Dick Groat era there. When Smith graduated in 1958, he wrote to every team in baseball inquiring about jobs. The only nibble was from Cincinnati, where GM Gabe Paul told Smith that if he could learn speed-writing he might have a secretarial job. Smith learned speed-writing and went to work for the Reds, at seventy-five dollars a week.

When Gabe Paul moved on in 1961 to head the expansion team in Houston, he took Smith as an assistant. Smith became Roy Hofheinz's right-hand man in the building of the Astrodome, and later his all-purpose baseball man in the front office. He left the Astros to join Gabe Paul in New York for two years in the mid-seventies, but then returned to Houston in 1975 when given the chance to be president and GM. There he remained until 1980, when he was unceremoniously dumped by new owner John McMullen.

At loose ends that winter, Smith was asked by the PRC if he'd help out the new Oakland owners. They were headed for salary arbitration with two top players, Mike Norris and Tony Armas, and they didn't have a clue what to do. Smith prepared and argued the cases, won both, and saved the A's $440,000. Then Jim Campbell asked if he could handle a Tigers case. He did and he won it. Other clubs took note, and suddenly Tal Smith was a hired gun for salary arbitration.

By the next arbitration season, in 1982, he represented six clubs and won seven of eight cases. Smith was something that many other old-line baseball men weren't: adaptable. He believed to his bones in the old-line values—scouting, farm system, and fundamentals—but he had the capacity for analysis and the stomach for battle that was required in salary arbitration. He also believed he was doing God's work—holding the line against the infidels. "He saw it as a crusade," said Steve Mann, an early member of Smith's team.

Smith came to represent, at one point, half of all teams in salary arbitration. For many of the rest, he was a sort of parish priest: dispensing free advice, providing solace, and taking confession. It was an outreach ministry, really, to the weak and fallen. Think of the baseball business as a big saloon. Think of Smith as the courageous prelate, ministering to the clientele there. Father Smith would walk in, working his way along the bar and counseling sobriety and sense. Everyone took time to listen, for he was supremely respected. But all too often, as Father Smith moved on to another member of the flock, the parishioners promptly tossed back another shot.

Smith put together the first computerized database of performance and salary statistics. His crack staff of analysts and lawyers showed up at hearings packing portable computers. They could put together sharp rebuttal arguments in minutes. But Smith's winning percentage didn't stay at those early dizzying heights. His own side saw to that. Clubs kept doing loopy things and agents kept using them to advantage in salary arbitration.

The proliferation of multiyear contracts had a particular impact. More than 200 of them were signed between 1981 and 1984 by players with less than six years' experience. Many of those contracts paid a premium price to ensure a player stayed put beyond his sixth year. Agents seized on those hefty contracts to argue cases for their own clients in salary arbitration. Tal Smith argued until he was blue in the face: multiyear deals that paid a premium to "buy out" free agency shouldn't be compared to the one-year contracts at stake in arbitration. Nonetheless, the player's side often prevailed.

"The problem wasn't so much that the arbitrator didn't understand," said Ed Wade, another Smith assistant then. "It was that the clubs didn't."

They would all too often do multiyear deals with young stars that didn't actually buy out free agency, but *paid* the players as if they were doing so. Al Holland got a three-year, $1.5-million deal from Philadelphia as a three-year man. Darryl Strawberry got a six-year, $7.2-million deal from the Mets after just a year in the majors. Another one-year man, the Yankees' Dave Righetti, got a five-year deal worth $2.9 million.

The Yankees had any number of ways to infect baseball's pay scale with their loopy deals. George Steinbrenner's early successes with Catfish Hunter and Reggie Jackson had addicted him to the free-agent quick fix, the splashy signing. The difference now was that his strong early front-office team—people like Gabe Paul (back to Cleveland), scouting chief Pat Gillick (off to Toronto as GM), and Tal Smith himself—had departed.

Steinbrenner surrounded himself with toadies and made his own deals.

After the Yankees' 1981 World Series defeat, for instance, he unilaterally decided the team needed more speed. As a onetime collegiate hurdler and assistant football coach, he respected that attribute and shunned all other considerations. At the winter meetings that December, he went after a man called by his agent "the fastest white man in baseball."

"You're going to have grandchildren one day," Steinbrenner told outfielder Dave Collins. "You have a choice. Those children can say, 'My grandfaher was a baseball player,' or 'My grandfather was a *Yankee*.' "

It wasn't so much the "Pride of the Yankees" spiel as the three-year, $2.5 million offer that hooked Collins. It was an incredible sum for a middling outfielder, though he'd stolen seventy-nine bases that year. Steinbrenner had forgotten just one thing. Collins had nowhere to play with the Yankees. He was gone after one year, though his pay was forever embedded in baseball's salary structure.

Steinbrenner's quest for a speed merchant also led to Omar Moreno, whose greatest asset as a player was having Tom Reich as an agent. Reich negotiated a legendary five-year contract for the outfielder, which not only paid an outrageous $600,000 annual base but an additional $214 per plate appearance. For baseball and fiscal purists, that only increased the pain of each at-bat of "Omar the Outmaker," as he was known.

Steinbrenner was such an easy mark for Reich that some owners wondered jokingly just what the agent had on him. Reich got Steinbrenner to bite for, among others, free-agent pitcher Ed Whitson. New York committed $4.5 million to him over five years, but traded him for, in essence, a bag of used baseballs after a year and a half. Whitson's ERA as a Yankee was at 5.38 at the time, and he was booed so mercilessly at the stadium that he couldn't pitch home games.

Another signature Steinbrenner contract was that of catcher Rick Cerone. Signed in November 1982, it paid him $2.2 million over four years, with an incentive clause. If Cerone was ever MVP, he got a $200,000 bonus. If he was runner-up, $150,000; third, $100,000; fourth, $75,000; fifth, $50,000; and sixth to eighth, $35,000. If he never made the MVP top eight, over the contract he got *$100,000*. In other words, Cerone was better off to be a bum than to ever be the league's fourth most valuable player.

All of this was grist for the salary-arbitration mill. All of this helped explain White Sox owner Jerry Reinsdorf's observation. "Baseball is the only industry," he once said, "where I have to pay someone what my dumbest competitor pays."

Reinsdorf devised a system to partially steer the White Sox clear of the process. Chicago would offer young players a multiyear contract that, through incentive bonuses, gave them a chance to quickly climb above the minimum salary. But it also gave the team an option year, preventing the player from going to salary arbitration his first year eligible.

The union screamed bloody murder, filing a grievance that protested the allegedly coercive tactics. But it lost and, indeed, Reinsdorf's only crime seemed to be excessive intelligence, by owner standards. The Lords had been left with but a few years when they still carried the whip hand on pay. Yet Chicago was one of the few clubs to use it.

More commonly, teams simply caved in the face of salary arbitration. The Orioles, Giants, Brewers, and Phillies skirted the process for years, by simply exchanging filings with their eligible players and always settling before hearings. They thereby established new, higher salary benchmarks for every comparable player to come along. The agents' formula was simple but effective. In the words of Tal Smith: "File high, create big spreads, create risk, and scare clubs into a settlement."

As the eighties wore on and salaries rose, the risks of each case did become higher. In 1979, the average spread was $19,000. By 1985 it was $163,000 and climbing. A GM facing several arbitration cases was rolling the dice on his whole budget.

Teams that avoided arbitration were afraid not just of the financial consequences but also of the process itself. They believed arbitration only caused hard feelings between player and club. "It's crazy," declared Edward Bennett Williams. "You spend all this time building up a kid, then use this process to tear him down."

It *could* get rough. The White Sox were particularly known for their bare-knuckle tactics. Tony Bernazard wouldn't speak to White Sox VP Jack Gould for years after his arbitration case. On another occasion, the White Sox got word that Ron Kittle's agent was rounding up some videotape at a Chicago TV station. Smelling a highlights film coming in Kittle's arbitration hearing, the club went out and produced its own "lowlights" piece: footage from an NBC *Game of the Week* telecast. It showed Kittle butchering a ball into some unearned runs, while Joe Garagiola groaned, "They say he's a terrible outfielder, and I guess he's worse than that."

The Cubs brought up Leon Durham's calamitous 1984 playoff error and brought on a tirade from his agent, Dick Moss. The one time Harry Dalton of the Brewers ever went to arbitration—with Jim Gantner—he was angrily confronted afterward by the infielder: "If you feel that way about me, why don't you trade me?"

(If a GM ever said anything nice about a player, on the other hand, a sharp agent might make him pay and pay. Whitey Herzog's book *White Rat* called Terry Pendleton "a jewel" and described the prime requirements of third basemen: "They've got to hit line drives with runners on, and they've got to give you good defense." The St. Louis GM's own words became the cornerstone of agent Jim Bronner's winning case for Pendleton.)

Arbitration hearings were actually not often so contentious. Jesse Orosco once fell asleep in the middle of his. But it was a great negotiating tactic, playing on GMs' fears they'd make the players unhappy and unproductive.

"They take advantage of a fundamental error in our thinking," said Andy MacPhail, who would go on to become the Twins' GM. "It's the height of vanity to think they're out on the mound thinking of the front office. It's about sixty-third on the list. They pitch for their families, their teammates, themselves."

What was true, however, was that players were now horribly money-conscious. It wasn't that they were greedy—though some were—but rather that salaries were the new basis of the pecking order. For ultra-competitive, ultra-proud players, it was how you measured who was the Big Dog. Marvin Miller had started it all by prying open the secrets of the payroll. Salary arbitration, 1980s style, ultimately made comparative pay an open, obsessive matter.

The pre-*Messersmith* player chafed at his shackles but joked about money. Asked how he'd spend his $75,000 salary, pitcher Tug McGraw said, "Ninety percent I'll spend on good times, women, and Irish whiskey. The other ten percent I'll probably waste." The ultimate post-*Messersmith* player was Fred Lynn. "Royalties are life-and-death matters," he said, "not baseball games." When in the same year Denny Walling won his arbitration case and Bill Doran lost his, Houston's spare infielder wound up being paid more than its regular second baseman. The pecking order was disturbed, and so, most assuredly, was Doran.

There was one other reason GMs were scared to death of salary arbitration. The results were about as predictable as a knuckleball. The hearings were sophisticated baseball arguments before an arbitrator who may or may not have understood baseball.

Some cases seemed doomed from the start. As Expos VP Bill Stoneman began his opening statement, an arbitrator once interrupted: "Montreal . . . that's in the American League, isn't it?"

Some cases seemed doomed midway through. During a break in Jason Thompson's hearing, the arbitrator approached the Angels first baseman. "Mr. Thompson, my son is a great fan of yours," he said. "Could I have your autograph?"

Thompson won.

It was widely believed that decisions were influenced by arbitrators' survival instincts. Baseball work was a plum assignment in arbitration circles. You were jetted to Los Angeles, Chicago, or New York for hearings. You achieved godlike status before your baseball-loving friends and neighbors. You added a sexy line to your résumé. You didn't even have to give a reason for your decision. All you had to do was pretty evenly divide your decisions, so neither players nor owners got mad enough to fire you. (The union and PRC jointly selected a dozen or so arbitrators each year to hear the cases.)

It was called "splitting the baby" among the cognoscenti, and it made every case a crapshoot. Ed Wade, an aide to Tal Smith, recalled one doubleheader before the same arbitrator. "We had Brett Butler in the morning, which in our opinion was a slamdunk for our side," Wade said. "Then in the afternoon we had Ron Darling, in a case where nothing supported our number. We figured we'd split. We did, but not the way we thought."

Butler won, and the Indians were out $250,000. (Cleveland had filed at $600,000, the outfielder at $850,000.) Darling lost, and the Mets were up $175,000. (New York had filed at $440,000, the pitcher at $615,000.)

It frustrated both sides, but it was to the players' advantage. A player might shoot too high and lose. But if he shot too high and won anyway, he hadn't just won big for himself. He'd set a new benchmark for every other comparable player. The agents would then seize upon that as "the market."

"It's a brilliant system," giggled one agent. "You don't have to win them all, or even most of them. As long as there are a few settlements or decisions that are high, the players can peg off that. The whole structure goes up."

It went up like an Atlas missile through the first half of the 1980s. Between 1980 and 1984 the average salary more than doubled, to $326,000. As an industry, baseball lost $277 million. The Lords had been crying poverty before the 1981 strike, but now some were really experiencing it.

Some teams, with big markets and big revenues, could make all the foolish moves they wanted and suffer all the inane arbitration decisions possible without much feeling it. (The New York Yankees were, and are, the prime example.) But others were whipsawed.

"You had a total and direct relationship between the clubs on the expense side, but not on the revenue side," said Oakland GM Sandy Alderson.

When Ron Davis won $375,000 in arbitration in 1983, in the noted Buoniconti "legal-pad decision," it began a $1 million hemorrhage for the Twins that year. Calvin Griffith had to borrow $750,000 just to meet his first payroll in 1984, and he had to start looking in earnest for a buyer.

The man Bill Veeck had called "the last dinosaur" sold the franchise for $34 million that year. A family whose baseball roots went back to 1888—when Clark Griffith started pitching— and whose ownership extended back to 1920 was out of the game. Griffith signed the papers with Minneapolis financier Carl Pohlad in pregame ceremonies at home plate and then, before 22,000 people, wept.

Carl Pohlad, the buyer, was typical of the new deep-pockets owner required by baseball. He owned banks and financed such eighties swashbucklers as takeover artist Irwin Jacobs. "I hear he's so rich he bought his dog a boy," said Twins manager Billy Gardner.

It was part of a whole wave of turnover in ownership that year. John Fetzer packed it in after thirty years, selling the Tigers for $52 million to Domino's Pizza magnate Tom Monaghan. And in December 1984, the Reds were sold to a Cincinnati auto dealer named Marge Schott. "You know how women are," she said in the first of many memorable statements. "At Christmas they buy things and charge it."

The dismal state of business was the final undoing of Bowie Kuhn. Having wobbled for two years in the face of growing opposition, he finally lost the confidence of even strong supporters like Charles Bronfman.

"The economics of the industry were in bad shape and Bowie wouldn't do anything to help," recalled the Expos owner. "As salaries started to escalate, you had to improve revenue streams."

Kuhn wasn't the man to do that. He was the guy who'd once scolded the Atlanta Braves for holding a Burger King Bat Day. (They were "prostituting" the game, he sniffed.) He was the guy who'd once refused to let a shaving-lotion company pay the holder of the season's longest hitting streak $1,000 a game.

The age of the romantic traditionalist was over. The age of Ueberroth was about to begin.

$ 16 $

PETER VICTOR UEBERROTH was born in the waning days of the Depression, the son of an itinerant building-products salesman. The story of his first forty years was both classic Horatio Alger and classic California hustler. It was also virtually unknown outside the Ueberroth family. That would all change in the eighties, an age of instant stardom well suited to his talents.

He was born in Chicago and grew up in an assortment of midwestern states, attending six elementary schools and three high schools. The Ueberroths finally settled in California, where he attended San Jose State College. He worked his way through college with a variety of jobs—including traveling seed salesman and chicken-farm egg selector—and with the help of a partial scholarship for playing water polo.

Ueberroth got his business degree in 1959 and quickly got down to business. He took his bride to Hawaii to go to work for financier Kirk Kerkorian's nonscheduled airline, which was based there. He moved back to the mainland at age twenty-four to begin his own business, a travel agency.

By the late seventies, Ueberroth's First Travel Corporation, which began humbly in his San Fernando Valley apartment, was grossing $300 million and ranked as the nation's second biggest travel agency. Then the Los Angeles Olympics Organizing Committee went out looking for a staff director. Ueberroth threw his hat in the rings.

The committee was looking for a big name, like Pete Rozelle or Alexander Haig. But this cool, self-confident entrepreneur with a broken nose (a water-polo souvenir) impressed the members. By the narrowest of margins (a 9–8 vote) he was picked for the job.

* * *

The Olympics had a sorry recent history. The 1972 Munich games had been marred by the slaying of Israeli athletes by terrorists. The 1976 games in Montreal had lost $1 billion. The 1980 Lake Placid winter games faced huge cost overruns, despite $100 million in government aid. The 1980 Moscow games were being boycotted by the United States. Ueberroth was determined that the 1984 games would run smoothly and corporately—and that he would be the CEO.

He demanded that corporate sponsors pay big fees—$4 million—to be associated with the Olympics. (Sponsorships for the Lake Placid games had gone for a paltry $10,000.) He commanded top dollar for TV rights—$225 million, by far the most ever paid for the games. And he screwed down costs relentlessly. He got corporations to underwrite construction of velodromes and swimming pools in exchange for blocks of tickets. He extracted concessions from contractors and got free labor from 50,000 volunteers.

Ueberroth had a saying: "Authority is twenty percent granted, eighty percent taken." He took it all, running the L.A. Olympics Committee with ruthless efficiency. From 1980 to 1983, its staff consisted of less than a hundred people, all of them pushed to their limits. One exhausted staffer heaved his way into the director's office one day.

"You know, I just can't go on, Peter," he said. "I've got to have some help."

Ueberroth looked up.

"What are you doing nights and weekends?"

He was a master at keeping subordinates off balance, alternately intimidating and charming them. He constantly put people on the spot: chewing them out in front of peers, as he pierced them with icy blue eyes, or giving them surprise tests on Olympic lore and international trivia. He cornered one staffer in an elevator and ordered him to name the six republics of Yugoslavia.

Ueberroth was simply pushing to get maximum effort from people and maximum command for himself. He once gathered a group of prominent L.A. businessmen whom he had recruited to oversee particular Olympic sports but who were now grumbling about various problems. At a showdown meeting, he stood on a stage and he coolly laced into them as they sat at their tables: "You've got all these great ideas how an Olympic Games should be run, and you're probably all smarter than I am, but the point is, I'm standing up here and you're sitting down there."

Ueberroth was also a public-relations genius who could see

the appeal of a cross-country torch run and created the feel-good image of the L.A. Games. He sometimes burnished his own image at the expense of the truth—claiming he'd been an alternate on the 1956 Olympic team, say, rather than a failed hopeful—but no matter.

It all worked. The 1984 Olympics turned a $222 million profit on revenues of $718 million. As an orgy of U.S. gold medals (in the absence of the Soviets and their eastern-bloc satellites), the games came to stand, in many minds, as a combined tribute to American muscle and American entrepreneurial spirit. It was what the Age of Reagan was all about. Ueberroth was *Time* magazine's Man of the Year. Now he was ready to move on to new triumphs.

The owners who were assigned the task of finding a new commissioner inevitably turned their eyes toward Ueberroth. They had flirtations with A. Bartlett Giamatti, Yale's president, and James Baker, then Reagan's chief of staff. But even before the magnitude of his Olympics triumph was known, Ueberroth was offered the job.

In March 1984, at an owners' meeting in Tampa, he agreed—with conditions. He wanted the commissioner's maximum fining authority raised from $5,000 to $250,000. The league presidents were to be brought under the umbrella of the commissioner's office. Reelection of a commissioner would just require a simple majority vote, not a supermajority as before. Finally, he required that Bowie Kuhn stay on until October 1.

Sitting upstairs in a Hyatt Regency suite, Ueberroth awaited the owners' response, together with his wife and Bowie and Luisa Kuhn. Finally, Bud Selig called with the word: yes. And it was unanimous.

Kuhn turned to Ueberroth. "I don't know whether to offer my congratulations or condolences," he said.

Ueberroth had been on the job two weeks in October when the umpires threatened to walk out of the National League playoffs. Richie Phillips, their contentious counsel, was at loggerheads with Chub Feeney over a new contract and felt he had some leverage.

The new commissioner stepped in, got it settled—on far more liberal terms than Feeney had offered—and got the umpires back to work. At a press conference someone asked if Ueberroth was concerned about what the owners thought of the generous settlement.

"The owners?" he said. "You can't find them. They're all out on their yachts."

Peter O'Malley read the quote in a Tokyo newspaper the next day and went wild.

"Don't put me in that category," he yelled at Ueberroth across thirteen time zones. "I'm in Japan promoting international baseball."

But that was only the beginning. Ueberroth meant to rule baseball the same way he'd ruled the Olympics. He would intimidate everyone in sight. He'd seize the 80 percent of authority that hadn't already been granted. He would countenance no shoddiness.

Upon the final out of the 1984 World Series, the stands at Tiger Stadium erupted. In a very different way, so did the streets outside. Mobs were soon running about; fires were burning, cars being overturned.

Ueberroth, his wife, Ginnie, and assorted baseball brass were trapped inside the stadium for three hours. Finally, a man named Harry Gibbs made a decision: they'd go for it. In the bowels of the stadium, a group of very worried people climbed into the commissioner's official sedan.

Gibbs was baseball's director of security. A retired FBI agent, he was in charge of investigating drug abuse, gambling influence, and other such threats to the game. He was also the commissioner's bodyguard. This part of the job used to involve mainly keeping Bowie Kuhn supplied with a fresh drink, or so the joke in baseball went.

Peter Ueberroth would demand more. A lot more. He was a control freak who wanted every contingency planned for and who wouldn't tolerate surprises. He'd made the Olympics work by hounding thousands of people into perfection. He expected baseball's biggest showcase to end in glory, not jeopardy. (The breakdown in crowd control was caused partly by an advancement test being held for Detroit policemen that day. It left the force short of supervisors, which baseball hadn't realized.)

The sedan inched through the mob, until it was sandwiched in too tightly to move. Halted, the car was rocked: back and forth, back and forth, the terrified passengers jostled in the seats. Suddenly, providentially, the rocking slowed and the driver was able to move forward again.

The threat was over. And so were Harry Gibbs's useful days with Ueberroth. The commissioner turned to a young man named Bryan Burns, a staffer in his office whom he'd identified as a comer.

"I don't want anything like that to happen again," he said. "I want you to take over the planning for postseason play."

(Burns, too, would eventually learn the hard way about Ueberroth's standards. He was sitting in the commissioner's box at the final game of the 1986 World Series, congratulating himself on how smoothly everything went. It hadn't been easy, but he'd truly thought of everything. Then, drifting down over Shea Stadium, he saw it: a parachutist. *He'd forgotten the air space!* "What are you going to do about that?" said Ueberroth, icily.)

In late November, Ueberroth prepared for his first winter meetings. He made his aides come in the Saturday before a planning session. He impressed on them that the meetings were to be run like clockwork and that the details would have to be all worked out before they left.

"We're like a train moving out of the station," he said. "It's going to be picking up speed, and it's eventually going to be moving very fast. Along the way, a lot of people will fall off the train. If there's anybody that doesn't like going at high speed they should get off now."

A man named Joe Podesta raised his hand to be recognized. Podesta was in the merchandising end of the commissioner's office and he had an idea for the winter meetings. The World Series scorecard cover was a montage of U.S. presidents throwing out first balls. Baseball had printed 2,000 enlarged copies of the artwork and advertised them for $200 apiece in the scorecard. So far, unfortunately, only four had been ordered.

Podesta, desperate to unload them, had an idea. They had a captive audience of hundreds of baseball people at the winter meetings. Why not display the original on an easel in the lobby and sell the prints? He described his idea to Ueberroth.

"How much do you sell them for?" Ueberroth asked.

"Two hundred dollars," replied Podesta, "but we'll give everybody a fifty-dollar break."

"How many do you have?"

"Oh, a thousand," Podesta lied.

"So how much is this worth?"

"A hundred, hundred-fifty thousand."

"Maybe if you added a zero I could get interested," said Ueberroth. He turned and walked out, leaving Podesta to twist slowly in the wind.

* * *

The meetings were in Houston that year. The five-day swirl of events included a dinner for Ueberroth hosted by the Gillette Company.

Gillette had been closely associated with baseball since 1939, when it paid $100,000 to be exclusive sponsor of that year's World Series radio broadcasts. Its sixty-four minutes of Series commercials yielded a gush of business that turned the Depression-ravaged company around. From 1946 to 1956, Gillette was the exclusive radio sponsor of the World Series and All-Star Game. When the World Series was first widely seen on TV, in 1948, Gillette was again the exclusive sponsor.

The company no longer had that kind of grip on baseball advertising, but it still sponsored All-Star balloting. Gillette paid about $250,000 for the rights and production costs. It was a small price to have the company's logo on millions of All-Star ballots and be the sole corporate sponsor associated with the midsummer classic. But then, Gillette had a special place in the heart of that traditionalist Bowie Kuhn.

The commissioner of baseball and the chairman of Gillette dealt with each other more as heads of state than as doers of deals. One year Kuhn would go to Boston to dine with Gillette executives and take in a game at Fenway Park. The next, the Gillette people would come to New York for dinner and Yankee Stadium. Recalled Seth Abraham, then a marketing man in the commissioner's office, "Bowie treasured that relationship."

Kuhn wanted to make sure baseball and Gillette remained entwined. Shortly before leaving office, he approached Coleman Mawkler, the company's CEO. You never know what might happen with future regimes, he said. He offered to nail down the All-Star arrangement long-term. Over a weekend at Martha's Vineyard, a group of Gillette executives worked out a ten-year contract with Kuhn and his people—"an incredible sweetheart deal," according to a participant from the baseball side.

Nonetheless, Gillette wanted to get off on the right foot with Peter Ueberroth. It hoped to have the same special relationship and took pains to make the Houston dinner first-class. As the new commissioner walked in, a Gillette official extended his hand and a warm greeting. Ueberroth responded with razor blades.

"When are you going to step up to an appropriate rights fee for All-Star balloting?" he said.

* * *

Ueberroth applied the same reasoning he had brought to the Olympics. Sponsors should pay a premium price for associating with a premium event. The All-Star Game was worth more like $1 million, as he figured it. He broke the contract and demanded the higher fee.

Gillette, fuming, took a walk. There were no other sponsors in sight. Ueberroth's staff quaked, but he was cool. "If somebody wants to get it, they can afford it," he said.

In 1985, baseball ran the All-Star balloting sans sponsor. But the following year it signed on *USA Today*—for $1 million. That was just the start of an all-out campaign to merchandise major league baseball.

The mechanism to do so had been in place since 1968, when baseball created the Major League Promotions Corporation, its merchandising arm, along the lines of NFL Properties. For years, however, it had drifted without direction, a pale imitation of its football model. Each club earned only about $40,000 a year from it. In the late seventies, pro football's licensing revenues were estimated to be ten times higher than baseball's.

The NFL had "league-think," as well as marketing savvy; baseball had local-think, and a healthy serving of inertia. Teams that did a nice business in caps and T-shirts, like the Yankees and Dodgers, hated to give it up to a central licensing authority. Teams that saw licensing as a nickel-and-dime novelty business didn't want to invest money from the Central Fund, the pool of cash dispersed by the commissioner's office.

Major League Promotions also had a tough time getting owners to approve corporate sponsors. Nobody was good enough for baseball. When Promotions tried selling the Lords on a Rolaids relief-pitching award, they got a chorus of groans: "Can't you find someone any more classy?"

Observed Seth Abraham, "Baseball was the most uncomfortable of all the major team sports in accepting that it was commerce. It carried the baggage of being the national pastime."

The beginnings of more sophisticated business practices came locally. Charlie Finley and Roy Hofheinz were showmen pioneers back in the sixties, of course. The Dodgers were always in a league of their own. But by the seventies, more teams were beginning to promote themselves.

The Twins ran TV ad campaigns to build player identification. One featured catcher Butch Wynegar homering in his first at-bat, making the All-Star Game as a rookie. The commercial, which played up his aw-shucks personality, finally cut to a smiling Calvin Griffith, saying, "I really like that kid."

The Royals had an adjunct sales force called the Royal Lancers, a group of one hundred Kansas City businessmen who hustled season tickets. They were rewarded with a variety of goodies, like cruises and VIP treatment at the park, and they produced. Kansas City had one of baseball's smallest markets and biggest season-ticket bases. (Aiding the cause was a well-spoken group-sales head named Rush Limbaugh.)

The Royals also effectively built a regional franchise. In the mid-seventies they expanded their radio network by 80 percent, to 110 stations, and tripled their TV network to fifteen stations. That extended their reach into the Plains, and they stirred wintertime interest with roaming caravans of players, making speeches and signing autographs. Eventually, 45 percent of the Royals' weeknight crowd came from at least fifty miles away, and 70 percent of the weekend crowd traveled that far.

The Orioles, too, flowered into a regional franchise under Edward Bennett Williams. They got broadcast deals that put them in seven states, dropped the word *Baltimore* from promotional materials, and made a big push into the Washington market. Eventually, 25 percent of their gate came from D.C. The Orioles used to define success along the lines of their 1974 slogan: "A million or more in '74." In 1983 they broke 2 million.

Teams revved up the stadium entertainment. Bill Giles dismayed his arch-conservative father, Warren Giles, by introducing the Phillie Phanatic, but the zany green mascot delighted the fans as it baited umpires and opponents. Between innings, Oakland fans rocked to Top-40 music on a Dolby sound system and roared at "dot races" across the scoreboard. The idea was to make baseball more fun for the casual fan. The rest of the baseball world had finally caught up to Bill Veeck.

To put it simply, rising payrolls had forced a rising standard for doing business. Teams needed new revenues and new fans and they got them. From 1976 to 1984, baseball's attendance climbed almost 50 percent and revenues more than tripled, to $625 million. "It was in this period that you saw clubs start to get more sophisticated," said Drew Sheinman, then an Orioles operative. "You started seeing different kinds of people come into teams' marketing departments."

It was Peter Ueberroth who would take that thrust national. He brought in an Olympics alumnus named Joel Rubenstein to pursue corporate sponsors for baseball at $5 million a pop. Soon

Equitable Life was sponsoring Old-Timers games; IBM was measuring "Tale of the Tape" home-run distances; Arby's was presenting awards to each team's RBI leader. (Arby's and RBIs . . . get it?)

Rawlings, the big sporting-goods maker, had been selling teams their uniforms and equipment for years. Now, Rubenstein informed the company, it would have to *pay* $1 million for the privilege of providing its merchandise. It did, and was duly made Major League Baseball's official equipment maker.

It was another matter selling teams' equipment managers on the change. Crusty and independent, some insisted they were still Wilson men and got bootlegged equipment from the rival sporting-goods manufacturer. In a similar vein, baseball's official soft drink, Coca-Cola, was to be the exclusive clubhouse cola. Imagine Coke's chagrin when a national wirephoto showed the star of one game drinking a Pepsi. An official investigation turned up six cases of contraband Pepsi in the bowels of the stadium.

Still, baseball kept adding sponsors relentlessly.

"Ueberroth had a sense of the real value of what we had," said aide Ed Durso. "He kept preaching, 'Don't be afraid to put a high value on it.' "

Nonetheless, in Ueberroth's early days, the gush of money going out to free agents overwhelmed the new revenue streams coming in. The new commissioner got a look at how the market worked during the Houston meetings.

That year's prize catch was Bruce Sutter. He'd just tied a major league record for saves (45) and recorded a microscopic 1.54 ERA. He'd been *The Sporting News*'s Fireman of the Year three of the past four seasons. His contract with the Cardinals was up, and he awaited the offers.

Ted Turner was first in line. He'd also made a hard pursuit of last year's premier free agent, Goose Gossage. It had come down to Atlanta and San Diego, and the two teams struck a quiet gentlemen's agreement to cap their bidding at a certain point. But the Padres reneged, got Gossage, and won the National League pennant.

Turner had fallen into this role of the unwitting stalking horse—jacking up the bids only to walk away empty-handed. He'd also fruitlessly pursued Pete Rose, Dave Winfield, Don Sutton, and Reggie Jackson. He was determined to get Bruce

Sutter. He threw out a big figure for openers: $7.5 million over five years.

Sutter's agents, Jim Bronner and Bob Gilhooley, countered with a proposition. How about a six-year deal at $1.125 million a year, with $5.5 million of the money funding an annuity. At 12 percent interest, it would pay Sutter more than $40 million over thirty-six years.

The ever-creative Bronner and Gilhooley would also soon do the so-called "lifetime contract" of Dan Quisenberry with the Royals. It plowed his salary into investments in co-owner Avron Fogelman's real estate operation. It guaranteed the pitcher a certain level of cash flow and exposed him to no risk. If the properties flourished, there was a huge upside. If they tanked, the Royals paid off the obligation. The deal was sometimes valued at $2 million a year, though it was so complicated nobody was quite sure.

Don Fehr once said, "It might well be the greatest contract ever negotiated." He didn't mean for the club. When Quisenberry later faded and fell into disuse, he asked Fehr if he had any recourse against the Royals. "Well," Fehr replied, "you could always buy them."

Turner's nose twitched. He was funding the rapid expansion of his TV empire with junk bonds. Big obligations down the road didn't bother him if they accomplished present objectives. He agreed to the deal in principle, though he had one suggestion: move the negotiations to Atlanta, get lawyers drafting, and let Sutter have a look at the city. Bronner and Gilhooley agreed.

They also informed the Cardinals' Lou Susman of their actions. It was a courtesy to the club for which Sutter had pitched for the last four years, a club that still had hope of retaining him. Susman hit the roof. He wasn't about to match Turner, but he would certainly do whatever he could to thwart him. In a National League ownership meeting, Susman introduced a resolution forbidding the kind of contract that Turner was dangling before Sutter. Since it was so clearly aimed at Turner, the Lords passed it.

The next day, the agents and Sutter met with Turner in his office. They were joined by a phalanx of Turner's lawyers. Everybody studied the resolution carefully and agreed: if they simply deposited more money up front they could still do it. But it would take some restructuring and fine-tuning to bring the contract into compliance. Turner pointed to an adjacent conference room.

"Go in there and make it happen," he told the lawyers.

Turner remained in his office with Bronner, Gilhooley, Sutter, and Sutter's wife. There he walked in rapid circles around the room, stopping only at the spittoon by his desk to expectorate. Everybody else tried to make small talk and study the office's assortment of sailing mementos, broadcasting awards, and pictures of Ted. Finally, Sutter couldn't stand any more of Turner's pacing.

"If you go around one more time, I'm going to give you the checkered flag," he said.

The lawyers emerged.

"I've got bad news," said one. "This is going to cost us another million."

"Christ, is that all?" said Turner. "Go ahead and get it done."

Later that day, he gave his Cable News Network the scoop: Bruce Sutter was a Brave for $10 million. Sutter, wearing an Atlanta cap, was all smiles at the press conference, as was Turner. "I finally got me one!" he cackled.

Ueberroth was appalled. It wasn't just the kind of money being thrown around, but the lack of thought that went into it. Owners were stampeded into moves by what columnists, talk-show hosts, and stadium banners said. "All these guys want to be well loved," said the Expos' Charles Bronfman. "You want to be admired in your town."

Pursuing free agents was often less a business decision than a civic cause. When the Royals were pursuing the second-hottest free agent of 1984, Rick Sutcliffe, they threw a dinner party for him that included Kansas City's mayor and Missouri's governor. "If Ronald Reagan walks in now, we give up," said Sutcliffe's agent.

Ueberroth saw little evidence of budgeting, of planning, of attention to the nitty-gritty. The owners knew their teams' won-lost records a lot better than they knew their balance sheets. They all wailed about losing money, but they didn't even know how much they were losing.

"Peter was surprised at the lack of focus these people put into the business," Bryan Burns recalled. "Owners would call and say they couldn't make a meeting. He'd say, 'What do you mean you can't be here? This is your *business*.' "

Under Kuhn, everybody and his batboy attended the ownership meetings—except the owners. Everybody knew the real business had already been done in the executive council. The meetings rambled on without focus or resolutions. Toward the end of one, Peter Bavasi slid a note in front of Ed Fitzgerald:

TODAY'S LINE SCORE
Decisions Made: 0
Committees Formed: 7

Peter Ueberroth stopped that cold. He announced he was doubling the ownership meetings to four a year. There would be just one seat per club in these quarterly sessions and he expected the owner to be in it. They'd deal with each other better, Ueberroth said, if they knew each other better. "If you're friends, why don't you act like friends?" he chided. "Why do you act like enemies?"

Ueberroth also informed them that baseball's real business would be done in these meetings. "The good news," he told Peter Bavasi, now the Indians' president, "is that I'm putting you on the executive council. It'll look great on your résumé, maybe the lead item on your bio. The bad news is that that committee will never meet as long as I'm commissioner."

No, Ueberroth wanted to play to the whole group. It was his forte. The meetings were to be his stage and he set it carefully. He assigned an advance man to scout out meeting sites. He wanted them at hotels, conference centers, anywhere *except* the usual spots. He would wield greater command if the owners were on unfamiliar ground. And Ueberroth had exacting specifications. He wanted amphitheater-style meeting rooms, so that the owners would be seated a bit apart. It kept them from talking to each other and kept their attention riveted on him.

Once a site had been chosen, Ueberroth fussed over details: the temperature of the room, the quality of his slide presentation, and, especially, the meeting's agenda. He wanted to get to the most important topics while everyone was still fresh. Sometimes, however, he would depart from the printed agenda and jump around randomly. He liked to keep everyone off balance and alert.

The setting allowed Ueberroth to slip into the role of the stern schoolmaster. He made owners raise their hands to speak, shushed their side conversations, scolded them for not doing their homework, embarrassed them if their attention strayed, cut them off if they rambled too long. "Sit down," he'd say. "I've heard all I want from you."

"Ueberroth loved to put the owners down, embarrass them any way he could," said Peter O'Malley.

No one was humiliated more than O'Malley himself. Ueberroth seemed to have it in for the Dodgers' owner from the start. They had operated in the same quarters for years yet came from vastly different backgrounds. Ueberroth was the self-made man, a lowly San Jose State grad who had built his own travel business. O'Malley was to the manor born, a Wharton School grad who was handed the Dodgers' presidency at age thirty-two.

Ueberroth had a visceral dislike for inherited wealth. He once airily dismissed O'Malley thus: "The only thing he really cares about are his two tickets to the opera."

And so the man who succeeded his father as Bowie Kuhn's power broker was now Ueberroth's punching bag. It was another effective way of establishing his authority: humiliate one of the most prominent owners and the rest will fall into line.

Actually, Peter O'Malley, though prominent, was no Walter O'Malley. He was bright and hard-working and had maintained the Dodgers' success, but he didn't have his father's command or charm. He was a distant man, who did, in fact, seem to prefer the art world to the bonhomie of baseball. (His wife was once chief costume designer for the Danish Royal Theater.) Some owners privately called him "Peter Brown," meaning that if his name wasn't O'Malley nobody would pay any attention to him.

But as the owner of baseball's most successful franchise and an intimate of Kuhn, he still had plenty of stature—until now, when he was Ueberroth's whipping boy. Once, as the commissioner was describing one of his initiatives, he noticed a disgruntled-looking O'Malley make an aside.

"If you've got an objection, get right up and articulate it," snapped Ueberroth. "Don't go out there in the hall and do it."

O'Malley sat stonily silent.

At another meeting, O'Malley interrupted a presentation by a staffer with a query.

Ueberroth jumped in. "That's a dumb question," he said. "The answer is in the tab in your hand."

Ueberroth flung the words *dumb* and *stupid* around a lot. He had studied the industry's economics, he informed the Lords, and concluded that they had only themselves to blame. He sometimes expressed his disdain in parables.

"Let's say I sat each of you down in front of a red button and a black button," he said at one early meeting. "Push the red button and you'd win the World Series but lose $10 million. Push the black button and you would make $4 million and finish somewhere in the middle."

He paused to look around. "The problem is, most of you would push the red one."

Ueberroth chided them for checking their business sense at the door. "You are so damned dumb," he'd say. "If there's a half-million-dollar decision in your other businesses, you'll go to the purchasing agent and make him justify it. In baseball, you'll make a five-million-dollar player decision and you'll say, 'That's not me. That's my general manager.' "

The stern schoolmaster frequently repeated his points, as though this were necessary to get things into the owner's heads. "He treated them like retarded children," said one baseball lawyer.

And they took it. They had, after all, put themselves in the hands of *Time*'s Man of the Year. They had hired him to show them the way.

The way led directly to new labor negotiations. The contract that concluded the 1981 strike was up in 1985. Ueberroth took the trouble to get acquainted with Marvin Miller. He was retired now but remained a power in the union. He'd already gotten his first successor fired for straying from the hard line.

That was Ken Moffett. The mediator of 1981 became the executive director of the union in early 1983. At first he seemed a natural. He had more than twenty years in the labor-relations trenches and his roots were on the union side. He'd become close to some of the players during the strike, jogging and joshing with them. Facing the end of his appointment as federal mediation director, Moffett advanced himself as a candidate, and the union's executive board chose him unanimously.

But with Moffett's arrival Miller didn't depart. He continued as a consultant, and he still came into the office. His old Steelworkers friend, Ben Fisher, visited and observed that Miller hadn't come to terms with retirement. He urged him to get some distance from the place, but Miller made excuses: he hadn't organized this, hadn't taken care of that, couldn't possibly leave.

"Marvin, get a suitcase or some big box and get your stuff out," said Fisher. "You can worry about it later."

Miller kept the office and kept getting more uneasy about Moffett. He hadn't taken a hand in choosing him, and he didn't like what he saw and heard. Miller was a workaholic, even at age sixty-six. Moffett had the work ethic of, well, a career federal employee. He commuted from Washington and lost office time traveling. He left arbitration hearings early. He took a vacation early on.

Moffett told the players, "No one ever wins a strike." Miller vehemently disagreed. In the two years since the 1981 strike, salaries had shot up 47 percent. Moffett told reporters, "It's time for labor and management to enter a period of labor peace." Miller, ever battle-ready, was dismayed. Moffett commented on baseball's new billion-dollar TV contract with a wide-eyed "Incredible!" Miller, conversely, was appalled. He had filed a lawsuit asserting the union's right to be involved in these negotiations. Moffett's naïve comments could only hurt it.

Miller tried to tell him that. He also wanted to warn him that the Lords might try to lengthen league playoff series as part of this deal. If so, the players should get a cut of the extra TV money. But Moffett was in Florida and didn't return calls. An angry Miller dictated a memo on those issues to go directly to the players. A Moffett aide, brought in from Washington, intervened. He bottled up the memo and told Moffett.

"I don't want you sending any letters, and I want you to stay out of the office," an equally angry Moffett told Miller. The locks on the union office were changed. Marvin Miller was suddenly an outcast. But he rewrote the memo at home, along with another one telling players what had happened. Then he mailed them.

"I knew it was just a matter of time after that," recalled Moffett. "I didn't have a base of support, and the players got scared. Marvin was their security blanket. They didn't want a guy in there as executive director who didn't get along with him."

He was fired after ten months on the job. Miller returned as interim director, and a loud message was sent. Those who deviated from the Great Emancipator's principles did so at considerable peril.

Miller had turned over the "interim director" title to Don Fehr now, but he hovered close at hand. Fehr was a baby-faced thirty-five-year-old lawyer who'd been with the union since 1977. He had been the union's local counsel when the Lords appealed the *Messersmith* decision in Kansas City. Fehr was just a pup out of law school then, but Miller was impressed with him. When Dick Moss left as general counsel, Fehr was offered the job.

Fehr was the cerebral sort; as a boy in suburban Kansas City he once read the *World Book Encyclopedia* cover to cover. Even now he read 150 books a year—an eclectic mix of physics and philosophy, economics and mathematics. "When we're on a plane, I watch the movie," a union colleague once said. "Don reads about string theory in *Scientific American*."

He was a precise, persnickety sort except when it came to his office, which was piled high with newspapers, briefs, law journals, books, and, for all anybody knew, last week's sandwiches. It fit right into the union's general office milieu, which had all the formality of a college newspaper. Its employees were young and wore blue jeans. The commissioner's office, four blocks away, was all middle-aged pinstripes. The difference in their career wins percentages spoke for itself.

Fehr was only mildly interested in baseball between the lines. His game was pool, a game of control and angles and anticipation. "If Marvin Miller is a Rommel, Don Fehr is an Eisenhower," said Skip McGuire, an outside lawyer for the union. "If he could, he would make sure every battalion, company, and squad is in place before he starts the offensive. He's very low-risk. He doesn't move until he's sure of his ground."

Fehr didn't have Miller's gift for concise talk with the players. He spoke rapidly, in long, winding sentences, examining matters from every angle simultaneously. "I remember telling him once, when he was in the middle of a thirty-line sentence at spring training, 'Don, you lost them,'" said Mark Belanger, who became a union staffer after retiring.

But he'd studied at the feet of the master and consulted regularly with him. There would be no revisionist "time for labor peace" talk from Don Fehr. The difference between Fehr and Miller was mainly one of style.

"Marvin wasn't reluctant to cut you off with 'Not in this world, not in the next,'" said Barry Rona, the owners' labor lawyer. "Don would discuss something exhaustively and have the patience and intellect to pick holes in it, so he could expose the deficiency in your position."

And so it was that Ueberroth decided to cultivate Miller and Fehr. Over a long lunch with both, he shared their acid assessments of Bowie Kuhn and compared notes on the state of the game. Ueberroth also got an earful on the past decade's labor warfare. Later, he would occasionally meet with Fehr at the Waldorf's Peacock Alley bar. His favorite topic, in these back-channels chats, was the owners, whom he universally dismissed as jerks.

Ueberroth put down the Lords in conversations with just about everyone. Around the office he called them "the twenty-six idiots." The half-dozen of them who called to complain about everything were known as "the whining, sniveling malcontents."

Ueberroth's contempt was partly for show. It helped him build a bridge with the union. It helped him establish alliances with the few owners he deemed more capable. ("You're the only one I can talk to; the rest of them are so dumb," he sighed to one owner—who was flattered until he found Ueberroth had said the same thing to six of the other Lords.)

In showing disdain and keeping a distance, he also maintained his aura of icy authority. "I'm not going to your kids' graduations or weddings or bar mitzvahs," he told them early on. "I'm not going to call you. The communication has to come from you, and I'll give you straight answers."

He made clear that he didn't care what the owners thought of him, though he once did ask the Expos' Charles Bronfman if he was doing a good job.

"Define your terms," said Bronfman. "If you define your job as you being the boss and we working for you, you're doing a great job."

Ueberroth smiled. "You know, I think you've got it right," he said.

But he made clear to the Lords that they were fools if they looked to him to solve all their problems—which, of course, they did. After all, they were edging ever closer to blind panic. Salaries had now broken the $2 million barrier. Since the start of the 1985 season, Ozzie Smith and Eddie Murray had signed huge contract extensions: Smith for $8.7 million over four years, Murray for $13 million over five years. "I'm tired of paying out all this money," Reds owner Marge Schott complained to a Ueberroth aide. "Why doesn't Peter do something about it? He's German."

The next chance to do something about the baseball economy came with the new labor contract. The PRC would push for some major structural changes: a cap on team payrolls, for one, and a cap on the maximum raise in salary arbitration. Lee MacPhail succeeded Ray Grebey as negotiator, and he pushed for the Lords to open their books. If the players saw the red ink, he argued, they'd see the need.

Ueberroth stepped in and appropriated the idea as his own. He ordered the Lords, over the vehement protests of some, to turn over their financial statements. ("It's none of their goddamn business," declared John McMullen of the Astros.) "Some owners wouldn't forgive me for that to this day," Ueberroth later reflected.

That was because of what the union did with the books. It turned them over to a Stanford University economist, Roger Noll, to analyze. As the Lords presented it, twenty-one of twenty-six teams lost money in 1984, for a combined operating loss of $41 million. As Noll saw it, baseball had *made* $25 million.

He found bookkeeping tricks at every turn. Turner's Braves were paid only $1 million for TV rights by Turner's Super-Station WTBS. They should have been getting at least the league average of $2.7 million. The Cardinals reported no revenue from parking and concessions, but another Anheuser-Busch subsidiary was raking in $2.5 million from that. The Yankees' $9 million loss included Steinbrenner's real estate investments in Tampa and $500,000 worth of charity contributions.

Noll saw more waste than distress. The A's had the highest loss—$15 million—but also the highest marketing expenses. He questioned why anyone would spend $4.2 million to take in gate receipts of $7.5 million. He noted the Dodgers' front-office payroll was four times the major league average. He estimated that L.A.'s $6 million profit could easily have been $3 million higher and called the Dodgers "baseball's answer to the Denver Mint."

The owners were furious. They had handed over their books for the first time ever and Noll had, in the words of a baseball lawyer, "urinated on them." They disagreed with his interpretations and they fumed as items leaked into the newspapers. *Los Angeles Times* readers, for instance, soon learned of Peter O'Malley's $1 million salary.

"If you can give them the books and use it for something, do it," O'Malley later said. "But we did it, and they just ridiculed it."

It was only the first Ueberroth move in negotiations that baffled owners. One moment he was coaching them on how to make money. The next he was slipping banana peels under them. When they proposed a salary cap, Ueberroth publicly called it "frivolous." In Cooperstown, at Hall of Fame induction ceremonies, he said owners should "stop asking for the players to solve their financial problems."

Ueberroth was supposed to be a great negotiator, but he had never negotiated with labor before. On one occasion when the PRC made a seven-point proposal, he ordered that it be printed up and distributed to the players and press. He didn't seem to know that, in the ebb and flow of bargaining, it would be outdated within an hour. Nor did Ueberroth truly understand the nature of the union beast. "Peter always thought a napkin-type deal was available," said Peter O'Malley, then a PRC member. "Marvin Miller doesn't do napkin deals."

Ueberroth sometimes appeared more interested in playing to the gallery than in accomplishing things. He liked to call himself "the fans' commissioner," and he seemed to care more about how things played in the press than how they figured into a labor agreement. The commissioner's office, it seemed to some owners, wasn't the highest one he aspired to. "I'll tell you what Peter Ueberroth wants in life," a friend of his told one Lord. "He wants to be appointed president of the United States."

Whatever his aspirations, Ueberroth certainly kept on grandstanding. At one point, he proposed finalizing negotiations on every other issue while continuing discussions on the pension contribution. The two sides remained far apart on this issue, the players wanting $60 million, the owners offering $15 million. Ueberroth proposed that it be bargained separately, with the $45 million difference put in escrow. For each day it wasn't resolved, $1 million would be deducted and donated to either amateur baseball or charity. The gimmick got some press, but no support from either side.

Negotiations dragged on well into the 1985 season. The union finally set a deadline: on August 6, no contract, no play. Baseball was again staring down the barrel of a strike. Emotions again ran high.

Astros owner John McMullen and his third baseman Phil Garner were out discussing the matter one day. McMullen fell into a predictable recitation of the party line about the need for big changes—salary caps and the rest. Garner finally interrupted him.

"John, what you're failing to see is that the players' union has made its gains over a period of twenty years," he said. "Why don't you project yourself out ten years from now and figure where you want to be? Now, if you can take one step to get there this time, then another step in the next negotiation, you might get where you want in ten years. The problem you owners have is you're not sure you're going to be around in ten years, so you want it all done today. That's why you walk in, you want to take it all away, and you get beat.

"I'll tell you something else. Free agency's not your problem. Salary arbitration's going to be your problem. You might as well leave free agency alone. It's not an issue you're going to change. It's cut in stone."

"You're a goddamned Communist!" McMullen roared.

End of discussion.

Garner, of course, was right. Salary arbitration *was* the key issue. The Lords' final strategy was to make a tradeoff: no salary cap in return for changes in salary arbitration. They wanted to change the rules to limit salary-arbitration raises to 100 percent and end the days of million-dollar deals for phenoms like Valenzuela. They also wanted players to wait three years instead of two before they were eligible for arbitration.

As the August 6 deadline drew near, the two sides reduced their negotiating teams to bare bones. For the owners, it was Lee MacPhail, Barry Rona, and Lou Hoynes. For the players, Don Fehr, Dick Moss, and, in a special return appearance, Marvin Miller. They hid out from the press, first in the Helmsley Building offices of the union's outside lawyer, then at Miller's Upper East Side apartment.

Miller still had the "no givebacks" mind-set of 1981, but the circumstances were far different in 1985. His union constituency had undergone a 50 percent turnover in the past four years. The players' average salary had nearly doubled, to $369,000. The issues were far less black-and-white than in 1981, and the players far less ready to fight. "We couldn't have gotten the '85 players to go out fifty days," said Don Baylor, then a union leader.

There was also a split between veteran players, who were willing to gut the two-year wait for salary arbitration, and young players, who didn't want to wait any longer than two years for the big bucks.

"There was a huge division," said Bob Boone, who was against going to the mats to keep the two-year threshold. It violated Miller's basic tenet of unity, he argued: "If thirty percent of the players don't want to strike, that's a losing proposition."

Boone, of course, was a thirteen-year veteran at this point. It was easy for him to argue against the young players on this point. But he also felt that his perspective differed from that of the younger guys in a broader way too. The union had suc-

ceeded beyond its wildest dreams, and the owners weren't trying
to grab control back this time. They were just asking for an adjustment.

"In the early days, I felt the players were always on the right
side," Boone said. "Now, for the first time, there was this gray
area, and I didn't know."

On Sunday, August 4, the baseball world celebrated two great
achievements. Tom Seaver beat the Yankees 4–1 for his 300th
win. In Yankee Stadium, 54,000 people cheered the great forty-
year-old pitcher. On the same day, in Anaheim, Rod Carew
stroked his 3,000th hit in a game against the Twins.

Two days later, the baseball world went dark. The two sides
met all day but conceded by late afternoon that they were still
far apart. That night's games were canceled, and the players' reluctant strike was on.

Ueberroth called Barry Rona that evening. He was going to
give them one more day to resolve this, he said. Then he would
toss the whole mess into binding arbitration. It was quite clear:
there was not going to be a protracted strike on the watch of the
"fans' commissioner."

The players would be more relieved than the fans. They had
painted themselves into a corner—a walkout they couldn't long
sustain—and here came Ueberroth to get them out. "We should
have fired him right then," one owner later spat.

The next morning, the negotiators had a new hideout: Lee
MacPhail's apartment. It was an elegant place on Fifth Avenue,
just up the street from the Plaza Hotel, overlooking Central Park.
They were sitting in his parlor, midday light flooding in through
the tall windows, when Ueberroth called.

"You guys have to make a deal," he said. "If you don't make
a deal by two o'clock, I'm going to walk down Fifth Avenue to
the apartment and take it away from you. You've got two
hours."

They all looked at one another. They could just see Ueberroth
striding down the boulevard, like Sheriff Buford Pusser in the
movie *Walking Tall*. Maybe, like the sheriff, he'd even be carrying a Louisville Slugger. Probably a media horde would be trailing along. They all agreed: Ueberroth was just confident (or
crazy) enough to do it.

"I think he's really going to come," said Lou Hoynes.

Barry Rona and Don Fehr retreated to a bedroom and started
negotiating, one-on-one, and fast. Everybody else stood around
admiring the apartment. Two hours later, Rona and Fehr

emerged breathlessly with an agreement: three years for arbitration, no cap on arbitration increases, and $33 million for the pension.

Ueberroth walked in twenty minutes later, loaded for bear. As he began telling them how he was going to solve this, he was interrupted. They had a deal. It was all over. Ueberroth called a press conference; the lawyers scrambled to get it all down in writing; and the next morning the New York tabloids told the story: "Ubie" had saved baseball.

Lee MacPhail wasn't at all sure that baseball was saved. He was planning to retire in a few months, at age sixty-eight. He'd been in baseball for forty-four years. His father, Larry, had been in it before him. His son, Andy, would be in it after him. He'd served and loved the institution well. But now he was more worried about it than ever.

The money ball just kept rolling. He didn't care what Roger Noll said—baseball was sick.

With the contract wrapped up, MacPhail had the leisure to give the Lords some final thoughts. He began to putter around at the computer, assembling some words and numbers. It turned into a full-fledged report, in which he observed that:

- Baseball owed $45 to $50 million to players no longer in the game. (They'd been released, but their guaranteed contracts went on and on.)
- Players with long-term contracts spent more time injured. (Of players on the disabled list in 1984, those with one-year contracts were out an average of twelve days, those with two-year contracts were out fourteen days, and those with contracts of three or more years were out eighteen days.)
- The performance of players with long-term contracts declined over the course of the contract. (He provided two tables showing the averaged performances of players with long-term contracts.)

Survey of 104 Hitters

	Games Played	HRs	RBIs	Avg.
Year prior to signing contract	133	13	63	.280
1st year of contract	124	11	56	.273
2nd year of contract	117	12	54	.267
3rd year of contract	118	10	53	.263

JOHN HELYAR

Survey of 57 Pitchers

	Games Played	Won	Lost	ERA
Year prior to signing contract	39	12	9	3.33
1st year of contract	36	10	8	3.63
2nd year of contract	37	9	8	3.56
3rd year of contract	35	9	8	3.91

MacPhail suggested clubs fill their final roster spots with kids up from the minors rather than "give in to the unreasonable demands of experienced marginal players." He noted some free-agent signings of the previous winter and published their dubious accomplishments in the 1985 season:

				1985 Record		
Player	Age	Signed in 1985 for:	Games Played	Avg.	HRs	RBIs
A	32	2 years	72	.207	3	9
B	36	3 years	59	.217	1	3
C	32	2 years	82	.188	4	13
D	34	2 years	68	.186	1	14

Pitcher	Age	Signed in 1985 for:	Games Pitched	Won	Lost	ERA
A	29	2 years	34	3	7	4.19
B	34	1 year	40	2	10	4.39
C	28	3 years	43	1	6	4.58

MacPhail also counseled clubs to be smarter about salary arbitration and to consider carrying rosters of twenty-four instead of twenty-five men. He finished with this conclusion:

These are some of the areas that I believe deserve your attention. Most important is that all clubs practice common-sense economic self-restraint. We must rely on the unilateral, self-imposed restraints of each individual club to do what experience and reasonable expectations indicate is in its own best interest. We must stop daydreaming that one free agent signing will bring a pennant. Somehow we must get our operations back to the point where a normal year for the average team at least results in a break-even situation, so that clubs are not led to make rash moves in the vain hope that they might bring a pennant and a resulting change in their financial position. This requires resistance to fan and media pressure and is not easy. On the other hand, the future health and stability of our Game depend on your response to these problems.

MacPhail sent it out in mid-October. When Ueberroth got his copy he scanned it with delight. Now, this was something he could use. He'd been in office a year now and he was ready to step up his attacks on "stupidity." He'd pushed for a watered-down labor deal partly because he didn't think the teams' salvation lay in such contracts. It lay in the Lords themselves. "He believed you had to make as good an agreement as possible in the nuts and bolts, and then it's up to the clubs," said one aide.

The Lords were more ready for his message than ever by the fall of 1985. It was partly, however, because Ueberroth had undermined their efforts to rein in salary growth during that summer's labor bargaining. "The thing that was called collusion," said one owner later, "grew out of the failure to get what we wanted in 1985."

$ 17 $

THE CROWDS POURED into St. Louis for the third game of the 1985 World Series. It was a perfectly glorious day for baseball, and the Cardinals and Royals were in the middle of a stirring Series. Kansas City had lost the first two games but would come back to win it in seven.

Baseball's owners filed into an auditorium at Anheuser-Busch, wondering if *they* could come back. The new labor contract was disappointing. The TV money was going down, they'd been told. And the commissioner's jaw looked particularly set today.

Ueberroth asked them whether they'd received Lee MacPhail's report. When several shook their heads no, he scolded them about reading their mail and distributed extra copies. He asked the outgoing PRC chief to say a few words.

MacPhail was his usual concise, understated self. It was time to stop blaming the union for all their problems and start exercising some discipline on their own. He reviewed the highlights of his report. Eyebrows shot up at the $50 million in salary obligations for nonplaying players.

"I suggest strongly we give Lee's remarks careful consideration," said Ueberroth.

This was the second round of his stepped-up campaign against their "stupidity." Last month, at an owners' meeting outside Chicago, he'd lectured about how three-year contracts didn't make "good business sense." He'd also urged them to take a more active hand in their clubs, not be "absentee owners." Develop some policies and procedures, for crying out loud.

"Look in the mirror and go out and spend big if you want," Ueberroth said, "but don't go out there whining that someone made you do it."

Now in St. Louis he returned to the evils of long-term contracts. Lee's findings were most instructive, the commissioner said. Who'd like to talk about their own experiences? Some owners started talking about their free-agent follies. Then they turned to the Sutter and Sutcliffe deals. The prize free agents of 1984 had developed bum arms in 1985. Bruce Sutter's ERA ballooned to 4.58, his saves withered to 23. Rick Sutcliffe spent the whole second half on the disabled list and ended up 8–8. Now the Braves and Cubs were on the hook to them for five more costly years. Yes, it was awful. Awful, awful, awful. When Royals co-owner Avron Fogelman tried to defend his "lifetime contracts" with George Brett, Willie Wilson, and Dan Quisenberry he was hooted down.

Ueberroth said he'd like to take a poll.

"As the CEO, I have to know what your policies are," he said. "I'm going to go around the room, and you have to tell me if you're going to be signing free agents. You're free to sign a free agent if you want, because we can't agree not to sign free agents. This is in no way binding and you have the right to change your minds. But I want to know those who are and those who aren't."

One after another, most said they wouldn't. Ueberroth interrupted at one point and turned to the lawyers—Lou Hoynes, still baseball's all-purpose counsel; Barry Rona, the new PRC director; and Jim Garner, the American League counsel. "Stop this discussion if at any point it smacks of collusion," he said.

They did not, and he continued to hector the owners. They needed to act like intelligent businessmen. Did they *have* a free-agent policy? Didn't they *care* about losing money? They'd put the whole industry in jeopardy. The networks wouldn't keep carrying them. NBC and ABC were losing money on baseball; they'd shown him the books. Next contract the TV money would go down.

"You, singular, are responsible for your own downfall, and if you are so dumb that you are paying all kinds of money to players that aren't playing so you're losing money and don't have money to pay players that are playing, please don't throw stones at anybody," he said. "It's your fault, Mr. So and So, don't rant and rave. Nobody is forcing you to do anything. It is your own stupidity.

"Look, you are intelligent businessmen or you wouldn't be where you are today. Let us try to operate in a businesslike way before we, as a sport, are bankrupt."

Finally, Ueberroth was through.

"Well, you are smart businessmen," he said. "You all agree we have a problem. Go solve it."

(The "go solve it" edict came from testimony in a later grievance hearing. In an interview, Ueberroth would later deny he said it.)

The next afternoon, Tom Reich looked forward to meeting with Bill Lajoie, the Tigers GM. He thought that talks regarding a new Lance Parrish contract were coming to fruition. Parrish had made $550,000 that year, a bargain for an All-Star catcher. But in one more year he'd be qualified for free agency. Reich was angling for a long-term deal with a package of real estate, deferred compensation, and annuities, like some of the Royals' contracts. They'd even talked about Parrish one day working in owner Monaghan's Domino's Pizza empire.

But as they sat down in his hotel room, Lajoie was clearly uncomfortable.

"Look, I don't know quite how to tell you this," he said, "but we have reviewed this and decided that the best we can offer is a two-year contract and not at the kind of money we have been talking about."

"Where did that bullshit come from?" Reich asked.

"We had some meetings and decided that these are the economics," said Lajoie. "Things aren't going so good after the championship season. This is the best we can do."

"Let's not beat the horse and let's not get hot," said Reich, trying not to get hot. "Let's just say that we're at an impasse."

They saw each other later on at a cocktail party. Lajoie told the agent he was surprised he didn't blow his top.

"Well, I don't know exactly what's happening here," said Reich, "but I don't hold you responsible."

(Lajoie would later maintain that the decision on Parrish was made well before the Series. There had been a long hiatus during which he didn't hear from Reich and he cooled on the idea. This was a period when Reich had moved his offices to Southern California and, it was said, "gone Hollywood." It was true that he was engaged to actress Jennifer O'Neill, for a time, and somewhat disengaged from his baseball affairs.)

Reich later called Parrish. "Something's up," he said. Soon after, he wrote a warning memo to his other clients. They were in for a mean season.

* * *

Shortly after the Series, the GMs gathered in Tarpon Springs, Florida, for their annual meeting. It wasn't enough for the owners to have the gospel according to Ueberroth. GMs made too many of the personnel decisions. So the commissioner preached directly to them:

- "It's not smart to sign long-term contracts. They force other clubs to make similar signings."
- If clubs wanted to sign a free agent, he personally "wanted to know the economics" that justified it. "I'm going to come down hard on sixty/forty," a rule that required clubs to have a ratio of 60 percent assets to 40 percent debt.
- He hadn't made any rule limiting contracts to three years, but they should look at what happened to players who had gotten long-term, guaranteed contracts in the past. Baseball was on the hook for $50 million in payments to players who hadn't performed.
- "Don't be dumb. We have a five-year agreement with labor."

Clubs quickly began demonstrating that they'd gotten the message. Nine of them soon had written policies that hewed to Ueberroth's recommendations: typically, no contracts longer than three years; none longer than two years for pitchers; none longer than one year for marginal players. Some of the clubs swore off free agents altogether. Then the clubs demonstrated they'd gotten the message in an even more meaningful way: in the market.

Kirk Gibson was an outdoorsman. There was no better way for a team to tell him they adored and wanted him than to invite him hunting. This the Kansas City Royals had done. They were the reigning world champions, but they were weak in right field. A platoon of Pat Sheridan and Darryl Motley had combined to hit only .224 with 20 homers and 60 RBIs.

Gibson could put up a lot better numbers than that. The last three seasons he'd averaged 28 homers and 91 RBIs, *with speed*—29 and 30 stolen bases, respectively, in the past two years. Gibson was a fiery competitor, a winner, and he was only twenty-eight. Here was 1985's primo free agent.

A Royals emissary had approached him as early as September. It was against the rules, but it was subtle enough: See you in November, big guy. Gibson's current team, the Tigers, had exclusive negotiating rights for two weeks after the Series. After that, it was open season. The Tigers had offered $1.1 million a year for three years, which Gibson rejected scornfully. He was looking for a minimum five-year deal at a minimum of $1.5 million per.

Gibson accepted the Royals' invitation to do some bird hunting, and prepared to begin his free-agent sweepstakes. He was still out in the woods with some Kansas City officials when his agent, Doug Baldwin, called Royals GM John Schuerholz. This outing, he said, was obviously the first step in Gibson's courting, so he might as well get things rolling. He was stunned at what he heard. "Yes, Kirk Gibson is a fine ballplayer," said Schuerholz, "but I really don't think we have any interest."

The agent was soon being rebuffed by every other team too. The Yankees were committed to a right-field platoon of Dan Pasqua and Gary Roenicke. (Not even a nibble from Steinbrenner?) The Cardinals were committed to Jim Lindeman. (Gibson couldn't beat out a triple-A prospect?) The Angels' priority was re-signing Ruppert Jones. (*The* Ruppert Jones who'd hit .231 that year?) The Braves went from hot to warm to unreturned phone calls.

At the winter meetings in San Diego, it was more of the same. "I felt like Moses," said Baldwin. "Every time I approached a group of GMs, they would part."

Other agents were befuddled as well. This wasn't the rich free-agent market they had expected. The only other quality players out there were Donnie Moore, Tony Bernazard, and Carlton Fisk. But of those, only Chicago catcher Fisk had gotten a single nibble—from George Steinbrenner, who'd dangled a three-year, $2.25 million offer during Thanksgiving week.

Fisk wasn't exactly tempted. It wasn't much of a premium over the $575,000 he'd been drawing, and he was a premium catcher. He was sure there would be better offers, and besides, his wife couldn't abide living in New York. Steinbrenner, in any event, did something un-Steinbrennerlike. He told Chicago owner Jerry Reinsdorf he'd made the offer and soon thereafter pulled it off the table.

It was, in a sense, the fulcrum on which something to be known as collusion turned.

"If you watch the patterns of baseball, everybody likes to justify their own stupidity based on somebody else being stupider first," noted one longtime baseball man. "I think clubs were saying here, 'I'm not going to be the first one; I'll wait for the Yankees or somebody to make a move.' "

The Yankees made no move. And neither did anybody else. The players had long feared something like this. Back in the winter following the 1981 strike, free-agent activity had slowed. Clubs were clearly reluctant to sign other clubs' players. So the union filed a grievance charging the Lords with "acting in concert." Such behavior, on either side, was explicitly barred in the first post-*Messersmith* labor contract—at the owners' insistence. The Koufax-Drysdale holdout was still a fresh memory in 1976. The owners wanted no such bloc bargaining by free agents. Nor did they want a Jerry Kapstein—an agent with a big client stable—orchestrating the movement of whole groups of players. Marvin Miller agreed to forbid the players from "acting in concert" as long as the owners were forbidden as well. The language had been renewed in each subsequent labor contract.

The 1982 grievance was an effective warning shot. The market picked back up. Still, the Lords continued to occasionally discuss among themselves how to rein in free agency, having been thwarted at the bargaining table. The Tigers' John Fetzer once tried to start a "buddy system," whereby anyone considering a big signing would call a brother owner to talk him out of it. It was a clever idea, but it didn't work.

The reason was simple. Nearly every owner thought he was just one player away from making the Series. Most thought a lot more about pennants than profits. And none trusted the others as far as he could throw them. "I wouldn't expect Sully [Red Sox general partner Haywood Sullivan] to tell me the truth," George Steinbrenner once said, discussing the ethics of trading. "I really wouldn't."

As Royals owner Ewing Kauffman put it, "You have twenty-six owners who are partners, and yet each owner tries to beat the other as much as he can in winning baseball games. So you're really not true partners, and you don't act like partners, and you don't run it like a partnership. You run it for the benefit of your own franchise."

But Ueberroth had effected an astounding change in the Lords' group dynamic. Suddenly they were less interested in improving their teams than in pleasing him. They'd been embarrassed into drawing their pursestrings closed. By early December, agents were calling Don Fehr. "What's going on out there?" they asked. "Do you have any clue?"

By the first week of 1986, Kirk Gibson was in a bind. If he didn't re-sign with the Tigers by January 8, under baseball's rules he couldn't sign with them until May 1. Much of his season would be wiped out. In the meantime, the Tigers had inched their offer up to $1.3 million a year for three years. If he got no other offers—and the silence was deafening—he'd be out of baseball.

In New Zealand, on a double honeymoon—he and best friend Dave Rozema, a former Tigers pitcher, had married sisters—Gibson took a call from his agent a half-hour before the midnight deadline in the United States. The four honeymooners sat in a restaurant, deadlocked, two to two, on whether he should take Detroit's offer. Gibson took out a coin to flip. It came down heads and he was headed back to the Tigers.

The final score of the 1985–86 free-agent season: of thirty-three free agents, twenty-nine went back to their old teams, having received no other offers. The four who did move on were marginal types whose former teams no longer wanted them: David Palmer, Al Holland, Juan Beniquez, and Dane Iorg. The free agents averaged just a 5 percent salary increase. Two thirds got just one-year contracts.

In the free-agent chill, other players caught cold. In the previous two off-seasons, seventy-five players had signed multiyear contracts that "bought out" their free agency. This year only fifteen got such deals. Suddenly, it seemed, clubs no longer saw the urgency.

Brett Butler was coming off a 1985 season in which he hit .311, scored 106 runs, stole 47 bases, and played a sparkling center field. He was a four-year man and looking for a multiyear deal with Cleveland. But when he and his agent, Dick Moss, met with Indians president Peter Bavasi, they were shot down cold.

"Our policy has changed," said Bavasi. "We're only offering one-year contracts to players with less than six years."

"Well, then my policy will be to leave Cleveland as soon as I can," said Butler.

"Fine, but you're going to find a different market out there."

Moss leaped to his feet. "What do you mean by that?" he asked.

"There won't be any offers," said Bavasi. "The market has changed, and it's not going to change back anytime soon. But don't worry; we'll take care of you."

The frozen free-agent market soon took its toll on salary arbitration. The Reich brothers, who had never lost an arbitration, suddenly lost all three of the cases they brought in 1986. Tom Reich had always possessed an unerring sense of the market. He projected how much salaries would rise during the winter and pegged his filing numbers accordingly. When the market stopped dead, this year, his numbers were high.

Gary Ward was a good outfielder for the Rangers. As a five-year man, he could readily compare himself with free agents. The Reichs hitched his wagon to Kirk Gibson. Tom originally figured he was good for at least $1.7 million. But Ward ultimately filed at $930,000. When Gibson had to settle for Detroit's $1.3 million, Ward was caught leaning the wrong way. Even at $930,000, his figure was too high.

Even before he lost, the Reichs found the tone of settlement negotiations quite different. They and the Rangers filed numbers only $65,000 apart on Ward. But when Reich tried to get a settlement—the circumstances seemed to favor one, considering the slim spread—Texas wouldn't budge. "We couldn't sell it," recalls Sam Reich. "The clubs knew we weren't going to get the help [from other signings] we had before."

Nonetheless, just as floodwaters crest only after the rains stop, the average salary rose another 11 percent in 1986, to $411,000. There was still much inflation to be wrung out of the system. And there was still evident distress: for example, the Pittsburgh franchise, which went begging until a coalition of business and local government stepped in to buy it. The Galbreaths were getting out of baseball after thirty-eight years. The "sportsman-owner" they epitomized seemed as quaint as Ladies Day.

Peter Ueberroth didn't let up. The price of fiscal progress was eternal vigilance. He kept assaulting the owners. ("I'd be embarrassed to be running a business that was losing this kind of money," he scoffed.) He kept preaching against long-term contracts. He still wanted to be informed if they were considering anything over three years. "I want you to come and tell me eyeball-to-eyeball that you're going to do it," he said.

Most important, he put them through rigorous show-and-tell exercises on their finances. As they came into the quarterly meetings, the owners were handed binders of salary data, organized team by team and detailing total payrolls, deferred pay, money owed to released players, and other data. Then, one by one, the owners had to stand up and discuss the numbers and the outlook. The exercise took up much of the session and kept everyone's feet to the fire.

Best of all, from Ueberroth's viewpoint, it was always guaranteed to get off to a good start. The clubs went in alphabetical order, which put the Atlanta Braves first. The players were listed from highest to lowest paid, so at leadoff was Bruce Sutter. In 1986, the sore-armed pitcher was paid $1.67 million to pitch a total of nineteen innings. "Now, that's what, around $100,000 an inning?" Ueberroth asked Ted Turner. "That's quite a bit, but, well, I guess he's worth it."

Yes, the Braves were the perfect case study of financial folly. They had baseball's highest payroll and they were in last place. They had an outfielder, Omar Moreno, who was getting paid by another team. He was signed after being released by the Yankees, who were obligated for most of his $600,000 salary. George Steinbrenner and Ted Turner tried to outdo one another in their confessions to Ueberroth. Cried Turner: "I don't care if you call us stupid. I've been the stupidest SOB here."

The commissioner followed an unrelenting Socratic method. "Perhaps I don't know much about baseball . . ." a question would begin, and then he would bore in—"but why did you sign Mike Greenwell for $500,000?" This he asked of Boston's Haywood Sullivan. "Here's a guy who isn't eligible for arbitration and you could pay him something close to the minimum if you wanted."

"I didn't want him to be mad at me," Sullivan mumbled, as the others tittered.

Ueberroth periodically turned to the lawyers, telling them to stop him if he got onto collusion grounds. They never did, though they did occasionally halt owners who got carried away in the raptures of "fiscal responsibility." That was the code word for abstinence, and the leading proselytizers were Jerry Reinsdorf, Bud Selig, and John McMullen. The Astros owner, stopped in the middle of a good rant, once retorted, "I'd rather go before a firing squad and be shot than die of cancer, which is what we're doing."

The lawyers reminded the owners of what the labor contract said: no "acting in concert." But if it was their *individual decision* not to sign free agents, there was no basis for collusion charges. There was certainly nothing wrong with exchanging information. The other side did. Then they waved Ueberroth on.

The commissioner would later deny that there ever had been anything resembling collusion. ("I don't think the owners are capable of colluding," he said. "They couldn't agree on what to have for breakfast.") But he did concede that his quarterly meetings had forged a new group dynamic. "Free agency had been a macho thing with the owners—taking pride in getting the other guy's players," he said. "I got them in a room together, and it was more difficult to do when they were eyeball-to-eyeball."

Some wondered just what Ueberroth did between quarterly meetings. He turned over the running of the commissioner's office to lawyer Ed Durso and TV chief Bryan Burns—two bright Kuhn holdovers in their early thirties. He spent so little time in the office that some called him the "Fed-Ex commissioner." The overnight delivery service did, indeed, make a lot of runs from 350 Park Avenue, New York, to Newport Beach, California, where he lived.

Ueberroth was much in demand in corporate America now, and he was looking after quite a few other interests. He was on several corporate boards, including Coca-Cola and E. F. Hutton. He actually negotiated the merger of Hutton and the Shearson brokerage firm on the side, pocketing a cool $900,000 for his trouble. He also invested serious time on his golf game.

Ueberroth saw little of owners between meetings. The Lords talked quietly among themselves about this man who had turned them inside out. "We used to call him 'the Gorilla,' because he does whatever he wants," one of them told Jerome Holtzman of the *Chicago Tribune*. "Now we call him 'the Lone Ranger,' because he rides at night and talks to nobody."

But between his aides, allies, and a crackerjack clipping service, Ueberroth always had great intelligence on what everyone was up to. He also had great capacity for retribution. He had demanded as a condition of his hiring that the commissioner's fining power be raised to $250,000 from $5,000—and he used it. If an owner made comments Ueberroth found "not in the game's best interests," he was fined. If an owner was slow to stop selling oversized beers—in accordance with a Ueberroth edict to reduce crowd rowdiness—he was fined. The fines weren't announced, leaving owners to stew privately, without the sympathy of their peers. They were an excellent reminder of his authority.

So was Ueberroth's cash-disbursal method from the Central Fund. That was the repository of revenues—principally network TV money—distributed to all clubs. It had always been divided equally among the clubs, but not under Ueberroth. He gave himself discretionary control over new income from areas such as licensing and merchandising. Thus he was free to give up to $500,000 extra to clubs on board with his pet causes, such as minority hiring and drug education. The ones who weren't would see up to $500,000 less.

Ueberroth rarely appeared at games. It was perhaps the one way some owners missed Bowie Kuhn. He loved baseball as a game—maybe too well to lead it as a business, but plenty enough to handle the spiritual aspects. The recurring rumor was that Ueberroth didn't much care for the sport.

His only real nonbusiness passion was fighting drugs. He'd headed off Olympics drug scandals with a tough testing program. He could see some political points to be scored. It was the heyday of Nancy Reagan's "Just Say No" campaign, and Ueberroth said plenty. Among other things, he got some attention by declaring that the United States should send in fighter jets to wipe out the Latin American drug fields.

Ueberroth had an exaggerated sense of his own importance in the drug war, but it was yet another way to impress the owners. "I'm going to hire more security," he told them once. "I've been informed the cocaine cartel is focusing on me and my family."

Baseball did have drug problems. It was a byproduct of players' new riches. The players attracted hangers-on who drew them (*some* of them) into a world in which the upscale drug of choice, cocaine, abounded. The 1986 Pittsburgh trial of a caterer–*cum*–drug trafficker called Curt the Chef implicated twenty-three players. Ueberroth threw the book at them all, imposing suspensions unless they agreed to: (1) donate a portion of their 1986 pay to an antidrug program; (2) submit to random drug testing the rest of their careers; and (3) perform community service.

This was also the bleak time when the Pirates sued Dave Parker for failure to perform up to his ability because of drug abuse and when three Royals players—Willie Wilson, Jerry Martin, and Willie Aikens—went to prison on drug charges.

Publicly, everybody agreed the situation was awful. Privately, baseball was ambivalent. It had a rich tradition of turning a blind eye to its players' peccadillos. In the 1920s, Babe Ruth's excesses were legend. In the thirties, Hack Wilson set an RBI record with whiskey on his breath. In the fifties, a bevy of Yankees drunkenly busted up the Copacabana. In the sixties, managers looked the other way as players gobbled "greenies" (amphetamines).

In the seventies, finally, when the drugs started getting scarier, some baseball men did sense danger. When San Diego GM Peter Bavasi heard that one of his players was on cocaine, he called him on the carpet. "You're getting off that stuff or you're getting off this team," he declared.

That night, the player came up as a pinch hitter in the ninth inning and rifled a line drive to bring in the winning run. The crowd went wild, and in the owner's box Ray Kroc was whooping as well. Only Bavasi was somber.

"Hey, what's wrong?" the owner asked.

"It's him," said Bavasi, pointing at the player being mobbed. "He's on cocaine."

"Well, goddammit, give *everybody* cocaine!" Kroc declared.

That was just baseball, where the saying went: "If you can hit the curveball, you can get away with murder."

But Ueberroth was determined to purge baseball of cocaine. It was a glaring problem and it was a potential coup for the self-styled drug warrior. Shortly before Opening Day 1986, he ordered mandatory testing of players four times a year. "It is imperative that we rid baseball of drug abuse—for the sake of our youth, who look to baseball for role models, and also for the future of our country," Ueberroth said. "Someone somewhere has to say 'Enough is enough' to drugs. And I've done that."

Don Fehr howled. Drug testing was a subject for collective bargaining, not unilateral decree. The union filed a grievance, and on July 30, baseball's arbitrator, Tom Roberts, found for the union. Ueberroth had overstepped his authority; drug policy would have to be negotiated. The Lords, finding the decision "shocking," fired Roberts on August 5.

The arbitrator was in the middle of hearing another case when he got word of his termination. The union had brought charges of collusion in the 1985–86 free-agent market. Upon the announcement of Roberts's dismissal, Fehr immediately fired off another grievance, protesting that action by the owners. An arbitrator couldn't be dismissed in the middle of a hearing, he argued. Fehr was furious. It seemed clear the owners were trying to derail the collusion case. If they had to start over with another arbitrator, a new hearing—and the decision—might be put off indefinitely.

In September, Roberts was restored as arbitrator, but the collusion hearings didn't resume until late October. In the end, they took thirty-eight days, filled up a 5,000-page transcript, and were augmented by 363 exhibits. Roberts didn't digest it all and make a ruling until September 1987. In the meantime, collusion was free to roll on.

* * *

It took a more virulent form in its second year. It had been an almost accidental conspiracy at first. Everybody was cowed into not wanting to be the first to sign a free agent. Nobody did, and it got to be habit-forming. It took on "a life of its own"—the phrase is invoked frequently by those involved.

Some of the owners had started to make money again. Most of them enjoyed turning the tables on the agents. As one insider recalls it: "The hardest part in the beginning was the mistrust"—suspecting someone would break ranks with a big signing. "By the second year they were seeing results. The feeling was, 'Hey, for the first time we acted smart last year; why not keep going?' "

Some *were* uncomfortable. Peter O'Malley would later call the period "the low point in baseball for me by far," a time that "set back our relations with labor a generation." He brought his attorney with him to an owners' meeting to observe the goings-on—the first time he'd ever done that. Afterward, O'Malley exchanged sharp words with Ueberroth. Ed Williams occasionally questioned Ueberroth and the lawyers closely on the meetings' practices: "Are you sure this is okay?"

But neither they nor anybody else with doubts threw themselves in front of the great, rumbling collusion machine. An associate of Williams who was privy to that owner's doubts said it best: "He wanted too much to be a member of the club." Besides, the lawyers kept insisting that the meetings were fine.

It was the market behavior that worried them. "Too many things put us too close to the edge," said Lou Hoynes. "It *looked* cooked. Economic sense is fine, but if the consequence was all those unsigned free agents, nobody would believe there wasn't a conspiracy even though there wasn't one."

Both Hoynes and Barry Rona would begin urging owners to make some bids and thaw the market, but with little to no success. Most of the owners and GMs were enjoying the free-agent boycott too much. A decade after the *Messersmith* decision, they were finally regaining control. They were also too scared of a confrontation with Peter Ueberroth. Said one: "We were a lot more concerned about doing the right thing in the eyes of the commissioner than the wrong thing in the eyes of the law."

It was the last weekend of the season in Montreal. After the Expos' Saturday game, Andre Dawson, his wife, and his agent, Dick Moss, went up to Charles Bronfman's private box. The outfielder's five-year contract was up. He'd had a great ten-year run with the Expos, but now he was looking at a not-so-great offer. After paying Dawson $1.27 million in 1986, Montreal wanted to go to $1 million for each of the next two years.

It was true Dawson had been hampered by bad knees the past three years. But even at the advanced age of thirty-two, Dawson had averaged 20 homers, 85 RBIs, and a .262 average over that time. He also remained a fan favorite, a clubhouse leader, and a superb right fielder. His ball-hawking ability earned him the nickname "Hawk." A million wasn't going to cut it, Moss informed Bronfman.

They'd been around the track together often. One of Moss's first clients as an agent was Steve Rogers. The Expos' star pitcher led Moss to numerous other Expos clients—at one time the club's whole starting rotation. Moss never settled for less than top dollar, and he came to do regular battle with Montreal. One of his contracts shook the franchise to its foundation—Gary Carter's six-year, $13.1 million deal.

"We ended up thirty to forty percent over where we wanted to be," said president John McHale, who eventually concluded that the Expos couldn't afford their star catcher. Four years into the contract, Carter was traded to the Mets for three lower-priced players. It wasn't a popular deal in Montreal, and Moss wasn't a popular figure in the Expos' front office. Owner Bronfman seemed to enjoy telling him the new ways of the world, and explaining how those new ways would affect the size of his offer to Andre Dawson.

"Times have changed," he said. "Certainly if we were having this discussion two or three years ago we would be talking about much higher numbers. But things are different now."

"The least you should do is let Andre get out with a proper number on his head," said Moss. "Why not give us a three-year proposal for $1.5 million a year? We can either treat it as a serious proposal or we won't. But it would set a higher market."

Bronfman wouldn't bite. Moss turned snarly. He said he'd heard something back-channels from inside the Expos. If Dawson didn't take whatever they offered, he'd play nowhere in 1987. Bronfman protested. There was no such threat.

Moss was unappeased. He wanted to see a better offer.

"You owe Andre Dawson that," he said. "You've had a good relationship. He owns more of the Expos' records than anybody. Given everything that's happened . . . *don't fuck with Andre Dawson.*"

* * *

At about the same time, Tim Raines sat down with a trio of Montreal's top brass: President John McHale, Vice President Bill Stoneman, and GM Murray Cook.

The star left fielder was about to wrap up the National League batting championship, with a .334 average. He had stolen seventy bases for the sixth consecutive season. He'd just turned twenty-seven, and he was eligible to be a free agent. The world was his oyster.

And yet he was getting a warning here: Try testing the free-agent waters and you might drown.

"You don't want to put yourself out on a limb," said McHale. "If things go wrong, you'll be the one affected by it. Tim, think of, number one, yourself and don't be fighting a battle other than the battle for what you want yourself."

Then McHale invoked the name of a player who'd taken on baseball sixteen years earlier and wound up exiled from the game.

"Don't be the martyr like Curt Flood," he said.

Raines quietly took it in. He'd had a good relationship with McHale, who, indeed, had personally driven him to counseling sessions when the player was being treated for drug problems. ("I think I saved Tim Raines," said McHale, who, in his own mind, was just trying to save him from trouble again.) But Raines saw this as a sort of dark Dutch uncle talk.

"Personally, he didn't want to see me hurt," said Raines. "But in a business sense he didn't want to let me go."

Journeyman players got the message pretty emphatically too. Shortly after the season, agent Tony Attanasio called Royals GM John Schuerholz about his client Rudy Law, a career .271 hitter, with great speed (77 stolen bases one season) and dependable outfield skills. He'd joined Kansas City that spring but missed part of the season due to an injury and only played 87 games, hitting .261. Now his contract was up.

Yes, the Royals still wanted Law, Schuerholz told Attanasio, but at a lot less than the $470,000 they'd paid him in 1986.

"In the past, we had to pay these players a lot of money to maintain the continuity of our club," he said. "The game has changed. That no longer has to be done. The owners have gotten smart."

"I don't quite understand," said Attanasio. "This is the organization that originated the lifetime contract and now you want to cut my guy because he was injured last year? He plays a decent game, and the ball game hasn't changed."

"The game *has* changed," said Schuerholz. "What was available before is not available anymore."

The Lords' resolve to just say no would be severely tested, however. There were so many free agents out there that winter. You could almost have fielded an entire All-Star Team of them: Lance Parrish catching, Bob Horner at first, Willie Randolph at second, Doug DeCinces at third, and an outfield of Dawson, Raines, and Brian Downing. The right-handed starter was Jack Morris; the lefty, Ron Guidry. That still left a bench of World Series MVP Ray Knight, All-Star catcher Rich Gedman, and Gold Glove catcher Bob Boone.

But now the system of collusion was more "efficient." GMs were freely talking with each other about whether or not they wanted players, and owners with owners. "Clubs are working together better, making fewer dumb financial decisions, signing fewer multiyear contracts," Toronto GM Pat Gillick reported to Ueberroth at the general managers' meeting that fall. The commissioner encouraged that spirit to continue. "Be honest with each other, exchange information," he said.

The owners began to exchange a new key piece of information at their meetings, too. As Ueberroth did his club-by-club financial reviews, owners disclosed one more item. For each player eligible for free agency, they revealed whether or not they wanted to re-sign him. To outsiders the signal might be as cryptic as that of a third-base coach. But to insiders it was crystal clear: hands off or have at him.

The term "fiscal responsibility" was now invoked repeatedly. It was a code word for short-term contracts, no free agents, and owner conformity.

"It was like an AA meeting," said one participant. "An owner would get up and say, in effect, 'Hi, my name is George. I was tempted to make this fiscally irresponsible signing, but I didn't.' Or an owner would get up and say his club had just conducted a further study of their past free-agent signings and what do you know: they'd all been terrible."

When the Atlanta Braves' new president, Stan Kasten, attended his first owners' session, at the 1986 winter meetings, he was startled. In the NBA, where he headed the Atlanta Hawks, trade talk dwelt on how players would help teams. "In baseball, all anybody wanted to talk about was salaries and money," he recalled. "Before you ever talked about a player's skills you asked, 'What's his contract like?' "

The winter meetings, long a fertile deal-making ground, were a bleak place for agents that year. The site was the Diplomat Hotel in Hollywood, Florida. The last time the meetings were held there, in 1981, agent Richie Bry had set up shop in a poolside cabana. There, reclining on a chaise lounge, smoking a cigar, he received bidders for his players. Now agents had to beg for audiences with a GM. "It was a casual indifference," said Randy Hendricks. "It was: 'You've got nothing to sell.' "

Rudy Law's agent, Tony Attanasio, was there trying to place the outfielder. The Royals had first offered $250,000—half his 1986 salary—and later inched up to $288,000. Attanasio was trying to drum up another offer. He was well liked in baseball, by agent standards, a former minor-leaguer with an easygoing manner and a modest stable of players. He tried to trade on his goodwill, wherever it had accrued, but got only one nibble on Rudy Law.

Tigers GM Bill Lajoie said he'd talk to him at the meetings. But once there, he made himself scarce. It was another Tigers official, Jerry Walker, who approached Attanasio to explain why.

"We're off Law," he said. "We're going another way."

Later, Attanasio ran into Lajoie. "What gives?"

"It's what I have to do," he said. "I'm going to pass on Rudy and that's it. I have to do what I have to do."

"In other words, you think he can help the Tigers."

"Rudy can play. He can run; he can steal some bases; but we are just going to go another way."

"What changed your mind?"

"I have to go to a meeting," said Lajoie, flustered. "I just don't want to talk about that."

Attanasio was continuing to troll the Diplomat lobby when he saw John Schuerholz walk through the revolving door. The Royals GM came over and pulled him aside by the Christmas tree.

"Here is the deal on Rudy," he said. "Let us make it and get it over with right now. I'll give you three hundred thousand, single room, no guarantees, no incentives, not a nickel more. You'd better take it."

"Why would I do that?" asked Attanasio. "Why would I want to take that?"

"Tony, look, the game has changed. You're not going to get anything better on the outside."

"John, you know that is not necessarily true."

"Believe me, take it. He can play for us."

Attanasio later called Law and urged him to take it.

"You are not going to get anything better than what we have right here," he said. "I feel it. I see it. I have seen it with other players. I feel the tempo of guys that I have known all my adult life. I know what is happening here, and I know you are going to be made into a proper point. So if you think you can make this ball club, this is a choice you've got to make."

Law knew it was a risk to go with a nonguaranteed deal. You never knew what would happen in spring training. But he told Attanasio to accept the offer.

"I know I can make that ball club," he said. "I was hoping I'd be able to get the guarantee, but if I can't, to hell with it." (Law was cut the following spring and never played major league baseball again.)

Dick Moss had had it by the end of the winter meetings. He represented Jack Morris, who'd won more games than any other pitcher in the eighties. Baseball's best hurler was being treated like a classified-ad applicant. Moss had sent a letter after the Series to every team in baseball but Detroit, which Morris wanted to leave. It said Morris was available for hire and wanted to talk. The replies varied from form rejections to letters emphasizing that they "would not get into a bidding war" to invitations for Morris to "make an offer" to which a club could say yes or no.

This last approach was a rote response a lot of GMs had begun making. The "make us an offer" line reversed the usual process, in which teams made the first financial move. It eliminated any chance of GMs starting out too high, and it minimized the maneuvering room of agents. It helped teams to just say no.

GMs continued to give Morris the swerve at the Diplomat. The Angels' Mike Port, for instance, had sent a "make me an offer" letter but now ducked Moss throughout the winter meetings. The only offer on the table was Detroit's: $1.2 million a year for two years. The money paled beside the three-year, $5.5 million contract Fernando Valenzuela had landed earlier that year. Moss argued that Morris should be at the same level. The Tigers offered an alternative: salary arbitration.

Moss took the offensive on the meetings' last day. He announced that Morris had chosen four preferred teams: Minnesota, California, Philadelphia, and the Yankees. They would set up a meeting with each and supply what had been requested: proposals that the teams could either take or leave. So they packed up and hit the road.

The first stop was Minnesota. Moss had put the Twins somewhat on the spot, seeing as how Morris was a St. Paul boy. The cameras and microphones were on hand to greet them at the Twins' offices, but it wasn't an unqualified PR success for Morris: he was wearing a full-length fur coat, which seemed to put a damper on public sympathy for the guy.

Moss and Morris spent hours sparring with GM Andy MacPhail and owner Carl Pohlad. They made a variety of proposals, ranging from a three-year contract matching Valenzuela's to a series of contracts to be settled in arbitration. MacPhail talked of his interest in making Morris "the highest paid Twin," a status currently held by Bert Blyleven, who was making $1.3 million. MacPhail and Pohlad caucused and decided they couldn't live with Morris's minimum target of $1.8 million.

"This was your show; we are left with your instructions—that we say yes or no," MacPhail told Moss. "Our answer is no, we can't accept any of these."

The pitcher and agent left for Tampa, to meet George Steinbrenner. Moss had a new wrinkle: go to salary arbitration for Morris's 1987 contract, then give New York rights to him for four additional years, either under new contracts or through salary arbitration. The Yankees wouldn't be saddled with a big, guaranteed long-term contract. Morris would be a no-risk free agent.

Steinbrenner phoned in his regrets the next day.

"It wouldn't be fair to Willie Randolph and Ron Guidry," he said, referring to his incumbent free agents, whom he purportedly wanted to deal with before Morris. "That's my first order of business."

Moss canceled the road show. They were out of time. It was December 18 and they had to respond to Detroit's salary arbitration offer by the nineteenth. They called the Phillies' Bill Giles and the Angels' Mike Port with proposals along the lines discussed elsewhere.

Nothing doing. Port mentioned he didn't like the risk of salary arbitration if Morris continued to compare with the top-paid pitchers.

"Well," said a disgusted Jack Morris, "I hope Mike Witt doesn't have another good year, so you won't have to pay him all that money."

The next day, he accepted the Tigers' offer of salary arbitration. "There we could at least get what a player like Jack should be getting," said Moss.

Morris won his case and $1.85 million—though angrily.

Some top players, however, refused to accept salary arbitration, and as January 8, 1987, approached, they faced a dilemma. If they didn't sign with their old team by that date, they couldn't sign again until May 1. To take their chances on the market meant taking their baseball lives in their hands. Tom Reich used to call January 8 "Cinderella Day"—when players left for the free-agent ball. Now they were a lot more likely to turn into pumpkins.

On that date, Bob Horner listened to his last offer from Atlanta. The Braves slugger, coming off a twenty-seven-homer season, was being offered a 30 percent cut from his pay of $1.8 million. "The days of the two-million-dollar contract are over," Braves GM Bobby Cox told him. "You're going to burn at the stake if you don't take this." (This is how Horner and his agent remember the threat; Cox only remembers using the word *burn*.)

On that date, Rich Gedman and his agent were trying to salvage a deal with the Red Sox. Boston had offered a three-year-contract at about $900,000 per. Gedman wanted at least $1.2 million, the kind of money catchers like Jody Davis and Tony Pena were making. He'd been an All-Star in 1986.

His agent, Jack Sands, made a proposal late that afternoon. They'd come down to Boston's level on money for a one-year contract that would allow him to be a free agent again next year. "We were willing to take a chance that collusion would end and Rich would get another shot," Sands recalled.

The two went home to sit by the phone for counteroffers that never came.

On that date, Bob Boone called Oakland GM Sandy Alderson: Would the A's be interested in him if he walked away from the California Angels? (He wanted a two-year contract; the Angels would only go one.) Yes, but at nowhere near the Angels' $900,000, said Alderson, who then called Angels GM Mike Port to relate the conversation. Believing they had him sewn up, the Angels wouldn't give Boone the last $12,000 he wanted as a sweetener.

On that date, Tim Raines, the National League batting champion, was looking at one offer: three years, $4.8 million from the Expos. It was only $100,000 a year over his old contract. It was an affront to his pride and goaded him on. "I was coming off the best year of my career, and I just wasn't going to cave in," he later said. "I felt like if I caved in, everybody else would have been hurt too."

Horner, Gedman, Boone, Raines, and four other players would come to be known as the "January 8 Eight": players who went beyond the signing deadline and into the teeth of collusion. They were more brave than hopeful, and with good reason. An owners' meeting lay just ahead, in February. The Lords would get fresh reminders of their "fiscal responsibilities," and the players would be left to twist slowly in the wind.

"For the guys who bought the program," Tom Reich later said, "it was a bitch."

On January 9, the Red Sox sent out a crystal-clear signal on Rich Gedman: a memo to every team on interoffice teletype, detailing the failed negotiations and concluding: "The Red Sox will continue to make every effort to sign Gedman."

Still, the catcher was hopeful he'd get a deal. In late January, he and Jack Sands flew west to meet the A's. The welcoming committee included manager Tony LaRussa, coach Rene Lachemann, and players Carney Lansford and Reggie Jackson. It was, said GM Alderson, like a "fraternity rush."

Oakland couldn't match Boston's $900,000 offer, Alderson said, but was open to a one-year deal that allowed Gedman to go free-agent thereafter. Baseball rules allowed players to become free agents just once every five years. But clubs could, if they wished, waive the so-called repeater rights.

Sands said he hoped the market would thaw by then. So too did the A's executive vice president, Roy Eisenhardt. "I sure wish some team would break the logjam out there," he sighed over a breakfast meeting. "It sure would be easier for us if some other team signed a free agent first."

A few days later, Alderson called Sands to scotch the deal. They had talked with Barry Rona, who was dead-set against waiving repeater rights. The team was still free to do it, Alderson said, but they were a small-market franchise—a "little fish" he called it—and didn't want to buck the big boys in New York on this one. "Jack, you must understand the political nature of the environment we are acting in today," Alderson said. "We cannot do this."

On the heels of that, Houston GM Dick Wagner called Sands and said he was about to make a "big offer" on Rich Gedman.

It turned out to be a rather modest one—a two-year contract at under $700,000 per, with an option for a third year. Gedman declined and went home to await more offers, which did not come.

The Braves found themselves backpedaling even more furiously than the A's in the strange case of Bryn Smith. The Expos wouldn't offer him a new contract after off-season arm surgery, making him a free agent.

Smith was attractive to a pitching-poor team like the Braves. He was a crafty veteran, who'd gone 18–5 with a 2.91 ERA as recently as 1985. When Braves GM Bobby Cox offered him a base salary of $100,000, with the rest of his earnings based on how much he could pitch, Smith tentatively accepted.

Then Cox ran the deal by higher-ups and was told to back off. Montreal still had designs on Smith, whom it expected to sign on the cheap after his discouraging journey through the free-agent market. And the Braves couldn't afford to make enemies. Ted Turner had gotten dangerously in debt through the rapid expansion of his TV empire. Now a group of cable-TV operators was bailing him out by buying a major stake in his company. If that were deemed a "change of control," it needed approval by nine of the other eleven National League owners.

Between the SuperStation, the free-agent follies (most recently Sutter), and Turner's big mouth, that approval would be tough. National League owners were usually down on Atlanta. In 1985, Turner made some comments in a TV interview that directly contradicted the Lords' labor stance. Ueberroth played the offending clip at an ownership meeting, and other owners ripped into the Braves' chairman, Bill Bartholomay. (He often represented the club in Turner's stead.)

"Enough's enough!" declared Ewing Kauffman. "I'm instructing my general manager: no more trades with the Braves."

Others echoed that sentiment. Still others ranted about how they'd refuse to play spring training games against Atlanta. Only the Indians' Peter Bavasi offered any support.

"Don't worry, Bill," he said. "I'll play you guys all you want."

Bartholomay brightened momentarily until he realized something. The Braves trained in West Palm Beach, the Indians in Tucson.

No, the Braves would have to remember their "fiscal responsibilities." Cox came back at Smith with a lower offer—a base of $62,500 and tougher performance targets. But instead of killing the deal, Smith accepted it. Cox tried again, offering only a minor league contract, to be renegotiated if he made the team. Fine, Smith said.

Now, with a February owners' meeting approaching, the Braves were frantic. Club president Stan Kasten could just hear the other owners: "Here these guys go again, they are out doing this free-agent stuff again," he said. "We don't like them. Let's vote them down."

Kasten personally gave the message to Jim Bronner, Smith's agent, just before the owners' meeting. He couldn't do business, period. The Braves survived Turner's restructuring unchallenged.

Bill Giles hated what was happening. He was participating in it because he was a get-along-go-along kind of guy. He also owed Peter Ueberroth. When the Phillies changed hands in late 1986, the commissioner insisted its president receive another 10 percent of the club's stock gratis. (He already owned 10 percent from the previous regime.) Ueberroth had any number of ways to get people in his pocket.

But the fifty-two-year-old Giles came out of another time, when baseball ownership was a more noble calling. He literally grew up in Crosley Field, when his father, Warren Giles, was the Reds' GM and later the National League's president. Baseball didn't pay players very well then, but it cared for them in other ways. They and the front-office people were all part of a fraternity, drawn to and bound together by this game. Now they were warring business factions. "The worst thing about this period was the animosity," Giles would later say.

Giles was known as a soft touch for players, particularly his favorites. Tony Siegle, Philadelphia's assistant GM, was once battling with Dick Moss over a new contract for Von Hayes. One day the agent smirked, "I hear we've got a deal." Hayes had seen Giles in the clubhouse and secured the deal he wanted, terms far superior to what Siegle was offering.

Giles kept Steve Carlton even after the once-great lefty had lost his stuff. He hurt his arm in 1985, and in 1986, when he was being hit hard, Giles urged him to retire. Carlton refused, but Giles was slow to part with a man who'd won 241 games for the Phillies over fourteen years. Only when the shelling went on until midyear did he finally, reluctantly, release him.

The Phillies had a home game the day it was announced. Before it, they showed a montage of Carlton career highlights on the scoreboard video screen. Giles, watching, wept convulsively for ten minutes.

He was a natural to break the free-agent freeze. Tom Reich thought so and made an approach.

Lance Parrish was on the market. The Tigers had offered $1.2 million a year for two years, but he wasn't interested. He was upset at the strong-arming of his friend Jack Morris back to Detroit and he thought $1.2 million was chump change for baseball's best catcher.

This he arguably was. From 1982 to 1985 he averaged 30 homers and 100 RBIs. He'd missed the second half of 1986 with a bad back, but logged 22 homers and 62 RBIs in just 91 games. The doctors had given him a clean bill of health in the offseason, and the Phillies clearly needed a catcher of this caliber. They'd finished second in 1986, but had to rely on a career second-stringer named John Russell to catch. A case could easily be made to Giles that Lance Parrish was the Pete Rose of 1987—the guy who could put Philadelphia over the top—and Tom Reich did so.

Giles conceded in a TV interview that he was interested in Parrish. The man was congenitally unable to keep quiet when a microphone or notepad was thrust in front of him. Some of the Lords called him "the designated leaker."

Now they were all over him. Tigers president Jim Campbell called to make clear he wanted to retain Parrish. American League president Bobby Brown said he'd hate to see an AL star go to the other league. Milwaukee Brewers owner Bud Selig suggested he check with the PRC before making an offer. And, finally, White Sox chairman Jerry Reinsdorf reminded Giles of his "fiscal responsibilities." (So Giles later testified, though Reinsdorf maintains he didn't say that. His version of what he said was: "Don't be stupid. Make sure you don't win by a whole lot.")

Giles checked with the PRC.

"You're free to do what you want," said Barry Rona. "No other club can tell you what to do." (He did, however, recommend the Phillies pay no more than a $700,000 base salary, with performance incentives on top.)

He also called Lou Hoynes.

"What do I do, Lou?"

"You sign Parrish," said Hoynes. "It's good for the Phillies and it's good for baseball. There's got to be *somebody* signing a free agent."

In late January, Giles set up his first meeting with Parrish and

Reich—tremulously. "I'm catching tremendous heat from all over everywhere," he told them.

"I can understand that," said Reich. "It takes some stones for you to be here right now."

Giles brought Phillies caps for Parrish's kids but bad news for the adults. The best he could do was a one-year, $1 million contract. Some baseball people were screaming they wouldn't trade with him anymore if he signed Parrish. And a million was more than the PRC wanted him to offer. He recognized, however, it was less than they wanted.

Damn straight, said Reich. Considering the Phillies' pay structure, they had something between Von Hayes ($1.3 million) and Mike Schmidt ($2.1 million) in mind.

Giles had another thought. If Parrish accepted a lesser amount, he could supplement it with side promotional and endorsement work.

"You'll just have to be patient for this year," he said. "I will do the best I can outside the contract. If he has good years for us, that can change. Next year, between the threat of arbitration and the fact that he'll have been a Phillie a year, we'll be able to accomplish what you're looking to accomplish this year. But I have to wait.

"Baseball as an industry has to lower salaries. It's like Eastern Airlines having to cut back across the board to stay in business. It's not collusion. It's just the owners finally understanding what is happening."

Parrish was willing to entertain the offer, under the circumstances. But then Giles threw in a new wrinkle. The player would have to sign a release promising that he'd never sue the Phillies over any of the circumstances surrounding the signing (read: that he'd never holler collusion). Reich balked. Talks came to a halt.

The pitchers and catchers were reporting for spring training a few weeks later, in mid-February, and Parrish was at loose ends. He hung around Reich's Sarasota condo and stewed. There were no other offers.

"You could see the pain in his face, even when he was doing something mundane like playing golf," said Sam Reich. "He couldn't focus at all."

The Phillies' lawsuit waiver became the subject of much jawing between lawyers for the PRC and the union. Finally, in mid-March, Giles dropped the demand. At the same time, however, he reduced the offer. Parrish signed for $800,000 plus the incentive of another $200,000 if he wasn't on the disabled list before the All-Star Game.

He reported for duty, drawing the same pay as he had with the Tigers last year.

At that kind of money, Parrish and the rest of the January 8 Eight weren't getting great public sympathy. The general reaction was: poor babies, condemned to being millionaires instead of multimillionaires.

But their plights and pay had to be viewed in this light: the sport that was still pleading poverty was actually exploding into prosperity. From 1984 to 1987, total attendance rose by 16 percent, setting records each year. In 1987, for the first time, it passed 50 million. Eight teams drew more than 2 million, an attendance level once reserved only for the Dodgers.

In the same time span, baseball's licensing revenues grew by more than 150 percent, to $450 million. This was partly thanks to Ueberroth. He had pulled licensing rights away from individual franchises and centralized them in Major League Properties, which could drive harder bargains with manufacturers on behalf of all of baseball.

It was also partly thanks to the explosion of the baseball-card industry. The cards had suddenly become one of the hottest collectibles of the 1980s. By mid-decade, Mickey Mantle's 1952 card was worth $2,000, Pete Rose's rookie card was worth $400, and a complete set of 1975 cards would fetch $220. The buying public, wanting to get in on the ground floor of the next hot card, bought new ones by the gross.

That's where baseball's big licensing money came from. Through the 1970s, Topps had a stranglehold on baseball cards through its exclusive contracts with players. But in 1980, a candy company named Fleer wanted to get into the market. It sued to break the monopoly and won. Starting the following year, Fleer and another company, Donruss, started churning out cards. Later, two more companies—Leaf and Upper Deck—got in on the action.

The companies vied to put out special sets, to showcase the cards of the hot rookies, anything to jazz up the baseball-card market. They churned out ever more cards for a market that was growing an estimated 300 percent per year by the late eighties. And for each pack of cards sold, about 9 percent in royalties went to Major League Properties.

Baseball eked out its first operating profit in eight years in

1986. The following year, with industry revenues *up* 15 percent (to $792 million) and the average player's salary *down* 2 percent (to $402,000), profits grew by nearly tenfold, to $103 million.

It was a stunning reversal of the post-*Messersmith* trend. The average salary of that winter's free agents—the most talented group since Kapstein's stable of 1976—declined by 16 percent. About three quarters of free agents signed only one-year contracts. Only seven players who *weren't* free agents signed multiyear contracts.

Young stars, once routinely inked to such long-term deals, were instead tossed scraps. Boston's Roger Clemens was given a take-it-or-leave-it offer of $460,000, after winning twenty-four games, the Cy Young Award, and American League MVP honors in 1986. Clemens, who didn't yet qualify for salary arbitration, held out. In late March, Ueberroth personally intervened to help reach a settlement: $650,000 for 1987, $1.5 million for 1988.

The upshot of the period was this: baseball was hot, but baseball *players* were out in the cold.

Dick Moss had begun the guerrilla method of free-agent marketing with Jack Morris. He would perfect it with Andre Dawson. On January 8, the outfielder walked away from Montreal's two-year offer totaling $2.4 million. He didn't plan to go back.

Soon thereafter, Moss met with Cubs president and GM Dallas Green. His pitch: Dawson loved Wrigley Field, whose natural turf soothed his knees, and Wrigley Field would love Dawson. He'd fix the Cubs' sub-par outfield production.

Green, at the age of fifty-two, was a classic baseball man, a hulking ex-pitcher who in 1980 barked and sparked the Phillies to a world championship. He loved gamers and he clearly admired Dawson. Equally clear, however, was that he wasn't buying. Green told Moss he had strict instructions from the parent Tribune Company: no more high-priced players until the Cubs jettisoned some of their current ones.

Moss hadn't gotten a nibble anywhere else by the time spring training opened. He called Green with an idea: Why not let Dawson report to the Cubs camp without a contract? They could check his knees, and they were under no obligation.

"I guess there's no rule against that," Green growled.

He called back thirty minutes later to say that, well, there was.

"It occurred to us all that maybe it wasn't such a good idea after all," he said. "If we get Andre over here, it's going to raise everybody's hopes, and if somehow it doesn't work out, everybody on the team is going to be depressed about it. So we'd better not do it."

Moss told Dawson what had happened. They were both low. Then the agent brightened.

"Why don't we just walk into camp?" he said. "Stir something up."

It wasn't Dawson's style. He was low-key and nonconfrontational. But he hated the thought of going back to Montreal with his tail between his legs. That's where this was headed. He finally warmed to Moss's idea. What did he have to lose?

It was a sunny early-March day in Mesa, Arizona, when Moss and Dawson walked into Green's office at HoHoKam Park. The Cubs' front-office secretary started at the sight. Um, Mr. Green was out and wouldn't be available—all week.

But Moss left an envelope containing a contract for Andre Dawson. A note was attached. It invited Green to fill in the blank in Paragraph 2: salary. Then he walked out and told the Cubs' beat writers what he'd done. The next day, the Chicago papers trumpeted the coming of Andre Dawson. The president of the Cubs exploded through the phone at Moss, furious at being put on the spot. "Dallas knows a lot of bad words," said Moss later, "and he used most of them."

Green did, however, agree to a private meeting with Dawson. Moss waited in a car while they chatted, then drove them to the airport. Dawson flew home to Miami; Moss flew home to L.A.

There he took a call from a Tribune Company lawyer. "Does that really mean what it says?" he said. "Can we put anything we want in Paragraph Two?"

The next day came a joint call from the lawyer and Dallas Green. They would agree to the contract and they'd filled in the blank: $500,000 plus $200,000 in performance incentives. Andre Dawson had a job, though at half his 1986 salary. In his mind, Moss ran through the Cubs' pay scale. No veteran would be making less than Dawson, except for spare outfielder Thad Bosley.

"Well, I am a little disappointed," he said. "We gave you a blank check, but I thought your definition of fairness would be a little more generous than this. But that was our offer and that's our deal."

"Well, you know I thought you were going to try some way to wiggle out of it," said Green, "but you're going to live up to your deal."

"That was our offer," said Moss.

"Okay."

Moss prepared to hang up so he could call Dawson with the news, but Green wasn't quite through.

"That was some PR campaign you ran," he said. "I didn't like it at all. You put us in a position where you got everybody in Chicago excited; you got everybody on the team excited, and there was no way we could say no."

Three days later, Green wrote a note to Barry Rona, relating the sequence of events. For a man who'd just signed a star at a deep discount, he was quite apologetic: "I was not quite as prepared to respond or handle this type of proposal as I probably should have been," he wrote. "I still feel, in the back of my mind, there is an ulterior motive to this sequence of events."

The rest of the January 8 Eight met varied fates. Tim Raines had flirtations with Seattle, San Diego, and Houston, where he had a one-on-one chat with owner John McMullen. McMullen offered the defending National League batting champion a 27 percent pay cut and an interesting rationale: "Once you're making a million," he said, "why worry about anything over that?"

Tom Reich sent seven teams the kind of "yes or no" proposal they all liked: take Raines for a flat $1.25 million or a $1 million base with $400,000 in performance bonuses. There were no takers.

Raines watched Opening Day on TV, worked out with a high school team, and waited. Finally, in mid-April, Reich set up a meeting with the Expos brass in Sarasota. There Raines agreed to a three-year contract, sweetened slightly beyond the January 8 offer of $1.6 million a year.

On May 1, he rejoined the Expos at Shea Stadium. He hit a grand slam home run to beat the Mets.

Bob Boone got no other bids and re-signed with the Angels on May 1 for the same amount they'd offered January 8. Later that season, the thirty-nine-year-old Boone set a record for most games caught and won his sixth consecutive Gold Glove.

Bob Horner's market value went steadily backward. The first baseman went from a $1.3 million offer from Atlanta to a $1.1 million offer from San Diego (just $800,000 of it guaranteed) to dead silence. Two months after rejecting San Diego's offer, Horner called back to accept. The Padres were no longer interested.

In early April, loathing a return to Atlanta and seeing no alternatives in America, Horner signed with the Yakult Swallows of Japan.

Doyle Alexander did return to Atlanta. He signed with the Braves shortly after May 1, for less than he'd been offered on January 8.

Rich Gedman spent February with his wife and their new baby, March working out with Roger Clemens, and April waiting. Then, May 1, he and agent Jack Sands went to Fenway Park to sign a new contract with the Red Sox. He looked forward to playing again, but it was not a happy day. "You felt like you came back like a beaten dog," he said.

Gedman felt like even more of one when he was through. The contract signing was easy: a two-year contract averaging $900,000. But then Boston's general partner, Haywood Sullivan, pulled Gedman and Sands into a conference room with co-owner Jean Yawkey.

Sullivan was old school. A former big-league catcher and manager, he'd parlayed being a favorite of the Yawkeys into various front-office jobs with the Red Sox and, finally, into a part ownership. He had signed Gedman ten years earlier, when he was a chunky kid from Worcester that nobody else wanted. He'd been proud of Gedman's development and hurt that he had been so willing to leave. He'd thought of Gedman as almost family, for Gedman was close to Sullivan's son, Marc, Boston's backup catcher. "I wanted to talk to him like I thought a parent would," Sullivan later said. "I didn't think he was getting the right advice."

He laced into Gedman about how he'd "let down all the little people who have been your fans." He'd been greedy; he'd been a dupe of the union; he "should have had second thoughts about becoming a test case."

Then Sullivan turned on Sands.

"You're to blame, and the union is definitely to blame," he said. "I know what you're thinking, Sands. You're thinking there's collusion going on." He let loose a string of profanities. "Of course we talk. We talk all the time, and you talk to people all the time, too."

Finally, his wrath spent, he ended with this parting shot: "I don't care who you tell about this." (Both Gedman and Sands testified to the accuracy of the foregoing. Sullivan, however, doesn't remember saying it.)

That about summed it up for the Lords. The tables had been turned, and there wasn't a thing, it seemed, the players could do about it.

* * *

In September 1987, arbitrator Thomas Roberts ruled on the union's first collusion grievance against the owners: guilty as charged. The damages to be paid by the owners would be assessed later. Now hearings on the 1986–87 free-agent crop were under way, in a new climate. "The clubs' case was obviously falling apart," said union lawyer Steven Fehr. "[Arbitrator] George Nicolau was asking tougher questions than *I* was."

The Lords took a new tack on collusion. It was called the Information Bank, and it was simplicity itself. A club making an offer to a free agent reported it to the PRC. That was called an information "deposit." A club wanting to know what others bid for a free agent could call the PRC and make an information "withdrawal."

The idea was to stimulate the market enough to blunt charges of collusion, while at the same time keeping a rein on the market. The signal was clear: Okay, guys, you can bid now. But don't top the other guy's offer by much.

A new labor lawyer was responsible for much of the change. After many years of angling for the baseball account, Morgan, Lewis, and Bockius finally got it. One of its Washington attorneys, Chuck O'Connor, became the PRC's principal counsel. Lou Hoynes and his firm of Willkie, Farr and Gallagher were reduced to a subordinate role.

O'Connor, a twenty-year veteran of labor wars with Teamsters, miners, and municipal workers, did what the lawyers before him wouldn't: he stopped Ueberroth's payroll-review drills at the meetings. He also instructed GMs and owners to stop talking with one another about player signings. The substitute market mechanism—the Information Bank—was, needless to say, his brainchild.

It *did* create the appearance of a more active market, though it often just amounted to churning. Oakland bid $1.3 million for Mike Witt, even though California, the team that was trying to retain him, had already bid $1.4 million. The Dodgers and Phillies were relentless matchers, but not toppers, of other clubs' offers. With this all-out caution, Los Angeles bid for Gary Gaetti, Mike Davis, and Dave Righetti; Philadelphia for Joaquin Andujar, David Palmer, and Danny Darwin. The bids were never successful, but, then, they were never meant to be.

Righetti set an American League record for saves in 1987 and, perhaps, an Information Bank record for "transactions." The Dodgers and Giants bid for him fast, but only equaling or underbidding the offers from his incumbent team, the Yankees.

Righetti accepted a salary-arbitration offer from New York and returned there.

Cleveland was the master of what the union called the "tight range" bid. The Indians offered pitcher Danny Darwin a deal that provided less in guaranteed money than did the Astros, who wanted to retain him, though, with incentives, a bit more in potential dollars. They offered Atlee Hammaker a deal that promised more in guaranteed money but with less upside potential. The idea, as Steve Fehr put it, was to "keep just a half-step ahead of the competition."

It was also the sort of bidding that continued to funnel players back to their old clubs. After a flurry of bidding activity, the incumbent team usually prevailed if it wanted the player. Mike Witt went back to California, Gary Gaetti to Minnesota, and Dennis Martinez to Montreal.

Some premier players continued to attract no interest at all. Jack Morris was sentenced to another two years in Detroit; Paul Molitor and Dave Smith returned to Milwaukee and Houston, respectively.

Yet also to be found in the Information Bank were the seeds of collusion's unraveling. The previous system had imposed a discipline of conformity; the Information Bank required *discretion*. It presented opportunities for mischief. Clubs were often late to report bids, prone to underreport bids, known to use the Bank to outright hoodwink other clubs. They were, in short, starting to revert to their old self-interested selves.

Consider the case of Jack Clark. The Cardinals first baseman was a monster power hitter who had an awesome 1987 season: 35 homers, 106 RBIs, and a .286 average, in just 131 games. Naturally, nobody else in baseball was interested in him.

Back during the 1985 season, Clark had been talking with St. Louis about a long-term contract at $2 million a year, which was in line with the rich five-year deal shortstop Ozzie Smith had just struck. That talk stopped with Ueberroth's 1985 Series meeting, but Clark still wanted a three-year deal at $2 million. The Cardinals wouldn't go beyond two years, and they wouldn't pay a guaranteed $2 million. Their limit was $1.5 million with incentive bonuses that, with continued top performance, could take him to $2 million.

By late December, Clark had come around on the length and the money, but was quarreling about a loan. He'd gotten into financial trouble through some bad investments. (Clark's spectacular mismanagement of money would later land him in bankruptcy.) The Cardinals had loaned him $250,000 and wanted it repaid. When the terms became a part of the contract negotiations, the first baseman exploded.

"Get me out of here," he told Tom Reich, his agent. "I'll go anywhere."

Reich, on reflex, picked up the phone and called George Steinbrenner.

"Jack Clark has broken off negotiations with St. Louis," he said. "Are you interested?"

He was. Profoundly. After making a strong run at the pennant in 1986, the Yankees had slid back to fourth in 1987. Steinbrenner had already hired Billy Martin for the fifth time in the off-season, and he was determined to recover in 1988.

"I'd love to have Jack Clark," said Steinbrenner. "But I'm not going to be able to be in a negotiation involving money."

The Boss meant he wouldn't exceed the Cardinals' offer, but he matched it precisely: two years at $1.5 million per, plus $500,000 in incentives. He did not, however, immediately inform the Information Bank.

Tom Reich, however, did let drop to the Cardinals' Lou Susman the fact that Clark was talking to someone else. He screamed at the PRC to find out who it was. John Westhoff, a young lawyer there, started calling around to see who it was. California, Oakland, Toronto, and Philadelphia all denied it was them. So did Yankee GM Bob Quinn.

"That would make no sense," he scoffed at Westhoff, and he wasn't lying. Steinbrenner hadn't told his "baseball people" what he was doing.

Only after Clark had already accepted the Yankees' offer did Steinbrenner call Westhoff. He had an information "deposit" to make. He laid out the terms offered and said Clark had until noon the next day to make a decision. It was, of course, a lie. Steinbrenner neglected to mention something else: a side letter promising a third year on the contract or, if things didn't work out in New York, a trade.

Steinbrenner didn't make the call until 11:00 P.M., but Westhoff immediately relayed word to St. Louis. Just as quickly, Lou Susman was all over Tom Reich. They'd drop the $250,000 repayment demand; they'd sweeten the terms; what did they have to do?

"It's too late," said Reich, with satisfaction. "I've given my hand."

Clark was in pinstripes and his experience was indicative of what was going on. "The blocks had started to loosen," said Reich.

The Yankees also tried to hoodwink the Angels out of Mike Witt by not reporting their true bid to the Information Bank. The Dodgers, in a similar vein, tried to trick the Twins out of Gary Gaetti. The Lords were reverting to form.

By the end of the Information Bank's first winter, in 1988, the Lords had lost all sense of urgency. The industry's operating profits would rise to $121 million that year and nearly double to $214 million the next. Almost everybody was making money. Almost nobody believed they could keep this going much longer. In August 1988, arbitrator Nicolau ruled on the second year of collusion: again, guilty as charged.

Nicolau and Tom Roberts, the first arbitrator, made a total of twenty-one players "second-look" free agents, able to test the market again. One of them was Kirk Gibson, who was signed by the Dodgers in early 1988. That year, he hit 25 homers, batted .290, led L.A. to the pennant, and was named National League MVP.

Then, in October, he hit one of the most dramatic home runs in World Series history. Though hobbled by hamstring and knee injuries, he managed to limp to the plate in the ninth inning of the first game to pinch-hit. Facing Oakland relief ace Dennis Eckersley with two outs, one on, and the Dodgers trailing 4–3, Gibson smashed a game-winning homer. He never played again in the Series, but the A's never recovered from that homer. The Dodgers—by far the weaker team—won in five games.

That, some thought, was the moment collusion really ended. Nobody who witnessed that scene—a fist-pumping Gibson rounding the bases, his teammates mobbing him at home, Dodger fans filling the night with a roar—could ever again say that no free agent was worth it.

As it all came crashing down around him, Ueberroth took no blame and professed only bewilderment.

"I never did anything wrong," he insisted over lunch one day with Lou Hoynes at the Racket Club. "I never said anything wrong."

"Technically you didn't," Hoynes told him. "The clubs heard your words, but they also heard the music, and it was martial music. They all fell into the beat."

$ 18 $

PETER UEBERROTH WAS on his way out. His term was up in 1989 and he had places to go, things to do. He would not stand for reelection as commissioner. The master of PR could trumpet his achievements in putting the profit back in baseball and getting the drugs out. The chickens hadn't yet come home to roost on collusion, for damages hadn't yet been assessed. It was time to declare victory and get the hell out.

But there was one more important piece of business. Baseball's network TV contract was up in 1989, and a new one was to be negotiated. Ueberroth wanted it to be the glorious final movement to the symphony of his commissionership. The owners *needed* it to be. TV money had become the Lords' lifeblood, the great equalizer in the baseball economy. One comparative statistic said it all. From 1971 to 1990, the average player salary grew 1,741 percent. In the same span, the revenue from national TV contracts grew 1,742 percent.

Baseball had come a long way from the days when TV was the enemy. It was certainly considered that in the 1950s. TV was blamed, at first, for slaying the minors. In 1949, when less than 4 million American homes had TV sets, 42 million people attended minor league games. By 1959, 80 percent of American homes had TV sets and 70 percent of minor league attendance had evaporated. Whole leagues disappeared, and old baseball men mourned.

Major league attendance also plummeted in TV's early years. From an all-time high of 20 million in 1948 it was down to 14.4 million in 1953. "The greatest fear I have about baseball is that we'll become a studio game," National League president Warren Giles wrote to his owners back then. "We'll be playing with only 500 people in the stands and everybody else watching on TV."

The Lords were fixated on gate receipts. Broadcasts amounted to "giving the game away." Before they were anti-TV, they were anti-radio. Larry MacPhail, it will be recalled, enraged his fellow New York owners in 1938 by refusing to renew an anti-radio compact among the three clubs. They wanted no games on the air, while the Dodgers' president wanted to broadcast them all. He considered radio a grand promotional tool.

While the Yankees and Giants stewed, MacPhail lined up 50,000-watt WOR to broadcast the games and General Mills, Mobil Oil, and Procter and Gamble to sponsor them. The other two clubs were forced to capitulate and put their games on WABC. Still, the way rights fees were arrived at for radio and early TV revealed the prevailing attitude in baseball toward those media. Clubs didn't try to calculate their games' value to the stations and then bargain aggressively. They tried to figure out how much attendance broadcasts were costing them and then charged just enough to replace lost ticket revenues.

Only a few teams saw TV's potential. The Brooklyn Dodgers telecast more than a hundred games a year in the fifties, and Walter O'Malley was exploring pay TV. The Cubs televised heavily from 1948 on, eventually putting all home games on TV. Phil Wrigley sold the rights for peanuts, reasoning that he was creating fans—housewives who watched while ironing, kids who flipped on the Cubs after school. Eventually, they'd get hooked and come out to the ballpark. "He said we should provide them with continuity," recalled Cubs business manager E. R. "Salty" Saltwell.

But as of the late fifties, five of the eight National League teams televised no home games at all. The franchise-hopping of that decade was driven far more by the promise of new stadiums than by the lure of vast TV markets. Milwaukee, Baltimore, and Kansas City were small cities, but they had big new ballparks. TV just wasn't a significant part of the revenue mix. Broadcast rights accounted for just 17 percent of baseball's total revenues in 1956.

Even in 1965, only four teams topped $1 million in local annual broadcast revenues: the Yankees, Mets, Dodgers, and Astros. (Houston was tops at $1.8 million. Roy Hofheinz made part of his fortune in radio and was an aggressive seller of rights. He even put together a Spanish-language radio network.) The Senators were on the low end, at $300,000 while the Twins, Cardinals, Cubs, and Reds represented the average, at $500,000.

It was in that year that baseball first started trying to harness its TV power. The Lords had granted *Game of the Week* rights, in various forms, since 1953. One year (1960) all three networks had a version. But the owners forbid their telecast in big-league cities, and the networks paid teams on a per-appearance basis. Thus, the 1964 Yankees reaped five times more than any other team: $550,000, compared to $100,000 for the runner-up Cardinals and Phillies.

John Fetzer changed all that. The Tigers' owner made his fortune in TV and radio stations, and he understood both baseball and broadcasting. He pushed the Lords to improve the packaging and distribution of their "product." "Mr. Fetzer got everybody together, and for the first time sold the rights to baseball as an industry," said Detroit GM Jim Campbell.

The result was a $5.7 million *Game of the Week* deal with ABC. It was no Rozelle-style masterstroke, but it was a major enhancement of baseball's TV income. That was because the Lords finally agreed to let the *Game* be televised in big-league cities, which were the nation's major TV markets. The deal was also significant in that it shared the proceeds equally. Each club would get $300,000, or at least three times more than any team except New York had seen previously. It was the starting point of the networks' economic importance to the game of baseball.

ABC got terrible ratings for the *Game* in 1965. That allowed NBC to swoop in and pick it up on the cheap. It captured baseball in toto from 1966 to 1968—the *Game*, the World Series, and the All-Star Game—for $11.8 million a year.

But from that unsure start, the network rights would climb geometrically. NBC paid $49.5 million for 1969–71, then $72 million for 1972–75. When bidding for the next contract came around, baseball divided the package between NBC and ABC for a composite deal yielding $92.8 million for 1976–79.

There was some grumbling about the networks' growing influence. In 1971, baseball started playing World Series games at night—just to appease the network. Viewers scoffed at the sight of Bowie Kuhn sans topcoat, pretending he wasn't freezing. Purists bemoaned the loss of a shared national experience: pressing ears to transistor radios and relaying scores through schools and offices.

But sponsors didn't pay for afternoon radio like they did for prime-time TV. And baseball needed prime-time money in the post-*Messersmith* era. The 1976–79 TV deal generated nearly $1 million per team, a powerful offset to rising payrolls.

Local broadcast rights were jumping too. This was partly because teams were learning the value of television games—even home games. As their marketing and ticket-selling operations got more sophisticated, they discovered that they didn't necessarily have to sacrifice attendance for TV. Indeed, some felt that if they played their cards—and cameras—right, TV could *help* attendance. "You could show the excitement of your fans screaming, of families having fun at the ballpark," said the Phillies' Bill Giles. "It was the best promotion you could have."

In addition, more clubs now had front-office specialists whose sole mission in life it was to maximize their TV and radio revenues. In 1975, Gene Kirby of the Red Sox ditched the club's flagship radio station of thirty years for one that would ante up a record $450,000 for rights.

It came as a blow to purists, for suddenly the Red Sox play-by-play was littered with plugs for sponsors. The new station had to pay the freight *somehow*. It was the beginning of a massive proliferation of commercial intrusions into baseball broadcasts. ("As the call goes out to the bullpen, how about calling Domino's?" and "While they're making a pitching change, Kendall Oil asks, 'Have you changed your oil lately?' ") But in the mid-seventies it was an unpleasant novelty, and Bosox announcers Ned Martin and Jim Woods were openly disdainful. Enormously popular with listeners, though not with sponsors, they were fired in 1978.

But even the fast-growing flow of local broadcast revenue couldn't keep pace with the gush of network money. In 1965, local TV generated three times more income for baseball than network deals. In 1980, for the first time, network revenue exceeded local TV rights. The 1980–83 deal doubled the old contract, yielding $190 million, or $1.8 million per team per year.

"The cry used to be that the game was too long; it was too slow; it was played in the summer," said Tom Villante, who negotiated the 1980–83 deal for baseball. "Strangely enough, all those negatives turned out to be positive."

The most positive of all was the summer part. Long a slack season for TV advertising, it perked up. Football once got all the car ads, as new models were introduced each fall. Now, with fierce import competition, new models came out constantly. So did ads. Chrysler glommed on to baseball, making Joe Garagiola its pitchman. The newly deregulated airlines were also embroiled in fierce competition. They turned to baseball to advertise for the peak summer-travel season. And, most of all, there was beer.

Nothing fueled TV sports like the Beer Wars. The first shot was fired in the early 1970s, when Phillip Morris purchased Miller Brewing. Armed with the tobacco giant's cash, Miller went after Anheuser-Busch hard. America's number-one brewer since 1957 was caught back on its heels.

The King of Beers was sent reeling by the introduction of Miller Lite in 1975. This was the first low-calorie beer, and it quickly tapped an enormous market. By 1976, Anheuser-Busch's market share had dipped from 23.7 to 19.4 percent. Miller had gone from a distant seventh to a strong second—and Gussie Busch had been ousted as chairman.

Miller used sports skillfully. Its pitchmen were glib ex-jocks, and its aim was to grab every possible TV spot for major sports events. Miller became the exclusive beer sponsor for *Monday Night Football*, the college football *Game of the Week*, the 1980 Olympic Games, the Indy 500, and yes, the World Series.

August Busch III, Gussie's son and successor, came back firing. He believed Anheuser-Busch rightfully *owned* sports. Certainly his father had positioned it that way, between the Cardinals and a host of sponsorships. Gussie Busch was by now a ceremonial relic, but young Auggie had inherited the fighting spirit, not to mention a calculating business head. If the infidels chose to challenge him on this ground, he'd make them pay dearly.

Anheuser-Busch poured 70 percent of its $400 million broadcast ad budget into sports. It also endeavored, at every turn, to push Miller out. The rival had snuck in to become sole beer sponsor of NBC's and ABC's baseball telecasts. It was galling, an Anheuser-Busch delegation told Bowie Kuhn, and they expected him to do something about it. The delegation, led by Gussie Busch's consigliere, Lou Susman, asked Kuhn to go to bat for them. He had the clout to force the networks to air Anheuser-Busch ads. Pete Rozelle, they pointed out, had gotten them onto *Monday Night Football*, where Miller was previously the exclusive beer sponsor. Kuhn primly refused. It was a network decision, he said, and he couldn't intercede in the middle of a contract. Susman gritted his teeth and made up his mind to *get* Kuhn. He would later lead the coup against Kuhn, using the company's TV sponsorships as leverage to gain support.

(When Kuhn did fall, his staunch ally, Peter O'Malley, ban-

ished Anheuser-Busch from Dodger Stadium and brought in
Miller. It slowed the flow of Bud at major league games only
slightly, however. Anheuser-Busch had locked up the concession
stands at every other stadium but Milwaukee, which went with
hometown Miller.)

What a difference a few decades made. Judge Landis refused
to allow beer ads on World Series radio broadcasts. Happy
Chandler turned down Brooklyn's Liebman Breweries as a sponsor for the first televised World Series. "It would not be good
public relations for baseball to have the Series sponsored by the
producer of an alcoholic beverage," he said.

By the 1980s, beer was the mother's milk of baseball.
Anheuser-Busch, which in 1976 sponsored the telecasts of
twelve teams, in 1986 sponsored those of all twenty-six. Its war
with Miller was also a huge factor in driving up the value of
baseball's broadcast rights. TV could pay big for baseball rights,
knowing Anheuser-Busch and Miller would pay big to advertise.
Baseball was summer; summer was beer; and beer was huge
money.

There was another reason TV bid up the broadcast value of
baseball. The networks had their own imperatives. Their identities were wrapped up in certain sports and their executives'
pride was on the line with each high-profile bid. (Men like
ABC's Roone Arledge had every bit the ego of a Lord.) Sometimes a network needed to win a high-profile sports bid just to
make a statement, no matter the cost.

Such was the happy case for baseball as it faced its next TV
deal in 1983. NBC was in a shambles in the early eighties. The
peacock was pulling up the rear in the Nielsens. It had recruited
Grant Tinker as its president, hoping the noted producer could
restore the old luster. At this low point in the network's history,
it wasn't about to lose baseball.

If football was the signature sport of CBS, as the Olympics
were at ABC, the national pastime belonged to NBC. It had enjoyed an exclusive lock on baseball from 1966 to 1975, and it
televised every World Series from 1947 to 1975. It presented
baseball deftly and lovingly. As an executive there once put it,
"Baseball is in the walls at NBC."

The old saw had been that baseball wasn't well suited to TV.
But with innovative camera work and top announcers, NBC
made it work for TV. Producer Harry Coyle developed the
center-field camera shot that became TV's standard vantage. He

originated the close-up shot—isolating key players' actions and reactions. When Carlton Fisk's twelfth-inning homer won game six of the 1975 Series, NBC's shot of him willing the ball fair, theatrically twisting and turning his body, heightened the drama. A record 76 million viewers tuned in to game seven.

NBC had the advantage of most-favored-network status with Bowie Kuhn. He was a lame-duck commissioner now, but nevertheless a member of baseball's three-man TV negotiating committee. Kuhn revered NBC's baseball connections, just as he did Gillette's. And he liked Arthur Watson, NBC Sports's genial president.

White Sox president Eddie Einhorn, another committee member, was also close to NBC, though he also had ties to CBS, for which he used to produce *CBS Sports Spectacular*. (He once taunted rival anthology shows with the immortal line, "Our shit's better than your shit.") But in the 1970s, Einhorn's syndication company provided NBC its entire menu of college basketball.

The third TV committee member was the Phillies' Bill Giles, a savvy user of the medium. He had, of course, employed his local carrier, WPHL, in 1978 to land Pete Rose. He was also the artful seller of a mix of cable and over-the-air rights that put Philadelphia among baseball's leaders in local TV revenue.

The committee called itself "KEG" (Kuhn-Einhorn-Giles) and it had a clear objective. It wanted to continue with at least two networks on the next contract—three if possible. Multiple networks spread the financial risks out, ensured greater promotion for baseball, and reduced hostile counterprogramming moves. A network that was in bed with baseball didn't run a blockbuster miniseries against the World Series.

But KEG did want one network to take the lead in the bidding process. "The strategy was to get one of them to go for the whole thing, to make the market," said Einhorn.

Baseball's leverage lay in a clause in the present contract. If either ABC or NBC made an offer on a new deal, it said, the other one could get half the package by matching it. It was simple: a bid from one would drag the other aboard. A network sports mogul would rather die than lose a major property. It was a loss of face, and it was tough to explain to network affiliates.

Finally, Einhorn got NBC to bite. It could least afford to lose the sport, and it had the most to gain. The "jewels," as the postseason and All-Star games were called, got big numbers, and the World Series carried particular importance. It was played at the same time when the networks' new shows debuted, and it provided a great opportunity to promote them.

Also, NBC's Arthur Watson didn't mind sticking it to ABC. He was still exercised about how that network had wormed away half the baseball package in 1975. (A man named John Lazarus was baseball's broadcast negotiator at that time. He came out of ABC Sports, remained in baseball just long enough to do the deal, then returned to ABC Sports. The cries of "inside job"—and worse—rang through the corridors of NBC Sports.)

ABC, it turned out, didn't even much like baseball. That network committed itself to Monday-night games, then carried them only sporadically when it became clear that other programs got better ratings. Baseball got its money, but not the showcase it desired. The sport also had to endure ABC's Howard Cosell, who, apparently uncomfortable with its rhythms, never seemed to *like* baseball. NBC's Vin Scully subtly enhanced a game; Cosell loudly got in its way.

In 1983, NBC came out with a "floor" bid that floored a lot of people: $475 million for half the package for five years. NBC would also guarantee to pick up the other half for $425 million if ABC didn't take it. The network was offering *quadruple* the amount of baseball's current contract. It was also putting ABC on the spot. As Watson's number two, Ken Schanzer, put it, "Either we succeeded in getting the whole package or we so crippled our competitor, we made his life hard."

With Watson and Schanzer on one side of the table and KEG on the other, they negotiated endlessly over the fine points throughout early 1983. To assure privacy, one meeting was held in the file room of the 21 Club. Another lasted long into the night of Valentine's Day, getting them all in trouble with Luisa Kuhn. All meetings were governed by a central ground rule: "We'd never let a lawyer in the room," said Schanzer. "We wanted businessmen, not a lot of verbiage and nit-picking." (In fact, Schanzer, Einhorn, and Kuhn were all lawyers, though none were practicing attorneys.)

Einhorn took the lead in shaping the contract's many intricacies. With his wide-collared satin shirts, medallions, and leather jackets, Einhorn looked like what he was—an unadulterated hustler. As a TV sports executive named Carl Lindemann once put it, "He's a street-smart guy, but not exactly the one you'd want making a presentation to the board."

But Einhorn was well versed in TV, through his syndication background and other ventures, and he loved doing deals—the more complicated the better. Fast Eddie's only shortcoming was a tendency to outrun the comprehension of others. In one meeting, he described a long, logarithmic formula he'd developed to split the package in new and exotic ways. He finished to a crashing silence. Watson and Schanzer looked blankly at Einhorn, then at each other.

"Would you mind if we caucused?" Schanzer asked KEG.

When they'd withdrawn he posed a question: "Arthur, do you have any idea what the fuck Eddie is talking about?"

"No," said Watson. "How are we supposed to respond? What do you think we should do?"

"We're pretty close to these guys," said Schanzer. "Maybe we should just tell them."

They went back into the conference room.

"Eddie, you're an old friend of ours; we've known you for years and we have to tell you," said Watson. "We've just listened to you for twenty-five minutes and we didn't understand a word you said."

He turned to Kuhn. "Commissioner, could you explain it?"

Kuhn cleared his throat and paused.

"I didn't understand it either," he finally admitted.

They all roared, except Einhorn, who just shook his head.

KEG finally took the offer to ABC. Roone Arledge passed. He told Einhorn he wouldn't go beyond $300 million. The proposed deal massively favored NBC, particularly since it gave the peacocks three World Series to ABC's two. Then Einhorn shopped it to CBS. He tried to stampede its sports chief, Neal Pilson, with a twenty-four-hour deadline to match NBC. Pilson wouldn't bite, either. KEG was left with NBC. Baseball still didn't want just one network. But if NBC was going to get an exclusive, Einhorn was going to demand a premium.

"The whole thing's yours for a billion," he told Schanzer and Watson.

The two looked at each other. Their original offer for both halves was $900 million. Watson mouthed one word: no.

"Eddie, we're tap city; there's no more money," said Schanzer.

Silence hung in the air for a moment. Then Schanzer continued.

"Look, there's enough money in this deal right now that if you have the discipline and will, you can re-create your business," he said. "There's one thought that's been plaguing me throughout this negotiation. I believe your owners will spend the money within a month of this deal. All you're asking me to do is pour more money down your sump hole."

The indefatigable Einhorn went back to ABC with a new idea. Baseball would extend the contract to six years and balance out the World Series to three each. Baseball was also willing to make changes to enhance regular-season games. For example, the networks could have exclusivity for the *Game of the Week*. Local baseball broadcasts would be forbidden while it was on. It could make a big difference in ratings.

Finally, Arledge bit. ABC paid $575 million; NBC paid $550 million; baseball popped the cork. It would reap $1.125 billion for the years 1984 through 1989. Each club was to collect $7.2 million a year—some improvement over the $1.8 million they got under the old contract.

"They're putting the wrong person in Cooperstown this summer," ABC's Dennis Swanson told one baseball executive. "They ought to put Eddie Einhorn in there for that deal."

Yet the surge of TV revenues in the eighties was not an unmixed blessing. The network cash was divvied up equally, of course, but the rest of the TV money fell like spot showers: heavily on some clubs and hardly at all on others.

The big variable was cable revenues. There hadn't been any to speak of as of 1975. But in the next decade, the number of American homes with cable TV would quadruple, to 40 million. By 1985, cable accounted for 12 percent of baseball's TV revenues. It was big money in places like New York, Philadelphia, and Boston. The Red Sox actually co-owned (with the NHL Boston Bruins) the outlet that carried its games, New England Sports Network. But in places like Milwaukee, Seattle, and Kansas City, cable money was virtually nil.

The Lords, in a rare instance of foresight, had prepared for this day. In the 1950s, Reds owner Powell Crosley got a measure enacted by National League owners that would require teams with pay-TV deals to share 25 percent of the proceeds with the visitors. Pay TV was no more than a gleam in Walter O'Malley's eye then, but industrialist Crosley had some broadcast interests. He anticipated that TV would one day come into the home by more sophisticated means than a rooftop antenna.

He also saw the danger. The teams whose cities were wired for cable and who exploited the medium would have a powerful new moneymaker. The teams who didn't would be disadvantaged. The baseball economy would be bifurcated even more sharply into haves and have-nots. He was a visionary, but the Crosley Act wasn't a panacea. The haves were clever enough to get around it.

The Mets, for instance, struck a $17 million-a-year cable deal in 1982. It was a record cable-TV deal at the time. But for contract purposes the seller of the rights wasn't the Mets. It was a dummy company called Leisure Productions. SportsChannel would pay the rights fees to Leisure Productions, which passed on only about 20 percent of it to the Mets. The result was that only a fraction of the loot was shared with the rest of the National League. Meanwhile, the dummy company, which reaped on the lion's share, belonged to Mets owner Nelson Doubleday, who was no dummy. (Many would quarrel with this assessment, and it is a fact that Doubleday was very much the heir, not the originator, of his publishing fortune. As one owner acidly put it, "The best decision he ever made was picking his parents." But Doubleday did keep sharp lawyers on retainer.)

Doubleday, whose publishing company had bought majority control of the Mets in 1980, was a typical new-boy owner. He liked to play up the fact that he was Abner Doubleday's great-nephew. But he was about as authentic a baseball man as Uncle Abner was a baseball inventor. He looked exclusively after his own interests and developed an increasingly poisonous relationship with Tom Villante, Bowie Kuhn's broadcast chief.

Villante was trying, among other things, to redraft baseball's archaic broadcast agreements. Doubleday saw this as a Trojan horse for more TV revenue-sharing and screamed bloody murder. "I paid twenty-one million dollars for this franchise based on a set of conditions," he bellowed. "You can't change the ground rules on me now."

Doubleday was one of the people Villante had in mind when he chided the Lords at a 1981 ownership meeting. They had a chance to get big money in the next network contract, he said. But they had to be willing to give the networks some things they wanted, like exclusivity for the *Game of the Week*. Villante said he'd heard a cascade of objections from owners who didn't want to sacrifice their own Saturday-afternoon baseball broadcasts. He urged that there be more concern for the good of the whole.

"You should cooperate to make the Central Fund as profitable as possible," Villante said. "What are our objectives here? We're doing this for everyone! There's one club in this room that would like to see the Central Fund disappear!"

Frank Cashen, the Mets GM, called out, "Identify that club!"
Villante hesitated.

"Name that club!" Cashen repeated. "You've made a charge,
now substantiate it for all of us."

"Nelson Doubleday," Villante said.

Doubleday, who was sitting immediately next to Cashen, had
been getting redder and redder throughout Villante's talk. Now
his face was the color of the Archbishop of Canterbury's vestments. Before he could start screaming, George Steinbrenner
started doing it for him. "You have no right to say that," scolded
the Boss, who also frequently quarreled with Villante. "You
have no right to say that."

Not even blood was thicker than this powerful new revenue
stream. While he was president of the Blue Jays, Peter Bavasi
once accompanied the club on a West Coast road trip. It brought
the Jays to Anaheim where Bavasi sat in the box of his father,
Angels GM Buzzie Bavasi. A TV producer popped in during the
middle of the game and handed the senior Bavasi a check.

"Geez, Buzzie, I'm sorry to be late with this," he said.

Peter Bavasi leaned over and saw the figure on the check:
$50,000.

"Is this a one-game payment?" he asked. "Are we on pay
TV?"

"Well, it isn't really pay TV," said his father. "You have to
understand. It's, uh, an experiment."

The young Bavasi well knew about the visitors' cut for pay
TV. In the American League, as in the National, it was 25 percent.

"You owe me twelve thousand, five hundred," he said.

"It's Gene's money," said the father. "It's to reimburse KTLA
[the club's main TV outlet]."

"It doesn't make any difference," said the son. "Autry owns
the club; Autry owns the station. The money's still going in his
pocket."

"That'll be enough," said the father, as if about to ground his
son for insolence. "That's all."

Peter Bavasi turned to the third person in the box and whined,
"Ma."

Evit Bavasi told them both to shush.

Weeks later, a check arrived in Toronto from the Angels. It
was for $6,250. Peter Bavasi called up Lee MacPhail to com-

plain he'd been shortchanged. What, as American League president, was he going to do about it?

"Buzzie's my best friend, but he's *your* father," said MacPhail. "You handle it."

The Blue Jays never did collect another cent.

There was no cause to weep for Toronto, however. It pressed hard for every TV advantage as well. Its 45 percent owner, John Labatt Ltd., had in a sense created the franchise for TV.

Labatt was Canada's biggest brewer. But in the mid-seventies its market share was stuck at 36 percent, while rival Molson was coming on strong. Labatt had actually slipped behind Molson in Ontario, Canada's most populous province. The two were waging the Canadian equivalent of the Bud–Miller beer wars to the south.

Molson had already gained the upper hand in sports. It sponsored the Canadian Broadcasting Corporation's *Hockey Night in Canada*, the immensely popular ice version of baseball's *Game of the Week*. It also sponsored the Montreal Canadiens' games and was the team's part-owner. For that matter, Canada's number-three brewer, Carling O'Keefe, was the Expos' sponsor on the CBC. Montreal's games—along with Carling's commercials—were broadcast across Canada throughout the summer beer-drinking season. Labatt was stuck with leftovers, like the Canadian Football League.

Labatt had paid $3.15 million to enter baseball and change all that. The company even would influence the naming of the team. (Out of 4,000 names suggested in a name-the-team contest, the one with "blue" in it was picked. "Um, Blue *is* our best-selling pilsner beer," one official noted.) The company would also be intimately identified with the team, as it poured a generous number of between-innings beer ads out for its TV viewers.

The Blue Jays quickly exploded in popularity. They were a dreadful team, but deftly marketed. They quickly developed a national following, in part because they were as Anglo as the Angels. To many in Canada, which remains deeply divided by language, the francophone Expos were a turnoff. The Blue Jays drew 1.7 million their first season, and their logo was on everything from pencils to pizza.

The Expos—and *their* beer sponsor, Carling—were alarmed. They had agreed, upon the Blue Jays' birth in 1977, not to telecast Montreal games into Ontario, Toronto's designated TV territory. The Blue Jays reciprocated by not invading Quebec, the Expos' territory. They could both broadcast anywhere else in the country.

But now it was clear that Toronto was a phenomenon. The Expos, who'd owned Canada for a decade, worried about going into eclipse. If Toronto kept them shut out of Ontario while pulling away in the rest of Canada, the Expos were left only with Quebec, which wasn't much.

Carling worried about going into eclipse too. Labatt had a good thing in the Blue Jays, and Carling was no longer associated with baseball in Ontario. It was suddenly being outflanked in the beer wars. The brewer screamed at the CBC TV network to get them back into Ontario. The CBC screamed at Expos owner Charles Bronfman. And Bronfman, who didn't need much encouragement, screamed at Bowie Kuhn for relief.

Toronto's Peter Bavasi tried to head off the confrontation.

"Pardon me for playing the other side of the checkerboard," he told Bronfman, "but why don't you use this situation to do some business with Labatt? Tell them you'll drop this dispute if they'll replace Carling as your beer sponsor. You'll have leverage and you'll make a fortune."

Bronfman and John McHale, the Expos' president, were proper sorts. They'd come out of another era and wouldn't think of ditching the incumbent sponsor. They arranged a hearing before Kuhn, bringing two CBC officials to help make their case.

But it was Bavasi who took the offensive.

"This is a beer war!" he declared. "We're talking about beer, not baseball. These guys shouldn't be here, any more than the Dodgers should make the case that they belong in San Francisco."

Kuhn's decision appeared to give something to both. He ruled that the Blue Jays could telecast eighteen games per season into Quebec, the Expos eighteen into Ontario. But the effect was to favor Toronto—massively.

"How could you do this to me?" wailed Bronfman, a longtime Kuhn ally. "You've ghettoized us into Quebec."

And indeed he had. Toronto would go on to become one of baseball's wealthiest franchises, Montreal one of its poorest. Such was the power of TV to swing fortunes. (Not surprisingly, Labatt's fortunes swung up with those of the Blue Jays. By 1986, its market share in Canada had climbed to 42 percent, leaving behind Molson, at 32 percent, and Carling O'Keefe, at 22 percent. Labatt eventually became the *Expos'* sponsor too.)

* * *

The biggest fortunes of all were being made by super-stations. As cable grew, so did they. As the *capacity* of cable systems grew, so did they. Between 1983 and 1988 alone, the number of channels available in the average American home rose from 14.6 to 27.7. The systems needed *something* to fill all those slots, and super-stations were just the ticket.

Several of the new super-stations were naked imitations of Ted Turner's WTBS: WGN, out of Chicago; WOR and WPIX, out of New York; and KTVT, out of Dallas. They all had the Turner formula down pat: reruns, movies, and sports. The fare was popular and the price was right for the cable operators: only 10 cents per subscriber. "We'll *give* it to 'em!" Turner used to declare. "We'll make it up on advertising."

Baseball had been very, very good to the super-stations. When the Braves opened the 1982 season with a thirteen-game winning streak, it was a national phenomenon and a shot in the arm for WTBS. The Braves had finally become a decent team—they won the NL West that year—which translated to bigger ratings and many new cable subscribers. WTBS, which had 20 million subscribers in the early eighties, had doubled to 40 million by 1987.

As the Cubs drove to *their* division title in 1984, WGN appeared on ever more cable systems. The Tribune Company owned both and enjoyed synergistic benefits throughout the eighties. WGN had 8 million subscribers early in the decade, 22 million by 1987. A Fairfax County, Virginia, cable system that discontinued WGN reversed its decision in a matter of days when it was inundated by protests from outraged Cubs fans. Such episodes flared up in other parts of the country as well.

As U.S. cable went international, so did the Cubs. A Cubs flag flew over a bar in Costa Rica. Cubs announcer Harry Caray was mobbed by fans during a Caribbean vacation. "Once the Chicago Cubs belonged to the city's North Side," a columnist wrote. "Now even North America wasn't big enough."

It was WGN's domestic omnipresence that bothered the Lords. Each of them had an exclusive territory for TV, but the super-stations flooded them all. In addition to WGN's Cubs and WTBS's Braves, WOR had the Mets, WPIX the Yankees, and KTVT the Rangers. In the summer months, super-stations seemed to *exist* for baseball.

It overloaded TV with baseball and undercut the value of everybody else's TV rights. The Reds figured that in 1986, 423 games appeared on TV in Cincinnati, only 11 percent of them their own. In cities with weak teams, a hot super-station club could overshadow the hometown nine. "Here are the Braves coming into Cleveland and doing no good for the Indians," said Tom Villante, baseball's broadcast chief. "People are walking around with Atlanta Braves caps."

Peter Ueberroth quickly moved to levy a "super-station tax" on Turner and the Tribune Company. They agreed, after sufficient hammering from him, to make annual payments to baseball. The total came to $8 million in 1985, with payments to escalate based on their growing subscriber base. The tax was distributed to the other twenty-four teams, but it failed to blunt the Lords' wrath. A study by the Ernst and Whinney accounting firm estimated that baseball was worth between $75 million and $84 million a year to the super-stations. Ueberroth's tax was a pittance.

John McMullen of the Astros raised ten kinds of hell. He even commissioned a *60 Minutes*-style documentary on the super-station menace to show to his fellow owners. It was called *180 Minutes* (referring to the approximate length of a game) and featured charts, interviews, and a narrator doing a fair impression of Mike Wallace. "Incredible as it may seem, a new television network of cable systems has grown up in America," he said. "It is broadcasting the games and not paying its full share. It hurts. And it's expensive."

But the Lords couldn't do much about it, though they *could* ensure no media mogul ever joined their lodge again. When Eddie Chiles proposed selling the Texas Rangers to Gaylord Broadcasting, his fellow owners set a league record for fastest no-vote. Gaylord owned super-station KTVT.

The Lords also couldn't—or wouldn't—do much about another pronounced trend: the gap TV was opening up between baseball's haves and have-nots. The business had always had both. While the Yankees' owners clipped coupons, in the early fifties the Boston Braves bought Hank Aaron on the installment plan. They couldn't afford to pay the Negro League Indianapolis Clowns $10,000 all at once.

But now the difference between the two classes was becoming greater, and it was all because of TV. In 1975, gate receipts accounted for 62 percent of baseball's revenues and TV 24 percent. By 1985, the gate had dropped to 43 percent and TV risen to 42. (The remainder came from a variety of other categories, such as concessions and parking.) But the rise in TV varied dramatically.

By the mid-eighties, the Mets were getting $17 million a year and the Royals $3.1 million. Kansas City was running one of baseball's best organizations, yet they were hard-pressed to keep up.

"It was somewhere in the early to mid-eighties that we began to feel the pinch," said John Schuerholz, then the Royals' GM. "We had small-market TV, but we had to fight the big boys and pay big-market prices for talent. We began to feel the effects of the system getting away from us."

George Steinbrenner was about to show Schuerholz and the rest of baseball that they hadn't seen nothin' yet.

Steinbrenner had amazed and ourtraged baseball for years with his ability to spend money. He'd set new salary plateaus with Catfish Hunter, Reggie Jackson, and Dave Winfield. He'd set new standards in free-agent folly—from Dave Collins to Steve Kemp to Ed Whitson.

It would turn out there was only one thing he was better at than spending money: taking it in. Steinbrenner would cash in on the TV age like no other owner. (A case could, of course, be made for Ted Turner, but he profited from the value baseball brought to TV, not from the cash that TV brought to baseball.) His critics—and there were a few—called it dumb luck. But as the cable age hurtled through the eighties, he managed to get the Yankees into the right spot at the right time for a big score. That was more than the other New York baseball team could say.

Both were dealing with a man named Chuck Dolan, a cable-TV pioneer as surely as Ted Turner. In a sense, Dolan was the man who inspired the super-station. He was the first to bounce a signal off the RCA broadcast satellite and create a national cable service, Home Box Office. He sold HBO to Time Inc., then settled into becoming one of the great hydra-headed sharpies cable seemed to spawn. Dolan ran a company called Cablevision Systems Corp., which operated cable systems in the Northeast. He also started and invested in ventures that sold programming to cable systems. Some called this a conflict of interest. Dolan preferred to see it as a *convergence* of interests.

His brainchild of the early eighties was a sports-only cable offering called SportsChannel. He went hard after every available New York team's TV rights. The aim was simple: gather up a ton of sports for SportsChannel and induce New Yorkers to pay a premium to watch it on his Long Island cable system, the nation's largest. It was the first of several regional SportsChannels Dolan would set up around the country.

In New York, one of the first teams in the fold was the NHL's Islanders. Their owner, John Pickett, was a friend of Nelson Doubleday. Pickett talked up SportsChannel to him and Dolan dangled big numbers in front of him. Dolan wanted the Mets very much, and Doubleday was primed to sign just when Tom Villante called from the commissioner's office.

He'd heard that the Mets were on the verge of a long-term deal with SportsChannel, he told Doubleday, and it concerned him. Villante told him to think carefully about a wholesale shift of games to pay TV. "It's a mistake to take too much off over-the-air TV," he said. "One, it has promotional value. And two, you must position pay TV as a supplement. If it looks like you're taking away from what's been on the air free, you'll get killed publicly."

Doubleday was unmoved, so Villante pressed forward with his other concern. If the Mets were going to make a deal, he hoped it was a good one. Cable TV was in a very fluid state, and you needed to play it smart.

"Can I ask just one thing?" he said. "Let me see your deal before you sign it."

"No way," said Doubleday. "We know what we're doing."

"Look, I've known Chuck Dolan a long time," said Villante. "He's a brilliant guy, but I know how he operates. He wants a lot of product and he wants it for a long time. He'll make small payments at the start and balloon it at the end. You should really work out a guarantee by which you'll work off of their subscriber base. If it takes off, you can participate in the upside."

"We can handle it," Doubleday repeated, irked. "Our guys know about this."

"Okay, I just want you to know my concern. I understand this is a twenty-year deal, and nobody's smart enough to see where TV is going that far out."

"Go fuck yourself," said Nelson Doubleday.

Villante was wrong about only one thing. It was a *thirty*-year deal. It paid $17 million a year, for which the Mets at first heartily congratulated themselves. In 1982, it was the biggest cable deal ever in baseball. But then cable started growing like topsy, and by the mid-eighties, the Mets' deal no longer looked so amazin'.

George Steinbrenner would, in fact, make it look just the opposite. He'd sold his cable rights to SportsChannel too, for $6.7 million a year in 1983. It granted the service one hundred Yankees games per season for the next fifteen years. (The rest of the games would go to WPIX.) But it also contained an escape hatch: after five years, Steinbrenner could buy out the remainder of the contract for $16 million.

The fifth year was 1988, a time when SportsChannel's archrival in New York found itself in a dilemma. Madison Square Garden Network (MSG) carried the games of the NHL Rangers and NBA Knicks. (The Garden, the network, and the teams were all owned by the Gulf + Western conglomerate.) MSG provided a steady, popular diet of hockey and basketball from fall through spring—but nothing in between. Its subscriber base was stuck at 2 million. "If we didn't get baseball, we'd hit the wall," recalled Bob Gutkowski, the network's chief.

Since the Mets were tied up long-term in their SportsChannel deal, that left just one team: the Yankees. All Steinbrenner had to do was exercise his escape clause at the end of the 1988 season, sit back, and watch MSG and SportsChannel go at it. It was vicious even before it got down to the bidding. Cablevision (SportsChannel's parent company) pulled MSG off its system's basic service in September, making it a pay channel. The move would diminish MSG's subscribers and severely hamper its ability to mount a big Yankees bid. MSG was still fighting Cablevision on that point—successfully, ultimately—when put-up time came in November.

Both MSG and SportsChannel started out at $400 million-plus for twelve years, then worked up from there. Then WPIX, the Yankees' longtime flagship station, jumped in. That goosed the bidding up. When the numbers reached $500 million, WPIX dropped out and decision time came. The two finalists were about equal, and it came down to who'd give Steinbrenner the best stroking.

That was no contest. He'd never liked playing second banana to the Mets on SportsChannel. Some Yankees games ended up being pushed into a leftovers bin called SportsChannel Plus. In addition, SportsChannel had taken the Yankees to court over its WPIX deal. (Steinbrenner had sold 100 games to SportsChannel and 75 to WPIX. Given a 162-game schedule, Chuck Dolan didn't like the math.) Steinbrenner was tight with Gulf and Western chairman Martin Davis, on the other hand, and he was going to be the Big Dog at MSG.

Madison Square Garden it was. The Yankees' TV money, already among the majors' highest, had tripled. The club's limited partners were so delighted with the $486 million, they gave

Steinbrenner 5 percent of it for his trouble. Steinbrenner, for his part, was so moved, he arranged a $100 million sweetheart loan to the partnership group, secured by the TV money. Naturally, 55 percent of it would go to the 55 percent owner. A smart businessman could do a lot with that kind of interest-free swag.

He announced the MSG deal on Friday, December 9. The rest of the Lords were stunned and dismayed. *George Steinbrenner with an unlimited bank account?* They would feel better inside a week, however. Another TV deal would eclipse even this, raining a torrent of cash on them all.

It looked for the longest while like baseball's network-TV money had topped out. The whole TV-sports machine sputtered in the mid-eighties. Even the NFL's rights turned downward in 1985.

The networks moaned and groaned about how much money they were losing on baseball. NBC had turned a profit in the deal's earlier years, but its payments escalated yearly and its bottom line had gone red. ABC had a terrible time from the outset, its profit on the "jewels" failing to cover its regular-season losses. "I can hardly wait for [the contract] to end," said Dennis Swanson, who succeeded Arledge as sports chief.

Ueberroth listened to the networks' tales of woe, looked at the books, and duly relayed word to the Lords. The TV money would be going down after '89; it was a certainty. This dire prospect contributed to the Lords' motivation to collude. They took little notice of what was going on just seven blocks away from baseball's headquarters at 350 Park Avenue.

There, turmoil shook the building known as "Black Rock." It was the headquarters of CBS, which succeeded NBC in the TV crapper. Its ratings had slid, and it was assaulted by a hostile takeover bid from Ted Turner from which it had to be saved in 1986 by a friendly investment from billionaire Laurence Tisch. Two years later, CBS was still struggling, and Tisch, now chairman, was still searching for answers.

Neal Pilson offered one. The sports chief, who had survived the purges at CBS, became one of the few holdover executives to gain Larry Tisch's ear. The forty-eight-year-old Pilson looked and acted like the man in the gray flannel suit. A Yale law school graduate, he put in six years as a corporate lawyer before joining Metromedia, and, later, the William Morris talent agency. He joined CBS Sports in the business end in 1976, and five years later became its president.

In the free-wheeling, free-spending world of TV sports, Pilson came on like an auntie at the orgy. In the early eighties, CBS Sports was pretty much confined to the NFL and NBA, and Pilson was content to turn out modest profits. He even made a speech chiding the other networks for paying "reckless prices" for sports rights. (ABC had just bid a record $309 million for the 1988 Calgary Olympics.)

But the TV world changed a lot as the eighties wore on, and so did Neal Pilson's mind. The networks lost 25 percent of their prime-time audience in a few short years. The only way to counter that, Pilson came to believe, was with what he called the "major event." One day, he commandeered a seat beside Larry Tisch for the train ride back to New York from a meeting in Philadelphia. He used the ninety minutes to explain his theory.

Pilson did it with numbers, the language a stock-market player like Tisch understood. Championship sports events were the only sure way to get a mass audience anymore. The Super Bowl had nine of the top ten ratings of all time. The Summer Olympics brought two weeks of twenty ratings in a world of tens. And although World Series viewership was down by 13 percent over the past decade, that was only *half* the erosion of other programming.

Larry Tisch nodded and listened. He was a very frugal man for a billionaire, and the only game that truly interested him was bridge. He didn't immediately warm to the idea of dropping bundles on sports. But he would learn that owning a network was like owning a ball club. It was a tremendously public enterprise. Dan Rather stalked off the news set in a huff and it was the talk of the nation. Firing 200 CBS employees got more attention than laying off 200,000 auto workers.

Like a baseball owner, too, Tisch read the papers, heard the talk of CBS's decline, and took it personally. As Edward Bennett Williams had once put it, "Even if you start out without an ego, the media make you into a genius or an idiot every morning. Your ego becomes involved for self-protection, for survival."

Tisch's ego was fully engaged by the spring of 1988. CBS was still third in the ratings. Its affiliate stations were up in arms. Rumors persisted that CBS was for sale. Tisch, the supposed savior, was getting murdered in the press. And now the 1992 Winter Olympics were up for bid. He was finally ready to buy into Pilson's "major event" strategy. The Olympics would tell the world CBS was alive. "Okay, fire the shot," he told Pilson.

In May, CBS bid $243 million for the Albertville games. That didn't just win, it lapped the field: $43 million above the minimum set by Olympics officials and $68 million more than runner-up NBC. They celebrated at Black Rock.

"They gotta be out of their minds," said Arthur Watson. For months, the NBC Sports chief publicly criticized CBS. There were now whole newspaper columns given over to TV moguls sniping at one another. (Rudy Martzke's, in *USA Today*, was a particularly prominent firing ground.) The business was that public and had become that competitive. Watson used those forums to keep up the attack. CBS couldn't possibly make a profit on Albertville, he charged. And it had only made things tough for the *responsible* networks.

"Mr. Pilson talks a lot," Watson said. "He talks of restraint, of keeping rights fees at reasonable levels. But then he goes out and overbids for the Olympics. What he says and what he does are two different things."

Late that year, the next round of Olympics came up for bid: Barcelona, 1992. The smart money was on CBS. Its production equipment would already be in Europe from the Albertville games. Its small setup costs in Barcelona gave it an estimated $15 to $20 million bidding edge. It was sitting on $3 billion from Tisch's sale of CBS's non-TV business. And the incentive remained great: CBS was still mired in third place.

But what happened at the New York Hilton on December 2 confounded the experts. The International Olympic Committee told the networks it had a number in mind. If nobody reached it, there would be a second round. The IOC opened the envelopes, and none contained the magic number, which turned out to be $350 million. The three were asked to dig deeper. CBS and ABC came back at about $360 million. NBC bid $401 million.

Arthur Watson gloated openly. He prided himself on his abilities as a cardplayer, a horseplayer, a strategist. Now he wanted to let the world in on a little secret. His blasts at the CBS Albertville bid had been a ploy. He had wanted to make CBS self-conscious and cautious the next time around. Then NBC could snap up what it *really* wanted—the Barcelona games.

"That wasn't a bad strategy, eh, coach?" Watson chuckled to reporters. "I thought we'd get Barcelona the moment after the Albertville announcement."

Peter Ueberroth watched Watson crow on the evening news.

Then he picked up the phone and called Bryan Burns. Ueberroth's young aide had been working on baseball's TV deal all year. He was carefully constructing a contract that would shape the next deal to baseball's liking and button down the myriad details that governed baseball's TV relationships. Burns had finally come up with a forty-two-page document that would be the guts of the new deal. But he didn't expect it to be put out to bid until next spring.

"I want to move everything up by months," Ueberroth told him now. "A window of opportunity has opened. At some point we have to jump through it. We've got to figure out when, because sometime it will slam shut."

He explained: CBS had $3 billion burning a hole in its pocket and, no doubt, a burning desire to get even with NBC.

"They've shown an aggressiveness before, and now they've been insulted on the evening news," he said. "Send out notices for the bid. Tell them all they have an equal chance."

CBS didn't believe it. Pilson had seen this all before. In 1983, Arthur Watson was supremely wired into baseball. There was no reason to believe he wasn't still.

The bid date was pushed up to Tuesday, December 13. The Friday before, Bryan Burns met Pilson's number two, Jay Rosenstein, for lunch. Amid the kimono-clad waitresses and soft Japanese music of a Midtown sushi bar, Burns tried to convince him that CBS indeed had a shot.

"This is a clear table, palms up; nobody's got a leg up," he insisted. "You make the best bid, you get the business."

Rosenstein was mildly encouraged by the message, but when he carried it back to Black Rock, most of CBS Sports remained skeptical. Pilson's crew was, nonetheless, crunching numbers for the bid at a breakneck pace. In a thirtieth-floor conference room, they projected advertising revenue and production costs. They tried to get their arms around intangibles, like the value of promoting new CBS programs in October during the Series.

Then Pilson pulled all the data together and went in to see Larry Tisch. He'd try to sell him on swinging for the fences: the whole baseball package.

NBC was worried too, though for a different reason. Ken Schanzer had a breakfast meeting with Burns and learned more about the contract. One part alarmed him. Baseball planned to cut back to twelve *Game of the Week* broadcasts. It didn't even want them to start until after the All-Star Game.

"The world has changed," Burns said. "People in Baltimore used to be able to see fifty-five Orioles games a year plus the *Game of the Week*. Now they get to see all the games they want of the team they want to see."

The *Game*'s ratings had declined for years, he explained, and it had become more of a headache for baseball than it was worth. Some owners bitched about changing game times. Some small-market owners complained that NBC only showed big-market teams. (In 1988, twenty-seven of the thirty-one games involved New York, Chicago, or Los Angeles teams.) They noted that the small-market players didn't get national exposure and didn't get voted onto the All-Star Team. It was time, Burns said, to severely trim it back.

Schanzer disagreed. One, the *Game* was good for NBC. It was reliable Saturday-afternoon programming. Even if the ratings were down to a four, that was better than anything else in that slot. It also provided more opportunity to recoup its rights cost. NBC didn't *want* to confine itself to the jewels. And baseball shouldn't, either, he further lectured Burns.

"This was the one national telecast of the week for baseball," Schanzer said. "Cable still wasn't a national medium. Only 60 percent of homes had it. And we'd always supplemented the *Game* with a high-quality pregame show."

Burns was unmoved, and Schanzer was frustrated. NBC was more interested in showcasing baseball than *baseball* was.

"It was all backwards," he later said. "If you're trying to promote a sport you want a network that's your friend, that's dying to do things for you. We venerated baseball."

He had one other disquieting thought, and he shared it with Arthur Watson back at the office. Starting the *Game of the Week* in July kept it from overlapping with the spring basketball playoffs.

"This was built for whoever's got the NBA," he said.

That was CBS.

It was like a Pentagon command post at 350 Park Avenue on Monday. The only difference was that the security was tighter. Each network's sports division was allowed to send in three people: its programming VP, its top bean-counter, and its chief attorney. They had one hour to read the contract and another hour to ask questions of a baseball lawyer, Tom Ostertag. The TV people could take notes, but they couldn't take a copy of the contract with them. They couldn't even go to the bathroom without a guard. They'd have to make big, quick decisions based on what they could absorb in two hours.

Schanzer returned to NBC's Rockefeller Center office sweating. He'd found the atmosphere offensive and the contract worrisome.

"Arthur, we're in trouble," he told Watson.

"Why's that?"

"The elements of the contract tell me they're affirmatively looking to go somewhere else."

Ueberroth was taking back rights NBC had long held. *Baseball* would now sell the star-of-the-game sponsor, not the network. *Baseball* would hold international TV rights, not the network. They sounded like fine points, but collectively they were integral to NBC's thinking about the bid.

Watson called up Ueberroth to protest the whole process.

"This is foolish," he said. "We're supposed to bid hundreds of millions on a contract we can't even see for more than an hour?"

"Arthur, don't worry," said Ueberroth. "We're not going forward in baseball without NBC."

The Big Three came in bearing bids Tuesday morning: first CBS's Pilson, then ABC's Swanson, finally NBC's Watson. Each met with Ueberroth one-on-one, then left. It was what he'd insisted upon: CEO to CEO, with no aides and no leaks.

Between his Pilson and Swanson meetings, Ueberroth stuck his head in Burns's office door.

"We're going to be okay," he said with a small smile.

"Are we in ten figures?" asked Burns, referring to billion-dollar territory.

"I'm not going to answer your question," Ueberroth said. "We're going to be okay."

That afternoon, after the sports chiefs had come and gone, he finally answered Burns. The three had been given their choice of any or all of four different bids: for the entire package; for one that would alternate between two networks; for the entire package minus the league playoffs, which would then go to cable; or an à la carte approach, in which a network could choose an individual season or a targeted piece of the package. Pilson had checked the first option and written a figure: $1.06 billion.

The four-year deal would *double* baseball's current TV package. And the number went more than $300 million higher than either NBC or ABC. It was all over.

"Let's get Neal back over here," said Ueberroth.

Pilson and his lawyer were there in a flash. Burns and Ed Durso joined the commissioner, who was poker-faced.

"We've asked you to come back because you've got a helluva shot to get involved with us," he said.

"Half of it?" asked Pilson.

"All of it," said Ueberroth.

An electricity raced through the room. Then Ueberroth, all business as always, moved on: "My records show you have concerns about fourteen things in the contract."

They went through them one by one, a few nits to pick in a forty-two-page document. That done, Durso produced a letter already written to Pilson. They shook hands all around, while Ueberroth asked everybody to keep quiet until the announcement was made the next day. And everybody did—until sometime that evening, when word began to leak out.

Peter Ueberroth was awoken from a sound sleep at 3:00 A.M. He heard the distant, muffled ringing of a telephone. Groggy and disoriented, he stumbled from bed. It was somewhere in his apartment, but he couldn't tell where. He wandered around while the phone rang and rang. Finally, he found it—in a guest room, in a drawer.

"Hello?"

It was Arthur Watson.

"Peter, you've got to give us a chance to overbid," he said.

"No," said Ueberroth. "Believe me, we've set down the standards and we can't get into that. The rule was: three envelopes across the table one time."

A desperate Watson kept asking in different ways for an opening back in. A firm Ueberroth wouldn't give him an inch.

"We can't do anything for you," he said, and finally wished him good night.

Everybody at the next afternoon's press conference was a lot jollier. Ueberroth brought a stack of white baseball caps bearing baseball's red-and-blue logo: a hitter—actually, Pete Rose—in silhouette. Tisch brought a stack of dark blue baseball caps bearing *his* logo: the famous CBS eye.

Both said all the right things. "It's a transaction that's good for baseball and baseball fans," declared Ueberroth. "There's risk in everything we do," admitted Tisch, "but this is a risk we love to take." Then Neal Pilson took Bryan Burns to Mickey Mantle's restaurant to celebrate.

In the warm glow of the moment, there was only one problem. As Eddie Einhorn put it, years later: "We spent the money before the ink was dry on the contract."

$ 19 $

"ALL I EVER wanted to be president of was the American League."

So said A. Bartlett Giamatti when named to be president of Yale University in 1977. There, in a nutshell, was the split personality of baseball's next commissioner. He was a distinguished scholar of Renaissance literature and a hopeless Red Sox fan, a pillar of the Ivy League and a sprightly wit.

At first blush, he was also a most unlikely successor to Peter Ueberroth. Giamatti had spent his first forty-eight years in the groves of academe, the son of a classics professor at Mount Holyoke College who then himself became a classics professor. He could, with equal facility, discuss Dante and Bobby Doerr, his boyhood hero.

But he'd never gotten any closer to the inner workings of the game than a lunch once with Lee MacPhail. After his "president of the American League" crack, MacPhail wrote him, offering to trade jobs. That note led, one day, to a pleasant get-together.

Otherwise, Giamatti scrounged for tickets at Fenway Park just like any other New Englander, though he would also pen an occasional highbrow piece on the game. In one of them, he referred to Edmund Spenser, the Elizabethan poet who, wrote Giamatti, thought he knew it all:

> He did not. He had never loved the Red Sox. While he knew of Eden and its loss, he knew nothing of the fall in Fenway. It is not enough to think, as he did, that only once were we to go east, out in the land of Nod. Such a passage occurs without end. It happens every summer, with a poignancy that knows no bounds, in that angular, intimate, ageless green space in Boston. There, whenever autumn comes, comes the fall again.

* * *

Giamatti would also hold forth in print on the Homeric roots of
home plate, the connection between baseball and America's rural
past, and why Tom Seaver's being traded by the Mets was like
The Expulsion of Adam and Eve, a fresco in Florence's
Brancacci Chapel. His thoughts on the game were all densely romantic and idealistic, never more so than in a piece he wrote
during the 1981 strike:

> Call it a symptom of the plague of distrust and divisiveness
> that inflicts our land, call it the triumph of greed over the
> spirit of the garden. Call it what you will, the strike is utter
> foolishness. O Sovereign Owners and princely Players, mas-
> ters of amortization, tax shelters, bonuses and deferred com-
> pensations, go back to work. You have been entrusted with
> the serious work of play, and your season of responsibility has
> come. Be at it. There is no general sympathy for either of
> your sides. The people of America care about baseball, not
> your squalid little squabbles. Reassume your dignity and re-
> member that you are the temporary custodians of an enduring
> public trust.

Marvin Miller read it on the *New York Times* op-ed page and
fired off a testy letter to Giamatti. He found his words fancy
window dressing for an uninformed viewpoint. This "squalid little squabble" concerned a vital issue in the players' professional
lives. When Giamatti himself became embroiled in a clerical
workers' strike at Yale, Miller congratulated himself on his restraint at not writing a follow-up. He was wondering what
Giamatti would say if he scolded him about "getting back to education."

(The two never met, content to dislike each other from afar.
Giamatti saw players as noble savages and performers of a valuable social rite. Miller saw them as professional entertainers
and members of a bargaining unit.)

Yale's persistent labor problems dragged on throughout 1983
and 1984. Giamatti's office was picketed by people bearing such
signs as BART, BART, HAVE A HEART! and BOOLA, BOOLA, WHERE'S
OUR MOOLA? Hundreds of people gathered outside his home late
one night to chant, "Bart can't sleep because Yale is cheap."

It was an awful time for Giamatti, who had little capacity for
conflict and yearned for a simpler, ivory-towered world. It

wasn't that he was stuffy. His courses on Dante and Spenser were counted among Yale's liveliest, the prof talking in street slang and sometimes wearing sunglasses. After Giamatti's stint as master of Yale's Ezra Stiles College, he was supposed to sit for the traditional portrait, to be hung in the dining hall. He refused, insisting a moosehead be mounted in its place. But Giamatti did have traditional ideas about campus civility and order, and he couldn't abide the sort of activity he was witnessing now.

Giamatti, chain-smoking Benson and Hedges, would age markedly in office. He would also grow bored with the non-crisis aspects of his job—stroking alumni for money and tending to Yale's physical plant. "Call me Bart the Refurbisher," he once told an interviewer. "I've spent twenty million dollars on deferred maintenance and will only be remembered by people who like to go through steam tunnels."

Out of the blue, in mid-1983, Giamatti was approached about his dream job. Bud Selig was leading the search for a new baseball commissioner, and asked if they could get together in New York. They were to meet at the Helmsley Palace, where Selig descended from his room at the appointed hour in foul temper. The Brewers had lost that day, and his moods closely tracked the team's results.

All of that fell away, however, as he got to know Giamatti over dinner. Selig thought he knew, better than anyone, what baseball meant to communities. He'd seen Milwaukee devastated by the loss of the Braves. He thought nobody could top Charles Bronfman in eloquence about baseball's sociological importance. But this man left them far behind: "Bart could articulate it; he felt it; he believed it."

Then he and Giamatti fell to just comparing baseball memories and discovered a common point of reference: the 1949 Red Sox–Yankees pennant race. Selig was fifteen that year, Giamatti eleven, and they'd both retained that season's every detail, as only baseball-mad boys can. Selig had been a Yankees fan, ever since their purchase of a former Milwaukee minor-leaguer named Herschel Martin. He'd idolized Joe DiMaggio in the late forties and Giamatti, of course, had idolized Bobby Doerr.

They left the restaurant and walked the streets of Manhattan, enjoying a lovely June night and replaying the season from their two perspectives. Eventually, they just walked around and around the block outside the Helmsley, talking about that last weekend, when New York won two games from Boston and the pennant. Only at 1:30 A.M., after comparing the joy and pain of Johnny Lindell's crucial homer, did they call it a night.

This, thought Selig, is one of the most remarkable men I've ever met. A few days later, he sent a ten-page memo to the search committee members saying just that. Giamatti had a remarkable grasp of the total baseball universe, he wrote, both its problems and its strengths. He understood the dynamics of this game and business better than people who'd spent a lifetime in it.

When Selig got back to Giamatti, to feel him out about taking the job, the Yale president was both flattered and tempted. He'd be immersed in his beloved baseball. He'd get a major pay hike. And he wouldn't mind shedding the petty politics and headaches of academia.

But Giamatti had been in office only four years. He'd promised the trustees seven, and he still had the labor problems to solve. He also wasn't sure he could face sneering academic colleagues if he went slumming in sports. And so, finally, hesitantly, he conveyed his regrets to Selig.

By 1986, when baseball came around again, things were different. Giamatti had just resigned as Yale's president and was at loose ends. He was mulling a Senate run and also considering going back into teaching, but he hadn't made any decisions. This time the approach came from Peter O'Malley. Chub Feeney was retiring as National League president. Was he interested in succeeding him?

This time the answer was a hearty yes. Giamatti took the job and no longer gave a damn what the academics thought. He had an answer for them: "I'm almost fifty years old and I've just fallen in love and run away with a beautiful redhead with flashing eyes whose name is baseball."

The allure of the job, however, was greater than its power. Franklin Roosevelt's first vice president, John Nance Garner, once declared the office wasn't worth a pitcher of warm spit. The same could be said, in 1986, of the National League's presidency. The office had been diminished under Kuhn and virtually gutted by strongman Ueberroth. Giamatti was limited to supervising umpires, disciplining players, interpreting the balk rule, and making ceremonial appearances.

But the job definitely had its moments. Before the fifth game of the Mets-Astros playoff series that year, a hard rain was falling in New York. The game's start was delayed, and still it kept pouring. It was up to the league president to decide whether to play. Finally, Giamatti walked out onto the field, turned to face the crowd, and flung his arms skyward in acknowledgment of heavenly powers. He was calling off the game. The crowd should have been disappointed, but it was such a fine, dramatic gesture that they cheered him. Giamatti's eyes shone; he held the pose; he loved it.

Giamatti was suddenly a *player* in this realm about which he'd long rhapsodized. He threw himself enthusiastically into his meager duties, handling with high dudgeon such offenses as Pete Rose bumping an umpire, Billy Hatcher corking a bat, and Kevin Gross sandpapering balls.

He suspended Gross for ten days and wrote a ten-page decision worthy of Oliver Wendell Holmes:

> Unlike acts of impulse or violence, intended at the moment to vent frustration or abuse another, acts of cheating are intended to alter the very conditions of play to favor one person. They are secretive, covert acts that strike at and seek to undermine the basic foundation of any contest declaring the winner—that all participants play under identical rules and conditions. Acts of cheating destroy that necessary foundation and thus strike at the essence of a contest.

It wasn't the sort of document Peter Ueberroth would have ever produced, but to the Lords that was Giamatti's charm. Ueberroth had worn rather thin on them after four years. The man had made the owners a lot of money, but he'd also made it clear to them, in time, that he was, as one of them later said, "more interested in his own image and where *he* was going."

Some key owners were ready for a return to leadership that didn't just steer the business but revered the game. Bud Selig was one such old-schooler. The owners could afford to revert to that ideal, of course, now that Ueberroth had them rolling in dough. In that atmosphere, Giamatti became the commissioner-in-waiting. In the fall of 1988, he was officially elected to succeed Ueberroth, effective April 1989.

He continued to cut a strange figure in baseball. This was not an intellectual crowd, and this goateed academic was, as Roger Angell put it, "a lifetime .400 talker." He once stopped an owners' discussion on super-stations cold by declaring, "What will come out of the welter and farrago of this remains to be seen." Yet, for an egghead, he had the common touch. He sought out the umpires to chat at every game he attended and had a special bond with them, as keepers of the games' order. (Also, they discovered to their delight that he could swear like a stevedore.) He was accessible, always sitting among the fans and always ready to talk with them. Giamatti once agreed to go on the air with the Red Sox announcers for a half-inning, then stayed on for five. Boston announcer Ken Coleman was so taken with Giamatti's feel for baseball that he finished his last broadcast each season by reading from the commissioner's essay "The Green Fields of the Mind."

Giamatti also recognized that a baseball man sometimes knew better how to handle things than a Renaissance scholar. He was once in the office of Bill White, his successor as National League president. White had been a standout first baseman in the fifties and sixties, and a longtime Yankees announcer thereafter. Now Giamatti was breaking him in as baseball's highest-ranking black official.

White took a call from Tommy Lasorda and put him on the speaker phone so they both could hear. The Dodgers manager was in a lather about Mike Scott. The Astros star pitcher was a flat-out cheater, asserted Lasorda. He scuffed the ball and the umps let him get away with it. How could they do that? How could his hitters touch that stuff? And so on—long, loud, and profane.

"Tommy, I'm glad you've gotten so righteous," White finally said. Then he called the honor roll of L.A. pitchers of his era who'd doctored the ball: "How about Phil Regan, Don Drysdale . . ." and so on, while Giamatti laughed silently in delight.

"We don't do that anymore," Lasorda huffed.

"Well, if you find out more about Scott, call back," said White.

Giamatti chortled after Lasorda hung up. "I really enjoyed that," he said. "You know, I couldn't have done that."

White came to be quite taken with Giamatti, as did virtually all the owners. Ueberroth scolded; Giamatti charmed. Ueberroth dictated; Giamatti listened. He revived the executive council; he brought the owners on the PRC back into the loop, he worked the phones. He also dropped the amphitheater meeting rooms Ueberroth had used to underscore his authority. Now they all sat at a round table, as equals.

His Yale background proved more relevant than anyone at first imagined. A college president must reconcile heady ideals with filthy lucre, referee petty disputes, and harness differing interest. Sounds not unlike a commissioner of baseball. Doug Danforth, the Pirates chairman who'd once chaired Carnegie Mellon University's board, saw the cross-over qualities in Giamatti. "He was genuinely liked by everyone, and he had the ability to build a consensus," he said.

One key point where consensus was invaluable was labor. The contract signed in 1985 was coming to an end. They had to set objectives and strategies for bargaining, which would begin in late 1989.

Baseball's profits were still soaring. The industry's operating profit would reach $121 million in 1988; its gross revenues would for the first time top $1 billion. The business was nearly three times the size it was at the start of the decade.

But the golden age of collusion was over. The Lords had already lost the two cases covering 1985–86 and 1986–87. A third collusion grievance was pending, and nobody expected to fare any better. The jig was up, and so, once again, were the players' salaries. By the 1988 winter meetings, some big free-agent deals had already been signed: Bruce Hurst to the Padres for a multi-year, $5.25 million deal; Andy Hawkins to the Yankees for $3.6 million; Scott Fletcher to the Rangers for $4.7 million.

Barry Rona, the Lords' labor negotiator, wanted a renewed salary-cap push. The PRC was also trying to develop a substitute for salary arbitration called "pay for performance." It would determine salaries of players with under six years' service by a statistical formula. PRC hard-liners like Bud Selig and Jerry Reinsdorf favored a lockout in 1990 if that's what it would take to achieve those ends.

It was a perfect example of one of the Lords' most reliable traits: seeing the glass as half empty. "The industry wasn't in bad shape right then," Rona admitted. "But any projection you made over the next four years showed that wouldn't last."

Rona, Reinsdorf, and Selig all lobbied Giamatti for his support. They knew from their own sad experience how crucial it would be. Ueberroth had played a mischievous role in 1985. Bowie Kuhn had opened the spring training camps in 1976 and scuttled all chance of a favorable settlement.

Every commissioner felt the same about work stoppages: "Not on my watch." Their interventions invariably aided the union. Lou Hoynes once told Kuhn, "You know, when we have a collective-bargaining year, we should send the commissioner on a wonderful six-month tour around the world."

Giamatti wasn't by nature confrontational. His every instinct was to be collegial and conciliatory. Nevertheless, he signed on to the lockout strategy. Indeed, Giamatti lined up Yale economist (later Yale president) Richard Levin to do economic modeling in support of the pay-for-performance idea.

He was, number one, still in the thrall of the Lords and of this scene. They'd opened up a wonderful new life for him and given him a $650,000 salary, six times what he made at Yale. For years, he toddled around New Haven in a yellow Volkswagen. Now he was driving a Mercedes.

As a creature of consensus, Giamatti was also a team player. If the Lords' best labor minds had come up with a hard-line approach, *he* was for a hard-line approach. "Bart was an organization man rather than a free-wheeler," said one baseball lawyer. "He repeatedly made the point that he wouldn't pull a Peter Ueberroth."

It still took Lou Hoynes by surprise. Hoynes was out of the loop on the PRC now, supplanted by Washington labor lawyer Chuck O'Connor. But he was still National League counsel and, as such, had worked closely with Giamatti. He considered himself Bart's *closest* adviser.

So it was with amazement, in December 1988, that he witnessed Giamatti's coming-out as a hawk. The winter meetings were in Atlanta that year. At one session, Barry Rona gave a summary of the bargaining objectives and gave a little pep talk on the possibility of a lockout. They had to be willing to stand firm this time. Giamatti followed with his own hearty endorsement.

Hoynes was dismayed. He thought the lockout strategy was folly and was hoping he could get Giamatti to see that. Somewhere along the line he'd lost him to the hawks. He only hoped it wasn't too late to get him back. No way could this man lead a 1930s-style J. P. Stevens action. He wasn't built for it. He could never withstand the pressures from politicians, the press, or the wavering owners—to say nothing of his horrified egghead friends.

He took Giamatti out to dinner that night to a Russian restaurant, Nikolai's Roof. Hoynes had also invited Chub Feeney and the league's secretary, Phyllis Collins, as a going-away party for Giamatti from his National League peers. As they nibbled caviar and threw back vodkas, Hoynes began working on Giamatti.

"You can understand why the small-market owners would want Armageddon," said Hoynes. "They figure it's the only way to keep from having to sell or move their team. But would that be the end of the world? Look at the broader picture. We're driving toward the cliff, and why? Even if you win, all you've done is sown dragon's teeth. You just bring back a vindictive union.

"This is like dropping the nuclear bomb at the next table. You're making a massive attack on the enemy, but it's going to take out your side too. This is a strategy that has no place in labor relations in the latter part of the twentieth century. It will look bad in the communities we operate in and I don't think it can be sustained by the owners. We may be able to withstand a strike when the *enemy* is coming across the line, but not when we're initiating the action against them."

Feeney and Collins, who agreed with Hoynes, backed his reasoning, and the three of them went on, while Giamatti listened. At evening's end, Hoynes suspected they hadn't reached him. The next day, he was sure of it. Giamatti was chilly toward him, and stayed that way through the meetings.

Later in December, Hoynes drove out to New Haven, where Giamatti was spending the holidays, to seek a Christmas amnesty. They repaired their relationship over a long lunch. They did not, however, close their schism on the labor matter.

"I think you're horribly wrong," said Hoynes. "But it's your decision to make and I won't get in the way."

As they walked out of the restaurant, Hoynes threw an arm around Giamatti's shoulder and they wished each other a Merry Christmas. Well, he'd lost that one, thought Hoynes. He didn't know he was also about to lose his status as Giamatti's number-one adviser. That title would go to a man named Fay Vincent.

Francis T. Vincent, Jr., was born in 1938, the same year as Giamatti and Ueberroth. The "Junior" was the hard part. Francis T. Vincent, Sr., was a Yale football and baseball legend and later an NFL referee. He cast a long shadow in Waterbury, Connecticut, where he raised his family.

Young Fay had his own dreams of athletic glory. He was a strapping six-foot-three and once spent a summer as an apprentice roughneck in the Texas oil fields. His buddy on the adventure was Hotchkiss School classmate Bucky Bush, whose older brother, George, owned the properties. But the winter after playing freshman football at Williams, Vincent had a terrible accident. Locked in a dorm room by pranksters, he tried to escape by crawling out the window and into an adjacent room. He slipped on an icy ledge and fell four floors, crushing two vertebrae. Vincent's legs were paralyzed.

The vertebrae were rebuilt with bone from his hip, and he spent the next year recuperating, sustaining his love of sports by watching nearly every Yankees game of 1956 that was televised. Vincent regained the use of his legs but would forever more walk laboriously.

He threw himself into intellectual pursuits, graduating from Williams cum laude and even considering becoming a Jesuit priest. The Jesuits turned him down, however, fearing that his injury would keep him from being able to perform mass. But Yale Law School accepted him. After he graduated in 1963, he began an unremarkable career as a corporate lawyer, and later as an SEC officer. Then an old Williams chum phoned him up.

Herbert Allen's family controlled Columbia Pictures, a company in turmoil in the late seventies. It was first shaken by the check forgeries of movie-studio chief David Begelman. Then it was racked by conflict about the handling of the scandal and the performance of Columbia's other top executives. The company and its board were rife with factions. Allen decided the only answer was a neutral outsider as CEO, a Mister Clean. He gave the job to Fay Vincent. "Nobody can lay a glove on him," he mused at the time. "We need a healer in this situation. We need a Judge Landis."

Vincent was certainly no Samuel Goldwyn. He was an owlish, moon-faced man who one day was a forty-year-old $47,000-a-year bureaucrat and the next was running a big entertainment company. He acted cautiously, not in the style of a movie mogul but, as one colleague put it, "as an arbitrator of demands for capital." The real power at Columbia remained Herbie Allen, which was, of course, precisely the point of placing one's obscure friend in the job.

Vincent was an activist, however, in his Mister Clean role. The movie business was filled with petty—and some not so petty—corruption which he tried to purge from Columbia. One production executive was fired for a transgression fifteen years past. Vincent tidied up accounting and accountability systems. "He was a man of deep moral conviction," said Guy McElwaine, who for six years headed Columbia's movie studio under Vincent. "That was the good news."

The bad news was that Vincent didn't know anything about

the movie business, which didn't stop him from getting deeply involved in it. "He was very concerned about the average cost per picture and began to get into decisions about production costs and ad budgets," recalled McElwaine. "These are decisions that are difficult to make even if you know what you're doing, and he'd develop opinions not based on facts."

It led to clashes with Hollywood pros like McElwaine and another Columbia studio chief, Frank Price, both of whom were fired by Vincent. There was an uneasy bicoastal dynamic at Columbia, headed by this New Yorker who'd never been to Spago and who much preferred curling up with a biography to watching a movie.

Actually, his low-key, intellectual manner made it hard to believe, on first impression, that he had an edge. His suits looked like they came off the rack at JCPenney; his only vice was pricey cigars; and his manner was self-deprecating. He liked to tell of his arrival at the Cannes Film Festival, when a photographer stuck his head in Vincent's limo, then yelled to the rest of the paparazzi, "Don't worry, it's nobody."

But if he didn't have a standard show-biz ego, big and blazing as the Radio City Music Hall marquee, he did have one like Carnegie Hall, home of the classier acts, which he favored. It was understated but nonetheless huge. Wherever he was, Fay Vincent seemed to feel he was the smartest person in the room.

Coca-Cola bought Columbia in 1982, and Vincent continued to head the company. He was credited with getting Columbia into the profitable TV syndication business and setting up the successful joint-venture movie studio, Tri-Star. It enabled Columbia to share movie production costs with HBO and CBS while satisfying his own fondness for "risk management."

But Vincent's revolving door of studio chiefs caught up with him. Columbia's movie business started dropping, and so did his stock. His earlier days had yielded hits like *Tootsie* and *Kramer vs. Kramer*. His latter days yielded *Ishtar*, one of cinema's all-time bombs. When Columbia and Tri-Star were merged into one company in 1987, Vincent was squeezed out and given a non-job at Coca-Cola. He left soon thereafter, with $20 million worth of Coke stock but no prospects. Then, for the second time in a decade, a friend beckoned from out of the blue.

Fay Vincent and Bart Giamatti had met in 1978 at a dinner party given by author Peter Benchley. Vincent was the new president of Columbia; Giamatti the new president of Yale; they agreed their jobs were impossible. Vincent admitted, however, that he did prefer his own.

"I make three hundred thousand," he pointed out, "you make a hundred."

Giamatti roared and they became instant friends, drawn together by their common love of baseball, literature, and Yale. They sharply differed only in their rooting habits. Vincent was a Yankees man. "He made me feel as if I had chosen to like yogurt instead of ice cream," Vincent said.

Every so often they talked about working together one day. They made a half-serious pact: if Vincent was ever in a position to hire Giamatti, he would, and vice versa. For years, the closest they ever came was when Vincent got Giamatti onto the board at Coca-Cola Enterprises, Coke's big bottling company.

Then Giamatti got his chance. He knew he had a weakness as commissioner: namely, his being a naïf about business. All the talk of super-stations and sponsorships rather lost him. He kept trying to bring owners' discussions back to the quality of the fan experience. Baseball had to do better at keeping ballparks clean and civilized, he lectured, or risk losing the family crowd. He lectured the Lords repeatedly about ballpark "ambience," though he took some kidding that *ambience* was a "Yale word."

As commissioner-elect, in late 1988, Giamatti knew he had to team up with a better business head. Fay Vincent was available, willing, and soon his deputy commissioner. The two of them were soon inseparable: attending almost every meeting together, taking breakfast and lunch together, going to games together. (Giamatti leaned over to him in one sun-splashed ballpark and murmured, "Don't forget. This is work.")

They were once walking along together slowly. Vincent's gait had worsened due to an arthritic hip, and he now used a cane. Giamatti had circulation problems, which, when they flared up, made him drag his feet.

"We're quite a pair," said Vincent. "The people who run other big-time sports must be in a lot better shape than us."

"Well, Fay, don't worry," said Giamatti. "We won't challenge Pete Rozelle to a race. We'll challenge him to a *think*."

Yet Vincent was less Giamatti's business guru than his soulmate. He, too, was poles apart from Peter Ueberroth. He, too, was more concerned with baseball's purification than its effective commercialization—as at Columbia, where making blockbusters seemed less important to him than purging evil.

"The new cast of characters was far more interested in the so-

ciological value of baseball than the business of baseball," said
Roger Werner, whose ESPN cable network had joined CBS as
the major TV partner. "The new regime felt that to mix commerce and the church of baseball was unholy. Those were the
problems of the money changers."

Soon, Vincent and Giamatti had a holy cause that illuminated
all their values and overwhelmed all else in the commissioner's
office.

Pete Rose had a gambling problem. He dropped bundles at the
track and he got in deep with bookies. As far back as 1978, the
Reds' Dick Wagner remarked to colleagues, "Pete's legs may
get broken when his playing days are over."

But baseball let him get away with it. GMs wouldn't mess
with a gold-plated gate attraction. Writers had no need to expose
the best quote in the business. And baseball's security director
then, Henry Fitzgibbon, limited himself to Dutch-uncle talks
with Rose. The player would nod at Fitzgibbon's warnings while
checking his watch to see if he could make post time.

The more Rose broke the records of baseball immortals—Ty
Cobb's 4,191 hits fell to Rose in 1985—the more he thought
himself above the rules of mere mortals. His entourage was the
darker side of Damon Runyon: a collection of low-life gofers,
memorabilia hustlers, and drug dealers. The same week he broke
Cobb's record, he accepted a cocaine dealer's $17,000 loan.

Rose, now the Reds' player-manager, needed the cash for his
gambling habit. He was hundreds of thousands of dollars in debt
to bookies. He became a regular on the baseball-card show circuit, collecting $8,000 to $12,000 per appearance. He'd sign autographs for two hours, collect his fee in cash, and take it home
in a bulging paper bag. That would keep another bookie at bay
for a while. Rose was also a fixture in the booming baseball-
memorabilia market. (That would lead to his later conviction on
income-tax evasion.) He sold his bat from the Ty Cobb–record-
breaking game for $125,000. He changed his uniform between
innings that game, the better to maximize his return on their
sale.

Rose's gambling was ultimately too blatant for baseball to ignore. Rumor had it he was in to the mob. It was even whispered
that he was betting on baseball. That had been a capital crime in
the game ever since the 1919 "Black Sox" World Series.

Peter Ueberroth, in his last days in office, called Rose on the
carpet. Rose tried to be buoyant, commenting on the photos of

baseball greats outside the commissioner's office. They included Roger Maris hitting homer number 61, Joe DiMaggio hitting during his 56-game streak, and Hank Aaron hitting his 715th home run. Asked Rose: "Why ain't I up there?"

Ueberroth wouldn't be charmed.

"We have only one purpose here," he said. "We've heard rumors about your gambling. We don't want to hear about betting on basketball or football. Did you or did you not bet on baseball?"

Rose and his lawyers fenced with Ueberroth. He flatly denied he'd bet on baseball or that he had problems with bookies. Nor had he won a bundle on a Pik Six racetrack jackpot, as had been reported. In the end, they fought to a draw and the meeting concluded.

Then Ueberroth did his part to cover up. He had only a month left in office and his plan was still in place: declare victory and get the hell out. He wanted no loose ends. When Murray Chass of the *New York Times* learned of the Rose meeting and called about it, Ueberroth said, "There's nothing ominous, and there won't be any follow-through."

Rose would not get off the hook so easily with Bart Giamatti. Three days after the meeting and one day after Ueberroth's kiss-off in the *Times*, he talked over the problem with his friend Vincent. They talked on the phone long into the night. Both agreed there should be a thorough investigation; the question was how to proceed. In the end, Vincent suggested that they get an outside investigator to untangle all these threads of rumor. And he had just the guy: a lawyer friend named John Dowd.

Dowd came from Brockton, Massachusetts, the same tough mill city that produced fighters like Rocky Marciano and Marvin Hagler. Dowd brought that same brawling spirit to the law. He had been a killer prosecutor with the U.S. Justice Department in the 1970s, heading a group called Strike Force 18. It went after mobsters, usually nailing them for their financial irregularities. He was also tapped to investigate then–FBI director Clarence Kelley on charges of accepting improper gifts.

Dowd wasn't much of a trial lawyer, but when it came to amassing a case, fellow lawyers looked on in awe. "If he went after the pope he'd bring him down," said one. He was both skilled at extracting information and zealous about going after it. "When John sees evil, the gloves come off," said another lawyer.

Vincent, who'd known Dowd from his Washington days, called him right after ringing off with Giamatti. He knew that Dowd was now *defending* people accused of white-collar crimes. Would he take the case? The old prosecutor's juices were instantly flowing. They immediately patched together a conference call with Giamatti and it was done. Dowd was baseball's Special Prosecutor.

Within days, he had a former Rose flunky, Paul Janszen, singing like a canary. A weight lifter and small-time steroids dealer, Janszen was a principal figure in Rose's entourage for two years. Then they had a falling out over $44,000 Rose owed him (for covering gambling debts). When FBI agents told Janszen he was about to get busted for drug dealing and income-tax evasion, they scared him into testifying against others. One of the others was Pete Rose.

The feds turned Janszen over to Dowd when they were done with him. In two days of interrogation, Dowd turned him inside out. Then he let loose a small army of attorneys and gumshoes on the leads he had provided.

Dowd reveled in the latitude afforded a baseball Special Prosecutor. A U.S. attorney had to abide by the niceties of the Bill of Rights. But the commissioner's lawyer was unshackled. He didn't need a search warrant or a subpoena. He had only to invoke the threat of retribution if a baseball man didn't cooperate with the commissioner. Even a star could be browbeaten into submission.

"It got progressively more heavy-handed as it went along," said Robert Pitcairn, Jr., one of Rose's attorneys. Whether required to produce a handwriting sample, put through an eight-hour deposition grilling, or forced to turn over documents, Rose got a constant reminder: any failure to cooperate would be grounds for suspension by Giamatti.

Dowd would later maintain he'd only played hard and fair by baseball's rules. "The commissioner has a right to everything." he said.

Then his own zeal got Giamatti in trouble. Another lowlife, bookie Ron Peters, had been of help by squealing on Rose. Now Dowd was going to be helpful to Peters, who was awaiting sentencing on a federal felony conviction. Dowd drafted a letter for Giamatti's signature to the sentencing judge. Peters, it said, had provided baseball with "significant and truthful cooperation" and been "candid, forthright, and truthful with my special counsel."

Giamatti casually scribbled his signature. It was a bad habit of his. In matters he didn't understand—whether law or labor relations—he put himself blindly in the hands of his handlers. Now he'd pay for it. Dowd, in his blunderbuss fashion, had worded the letter more strongly than the standard such document. If Rose's lawyers got ahold of it, they'd claim Giamatti had prejudged their man.

They did. Judge Carl Rubin, the Cincinnati jurist handling Peters's disposition, was furious. One, he resented the intrusion of baseball, which wasn't a party to this case. Two, he was a Reds fan, and Giamatti was clearly trying to railroad the great Pete Rose. Judge Rubin disclosed and denounced the letter to everyone who would listen: his old friend Reuven Katz, who happened to be Rose's agent; the assistant U.S. Attorney who was prosecuting Peters; and then the press, who put it all in big headlines.

Cincinnati was in an uproar, and, what's more, Rose's attorneys had ammunition for a counterattack. Lou Hoynes begged Giamatti to disown the letter—let the world know he'd signed it not because his mind was made up but because his lawyer told him to. Giamatti wouldn't do it. He was loyal to Dowd.

That was in April. In May, Dowd delivered his report: 225 pages, plus more than 2,000 pages of transcribed interviews and exhibits. It cost baseball $3 million to learn that Rose had, indeed, bet on baseball. In June, just before Giamatti's scheduled hearing on the matter, Rose's lawyers sued him. They asked that the hearing be enjoined and the commissioner be forced to pay damages for besmirching Rose's reputation.

A Hamilton County judge granted the injunction, declaring: "It appears to this court at this point that the commissioner of baseball has prejudged Peter Edward Rose. We further find that the hearing set for tomorrow in New York before the commissioner of baseball would be futile and illusory and the outcome a foregone conclusion."

That night, a banner in Riverfront Stadium read: PETE 1, BART 0.

Throughout the summer, Rose's lawsuit careened between various Ohio courts and took a terrible toll on Bart Giamatti. He'd been badly mauled in a deposition by Rose's lead lawyer, Robert Stachler. He was dazed by the glare of public scrutiny and dizzy from the whirl of nonstop meetings. Chain-smoking more furiously than ever, Giamatti was no more built for conflict now than before.

Dick Wagner once came out of 350 Park Avenue and saw Giamatti leaning, exhausted, against the front wall. He looked awful. He'd gained weight, had deep black circles etched under his eyes, and had grayed markedly.

"Hey, you look like you're holding up the building," joked Wagner, now an American League official.

Giamatti laughed weakly.

He was, among other things, torn by conflicting advice. On the one hand, there was Maximum Fay. Vincent wanted to crush Pete Rose—more so with each passing day. He was leading the legal defense of the Rose suit and it frustrated him. Rose's lawyer, Stachler, was a spray-hitter, much like his client—belting drives into every court he could find and hoping for a hit. He was also cagily shifting the focus away from Rose and onto the process.

Vincent liked the idea of both breaking Rose with legal bills and busting him out of baseball for life. Vincent wanted to make him pay for desecrating baseball, and he didn't care how long it took. "Mr. Stachler," he once told the lawyer, "you have done more harm to baseball than any single person in seventy years of the game's history."

On the other side was Lou Hoynes. He still had Giamatti's ear, and he favored a swifter, softer resolution. Get Rose out without making a federal case of this any longer, he urged. It was time to get on to other things.

The two vied for favor with Giamatti and argued incessantly with one another. They hadn't much liked each other from the start, and now it was war.

Barry Rona did his best to offer objective guidance, and he observed a change in Giamatti.

"It became apparent that he was beginning to have legitimate, serious questions about Fay's positions," Rona recalled. "He was moving from blind faith in Fay toward asserting himself."

While Giamatti pondered, the standoff continued for two months, partly a game of legal chess, partly a game of chicken. If it came to a trial, Rose would look terrible, all his sleaze and lies bared. But so would baseball. Its governance, as portrayed by Stachler, would make the game seem less like apple pie and more like a can of worms.

Finally, *both* sides blinked. Settlement talks began in mid-August, with Vincent's first offer: a ten-year banishment. Rose's agent Reuven Katz pressed for a lighter sentence. He also wanted no finding that Rose had bet on baseball. He envisioned the sort of consent decree that Vincent would know from the SEC: the accused admitted no offense and agreed never to do it again. Vincent countered with a seven-year banishment. Katz refused again.

Ultimately, they agreed to put him on the "ineligible list." It would be termed a permanent suspension. But under baseball's rules, Rose could apply for reinstatement after one year. And Katz got one sentence he very much wanted in the five-page agreement: "Nothing in this agreement shall be deemed either an admission or a denial by Peter Edward Rose of the allegation that he bet on any major league baseball game."

Rose signed the document and flew off to Minneapolis to be on a cable-TV home-shopping show. There he sold autographed balls for $39, bats for $229, and jerseys for $399.

The next morning, August 23, exactly six months after the Rose investigation started, Bart Giamatti took the podium at the New York Hilton to announce its denouement. It sounded more like an address to graduating seniors than a briefing for baseball writers:

"Let there be no doubt or dissent about our goals for baseball or our dedication to it," he said in conclusion. "Nor about our vigilance and vigor—and patience—in protecting the game from blemish or stain or disgrace. The matter of Mr. Rose is now closed. It will be debated and discussed. Let no one think that it did not hurt baseball. That hurt will pass, however, as the great glory of the game asserts itself and a resilient institution goes forward. Let it also be clear that no individual is superior to the game."

The high-minded statement completed, the writers cut to the chase with the first shouted question: Had Rose bet on baseball?

"In the absence of a hearing and therefore in the absence of evidence to the contrary," Giamatti began, looking down, shuffling his papers, then looking back at the questioner, "I am confronted by the factual record of Mr. Dowd. On the basis of that, yes, I have concluded he bet on baseball."

Pete Rose and Reuven Katz, watching the press conference on TV in Katz's living room, were stunned. After days of careful negotiating over the wording and meaning of the agreement, it had been casually trashed on national TV. Giamatti and Vincent congratulated each other for vanquishing evil and prepared to finally take a vacation.

Vincent was basking in the sun on the deck of his Cape Cod summer place eight days after the Rose announcement. He was enjoying a cigar and a book in midafternoon when the call came from American League president Bobby Brown. Bart Giamatti had suffered a heart attack at his own summer place on Martha's Vineyard.

Vincent tried numbly to get some details from Brown, himself a cardiologist, but he knew none. Within an hour the details would make no difference. Giamatti was dead.

The baseball world—except, perhaps, for certain parts of Cincinnati—went into stunned mourning. Ken Coleman, the announcer, moved up his traditional reading of Giamatti's "Green Fields of the Mind" from his last postgame show of the season to the pregame show of that night's Red Sox game.

> It breaks your heart. It is designed to break your heart. The game begins in the spring, when everything else begins again, and it blossoms in the summer, filling the afternoons and evenings, and then as soon as the chill rains come, it stops and leaves you to face the fall alone. You count on it, rely on it to buffer the passage of time, to keep the memory of sunshine and high skies alive, and then just when the days are all twilight, when you need it most, it stops ... And summer is gone.

The outpouring of grief from the Lords was genuine. Giamatti was deeply flawed, but he was also the deepest thinker and strongest spiritual leader ever to hold that office. He appealed, in stark contrast to Ueberroth, to their better selves. "The best friend I ever had," said Bud Selig. "We lost a great voice for the game," said Bill White. "Aw, Jesus," said George Steinbrenner, who'd been talking jovially by phone with Giamatti just before his collapse, "everybody should pray for this man."

His death also created a vexing practical problem. Labor negotiations were now just months away, and preparations for a lockout were moving along. Giamatti had signed on to the program, of course. The hawks pushing the strategy—Bud Selig and Jerry Reinsdorf—thought they'd sold Fay Vincent too.

They settled on Vincent as the next commissioner. To search for anyone else risked getting a dove. Certainly to start a full-scale search, at this late date, might derail the strategy. Also, if the throne were to stay empty very long, the players might take it as a signal that the lockout was an empty threat.

Vincent had also come off as a passable business head in the few meetings they'd observed him in. Certainly he was a faithful extension of Bart Giamatti. In the days after his death, Vincent's sentences were laced with "Bart said" or "Bart and I" or "Bart would have . . ." When Reinsdorf and Selig talked to him about the commissioner's job, he was blunt as could be: "Bart's agenda is my agenda." It was a major selling point for them with the rest of the Lords. The one comfort they could take in Giamatti's passing was that his deputy, Fay Vincent, would carry his standard.

It was this strange conjunction of motives—of keeping the lockout on track, and of keeping Bart Giamatti's memory alive—that swept Fay Vincent into office. Selig and Reinsdorf worked the phones hard on his behalf right up to the September 13 ownership meeting. They wanted to vote to come then and implored: "We can't afford a gap."

Selig and Reinsdorf even enlisted George Steinbrenner to lobby for Vincent. As the most unpopular owner in baseball, Steinbrenner didn't have any chits to call in, but he did have indefatigable energy once he got behind a cause. Steinbrenner decided to make Vincent, a fellow Williams man, his cause.

"Not so fast," cautioned Arthur Richman, the Yankees' senior vice president, when he heard of Steinbrenner's lobbying. "You don't know anything about this guy; he's never been in baseball. Why did they let him go at his last job? Why did he leave?"

"Mind your own business," Steinbrenner snapped.

(Later, when Vincent turned against Steinbrenner and the Boss found himself under a lifetime ban, he would turn on Richman. "Why didn't you tell me?" he screamed.)

And so, when the Lords gathered at Milwaukee's Pfister Hotel in mid-September it was less for an election than a coronation. Selig and Reinsdorf had done their work well, with Steinbrenner's assist. As the Fay Vincent bandwagon rolled out, only one owner tried to put on the brakes.

"We're all in shock and we ought to go slow," said Peter O'Malley. "Let's face it. We don't know much about Fay. Why don't we take the time to look? Why not make him the acting or interim commissioner?"

O'Malley was making good sense. Some heads were nodding in agreement. Then he went too far.

"And what about his health?" O'Malley asked. "In his condition, can he work a full day, get around as much as you need to in this job?"

Now, baseball doesn't have much truck with political correctness, but O'Malley had stepped out of bounds.

"That's not fair," said Jim Campbell of the Tigers. "I worked for someone for years who was in a wheelchair [John Fetzer]." Someone else harkened back to FDR. Suddenly O'Malley was on the defense for mugging a cripple.

The moment for doubting Fay Vincent had passed. The arguments Selig and Reinsdorf had seeded among the Lords began to be echoed around the room: continuity, Bart's legacy, and all that. Still, O'Malley's points had taken hold with some.

"We *are* moving quickly," said the Royals' Ewing Kauffman, "and it makes me wonder about something. Suppose he doesn't work out. Shouldn't we know if there's some way of getting rid of a commissioner if we need to? Peter Ueberroth always said he couldn't be fired, but I don't know if that's true. Maybe we should amend the agreement to lay out some kind of procedure."

He was referring to the Major League Agreement, the 1921 convenant between Judge Landis and the owners. It laid out the commissioner's powers and had survived to that moment as baseball's basic governing document. Reinsdorf said he'd sound out Vincent about it.

The meeting recessed and Reinsdorf went to Vincent's room. He told him some owners apparently thought they needed to establish a procedure for firing a commissioner as well as hiring one. God forbid they'd ever need to use it, but what did he think?

"I'd really rather not put that in the agreement. It weakens the office," said Vincent. "But I can assure you that if a clear majority of the clubs don't support me, I would have to resign. No commissioner can serve without the support of the clubs."

(That, at least, is the way some owners recall it. Vincent only remembers being asked what he thought of a procedure to remove a commissioner convicted of a crime. He said he wasn't against that, but he was against enacting it in the emotion of the moment.)

Reinsdorf carried the word back.

"We don't need to amend the agreement," he said. "He said he'd leave voluntarily."

By acclamation, Fay Vincent was made baseball's eighth commissioner.

$ 20 $

IT WAS 5:04 P.M. in San Francisco, October 17, 1989, about a half-hour before the third game of the World Series. Fay Vincent was standing in his field box, chatting with a friend, when something caused him to lurch off balance.

He grabbed for the box's railing, thinking that his legs had failed him again, and that the noise he heard was just a low-flying jet. His wife, Valerie, told him otherwise. "It's an earthquake," she said.

Candlestick Park swayed, concrete crumbled, people screamed. Fifteen seconds later, the shaking finally stopped. So did the World Series. Players scurried to the middle of the field and confusion gripped the crowd, fast approaching the stadium's 62,000 capacity. At first the earthquake-inured fans of the Bay Area demanded to get on with it, chanting "Play ball! Play Ball!" The urgency of the situation became evident only when a loudspeaker-equipped police car began circling the field, issuing orders to exit. (The stadium PA system had been knocked out.) By 6:30, amazingly enough, Candlestick Park had emptied without incident or injury.

The crowd walked out into a tableau of destruction. A few miles away, the upper level of the Nimitz Freeway had collapsed into the lower level, crushing cars and people. In San Francisco's Marina District, houses had buckled and a fire raged. The San Francisco–Oakland Bay Bridge had snapped. It was the worst earthquake there since the massive 1906 tremor.

The power was still out the next day at the St. Francis Hotel, baseball's headquarters hotel. That morning Fay Vincent walked into a ballroom packed to the rafters with media people and lit only by candles. He was to report on a meeting he'd just had with people from the San Francisco police, the A's and the

Giants, and ABC. The new commissioner slowly made his way to the podium, his gait, as always, tortured. Then he began speaking, and the awkward man turned elegant.

"It has become very clear to all of us in major league baseball that our concerns, our issue, is a modest one in this tragedy," he said. "Baseball is not the highest priority to be dealt with. We want to be very sensitive as to the state of life in this community. The great tragedy is, it coincides with our modest little sporting event.

"We don't want to be conducting baseball while the hunt for victims is going on, and while the community is still in a very serious stage of recovery. So from my point of view, it is far better to wait here, recognizing that we support the community's effort. We'll try to be as helpful as we can, and we won't be in the way of that effort.

"There is so much to learn at a time like this. We have to know the degree of dislocation in the community, guided solely by city and state officials. We cannot put baseball ahead of these things. We are very mindful that we are only a very small part of a much larger problem. We know our place, and it would be totally inappropriate to think of playing right now, even if we knew about the condition of the park.

"Of course, we want to do everything in our power to finish this World Series, but we will not intrude on the dignity of this community."

Vincent's early reputation had been made. He was at once calmly understated and truly statesmanlike. Backlit by the eerie candlelight, he had shone brightly. "If ever the business of fun and games was put in proper perspective, Vincent did it," wrote *USA Today*'s Hal Bodley in the cascade of favorable press notices.

Behind the magnanimous public face, however, there was a more steely side to Vincent. By late that week, he was restless to resume the Series. He had in mind Tuesday, which would be one week's hiatus and time enough, he believed, for the Bay Area to regroup. He'd talked it over with San Francisco police commander Isiah Nelson, who thought a Tuesday game doable.

But approval had to come from Mayor Art Agnos, with whom Vincent met on Saturday. They were at Al Rosen's downtown apartment, with Rosen and Giants owner Bob Lurie and executive vice president Corey Busch on hand, too.

Vincent made a few murmurings of sympathy to Agnos, then

got to the point: "Baseball and the World Series need to get started. I want to get going Tuesday."

"That's impossible; I'm not going to authorize it!" Agnos exploded. "We haven't had an opportunity to complete an evaluation of Candlestick's structure. All our engineers are overwhelmed with public buildings, bridges, trolleys, and all the other things that are priorities. Our police are overwhelmed; they can't be directing traffic at the stadium."

"That's not what your police commander said," Vincent replied. "He said Tuesday would be okay."

"Who's he speaking for?" asked Agnos. "He's responsible for Candlestick Park, not the entire city. I don't want it started again until two weeks have passed. It's important to show respect for the people who have been affected by this."

"Well, it's important to get baseball going, too," said Vincent. "We can't have a huge break in the Series. I'd hate to be the mayor who canceled the World Series. That would be hard."

"No, it's not hard at all," said Agnos. "I'd hate to be the commissioner who took baseball to an unsafe stadium when we were still digging up bodies out of a collapsed freeway."

They volleyed words back and forth in that vein, each wearing tight smiles. Vincent said he could always move the Series out of San Francisco. (Lurie about passed out. This was the first World Series there since 1962; it was the moment he'd waited for since buying the Giants in 1976.) Agnos told him to do what he must. He had bigger concerns than baseball. The meeting broke up with Vincent and Agnos snarling mutual "I'll get back to you's."

In the end, it was a compromise. The Series resumed neither as soon as Vincent wanted nor as late as Agnos did. On Friday, October 27, the Giants took the field before an emotional Candlestick throng, and the A's resumed their sweep.

There was one other piece of backstage unpleasantness. Vincent had made one gesture Agnos appreciated: donating $1.3 million on behalf of baseball to the earthquake relief effort. But Vincent had done it without consulting the owners and some called to object, most vociferously Peter O'Malley.

"That'll cost me fifty thousand bucks," he said, referring to the amount each club would kick in. "I've never given fifty thousand bucks to anybody or anything. I'd like to have some say before you do it for me."

Vincent was taken aback.

"I give fifty thousand dollars to a number of charities every year, and I'm not worth as much as you," he said.

O'Malley later apologized, and it only amounted to a minor quibble in a major triumph for Vincent. A national poll found 85 percent approval for the way the sport handled the earthquake. Much of the acclaim was based on astonishment. It was so rare for baseball to behave with any grace.

It was at once the high point and turning point of Vincent's regime. Until then, he was a virtual unknown outside ownership circles. Pete Rose, asked once who had accompanied Giamatti to a meeting, referred to him only as "the crippled guy." A San Francisco TV news anchor called him "Commissioner Vincent Fay."

The earthquake changed all that. The press had been plentiful, it had been positive, and *he liked it*. "The earthquake gave him national exposure, 110 percent of it favorable," said one confidant. "It gave him a new level of confidence. It was the beginning of the transformation of his role. He started to look for issues."

One began to swim into focus a month after the Series. On the day before bargaining talks were to begin, Vincent fired Barry Rona as chief labor negotiator. Chuck O'Connor, the PRC's general counsel, was elevated to take his place.

There wasn't a dime's worth of difference between Rona and O'Connor on labor strategy. But Rona had been the PRC's point man through the collusion era, so Vincent presented his head to Don Fehr as a goodwill gesture.

"Every commissioner wants to have an image, leave a legacy," Rona would later say. "Bowie Kuhn took care of the game. Peter Ueberroth brought business sense. Bart was trying to take baseball back to a non-crass business. And Fay wanted to be the labor-relations commissioner."

Vincent made another player-friendly gesture at about the same time, hiring Steve Greenberg as his deputy commissioner. The son of Hall of Famer Hank Greenberg, the forty-year-old lawyer appealed to Vincent on several grounds. He was a reputable agent, as agents went, whose clientele included Mark Langston and whose relations with Don Fehr were warm. He had administrative experience, managing a big Los Angeles law firm whose name partners included Mickey Kantor, the West Coast Svengali behind Bill Clinton. Greenberg was also a member in good standing of the Yale-Hotchkiss connection. An alumnus of both, he'd studied English Lit under Bart Giamatti and served on the Hotchkiss board with Vincent.

But even as Vincent was making his peace offerings, the PRC readied for war. The hawks had ever more reason to be hawkish. Salaries were taking off again, and the labor contract was the last best chance to keep them in check.

For three years, the top salary level had moved little above the $2 million plateau, reached in 1985. It was one of the great triumphs of collusion. Then, in early 1989, a group of elite pitchers took turns reaching new highs. First Dwight Gooden signed a three-year contract averaging $2.3 million per; then Roger Clemens came along with a three-year contract averaging $2.5 million. Finally, Orel Hershiser and Frank Viola signed matching pacts: $2.6 million a year for three years.

But late that year, other top-level players would make a shambles of the old salary standards. Between mid-November and mid-December 1989, four of them smashed through the $3 million mark: outfielders Kirby Puckett and Rickey Henderson, then free-agent pitchers Mark Langston and Mark Davis. New salary records were established almost daily, and Oakland's Henderson never would get over being eclipsed so fast and by so much. He would pout and complain through his entire four-year contract.

Non-elites cashed in too. Pascual Perez's 9–13 season and drug-plagued career qualified him for $5.7 million over three years with the Yankees. (He was a Tom Reich client, naturally.) Bryn Smith, who'd gone begging for a job during collusion, signed a three-year, $6 million deal with St. Louis. Walt Terrell, loser of 34 of 52 decisions the past two years, got a three-year, $3.6 million contract from the Pirates.

One might have said the signings went off like a string of firecrackers, except that the Lords viewed them more as nuclear bombs. In early 1990, Lou Gorman, the Red Sox GM, wailed, "This is insanity. Where is it going to end?"

Ah, but it was only beginning. There is a predictable response to any lifting of restraints: a geyser of pent-up demand. So it was with the end of collusion. And there was still lots more cash to come. The CBS deal—and the companion ESPN contract—would begin in 1990, doubling each team's TV money to $14 million. The Lords, flush with $214 million in 1989 operating profits, could moan all they wanted about the salaries, but for now they could afford them. Even PRC chairman Selig, who woke up each morning moaning about the baseball economy, had lavished $3 million salaries on Robin Yount and Paul Molitor.

For this and other reasons, Chuck O'Connor was behind the eight ball from the start. He was a bear of a man—forty-nine years old, six-three—who'd lawyered for the PRC for just two years, though he had a twenty-year background in labor relations. He also had a long stint as the PRC's "shadow counsel." O'Connor's clients included Anheuser-Busch, and starting in the early eighties, Gussie Busch's lawyer and adviser, Lou Susman, assigned O'Connor to follow baseball's every labor move. It gave Susman ammunition of his own. It also positioned O'Connor's firm to angle for the PRC account, which it eventually won.

O'Connor was a pro: Boston-Irish and shrewd. But he'd formally taken the reins on the eve of the talks, just two and a half months before the lockout deadline. If there was no agreement by February 15, the Lords would lock the players out of spring training.

Normally, that kind of lead time wasn't so terrible. Labor negotiations were notorious for meaning little until the last minute. But in this case the PRC was bringing some novel ideas to the table. Their proposed salary cap was more sophisticated than the one of 1985. O'Connor preferred to call it "revenue participation," with players getting 48 percent of the gross. It was modeled on the NBA's 53 percent cap formula, but with all sorts of caveats and codicils attached. It would take time to explain and evaluate. Then there was pay-for-performance, which would rank (and pay) younger players according to their stats.

The union wasn't excited about either proposal. Its associate general counsel, Gene Orza, dismissed pay-for-performance as "Rotisserie Baseball for lawyers." Will Clark had just cut a deal that made the proposal even less appealing: the Giants first baseman, a three-year man, signed a long-term contract at $3.75 million a year. If the union agreed to pay-for-performance, even a star like Clark would max out at less than half that.

Nor did the players fancy a salary cap. Marvin Miller, still very much an influence, still hated the NBA's version. He said it over and over: no mechanism that limited a player's earning power was acceptable.

Not wishing to jaw about the cap more than absolutely necessary, Fehr got right to the bottom line with O'Connor and Co.: "In the aggregate," he asked, "does this produce higher, lower, or about the same pay?"

A collective mumble came back at him from across the table: "We don't know."

Fehr didn't believe that for a nanosecond. It had to be less or the Lords wouldn't be offering it. "They were saying, 'We want you to agree to this, and we'll spend ourselves into oblivion if you don't.' "

There was another reason the players didn't care for any mechanism to limit their earning power. They'd already had experience with one: collusion. The pall of that era still hung darkly over the bargaining table. "You have to remember," Don Fehr later said, "the damages on the collusion cases hadn't yet been settled, and we were ready to shoot them all."

Fay Vincent had begun reaching out to Fehr in private chats, but these were different from Ueberroth's old Peacock Alley cocktail chats. Ueberroth had used those meetings to send the union a message. Before heading over, he'd ask his labor strategists, "What do you want me to leave him with?" Vincent just wanted to make nice. "He didn't have an end result in mind," said one baseball lawyer. "It was just communication for communication's sake."

"He'd talk in terms of conclusions," said another. " 'I've got a great relationship with Don Fehr, ergo I'll make a great deal with him.' "

Once again, the union's experience and continuity would contrast sharply with the Lords'. Vincent, like Ueberroth before him, would be climbing a steep, slippery learning curve. Joe Cronin would be rolling in his grave. He'd once recited the old saw to Marvin Miller: "Players come and go, but the owners stay on forever." Now it was the reverse.

More than two decades later, Marvin Miller was still there and working over his fifth commissioner. At the age of seventy-three he was no longer directly involved in bargaining sessions or player meetings. His name, ironically, meant less to the current crop of players than it did to the owners. But he was still a union consultant and its gray eminence. Gene Orza once gave a speech at which someone asked what he thought of Marvin Miller. Orza didn't answer with words. He genuflected.

Fehr wasn't a blind acolyte. He was increasingly his own man, and he sometimes argued vigorously with Miller. But he did still turn to him often for advice, and he knew the price of ignoring it. Miller didn't hesitate to publicly criticize him if he thought Fehr erred. He scolded him in the *New York Times* after the 1985 contract for allowing "givebacks," the dirtiest word in Miller's vocabulary.

If Fehr had his own set of reasons to stand firm in 1990—and he did—Miller's kibitzing gave him one more. Most prominent on Fehr's own slate of proposals, indeed, was restoring salary arbitration rights to two-year men. In Miller's eyes, raising that threshold to three years had been the most grievous "giveback."

Lurking in the wings, too, was Dick Moss, who remained close to union affairs. He'd taken Don Fehr's brother, Steve, into his agenting practice. He had clients like Brett Butler, who took active roles in the union and took their cues from Moss. Moss, like Miller, counseled Fehr against any dangerous trends toward moderation.

"Don can be wooed," said Moss. "He can be invited into the commissioner's suite and flattered and made to feel full of himself. Don entertains all these thoughts on how he'd fix management."

In the fervent eyes of its founders, that wasn't the union's job.

There was just a week left until pitchers and catchers were to start reporting to spring training. The Lords met in Chicago to decide whether they'd be allowed to.

Some were optimistic that the rich, fat players could be brought to heel in quick order. Others took comfort in the words of American League president Bobby Brown, a fifties-vintage Yankee. "The players want to go to spring training," he assured them. "They can only sit out so long."

Chuck O'Connor had grimmer counsel. This was still a tough and determined union. "We've got to be prepared for this thing to go to Memorial Day before the players are prepared to come to the table," he said.

The twenty-six owners voted unanimously for a lockout.

The union was underwhelmed. "It's real easy to take a hard line in February," Fehr mused, noting that nobody was losing any money or taking any heat from the fans in the dead of winter. "It's a tribal show of solidarity."

Yet the state of solidarity in his own camp was suspect. Just as in 1985, many veteran players didn't want to go to the mats on salary arbitration, the issue that affected young players. Bob Boone, now forty-two and entering his last major league season, was hearing it over and over: "Why don't they make a deal? Why don't they make a deal?"

Finally, he called Don Fehr. "For what it's worth, here's what

I'm hearing," he said. "You have a membership that's divided and weak on this issue. I'd hate to have the union crumble in the face of it. I think you should make a deal."

"Bob, I've had twenty-five calls today and you're the only guy who has that opinion," said Fehr.

Their conversation, chilly and perfunctory, ended.

Boone hung up and his phone began ringing. The players who weren't calling Don Fehr were filling Boone's ear.

The only side that was in bigger trouble was the Lords'. Within days of the vote, their icy resolve was melting faster than a snowman in August. Fay Vincent's phone was ringing with pleas—from Eli Jacobs of the Orioles, Fred Wilpon of the Mets, Peter O'Malley, Walter Haas—to short-circuit the lockout.

The specter of Memorial Day had affected them powerfully— and Vincent too. "I don't think we can get a revenue participation," he told O'Connor. "What's our fallback?"

O'Connor was stunned. Vincent was ready to pack it in, just like that, on their number-one issue? "This was his first turn on the watch and it wasn't acceptable [to have a stoppage]," he later reflected. "He panicked."

Vincent had already sat in on a few negotiating sessions as an observer. Now he started calling around to PRC members, asking if they'd mind him becoming more active. It was mid-February, after all, and they were becalmed at the bargaining table. The key call was to Bud Selig, the chairman.

"Do you want me to enter the process?" Vincent asked.

"Why not?" Selig replied.

In the blink of an eye, Vincent *was* the process. The talks moved from a hotel to the commissioner's Park Avenue office, decorated by a row of signed baseballs, a blown-up version of Whitey Ford's baseball card, and a portrait of Giamatti.

There the union began talking past Chuck O'Connor and addressing Vincent. As one of the Lords' men noted, "Once you've been shaved by the head barber, you don't move down to the second chair." Vincent himself shrugged: "You can't just dip your toe in."

More significant than the formal bargaining sessions was a series of off-the-record, let-your-hair-down talks with Don Fehr. In the meetings, which also included a handful of other union and management officials, Fehr poured out his rage at the events of recent years. Ueberroth had played him for a chump in 1985.

He'd gotten him to agree to a rollback of the players' salary arbitration rights, then stabbed him in the back with collusion.

"Look, we've been down this road," said Fehr. "Last time it was, 'Do this and we'll have a great partnership.' Well, we saw what happened. We've got a pound of flesh coming, and we've got to be paid. If you think we're going to go for the things you're proposing, in the meantime, you're out of your mind.

"You've got to understand the depth of the feeling here," he continued, addressing Vincent. "Whatever the merits of these positions, you have to understand the background. This is being taken as another vehicle to screw the players."

Fay Vincent listened and nodded and made a decision. There was no way a salary cap or pay-for-performance would fly with Don Fehr. Somehow, he thought, nobody had calculated the bitter fruits of collusion into this negotiation. And so, just one week after the Lords' lockout vote and two days into the actual lockout, he pulled the revenue-sharing and pay-for-performance proposals off the table. He substituted his own nine-point plan, including:

- Minimum salaries of $75,000, $125,000, and $200,000 for players in their first three years.
- A 75 percent cap on raises in salary arbitration.
- A joint committee to study revenue-sharing, with a report due in April 1991.

The Lords were stunned. Fred Kuhlmann, the Cardinals' president and the one owner of the PRC with a labor background (at Anheuser-Busch) was enraged. So was Jerry Reinsdorf, who'd already been mystified at Vincent's modus operandi: the commissioner kept citing the opinions of George Will, the Washington savant and an Orioles board member, who called him frequently.

Now Reinsdorf admired Will as a political pundit, but severely doubted his credentials in baseball labor relations. "Who the fuck is George Will?" he finally exploded. "I like to watch George Will on Sunday mornings, but who cares what George Will thinks?"

Reinsdorf knew what *he* thought, in the wake of Vincent's unilateral action: "We were fighting over nothing."

The two sides would nonetheless fall into a long stalemate centered on salary arbitration. Nor did they make much progress on a laundry list of other issues: pension contribution, minimum salary, collusion-protection language. (The union wanted treble damages if the owners ever "acted in concert" again.) They couldn't even agree on what they had agreed on in the 1985 contract. Because of the frantic ending of the two-day strike, in which Ueberroth put a press conference ahead of drafting final terms, the Basic Agreement never was printed up.

"They weren't bringing *anything* to the table," recalled pitcher Danny Jackson, a member of the union's bargaining team. "I could have missed all those meetings from December to February and just waited until March. I'd spend hours flying around to meetings, and they'd bring in the same old things with different language. It was quite upsetting."

By February 25, ten days into the lockout, Don Fehr had had it too. He called a recess and flew west for a series of regional player meetings. First it was Phoenix and a crowd of about a hundred players: Don Mattingly, Dave Winfield, David Cone, Dave Stewart, Mark Langston, Ryne Sandberg, and many more. Then it was on to Los Angeles and Tampa and more briefings.

They were "good pump-up meetings," as Mets player rep Ron Darling put it. But they still couldn't patch up the union's fault line: the division between young and old players on salary arbitration. George Brett popped off about the issue not being worth it. So did several Pirates players. One veteran player and union activist waxed nostalgic. "Back then, unity was easy, because we were going for something," he said. "Now it's a more abstract thing of supporting the system. And the money is so big, you can't go out and re-create the income from this job."

After that winter's free-agent frenzy, twenty-seven players now made more than $2 million. About 150 players—25 percent of all major-leaguers—were making over $1 million. Unlike the days of the 1976 lockout, few players missed their "Murphy money." For this they had baseball cards to thank. That booming industry yielded each player $80,000 a year in licensing royalties. On top of that, the union had socked away a reserve fund of $80 million. In mid-March it would distribute $5,000 from it to each player—"dog-track money," one called it.

After a ten-day break, talks finally resumed on March 6. Don Fehr presented what he thought to be a breakthrough compromise offer. The union would go for just 50 percent of the two-year players being eligible for salary arbitration. The Lords, insisting on a three-year threshold for everybody, wouldn't touch it.

Two days later, Vincent made his own proposal: that the owners lift the lockout in exchange for a no-strike pledge by the players. The Lords embraced it; the players spat upon it. "No self-respecting union gives away the right to strike," snorted Gene Orza. "They knew in advance the answer we would give. It wasn't asked to get an answer. It was a public-relations event."

It wasn't even good PR. At the press conference announcing the proposal, the writers ended up shifting their questions from Vincent to the squirming Bud Selig and Chuck O'Connor. Who was in charge here? When were negotiations ever going to get off the dime? Could the season possibly start on time? Indeed, this now matched the length of the 1976 lockout—twenty-three days—with no end in sight.

Backstage at the PRC, tempers were short. Vincent wasn't expediting a settlement; he was muddying the waters. It had been convenient, at first, to let him get involved. Bud Selig was unwilling to come to New York and be an activist in negotiations. Chuck O'Connor had been thrust into his job at the last minute and, in any event, was less a leader than a barrister. They were relieved, at some level, to have Vincent at the table.

But his lack of experience and savvy in this arena was now evident. They had to get O'Connor back in the lead. On Thursday, March 8, the owners on the PRC told Vincent, in effect, to back off. They also agreed to play it cool for the next few days.

"Let's take the weekend off," said Chuck O'Connor. "If they try to call us over the weekend, just don't take it. We'll wait until Monday or Tuesday and come back fresh."

The rest of the PRC agreed. The hiatus could help shift Fehr's focus away from Vincent and get things back on track. The commissioner also seemed to concur. He also swore that whatever his role now, it was no more Mister Nice Guy for Fay Vincent. "From now on," he said, "I'm going to be known as Conan the Commissioner."

Chuck O'Connor was at Madison Square Garden Saturday afternoon watching the semifinals of the Big East basketball tournament. It was a rare break from the lockout grind and a welcome chance to spend time with his son.

At halftime, a TV reporter approached him. "What's Fay meeting with Don Fehr for?" he asked.

"He's not," O'Connor said. "He's in Greenwich."

"You're half right," the reporter said. "He's in Greenwich meeting with Fehr."

O'Connor went off to find the nearest phone, fuming. He furiously pounded the digits for Bud Selig's home number. *Selig.* He must have known about this and condoned it. *How could he?*

But Selig was equally baffled. "What? What?" he muttered.

Don Fehr had been surprised to get the call from Vincent at home, but he was receptive to the invitation to meet. He lived just one town over from Greenwich, in Rye Brook, New York. It was a ten-minute drive to Vincent's home, and why not? "I wanted to see whether something more productive might come out of a meeting in that setting," he later said.

Nothing did. The only thing Vincent accomplished that weekend was to gut the PRC's objective. He hadn't stepped out of the negotiator's role, but rather jumped back into it with both feet. "The ability to redirect Don was destroyed," said one baseball lawyer. "So was all internal trust and cohesion."

By next Wednesday, March 14, it was Fehr's turn to be anxious. That evening, Peter Gammons had reported on ESPN that peace was near at hand. Bud Selig and Paul Molitor had met privately, according to Gammons, and agreed on the outlines of a settlement. The PRC would soon be making a new offer.

It was mostly fantasy, but it had just enough fact to bother Fehr. Molitor was the American League player rep and a longtime union activist. But he'd joined the Bob Boone camp on salary arbitration. Fehr knew that Boone, who'd withdrawn from the union's inner circle, was stirring up dissent among the troops. He'd heard the veteran catcher's line from enough players: "Is one year of salary-arbitration eligibility worth losing an entire year's salary over?"

Fehr was furious. He thought Boone was being selfish. The real message coming from Boone, Fehr thought, was that this issue wasn't worth it to an eighteen-year veteran who'd signed a $1.9 million contract for 1990. And for that matter, Molitor was a twelve-year man who'd just signed a three-year, $9.1 million contract. He doubted the Brewers' star was trying to make any unilateral deals with Selig, but Molitor was close to Selig and could be sending signals that undercut the union. Certainly the owners had learned there was dissent among the players.

The union's central ethos, as always, was unity. If it was being undercut thirty days into the lockout, that was dangerous. It was time to trot out the old warhorse. Fehr called up Marvin Miller Thursday morning and filled him in on what was happening. There would be a showdown meeting between Boone,

Molitor, and the negotiating committee Friday, and an executive board meeting Saturday. Would he come to them?

Miller, with some misgivings, said he would.

A foul mood hung over the union meeting. The PRC had finally sent over the proposal Gammons had trumpeted. But while flitting around with other issues, it failed even to address salary arbitration. And everyone was on edge about the rift in their own ranks.

Molitor led off, denying the ESPN report. Yes, he'd met three or four times with Bud Selig in the past week. But only to urge him to put some serious proposals on the table. He did admit to teaming up with Boone on the salary-arbitration issue. Between them they'd phoned scores of players.

Now it was Boone's turn on the griddle. His old mentor went after him first.

"In the 1981 strike you were magnificent," said Marvin Miller. "I have to conclude from your actions now that you aren't the same man I knew then."

"I *am* the same man," Boone said. "It's the issue that's different here. We have free agency; we have salary arbitration. Why risk the season for a question of one year's salary-arbitration eligibility?"

"I think you've forgotten how important principle is in these cases," Miller replied. "In 1981, it was a strike for principle by the overwhelming majority of players, not money. It was for the benefit of the younger players and those to come after them."

One by one, the rest of the players joined in blasting Boone for undermining their negotiating strength.

He fired back. The first principle he'd learned from Marvin Miller was to establish positions the players could all support. Now, it seemed, the union leaders were trying to dictate positions. Yes, he'd polled players, but it was because the union apparently hadn't.

"You're either not in touch with the pulse out there or you ignored it," he said. "I talked to my fellow players, and their opinion is like mine: this is not an issue to stop baseball over. This is something we can't win in an extended lockout.

"You tell me what I did was wrong. Do you mean we're not allowed to have a dissenting voice in our union? Do you work for us or do you dictate to us? Shame on you for putting me in this position. My goal was simply to find out what the guys want. If the day comes that a player can't talk to his peers, this isn't the union I want to be in."

On and on the stormy session went. But the players ended up together on one thing: a unanimous vote to reject the PRC's latest proposal. Bob Boone and Paul Molitor added their hearty concurrence.

There was a bigger union gathering Saturday. The player leaders held a summit meeting that afternoon at, appropriately enough, the Summit Hotel. The executive board's usual group of thirty was swollen to double that number by players who'd flown in from around the country.

Marvin Miller was there too. This was the meeting Don Fehr had particularly begged him to attend and address. They might be near a settlement, but they needed more solidarity. So many younger players had no sense of history. They didn't know the origins or importance of salary arbitration. They didn't know how the union had struggled for its gains, nor, therefore, that struggle was required to keep them. Could Miller recount the old battles and recite the eternal verities?

He was older now, but never better—an oracle summoned from 1966. Miller still spoke quietly, and you could still hear a pin drop. He could still take the players by the hand and lead them down the compelling path of logic. There were some who said this fight wasn't worth it, he began. They were wrong.

"When we negotiated salary arbitration in 1973, it was the first big breakthrough for the players' union," said Miller. "Before then, the owners told the players what they would get. It didn't matter if you were a marginal player or Joe DiMaggio. If you didn't like it, all you could do was find a new line of work. Jimmie Foxx won the American League Triple Crown one year and was forced to take a pay cut the following year."

He went through the history of how many times the owners had tried to scale it back and how many times they'd defended it: 1976, 1980, and again in 1985. Those who wanted to cave on salary arbitration were ignoring past history, future well-being, and their fellow players. The owners were using the salary-arbitration issue as a ploy to divide the union. They shouldn't fall for it.

"It's not my place to tell you what to do," he continued. "But it's clear to me that what's happened the past few days has hurt. The dissenting remarks by some players have given new strength to the owners' resolve. A settlement has already been delayed, and the settlement you get won't be as good as it could have been.

"But whatever happens, you'll get a better deal staying together. I'll tell you what I've told players from the beginning. Stay solid, because you are irreplaceable. Stay solid, and you can have anything that's reasonable and fair.

"Failing to support the democratically arrived-at decisions of your negotiating committee, your executive director, and your staff can have only one result: a permanent loss of credibility. If you waver, you can count on one thing: the owners will never again take the player reps seriously. The issue here is no longer just salary arbitration. It's the future effectiveness of the union."

Marvin Miller, concise as always, had said his peace inside a half-hour. Then he walked out the door.

There followed more than four hours of arm-waving and speechifying. Dave Winfield, one of the few who went back to the bad old days, gave a hearty amen to Miller. Boone, Molitor, and Pete Incaviglia (the Rangers' player rep) defended their positions and ducked more brickbats. The meeting was mostly packed with supporters of the union line, including a group of Mets who came en masse from Florida in a show of force: Bob Ojeda, Howard Johnson, Barry Lyons, Tim Teufel, and Keith Miller. As Don Fehr would later put it, "All our executive board meetings are like family fights."

But in the end, the executive board's vote was unanimous, and the executive director went out to announce it to the media.

"Well, we finally received the ESPN offer," said Fehr, to laughter. And, he added, they had roundly rejected it. In a press conference that lasted fully half as long as the meeting itself, player after player testified in one voice. As Fehr later summarized it: "There are no loose pieces here. If they want to fight some more, they'll get a fight."

The next day, the Lords—who could, after all, read the newspapers perfectly well—began to hustle toward a settlement. The movement had really begun Saturday, when Don Fehr came over to 350 Park Avenue before the summit meeting. He wanted them to know that their latest offer wasn't flying, and that the union's offer of ten days ago was still on the table: 50 percent of the two-year class eligible for salary arbitration.

After he left, Vincent looked around at the owners on the PRC: Selig, Reinsdorf, Kuhlmann, McMullen, Pohlad, and Wilpon.

"I beg you to take this deal, I beg you," he said.

They wouldn't do it. Some could barely disguise their contempt. *Beg them?* Anybody with a feel for the rhythm of a negotiation knew there was plenty of endgame to play out yet.

By Sunday, that rhythm was picking up. Don Fehr and Gene Orza came to 350 Park Avenue around noon with a new proposal: make 20 percent of the two-year players eligible the first year of the agreement, 25 percent the second year, and 35 percent the third. Chuck O'Connor, who'd resumed negotiating command as they got down to the short strokes, made a counteroffer: a flat 12 percent for all three years.

Within hours, the players were back with a new formula—two of them, actually. Take your pick, they told O'Connor: making 18 percent of the two-year guys eligible the first year, 21 the second, and 30 the third; or a schedule of 18, 22, and 29 percent.

The PRC inched up to 15 percent across the board. The players came back with 20. And finally, late Sunday, they compromised at 17 percent. It was something to shake hands on, if not shout about.

Indeed, some of the Lords would only shout in anger. PRC member John McMullen, who'd left to attend a Les Aspin fundraiser (oh, the obligations of a defense contractor), returned to a galling scene. Not only had the union decisively won, in his view, but the bastards had taken over the commissioner's office. Don Fehr was sitting at Vincent's desk, looking like the cat that ate the canary. The players were jovially passing around and signing a baseball, at Vincent's request. He would display it on an office shelf, beside the one autographed by Babe Ruth.

Shortly after 1:00 A.M., with all the details completed, everyone trooped over to the Helmsley Palace for the announcement. For such a happy occasion and such a well-spoken man, Vincent's announcement struck everyone as rather flat.

"Finally we have reached what we all sought," said Vincent, only a flicker of a smile crossing his face. "Despite the travails, despite the difficulties, this is the proper way for baseball to resume."

What the writers didn't know was how Vincent spent most of his day. He had plenty of time to kill between the swapping of proposals. He passed some of it discussing Greek and Latin classics with union lawyer Gene Orza. He also thoroughly read the Sunday newspapers. He was normally a *Times* man, of course, but today the *Daily News* grabbed his attention. It had broken a front-page story about a character named Howard Spira who had shaken down George Steinbrenner for $40,000. Spira was what was called in baseball a "known gambler."

Vincent shook his head as he read and reread the story. Another crisis was shaping up even as this one wound down.

$ 21 $

In the beginning, there was Al Frohman. At five-four and 220 pounds, he looked, as one writer put it, "like ten pounds of Malt-O-Meal stuffed into a five-pound bag." He dressed worse, wearing sweaters singed by the cigarettes he chain-smoked. Frohman, the son of a rabbi, had left a career as a caterer in New York to move to the West Coast, where he had gotten into the T-shirt business. His specialty was manufacturing ones that bore pictures of athletes' faces.

That's how he met Dave Winfield, who couldn't have been more his opposite if he'd come from Mars. Actually, Winfield came from Minnesota, where he was such a great and versatile college athlete that he was drafted not only by the San Diego Padres but also by the NBA's Atlanta Hawks and the NFL's Minnesota Vikings. He chose the Padres, went directly to the majors, and became the toast of San Diego. The sleek, six-six Winfield spoke, dressed, and dated elegantly, doing the town with models.

He met Frohman, always on the lookout for T-shirt opportunities, and, unaccountably, the two hit it off. Frohman became a father figure to Winfield, who'd grown up without one. He spent vast amounts of time with him and taught him about business, with an emphasis on his personal credo: "Don't think small, don't think cheap. Think smart and intelligent. Think Jewish."

Winfield first became a free agent in 1977 and was represented by Frohman, who drove Padres GM Buzzie Bavasi absolutely crazy. He'd light a cigarette, then rummage through Bavasi's desk looking for an ashtray. He'd blow his stack regularly, waving his arms and shouting *"Vot is dis, vaddaya mean, you givin' me nottin',"* in Garment Districtese.

They came to terms with the Padres in mid-1977 for $1.3 million over four years. As part of the deal, Winfield would actually

454

pay the Padres $100,000 over four years to buy 100,000 bleacher seats for kids. He'd begun to get heavily into charitable work through something he named the David M. Winfield Foundation.

The foundation raised and spent money for entertaining poor kids. It hosted thousands of them at a party before the 1978 All-Star Game in San Diego. It threw a bash for 8,000 local children at the 1979 All-Star Game in Seattle. By 1980, the All-Star Party in Los Angeles was up to 10,000 children, with the kids getting not only autographs from players but physicals from doctors.

"Dave really was sincere with his efforts for the foundation," recalled Bavasi, though he sometimes wondered just how it worked. He once went to the hospital to visit Frohman, a sickly man who always seemed just one doughnut away from his next heart attack. The GM found him in a palatial suite.

"Ray Kroc stayed here once," Frohman bragged.

"Yeah, but he's a billionaire," said Bavasi. "How are *you* affording this?"

"The foundation's paying for it."

Oh.

Frohman remained Winfield's agent in sickness and in health. His main qualification was total devotion. Winfield once charged Nolan Ryan after a duster, inciting a brawl. Frohman jumped out of the stands and waded right into it. Before the All-Star Game in San Diego, Peter Bavasi noticed Frohman standing by a fancy car in the parking lot. Hey, Al, whatcha doing? "This is Dave's car," said Frohman. "I'm guarding it."

Winfield tried to fix Frohman up with other clients, to no avail. He hung around Jack Murphy Stadium constantly and they knew him too well. The checks he wrote them sometimes bounced and the fine clothes he often promised for their wives or girlfriends (or both) never materialized. In the clubhouse, he was thought of as Dave Winfield's cross to bear.

Winfield was up for free agency again after 1980. Over the past four years, he'd averaged 26 homers, 99 RBIs, and a .292 batting average. Just twenty-nine years old, with a cannon arm, he was a red-hot property.

He was also no dummy. He got some negotiating backup for Frohman, who was a great mentor but no superagent. One adviser was a man named Bob Erra, whom he'd met through one of Frohman's cockamamie schemes. (The idea was something called Superstar Village, a resort where pro athletes would be the draw, putting on sports clinics and mingling with the commoners. Winfield and Frohman took the idea to the Scripps Clinic, an elite San Diego medical center they thought might like to invest. Erra, the clinic's chief financial officer, thought not. But he did become friendly with Winfield.) The other backup was the formidable Dick Moss.

The game, as Moss saw it, was to get to George Steinbrenner. After three straight American League pennants, 1976 through 1978, he hadn't gotten to the Series in the past two years. "Winning a hundred and three games is like kissing your sister," said Steinbrenner, after the 1980 Yankees won that total but lost the league playoffs to Kansas City. "It's nice but it doesn't pack the wallop that kissing your girlfriend does."

Steinbrenner clearly lusted for Winfield but was handicapped by those 103 wins. With the majors' best regular-season record, the Yankees drafted last. Since only thirteen teams could draft a player, Winfield's negotiating rights might be gobbled up before it was the Yankees' turn.

Moss had to discourage the riffraff. He sent out letters to clubs, spelling out Winfield's requirements: a long-term contract, a winning team in a major market, a natural-turf stadium, and support for the Winfield Foundation. Anybody who couldn't step up to the plate on those needn't bother drafting him.

It worked. In the November free-agent draft, ten clubs picked him, one of them the New York Yankees. Steinbrenner immediately applied the full Reggie treatment. As Winfield would later recount: "Flowers, Broadway shows, dinner at the 21 Club, chauffeured limousines. Even telegrams in the middle of the night—'We want you in New York.'"

All Winfield need do was find some other obliging suitors to gig up the price. He found ideal ones in the Braves and Mets. Ted Turner threw a big number on the table and the Mets threw a big scare into Steinbrenner. He'd rather see one of his ships sink than lose Winfield to his Flushing Meadows rival. He made a huge offer:

- A $1 million signing bonus.
- A ten-year contract at $1.4 million per.
- A cost-of-living escalator, matching the inflation rate at up to 10 percent per year.

To Winfield and Co., the cost-of-living clause was vital. Inflation was going through the roof in the early eighties. The escalator helped protect the value of the contract and potentially added many dollars to it. Steinbrenner, in a lather to get the deal done, failed to grasp its significance.

The deal was almost done when Steinbrenner asked for a buyout option. After eight years, he wanted to be able to buy out Winfield's last two years at 50 percent, or $700,000 a year. He clearly considered the two to be one and the same thing. Bob Erra was clearly amazed when he caucused with Winfield.

"I can't believe it," he said.

"Believe what?" asked Winfield.

"The guy's a big wheeler-dealer but he doesn't know how a cost-of-living escalator works. He doesn't realize it *compounds*."

"Meaning?"

"Meaning if inflation's more than ten percent and you compound one-point-four million at ten percent a year, the eighth year of the contract your base salary could be two-point-five million, and a fifty percent buyout would be . . ."

It didn't take them long to do the math. Nor did it take them long to get back to Steinbrenner.

"Sure," said Erra, "we'll agree to give you the option of buying out the contract at fifty percent over the last two years."

The deal was done. It was only when he saw the next morning's *New York Times* that Steinbrenner realized what he'd really done. Someone had clued the *Times*'s Murray Chass in to the wonders of compounding. Steinbrenner had gone to bed thinking he'd signed a $16 million deal. He woke up to read it was potentially $23 million.

The phone rang at Bob Erra's bedside at 6:00 A.M., California time.

"Erra!" George Steinbrenner shouted into his ear. "What's going on here? We don't have a twenty-three-million-dollar deal!"

"You're in the shipbuilding business," Erra said. "When you give your employees a cost-of-living increase, doesn't it compound?"

Silence on the other end.

"Well, the compounding effect of a cap of ten percent could make Dave's contract worth twenty-three million."

Steinbrenner hung up. Dave Winfield, without yet donning pinstripes, was off to a terrible start with the Boss.

The even bigger hang-up would come later. Steinbrenner had made a side agreement with Erra, typed it up himself. He'd contribute $300,000 a year—$3 million above and beyond the contract—to the David M. Winfield Foundation.

* * *

Winfield was a 14-carat star in the New York firmament. He made the All-Star Team his first eight years there. He drove in 100 runs or more for five straight seasons. His 37 homers in 1982 were the most by any right-handed Yankee batter since Joe DiMaggio. His New York years would be the cornerstone of a certain Hall of Fame career.

And yet George Steinbrenner despised him. It began with the contract, on which he felt snookered. It grew with the 1981 World Series, when Winfield got just one hit and the Yankees got beat. (Steinbrenner sarcastically referred to him as "Mister May," in contrast to postseason dynamo Reggie Jackson's "Mister October" monicker.) The relationship deteriorated from there, with the continuing assistance of Al Frohman.

Frohman headed a Winfield-created company called Top Hat Inc., which was to market the player's services and baseball memorabilia. Steinbrenner somehow agreed to be a 50 percent partner. He and Frohman soon fought like cats and dogs and the business went bust.

Quite apart from that, Frohman's legendary tact could only make a bad situation worse. Once in the midst of a Winfield slump, Steinbrenner ran into Frohman and said, "You better tell your boy to start hitting."

"He's not a boy," said Frohman. "Go fuck yourself."

Steinbrenner began withholding payments to the Winfield Foundation, leading a running legal battle that lasted for years. But the foundation continued its activities. In August 1981, it threw a party for 20,000 poor kids at Randalls Island Park in New York, with a free baseball clinic, autographs, and bag lunch. In September, when he played for the first time in his hometown of Minneapolis, he gave a free baseball clinic, free physicals, picnic supper, and tickets to the game for 1,500 poor kids.

Unfortunately, the foundation wasn't just about helping poor kids—or covering Al Frohman's medical expenses. It was also a paycheck for assorted groupies. One of them was Howard Spira, a man once described as "the Babe Ruth of greaseball hangers-on."

The twenty-one-year-old Spira became a gofer at the Foundation in 1981, fresh from a stint as a gofer at NBC Sports. He was Dave Winfield's all-purpose lackey, a fixture around the Yankees clubhouse whom one player described as a "buzzing fly." At the same time, Spira had developed an expensive gambling habit and deep debts.

He was into a chap named Joseph Caridi for $57,000 when the chief of the Colombo crime family's gambling division took him for a little ride. As they drove around in his limo, Caridi demanded repayment and Spira tried to stave him off with Winfield souvenirs. He produced a baseball signed "To Anthony from Dave Winfield," for Caridi's son. He pulled out two glossies of Winfield signed the same way. Caridi, unimpressed, lifted Spira by the front of his shirt through the limo's sunroof, then partially closed the roof. There was Howard Spira, riding through the streets of Manhattan, his head outside the car.

It was enough to focus his mind on debt service, and Spira pleaded with Winfield for help. In late 1981, he gave Spira a check for $15,000. It would later become a point of contention, Spira claiming Winfield knew damned well what it was for, Winfield saying he didn't.

The two, in any event, fell out over time. Spira, in the manner of all scorned hangers-on, became bitter. He'd seen to the great man's every whim, then been discarded. By late 1986, he was down on his luck, short of cash, but still possessed of a keen eye for an angle.

George Steinbrenner was still locked in mortal combat with Winfield when Spira approached him with an enticing offer. He had great dirt on Mister May. That "death threat" he blamed for his terrible '81 World Series performance? A phony, concocted by Frohman. The foundation? A den of iniquity through which Winfield and Frohman ran funds for their own purposes. He also told of his own gambling debts, which put him in deep with mob types, and of Winfield's loans to help him out. It was a blend of fact and fantasy, for, as one lawyer who knew him estimated, "Howard probably lies fifty percent of the time." But it was good enough for George Steinbrenner, who took the tale to Peter Ueberroth. Three times he met with the commissioner to harp on Spira's allegations and urge that Winfield be investigated. Three times Ueberroth in effect kissed him off, telling Steinbrenner to "keep me posted." The owner hired his own private eyes to follow Spira's leads.

Ueberroth was not inclined to give much weight to Steinbrenner's tale. He'd heard so many. The entire commissioner's office, indeed, was inured to the Boss's whinings. Among other things, he constantly protested umpires' calls. Yankees GM Bob Quinn brought in so many videotapes of offending plays that staffers would crack, as he walked through the door, "Here comes Metro-Goldwyn-Mayer again."

Baseball's security chief, Kevin Hallinan, did finally take a look at the Yankees' gumshoe files but didn't pursue the matter. Steinbrenner next got the New York District Attorney's office to start investigating the foundation. But then the man who was to be the primary target dropped dead. Al Frohman suffered a massive stroke and died in late 1987.

The Boss and the player kept fencing. Steinbrenner forced an audit of the David M. Winfield Foundation and publicized the embarrassing findings. In 1986, it had spent about $6 for every $1 it gave away. Winfield, after a flurry of suits and counter-suits, nonetheless forced Steinbrenner to pay up $375,000 in 1987. Two years later, after another series of legal battles, Winfield was forced to admit that he too was short on his required contributions. He kicked in $230,000; Steinbrenner grudgingly released $600,000 he'd held in escrow.

Then, after a long hiatus, Howard Spira reappeared. He showed up one day at the commissioner's office in February 1989 and demanded to be interviewed. He unburdened himself on Kevin Hallinan, holding forth for 189 pages of transcript on everything from how Dave Winfield screwed his way through the '81 Series to how Frohman's driver placed bets with a Genovese crime-family figure named Little Al. Oh yes, and also how he planned to hit up George Steinbrenner for $150,000, a job, and a place to live.

Again, Hallinan let it slide. This twerp's allegations of long-ago deeds and a dead man's misdeeds didn't seem to constitute a clear and present danger to baseball.

But Spira would not go away. It had been two and a half years since he had talked with George Steinbrenner, dealing since then only with his minions. He was forever calling the Boss's security man, ex–FBI agent Phil McNiff. He was a pest, but if his tips ever led to genuine dirt on Winfield, it would be paydirt for the Boss. But finally, in September 1989, Spira again phoned Steinbrenner.

"I've been waiting," he said.

"Waiting for what, Howard?" said Steinbrenner. There was silence on the other end. Steinbrenner repeated, with rising volume, "Waiting for what, Howard? Waiting for what?"

Spira admitted that he'd never been promised anything for the Winfield dirt. This conversation would mark the start of a long shakedown campaign. Just as he'd whined of being unappreciated by Winfield, Spira now whined about being badly used by Steinbrenner. He still needed money, and if he had to get nasty to secure it, he would. In calls over the next few months, he threatened to go public with damaging disclosures about certain Yankees employees. He told Steinbrenner he had tapes of their phone calls discussing Winfield. He also suggested, in his best tough-guy impersonation, that the owner might want to beef up his personal security. The owner took the menacing advice, stationing security guards at his home and at those of his children.

In the end, however—January 1990—Steinbrenner paid Howard Spira $40,000. It was not brave and it was not anything Steinbrenner ever wanted known. But, in his mind, it was a small price to get this twerp out of his life. He'd paid a lot more for washed-up relief pitchers. "A little man with a gun is a big man," he later told Fay Vincent.

Steinbrenner had Spira sign a two-page agreement promising not to "seek or create any publicity or make any public statement with respect to the nature or substance of this matter." Then he heaved a sigh of relief.

But the $40,000 didn't take Spira very far. He kept hounding Steinbrenner, demanding another $110,000 to keep him from going public. He was already, unbeknownst to Steinbrenner, trying to sell his story to New York newspapers for $50,000. Finally, Steinbrenner reported Spira to the FBI. On March 23, a Florida grand jury indicted him on eight counts of extortion.

When the *Daily News* broke the $40,000 payment story the same week, however, it was Steinbrenner who was in trouble— with baseball. The commissioner was "shocked" to learn he'd been consorting with a known gambler. (The commissioner's office had only been apprised of the relationship three years earlier.)

Roland Thau was sitting in his office off Federal Square in Lower Manhattan on that March Saturday when the call came. He was annoyed to be interrupted, as he was trying to catch up on paperwork, but he was the only one in the Legal Aid Society's office. The call was from someone at the Federal Magistrate's office.

"We've got a removal case here," he said, "someone who's been arrested on charges in Florida. Can you come over to represent him?"

"If the judge doesn't mind me being in dungarees I'll be right over."

Thau jammed his hands in his pockets and walked across the street to the Federal Courthouse. With his white beard, rimless glasses, and thinning wisps of hair, he had a professorial air, but Roland Thau was perhaps the city's most dogged defender of the indigent accused. He would soon be honored by the New York Criminal Bar Association for his twenty years of work as a federal defender.

Compared to the Midtown swells, he made little money. But Thau, a wartime immigrant from France, had sustained an idealism about his role in the legal system. He genuinely hated people being railroaded by the system, and he fought hard—made himself a thorough pain in the butt, in fact—on their behalf. Nevertheless, Thau also had his share of humdrum cases in which his only role was to see that the process was followed correctly.

Such was the case with Howard Spira. He'd been arrested the day before and spent the night in jail. Now Thau sat down with him and went over his two options: fight extradition in a removal hearing or agree to surrender in Florida. Spira told him he'd waive the hearing and surrender. The two stood before the magistrate; Thau said he'd make surrender arrangements with Florida authorities; and Spira was free on bail.

No sooner was he out than he got a call from Kevin Hallinan, the commissioner's security director. The man with no interest in Spira's tales thirteen months earlier was now most interested.

"We'd like you to work with us in our investigation," he said. "This is your chance to get back at Steinbrenner and even the score."

Hallinan called him back Sunday with the same pitch, and Spira said they could meet Monday. But when he told Roland Thau about his appointment, he was counseled against it. Until he went to Florida, Thau was still his lawyer, and he warned him of the danger.

"Anything you tell him is discoverable for your trial," he said. "It could be used against you. Let me call him."

He got Hallinan on the phone and told him Spira wasn't coming in. A disgruntled Hallinan replied that a lawyer from baseball would be in touch.

The next call to Thau was from John Dowd. He was back in the saddle again as special prosecutor. He'd already subpoenaed a boxcarful of records from the Yankees, and, he explained to

Thau, he was going to get to the bottom of the Steinbrenner-Spira relationship.

"I'm very interested in talking to Spira," he said.

"I understand your interest, but I have my interests too," said Thau. "I don't want my client interviewed, and I'm going to advise him not to talk with you."

"I understand your concerns; they're legitimate," said Dowd. "But I'd like us all to get together so that I can let Mr. Spira know my areas of interest."

"What for? If he abides by my instructions, he won't have anything to say."

Dowd said he would consider it a worthwhile meeting even if Spira didn't say a word. He wanted him to know his areas of interest. Thau weighed what to do. He could easily tell Dowd to go to hell. But it might be beneficial to have a cordial relationship. No doubt the commissioner's office had a big file on Steinbrenner. That could be useful to Spira later on in his extortion defense. He invited Dowd over.

John Dowd, Kevin Hallinan, and another baseball security man, Ken Springer, trooped into a conference room at the Legal Aid Society that afternoon. Thau again counseled Spira not to say anything substantive and Dowd began a high-minded talk. He was assisting the commissioner in protecting the good name and integrity of baseball. The commissioner had an open mind in this investigation and wanted to be fair to Steinbrenner.

Thau was wondering where this bland little speech was going when Dowd asked whether they could meet privately for a moment. They walked down the hall to his cluttered little office, where Dowd changed tone 180 degrees.

"Only the commissioner can bring George down," he said. "That arrogant son of a bitch has gotten away with a lot of shit for years and it's high time that he be dealt with. I believe Spira's got a lot of information on Steinbrenner, including tapes, and that's of considerable interest to me."

"Look, I'm representing Spira for just a short time, until he surrenders in Florida," Thau said. "There might come a time when his permanent counsel considers it in his interest to trade information with the commissioner's office. But that's a decision for his permanent counsel in the future."

"Who's representing him in Florida?" asked Dowd.

"He declared indigency here, so he'll probably request that a lawyer be assigned to him."

"I've got a friend who's an excellent criminal lawyer in Florida," said Dowd. "I'd suggest you contact him, and he might be of assistance."

Thau was uncomfortable. He was trying to keep Spira at a distance from the baseball people, and Dowd was trying to jostle closer. But he decided to let Dowd proceed for a bit, just to see how this played out. He called a Washington lawyer to get the Florida lawyer's number, then gave it to Thau. By the time he was done, the lawyer decided he truly didn't like the smell.

"I think this is a conflict of interest for you to recommend or get counsel for him," he said. "I won't have anything to do with putting him in contact with this person."

Little did he know that, down the hall, Spira was already in contact. Before the meeting, Dowd had given Springer the Washington lawyer's card and an order: "If you get an opportunity to give this card to Howard, this is someone who may be able to represent him."

While Kevin Hallinan stood outside the conference room, talking on a cellular phone, Springer did so.

"Don't tell Thau about this, but call him and he'll help you," he told Spira. "I'm speaking for the commissioner. If you help get George Steinbrenner thrown out of baseball, I promise you won't spend a day in jail. You know, baseball's been looking for an excuse to get George, and this is the opportunity they've been looking for. If anyone could pull this off, you could."

"Look, I've just been arrested," said Spira. "I've only known a lawyer for a day and a half, and I'm not sure what to do," said Spira.

"If you work with the commissioner," said Springer, "you'll never see the inside of a jail cell again."

Spira took the card but did not keep it to himself. He later told Thau, who hit the roof. He called Dowd and Hallinan to complain bitterly. He got no satisfaction, and Dowd eventually succeeded in getting Spira a Florida lawyer. The railroading of George Steinbrenner was under way.

But the man who detested railroading—Roland Thau—would eventually have his day. He would later press for perjury charges against Dowd and Hallinan, after both swore nothing untoward had happened that afternoon. But the bulldog Thau had meticulously documented the incident. Later, when the cheering for Steinbrenner's exile died down and the way it was done examined, it would provide a damning starting point.

(Dowd continues to deny impropriety in trying to line up Spira with counsel and also denies making anti-Steinbrenner statements to Thau. Nor does he recall any of the other statements, produced by Steinbrenner's lawyer, which made him look biased from the beginning. "They were going to investigate the investigator, which is the way you try to throw people off the track," Dowd said. "It was a lot of baloney and a waste of time. There was no lack of due process."

The statements and actions presented here are allegations submitted in various proceedings by Steinbrenner's lawyers.)

It was to be a replay of the Pete Rose process, as Dowd was quick and proud to acknowledge. Questioning one of Steinbrenner's private detectives, Dowd asked if he was aware of the Pete Rose case. Sure, said the gumshoe.

"Well, Kevin [Hallinan] and I were the ones who did that investigation," said Dowd. "Pete Rose doesn't belong in baseball, and neither does George Steinbrenner."

Even with the Boss's lawyers, Dowd was about as subtle as Rocky Marciano. One of them met the special prosecutor for the first time and said, "Hi, I'm Bob Banker. I represent George Steinbrenner."

"Hi, I'm John Dowd," he replied. "I never met a man who liked George Steinbrenner."

Later he went even further, telling Banker he considered Steinbrenner a "career criminal." Winfield was the finest player the Yankees ever had, he said, and it was an outrage what the owner had tried to do to him.

Fay Vincent was about as neutral. For seventy years, baseball's Bill of Rights had been the "Rules of Procedure." They governed investigations and were concerned with the right to counsel, rules of evidence, and other due-process requirements. Vincent summarily abrogated the Rules, in effect declaring martial law for the Steinbrenner investigation. The owner was forced to waive his attorney-client privilege or face being immediately suspended. (Vincent maintained that the Rules of Procedure were only meant to govern disputes between parties, not investigations by the commissioner.)

Dowd was an information vacuum cleaner, interviewing dozens of witnesses and reviewing the paper trail. But, as *Sports Illustrated* would later put it, "he chased evidence relating to Steinbrenner like a hound but didn't always pick up other scents."

He would relentlessly probe Steinbrenner's payment of $40,000 to a "known gambler" (who didn't gamble anymore), and his use of Spira's dope to pursue his Winfield vendetta, and how he'd done it all behind the commissioner's back. Yet Dowd would hardly acknowledge the implications of Winfield's $15,000 loan to help Spira with his debts to the mob. Dowd's deposition of Winfield lasted thirty minutes.

(There was a big difference between the actions of the player and owner, Dowd later explained: "Winfield wouldn't have anything to do with Spira after he found out he was a gambler.")

Steinbrenner's lawyers were permitted to be present only at the depositions of Yankees employees and only on the condition they not open their mouths. Otherwise, they had to content themselves with reviewing transcripts somewhat later— transcripts slightly altered by Dowd.

The lawyers weren't allowed to depose Winfield, on the grounds that he'd already told Dowd what he knew. They had a three-hour time limit with Hallinan, whom they wanted to grill about Spira's early approaches. Steinbrenner's lawyers also wanted to establish that Ueberroth knew of and condoned the owner's early Spira contacts. After pressing for a deposition for months, they heard from the commissioner's office later one afternoon: Ueberroth would be available the next morning for fifty minutes by phone. It was a waste of time, as Ueberroth remembered and offered little.

Neither were Steinbrenner's lawyers allowed to see the so-called Dowd Report, which, as in the Rose case, was one long snarl against the accused. "This wasn't a balanced investigation, it was an indictment memo," said one baseball lawyer, no friend of Steinbrenner's. "It was a document that shapes everything so a decision-maker has a clear path to follow."

By the time the formal hearing was convened, on July 5 and 6, the Steinbrenner camp was pretty sure where this decision was headed. They were deeply skeptical when Vincent began by saying they could rely on his having an open mind and his being "a man of honor."

Paul Curran, one of Steinbrenner's lawyers, started. He had the acute bullshit detector of a U.S. attorney, which he once was. He leaned toward a colleague and whispered, "We're in trouble."

They were. Steinbrenner had been promised he'd be able to call his own witnesses and present other evidence. Steinbrenner himself turned out to be the only witness. In a session that lasted all that Thursday, the fifth, and spilled over to Friday, he was questioned by Vincent and then engaged by him in a colloquy on the meaning of the "best interests of baseball."

Then Dowd dumped 258 exhibits into the record—every document, transcript, and scrap of hearsay he had—and the hearing recessed. Steinbrenner's lawyers, laboring under the delusion it would be re-opened, struggled to digest it all and gagged when they woke up on July 15 to read their *Times*. It reported that Vincent was at his Cape Cod summer home to mull over his decision on Steinbrenner. He would later be joined for consultation by a trio he called his "partners": deputy commissioner Steve Greenberg, outside counsel Harold Tyler, and John Dowd.

"When you hear the judge is deliberating with the prosecutor you know you're in trouble," said Curran.

Harold Tyler hastened to reassure Steve Kaufman, another Steinbrenner lawyer. "The commissioner doesn't really want to hurt George," he said. "Maybe we can give you a preview of the decision and a chance to respond."

That gave the Steinbrenner camp some comfort. Tyler, a former federal judge, was known to be a straight shooter. He seemed to be saying a settlement was available in place of a Vincent thunderbolt. Still, the lawyers continued to work feverishly on Plan B: a suit against Vincent. They wanted it ready to go in a heartbeat if this came down ugly. Steinbrenner's Star Chamber experience made Rose's look like the Warren Court. They too would love to put the process on trial.

It was with some surprise and bewilderment that Kaufman took Harold Tyler's next call. It was late Friday afternoon, July 27, and he wanted Steinbrenner *et al*. at the commissioner's office on Monday morning at nine.

"What's this about?" Kaufman asked.

Tyler said he didn't know.

"Is is about a settlement?"

Tyler again pleaded ignorance.

Nonetheless, Steinbrenner and Kaufman walked into 350 Park Avenue Monday morning assuming that they'd get a tentative reading on Vincent's decision. They were handed a fifty-three-page document containing his final decision. Numbly, they sat down in a conference room to read it. The nub of it was that Steinbrenner would be suspended for two years, followed by three years' probation.

A shaken Kaufman called Curran. "You and Aaron [Rubinstein, a law-firm partner] had better get down here," he said.

Curran raced to join them, ready to pull the trigger on the suit. He thought the penalty draconian and the grounds, as outlined by Vincent, spurious. On top of that, the process had stunk.

Steinbrenner wouldn't hear of suing. Sure he could fight it, he said, but it would be hanging over him for years. Meanwhile, Vincent would be beating him up every chance he got, and he'd be under a cloud. Steinbrenner was particularly obsessed about what this would do to his standing with the U.S. Olympic Committee. He loved being its vice president, and he might have to surrender the post with a baseball suspension pending. No, what he wanted was a deal that would keep some of his ownership rights and keep out the word *suspension*.

They emerged to meet Vincent.

"I can't live with a suspension," he said. "It would hurt me with the Olympic Committee. I wouldn't mind not being general partner; I'm phasing out of the Yankees anyway. But I don't want you to call it that."

"If there's some alternative that's comparable, I'm willing to consider it," said Vincent. "But I'm not going to whitewash it. Why don't you go off into the conference room and see what you can work out with Steve [Greenberg] and Judge Tyler?"

The day wore on, with the two sides batting proposals back and forth. There was endless nit-picking and long waits as the latest drafts were sent out for typing.

They haggled over what aspects of the baseball business Steinbrenner could remain in, settling on broadcast contracts, concessions, lease negotiations, and financing. They worked out language that allowed Steinbrenner to make one of his sons a general partner if he so desired. Steinbrenner seemed almost relieved, noting several times he was sixty years old and had been doing this for seventeen years. It was time to turn this over to his son Hank, who was thirty-three.

Then the big one: Steinbrenner agreed to go on baseball's "ineligible list." This would forbid him from associating with anyone in the game without the commissioner's explicit approval, and it was an open-ended banishment, putting him in baseball purgatory with the likes of Pete Rose. But it removed the word *suspend*.

Vincent had originally set a five o'clock deadline. The negotiating took them beyond that, and it was still dragging along when Vincent's patience ran out. It was about seven, and he'd scheduled an 8:00 P.M. press conference at the Helmsley Palace

Hotel. They'd have to leave soon and he was irritable, exploding at Paul Curran when he tried to rejoin the negotiations.

Vincent looked up from his desk and said, "You're not welcome here."

Curran bit his tongue and walked out.

Steinbrenner and his lawyers were caucusing in the conference room, trying to make a final decision about signing, when Vincent rapped on the glass door. Behind him was a dolly on which rested boxes of his fifty-three-page decision. They were on their way to the Helmsley.

"Time's up," he said. "Apparently you're not going to sign, so we're going to release my decision. If you think differently about it tomorrow or next week or whenever, I'll take your call."

He hobbled down the hall, Greenberg, Tyler, and the box-laden dolly trailing behind. They waited a moment at the elevator bank for the next one down. Then they entered, punched the button for the ground floor, and were watching the doors begin to close when a hand came flying through.

Within a foot of being shut, the doors opened back up. Steve Kaufman was standing there.

"He'll sign," he said.

After just a few more minor changes, he did. The commissioner's lawyers ran off fifty copies for the press and Steinbrenner shouldered his way through the crowds of reporters waiting in front of 350 Park Avenue.

"We're pleased," he said, keeping a promise to low-key it.

Steinbrenner *was* pleased—under the circumstances. He'd preserved his ability to stay involved in important financial areas and he'd kept the franchise in family hands. "George wasn't happy with it, but he could live with it," said Curran.

Then came the press conference. With but little prodding from reporters, Vincent laid out the whole progression of the day's events. He called Steinbrenner's decision "strange" and blurted out the very word he'd just spent nine hours of negotiating to avoid. "Mr. Steinbrenner will have no further involvement in the management of the New York Yankees," said Vincent. "This is a suspension, if you will, on a permanent basis."

Steinbrenner was furious and got more so as Vincent gave follow-up interviews over the next two weeks, rubbing the banished owner's nose in his punishment. "Anybody who [talks with him] is risking his baseball life," he told one interviewer. "The man can't do *anything* without my permission," he told another. "He can't go to spring training without my permission."

Vincent was a hero in precisely the circles he wished to be one. In New York, the announcement touched off a ninety-second standing ovation at that night's Yankees game. Among the Lords, the huzzahs were private but no less heartfelt. They ranked Steinbrenner right up there with Marvin Miller as father of the modern salary structure. There would be no more Pascual Perez horrors out of the Bronx.

That matter dismissed, Fay Vincent was having a marvelous time. He aimed to visit every major league park that season, and he would succeed. Vincent said he wanted to take the game's pulse and check the stadium ambience—Giamatti's word—but mostly he seemed to be thoroughly enjoying himself.

Vincent had a pregame ritual: sitting on a golf cart near the batting cage, answering the local writers' questions, bantering with players and managers, then visiting the umpires' dressing room. He also had a game ritual: hot dogs in the second inning, ice cream in the sixth, and scrupulous neutrality throughout. His only show of support was applauding both teams' home runs.

Like Giamatti, he loved rubbing shoulders with people he'd long admired from afar. When Vincent sat through an Orioles game with Joe DiMaggio, he was reduced to a schoolboy, questioning the legend about everything he'd always wanted to know: the toughest pitcher he'd faced; the way he guessed what pitch was coming; how he hit the knuckleball. Then he rushed to write it all down in the daily journal he kept. Vincent was also tickled to witness a debate between Ted Williams and Warren Spahn on who was dumber, pitchers or hitters. And when Boston catcher Tony Pena pulled a practical joke—coating his palm with pine tar before shaking hands with Vincent—the commissioner was giddy with delight at the one-of-the-guys treatment.

Some owners weren't thrilled with his grand tour of the parks. They considered it a waste of valuable time and wondered if their leader wasn't just a little star struck. Vincent attended Nolan Ryan's three hundredth victory and later talked about the thrill of sitting in the dugout next to him.

"Nolan Ryan's a player," Jerry Reinsdorf told him. "You're the commissioner of baseball. You can't be in awe of a player, I don't care who he is."

But overall, between crises, life was good. Vincent would get calls from top executives he knew, offering to exchange jobs. He turned them down flat. "This is the best job in Western civilization," he declared, "and nobody sits in front of you at the games."

The only seriously discordant note was George Steinbrenner, lurking in the shadows and tossing an occasional rock. Under the terms of their agreement, he couldn't sue Vincent. But he could put up surrogates to sue. Two Yankees limited partners filed suit. So did Leonard Kleinman, whom Steinbrenner nominated to be general partner but whom Vincent rejected.

Steinbrenner was also thought to be the source of gossip-column items that kept popping up about Vincent in the New York newspapers. One, in Cindy Adams's *New York Post* column, told of a lavish Palm Beach party Vincent had supposedly thrown for friends, all paid for with baseball money. In truth, there was a Palm Beach soiree, but it was put on by Major League Properties for its top customers. Vincent was nowhere near it.

Vincent shrugged off Steinbrenner's attacks, variously comparing them to a sinus infection ("It's better some days than others, but it never goes away") and Wagner's music ("It's not as good as it sounds"). Even people who didn't know Richard Wagner from Honus Wagner could enjoy Vincent's dismissive wave of the hand.

One rock did do some damage, however, though it wasn't evident at the time. Steinbrenner's lawyers petitioned the executive council to review his banishment. They laid it all out, from the Roland Thau incident at the start to the rubbing it in at the end. They detailed how Dowd had investigated and Vincent adjudicated and complained bitterly about the mockery they made of due process. They invited the owners to check for themselves—and Jerry Reinsdorf and Bill Bartholomay did.

Bartholomay read their report to the council, and nothing came of it. The aggrieved party was Steinbrenner, after all, and the council wanted to provide no more fodder for his compatriots' suits. But the owners had a universal reaction.

"This is terrible," said Peter O'Malley. "We should destroy the report."

And they did.

$ 22 $

ON THE WALL of Jeff Smulyan's office is a picture of himself careening down white-water rapids in a raft. The terror of the moment is etched in his face; the river churns around him.

That was nothing compared with Smulyan's two and a half years in baseball. He had arrived in Seattle in 1989, a prosperous yuppie with a new toy called the Mariners. In 1992, he left town practically in a barrel, one step ahead of his creditors and two ahead of a lynch mob.

"If somebody had told me any one of a thousand facts I didn't know in August of 1989, would I have bought the Mariners?" he later reflected. "Of course not."

Jeffrey Howard Smulyan was a creature of the eighties. In the first year of that decade, he was a thirty-three-year-old entrepreneur with a crazy dream. He would parlay his experience managing a failed Indianapolis talk-radio station into a radio empire. It was the eighties. There was boundless optimism, endless credit, and wide-open opportunities for a hustler.

In 1980, Smulyan formed a company called Emmis Broadcasting Corporation, which began by purchasing an Indianapolis radio station. Then, in rapid succession, through heavy borrowing, he bought another dozen of them—in Minneapolis, St. Louis, Los Angeles, Washington, and assorted other cities. He capped off the spree in 1988 by acquiring all of NBC's radio stations. Smulyan now had the biggest privately owned radio-broadcasting company in America.

Yet he was still basically an unknown, possessing just three minor claims to fame. He'd given David Letterman his start in talk-radio in Indianapolis. He'd once been *Cosmopolitan*'s Bachelor of the Month. And he'd invented the all-sports radio format, converting New York's WNBC to WFAN. That station became the Mets' radio outlet and gave Smulyan his first taste of the baseball business.

He wanted in. He wanted to tell the world he'd arrived. Ever more, that was the motive for owning a baseball team. Even Peter Ueberroth, who exhorted owners to run their teams like any other business, acknowledged that club ownership was, as he called it, "a vanity investment." The other new entries to Lordship in 1989 illustrated this perfectly.

Eli Jacobs, the new Orioles owner, was a New York leveraged buyout artist. Some rich folks collected Picassos; he collected Washington big shots. His companies' boards were laced with people like Howard Baker, Robert Strauss, and Vernon Jordan. What better venue to collect and cultivate friends than the Memorial Stadium owner's box in Baltimore? On one memorable evening, he would entertain Queen Elizabeth, Prince Philip, President Bush, and a host of other dignitaries. The Orioles' 6–3 loss was rather overshadowed.

The president's son, also named George Bush, led a group that bought the Texas Rangers. Lost for years in the shadow of his father, the First Son's ownership of a baseball team suddenly made him a personage. Actually, he was only one of two general partners, the other one being the brains of the operation. That was Rusty Rose, a Dallas sharpie who'd made a fortune short-selling stock. (He was sometimes called "Rusty the Mortician.") But Bush was the out-front guy, a role in which he exulted.

"Does he know that he doesn't really run this team?" a writer once asked a Rangers official.

"No, no," said the official, "and don't you dare tell him."

Jeff Smulyan did genuinely love baseball. As a boy in Indianapolis, he lay in bed at night listening to two things on the radio: rock music and the San Francisco Giants. His idol was Willie Mays, and he followed his exploits wherever he played, tuning in powerful stations from around the country: WCAU in Philadelphia, WABC in New York, WWL in New Orleans, and more.

Now, at age forty-one, he had the money to play the game as an owner, and Seattle was for sale. It took a brave or foolhardy man to look past its history as a baseball town. The Seattle Pilots, a 1969 expansion team, went bust after one year and moved to Milwaukee. The Seattle Mariners, established in 1977, had never enjoyed a winning year. They'd never even finished the season at the .500 mark. They played in a dreary domed stadium and had never drawn more than 1.3 million.

Smulyan consulted with some of the Lords, including, at great length, Bud Selig and Jerry Reinsdorf. They tried to discourage him, particularly at the asking price of nearly $80 million. "You're getting into something you can't win," they told him, in echoing words. "We don't think baseball can survive in Seattle."

Still, Smulyan heard what he wanted to hear—that some part of the problem in Seattle was owner George Argyros. He was despised as an arrogant, absentee, and tight-fisted owner. His successor would reap enormous goodwill just for not being Argyros. He had jettisoned top players like Mark Langston, cut the payroll to the bone, and didn't much care how anybody felt about it.

"I thought with a little TLC and a totally different approach you could finally make it perform," Smulyan recalled. "I subscribed to the ABA theory—anyone but Argyros. I was wrong."

Smulyan's first mistake was to pay Argyros's price—$77.5 million. His second mistake was to come in at the crest of the baseball economy. The CBS deal would kick in next year, the industry was flush with cash, and he figured the rising tide would lift even a small, leaky ship like Seattle. The third mistake was to believe what he heard about collusion.

The Lords and their lawyers believed that collusion damages wouldn't amount to more than $1 million per club. Based on that assurance, Smulyan didn't try to keep Argyros on the hook to pay them. When the damages came in at $10.8 million in 1990, Smulyan's screams could be heard all up and down Puget Sound.

(The Lords had only themselves to blame, as usual. Their 1989 spending binge handed the union all the ammunition it needed to make an argument: See where salaries would have gone if not for collusion? The higher the post-collusion market went, the bigger the damages got.)

Smulyan wasn't the only new owner to pay for the sins of his predecessor. The Bush-Rose group actually got the Rangers' seller, Eddie Chiles, to agree to contribute on damages but capped his liability at $500,000. They, too, never believed the tab would amount to more than a million per team.

For the Mariners, however, the blow was proportionally bigger than for other clubs. Texas saw about $53 million in annual revenues and turned an annual operating profit of about $3 million. Seattle's revenues were only $35 million—baseball's lowest—and it was harder pressed to cover the unexpected hit.

What was worse, Smulyan soon discovered that he couldn't make the revenue needle move up.

Being a broadcast guy, he was certain that that was one area where he could improve. The team was paid nothing at all for TV rights by its flagship station. It telecast sixty-five games, but the Mariners' only revenues came from selling the beer sponsorship to Anheuser-Busch, for about $1 million. The team had no cable-TV deal, and its radio rights fetched only another $2 million. The grand total of $3 million represented baseball's lowest broadcast take.

Since the city was right in the middle of the fourteen-team American League in TV market size, Smulyan saw no reason he should be bringing up the rear in broadcast revenues. Early on, however, a friend in the TV business gave him the facts of life. "The good news is that you've got a booming market, great disposable income," he said. "The bad news is that the over-the-air guys are Kelly and Gaylord and the cable guys are TCI. They may make you old before your time."

TCI stands for Tele-Communications Inc., the nation's biggest cable company. Like Cablevision in New York, TCI worked both sides of the street. It operated Seattle's cable-TV system and also owned the regional cable-sports channel, Prime Sports Network. But unlike the situation in New York, there was no competing sports service. Prime Sports had no motive to pay up for Mariners games. In fact, it had no interest in paying for them or putting them on at all.

With Smulyan unable to make any inroads on a cable package, he turned his attention to "free" TV, determined to present the stations with some innovative ideas and increase his rights fees. He did some research into other teams' past deals and found that the one he really liked was the Phillies' "Pete Rose play" of 1978. Bill Giles, it will be recalled, got his flagship TV station to put up $600,000 to help the club sign Rose.

Smulyan took a similar idea to a Seattle station.

"We'll buy a free agent, you buy a free agent," he suggested. "You can market the free agent as the Channel Eleven Superstar. That'll be your contract extension. We'll win more games with two new players. Your ratings will go up and you'll make more money."

The reaction? "They yawned," said Smulyan.

He decided he'd have to "induce demand." If he could actually get people excited about the Mariners—a Seattle first—and if he could get attendance up, TV would come around. The stations would *have* to see the value of the games.

Smulyan livened up the Kingdome, splashing more color around it and playing rock music throughout the games at every opportunity. He signed free-agent first baseman Pete O'Brien, which made neither baseball sense (the team already had a good first baseman, Alvin Davis, and another one coming up, Tino Martinez), nor fiscal sense ($7.6 million over four years). But it did signal to fans that Smulyan, unlike Argyros, meant to be competitive. Attendance crept up to 1.5 million in 1990.

Then the Mariners started doing some of the snazziest—certainly the funniest—advertising in baseball. They met head-on what they saw as a central problem: it wasn't hip to be a Mariners fan.

One TV spot was constructed around a clip from Sergei Eisenstein's 1925 silent film *Potemkin*, with the peasant leader shouting a dubbed-in command: "Let's go to the Mariners game!" The peasant masses put their hands on their heads in despair, refusing to go. The leader then talks up new Mariners' players and the newly spruced-up Kingdome. Finally, the masses march happily off to the ballpark.

Another ad played on the fall of the Iron Curtain, with a man saying, in a thick East European accent: "For years we lived without hope. Our lives were so miserable. All of a sudden last year there was a new spirit in the land. There were fireworks, and children were laughing. Even the moose danced on the dugout. Ah, Mariners baseball. What a wonderful time to be alive."

The club's $1 million worth of marketing—moose mascot and all—yielded a record 2.1 million attendance in 1991. (It also didn't hurt that the team posted its first-ever winning record, 83–79.) But it was a record with an asterisk. Between heavy promotion costs and deep discounting (about 950,000 tickets were bargain-priced), said Smulyan, "That was the most expensive audience in the history of the world."

What was worse, the Mariners were falling still further behind financially. When he bought the club, Smulyan figured it was $6 to $9 million below the league average in revenues. By 1991, it was $20 to $22 million below the average and dropping like a stone. And as if the Mariners' handicap in broadcast revenues wasn't enough, a spate of new stadiums was radically changing baseball's economics. As they came on line, Jeff Smulyan made it a point to visit them.

* * *

It was like Dorothy landing on the other side of the rainbow. Toronto's SkyDome was as removed from Seattle's Kingdome as Oz from Kansas. Blue Jays president Paul Beeston gave the grand tour, pausing only to resuscitate Smulyan.

The scale of the place hit him first. At its peak the retractable dome was thirty-one stories high. The DiamondVision scoreboard, designed to hook the video generation, was three times the size of anything he'd seen before. And the 50,000-seat capacity was only the beginning. SkyDome had 168 luxury-suite skyboxes, 7,000 club seats (with waiter service and other amenities), and a Stadium Club with 1,800 members. Then there was a 350-room hotel and acres of restaurants, including a Hard Rock Cafe and North America's biggest McDonald's.

The SkyDome had been built by a consortium of government (the province of Ontario and the city of Toronto chipping in $30 million) and corporate Canada. About thirty Canadian companies—including all three major brewers—contributed $5 million apiece. For their investment, the companies got skyboxes, "preferred-supplier" status, and the privilege to spend still more on stadium signage.

Smulyan noticed a sign on the videoboard for Microsoft, the Seattle-based software giant.

"What's the deal here?" he asked Beeston. "What's that cost?"

"Well, I think the ad is three hundred thousand a year, and they bought a suite." (That would be another $80,000 a year.)

Later, Smulyan called Gary Kaseff, the Mariners' president.

"Gary, how much does Microsoft spend with us?" he asked.

"Let's see, they buy six season tickets a year and they do Microsoft Night, which is 6,000 tickets at three dollars. That's $19,821."

Smulyan would later kvetch at Microsoft. How could they spend so little on baseball in their headquarters town and support it so royally in Canada?

"Well, it's *important* in Canada," the man from Microsoft replied frankly. "Our Canadian division needs to be in there."

He was right. In Toronto, the SkyDome had become a civic monument and the Blue Jays a secular religion. It was a wonderful confluence of circumstance for the franchise, which was engulfed in a torrent of new money. The Blue Jays doubled their gross the SkyDome's first year (in 1989) and became the first franchise to draw 4 million fans (in 1991).

"I'd seen the ultimate marriage between government, which

builds these facilities, and the corporations and the people who tie into them," said Smulyan. "You take the suites, the signage, throw the media on top, and you have an economic juggernaut."

In most cities, however, it was a shotgun marriage. These wondrous new stadiums were often the product of teams' ominous threats to leave. Cities desperate to be "big league" and politicians desperate to avert civic catastrophe were putty in owners' hands. A study would be ordered up proving baseball's importance to the local economy, and the ransom—a new stadium—would then be paid.

Skeptics debunked the economic-impact figures that claimed that teams generated from $50 to $140 million a year in new local spending. Studies done for a Chicago think tank, the Heartland Institute, tore to shreds the conventional wisdom about teams' civic benefits. "One of the most unfortunate wastes of tax dollars today is the subsidized construction of sports stadiums and arenas," said Joseph Bast, the institute's president. "These facilities have become the pyramids of the twentieth century: monuments to the pride of a few, financed by taxes of the many."

But try telling that to a metropolis in the grip of a sports identity crisis. Such a city, in the mid-eighties, was Baltimore. When football's Baltimore Colts literally slunk out of town in the middle of the night in March 1984, its mayor, the flamboyant William Donald Schaefer, was beside himself. Baltimore had earlier lost another big-league franchise, the NBA Bullets. This left them with only one, the Orioles. Baltimore's status as a big-league city was hanging by a thread, and Edward Bennett Williams was refusing to sign anything longer than a one-year lease at Memorial Stadium. The recurring rumor—ever since his 1979 purchase—was that this Washington power broker would ultimately move the team to D.C.

In 1985, Schaefer ordered a task force to get cracking on a new stadium for the Orioles. In 1986, he moved into position to do something about it. He was elected governor of Maryland and quickly began pressing for a new state-funded baseball stadium in Baltimore. Ed Williams, dying of cancer but still formidably persuasive, made his own appeals to the legislators.

The stadium was sure to be costly, and it was highly controversial. "If blackmail is a crime, how come rich and powerful people seem to practice it around here without any problem?" wrote *Baltimore Sun* columnist Roger Simon. "How can we be told that, unless this state builds EBW a new baseball-only stadium, he'll leave town?"

But the stadium passed, to be funded by a new state lottery, and it was soon coming out of the ground. In design, it was diametrically opposite Toronto's. The SkyDome was futuristic. Oriole Park at Camden Yards—the hybrid name finally selected—was a throwback. It was no accident. In planning for the facility, the Orioles brass had looked around the majors and come to a conclusion. The special relationships fans enjoyed with teams like the Cubs, Red Sox, and Yankees stemmed, in some part, from their stadiums: quirky, baseball-only facilities. "The most stable, prosperous, storied franchises had parks with character," recalled club president Larry Lucchino. "We decided that was no coincidence."

The Orioles had to fight for that. The first proposed design came in for a generic 1970s-style stadium. Before a meeting of the Maryland Stadium Authority, where it was to be considered, an agitated Lucchino put brochures for the Yugo automobile at each member's seat. "We don't drive Yugos and we don't want to play in a Yugo," he said. "We want a ballpark."

That was what the Orioles eventually got. It was still under construction as Jeff Smulyan walked the grounds with Lucchino. But from what could already be seen and what the drawings showed, he could tell it was special. There would be a double-decked stadium but with the feel of a low-slung grandstand. The façade and the seats would be a traditional green, and every aisle seat would bear a reproduction of an 1890s-vintage Orioles logo. A huge videoboard would rise above the center-field bleachers, but it would be topped by an old-style clock, to be flanked by two Orioles weather vanes.

The foul territory would be small in this asymmetrical field, keeping fans near the action and reducing dead space to a minimum. Camden Yards had a short right field guarded by a twenty-five-foot-high wall bearing old-fashioned ads and out-of-town scores. Beyond the right-field bleachers loomed the ninety-four-year-old B&O Railroad warehouse. Its proximity would be the capping touch in re-creating a turn-of-the-century, inner-city ballpark.

Yet it was, in the words of one writer, "as if you crossed Fenway Park with a Hyatt Regency hotel." Camden Yards had 72 luxury suites, renting for between $55,000 and $95,000 per season. It included 5,000 club seats for season-ticket holders, which were served by waiters and handy to air-conditioned lounges, if the game or weather grew dreary. For another $500 apiece, the suite-and-club-seat crowd joined the Camden Club, atop the B&O warehouse. (Those who couldn't afford the high life all season could always rent out the stadium's "Frank Robinson Party Suite" by the game.)

Smulyan couldn't help thinking of his pitiful forty suites back at the Kingdome. Only half of them were leased, and only 10 percent of the rental revenue went to the Mariners. These boxes were an afterthought, and looked it, sandwiched under the upper deck so that the overhang made it tough for occupants to follow fly balls. And that, the front-office staffers joked, was the problem with trading away Bill Swift for Kevin Mitchell. They needed sinkerball pitchers like Swift for the sake of skybox fans.

The upscaling of the new baseball parks did draw some criticism. *Washington Post* writer Jonathan Yardley would call Camden Yards "a rich people's park." One stadium architect referred to the separation of the fat cats from the masses as a virtual "caste system."

But at Camden Yards, life wasn't so bad even for the commoners. The stadium had three big deli bars, providing tasty if pricey alternatives to a hot dog. The better fare and the greater number of food stands in the park allowed the Orioles nearly to double their per-capita concession revenue to $9.33, which translated to $13 million a year.

Companies clamored to advertise in the trendiest new spot in Baltimore, to which the Orioles drew 3.6 million fans in their first year there. Stadium signage yielded the Orioles a whopping $5 million a year. The *Baltimore Sun* alone paid $650,000 to be atop the center-field scoreboard. Still, it was another center-field advertiser that presented the ultimate symbol of this park's old-time look and new-age profit. It was for CellularOne, "The Official Cellular Carrier of the Baltimore Orioles."

Finally, Smulyan would visit Chicago and the new Comiskey Park. It was just across the street from the old Comiskey but towered above it both architecturally and in profitability.

For years, the White Sox had been a dicey business proposition. The Northside Cubs were Chicago's fashionable and profitable team. The Southsiders played to blue-collar crowds in the decaying Comiskey Park. The place resonated with history. Mike Veeck once found Shoeless Joe Jackson's original contract in an elevator shaft. But it was of Wrigley Field's vintage without its charm. Comiskey had thousands of obstructed-view seats and needed millions of dollars in refurbishing. Jerry Reinsdorf and Eddie Einhorn poured $20 million into it in their first few years.

Between that investment, Einhorn's failed pay-TV effort, and a sagging attendance, the White Sox were struggling by the mid-eighties. Fan support spiked up to 2.1 million in 1983, when the team won the American League West, and it stayed at that level in 1984. But then it dropped back to 1.4 million in 1985 and slid from there. The White Sox were going so badly that Reinsdorf bought the NBA Chicago Bulls as a hedge.

He also began maneuvering to improve his lot in baseball. Reinsdorf and Einhorn hosted Illinois governor Jim Thompson on Opening Day 1985 and brought up the subject of their Comiskey problem. "Big Jim," as the hulking pol was known, had graduated from Northwestern Law School a year ahead of them. He'd worked on the law journal with Einhorn and kept in touch. He listened closely and sympathetically.

He agreed they needed a new park and said he'd help. But, he added, there was one thing they had to know: "You'll never get one built unless there's a crisis—unless people think you're going to leave if you don't get one."

Chicago got a stadium bill before the Illinois legislature in 1986, but it was turned down flat. The same year, voters in Addison, a suburb west of the city where Reinsdorf had bought land, turned down the opportunity of hosting a stadium. The legislature did approve forming a stadium study committee, but half its members were Jim Thompson appointees and half were Chicago mayor Harold Washington's. It was deadlocked and doomed by politics.

But business was business. Reinsdorf was not the profiteering shark he was widely thought to be. The reputation came largely because, as was once said of Walter O'Malley, he *looked* like capital—a roundish real estate syndicator who smoked big cigars. In truth, Reinsdorf had already made his fortune, selling his Balcor Co. to American Express for $103 million. "I'd rather break even and win than not win and make money," he once explained.

He was in baseball because he thought he'd enjoy it and because, as with Smulyan, it screamed out that this poor Jewish kid, the son of a sewing-machine peddler, had made it. No, Jerry Reinsdorf didn't care about making a lot of money. But sitting around and passively losing money went totally against his grain.

Reinsdorf listened to pitches from Denver, New Orleans, Buffalo, and Washington. But the one that really intrigued him was St. Petersburg. It seemed, at first blush, an unlikely big-league city, known for septuagenarians and somnolence—or, as one wag put it, "a town so dull the roosters sleep till noon." But while Chicago was getting precisely nowhere on a new ballpark, St. Petersburg had built a $100 million domed stadium on spec. Let the economists scoff. St. Pete saw that kind of value in attracting a team and entering the mystical realm of "big league." The Pinellas County Sports Authority had been founded in 1976 for the main purpose of courting major league baseball.

This city was also more than a blue-hair ghetto. It was a gateway to Florida, lush virgin territory for major league baseball. California had five teams; the nation's fourth-biggest state had none. Whoever was in there first owned Florida, for TV purposes. St. Petersburg saw at least $10 million a year in TV money for the White Sox.

By 1988, Reinsdorf was talking seriously to the St. Petersburg crowd, a mix of city-government and private-sector people. (One was his ace reliever Bobby Thigpen's father-in-law, who happened to be president of the local electric utility.) He also let Chicago know just what he was doing. Public passions became aroused. *Chicago Tribune* columnist Mike Royko urged his readers neither to drink Florida orange juice nor to take Florida vacations. When the *Tampa Tribune* suggested their readers retaliate by sending Royko orange seeds, the columnist replied: "Let them send me their orange seeds. I've been to Tampa and St. Petersburg. Everybody down there looks like George Burns. I'd be far more concerned if they sent me their spare teeth."

But it was all going St. Petersburg's way. The Florida legislature authorized $30 million to complete the Suncoast Dome, as the stadium was called. (The city had built the basic structure, but needed the money to fit it out with videoboards, concessions stands, luxury suites, and such.) The White Sox did their own study of the TV market and were even more bullish than the locals. They saw at least $16 million a year, which would vault them into the majors' top ranks of TV revenues. "The greatest opportunity in baseball since Walter O'Malley took the Dodgers west," said one White Sox official.

The analogy seemed apt as the Illinois legislature came down to the last day of its session, June 30, 1988. It had before it a bill authorizing a $150 million stadium for the White Sox. But the chances of passage seemed dim as the day and evening wore on.

Florida TV carried the session live, and the bars in St. Petersburg and Tampa, across the bay, filled up with people watching in giddy anticipation. By Illinois law, no bills could be enacted after midnight, June 30, and the hour was fast approaching.

It was 10:30 P.M. when Big Jim Thompson strode onto the floor of the Senate and started twisting arms. An hour later, the stadium was approved there, 30–26. Thompson raced across the capital rotunda and into the House chamber. He threw off his coat, rolled up his sleeves, and began calling in every damned chit that was owed him.

But at 12:00 A.M., Central Time, Thompson was still short of the sixty votes needed. Cheers rang across Tampa Bay—but Florida didn't know Illinois politics. The clock on the House floor had been turned off, the deadline ignored. A few minutes after midnight, Thompson picked up his sixtieth vote. The stadium was approved, 60–55, and the House Majority Leader declared the time 11:59 P.M.

Big Jim Thompson wore an ear-to-ear grin. The good people of St. Petersburg looked on in stunned disbelief. Jerry Reinsdorf got the gold mine, and they got the shaft.

The lease Reinsdorf got from the Illinois Sports Authority deserved immediate induction into the Sweetheart-Deal Hall of Fame. The White Sox would get the new Comiskey rent-free up to 1.2 million in attendance each year. Above that, the Illinois Sports Authority got $2.50 a ticket. The White Sox would also give the authority 35 percent of its broadcast and advertising revenues over $10 million. But the White Sox got back $5 million a year for upkeep, repairs, and insurance. After the first ten years of the twenty-year lease, the authority would buy 300,000 tickets if attendance fell below 1.5 million.

There seemed little danger of that, judging from the new Comiskey's inaugural season, when the White Sox drew a club-record 2.9 million. The key wasn't the total number of tickets sold, however, but the *kind* of tickets sold. Old Comiskey had only 7,000 seats good enough to command premium prices; new Comiskey had 22,000. Old Comiskey had 36 luxury suites, new Comiskey 85, with the capacity to expand to 106.

The bad news was for the Joe Sixpacks of Chicago and environs, once the franchise's bread-and-butter. All those box seats extended Comiskey's lower deck way back from the field. All those luxury suites were sandwiched on two levels between the lower and upper decks. The poor slobs up top were halfway to

Addison. The last row of seats in old Comiskey's upper deck was closer to the field than the first row of new Comiskey's upper deck.

Anyone who tired of following the little figures on the diamond could always go downstairs to one of the two big retail outlets. There he could browse for White Sox Christmas ornaments, White Sox shot glasses, White Sox trash cans, White Sox inflatable baseball bats, or actual bricks from the old Comiskey, at $12.95 each.

"Comiskey is a baseball emporium for the nineties," wrote one scribe, not completely in admiration, "a baseball mall, a place where you can root, root, root for the home team while the home team roots through your pockets, searching for the treasure it needs to pay $5 million for a pitcher."

Jerry Reinsdorf read and heard the barbs, and they bothered him not a bit. He'd been rich and he'd been poor and rich was better. In new Comiskey's first season, he cleared a $22 million operating profit. After years of struggling to break even, he had baseball's second most profitable team in 1991.

Jeff Smulyan thanked him for the tour, bade him farewell, and returned to Seattle, shaken.

"I had seen the future," he later said, and he was scared to death *he* was history. Still more of these new mega-parks were coming on line. He hadn't even seen what was happening in Cleveland, Denver, or Arlington, Texas, all in earlier stages of development. *My God*, he thought, *we could be $40 million below the average revenues. It's an economic nightmare.*

Nonetheless, he was determined to try to succeed. The priority was to take another crack at TV, and he saw a window of opportunity. The 1991 Mariners had their first-ever winning team—had even surged briefly into pennant contention. Ken Griffey, Jr., was emerging as a superstar. The crowds, albeit at discounts, packed the Kingdome. The TV ratings, which languished at around four in 1989 and rose to about seven in 1990, were now coming in at eleven and twelve. Smulyan thought he could surely get a better deal now.

But during a late-May series against the Rangers, with first place at stake, he sat in his owner's box and heard the brutal truth from the man from Seattle's biggest TV station: $20,000 a game for forty games was all he could do. Smulyan didn't need a calculator to figure the total: $800,000. That was even behind where he was now.

"I don't get it," he said. "George Bush just got a hundred thousand dollars a game for the Rangers! Baseball has no value here? If that's the best you can do, I'd rather take snapshots and walk around downtown with them, telling people about the game."

The reality was that baseball still had little value there as TV programming. It wasn't that it was a bad sports town. The NFL Seahawks had a waiting list of 20,000 for season tickets. The NBA SuperSonics would draw an average of 14,313 per game that year, in an arena with an official capacity of only 14,253. But fifteen years of godawful teams doomed the Mariners. Perhaps teams in old-line baseball-mad cities could go through such a fallow run and still have a following. But not in Seattle.

"It's not you, Jeff; it just doesn't matter out here," one corporate executive told Smulyan. "It's not an enterprise that people wrap themselves around out here. If you won four or five pennants that would be another thing."

While Seattle's revenues were stuck at $35 million, its costs were soaring. Argyros had reduced the team's payroll to a rock-bottom $8 million in 1989, for quick sale. By 1992, it was up to $23 million. Smulyan hadn't gone wild in the free-agent market, except for the Pete O'Brien misadventure. He'd merely been caught in the updraft of the greatest, quickest run-up of baseball salaries ever.

In 1989, when he bought the Mariners, the average baseball player's salary was $489,000. By 1991, it had risen 80 percent, to $880,000. By 1992, the average salary would reach $1 million. That year, 174 players made more than $2 million, up from only 29 in 1990. It was a hyperinflation worthy of Bolivia.

The biggest economic shocks came in 1990 and 1991, when even average players joined superstars in the penthouse and salary arbitration became still more monstrous.

Jose Canseco set the tone in mid-1990, flying past the $4 million barrier only seven months after the first breaching of the $3 million mark. He signed a five-year contract with Oakland averaging $4.7 million per, and Darryl Strawberry nearly matched it in November with a five-year contract with the Dodgers averaging an annual $4 million.

But the truest indicator of hyperinflation was a certain mediocre thirty-three-year-old pitcher. He'd compiled only a lifetime record of 83–82 with a 3.70 ERA, yet in November 1990 San Francisco signed the lefty to a four-year contract worth $2.5 million per season. The 1990–91 signing season was to become known as "the Bud Black market."

It was incredible. A year earlier, Orel Hershiser and Frank Viola were baseball's top-paid pitchers. Suddenly Bud Black was their salary equal. Other pitchers moved quickly to cash in, using the baseline he'd set. On one November day, Tom Browning, Mike Boddicker, and Danny Jackson signed contracts that guaranteed them a combined $32 million. Dennis Martinez and Jose Rijo signed multiyear $3 million-plus deals soon thereafter.

In fairness, it could just as well have been called "the Darren Daulton market." In early November, the oft-injured catcher and career .227 hitter signed a three-year $6.75 million deal with the Phillies. That just as surely set a standard for better players to top—like 1990 batting champ Willie McGee (four years, $13 million), 1989 MVP Kevin Mitchell (four years, $15 million), and Gold Glove third baseman Terry Pendleton (four years, $11.2 million).

Bud Black was the preferred symbol, however, because his contract was the handiwork of Al Rosen. The Giants' president was considered the Typhoid Mary of GMs. His loopy contracts could—and often did—infect a whole winter's signings. Since Rosen refused to go to salary arbitration, feeling it only caused hard feelings, the lofty contracts he negotiated instead hurt every other owner's arbitration cases.

There was, for instance, the Jose Uribe signing, when the Giants shortstop was coming off 1989 numbers of .221 and 30 RBIs. He was a decent shortstop, but was he really worth $3.85 million over three years? At about the same time, his double-play partner, Robby Thompson, inked a four-year, $5.9 million deal. They were staggering figures for mediocre middle-infielders, promptly raising the salary bar for all stripes of middle-infielders.

Rosen's 1990 contract with Will Clark raised the high-water mark for salaries at the time—$15 million for four years—and raised eyebrows all over baseball. Clark was a legitimate star, but he was also just a three-year man. If the idea behind long-term deals was to lock up players and prevent free agency (as most GMs thought), the deal defied logic. It only deferred Clark's ability to walk for one year. It was an incredible premium to pay to keep this first baseman wrapped up through his seventh year instead of his sixth.

Rosen's Matt Williams deal was also a wonder. He gave the third baseman a two-year, $2.6 million contract after just two years in the bigs: $600,000 for 1991 and $2 million for 1992. The first year was particularly high, since Williams wasn't even eligible for salary arbitration. Naturally, every third baseman who *was* eligible for salary arbitration keyed off those numbers.

Rosen was an agent's best friend, the go-to guy when a pigeon was needed. Agent Dennis Gilbert was once talking with an owner about the big salary he hoped to fetch for a client. He admitted, since the owner was a disinterested party, their target figure was starting to look too high. Then, as they spoke, word came in of another Giants mega-signing. Gilbert let loose with a heartfelt "Thank you, Al Rosen."

One theory was that, as a former player, he simply liked players too much. Rosen played a fine third base for the Indians for ten years and was American League MVP in 1953, when he led the league in homers and RBIs. But that alone didn't explain it, since lots of former players were mean as snakes as GMs (see Paul Richards, Ralph Houk, Eddie Lopat, *et al.*). The alternative theory was that he'd been trained in the negotiating art by George Steinbrenner, for whom he'd worked in the late seventies as the Yankees' president.

Suffice it to say the other GMs didn't quite know how to react when, at the 1990 winter meetings, Rosen addressed a press conference and lamented runaway salaries. Laugh? Cry? Go right for his throat? The man who'd just committed $33 million to three players—including Bud Black—was heard to say: "For a hundred years we couldn't find a way to destroy this game, but now I think we've found the key. It's disastrous."

It was hypocritical blather, of course, and dismissed as such.

The more meaningful commentary here would come behind closed doors. After twenty-two years as the Expos' owner, Charles Bronfman had decided to get out. It wasn't because he could no longer afford it. He did have the Seagrams distilling fortune to fall back on. It was because he could no longer stand it. Between the never-ending battles with players and the growing discord among owners, this was no longer fun.

"Today baseball is big business," he said in a farewell address to the Lords. "Revenues are exceedingly strong, but expenses may soon choke many of us. Players' salaries at the major league level have lost not only all sense of proportion but sense of reason. Occasionally one gets lucky, as did the Dodgers with Kirk Gibson. But the financial enticement to win is so strong that we all roll the dice every year to the benefit, at the end of the day, of very few indeed.

"Surely we are not so arrogant that we cannot learn from others. The NBA has evolved a formula. It may not be perfect, but it works. I beg you. Take that formula, refine that formula, share revenues with the players, and reward them handsomely on a basis that is economically fair to all—club, player, and public. There is so much more than economics to be considered. There is our society."

Bronfman would get a strong round of applause but no appreciable action. As he reflected on baseball, two years after leaving it, the battles still raged and his disgust was still evident.

"I have regretted it always," he said, "not only that we get into bitter disputes but that both sides are so silly. We get into an adversarial posture over something neither side owns. The owners don't own the game; the players don't own the game; the North American public owns it."

The financial consequences of that winter's salary-arbitration season would be particularly great. The biggest paycheck ever to come out of arbitration, until then, was Don Mattingly's 1987 win: $1.975 million. In 1991, *eleven* players would shoot to top that.

The biggest number of all, $3.35 million, was on the head of Doug Drabek. The Lords thought it audacious. There was no question that the Pirates pitcher had been great in 1990. He won the Cy Young Award, going 22–6 with a 2.76 ERA, pitching Pittsburgh to the National League East title. He'd put together three consecutive stellar seasons, in fact, and was a great competitor with a nasty slider.

But he was also just a four-year man, and now he wanted to triple his 1990 pay of $1.1 million. Pittsburgh was only willing to double it, to $2.3 million. When the numbers were filed, the baseball world gasped. The million-dollar spread was the biggest ever in salary arbitration. As recently as 1984, the total spread for a whole *season* of salary-arbitration cases was $1.3 million.

Drabek was represented by the redoubtable Randy Hendricks. His aim was to break his client loose from being compared to other young pitchers, who indeed did not make that kind of money. In the 1985 labor contract, the Lords had moved to prevent any more Bruce Sutter–style breakthroughs. They insisted—and the union agreed—that players could only be compared with others in their "class" (that is, four-year men with four-year men) or with players just one class up from them.

There was one exception: players of "special achievement" could have more latitude.

And this, according to Randy Hendricks, Doug Drabek was. He and his staff, which now included stats whiz Bill James, would spend months preparing exhibits to prove it. The sophistication of arbitration cases had accelerated, with a massive arms buildup of computer software on both sides. Advocates for both player and club could make the numbers sing, dance, and prove just about anything they wanted. Both sides brought 40-megabyte laptop computers to the hearings, the better to develop instant killer rebuttals. In the words of Padres GM Joe McIlvaine, "It was a statistical orgy."

Hendricks realized that in order to portray Doug Drabek as a "special achiever," he would have to fashion statistical categories that put his client in the best light—and in the company of high-paid veteran pitchers. One was "pitchers with career winning percentages of at least .600" (with a minimum 1,000 innings pitched). Drabek, at 69–45 and .605, was just behind high-paid vets Dwight Gooden, Roger Clemens, Teddy Higuera, and Bob Welch, and just ahead of Tom Browning and Orel Hershiser. Another was Hendrick's "Iron Man" category—pitchers who'd logged at least 675 innings the past three seasons. Ranked in ascending order of ERA, Drabek was number two to Clemens. The rest were also high-paid vets: Dennis Martinez, Frank Viola, Dave Stewart, Bruce Hurst, and so on down the line.

Hendricks would also haul lesser pitchers into his argument in order to show the pitiful inadequacy of the Pirates' $2.3 million offer. How could anyone, he asked, put Doug Drabek on the same salary plane as Zane Smith ($2.65 million) or Jim Deshaies ($2.1 million)? He also skillfully wove in the one-year, $2.4 million contract the Cubs had given Greg Maddux last year. It was a positively Al Rosen-ish contract, since Maddux was only a three-year man, but it was another brick in Drabek's case.

Then Hendricks put the finishing touch on his Drabek preparations. He approached the agents' other favorite pigeon, Lou Gorman. He'd been a front-office operative for nearly thirty years, with stops in Baltimore, Kansas City, Seattle, and New York (the Mets), before being named Boston's GM in 1984. He, no doubt, would have been perfectly fine for the job in pre-*Messersmith* days. Gorman was once a farm-system director for the Orioles and Royals, a good evaluator and developer of talent.

But when it came to the GM skills of the nineties, he was hopeless.

Mike Greenwell's agent once landed him a big contract by presenting Gorman with the Elias rankings, a composite statistical analysis, compiled by the Elias Sports Bureau. It ranked him number seven among the AL's outfielders, first basemen, and designated hitters. No matter that nobody paid much heed to the Elias rankings, or that Greenwell was only a two-year man. Greenwell got an easy, and for then princely, $500,000.

Gorman was just an affable sort, whose temperament was ill suited to confrontations or hardball negotiations. (He was known around baseball as "Good-Good," which were the words he constantly murmured.) In salary-arbitration hearings, he had to be restrained from nodding along in agreement as the player's side presented its case.

If an agent needed to make a market, Lou Gorman was his man. The Red Sox were rich and he was easy. The Boston club once shot a $3 million-a-year offer at Kent Hrbek, which the first baseman leveraged into a handsome five-year contract extension with Minnesota. They floated a $33 million offer for Kirby Puckett, giving him all the ammunition he needed to wiring another $2.5 million out of the Twins. (Minnesota only wound up at $30 million, but it was there, not Boston, that Puckett really wanted to play.)

There was only one way to get richer than by using Lou Gorman as a straw man, and that was to get signed by Lou Gorman. He gave Al Rosen a run for his money at the 1990 winter meetings, committing $27 million to three free agents: pitcher Matt Young, who was 51–78 lifetime with a 4.26 ERA; Jack Clark, whose offensive pop was waning at age thirty-five; and Danny Darwin, a thirty-five-year-old hybrid starter-reliever who'd never had more than 13 wins or 8 saves in a season. Darwin got the biggest contract of all, four years and $11.8 million. His agents were the brothers Hendricks.

Now Randy Hendricks turned to Gorman on another front. Boston's Roger Clemens was another client, and his contract was up after the 1991 season. At $2.6 million a year, it was baseball's biggest when signed two years before. Now it was only the fourth-biggest salary on his own team.

Hendricks had a little message for Gorman. It was now or never. Either they worked out a contract extension over this winter or Clemens would rocket off to another team as a free agent at the end of 1991.

Clemens was, in a word, the Franchise. His lifetime 116–51 record was the best winning percentage in Red Sox history. He'd gone 21–6 in 1990 with a 1.93 ERA, the lowest in the American League in twelve years. He was a big star on an otherwise blah club.

In fairness, this message wasn't first delivered on the eve of arbitration. The brothers Hendricks and the Boston GM began seriously talking contract at the winter meetings in early December, though they were far apart. The agents wanted Clemens to become baseball's highest-paid player again, eclipsing Jose Canseco's $4.7 million. The Red Sox were offering to make him baseball's highest-paid *pitcher*, a difference of $1 million a year.

They kept talking, meeting the day of the Boston baseball writers' banquet in early January, but remaining apart. Later that month, Hendricks also pressed Boston's general partner John Harrington to "get it done," and the gap started to narrow. Finally, Lou Gorman did what he did best: caved. On February 8, Clemens signed a four-year deal for $21.5 million, restoring him to baseball's penthouse as the first $5 million-a-year player. Boston fans, who'd been agog in 1968 at Carl Yastrzemski's $100,000 salary, would now watch a man who earned that much in a week.

Doug Drabek's arbitration hearing was five days later. The Clemens signing wasn't the cornerstone of Randy Hendricks's case, but it was a wonderful capstone. It underscored his central point: premier pitchers commanded premier salaries. It reinforced all those comparative charts that put Drabek alongside Clemens. Indeed, it made Drabek's $3.35 million filing seem downright reasonable. Drabek won the case.

It was 70 percent higher than Mattingly's old salary-arbitration record, and it immediately set other dominoes toppling. Greg Swindell, an Indians pitcher and fellow Hendricks client, won his arbitration case and $2 million. Chuck Finley, an Angels pitcher and fellow Hendricks client, settled his case on highly favorable terms, for $2.5 million.

All across baseball, the Lords screamed bloody murder. The brothers Hendricks had filed the big salary-arbitration numbers, knowing Clemens's contract would support them. Nobody denied Randy Hendricks's formidable powers in a hearings room—he hadn't lost a case in six years—but in the words of Frank Casey, the lawyer handling the Swindell case for the Indians, "One Clemens signing was worth five Clarence Darrows in the hearing room."

The Drabek decision was a body blow to the Pirates, a club whose revenues ran barely ahead of Seattle's. They *won* their arbitration cases against Barry Bonds and Bobby Bonilla but still gave them raises of 170 and 92 percent, respectively. The 200 percent raise for Drabek would blow their 1991 budget out of the water.

Drabek's $3.35 million mark would also set a high baseline for next year's top players in salary arbitration. In 1992, three players would eclipse Drabek's record, topped by Ruben Sierra's $5 million. The agents could hardly wait.

Stan Kasten, the Braves' president, liked to explain it with a parable—whenever, that is, he wasn't expressing it in a primal scream. "A king grants a wish," he said. "He will give his subject a penny and double it every day for a month. Do you know what the last payment is? *Five million dollars.* That's what happened here. Once the ball started rolling, it just picked up steam."

The Pirates were one of ten teams that slid into the red in 1991. The baseball industry as a whole was breaking even, but the fortunes of its haves and have-nots were growing ever further apart. Between the wildly different stadium and TV deals, the gap between the team with the biggest gross (Los Angeles) and the smallest (Seattle) had now grown to $80 million. In 1980, the difference was $10 million. The payrolls of three teams—the A's, the Red Sox, and the Dodgers—now exceeded the Mariners' total revenues.

By late 1991, Jeff Smulyan was tapped out with his bankers, who had demanded a $39 million loan repayment by early 1992. He was also hurting at his Emmis Broadcasting, which was suffering through the same ad slump that had cut into his TV revenues. And he was just plain tired of trying to make an impossible situation work. The eighties were long gone, and the nineties looked ugly, particularly in a small-market baseball town.

Smulyan had adopted Jerry Reinsdorf as his rabbi and role model, and now he would adopt the Reinsdorf approach. He told the city's business leaders he needed a guaranteed $13 million-a-year revenue increase or the Mariners as a team would become a "free agent." Then Smulyan did something else. He began secret meetings with the good people of St. Petersburg.

They were, as always, motivated. The Suncoast Dome remained empty, following the city's stunning failure to get a National League expansion team. Yes, St. Pete was told, this was a great market and a fine facility and their turn would come. But the fellow with the video chain in Miami had more money. That was, after all, what the expansion process was about—who could fork over the most money. That was also why it aroused the Lords' passions so and began to turn a whole passel of them against Fay Vincent.

$ 23 $

BASEBALL NEVER HANDLED expansion very well, mostly because baseball didn't *like* expansion. For sixty years the majors comprised sixteen teams, and the Lords liked it just fine that way. From 1961 to 1993, that number would grow by 75 percent—though grudgingly at each step along the way. To baseball, expansion was never the pursuit of new opportunities; it came always as a response to a problem.

The first round of it could be traced directly to the flight west of the Dodgers and the Giants. New York was trying to rustle up a new team; congressional committees were investigating the deed; and in the ferment, something called the Continental League emerged. It was the first serious effort to form a third major circuit since the demise of the Federal League in 1915.

The brand-new eight-team Continental League seemed ready to go in the late fifties, and it had the Lords spooked. Branch Rickey was involved—it was his last hurrah, his little revenge on Walter O'Malley. Also in on it was William A. Shea, a powerful New York lawyer who knew how to shake the money tree. Finally, to get the Mahatma and the Congress off their backs, the Lords agreed to add four teams in 1961 and 1962. The Continental League never did play a game (though, in the process, Shea got a stadium named after him), but it changed the face of baseball.

Later in the decade, Charlie Finley was the culprit. After his 1968 move of the A's to Oakland brought down the wrath of Missouri senator Stuart Symington, the American League got an expansion team into Kansas City faster than you could say "antitrust exemption." The owners hastily put a companion team in Seattle, at the same time, in 1969, which was a mistake. The Seattle Pilots went bust after a single season, after which they moved to Milwaukee and became the Brewers.

That touched off a long-running lawsuit against baseball by

Seattle (King County, to be precise), which forced another round of expansion in 1977. The Seattle Mariners were created that year to make the suit go away.

Now Congress was forcing a new round of expansion. Peter Ueberroth had committed to it on Capitol Hill in the mid-eighties. By the late eighties, senators from baseball-starved states were pressing the Lords to make good. The "A-word" was occasionally mentioned.

Bart Giamatti was grilled by them less than a month before he died, taking time out from the Pete Rose wars to attend a hearing. The Senate was actually pressing for *six* new teams. Giamatti fenced with them in his inimitable style, citing the dilution problems they faced.

"Hitting a major league fastball, sir, is perhaps the most difficult act in American sport," he told one congressional interrogator. "Major league baseball players of the kind of quality the American people have had every right to expect since 1876 are scarce items. One must be responsible, deliberate, and prudent."

Responsibly, deliberately, prudently—and totally unenthusiastically—the National League later that year announced a two-team expansion, to take place in 1993.

There were many reasons for the Lords to loathe expansion. It spread a thin talent pool even thinner, which drove up demand for players and increased the upward pressure on salaries. It removed some of the scarcity that undergirded the value of the franchises. When a city without a team—like St. Petersburg—made a play for another city's team—like the White Sox—it opened up delicious possibilities, as we have seen. When that former "open city" was blessed with an expansion team, however, a handy source of leverage was gone.

Expansion teams forced baseball to cut up the national-TV pie into ever thinner slices. The new clubs packed crowds in at home—at least until the novelty wore off—but they were death on the road. Teams loved to host the Yankees, whose appeal couldn't be diminished even by George Steinbrenner. But they couldn't get people in for a Mariners game at gunpoint. Midway through Toronto's first season, the club's president, Peter Bevasi, observed, "We've been through thirteen Bat Days so far this year."

To revenge themselves on the expansion teams, the Lords made sure the newcomers were put at a severe disadvantage. The 1977 entries didn't receive network TV money their first three years. The 1993 entries only had to go one season without network money, but it was a big one—the last year of CBS's mega-contract. In the amateur draft, the talent-starved expansion clubs got the last picks. In the assignment of minor league affiliates, they got the leftovers. A club in Miami would be stuck with a triple-A affiliate in Edmonton (that's right, in Alberta, Canada). "The name of the game in baseball," said Carl Barger, the Miami club's president—until he died of a heart attack at the '93 winter meetings—"is 'do it to the expansion teams.' "

It became as durable a baseball tradition as the seventh-inning stretch. The owners didn't perfect "doing it to the expansion teams" right off. The American League mistakenly made the rules for its first expansion draft too liberal, and the expansion Angels grabbed such good players as shortstop Jim Fregosi and pitcher Dean Chance. They made a good run in 1961, finishing with seventy wins, and shot all the way up to third place their second year.

The National League owners went to school on that. They weren't about to part with any of their clubs' good players, and they restricted their expandees to picking from only fifteen available players per club—the designated dregs. Paul Richards, the new Houston team's GM, walked out of the owners' meeting after hearing the draft rules and into a group of waiting reporters. "Gentlemen," he announced, "we've just been fucked."

That draft produced the 1962 Mets, who went 40–120, finishing sixty and a half games out of first place and eighteen games out of ninth. They began the season by losing nine straight and ended it by hitting into a triple play. This was the team of Casey Stengel, Marvelous Marv Throneberry, Choo Choo Coleman, and two pitchers named Bob Miller, who went a combined 3–14. To the fans, the Amazin' Mets were lovable buffoons. To the Lords, they were a hearty new colony of the "do it to the expansion teams" ethos.

The rites of expansion were one of the few things the Lords could unify behind—until 1990, that is. The problem was the newcomers' entry fee, which in past drafts was modest: $2 million in the early sixties, and still only $7 million as late as 1977. The fees were divvied up within the expanding league; it made the owners feel a little better about welcoming the new lodge members.

The ante would rise sharply for the 1993 National League entries, and for two good reasons. First, the incumbents needed the money. And second, the incumbents wanted to boost the value of their own franchises at the expense of the expansion teams. The expansion fee was arrived at in baseball's usual scientific manner. A four-member committee (three owners and Bill White) oversaw the expansion process. At one meeting, each wrote a suggested fee on a slip of paper and tossed it onto the table. Their figures ranged from $50 to $100 million; the committee settled on $95 million.

It was a wildly high number—only one team had ever sold for that much: the Mets, for $100 million—and the American League owners, when they saw what was developing, were desperate to get a piece of that $190 million. They needed the money, maybe even more than the National Leaguers. Two thirds of the American League was made up of small-market clubs. Getting a cut of the NL's beefy expansion fees wouldn't solve their fundamental problems, but it would help until a meaningful solution could be found.

The National League told them to get lost. They hadn't even *wanted* to expand. If this was going to be their cross to bear, it would be their money to keep. Peter O'Malley and Bill White were particularly adamant. "If there'd been a vote, [expansion] would have been turned down," said White, who summarized his first reaction to the American League this way: "Okay, if you guys want to expand, *you* do it and keep *all* the money."

But since that wasn't an option, the National League owners finally agreed to try negotiating a split. The AL had to give its assent on new cities, after all, and could throw a monkey wrench into the process, if sufficiently peeved. The Pirates' Doug Danforth and the Padres' new owner, Tom Werner, would carry their banner; the Brewers' Bud Selig and the Orioles' Eli Jacobs the American League's. If they couldn't agree on anything by June 1991, the dispute would be dropped into Fay Vincent's lap.

That was when two new teams were to be selected. Baseball tried to make the expansion process sound scientific, with much talk of TV markets and demographics, but it was permeated with politics. H. Wayne Huizenga, the Miami hopeful, was a great pal of Pirates president Carl Barger, who was on the board of Huizenga's Blockbuster Entertainment Corporation, the video chain that had just struck a great deal (for baseball) to distribute highlights tapes. Herb Kohl, the key man in a St. Petersburg ownership group, was one of Bud Selig's oldest, dearest friends. They'd gone together to the first game the Braves ever played in Milwaukee.

The winnowing process was also marked by a few personal quirks. The owners were having one meeting to review the early candidates, when Gene Autry took the floor.

"Buffalo," he said. "I played in Buffalo in 1939 and we had twelve thousand people and it was a very good crowd." He went down the whole list, rating each city according to how he was received during his touring days. Everybody gave him a nice hand at the end.

Picking the cities (Miami, because Huizenga could "write the check," and Denver, because it was virgin western territory) was easier than settling the internecine fee war. The American League offered to contribute 50 percent of the players for expansion in return for 50 percent of the fees. The National League replied, "Forget it."

Talks dragged on. It turned out that the Lords didn't negotiate with one another any better than they did with the players. The negotiating teams had to bring each proposal and counterproposal back to be mulled by the whole group, where debate would shoot off on tangents or dissolve into *ad hominem* attacks. "One of your guys cost us eleven million apiece," screamed the American Leaguers, referring to Philadelphia's Bill Giles. (He'd given all-too-candid testimony during the collusion hearings, in the eyes of some fellow owners. This somewhat overstated the testimony's importance, but that made no difference to scapegoat-minded Lords, who were out that sum in damages.)

The National League's last, best offer was to share 30 percent of the fees. The AL owners, thinking they could do better by Vincent, turned it down. He'd given every sign of being sympathetic to their side. After voicing his opinions on the subject at some meetings, Vincent was privately, snidely called by the National Leaguers "the American League counsel."

So into Vincent's lap it dropped. He held a three-hour hearing, at which AL president Bobby Brown led the argument for his constituents, NL counsel Bob Kheel for his. When it was over, Vincent was urged by some—including Mets president Fred Wilpon—to throw it right back into the owners' court. This was clearly a no-win situation for him.

But Vincent loved playing the judge. He wallowed in the quasi-judicial process of the Rose and Steinbrenner affairs, and delighted in penning long, legalistic opinions. He inserted himself into a discipline case against umpire Joe West, overruling the decision of a livid Bill White. Vincent was disgusted with the owners' inability to work things out but had no capacity to resist getting involved.

In mid-June, at an owners' meeting in Santa Monica, he issued his decision. It was seven pages long and read, as always, like the opinion of an appellate court. The owners ignored the elegant reasoning and went right to the bottom line. Vincent had given 22 percent of the expansion fees to the American League. Each club would get $3 million and lose three players in the expansion draft. In the future, he wrote, expansion fees were to be split fifty-fifty.

The air was blue in the American League owners' caucus. They'd turned over the decision to Vincent, sure they'd get a better deal, and they'd come out worse. They were giving up 54 percent of the players and getting 22 percent of the cash. Where did he come off with that *future* fifty-fifty split? They hoped to hell this was the last expansion in their lifetime. There was talk of blocking the National League's entry to Florida, since it required majority assent of the American League. There were mutterings about firing Vincent. Bobby Brown—angry too, but ever courtly—tried to get them to calm down.

Some never would. Jackie (Mrs. Gene) Autry, running the Angels in the Cowboy's dotage, turned against Vincent for good. So did the Twins' Carl Pohlad, who'd been dismayed at Vincent's lockout performance and was now appalled at his expansion reasoning. Pohlad had formed a caucus of small-market owners who met regularly and wrung their hands furiously. ("It kept growing," cracked charter-member Smulyan, "basically because it consisted of clubs losing money.") It was those owners—even Vincent's good friends Eli Jacobs and George Bush—who were most upset.

Pohlad's GM, Andy MacPhail, exploded in public and framed the issue at length in Peter Gammons's widely read *Boston Globe* and *Baseball America* columns:

"This is a calamity to the small-market clubs that have to depend on hard work and development to survive," he said. "To clubs like ours, Texas, Cleveland and Seattle, which don't have the market size to afford—like the Dodgers and Red Sox—to write off mistakes, this is a blatant slap in the face. I love baseball, but my entire life at the ballpark has been in a working capacity, both growing up with my father when he was a general manager and since I've been in the game. It's been business, so I've never had the luxury of viewing the game from the romantic and aesthetic standpoint. I really don't think Fay thought this out. It shows the need for him to get someone in the office with a more practical baseball understanding.

"What is equitable about this? We provide 54 percent of the players and get $1 million a player. The National League clubs get $6 million a player to replenish their coffers and make up for the cost. We spend $6 million a year in scouting and development, and if we produce two good players a year, we are doing our job. Losing three players in a small market and not getting compensated is a major loss. The Dodgers or Red Sox can eat the losses. We can't. We couldn't afford to gamble $800,000 on a John Candelaria; we wanted him, but we couldn't afford $800,000. Texas has had to juggle its roster and payroll to keep at $20 million.

"Fay has polarized the leagues and the conflicts within the leagues. But maybe he doesn't understand the cost of replacing the players."

MacPhail was a much-respected GM, en route to winning it all that year. He took some calls congratulating him on the blunt words. Then he took another one in his Cleveland hotel room, where he was on the road with the Twins.

"I want you here Tuesday," said Fay Vincent.

"Well, I'm going to be there starting Thursday for a Yankees series," said MacPhail. "Can't it wait?"

"No," said the chilly voice. They set up a time for Tuesday.

Andy MacPhail walked into 350 Park Avenue nervous but ready. He'd had his office fax him data that documented their scouting and development costs and their farm system's yield. Maybe he could have a productive dialogue.

He did not.

First, Vincent upbraided him for going public with Gammons. "If you've got a complaint, pick up the phone and call me," he said.

Second, he disagreed with MacPhail's analysis. "If you put eight hundred thousand dollars into your house, that doesn't mean it's worth eight hundred thousand," he said. "It's what somebody wants to pay you."

MacPhail tried to recite the facts he'd brought with him and to make his points about small-market economics. He didn't get far.

"I know what I'm doing," said Vincent. "*I know what I'm doing.* I can have you fined and suspended for criticizing the commissioner. I can show you the rule."

MacPhail felt anger surge through him. *What goddamned country am I in here, anyway?*

"Do what you're going to do and let me out," he said.

Vincent backed off, and they managed to complete the meeting more or less civilly. The commissioner obviously wasn't going to hand the GM his head, and the GM obviously wasn't going to change the commisioner's mind. But MacPhail did try to impress upon him that he wasn't just idly popping off.

"I'll tell you how strongly I feel about it," he said. "I'll give you back the three million dollars and I'll take the players."

MacPhail was not the only American Leaguer to make that offer, but it did no good. The deal had gone down, and so had Vincent's stock.

Up until then he was on good terms with most of the American League owners. Selig and Reinsdorf had swept him into office. Jacobs and Bush were good friends. Walter Haas and Ewing Kauffman were old-school gentlemen who meshed well with the Hotchkiss-Williams commissioner.

Previously it was the National League that was taking some potshots. John McMullen had never forgiven Vincent for the lockout. Now he was miffed at interference in his efforts to sell the Astros. Vincent had told him—and, worse, the Houston press—that he didn't want the club sold to out-of-town interests. McMullen was on the phone with Bud Selig at least three times a week proclaiming Vincent "a disaster." Peter O'Malley had testy relations with Vincent from the start. Vincent was also at odds with Ted Turner and the Tribune Company in Washington, where he was lobbying to rein in super-stations.

"He figured he could count on Selig's support in the American League, but he'd better make some friends in the National League," Jerry Reinsdorf later said. Instead, the decision lost American League allies without adding any National Leaguers. They believed all along the whole expansion pot rightfully belonged to them.

Some neutrals—commissioner's office staffers—were more bothered by Vincent's attitude than his decision. Between his disgust with the owners' actions and his certainty about his own, Vincent seemed hardly to listen to anyone anymore. "He was moving from leading to ruling," said one lawyer.

In short, everyone wound up disgusted and divided over a $190 million windfall, not least of all Vincent himself. The text of his expansion decision concluded: "I am disturbed by the apparent unwillingness of some within baseball to rise above parochial interest and to think in terms of the greater good of the game. The squabbling within baseball, the finger-pointing, the tendency to see economic issues as moral ones . . . all of these are contributing to our joint fall from grace."

He hadn't yet seen the half of it.

$ 24 $

FAY VINCENT WAS cool to the new labor chief from day one. His name was Richard Ravitch, and he was the owners' latest Great White Hope, the man who might knock out the union. The fact that he was the fourth PRC chief in the past six years should have told them something about his chances, of course. The players had the enormous advantage of just one leader in that span, Don Fehr. They never strayed into the strategy-of-the-month syndrome.

Vincent's problem with Ravitch began with money. He was making more of it than the commissioner. The new PRC chief had been hired in November at $750,000; the commissioner was making $650,000. Vincent fell into a funk worthy of Rickey Henderson.

Bitch, bitch, bitch. That's what Vincent did to everyone who would listen. It was a slap in the face. It was grossly unfair. It was, finally, a diatribe some found unseemly. "This guy's been saying he doesn't need the job, he's got twenty million dollars' worth of Coke stock," muttered one owner. "Now suddenly he's squabbling about money?"

Bud Selig, the PRC chairman and the man who'd hired both of them, insisted there was nothing of substance to the salary discrepancy. That was just the kind of money it took to get a man of Ravitch's caliber. It was no doubt true that he didn't work cheap. Yet, still, said one ally of Vincent's, "It was intended as a slap at Fay and taken that way."

But Vincent was threatened by Ravitch for other reasons as well. Unlike the low-profile O'Connor, whom he replaced, Ravitch was a New York man-about-town. He'd shuttled back and forth for years between high-profile private and public-sector jobs. As a businessman, Ravitch had run his family's construction company, chaired the Bowery Savings Bank, and cut deals for the Blackstone Group, a small but high-powered investment banking firm. But he'd really made his name for himself as the Mister Fix-It of New York politics. In the mid-seventies, he was recruited to save New York's Urban Development Corporation, an organization chartered to build publicly assisted housing but at that time listing toward bankruptcy. His success led to being drafted for another mission impossible—chairing the city's Metropolitan Transit Authority.

Ravitch did an enormous amount to upgrade New York's public transit, though it was a thankless job. One of his most vivid memories of attending a baseball game came during the 1981 World Series, when he left his seat at Yankee Stadium to get a cup of hot chocolate. He was recognized by nearby fans and accosted with, "What are you going to do about the subways, you fucking bum?"

Ravitch's other great baseball memory was watching Jackie Robinson's first game in New York, an occasion that spoke more to his politics (liberal) than his fandom (slight). He wasn't the least bit interested in entering baseball when he was first approached about the PRC job. Though at loose ends—defeated in the New York mayoral race and departed from Blackstone—he shunned Bud Selig's first advances. When he told his children he'd done so, they were horrified.

"Dad, you're crazy," said one. "Everything you've done has been so purposeful and weighty. Now here you have a chance to get into *baseball* and fix the economics."

And so Ravitch changed course and agreed to discuss the PRC job, though he did wonder about its autonomy and authority. "What's the relationship with the commissioner?" he had asked Bud Selig.

"Oh, you don't work for the commissioner," Selig assured him, "you work for us. The commissioner has agreed to stay out of labor."

Ravitch made his first mistake. He took Selig's words at face value. These words were as true as when John Gaherin had been wooed twenty-four years earlier: the PRC chief technically didn't have anything to do with the commissioner. They were also just as false. The commissioner was, of course, a monstrous force in labor. Blinded by the light of the national pastime, sweet-talked by Selig, Ravitch would later admit, "I didn't do my homework."

Hired in late 1991, Ravitch tried at first to be friendly with

Vincent, chatting about mutual chums and goals. But Vincent made every effort to discourage him.

Vincent to Ravitch on his own omniscience: "When baseball isn't played, the pressures become brutal. You've got the press, the Congress, the public. The commissioner has to intervene."

Vincent on the treachery of owners: "They're going to pull the rug out from under you."

Vincent on the futility of any tactic Ravitch might mention, from "reopening" the labor contract (as the 1990 pact allowed for, if so desired by either party, after the 1992 season) to taking another run at the salary cap: "Don't think you're going to be able to accomplish anything. In the end, you know, I'm going to have to come in and settle it."

Before long, Ravitch gave up trying. He stayed on the eighteenth floor, Vincent on the seventeenth, and rarely did the twain meet.

Ravitch actually had skimpier labor-relations credentials than anyone to head the PRC, except for Lee MacPhail. He'd dealt with unions in construction, of course, and he'd had some monumental go-arounds with the Transport Workers Union, including an eleven-day strike. But only a small aspect of his long résumé involved collective bargaining.

What did qualify Ravitch was his tenacity and energy. Ravitch took and made phone calls even faster than he lit and snuffed out Kent cigarettes. ("Dick has this thing of being almost unable to refuse a phone call," a colleague once declared.) He had political skills that Selig hoped might unite the fractious owners on labor.

When Ravitch wasn't on the phone in those early days, he was on the road. He was determined to meet with all twenty-six owners and immerse himself in the business. He wanted to take each club's temperature; take the measure of what each owner wanted and of how far he was willing to go in the next bargaining round; get a sense of the baseball economy.

The tour opened his eyes. He found out just how tough the issues were—and how little he'd known going in. Fay Vincent had reason to be smug. A common thread ran through almost every labor negotiation of the past twenty years: commissioners' intervention. The PRC chief had titular authority, but the czar had his "best interests" power—and absolutely no capacity to resist using it, even if it meant undermining the Lords. "I call it 'commissioneritis,' " said Fred Kuhlmann. "Almost invariably, the degree of it grows while they're in office."

Ravitch would hear the term several times over and hear all the horror stories: Kuhn and the 1976 lockout; Ueberroth and the 1985 strike; Vincent and the 1990 lockout. By the time he'd completed his fact-finding mission, he was firmly convinced: "commissioneritis" was a deadly virus.

"It's a crazy system," he told anyone who would listen. "Don Fehr will never take anyone in his job seriously as long as Fay is here." Ravitch, a great reciter of epigrams, invoked one from Napoleon: "Better to have one bad general than two good ones."

Ravitch wasn't the first PRC operative to seek alternatives to this flawed system. John Gaherin had constantly searched for a better model, to little avail. He once found one he liked and brought it to Bowie Kuhn. "The Bituminous Coal Operators Association," he announced. "It's management's trade association for both industry policy and labor relations."

Kuhn looked at him as if he were a cat who'd proudly placed a dead mouse at his feet. Emulating the sooty mining business? Admitting he was less czar than trade-association toady? "I'm not part of management," he sniffed.

Ravitch was, however, the first to push aggressively for change. He talked at great length with Bud Selig, urging an end to the commissioner's ambiguous role in labor. He'd like to see the commissioner cut out of labor. But he'd settle for simply better defining the commissioner's role. "Why not clarify it one way or another once and for all?" he asked.

Selig listened and questioned and murmured empathically, all of the things he did best.

In twenty-five years, Allan H. Selig had gone from the ultimate baseball outsider to the ultimate insider. He grew up amid modest wealth, the son of a Ford dealer in Milwaukee, and he grew up baseball-crazy. He could still describe the homer he saw Billy Bruton hit off Gerry Staley in the Milwaukee Braves' first-ever game in 1953. He could also describe the way his heart was ripped out and stomped flat when the Braves left town in 1965.

Selig, then in his early thirties, became immersed in the drive to get the city another franchise. Wherever owners gathered, recalled one baseball executive, "There was Bud, lurking behind a potted palm." It was a long, hard road, since baseball was sore at Milwaukee for contesting the Braves' move. The city had to prove itself all over as a market, hosting exhibition games—in one year, ten White Sox games.

Milwaukee nearly landed the White Sox, but then new ownership emerged in Chicago. Then the city was bypassed for expansion in 1969. But when one of the expansion franchises—the Seattle Pilots—faltered and failed, Milwaukee swooped in. Selig was part of a group that agreed to buy the bankrupt team for $10.6 million. Seattle's King County tried to block the sale just before the start of the 1970 season, and the Pilots' fate hung in the balance. A truck driver hauling the team's equipment north from its Arizona spring training camp was told to drive to Utah and await further instructions: west to Seattle, or east to Milwaukee. When a bankruptcy-court judge gave the team to Milwaukee, the truck headed east and Bud Selig entered baseball.

For years he would be overshadowed by Ed Fitzgerald. Selig operated the club, but Fitzgerald represented it in the Lords' councils. Fitzgerald was considered Milwaukee's heavyweight, chairing the PRC and serving on the executive council. Selig was considered a lightweight. "Couldn't piss straight without a road map," as one insider tartly put it.

It was only after the 1981 strike, when the old guard fell and Fitzgerald left baseball, that Selig emerged. He led the search for a commissioner to replace Bowie Kuhn, became chairman of the PRC, and went on the executive council.

Selig loved the game of baseball no less as an owner than as a fan. His mood was closely tied to whether the Brewers had won or lost their last game. He waxed rhapsodic about the traditions and rhythms of the game. It was why he'd been so drawn to Bart Giamatti. He was close to his players, retaining some of his little-kid awe at their abilities and enjoying their jock camaraderie.

But Selig was a hawk on labor matters and an apocalyptic voice on the baseball economy. He viewed the world through the prism of a small market, with the eye of a man not born to fortune. Addressing ownership meetings, his hands outstretched or wringing in agony, he would decry the latest "insidious" development. (It was a favorite word.) To Selig, disaster lay forever just around the corner.

Some peers declared him "the best crier in baseball." In an industry where every owner cried readily, profusely, and expertly, it was quite a tribute. Yes, ol' Bud climbed into the sackcloth one leg at a time. But some doubted his alleged poverty. The Brewers had a sweet stadium deal. Their president was known to his staff as "Budget Bud," cutting costs to the bone. The Brewers made a tidy profit, despite their tiny market.

The Brewers, in fact, contributed to some of the very salary abuses Selig deplored. He had just cried his way magnificently through an ownership meeting in 1978 when he was handed a message on his way out. Brewers GM Harry Dalton had phoned to say he'd signed pitcher Jim Slaton for $1.2 million over three years.

A companion saw the figure, a large one for 1978.

"Hey, Bud, what gives?" he asked.

"Oh . . . well," said a flustered Selig, "I'll have to talk to Harry about this."

To some there was no statement more damning about the baseball business than the fact that Bud Selig was a leader. Detractors called him Bud Light and invited a look at the record. Selig had, for instance, chaired the PRC since 1985 and overseen countless labor misadventures. Yet blame always slid off his back and directly onto the backs of others. Ronald Reagan should have had such Teflon.

Selig assumed ever more responsibility because nobody else cared to ("We're like a country club in that respect," as one peer put it). He'd be on any committee, put in any amount of time, and almost by default emerged with stature. Selig also became a one-man clearinghouse for gossip and opinion, spending 80 percent of his time on the phone with fellow owners or other ranking baseball people.

Good old Buddy seemed sympathetic to every point of view. If detractors felt he had all the sincerity of a car salesman, they still probably talked to Selig. He was an indispensable listening post. "He's a very good listener; there's nobody that doesn't feel they can talk to Bud," said Sandy Hadden, the longtime aide to Bowie Kuhn. "He could even talk to Finley."

As a leader, he was far less Walter O'Malley than George Gallup. Selig was a poll-taker really, taking soundings as he worked the phones and sensing when a body of opinion had reached critical mass. Only then did he jump out in front of it. Of course, this gave Selig splendid deniability if something went awry. It hadn't been *his* idea. As one baseball executive put it: "Selig has survived as a leader by not doing anything."

Nobody talked to Selig more than Jerry Reinsdorf. They were on the phone constantly, like a couple of old washerwomen chattering across the backyard fence between Chicago and Milwaukee. Reinsdorf kept trying to enlist Selig in a holy war he was itching to fight: the ouster of Fay Vincent.

He'd accumulated so many grievances that he actually wrote his own list of "Bad Things Fay Has Done." It included: being a labor wimp; being a press hound and compulsive leaker; and being an ineffectual leader. To Reinsdorf, Vincent fiddled with little issues and traveled to every ballpark while the baseball industry burned.

There was something visceral involved, as well. Vincent wasn't to the manor born—he was a scholarship kid at Hotchkiss, Williams, and Yale—yet he'd adopted the manner of the upper crust he met there. He gravitated toward clubby old boys from those schools or places like them.

Reinsdorf had gone to a public high school in Brooklyn and didn't really care where anyone had prepped. He belonged to no clubs and had no truck with anything but ability. He'd come to believe that Vincent, cloaked in that Ivy manner and advanced in life by his Ivy friends, was a fake.

Seattle was the latest addition to Reinsdorf's "Bad Things" list. Jeff Smulyan never got the $13 million in revenue commitments he demanded, and in late 1991 he put the Mariners up for sale. His Kingdome lease gave the city of Seattle ninety days to come up with a local buyer. Otherwise they were on their way to St. Petersburg.

In January, the city produced one. A group led by the Japanese video-game giant Nintendo made a $100 million offer for the Mariners. The commissioner, when called by the press for comment, issued a statement: "Baseball . . . has developed a strong policy against approving investors from outside the United States and Canada. It is unlikely foreign investors would receive the requisite baseball approvals."

Vincent had touched off a firestorm of controversy. Japanese interests had recently bought two movie studios (including Vincent's former employer, Columbia), Rockefeller Center, Pebble Beach, and, it seemed, half the rest of America. To some, buying into the national pastime was the ultimate symbol of Japanese incursion. To others, however, the institution of baseball came off as xenophobic and hypocritical. Since when did it require a local owner? Smulyan hadn't been one. How dare baseball deny Seattle its savior?

Vincent hadn't created baseball's policy. He'd only recited the one recently developed by baseball's ownership committee. That was a group of Lords charged with screening would-be buyers and setting standards for ownership. Vincent, seeing that xenophobia wasn't playing well in the press, adroitly renounced the ownership committee's policy and began working with the Nintendo group to shape an offer acceptable to baseball.

Meanwhile, the ownership committee fumed. One member was Jerry Reinsdorf, and he felt strongly that this committee— not the commissioner—was empowered to act on ownership applications. And this idea of the Japanese . . . he didn't like it, and he wrapped himself in the flag. To one committee meeting Reinsdorf even brought a clip from *Field of Dreams* in which James Earl Jones rhapsodizes on America and baseball. (The real reason for Reinsdorf's stance, thought some skeptics, was his resentment of a sad-sack franchise being bought for top dollar by a deep-pockets owner. How would the union ever be convinced of baseball's economic peril? Invoking the Yellow Peril was the only answer.)

In the end, Reinsdorf couldn't stop Nintendo, but he could hold the buyer to strict conditions. Nintendo's voting stock in the franchise would be less than 50 percent and the Mariners' operating chief would be a local hand. It turned out to be a Seattle utility executive named John Ellis. Reinsdorf thus limited Nintendo's involvement and caused that investor to pay dearly for its license to lose money. But this partial victory didn't make him like Fay Vincent any the more.

Nonetheless, he extended Vincent the courtesy of a meeting to go over the final shape of their Nintendo requirements. Reinsdorf and Kuhlmann met him in Washington, where he was doing some politicking. They were thus startled to read in *USA Today* they'd been "summoned to Washington" by the commissioner, who'd ordered the Mariners transaction completed.

USA Today's Hal Bodley was one of a trio of Vincent's primary press outlets. The others were Murray Chass and Claire Smith of the *New York Times*. The paper of record was so reverential toward the commissioner that, as *Daily News* columnist Mike Lupica once wrote, "it treats Vincent like a Sulzberger."

It infuriated the Lords, who begrudged Vincent his savvy with the press. Vincent's media manipulation was, in fact, designed at 350 Park Avenue. "We felt if he was honest and accessible and nurtured relationships, we'd get a fair shake when we needed it," said Rich Levin, the commissioner's PR chief. "My experience in 1985 was that management got killed in the press during a tough labor situation."

Reinsdorf, for all his gripes about Vincent, still couldn't get his friend, Bud Selig, to turn on Vincent. The commissioner's approval rating still wasn't that low, and Selig still operated on the George Gallup principle. He was also, by reflex, a defender of the establishment. Between the implorings of Reinsdorf and Ravitch, however, Selig did finally agree to back a limited action: getting Vincent out of labor.

"Go ahead and draft some changes to the Major League Agreement," he told Ravitch. "But this is too sensitive an issue for you to address firsthand with Fay. Let me bring this to him."

Dick Ravitch went to work on the amendments with Chuck O'Connor, who'd remained the PRC's counsel. It was a relatively simple task: five changes to the seventy-year-old document that would assert the PRC's sovereignty in labor and cut the commissioner out of it. The hard part, of course, would be selling it to Vincent. The Major League Agreement forbade any diminution of the commissioner's powers without his assent.

O'Connor had known Vincent for years. He knew his ego, and he knew this would never fly if it looked like Vincent's balls were being stuck in Ravitch's back pocket.

"Let's present this in a way that the idea seems to come from Fay," O'Connor suggested.

Sold, said Ravitch. He drew up a press release, consisting of a statement to be attributed to Vincent. It began:

> I have today proposed that the Clubs amend the Major League Agreement to make clear that labor negotiations and labor relations are the sole and exclusive responsibility of the Player Relations Committee and that the Commissioner has no authority or responsibility over such matters. If adopted by the Clubs, the amendments should end all speculation with respect to the Commissioner's role during all future labor negotiations.

After one and a half pages of careful verbiage, it concluded with a little treatise on why the amendments were necessary:

> In all negotiations, and particularly labor negotiations, it is imperative that the participants at the bargaining table understand that the person sitting on the other side has the responsibility and authority to conclude the negotiations. If one side believes that the person on the other side represents just the

first step to reaching an agreement, serious bargaining will not take place until the ultimate authority becomes involved. By proposing these clarifying amendments to the Major League Agreement and by announcing that I will play no role in the next labor negotiations, the Players Association, the Clubs and the public will understand that the sole and exclusive authority and responsibility for labor negotiations rest with the PRC and not with the Commissioner's Office.

What happened next is a matter of disagreement. Selig would later maintain he called Vincent with words that were something less than a directive and something more than friendly advice: "Fay, you've got to either get in or get out of labor. The way we're running it now is like being a little pregnant; it doesn't work well. We need a better-defined process, and you should either run it yourself or step out of it. I don't care which it is, but we should end the ambiguity."

Vincent remembers the issue surfacing only when he learned about the Major League Agreement amendments from the Rangers' George Bush. He angrily confronted Selig: "How dare you? This is outrageous and I'm going to go after you."

Both men deny the other's version, but one thing is clear: Vincent wasn't at all receptive. His response sounded like something out of King George III. "This is seditious activity," he said to one baseball lawyer. "I'll fine anybody who has a meeting to discuss it."

Selig did finally have a full-blown meeting on the subject with Vincent in New York. It was mid-May, but the atmosphere in the commissioner's office was as warm as that of an October night game. Vincent wouldn't even read the proposed amendments. "This is bullshit," he said.

Selig had brought along Fred Kuhlmann, to try to keep things calm and to emphasize that this wasn't just a Dick Ravitch–Bud Selig crusade. Lots of owners disliked the current labor-relations structure.

Kuhlmann was on almost as many baseball committees as Selig. Retired as vice chairman of Anheuser-Busch, he had time on his hands and a wise head on his shoulders. He was a calm voice in emotionally charged meetings, and he'd been neutral on Vincent for some time. He was quietly appalled at his amateur tactics during the lockout. He wasn't impressed with Vincent's grasp of the business or his running of meetings. Peter Ueberroth ran a crisp agenda and delivered a message. Vincent's meetings were like church services, where they talked about the good of baseball.

Still, Kuhlmann wasn't the sort to stir up dissent. He was an orderly gentleman, a lawyer who'd been the brewery's general counsel for sixteen years. He was also seventy-three years old, and had no appetite for palace intrigue.

The Mariners–Nintendo controversy changed that. Kuhlmann chaired the ownership committee and resented Vincent's intervention. Then he discovered something that he resented even more. Vincent was telling people that Kuhlmann wasn't up to the job of chairman. He was getting old and forgetful. To his face, however, Vincent said, "You're doing a great job, Fred."

Kuhlmann looked on as Selig hastened to smooth things over with Vincent. "Don't take this personally," he said. "Baseball has changed a lot since the 1920s. We should recognize that and change the Major League Agreement to reflect that."

Vincent disagreed. He was a strict constructionist on the compact, which was originally drafted by Judge Landis and the owners of the day. In its brevity and simplicity, he regarded it a brilliant governing document. He wasn't going to tinker with it for the sake of Dick Ravitch. Said one friend, "He viewed the Major League Agreement almost as the tablet of God handed to Moses."

"But, Fay," said Selig, "how are we ever going to negotiate a decent labor contract when the union knows the commissioner will just step in at some point? We're not trying to weaken the office; we're trying to strengthen our hand in labor."

"I have no intention of opening the camps," said Vincent. "I also don't have any intention to be the person who in any way caused the diminution of the commissioner's power."

They talked about it for a while, then Selig excused himself to go to the men's room. Vincent and Kuhlmann sat there looking at each other.

"Fay, I know you're not going to sign this," said Kuhlmann, "and if I were in your shoes, I wouldn't either."

"You're right," said Vincent.

The exchange led to a little thawing by the time Selig returned.

"What are you driving at here?" asked Vincent. "What's your fear?"

"Look, commissioners have repeatedly taken actions that undermine owners' position," said Kuhlmann. "There are some areas we'd like you to stay out of. Maybe there's another way to go at this—perhaps if we could get some commitments instead of amendments."

He listed three, right off the top of his head:

- Don't talk with Don Fehr without the PRC's permission.
- Don't be commenting to the press about labor matters.
- Stay out of any lockout or other labor confrontation, unless you're invited to do so by the PRC.

"I'll give you my word as a gentleman," said Vincent. "I can abide by all of those."

It did not put the issue to bed. Vincent was at the next PRC meeting, in Chicago in early June. So were the amendments to the Major League Agreement.

Around the table, one member after another stated his position.

The league presidents, Bill White and Bobby Brown, came down for getting the commissioner out of labor. They themselves had been cut out of the process by Vincent in 1990, and they had no use for the man. They'd be glad to have Vincent experience the joys of being neutered.

White in particular was in a constant state of fury with him. The league presidents, diminished by previous commissioners, were about as powerful as clubhouse boys under Vincent. He'd usurped White's lead role in negotiating the umpires' new contract in 1991, and White wouldn't even sign the finished document. "It's your agreement," he told Vincent, shoving it back across the table at him. He'd almost resigned on the spot when Vincent overruled and publicly humiliated him, as he tried to rein in an umpire named Joe West. (The sometimes pugnacious West had been involved in a series of on-field altercations.)

White had spent his life in baseball and thought this newcomer had neither a clue what the business was about nor an interest in learning. While Giamatti had tried to learn from the insiders, Vincent lectured them or ignored them.

Like Reinsdorf, White saw in Vincent a misguided activism. The commissioner once came to him on the warpath about Tim Leary, a pitcher who'd been caught by TV cameras as he swallowed a mysterious substance. Apparently he'd been doctoring the ball.

"We've got to go banish this guy," Vincent declared.

"Why?" said White. "He's got four wins. Who's he hurting?"

The only satisfaction White took in the relationship was screaming at Vincent privately, which he did often. Beginning with the labor issue, he'd manage to find other ways to combat the commissioner.

Selig, Reinsdorf, and Kuhlmann were also for the amendments, of course. So was Carl Pohlad. The only two opponents on the eight-member PRC were Wilpon, long Vincent's closest friend in baseball, and John McMullen, Vincent's newest friend.

After two years of screaming for Vincent's head, McMullen had abruptly stopped. The key event was Vincent's visit to Houston the previous week. There he scolded the local press and fans for vilifying McMullen, who'd been blasted for stripping the Astros of stars and dooming them to last place as he tried to unload the team.

"By demeaning John and by failing to support the team, I wonder whether the people of Houston have not made the sale more difficult," he said at a press conference, as McMullen looked on beaming.

The Houston media called Vincent "the commissioner from wonderland" and worse. "Whether he knows it or not, the commish has put those of us in the news business on quite a spot," wrote Ray Buck, a *Houston Post* columnist. "We can write only nice things about McMullen from now on. If we don't, we could get stuck with him for life."

But it did wonders for Vincent's relationship with McMullen, whose attitude in Chicago could be termed "live and let live." He said, "I think Fay should get out of labor, but if he's not going to, we should just move on."

Vincent listened calmly to the arguments for absenting himself from labor. Then he responded—civilly but no less adamantly than ever. Certainly he understood their concerns. Certainly he would consult with them in the unlikely event he wanted to insert himself. But, he said, "I'm not going to do it. There's no way I'll agree to a diminution of my powers. Besides, you're much better off with my word than with a piece of paper."

Furthermore, Vincent said, he disagreed with the premise that the industry's CEO should pretend that one of its most vital problems didn't exist. "This is something a commissioner should be responsible for," he said, "unless you think somebody else should be the commissioner."

"Yes, I do," said Jerry Reinsdorf.

* * *

Bud Selig was in New York the following week for the owners' quarterly meetings. He awoke early his first day there, and was well into the *New York Times* by six-thirty. He reached the sports section and the lead story hit him like a gut punch: VINCENT REPELS MOVE TO CUT HIS POWERS ON LABOR.

Murray Chass presented a version of the Chicago PRC meeting that one anonymous source had called "the putsch that failed." The effort to get Vincent out of labor was, Chass wrote, part of "an attack from a small group of critics in baseball, mostly nestled in the American League." Selig and Jerry Reinsdorf were specifically mentioned. So was Dick Ravitch, who, according to the story, aspired to Vincent's job.

Selig was beside himself. *What putsch?* He'd tried everything possible to gently persuade Vincent. *What failure?* The story made it sound like Vincent had thwarted a deadlocked PRC. In reality, its members overwhelmingly favored removing him from labor. This was clearly a version put out by Vincent or his spin doctors.

By seven o'clock, Selig was on the phone with Vincent at home, giving him the gist of the *Times* story.

"Fay, what the hell is going on?" he demanded.

There was a silence.

"I don't know where he got that," said Vincent.

Selig did not believe him. The two had remained on good terms, even after Vincent's 1990 lockout performance, which had dismayed Selig; even after Vincent's expansion decision, which had stunned him. But now Vincent had hurled down the gauntlet in the press, which was anathema to the extremely press-conscious Selig.

The rest of their conversation was perfunctory and unsatisfactory. At its end, something deep inside Bud Selig had shifted and the ground beneath Fay Vincent had grown shakier. Yet this was no San Francisco earthquake. It was so subtle neither of them yet knew it.

The Chass story had also charged the air at the owners' meetings, held at the Waldorf-Astoria Hotel. The PRC assembled that morning to go over the amendments again. They would later be presented to the full ownership group. Vincent couldn't abide sitting through it again. His back was killing him and the owners were disgusting him.

It wasn't just the unrelenting attacks of some, it was the unrelieved stupidity of others. Vincent was still shaking his head at the call from Cleveland's Dick Jacobs in April. The Mets 'had signed Dwight Gooden to a three-year contract averaging $5.15 million, and Jacobs was enraged. He wanted Vincent to fine the Mets for agreeing to such a deal.

"In Hollywood, the level of venality is much higher," Vincent would later say. "But in baseball the quality of thinking is so poor." He sent Steve Greenberg to the PRC meeting as his proxy.

But the meeting had barely begun when Bill White spoke up.

"Let me ask something," he said. "Do you think Steve should be here?"

"What do you mean, 'Should I be here?' " asked Greenberg. "I always come to the PRC meetings."

"I don't know if it's appropriate," said White. "He's the commissioner's deputy and we wouldn't want the commissioner here."

Bud Selig tried to head off a confrontation.

"I don't think it really matters, does it?"

But White pressed: "Steve, when you didn't want my legal people in your meetings I acquiesced to it."

"Wait a minute," said Reinsdorf, searching for a face-saving out for everybody. "Steve, if we asked you to leave, you'd leave, right?"

Greenberg was red-faced.

"Jerry, you don't have to ask me to leave," he said.

Greenberg stood up and began scooping things into his brief-case, papers flying, binders clunking. He snapped the briefcase shut and walked out, slamming the heavy oak door behind him.

None of this changed a thing at the meeting. The only thing the PRC did differently was vote instead of just talk. It was 6–2 in favor of the amendments. It meant nothing without Vincent's assent, but it was something to take to the full group.

That afternoon, at five o'clock, the leagues held a joint meeting. Both Vincent and Ravitch were invited to address it, but only the PRC chief came.

"There's a basic principle in labor negotiations," said Ravitch. "Two people can't be involved or the other side will divide and conquer. As long as the commissioner can be involved, there's no reason for the union to think they have to deal with us."

No sooner had he stopped speaking than Nelson Doubleday ripped into him.

"What right do you have to raise these questions?" he said.

"You should have known the commissioner had the right to be involved when you took this job. If you didn't think you could work with Fay you shouldn't have taken it."

"This has nothing to do with who's commissioner," said Ravitch. "If I was commissioner, I'd do the same thing. It's a structural problem. We have no leverage as long as the union knows the commissioner will step in."

Doubleday would not be satisfied. "It's wrong to try doing this to a commissioner in the middle of his term," he said.

Doubleday accused Ravitch of wanting Vincent's job. He attacked Selig for having set this in motion. He went after Jerry Reinsdorf as the supposed leak for the *New York Times* story.

But when the floor was thrown open, Vincent had few vocal defenders: Doubleday's partner, Fred Wilpon; the Orioles' Larry Lucchino, and the commissioner's new best friend, John McMullen. Every other owner who spoke bought into Ravitch's reasoning. The commissioner should butt out on labor. Peter Widdrington, the Blue Jays' chairman, finally stood up. Alluding to the scant three voices opposing Vincent's removal from the process, he said, "There are twenty-five clubs that support the PRC, and we're going to tell the commissioner that," he said. "Is there anybody who doesn't agree?"

Silence.

"We should communicate back to the commissioner," said Widdrington.

That evening, Vincent finally made his first appearance, at a tense dinner of the owners. It was George Bush, the old family friend, who did the communicating. "An overwhelming number of the clubs want you out of labor," he told Vincent, adding that he thought this called for a prompt and ameliorative response. "Your survival may be at stake here."

Vincent and Greenberg went back to 350 Park Avenue that night, to draft a speech for the next morning.

"We are at a crossroads," Fay Vincent began, looking out at the owners. "Baseball has never been in a more fractious state. Perhaps it is not surprising in a presidential election year in which we have three candidates and voters appear to be prepared to abandon their traditional party allegiances in numbers unprecedented over the last century. There is a certain ugliness in the public consciousness.

"But for me to chalk up baseball's unruliness as a sign of the times is too facile and ultimately not helpful. Like a team that shows up for a game to find poor field conditions, a strong opponent, and a hostile crowd, you—baseball's ownership—are currently confronted with a great many difficult obstacles, some seemingly insurmountable. However, like the team in my analogy, we have a choice between two alternatives.

"One, we can look for excuses, even to the point of blaming others in an attempt to avoid personal responsibility for our side's failures. Or, two, we can come together and commit to winning, to success. So let me talk to you this morning about the tragic state of affairs in which we find ourselves and about a common approach to dealing with a number of our problems.

"I am no naïf. I know how unprecedented unity is among all of you. But again, there is no choice. Perhaps you have hit bottom. Perhaps you are frightened enough—I know I would be—to finally begin to work together.

"It may be that never before has baseball been in such a sad financial state. Perhaps as many as ten teams are for sale, with few buyers in the marketplace. Many of you are losing lots of money. There is no liquidity. Banks are out of the business of lending to us. Revenues seem poised to fall sharply.

"Unfortunately, serious economic problems frequently have a way of breeding irrational behavior. We have seen some examples of that already. Perhaps the common cause is fear, as Jackie Autry has said. Poorly thought-out public statements and ill-conceived actions have the ability to bring disastrous results just at a time when we need a unified approach to common problems. Our challenge is to be constructive during these tough times. And is there any comfort or hope without unity? I don't think so. We must help one another.

"A new and restructured labor agreement is vital. But we need more than that. We have to begin to run this business better. The process by which we deal with our problems—including labor—simply has to be improved. Could it be any worse?

"And so I come to labor and to the recent drama with the PRC. Who can disagree that a restructuring of our player-compensation system during the next round of bargaining with the Players Association is an essential element in dealing with our financial troubles? And who can disagree that solidarity—a term more often associated with union activities than with ownership—is a key ingredient to our success? This time, you—and we—must stick together in every sense.

"You all know of the PRC decision to ask me to agree to a major change in the Major League Agreement to eliminate the role of the commissioner in labor. Believe me, I can fully understand the concern the PRC has. I gave the PRC request careful thought.

"However, Article Nine of the Major League Agreement specifically provides that the commissioner's powers shall not be diminished during his term in office. Leaving that aside, it is my belief that baseball would not be well served by the enactment of these amendments. Accordingly, as you know, I have advised the PRC that I have no intention of agreeing to these amendments.

"I do not think this change would serve you or baseball well—and I am totally opposed to any such major change being made in the heat of battle, without lots of time for debate and careful thought. This issue, however, requires more attention. I want to help. So I have been thinking about it and about you. I will continue to do so.

"First, I reemphasize my belief that the player compensation system is fatally flawed and must be changed. And I pledge to be helpful to the PRC in the course of whatever labor confrontation may lie ahead. Toward that end—at Fred Kuhlmann's request—I have given the PRC a series of commitments. Let me repeat—and renew—those commitments that I have made:

"One, I will not meet with or communicate with Don Fehr on any issue falling within the responsibility of the PRC, as broadly defined.

"Two, I will not make any public statements in the press or otherwise adverse to the negotiating position of the PRC.

"Three, I will not take any action in the labor area, without full discussion and disclosure to the PRC and will act, if at all, only in the most dire of circumstances.

"And let me add a fourth pledge, one that I hope will alleviate your most important concern. I will not take any action, ever, to open spring training camps or to bring about an end to a lockout, absent a new labor agreement. These commitments by me should not be taken lightly, for you must understand that I share your desire to achieve our common labor objectives."

Vincent went on to scold the owners about divisions between big-market and small-market clubs, to urge the two leagues to cooperate, and to ask that they "not engage in vacant prattle."

"We must strive to replace selfishness and defiance with a sense of kinship and compatibility. In the final analysis, our greatest and perhaps our only strength is in unity. Our downfall is guaranteed if we permit ourself to slide into a state of internal discord. The choice is ours to make.

"Sometimes I wonder why you and I put up with all we do. Obviously we care about this great game. We know we have duties beyond ownership. And so if we are in trouble—and we surely are—we must get out of it. We must make progress. We simply must get off the floor. You should want to help. You must help if we are to succeed. I will do my best. I am sure you will, too."

Fay Vincent laid down his text and was bathed in a great, sustained round of applause. Jerry Reinsdorf ran into Dick Ravitch afterward. "Well," he said, "I think you got everything you needed."

Vincent invited some writers over to his office for postmortems. The group included his regular Boswells: Chass and Smith of the *Times* and Bodley of *USA Today*. But it also included some others, like veteran baseball writers Jerome Holtzman of the *Chicago Tribune* and Frank Dolson of the *Philadelphia Inquirer*.

The stories in the next day's papers—and for several days afterward—lionized Vincent.

VINCENT SAVES THE GAME AGAIN, blared *USA Today*. "When baseball's most recent palace revolt was aggressively rebuffed by Commissioner Fay Vincent last week, those who care most about the game—Vincent's one of them—were huge winners," wrote Hal Bodley. "Not only did Vincent put down the coup, he might have saved the game for 1993."

OWNERS ARE SWAYED BY VINCENT'S SPEECH: "HE'S IN TOTAL CHARGE" read the *New York Times* headline. "Adopting a firm but conciliatory and statesmanlike approach, Commissioner Fay Vincent addressed baseball's owners yesterday and defused the volatile conflict that flared over a failed attempt to wipe out his authority in labor matters," wrote Murray Chass.

VINCENT'S CANE IS NOW HIS SWORD, topped the Dave Anderson column in the *Times*. "Maybe it's the cane," he wrote. "Because of his torturous back ailment, Fay Vincent needs to walk with a cane. Maybe some baseball club owners considered his cane to be a sign of weakness, a sign of a commissioner who would surrender to a palace coup. Instead, those owners surrendered.

"As soon as Fay Vincent waved his cane as if it were a sword, they slunk back into the shadows whence they came. They discovered that while he is their employee, he's not their stooge. More than anything else, the commissioner is the conscience that some club owners don't seem to have."

It seemed to be Fay Vincent's finest hour. The *New York Times* said so. But it turned out to be the starting point for a long, hot summer.

Vincent had said all the right things in the meeting, but his opponents had discovered something in the straw vote: his core of support was gossamer-thin. "That's what really smoked it out, when we saw that out of twenty-six existing clubs, twenty-three didn't want him in labor," said Reinsdorf. "I think we got bolder after that."

Vincent had also said all the wrong things *after* the meeting. His speech had turned from conciliatory promises about labor to a bold tongue-lashing of the Lords. His image-burnishing habit, long just annoying, was now infuriating. If Vincent could so twist the meeting's spirit, how could they trust his word? If he was so contemptuous of them, who the hell needed him?

"It appeared to be a tremendous victory for him," said one baseball executive, "but it was really the beginning down the slippery slope."

The National League's divisions had offended geographical sense for twenty-three years. Two Western Division clubs, Cincinnati and Atlanta, were in the *Eastern* time zone. Two Eastern Division clubs, Chicago and St. Louis, were *west* of them, in the Central time zone.

Like most gerrymandering, it was the product of a deal. When the National League split into divisions in 1969, the Mets were unhappy at losing dates with the Giants and Dodgers. The expatriate clubs still had strong New York followings. As a sop, the National League threw two other venerable teams into the division, the Cubs and Cardinals.

After just one year of divisional play, Cubs owner Phil Wrigley urged realignment. "Isn't it silly for Atlanta and Cincinnati to fly over Chicago and St. Louis to go to California?" he asked. "The only ones getting rich are the airlines."

But the divisions remained the same, and the ownership of the Cubs changed. By the 1990s, the Tribune Company wouldn't dream of realigning. The Cubs liked to clothe their Eastern Division preference in talk about their great rivalry with the Mets. But this was assuredly about ratings. The Cubs' night games in the East started at six-thirty Chicago time. They provided good early prime-time programming and they led in nicely to WGN's high-rated *Nine O'Clock News*.

Bill White decided to make realignment his cause. Since most of his functions had been stripped, the National League president had time on his hands. He drew up a plan to send the Cubs and Cardinals west and bring the Braves and Reds east. Then he began going around to each club affected, trying to sell it.

Atlanta was easy. As surely as the Tribune Company's superstation hated having more games in the West, Turner's superstation loved having more games in the East. The Cardinals weren't crazy about it, since they'd run the numbers and saw this would cost them a little money. But they were willing. Cincinnati took some cajoling, since Marge Schott had a congenitally difficult time accepting change. But once she saw she could save money on travel, she came around.

That left Chicago. White finally approached Stanton Cook, the sixty-seven-year-old chairman of both the Cubs and the Tribune Company, whose white hair and distinguished bearing gave him the nickname "The Senator." Courtly as he was, Cook protected his business interests with the ferocity of a she-bear. He did not like realignment in general, and he particularly did not like it now. He saw it as the second part of a two-pronged attack by baseball on his company.

It was true that Fay Vincent was going after super-stations, for he saw them more than ever as monstrosities. Turner's WTBS was up to 57.6 million subscribers, WGN had 34.9 million, and WOR had 13.5 million. The more cable systems they were on, the more value they sucked out of every other team's TV rights. By one estimate, WGN and WTBS were costing baseball $250 million a year in TV revenue. The Cardinals' flagship station, for instance, estimated that its viewership for their games fell 30 percent when they went up against WGN games and 15 to 20 percent against WTBS games. Lower ratings translated into lower ad revenue and lower payments for TV rights.

The so-called super-station tax developed by Peter Ueberroth hardly offset the damage. Turner was paying about $15 million a year and the Tribune Company $5 million in the early nineties, a fraction of baseball's programming value to them. Vincent wanted the Tribune Company's levy raised particularly sharply, into the $20 million to $25 million range. Unpleasant negotiations were continuing.

In Washington, Vincent was trying to get Congress to repeal something called the compulsory license, a federal regulation allowing TV stations to take their signal nationwide without permission or appropriate payment from the holders of their programs' copyrights. Vincent knew compulsory license repeal would gut the super-stations. He also had a backup position. Baseball would seek to require that cable systems black out super-station games when there was simultaneous TV coverage of a local game.

It all came to a head in a cable reregulation bill, to be voted on in the summer of 1992. Tribune Company lobbyists worked the back alleys of Capitol Hill, angling to nullify the compulsory license attack. (They would make sure some key language was inserted: No business with an antitrust exemption could benefit from compulsory license repeal.)

The Tribune Company also reminded certain parties of their constituents' rooting interests. "You know," the company's lead lobbyist, Shaun Sheehan, told Dennis DeConcini, "if Vincent gets his way, the Cubs games could no longer be brought into Arizona."

The Arizona senator looked at his aides: "Is this true?"

It was, sort of. Arizona was shared TV territory for the Giants, Dodgers, and Padres. Among the three, there would almost always be a televised game triggering the WGN blackout. Arizona was home to many Chicago expatriates who retired there to be near the Cubs' spring training camp in Mesa. DeConcini, a key member of the Senate subcommittee reviewing the compulsory license matter, suddenly knew where he stood on this issue.

Ted Turner's lobbyists, meanwhile, opted for an all-out public assault on Vincent. In the midst of calling the play-by-play during one game, announcer Skip Caray digressed into describing the action in Washington and the imminent threat of Braves blackouts. "We may be going through the pennant race with many of you missing a lot of it," he said.

Caray urged viewers to call a toll-free number if they wanted to protect their constitutional right to unlimited baseball. The number was displayed on the screen along with a message: "Let your voice be heard!" Every call triggered an anti-blackout telegram to the viewer's congressman—approximately 6,000 of them in all, it turned out.

And so, in the end, the super-stations put Fay Vincent to rout in Washington. This did not, however, make Stanton Cook any more disposed toward being a statesman about realignment when it came along. To him it seemed like simply another assault on the Tribune Company's coffers.

"If I were you, I wouldn't do it either, from an economic standpoint," Bill White conceded, as he tried to sell Cook on his proposal. He argued that this was better for the league overall, however, and he threw Cook a sop: seven o'clock game times on the West Coast. That would translate to nine o'clock starts in Chicago, and that wasn't so terribly late, was it?

It still conflicted squarely with the *Nine O'Clock News*, however, and it wasn't as though the Tribune Company responded to interests beyond its own. They had acquired a reputation, on merit, for not caring one bit about the effects of their actions. In the spring of 1992, the rest of the Lords were up in arms about Ryne Sandberg's contract, personally negotiated by Stanton Cook. It was a four-year deal averaging $7.1 million and represented a huge jump past the previous high-water mark (Bobby Bonilla's $5.8 million). "Don't you know there's a number between five and seven?" John McMullen screamed at Cook. "It's six!"

And so the Cubs did just as Bill White had feared they'd do: vetoed realignment. The measure passed 10–2, but a no vote from any of the affected teams effectively scotched it. (The Mets joined the Cubs in opposition, a professional courtesy extended from one self-centered big-market club to another.)

Some of the National League owners were apoplectic. The normally placid Bob Lurie ranted at length about the Cubs' selfishness. Still, only half the National League owners favored inviting Fay Vincent to intervene, using his "best interests" power to impose realignment. To Bill White, that wasn't nearly enough support for the drastic step of overriding the National League's constitution.

White suggested to Vincent, in an informal jawboning session, that there was more than one way to skin a cat. Bob Kheel, the veteran National League attorney, had apprised White of some relevant history, and he passed it on. In 1976, Bowie Kuhn was pushing hard for National League expansion into Toronto and Washington. The league's owners approved it, 10–2, but expansion then required a unanimous vote. Kuhn simply used his powers to change the rules, rather than impose a result. Henceforth, he ordered, only 75 percent approval was needed. He was thwarted anyway, because the second vote was 8–4. But, White noted, it provided a model for what Vincent might do.

It wasn't Vincent's way to use subtlety, however, when he

could use a blunderbuss. "My God," he told advisers, "if we can't resolve easy issues like this, how are we going to get anywhere on the big ones?"

And so, ignoring both White's informal suggestion and his written request to keep out, Vincent ordered realignment. All hell immediately broke loose. The Cubs sued. Peter O'Malley decried this "dangerous precedent." And Bill White pumped gallons of gasoline onto the flames, hoping they'd engulf Vincent. The commissioner and "The Senator" squared off in one explosive meeting, from which Cook emerged looking, in the words of one observer, "like he'd been in a war."

In a sense he had, for this was the beginning of one.

"The issue had ceased to be realignment," said one Vincent supporter watching the unfolding events with trepidation. "It was 'We have a commissioner who's out of control.'"

$ 25 $

THE DECLARATIONS OF war came crawling out of a fax machine in Milwaukee, each a simple but powerful statement: the undersigned had no confidence in Fay Vincent. It was the price of admission to a weekly conference call on how to get rid of him.

Bud Selig had finally signed on to the insurrection. That would give it crucial impetus. Selig gave the dissenters an imprimatur of legitimacy and attracted fence-sitters to their ranks. The run of Vincent-inspired stories, from his repelling of the ersatz putsch to his supposed tongue-lashing of the Lords, had pushed him over the edge. A dismayed Selig also read the stories about his Brewers tapping baseball's credit line for the maximum $35 million. It was true; it was embarrassing; and it smelled like another leak from 350 Park Avenue.

"Bud was livid," said one insider. "His feeling was, 'This man is willing to put himself above the institution to trash us.'"

Selig was also bothered by other developments shortly after the New York meetings. Ravitch had sent Vincent an "eyes only" memo, which was soon circulating all around baseball. The leak smacked of a retaliation against the PRC chief. Vincent wrote a memo of his own, reiterating to the Lords he'd stay out of labor. But to the careful or suspicious reader, it seemed to give him some outs for breaking the pledge. A second wave of reaction to Vincent's pledge speech was now forming: he'd said it, but he didn't necessarily mean it.

The original set of conference-call conspirators numbered about ten. The Cubs quickly faxed in their no-confidence vote and became a ringleader. The Tribune Company was no better respected now as a baseball citizen, but it had earned its spurs as a Vincent-hater. Its influence had also increased, which, in baseball, was even better than having respect.

Tribune stations now held the TV rights of seven teams—25 percent of all baseball. Its stations already carried the White Sox, the Angels, the Yankees, and, of course, the Cubs. They had recently negotiated deals to add the Colorado Rockies, the Phillies, and the Dodgers in 1993. (L.A.'s contract would pay the team a hefty $75 million over five years.) Most of those teams' owners were anti-Vincent to begin with. But the influence of the Tribune Company was clearly felt on a start-up outfit such as Colorado, and it could stiffen the resolve of others.

Stanton Cook volunteered Tribune's lawyers to draw up articles of impeachment for Vincent. It would, he said, be a pleasure.

The heart of the document they drafted was its Section I, "Reasons for This Action":

The election of the Commissioner is a compact of trust with the Leagues and baseball clubs. The basis of that trust is the understanding that the Commissioner will conduct his office effectively and professionally to advance the best interests of baseball. The present Commissioner has failed to do so in numerous respects:

1. Inability or unwillingness to build a reasoned consensus with or among owners on fundamental issues facing baseball.
2. Failure to manage relationships with outside parties important to baseball (e.g., television networks) in a constructive manner.
3. A lack of judgment regarding major actions in office, particularly evident in recent months.
4. Inconsistency and lack of directness in communications with owners, which has tended to divide owners and set them against one another, often based on misunderstanding or misrepresentation of owners' views.
5. Premature or inappropriate contacts with media which work against baseball's interests in negotiations with third parties, or unfairly present the Commissioner's personal view as the position of Major League Baseball.
6. Lack of objectivity has eroded the office's ability to function as arbitrator in disputes among parties, which is one of the most important functions of the office.
7. Practice of intervening in actions that have been delegated to other groups (e.g., Ownership Committee, Player Relations Committee) has undermined the effectiveness of those entities and compromised baseball's interests.

In these circumstances, out of respect for the Office of Commissioner and to protect that important position from further damage, the undersigned baseball clubs believe it is essential that the current Commissioner resign and be replaced by someone better able to manage the affairs of the office in the best interests of the game.

The recitation of failings and the uprising were not altogether fair. Fay Vincent might have been a passably acceptable, conventionally mediocre commissioner at another time in baseball's history. But he'd come along when the business was imploding before the owners' very eyes. "Virtually every aspect of baseball's institutional deficiencies combined to get Fay," said one baseball lawyer. "It was like he hit every exposed rock out there."

The list of conference-call regulars showed how Vincent was the lightning rod for thunderbolts of discontent all over. They were an odd mix of clubs, united only by their despisement of the commissioner.

Five were have-nots: the Brewers, Twins, Pirates, Padres, and Indians. They were scared to death that Vincent was doing nothing to prevent their going down the drain.

Seven were haves: the White Sox, Dodgers, Cardinals, Angels, Yankees, Blue Jays, and Cubs. They were scared to death that Vincent *would* do something. Anybody so enamored of his "best interests" powers might well declare martial law and impose revenue-sharing.

Both groups had some basis for their fears.

Vincent had done precisely nothing to aright the baseball economy, which was now badly listing. At least two thirds of the clubs would lose money in 1992 and eighteen of twenty-six teams were beginning to post declines in their attendance figures. No sooner did baseball get a new $260 million line of credit than ten cash-starved teams gobbled it all up. The Tigers had to tap it just to make payroll.

Even the silk-stocking clubs had a squirrelly edge of panic about them. The Yankees dropped their teams in the Florida Instructional League and the Florida State League. The Dodgers trimmed their power bill by cutting back on elevators, escalators, and scoreboard clocks. They ordered scouts off the road. Then the ultimate: they cut off desserts in the press lounge.

Vincent saw the numbers, listened to the howls, and intellectualized it all into indecision. He addressed even the simplest matter by beginning, "That's a very difficult issue." He would then proceed to circle all around the subject in a dance of multisyllabic avoidance before coming to a conclusion—*maybe*.

It wasn't *his* fault, he sometimes said, that trouble came looking for him. The truth was, he sat passively waiting for issues to become a mess instead of getting ahead of the curve on them. CBS, for instance, approached him about extending and restructuring its contract. It would lower the network's rights fees but still lock in a healthy level of TV money for baseball beyond 1993. That would almost surely beat whatever came out of a new bid.

Neal Pilson put it to Vincent straight. The golden goose was dead. The Beer Wars were over. Anheuser-Busch had finally and utterly defeated their main rival, Miller. Neither of them was buying TV time like they used to, and overall demand was listless as well. There was also far too much TV-sports "inventory," as he termed it. Sports programming had mushroomed, between the huge increases in some sports' exposure—the NFL had extended its schedule and expanded its playoffs—and the continued growth of sports-oriented cable. Baseball was looking at a 33 to 50 percent drop in its network TV rights on the next contract, Pilson warned.

Given the same message and opportunity, NFL commissioner Paul Tagliabue went for the extension (though his owners eventually vetoed it). Vincent did nothing. Nor did he do anything to cultivate relationships at the other two networks—his best hope for stirring up expensive bidding. NBC Sports's president, Dick Ebersol, let his friends in baseball know he detested the aloof Vincent.

Vincent was presiding over a baseball economy that was starting to resemble that of a banana republic—a few rich teams and a whole lot of poor ones. Carl Pohlad's small-market caucus—the Pohlad Group, as it was known—was up to eighteen clubs. That was a pretty fair barometer of how many teams were seriously worried.

Some big-market owners, in turn, fretted about the Pohlad Group, certain that its meetings were full of talk about how to take from the rich. Vincent fielded occasional calls from a distraught Peter O'Malley. "They met again," he'd report. "Use your authority to stop them."

"Look, Peter, *I* know these meetings are going on," Vincent replied. "How can I tell them not to meet?"

He finally assembled a bipartisan committee to hash over the issues. It was one of Vincent's favorite alternatives to action. He'd created an economic-study committee as part of the 1990 lockout settlement. It was a blue-ribbon panel appointed equally by union and management that included heavy hitters like Paul Volcker, the former Federal Reserve Board chairman, and Peter Goldmark of the Rockefeller Foundation. Vincent insisted this was the way for players and owners to come to a common understanding on the baseball economy.

But it was doomed to be a waste of blue ribbon, if the performance of the so-called Big Market–Small Market Committee was any indication. There were eight members (four big-market, four small-market) and little came of their meetings. Partly it was because the owners' own house rules barred them from sharing financial data. Partly it was because the committee was gridlocked by design.

Vincent's greatest friend and ally was Fred Wilpon, who would rather sacrifice his firstborn than surrender another dime of Mets revenue. His second-greatest friend and ally was Eli Jacobs, whose Camden Yards park had transformed the Orioles from a have-not to a have. Vincent bought their arguments against revenue-sharing, being something of an economic royalist himself.

"Why should we take money from the wealthy clubs just because they're wealthy?" he asked. "If the industry is losing money as a whole, this just levels out the losses. Player compensation is the problem, not revenue-sharing."

The Pohlad Group, seeing no help coming from 350 Park Avenue, went out and hired a consultant from Arthur Andersen to come up with a revenue-sharing model. That only hardened the lines between the haves and the have-nots, although it did get Vincent's attention.

He had baseball's chief financial officer, Jeff White, make a call to Carl Pohlad. "You know," said White, "we're really going to start focusing hard on revenue-sharing."

Vincent, aware that mischief was afoot, made a few other gestures to shore up support. He put the Blue Jays' Peter Widdrington on the ownership committee. He awarded the 1996 All-Star Game to Montreal, whose president, Claude Brochu, was a fence-sitter. (Bill White got that rescinded, however, by complaining that Vincent had subverted the usual selection process.)

But overall Vincent did little to counter the increasingly active dissidents. His supporters were dismayed at how lightly he took them.

"I likc Fay," said Larry Lucchino of the Orioles. "He's very bright, very thorough, and we had enormous respect for his integrity and love of the game. But the job requires political instincts and acumen, and that was not his strong suit."

"Fay found it unseemly to have to fight this kind of fight," recalled George Bush. "To his credit, he found it beneath him."

The Rangers owner admired Vincent's principles, but told him straight out: "If you're willing to fight, I'll fight with you. If you're not, I can't do it for you."

Vincent waved off this and all other warnings about his enemies massing for war. He had the serene self-confidence of a man about to get blindsided. "You'll see," he said. "There aren't a half-dozen owners who care about this."

He preferred, as usual, to spend more time playing judge and avenging angel. He turned to be open-and-shut case of Steve Howe.

Steve Howe was a six-time loser. A Rookie of the Year with the 1980 Dodgers, he'd flamed out as a star and drifted in and out of baseball over the course of a decade. He could throw a ball ninety miles an hour, but he couldn't kick a cocaine habit. It landed him in such remote baseball outposts as the California and Mexican leagues, and, finally, after his sixth drug-related suspension, out of the game altogether.

In 1991, he applied for reinstatement; Vincent granted it; and the Yankees gave him one last shot. He was brilliant. Howe was thirty-three and no longer of full-time closer caliber, but he finished at 3–1 with a 1.68 ERA. He swore he was finished with drugs, but in December 1991 he was arrested in Montana in the process of buying cocaine.

When he ultimately pleaded guilty to attempting to buy the drug, Fay Vincent said enough was enough. On June 24, 1992, Steve Howe's seventh drug violation got him kicked out of baseball for life.

The players' union filed a grievance. Yes, Howe was guilty, but only of "attempting to possess" the substance. He'd been clean in repeated drug-testings during the season. Vincent had gone too far, the union argued.

Dick Moss, Howe's agent, would argue the union's case. It was built around the contention that Howe had a medical problem—adult attention deficit disorder. It was a new theory for explaining cocaine addiction in some people, tracing it back to childhood hyperactivity. In addition, Moss asked three members of Yankees management—manager Buck Showalter, GM Gene Michael, and a vice president named Jack Lawn—to be character witnesses for Howe.

At the hearing, held on Tuesday, June 30, Moss asked them innocuous questions about Howe and they gave innocent answers. The trouble came on cross-examination. Representing baseball was a lawyer named Bill Cavanaugh. Chuck O'Connor, who normally handled grievance cases, was, in effect, himself suspended by Vincent, for having fallen in with the commissioner's enemies. Cavanaugh was a junior partner of Harold Tyler's, the former federal judge who'd become Vincent's all-purpose lawyer.

Inexperienced in this setting, he committed the lawyer's cardinal sin. He asked a question without knowing the answer. It was the same one to all three: What did they think of baseball's drug policy? He got variations on the same answer from them all: lifetime suspensions for a circumstance like Howe's weren't always appropriate.

They were opinions, of course, with no factual bearing on Howe's case. Moss took little note; the hearing recessed; and he prepared for the next round of testimony.

At nine-twenty Wednesday morning, Buck Showalter was in his office, preparing for the Yankees' one o'clock game with the Royals. The thirty-six-year-old rookie manager approached each game as though it were a final exam: poring over scouting reports, computer data, videotapes, organization reports. Later he would call in players for one-on-one meetings.

His regimen was interrupted by a ringing phone. A woman's voice on the line said, "One moment, please, for Mr. Vincent."

Fay Vincent's flat voice came on.

"We have a problem with your testimony yesterday," he said. "I want to see you in my office at eleven if your schedule allows."

"I've got a one o'clock game," said Showalter. "I don't think I can do it."

"Be here," said Vincent.

Showalter was stunned. He was new in the big leagues. He went looking for somebody—anybody—to talk to about what just happened. The first person he saw was Yankees PR man Jeff Idelson. Showalter stammered out his exchange with Vincent. What the hell should he do?

Idelson called Gene Michael at his New Jersey home, re-counting what Showalter had told him.

"That's crazy," said Michael. "Let me call and straighten this guy out. He must not know we've got a game."

He called the commissioner's office and got right through to Vincent. "What's going on with Showalter?" he asked.

"I've got serious problems with his testimony yesterday, and yours and Lawn's too," said Vincent. "I want to see you all in my office at eleven."

Michael looked at the clock. It was already 9:35.

"But we have a game at one," said Michael. "Buck needs to prepare for it."

"I told you to be here at eleven."

Michael had just been through it with Vincent on another George Steinbrenner case. The commissioner's office had inves-tigated charges of illicit contacts between him and Yankee em-ployees. Steinbrenner was cleared, but Michael was still peeved at the way he had been treated. Vincent had denied Michael the lawyer of his choice. Vincent didn't like the fellow, because he had represented another Yankees exec in one of the nuisance suits that were filed in the wake of Steinbrenner's banishment. Now, Michael, having a bit of a short fuse anyway, fired back.

"Look, it's almost quarter of ten," he said, his voice rising. "I don't *know* if I can be there at eleven."

"You'll both be here at eleven," said Vincent.

"I just told you, I don't know whether I can be there at eleven!" shouted Michael. "I'll be there when I can be there."

Michael tore out of his house and into his blue Chrysler New Yorker. As he screeched out of his driveway and toward the city, he picked up his car phone and called David Sussman, the Yan-kees' general counsel. He told him what was happening and that he was on the way to the stadium to pick up Showalter and Lawn. He asked Sussman to try to find out, in the meantime, what the hell was happening. And could he bring a lawyer?

Sussman, stunned, hung up and called Steve Greenberg.

"I understand the commissioner wants to see Stick and Showalter in connection with the Howe case," he said. "Could you tell me what this is about?"

"He wants to see Lawn, too," said Greenberg. "We have some problems with their testimony."

"Should I be there?"

"No, that's not necessary."

Michael arrived at the Stadium, picked up the others, and

headed for 350 Park Avenue. To understand how Michael could make his way over the George Washington Bridge, along the Cross-Bronx Expressway, off to the stadium, and into Midtown Manhattan in an hour and a quarter, it is necessary to know something about his driving style: Gene Michael scares New York taxi drivers.

As he careened along, Lawn and Showalter hanging on for dear life, he called Bob Costello, the lawyer he'd been denied last week. He told him he might need him again.

"Let me call you back," Costello said. "Let me call the union office and find out if there's a transcript. I'll try to get one right away and meet you at the commissioner's office."

Costello found that there was no transcript and told Michael they shouldn't go in without a lawyer. The GM protested. They'd done nothing wrong, and he didn't want to make it a bigger a deal than it was already.

"You don't understand this guy; you don't know the way he operates," said Costello. "You're crazy to go in there without a lawyer. But if you choose to do so, be advised: there is no transcript, so don't make any comments about your testimony. Simply tell the commissioner you'll be happy to answer any questions after you see the transcript.

"I guarantee you that when you take that position, he's going to get very irritated. He's going to threaten you with discipline. Keep in mind when you're in there that there's only one reason to call you on such short notice. Whatever you said yesterday displeases this guy. He wants to bring you in there and have you contradict what you said—and if you do, you can be guaranteed you'll be called back in there as a witness for his side.

"The bottom line is, he wants you to change your testimony. He will not ask you directly to do that. He's not that foolish. But he will do things that will cause this idea to enter your own mind. And I'm telling you, when you decide not to talk about what your testimony was, he's going to threaten you with discipline."

Costello told the same thing to all three men in the car. They handed the phone around and heard the same speech. And they all had the same reaction.

"Oh, that's crazy," said Lawn. "He'll never do that."

"Mark my words," Costello warned.

Showalter was the first to be shown into Vincent's office. The commissioner was sitting at his desk, smoking a cigar and looking grim. Showalter took a seat in front of his desk, as surrounded as a pitcher with the bases loaded. To Vincent's right sat an equally grim Steve Greenberg. On either side of Showalter and behind him sat Harold Tyler and Tom Ostertag, baseball's general counsel.

"We have some real problems with your testimony," Vincent began. "I want to go over what happened."

He reviewed the questions Showalter was asked about the Howe banishment and baseball's drug questions, concluding, "How did you respond?"

Showalter's anxiety, mounting fast, forced Costello's advice from his mind. He recounted his answers as best he could remember. When he was through, Vincent let him have it.

"Well, you effectively resigned from baseball when you testified," he said.

Showalter spent the rest of the meeting in a daze, stunned by Vincent's pronouncement and sickened by the cigar smoke. He would later only remember a jumble of other statements from Vincent: "Dick Moss set a trap for you fellows and you fell right into it. . . . You work for baseball; you work for this office when you sign a contract. . . . We cannot have people who disagree with our drug policy. . . . We've talked with Joe Malloy and Mr. Steinbrenner and they are aware of this situation and they are not happy with it. . . . Your testimony was a kick in the balls to the commissioner's office."

At least three more times Vincent would tell Showalter he had quit baseball with his testimony. But he finished by telling him he'd hold off and officially take action in a few days. "You will have to sweat it out until Monday," he said.

Gene Michael was next.

"I have serious problems with the testimony of you three Yankee people," said Vincent. "When you signed your contract, you became bound by the policies of the commissioner. By your testifying for Dick Moss, you effectively resigned."

"I didn't testify for Dick Moss," Michael protested. "I testified for Steve Howe."

"By speaking against baseball, you have effectively resigned from baseball. You just quit your baseball job."

Vincent began firing questions about yesterday's testimony. But Michael hewed to Costello's line. He didn't remember exactly and wanted to see the transcript before answering.

His inquisitors persisted. Greenberg asked about a cross-examination question Michael had been asked, about whether he thought permanent expulsion was a useful deterrent. "Cavanaugh threw you a soft pitch right down the middle, a pitch you couldn't miss, but you missed it," he said.

"This [the arbitration hearing] is where you needed an attorney, not last week," said Vincent. "The Yankees didn't brief you well. Yankee lawyers have not served you well."

Michael still wouldn't discuss his hearing answers, though he told Vincent he would say one thing about his testimony and his view of drug addiction: "I said what I believed. I have compassion for people. I've learned they have little resistance. They fall off the wagon without a good support system."

Vincent was visibly annoyed. He began telling Michael again that he had quit, resigned.

"I haven't quit," Michael shot back. "I didn't resign."

He sat there with a small smile, shaking his head back and forth slowly.

"Do you think something is funny here?" asked Vincent.

"No, I didn't mean it that way. Nothing's funny here. But that's what your guys were doing from the other side of the table yesterday when Buck was testifying. Smiling and laughing."

As the session was winding down, after more than thirty minutes, Vincent made one last effort to grill Michael about his testimony. Michael stuck to his guns: not without a transcript.

"Well," said Vincent, dismissing him, "maybe you'll remember your answers on Monday when I discipline you."

It was twelve-thirty. Michael and Showalter dashed for the stadium. It was Jack Lawn's turn.

"I have great concern that you three would testify without getting clearance from anyone," said Vincent.

"Well, I did," said Lawn, "from Joe Malloy and David Sussman."

"No, you should have gotten it from me," said Vincent.

He looked at Lawn coldly and delivered the same message he had given to the others: "You effectively resigned when you agreed to appear at the hearing."

"I was sworn to tell the truth," said Lawn. "I only testified in accordance with my conscience and my principles."

"You should have left your conscience and your principles outside the room," Vincent said.

Lawn, stunned, fumbled in his shirt pocket for something to write on. He wanted to remember Vincent's words precisely. He was no babe in the woods. He was a former Drug Enforcement Administration head, the kind of G-man Steinbrenner loved to hire. Lawn found an index card and jotted them down. This also gave him time to regroup mentally. He went on the offensive.

"I supported the drug policy when asked, and I also acknowledged the power of the commissioner to suspend," he said. "What's the problem?"

Greenberg replied, "Well, I interpreted your testimony as—"

"Your interpretation means nothing to me," Lawn interrupted.

"What you did was stupid," Vincent said. "You were stupid. You were led into a trap by Dick Moss, and you were all a bunch of lambs following him. You should not have testified for the other team."

It was no act of disloyalty to testify, Lawn maintained.

"I could have been subpoenaed," he said. "I testified in the Noriega trial because I was subpoenaed by the defense."

"That's the difference!" Ostertag said, jumping in for the first time.

"You said too many things," said Greenberg. "Based on your experience, you should know when you testify that you should say only certain things."

"What do you mean?"

"If you were called to testify before Congress and you knew your testimony would be used against the administration, you wouldn't go."

"You don't understand," said Lawn. "If you're called to testify, you testify and you tell the truth."

"You should not have testified on behalf of the Players Association," said Vincent.

"It was not the Players Association. I testified for Steve Howe."

"I could not believe that you all would testify because of your interest in seeing Steve Howe in a Yankee uniform," said Vincent.

"That's not why we testified. We testified to tell the truth."

"But then why would you want to testify?" asked Vincent.

"If a month from now I pick up a paper and see that Steve Howe killed himself, at least I would have known I tried to help."

Vincent had had enough of the debate. He signaled it was over—as well as Jack Lawn's short career with the Yankees.

"While you might think you work for the Yankees, you all work for Major League Baseball," he said, "and you have effectively resigned from baseball."

Greenberg wasn't quite ready to let it go.

"Why did you continue to talk about addiction being a disease?" he asked.

Lawn began explaining what the latest research in the field said—until Judge Tyler broke in.

"In my court," he growled, "addiction was not an excuse for breaking laws."

"Why did you do this for Steve Howe?" Greenberg asked.

Lawn looked at him.

"Well, as I learned in the Marine Corps, you don't abandon the wounded."

Michael and Showalter debriefed on the phone with Costello as they drove back to the stadium. Showalter wondered: Could he even suit up?

"Look, let Buck go up and manage the game," said Costello. "I'll meet you at the stadium, Gene. Buck needs a lawyer. I'll get a guy I know very well, and who knows Vincent very well."

Costello called Dom Amorosa. Together they'd tangled with Vincent on previous Yankees matters.

"Dom, you're not going to believe what this bully is up to this time." He filled him in.

"You've got to be kidding," said Amorosa. "This can't possibly be accurate."

"I'm telling you, this is what happened before they went into the meeting; this is what they tell me happened at the meeting," said Costello. "This guy has finally cooked his own goose."

Michael pulled into the stadium parking lot at 12:56. The first pitch was in four minutes.

Showalter tried to shoulder his way past waiting reporters, saying, "I have a game to get to." Some, noticing his ashen face, asked if he was okay. He tried to deflect the questions and leave them laughing.

"You ever ride with Gene?" he asked.

Showalter stopped in David Sussman's office before suiting up.

"How did it go?" asked Sussman. Then he noticed Showalter's face and already knew the answer.

"He said I've been kicked out of baseball," Showalter said. "I can't believe this. I'm out of baseball. Who's going to manage the club? What am I going to do for my family? I've got a wife and a little kid. Thank God I have a college degree. I can probably get a high school coaching job."

By the time he reached the dugout it was the top of the second inning. The Yankees were already behind 6-0, but he was happy to see the lush green grass and the great blue stadium. It was like coming home after a long, strange journey through the looking glass.

Bob Costello headed for the stadium to meet Gene Michael. Upon arriving, he ran into a man he recognized as Jack Lawn.

"Jack, Bob Costello," said the lawyer, extending his hand.

They fell into step, walking toward the stadium entrance.

"Did you get the same word as Michael and Showalter?" asked Costello. "That you're out of baseball?"

"Yeuh."

"Were you told you quit baseball?"

"Yeah."

"That you effectively resigned from baseball?"

"Yeah."

"Well, what's your reaction to this?"

Lawn stopped and looked at Costello.

"Fuck *him*."

Inside, Costello met with Michael. They were joined by Amorosa and, after the game, Showalter.

By now it was a media event: The Case of the Tardy Manager. The Yankees had come back to win a stirring 7-6 game, but all the writers wanted to know was what had happened off the field.

From a walkway in back of the press box, they could see into Michael's office. They were pounding on his window and mouthing the question: "What happened?"

They pulled the shade and debated whether to lay low or go public. They decided to come out shooting, with Amorosa leading the way. Fay Vincent, he said, had tried to get Showalter to change his testimony.

"Buck Showalter will not give in to intimidating tactics by Commissioner Vincent," he said. "Mr. Showalter intends to protect his rights and protect the Yankee organization. Obviously, Vincent takes issue with anything that contradicts his position and as a result tried to intimidate these Yankees into changing their testimony."

Costello jumped in with more of the same, and it all played very big in the New York tabloids. They were all over Vincent, who could stomp George Steinbrenner all day, as far as they were concerned, but who was way out of line on good guys Showalter and Michael.

Two days later, the Monday meeting was canceled and the discipline threat dropped. Between the media firestorm and the pointed words of arbitrator George Nicolau, Vincent backed off.

The union filed a National Labor Relations Board complaint against Vincent, later settled by requiring that a notice be posted in each clubhouse. Its message: everyone in baseball should feel free to testify candidly in grievance hearings "without fear of discipline, retaliation, or other discrimination."

Vincent had been let off the hook easy, as some saw it. The union could have made more of his flogging of Showalter, Michael, and Lawn. But he was too valuable a foil as commissioner, for labor purposes, to engage him in full combat. Vincent was a buffer against bellicose owners like Reinsdorf. He was a check on Ravitch's ambitious and dangerous designs. He was the union's go-to guy in a crunch.

Vincent would not be in that position for much longer, however, if a growing number of owners had their way. If anything gave impetus to the growth of the Dissident Dozen, it was the manhandling of the Yankee Three. More no-confidence memos came across the Milwaukee fax machine. The conference-callers turned to two big questions. One: How much support did they need to fire Fay Vincent? Two: Could they legally fire him?

It was part of the received wisdom of baseball: a commissioner couldn't be fired. As legend had it, Judge Landis had insisted on Article 9 to ensure that he couldn't be undercut or thrown out. The key passage held that "no diminution of the compensation or powers of the present or any succeeding Commissioner shall be made during his term of office."

When people started talking about firing Vincent right out loud, it was to Article 9 that Fay Vincent quickly pointed as proof positive that they couldn't. Getting fired was the ultimate "diminution," and it was forbidden by the framers. (Commissioners had been cashiered, of course, but they had ultimately resigned and gone voluntarily.)

So many lawyers had been drawn in by the dissidents that they had to have their own separate conference calls: Bill Webb of the Phillies, Sam Fernandez of the Dodgers, David Hiller of the Tribune Company, Paul Jacobs of the Rockies, and Bob Dupuy, the Brewers' outside lawyer. In addition, NL counsel Bob Kheel and AL counsel Bill Schweitzer were usually on the line—nervously. They were concerned about being part of a "plot." But, they rationalized, there was nothing wrong with being on hand to answer questions from league members.

Dupuy would be on the line for the owners' calls, then relay the legal questions to the lawyers' group. Then they would all scurry off to work on the issue of the week.

Jerry Reinsdorf wanted just one more lawyer—his own guy—to dig into the question of firing. Vincent had obviously forgotten their little chat at the Pfister Hotel, when he said he'd go quietly if he lost support. Reinsdorf turned to a law-school classmate and longtime counselor of his, Jerry Penner, and asked him to "figure out history here."

Reinsdorf knew there were transcripts of the owners' meetings in which Landis was chosen as commissioner and the Major League Agreement drafted. They'd been used by baseball's lawyers to defend Bowie Kuhn, when Charlie Finley challenged his "best interests" powers after the Rudi–Fingers–Blue decision. Reinsdorf suggested that Penner track down those seventy-year-old documents.

The lawyer quite agreed. If he could find out what the framers intended in Section 9, perhaps they could better counter Vincent's argument. He finally located the full transcript in the files of Baker & Hostetler.

On a Sunday afternoon, Jerry Penner settled down at home to read all 700 pages of it. The owners had employed a court reporter to take down their deliberations. It was as though Judge Landis and his times had been brought alive before Penner's eyes.

They were a lot like these times, actually.

An impassioned speech by Dodgers owner Charles Ebbets jumped out at Penner. Ebbets talked about the failure of the three-man National Commission that had tried to run baseball but consistently broken down into self-interested squabbling. He argued for a strong commissioner and stable governance:

Animosities, petty jealousies and peanut politics should be dropped and ignored. I believe it is our duty here to the great American public, not so much to ourself as trustees, not to pass on professional baseball because we are financially interested, but if we are broad-minded people we should look further ahead to the public that we have encouraged to enter our gates, millions of people who have come to us and have become kids again when they got into our gates.

They are grown people but at the game they are kids and they look to us for entertainment and attraction, and they are the people who are looking to us today. They are the people we have got to consider—not so much our money but that great American public that we have brought up to entertain and who look to us to continue this great American sport along professional lines.

The game itself will last as long as eternity lasts. It can never be done away with. As kids, you and you and myself, I in my kid days 50 years ago played "Old Cat," used to go to Elysian Fields and come back in a stone fight against New Jersey, and the feeling that pervaded you in your kid days is the feeling of the kids today, and you can't take the game away from them. But you can improve this game and broaden it in the minds of the people who come into your gates and into my gate, and those are the people we have got to consider. Those people are looking in the direction of this room today to see what we do.

Colonel Jacob Ruppert, the brewer who owned the Yankees, decried the squabbling between the two leagues:

We have come to the point where we must do something. You go to one side and hear one story and then go to the other side and hear another story. What is the result? What has baseball got out of it? We have been acting like a lot of schoolboys.

It is too bad for men to mistrust one another in baseball or no matter what it is. Baseball is aired in the newspaper. Everybody knows about it. Our business is an open book. We are delighted for them to know our business. The public have become enthusiastic over our business. Still we are in a room where everybody interested in baseball is looking at the other man and saying, "The more I see of this American League man," or "The more I see of this National League man," the bigger damn fools I think they are.

When I was interested in baseball years ago, I got so disgusted reading about politics in baseball I would not go to a baseball game any longer. The time will come when it will be too late to remedy conditions and again a great many will stay away from baseball and it will take considerable time to get them to come back again.

As Landis talked with the owners, Penner discovered, he was preoccupied with the length and term of his contract. He never mentioned a thing about not being fired. He just wanted to be sure he was paid. (Eight years at $50,000 a year, if you please. The owners prevailed for the first and only time with Landis, getting him to accept seven years.)

The owners, for their part, spent much more time on the rules for drafting, signing, and optioning players than on the grand design of the Major League Agreement. A Philadelphia lawyer named George Pepper kept ducking in and out of the owners' meetings to check on various points. He was clearly the real drafter of the Major League Agreement, and he would finally go over it with the owners and Landis, section by section.

When he came to Article 9, he said, "I would like to take entire responsibility for suggesting that there ought to be a provision binding the parties that the powers and compensation of the commissioner should not be diminished during the term of his office."

So—Judge Landis hadn't handed it down on tablets after all. It was all the idea of a Philadelphia lawyer trying to *ingratiate* himself with Landis.

When Section 9 was read aloud again later, it drew not one comment from the owners. A long and vigorous discussion did ensue, however, on whether the proper draft price for minor-leaguers was $5,000 or $7,500.

No matter. Jerry Penner had found what he needed to know. He finished and plunked down the transcript. If it wouldn't have shattered the suburban hush and been so corny, he'd have shouted "Eureka!"

He did the next best thing. He called Jerry Reinsdorf.

Now the conspirators felt secure on both historical and contract-law grounds. Vincent could be fired as long as he was paid for the duration of his term. What still wasn't clear was how many votes it took to fire him. Nowhere was it spelled out and no one knew for sure. All they knew was that the number of conference-callers was steadily increasing.

The Colorado Rockies came aboard, appalled at the lack of direction and leadership in their early ownership meetings. The Mariners' new chairman had the same reaction, though he hadn't joined the conference-call conspirators. John Ellis emerged, dazed, from his first owners' meeting and said to Dick Ravitch, "Is this it?"

"This is it," Ravitch grinned.

The Braves finally came aboard, another super-station voting its economic interest. Bill Bartholomay and Stan Kasten, their chairman and president, had been down on Vincent for some time. It took time to bring around Ted Turner, who didn't want to burn any bridges before he needed to.

When the Giants' Bob Lurie turned against Vincent, the conference-call group was up to sixteen. Lurie was steamed that Vincent had invited him to "explore his options"—including moving—and then pulled the rug out from under him when he tried to sell to St. Petersburg interests.

But there the number stuck. Reinsdorf and Selig couldn't win over anybody else. Vincent had his staunch core of support: Fred Wilpon, Eli Jacobs, and George Bush. He had other supporters by default. Vincent spent a lot of time at Fenway Park, because of his Cape Cod place, and had friendly relations with Haywood Sullivan. Wayne Huizenga was no admirer, but he was grateful for Vincent's role in keeping the Giants out of St. Petersburg. Wally Haas, president of the A's, had no use for Vincent, but Walter Haas, Sr., the patriarch, was friendly with him.

Reinsdorf had always figured the magic number was twenty-one. That was the three-quarters no-confidence tally that would be beyond reproach. When it became clear they couldn't reach that, his fallback was eighteen—still a healthy two thirds. In any event, he wanted the vote to come by the next quarterly owners' meeting, on September 8. If it passed, so might the moment for dethroning Vincent.

Some owners who'd signed on to the conference calls but remained on civil terms with Vincent urged him privately to resign. Doug Danforth of the Pirates visited him at 350 Park Avenue in early August. The retired CEO of Westinghouse was establishment through and through—Duquesne Club, Business Roundtable, the works. Establishment men hated scenes, and he personally liked Fay Vincent.

But he couldn't stand by and watch his franchise go down the drain. The Pirates had hired bright young men to run both the business and baseball sides. The team was en route to winning a third straight National League East title and they'd drawn 2 million last year. Yet the club was losing money and in the process of losing its best players—Bobby Bonilla had already departed—because it couldn't afford to keep them. There was something wrong with this picture and Fay Vincent, in Danforth's view, was doing nothing to address it.

"Fay saw that revenue-sharing would have to happen, but he wasn't spending time approaching it," he would later reflect. "It's something you have to look at and build a consensus."

The Pohlad Group was a reaction to that, and while Danforth participated in it, he could see the downside of it. It made the divisions between the haves and have-nots sharply political as well as financial.

Danforth settled into Vincent's corner office on the seventeenth floor.

"Fay, in my judgment you've lost the confidence of the majority," he said. "Have you thought about bagging it?"

Vincent hadn't and wouldn't. For more than two hours, Danforth tried to soft-sell resignation. The problems were overwhelming. The owners were louses. Who needed this aggravation? The worsening condition of his back gave him every reason to resign for the sake of his health. It was a graceful out, and it was true: Vincent faced an operation to try to stem the deterioration.

"Say it's your health; say these guys are a bunch of assholes and don't appreciate you; say whatever you like," he said. "But I think you should resign."

Vincent wouldn't budge. Nor would he respond to the Phillies' Bill Giles, who also paid a visit.

"Fay, you know I've been supportive of you, but I think it's time to step down," he said. "You just don't have the support of enough clubs in the American League. There are eight or nine owners who have never recovered from expansion. You can't govern the American League."

"Well," said Vincent, "what did you think of my decision?"

"I thought it was perfect, just right. But you can't lead if there are too many people against you."

Vincent didn't take their advice. Asked to call an ownership meeting to review his status, he flatly refused to do so. In a letter, he said he took his "moral leadership" responsibilities too seriously and his employment contract too literally to accede to this. He'd been retained to serve until March 31, 1994, and, by God, would do so.

"I will not resign—ever," he wrote on August 20. "Even if there is a meeting and a vote to remove me from office, or an attempt to limit my powers . . . I will not leave. I will continue to carry out my responsibilities until such time as the highest court of this land tells me otherwise."

In case they wanted to make something of it, he concluded, he'd retained a lawyer named Brendan Sullivan. Oliver North's old pit-bull attorney would be glad to take them on.

The letter, dripping contempt and anger, was surely a cathartic exercise for Vincent. It was, however, his final political misstep. Reinsdorf and Selig were still having trouble screwing up a lot of owners' courage to take the last step. It was one thing to fax in their no-confidence complaints and grouse on the conference calls. It was quite another to get out the long knives. It would be ugly and, one way or another, there would be major repercussions. But Vincent's haughty letter gave a shot in the arm to the opposition. "When you're faced with an opponent who's shown a lack of resolve, you throw him a bone, give him an excuse to back off," one of the lawyers involved would later reflect. "Instead, Vincent said, 'In your face.' He challenged their manhood."

Vincent's refusal to call a meeting would not, in any event, prevent the owners from having one. They simply turned to the league presidents and asked *them* to call for one. Bill White and Bobby Brown gladly did this.

"Well," Nelson Doubleday said to White, "I guess the Jewboys have gotten to you."

Now the groundwork was laid for the final confrontation. The conference-callers decided to split the showdown into two meetings—one on September 3 in Chicago, the other on September 8 in St. Louis, the site of the quarterly ownership meeting. If the first one produced a big enough no-confidence vote, perhaps Vincent could be convinced to resign before the second. They hoped to avert the still-unanswered question: How big a vote was needed to fire him?

Indeed, Reinsdorf and Selig were nervous as cats in a string factory. They were still stuck at sixteen votes of no-confidence. It was a rock-solid bloc, made up of people who, in the words of one, "don't want to fire Fay, we want to kill him."

But the magic number was eighteen. They *thought* they could pick up two more in the meeting. John Ellis of the Mariners seemed to be leaning their way, though he wouldn't sign on to the conference calls. Mike Illitch, the Tigers' owner, was brandnew to baseball but not to this kind of dustup. As the Detroit Red Wings' owner, he'd been through the changing of the guard in the NHL a few months back (when president John Ziegler and chairman Bill Wirtz were rather gracefully slid out of office). At least he wouldn't be afraid of the issue. Selig and Reinsdorf were also trying to get John McMullen to rejoin their camp and bring Ewing Kauffman aboard. Kauffman didn't care for Vincent, but he feared a long legal fight. Selig and Reinsdorf hoped that between these four they had two more votes. But they hated to rely on hope rather than assurance.

They tried to orchestrate the meeting to maximize their strength. Seats would be assigned. The pro-Vincent owners would be kept isolated, flanked by strong anti-Vincent stalwarts so that they wouldn't be able to solicit votes from undecideds or plot strategy among themselves. The Mets and Orioles would be off in the left- and right-field corners of the room.

They also paid careful attention to the batting order for taking their whacks at Vincent. Paul Beeston of the Blue Jays, who would chair the meeting, would control that. The grayer heads would go first, to keep things as statesmanlike and cool as possible. Beeston, working his way down a list, would recognize them in preset order.

Beeston was also tutored by lawyer Bob Dupuy on Roberts Rules of Order. He instructed him not to get flustered if Vincent's supporters tried a parliamentary maneuver. He was particularly wary of Orioles president Larry Lucchino, the brightest of the loyalists and a lawyer. Beeston would be flanked by the two league lawyers to advise him, and, Dupuy reminded him, the chairman always had the power to call for a temporary adjournment if he was thrown a curve.

The dissidents had some divisions on basic points right up to the very morning of the meeting. Jerry Reinsdorf, who'd taken a suite overnight at the O'Hare Hilton, hosted a breakfast council of war there.

Over coffee, Selig, Tom Werner of the Padres, and Peter Widdrington of the Blue Jays argued for a softer version of the resolution. Have a no-confidence vote, they urged, but don't demand that Vincent resign. They thought that might pick them up some more votes.

Reinsdorf disagreed.

"If we don't ask him to resign, will we really pick up any more votes?" he asked. "And if we don't ask him to resign, you know what will happen? He'll get this resolution, look at it, and say, 'They didn't ask me to do anything.' "

The group analyzed the fence-sitters and ultimately agreed with Reinsdorf. If they picked up neutrals, it would be for reasons other than the wording. And if they whacked Vincent over the head with anything less than a two-by-four, he wouldn't deign to notice.

The Lords filed past a phalanx of writers into the meeting

room and into their assigned seats. Doug Danforth was recognized by Beeston and arose.

"My interpretation is this," he said. "Fay has lost the confidence of the majority of owners. Because of that, it would be very difficult for him to govern effectively."

Then Danforth made clear where *he* stood.

"I personally have no confidence in Fay's leadership," he said. "Players' salaries are too high; clubs are on the verge of collapse; and there's no planning. Media leaks come out of his office, and he's intervened in areas he had no business getting involved in.

"The commissioner is the leader. He has to take the blame for how bad things are. Baseball cannot move forward under his leadership. The office is in disarray, and he is not able to build consensus among owners."

Then he read the no-confidence resolution.

Beeston went through the remainder of the graybeard lineup: Fred Kuhlmann, Bill Giles, Stanton Cook, Peter O'Malley.

The Dodgers' owner had cautioned them two years earlier that they didn't really know Fay Vincent. Now he was saying that they knew him only too well.

"Fay Vincent holds us in low regard," he said. "He's always saying something negative about one owner to another owner. I don't know what he said about me, but I know what he said about every one of you."

Carl Pohlad poured out his frustrations.

"Fay is not an effective leader," he said. "All he's interested in is having the spotlight on himself. He loves to go to ballparks, sit on the field, and sign autographs instead of being in the office getting his job done."

He ticked off a list of qualities needed to be a good CEO and concluded that Vincent didn't have them.

"Fay's incompetence is a cancer," he said.

George Bush was the tenth owner to speak and the first to defend Vincent.

"I'm sad we're here," he said, looking around. "I don't agree with the first nine speakers. Fay has integrity and backbone. His word is his bond. He makes tough calls. Even if George Bush doesn't agree with them, he respects them.

"Fay doesn't play politics. Those who have spoken have been inconsistent with their criticism. Fay believes in principle and is digging in. He won't quit. He will go to court to retain his position; I assure you of that. There's no point in firing him, because he's not leaving.

"I'd like you to think about something else, too. Baseball can suffer the consequences of causing a good man to walk through the klieg lights like this. How can we ever fill this position if you do succeed in removing Fay like this? Let him at least serve out his term."

The Orioles' Larry Lucchino echoed Bush.

"The commissioner will always alienate some people," he said. "This resolution doesn't mean anything. It doesn't terminate the commissioner. He can't be fired and he won't resign. We should take the high road and honor the contract. We lack integrity if we try to terminate it. The Orioles have the right to have a commissioner for the balance of his term."

It struck some as a thinly veiled threat that the Orioles would sue if Vincent were axed. But Lucchino didn't try the parliamentary maneuvers they'd feared. The closest thing to any such effort came from Boston's Haywood Sullivan. He moved to amend the no-confidence motion so as to gut it. Reinsdorf quickly moved to table it, and got the votes to do so.

Fred Wilpon made the only other run at staving off the no-confidence vote.

"We're like two trains on a track running at each other," he said. "We cannot allow them to collide. Even if the anti-Vincent group is right, we cannot achieve our goals. It's a lose-lose situation because the legal fight will be too long. We must reach a compromise, and I would like to propose one."

It covered four points:

- Vincent would stay in office but agree in even stronger terms than before to stay out of labor.
- The owners would form a restructuring committee to recommend changes in baseball's governance.
- Neither side would derogate the other to the press.
- Vincent would make a promise of no retribution.

About the only response Wilpon drew was raised eyebrows at the last point. Why did he think it necessary to assure them of no bloodbaths? What did that say about his friend Fay Vincent?

Jerry Reinsdorf would have added that to his list of "Bad Things Fay's Done" (under the heading of "Heavy-handedness"), except he already had so much material. He'd separated Vincent's failings into ten categories and was down to his banning of Minnie Minoso (in the "Needless Actions" category) when he realized he'd already prattled on for twenty minutes. He chastised himself later, knowing he may have risked losing votes on account of excessive vehemence.

Reinsdorf cut himself short. "I've probably talked too much," he admitted.

"That's right," said Selig. "Give 'im the hook."

Selig's own talk was short but emotional.

"My best friends in the whole world are in this room; this is a very traumatic day," he said. "In the beginning, I considered Fay an appendage to Bart, the best friend I'll ever have. I wrote a memo after the 1990 labor negotiations, which was highly critical of the commissioner. John McMullen called me and said it was far too easy on him. The Wilpon plan is many months too late. It would have been acceptable much earlier, but not now.

"I've always been a great defender of the establishment. Fay has had an opportunity to propel us forward, but instead he's held us back. Band-Aids won't work for the next eighteen months. Only a commissioner can lead. I was one of the last to come to the conclusion that Fay must go, but he doesn't really care for the institution. While this is a tragic circumstance, it damages the office further if we continue in the vein we're in today. There will be less damage if we make a change and move on so we can propel the industry forward."

Selig and Reinsdorf began to breathe easier when Detroit's Mike Illitch, attending his first ownership meeting, said he wanted to be "a good partner" and backed the resolution. They heaved a sigh of relief when Seattle's John Ellis got up.

"My relationship with Fay has been very good; Fay has been very helpful to me," he said. "But it's clear our existing situation is intolerable. A large majority of the clubs have lost confidence in the commissioner. I am going to vote for the resolution for that reason. A commissioner cannot be the commissioner without support. I ask for the largest majority possible in support of the resolution."

They had their two-thirds majority. The no-confidence resolution passed 18–9, with one abstention. (The abstention was Marge Schott, who'd given the meeting its one moment of comic relief. When her turn came to weigh in on Vincent, she said, "What's all this about the Tribune Company getting TV rights with so many clubs? What's this mean? Does it mean that every time the Tribune gets a new team it creates a new super-station?" Beeston declared it a little off the point, and they moved on.)

The meeting was over. Bill White went off to call Vincent with the results. Bud Selig briefed the press. Everybody else raced for the airport for homeward flights—and braced for an ugly confrontation in St. Louis, five days hence.

Publicly, Vincent vowed to press on. Privately, he was crushed. Some owners had told him one thing and voted the opposite—not a first in the baseball business, but still a shock to Vincent. ("I'm with you," Ted Turner had told him to his face.) Some of the owners' votes he found unfathomable. He'd campaigned for a San Jose stadium for Bob Lurie. He'd had warm relations with the Toronto people. As for Seattle, where he'd shepherded the Nintendos through all the obstacles, he could only say, "*Et tu*, John Ellis?"

At his Cape Cod retreat that weekend, Vincent mulled over what to do. Wayne Huizenga of the Marlins urged him to come to St. Louis and knock 'em dead with another speech. But most of the advice from allies was to give it up. They were a broken record: "There's no point in continuing."

Steve Greenberg was with Vincent at the Cape, dutifully but reluctantly working on a speech for St. Louis. "It makes no sense to be litigating and fighting for the right to do a job you don't want to do anymore," he said.

The owners' side was also girding for battle, on the assumption there would be one. On Labor Day afternoon, Jerry Reinsdorf, Bill Giles, and Selig's lawyer, Bob Dupuy, were in a mini–conference call preparing for a mass conference call later on. They were again weighing the best procedures, discussing the best ways to forestall challenges, when Bill Giles broke in.

"He's resigned," he said. "It just came over the wire."

A massive sense of relief oozed through the phone lines.

The St. Louis ownership meeting turned from a tense confrontation into a three-day celebration. Bud Selig became, in effect, acting commissioner. He extended an olive branch to Fred Wilpon, making him co-chairman of the restructuring committee he'd proposed. There was grand talk of seizing control of their destiny and of bright new days.

For the first time in ages, the old bonhomie seemed to be back. At the end of one day's meetings, the Busches hosted a party at their Grant's Farm. It was as opulent as in Gussie's day, and it was a magnificent evening in every way. A thunderstorm raged outside, accentuating the warmth and good cheer inside. The Lords swilled beer and cocktails and listened to Gene Autry sing his old songs.

They were back in the saddle again.

$ 26 $

FAY VINCENT, IT turned out, would be the last thing the Lords agreed on for a long time.

First they splintered on labor strategy. Dick Ravitch was pushing to renegotiate the labor contract, which under the 1990 settlement could be reopened at either side's initiative. The deadline for doing so was December 1992.

Plenty of small-market clubs, facing mounting losses, agreed with Ravitch. In 1992, the Pirates lost $10 million and two more star players, Barry Bonds and Doug Drabek. Team president Mark Sauer once tried explaining to his shortstop, Jay Bell, why the system needed revamping.

"Jay, the point is you guys have won," he said to Bell, the National League player rep. "But now you have to decide whether you're going to burn the bodies, bury them, or put us in intensive care. What are you guys going to do?"

Bell and most other players listened skeptically to these plaintive cries. For years, they'd heard the same story: baseball was on the verge of collapse; salaries had to be reined in. Yet somehow owners kept laying out money—and more money—without ever going bankrupt.

"You're hearing a lot of talk about how bad off the clubs are," Don Fehr told the players earlier that year as he made the rounds of spring training camps. "I'd like to give you a fact. If they paid every major league player one million [dollars], they'd only have seven hundred fifty million left over." It never failed to get a gasp and a laugh. (It did, however, ignore certain other significant costs, like taxes, lease payments, farm systems, and front-office payroll.)

Ravitch held a series of regional meetings that fall on the reopening of the labor negotiations. He argued that it was the only way to change the game's economic course. He showed the owners some gruesome charts that projected how far they'd be underwater by 1995 if they waited that long to reopen. They'd be taking a chance by reopening, Ravitch acknowledged, "But without risk there's no leverage."

Shadowing him at each meeting were two owners who vehemently disagreed, the Mets' Fred Wilpon and the Orioles' Larry Lucchino. The weak clubs wouldn't be aided by a reopener and work stoppage, the two maintained; they'd be killed. Baseball would close the doors on revenue they desperately needed and jeopardize the last year of the lucrative CBS contract.

Wilpon and Lucchino were protecting their own big-market interests, of course. The Mets were potentially the most lucrative franchise in baseball (they minted cash during the team's late-eighties glory days), but they had to play to profit. The Orioles loathed losing a single sellout at Camden Yards.

The two developed an economic argument worthy of Milton Friedman: *Let the market do the job.* Don't tender players contracts. Don't offer salary arbitration. Don't be afraid to cut players loose. If the market was flooded with players, it would drive down salaries and send a powerful message to the union. The party was over. Baseball didn't need a lockout, argued Wilpon and Lucchino; it needed a "market correction."

The free-agent market opened, and the news of big signings began pouring into Ravitch's 350 Park Avenue office: John Smiley to Cincinnati for $18.4 million; Doug Drabek to Houston for $19.5 million; Jose Guzman to Chicago for $14.3 million. Ravitch and Jerry Reinsdorf developed a running joke about it. Whoever got word first of the latest megasigning would call the other with an announcement: "We've had another market correction."

Wilpon's economic theory may have been flawed, but he'd cast doubt in the minds of many militant-leaning owners.

As the winter meetings rolled around, no one knew which way the vote would go.

The gray December sky hovered over Louisville and refused to lift. An icy wind cut through the walkway between the Galt House hotel's two towers and twirled through the revolving door into the lobby. Rain occasionally pelted the hotel's windows, smearing and blurring the downtown skyline.

The weather was the good part.

The furies had descended on baseball's 1992 winter meetings, assuring that the year would conclude in the only appropriate manner: absolute chaos.

While owners sat in one room mulling how to restore fiscal sanity, general managers sat in various others, signing free agents to $230 million worth of contracts. The biggest deal of all came right at the start. Jerry Reinsdorf called Dick Ravitch, who was still in New York, with the news.

"We've had another market correction," Reinsdorf announced. "Barry Bonds to the Giants. Six years, forty-three million."

Ravitch gulped. Then he wondered: "Well, who's obligated to pay for it?"

The Giants' current owner, Bob Lurie, had agreed to sell the team to a group led by Safeway supermarket magnate Peter Magowan. But the $100 million sale hadn't yet been approved. And it was Magowan who'd made the deal with Bonds. What if the sale wasn't approved? Who'd be on the hook, Lurie or Magowan?

No one seemed to know the answers to Ravitch's questions. A press conference announcing the deal was called off, and the parties spent the next forty-eight hours reconstructing the terms. In the end, after they'd succeeded in doing so, a haggard Dennis Gilbert, Bond's agent, joined a beaming Bonds, who proclaimed it "the greatest moment of my life."

It was that kind of week. Carl Barger, president of the Marlins, dropped dead of a heart attack. Marge Schott insulted every ethnic and racial group in America, creating baseball's worst affirmative-action flap since Al Campanis aired his views on swimming. Jesse Jackson showed up to denounce baseball, demand a meeting, and of course make every TV network's evening news. Bud Selig dashed around so frantically between meetings that a group of agents, discussing a movie adaptation of the follies, had no problem casting him. "Jack Lemmon," said Randy Hendricks. "We want that *China Syndrome* feel."

A core-meltdown comparison seemed apt, though Twins GM Andy MacPhail wasn't laughing. He was a third-generation baseball man who, for the first time, questioned whether he belonged in the business. "I wonder if it's appropriate to participate in something that has almost become decadent," he said. "Everyone in the game would benefit if they would take one step back and understand the fundamental elements of the game that made it such an integral part of America. We should not jeopardize that, but that's what we're doing. We're infecting the game with acrimony, and there's no reason for it. Someone has to take the first step. Someone has to have the courage to say, 'Hey, this is wrong. We're perverting one of our institutions.' "

The acrimony was assured of continuing, however, when the Lords finally voted on the labor-contract reopener. Dick Ravitch got what he wanted, but by a vote so close, 15–13, that it was hardly a mandate. Indeed, it suggested fissures among the owners more than a day of reckoning for the players.

Ravitch had planned to make his lead-off item on the bargaining agenda a salary cap. It was something the owners could unite behind, maybe even hang tough on. But Wilpon and Lucchino had done well in scaring the weak clubs with talk about a lockout. The have-not small-market clubs put a huge condition on supporting the reopener. Ravitch would first have to forge a revenue-sharing agreement among the owners. They demanded not just salary limitation but resource redistribution. And thus was Ravitch's original strategy stood on its head.

Don Fehr, in Louisville for a joint management-union meeting on AIDS, was visibly dismayed by the vote. It wasn't that he lacked confidence in the players' ability to handle what might come. It was the owners that concerned him.

"They are utterly disorganized and have no plan," he said, shaking his head. "But they've created the conditions where things could get out of control."

That's more or less how a member of the Economic Study Committee put it, too. The committee released its long-awaited report that week and provided one more clue to why Fay Vincent was an ex-commissioner. He'd put great stock in the committee's ability to forge a consensus view between owners and players on the state of baseball's economy. Instead it produced a classic in the genre of writing by committee. The tortured compromise language obfuscated rather than clarified the issues.

Tucked away in the back, however, was one glimmering piece of insight. Committee member Henry J. Aaron was best known as a health-care economist at the Brookings Institution. But his short, blunt minority report just about said it all on the baseball industry:

Through roughly 9,000 words of text . . . the majority report leads readers up one blind alley and down another, suggesting that an industry whose companies are valued in the market at prices as high, or higher than, ever before is on the brink of some vague sort of economic trouble.

The industry of baseball *is* in political chaos, bereft of any governing mechanism by which clubs can agree to share revenues among themselves in a fashion that will permit all clubs both to compete equally on the field and to have an equal chance to make positive operating revenues. No such concerns arise in most other industries, where increased market share goes to the strongest companies. In baseball, however, more "companies" in more cities make a stronger industry able to bring the pleasures of baseball to more fans. Thus, a governance structure of professional baseball clubs that is incapable of enforcing greater revenue sharing is *the* problem. Unless that problem is addressed and solved, labor-management peace will never come to baseball.

Revenue-sharing had been a thorny issue since the dawn of baseball. In the 1880s, one of the charter National League owners—Frederick Kimball Stearns of Detroit—spent $25,000 to assemble a top team. The Detroit market alone wouldn't support that huge investment. But Stearns was sure he'd draw big on the road, where he got 30 percent of the gate.

The other owners realized this and simply changed the rules. Instead of getting a percentage of the gate, Stearns could collect only a fixed $125 per game.

Revenue-sharing had operated more or less the same ever since. The issue was often debated in high-minded terms, but it all came down to pocketbook interests and haves versus have-nots. One of Brooklyn's early owners gave the back of his hand to visitors clamoring for a bigger cut of his gate. Why, he asked, should small-city teams leave his park "with a good fat pocketbook," while he received only "small change" when visiting them. Conversely, Bill Veeck once pressed the Yankees for half their radio/TV revenues for broadcasts of their games with his St. Louis Browns.

"We're half the attraction," he argued.

"Would you have agreed to this when you had the Indians?" asked Yankees GM George Weiss, referring to Veeck's prosperous former club.

"Circumstances alter cases," Veeck replied.

He got nowhere. Neither did Charlie Finley, even when he once threatened to skip a series in Yankee Stadium if he didn't get a cut of the TV money.

The haves royally swatted away the impudent have-nots at every turn, making them out to be welfare chiselers. Walter

O'Malley used to quickly dismiss all talk of revenue-sharing, saying, "That's socialism." Boston's Haywood Sullivan once averred, "If we took a socialistic approach, we'd have everyone out fishing. People would say, 'Oh, the Dodgers will carry me.'"

George Steinbrenner's standard denunciation began with the declaration, "*Comrades*, I want to make it clear I'm not going to pay anyone for not working." He tore into Calvin Griffith once, after the Twins' owner had implored the big-market teams to spread the wealth. "If you let me get rid of all the relatives on your payroll," said Steinbrenner, "I'd be glad to give you some of my TV money."

And so, in baseball, the subject of revenue-sharing became something like the weather: everybody talked about it, but nobody did anything about it. Bart Giamatti once asked Lou Hoynes what he saw as baseball's top business priority. "To more evenly distribute its revenues," Hoynes replied. "You don't have to be a genius to figure that out, but you do have to be a genius to figure out how."

Revenue-sharing was so intractable that there was even a joke about it. An agent was out taking a walk one day when God came up alongside him. The two started to chat about baseball.

"God, when will we ever see another four-hundred hitter?" the agent asked.

"Not in your lifetime," answered God.

"What about a thirty-game winner. When will that happen again?"

"Not in your lifetime," answered God.

"What about revenue-sharing? When will the big-city owners agree to revenue-sharing to help the teams in smaller cities?"

God smiled and said, "Not in my lifetime."

There was some revenue-sharing in baseball, of course. Every team equally shared the network-TV and licensing revenue. But otherwise, compared to the NFL, it was sparse. In the American League, visitors got 20 percent of the gate; in the National League, 46 cents per ticket. The visitors' take in the National League had risen only 31 cents per ticket since 1885.

The formula for sharing local TV revenue was nearly as antiquated. The National League Broadcast Agreement, drawn up in 1956, carved up the country into exclusive territories for TV purposes. It also required teams with games on pay-TV to share 25 percent of the revenue with the visitors. Though the document has a fifties-era vision of pay-TV (referring to "closed-circuit theater television"), it became the basis for sharing local cable-TV revenue. The American League used a roughly equivalent formula.

But there were more holes in those broadcast agreements than in the 1962 Mets' infield. The teams on super-stations, for instance, didn't qualify as cable TV. Stations like WTBS and WGN were technically just local broadcast outlets. The fact that their signals were picked up by cable systems across the country was irrelevant, for the purposes of the National League Broadcast Agreement. Nor did teams with big non-cable TV deals have to share revenue. The Dodgers, for instance, had no cable, but sold their over-the-air TV rights for $15 million a year.

A small-market team like Montreal, with a small cable-TV contract, was actually writing checks to a big-market team like Los Angeles. "The rich are being subsidized by the poor; it's outrageous!" exploded Claude Brochu, the Expos' president.

Brochu and the National League's other small-market owners had been smoldering ever since their 1991 failure to obtain modest gate-splitting reform. Bill White had proposed a formula that would net them 75 cents a ticket. It wasn't a windfall, but it was better than 46 cents. The big-market owners became vexed, however, when the Pirates' Doug Danforth pressed for a greater raise—a 20 percent visitors' share, matching that of the American League. They decided to put the have-nots in their place by voting down raises of *any* magnitude.

The small-market owners found their means of attack in the National League Broadcast Agreement. For years the document was routinely renewed, and for good reason. Besides establishing territories and cable-TV rules, it established reciprocal broadcast rights from each other's ballparks. The alternative was negotiating separate agreements among all the teams. Therein lay potential chaos.

Therein, the have-nots finally decided, lay their revenge. In December 1993, five NL owners served notice that they would refuse to sign the 1994 Broadcast Agreement. (It took one year's notice to dissolve the pact.) They were Montreal's Brochu, Pittsburgh's Doug Danforth, San Diego's Tom Werner, Houston's Drayton McLane, and Miami's Wayne Huizenga.

If TV access was to be negotiated team-by-team, the small-marketeers intended to extract a stiff price. They wanted to divvy up *all* the local TV money, not just that from cable, and they wanted the Braves and Cubs to pay much more than the

$20 million in "super-station taxes" they now contributed. They would also try to use the Broadcast Agreement as their weapon to change the gate split and get a piece of the haves' luxury-box income. In sum: the big boys would jolly well pay up or the small marketeers would take their bats and balls and go home.

The American League have-nots missed the notification deadline for 1994. But nine of them soon spelled out their Broadcast Agreement plans for 1995: o-u-t. "These guys figured out, 'We have our own deck of cards to play,' " said one baseball-broadcast expert. "They finally said, *'No mas.'* "

The haves snarled back. Okay, they said, end the Broadcast Agreement. But that would end the exclusive territories, too. How about a national Yankees network? Or how about the haves only signing TV contracts with one another? What kind of a TV package would the Expos have if they could show the Florida Marlins and Houston Astros but were frozen out of the Braves, Cubs, and Dodgers?

One small-market owner summarized the lofty tenor of the debate this way:

> BIG GUY: If you try to steal our money from us we'll sue.
> LITTLE GUY: But we aren't going to survive without changes.
> BIG GUY: Well, go ahead and die. You might not be here, but there'll still be another pigeon to take your place.

It was in this environment that poor Dick Ravitch had to operate. He wasn't naïve about the task, which he privately admitted was a bear. He liked to describe his job with a joke: "A guy was driving down the street in a panel truck and every time there was a red light he'd jump out, run around to the back of the truck, and hit it three times with a baseball bat. The guy driving behind him couldn't contain his curiosity any longer, and said to the other guy, 'Why are you hitting your truck with the bat?' He says, 'This truck has a two-ton capacity. I got three tons of birds in the back, and therefore I have to keep one ton flying at all points in time.' "

Ravitch's task was particularly formidable because he actually had to get the Lords' agreement not only on revenue-sharing but on the accompanying salary-cap formula. He called the two, with good reason, "the Siamese Twins." The big-market owners would only accept revenue-sharing if their payrolls were sliced by the salary cap. Small-market owners would only accept a salary cap if they got enough revenue-sharing. (A salary cap set a maximum on teams' payrolls, but also a minimum. That could be a problem for strapped franchises.) If he pulled all that off, of course, he still had to sell it to the player's union.

If anyone had a shot at delivering the Siamese Twins, said some admirers, it was Ravitch. But how much of a shot? "Dick is incredibly effective and hard-working," said one baseball executive. "That takes his chances from zero to five percent."

Ravitch had only the smallest of windows during which to get all this done—before spring training. Only until then would the owners have the leverage of a lockout threat. Ravitch also had only the slightest chance to sell it to a skeptical Don Fehr.

He'd tried to get to know the union chief over a series of friendly lunches. They had an economic conundrum in common, Ravitch maintained. Just as only a small portion of owners made all the money, so, too, with the players. By 1994, Ravitch projected, 10 percent of the players would be making 50 percent of the total pay. The peasants in both camps were about to rise up in arms. "I've got a problem with my constituency, you've got a problem with yours," Ravitch said. "We could really change the system."

It was true that star players cashed in, that winter of 1992–93, while secondary players got whacked. Kevin Bass signed with Houston for 25 percent of what he'd made with San Francisco in 1992 ($500,000 versus $2 million). Ellis Burks changed Sox (Red to White) at about the same discount ($500,000 versus $2.3 million). Boston refused to pick up the option on Billy Hatcher's contract at $1.6 million. He was released, then the Sox promptly re-signed him to a new *two*-year deal at $1.4 million. The Dodgers retained Eric Davis but trimmed him back from $3.6 million to $1 million.

The list went on and on. By mid-January, fully four dozen veteran players had signed for substantial cuts. Many more would later sign minor league contracts just to get their feet in the door for spring training tryouts. "We're headed toward a star system," said Tal Smith, "where the marquee players get whatever the market will bear and the supporting players scramble for what they can."

Still, the bifurcated baseball economy didn't represent nearly as much of a problem for Don Fehr as it did for Dick Ravitch. Yes, his union's membership was stratified. But the $3 million players wanted no change in the system, for obvious reasons. Neither did the $109,000 players. Each rookie was totally confident he'd be a star some day and cash in big. The $1 million veteran in the middle who'd been squeezed out didn't count. He was basically out of baseball and thus out of the union.

So Fehr wouldn't buy Ravitch's argument and he resisted Ravitch's efforts to cozy up to him one-on-one. As a matter of policy, he negotiated with nobody from the Lords' side unless players were present. As a veteran of fifteen years, he'd heard all these "disaster is nigh" arguments before. Fehr walked away from each lunch with the same thought: "He sounds just like all the other guys, and he thinks he's different."

On Friday, January 9, Ravitch invited Fehr and Gene Orza over to his office and hit them with a surprise. He told them they *had* to get a contract done by mid-February, when spring training opened. With so many complex issues on the table—revenue-sharing, salary caps, and the rest—he wanted to work out an accelerated negotiating schedule.

To Fehr and Orza, a mid-February deadline screamed out one word: lockout. But they weren't about to let Ravitch dictate the pace of this game. The time frame was totally unrealistic to discuss a complete restructuring of the baseball business.

"This is a setup for a confrontation," Fehr said. "If you want to do it, go ahead, we can't stop you. But it won't affect our bargaining posture at all."

As they left, Ravitch handed them a letter that put his speed-up request in writing. The two sides agreed on only one thing: they'd see each other next Wednesday for the first negotiating session. Fehr and Orza hustled back to their office to get the word out to player reps: the war drums were beating again.

Any appetite Dick Ravitch had for hardball on Friday, however, was gone four days later. A Monday and Tuesday ownership meeting in Dallas was no council of war; it was a Chinese fire drill.

Ravitch spent much of his time there trying to counter yet another Fred Wilpon foray against him. The Mets' president headed the restructuring committee, organized upon Vincent's ouster and charged with reinventing baseball's governance. Its latest draft recommended that the PRC chief—Ravitch—report to the commissioner. "Over my dead body," Ravitch told every owner who would listen.

Meantime, it was business as usual for the Lords: the commissioner search committee had produced nothing; the Marge Schott mess kept dragging on; and the TV committee hadn't even begun any negotiations for a new network contract. In the words of one disgusted participant, "It was simultaneous gridlock and chaos."

One moment was particularly illuminating. Both Ravitch and Jeff White, baseball's chief financial officer, were to make progress reports. White went first, reporting the financial results for 1992 and forecasting 1993's. Among other things, he projected that the teams would pay a total of $830 million in player salaries and another $55 million in benefits.

Then it was Ravitch's turn. He projected 1993 salaries and benefits of $975 million. A question immediately came from one of the Lords: why the $90 million discrepancy? "Jeff," Ravitch asked, "was your number based on what they [the owners] told you or on the actual contracts signed?"

It was what the owners told him, White said, and a smile immediately split Ravitch's face. "You lied!" he informed the Lords. "Your projections come out low every time!"

Ravitch dragged himself back to New York Tuesday night and turned in early, trying to rest for the players' meeting Wednesday morning. He awoke at 4 A.M. with a thought. His mind-set had been changed by the Dallas meeting, though it hadn't crystallized until now.

"The owners don't want to negotiate; the union doesn't want to negotiate; only *I* want to negotiate," Ravitch said to himself. "Let's call off the charade. I've got no leverage and Don knows it."

If he went in with a poker face, followed by the usual press-conference rhetoric, there would be another round of lockout-speculation stories. If he went in and made a clean breast of it—no lockout—they could skip the charade, get down to business . . . and maybe get something going. Ravitch went back to sleep happy.

He walked into a conference room six hours later, where seven union staffers and nine players had gathered to meet him.

"I'd like to make an announcement," he said. "I am not going to recommend a lockout."

He looked around the room, as though he'd expected an ovation. There was no reaction at all, only silence. Finally, Don Fehr spoke.

"That's constructive," he said.

Mostly, Fehr was startled. Ravitch had totally reversed field. Had the owners called him off? Had it all been a bluff? What was the man up to? Did he have any idea?

The players at the meeting were also nonplussed. Ravitch said he wanted to educate them on the sad state of the industry, and produced a stack of chart-laden slides for an overhead projector. "I've got the information on these transparencies," he said.

"Transparencies," Texas pitcher Kevin Brown spoke up. "Well, that's a good word for it."

The transparencies—also known as Ravitch's traveling slide show—became the centerpiece of a push by the labor chief to talk past Don Fehr and directly to the players. He held four meetings with various groups of them during spring training in Arizona and Florida, flashing charts that showed baseball going straight to hell:

- Baseball's declining ratings on both network TV and local broadcasts.
- Baseball's declining demographics—an older, poorer audience than that of the NBA and NFL.
- Baseball's rising ticket and concession prices. (The cost for a family of four to attend a game had crept over $100 at some parks.)
- Baseball's rising salary burden (growing to 63 percent of the gross by 1993) contrasted with its falling revenues (a projected 50 percent drop in network TV revenue after that year).

At the first meeting, in Phoenix, Don Fehr watched the numbers and wondered privately why Ravitch had used some of them. He had projected, for instance, that 263 players would be making $3 million by 1994. Fehr did some rapid division in his head. That worked out to about nine players per club. "They might not react to that with fury," he thought.

Fehr openly jousted with Ravitch on other points. How did he square owners' cries of poverty with their market behavior? Take the megacontract Cecil Fielder had just signed, which featured a $10 million signing bonus.

"All these owners say Fielder's not worth thirty-six million," he lectured. "What they really mean is Cecil Fielder isn't worth thirty-six million to *me*. Every signing means that player is worth that amount to somebody. Otherwise you're trying to convince us that the owners are not rational people, that they're all fucking idiots."

At one point, one of the thirty players attending the meeting injected a question. "I don't understand," he asked Ravitch. "Why don't you just market the game better?"

Ravitch said he thought the owners *would* do a better job if they reached a state of economic equilibrium. But he agreed that they *had* to do better. "The public doesn't like you and they don't like us," he said.

It was true. Baseball had ousted Fay Vincent, locked out players, shaken down cities—and alienated America.

It was documented in excruciating, embarrassing detail. A Harris poll found that 18 percent of those surveyed named baseball as their favorite sport, down from 23 percent in 1985. (Basketball's "favorite" status doubled to 12 percent in that time.) Another survey found that 42 percent of respondents called themselves baseball fans, compared to 60 percent four years earlier.

Since 1989, baseball's TV viewership among twelve- to seventeen-year-olds had fallen 24 percent, while the NBA's had risen 31 percent and the NFL's 16 percent in that category. In an ESPN survey of one hundred children aged ten to twelve, only six named baseball as their favorite sport and four named a baseball player as their favorite athlete.

A *Sports Illustrated* poll identifying the twenty American athletes that kids most admired listed only one baseball player—Bo Jackson. (He was, in fact, a combined baseball-football entry at the time.) A New York firm that matches companies with celebrity spokesmen ranked more than 300 athletes in terms of "likability." Only two active baseball players, Jackson and Nolan Ryan, made the top seventy-five. (Some retired players did considerably better in these so-called Q-ratings. Willie Mays was rated number four and Mickey Mantle number six.)

"When people talk about spoiled, overpaid athletes these days, they're talking about baseball players," said David Burns, whose Chicago company matched athletes with products. "Compare the reputation of Roger Clemens and Jose Canseco with squeaky-clean Joe Montana or patriot David Robinson or good-guy Wayne Gretzky. Other sports superstars appreciate their role, but baseball's best seem to be foaming at the mouth."

A sour feeling lingered about the game, one not dispelled by soft summer evenings at ballparks or taut pennant races. Even by the big-money standards of other pro sports, baseball was obsessively money conscious. For one thing, it was the only sport with salary arbitration. Those cases filled sports sections each

February and alienated fans everywhere. "Here's a country in the throes of recession," said Pirates president Mark Sauer, "and we're throwing brickbats over salary arbitration."

Baseball was also the only sport with unfettered free agency. That created huge player movements each winter, which created huge interest and lots of press. But it was also a system designed to rend the old bond between players, teams, and fans. As the money got bigger, free agents were less apt to re-up with their old teams and more likely to move on.

The day after Jack Morris pitched a ten-inning shutout to win the thrilling 1991 World Series, he filed for free agency from the Twins. No sooner had Dave Winfield won the 1992 World Series, with an eleventh-inning double, than the Blue Jays cut him loose. Pittsburgh won its third straight National League East title, then bid farewell to cornerstone players Barry Bonds and Doug Drabek. Pirates president Sauer, ruing the age of the "migratory player," said he was more concerned with rebuilding the fan base than the ball club.

Baseball was also the only sport where newspapers compiled full-page tables listing each player's salary and toting up the current number of millionaires. It was the ultimate mutation of Marvin Miller's wish that each player know, as a basic bargaining right, what his peers made.

Now everybody knew and everybody had an opinion. The public scrutiny of every aspect of athletes' pay and performance was obsessive. It was fueled by all-sports radio, all-sports TV, and the death-struggle of cities' daily newspapers to survive. They had to have raw material to survive, and baseball, with its eight-month season and 162 games, provided it.

Call-in radio resonated with talk of teams' salary structures and players' incentive clauses. There were fifty-one all-sports radio stations in the country in 1993, each spending many hours a day hearing from the public. In his final days with the Mariners, Jeff Smulyan took a regular beating on one such Seattle station. "Jeff," a friend kidded the format's creator, "you have been hoisted by your own petard."

The dissemination of games' scores and highlights was so instant and pervasive that the media were left to traffic in speculation and compete for scoops. Joe McIlvaine, back with the Mets as GM, despaired about what he called "the *National Enquirer* mentality" that had seized baseball writers. "I beg them to write about what's going on on the field and they look at me like I'm from Mars," he said.

The money in baseball both fascinated and repelled fans, in a way that the money in no other sport did. They could understand a seven-foot center or a 260-pound linebacker having superhuman physical traits that commanded superdollars. But baseball players didn't *look* any different from the average Joe. And they didn't come through, all that often, in superhuman fashion, for the game was predicated on failure. Even the best hitters were retired seven out of ten times. And so, with little provocation, fans turned on these symbols of inequitable income-distribution.

"The economic disparity between the players and the guys who sit in the stands was so much less in my dad's day," said Steve Greenberg, the son of Hall of Fame slugger Hank Greenberg. "The average fan felt much closer to the players. They were working stiffs like them. There was a sense of sympathy and empathy. Now fans say, 'Who can relate to a guy who's making five or six million dollars?' "

As deputy commissioner, Greenberg headed a task force to upgrade the image of players. The group did produce a rare joint venture between the commissioner's office and the player's union, called the Rookie Career Development program. For three days each winter, top prospects from each team attended classes on handling life in the fast lane, with a heavy emphasis on handling money, fame, and the media.

It was, by all accounts, constructive, though far short of a solution. The sad truth was that some of the game's biggest stars were also its biggest jerks. Jose Canseco's rap sheet was nearly as long as his tape-measure home runs. Bobby Bonilla sulked about official scorers' decisions and menaced writers who displeased him. *Sports Illustrated* captured the essence of Barry Bonds with a cover story headlined I'M BARRY BONDS, AND YOU'RE NOT.

It all greatly resembled the final scene in George Orwell's *Animal Farm*. The pigs, who'd once led a barnyard rebellion against the oppressive farmers, now shared many of their traits and, at the end, were sharing a sumptuous meal with them. Wrote Orwell, "The creatures outside looked from pig to man, and from man to pig, and from pig to man again; but already it was impossible to say which was which."

Still, in some large part, it was the owners' own damned fault. Michael Jordan was no less self-centered and no more virtuous than any baseball player, and his income was considerably higher. Yet the NBA had marketed him beautifully as a genial Superman in designer sneakers.

Baseball owners, obsessed with denouncing the overpaid players, never did that. As agent Scott Boras once put it, "If the players were a can of Campbell's soup, the owners would roll it down the aisle, step on it, kick it, call it overrated and overpriced, and then stick it on a shelf and try to sell it."

Baseball had also utterly failed to use TV to enhance the game. The *Game of the Week* had been severely scaled back. The best efforts of CBS to do creative production work were rebuffed. ESPN went through ten kinds of hell trying to produce state-of-the-art broadcasts. (Clubs took care of their local TV interests first, last, and always. ESPN, which could greatly enhance baseball's national image, had to beg for cooperation—and rarely got it.)

Baseball took only one major step to accommodate network TV. It started World Series games at nearly 9:00 P.M., the better for CBS to dominate prime time. But it meant the games lasted until midnight, often long past when America's children had gone to bed. The Lords didn't concern themselves with losing a generation of fans. That would be thinking ahead.

"Baseball saw network TV as a means of acquiring capital," said Ken Schanzer of NBC Sports. "The NBA saw it as a partner and a tool for promoting and extending the game. [Commissioner] David Stern wanted an NBA game on every week and he wanted the Saturday show, *Inside Stuff*. He saw the value of having a consistent focus."

In mid-1993, the NBA secured a 25 percent increase in its TV rights—$750 million over four years from NBC. Two weeks later, baseball reached *its* new network deal—for no guaranteed money. Rather, it formed a joint venture with NBC and ABC that would reap 80 to 90 percent of the advertising revenue generated.

It doomed baseball to its first-ever dive in network-TV money, an estimated 50 percent in 1994. (ESPN would also later slash its payments to baseball by around 50 percent, reaching a six-year, $225 million agreement.) Some owners put the best face on it, talking of baseball's new ability to "seize control of its destiny." Eddie Einhorn was particularly enthusiastic, but then this deal was Fast Eddie's idea. He'd dreamed up a similar approach for the U.S. Figure Skating Association, providing one-stop shopping for TV advertising, corporate sponsorships, and other marketing tie-ins.

It had worked nicely for the triple-axel set, but it elicited profound skepticism for baseball. "It's crazy," said Tom Villante, the BBDO ad-agency veteran and former baseball broadcast chief. "Advertisers buy baseball as a package with other sports. They want assurance that if ratings fall short, they can get make-goods [free compensatory ads] somewhere else on the network. You can't do either of those with this setup."

Ken Schanzer was brave enough to sign on to run it and optimistic enough to believe that baseball's sag in popularity was temporary, and illusory. "There's nothing wrong with baseball," he said during his early days on the job. "CBS just paid too much for it. Baseball has as many young people watching the World Series as the NBA does its finals. But it's been *perceived* differently. You're talking about a game with the most profound roots in American culture. We simply have to tap in to that strength."

There was at least one good thing to be said about the TV deal. It played right into Dick Ravitch's hands. If anything showed the need for dramatic restructuring in the baseball business it was the loss of at least $7 million per club per year in network money. He turned up the volume on his message to the owners. They could no longer look to the golden goose of TV; they had to look to each other.

Ravitch did get the owners to vote approval of revenue-sharing in principle. Getting them to agree on the nitty-gritty of a formula, however, was another matter. "One day, I heard from the big-market clubs that I was conspiring with the small-market clubs," he recalled. "On the same day, I heard from the small-market clubs that I was in the big markets' pocket."

Ravitch went into overdrive. He got clubs' chief financial officers to develop a system for putting their books in a standard format and enabling the Lords to compare them. (The owners had agreed to waive the old prohibition against sharing business data.) He jawboned owners until his jawbone ached, going particularly hard after the new, more educable ones like Seattle's John Ellis and Detroit's Mike Illitch.

Ravitch's girth, which tended toward heavyset anyway, expanded weekly, as too many meetings over too many meals took their toll. Some days he would nearly succumb to sleep during his last meeting of the day. Alternately gregarious and brusque in the best of times, Ravitch's temperament had turned ragged. He particularly exploded at reporters and academic "experts" who suggested the owners weren't losing money, just cooking the books. "They aren't crooks," Ravitch explained to one, "they're assholes."

It was, all in all, a fine campaign by an experienced politician. Yet Ravitch made painfully slow progress. Nothing better illustrated why than the two teams that dominated baseball-business news that summer. They were on opposite coasts and on opposite ends of the spectrum.

In Baltimore, baseball was robust. Crowds jammed into Camden Yards, while bidders prepared to jam a courtroom, each hoping to purchase the Orioles. The franchise was on the block, en route to being sold for the highest sum ever fetched by a sports franchise.

The value of the Orioles had moved inversely to the personal fortunes of their chairman, Eli Jacobs. In 1990, his first full year as owner, the team had an operating profit of $2.1 million. In 1991, when the Orioles made a pennant run, it increased to about $7 million. In 1992, when they moved into Camden Yards, it quadrupled to $28 million.

They were easily the most profitable team in baseball that year. Though they made slightly less in 1993, Baltimore had firmly established itself among the game's financial elite, with revenues projected to top $90 million.

Eli Jacobs was otherwise going down the drain. His business empire, built with junk bonds in the 1980s, had collapsed under debt in the 1990s. A bank foreclosed on his mansion. A retiring man in the best of times, he retreated during Camden Yards games to an owner's box so secluded that employees called it "The Bunker." Suddenly, the team he'd bought for amusement and status was his prize asset. Jacobs took money out of the Orioles to fend off creditors, and by late 1992 he was earnestly looking to sell the team to raise cash. The team he'd bought for $70 million in 1989 was now worth twice as much.

That, at least, is what a group headed by one William O. DeWitt, Jr., was willing to pay. His interest lay partly in the Orioles' lineage—the old St. Louis Browns. His father had once owned the Browns, and Bill DeWitt, Jr., was the team's batboy when Bill Veeck pulled his most famous stunt. The youngster's uniform was used to outfit midget pinch hitter Eddie Gaedel.

"I've got a soft spot in my heart for the Browns," said DeWitt, who also admitted to a soft spot for cash flow. His Cincinnati investment firm was involved in a variety of businesses, ranging from computers to restaurants, and he wanted to add baseball to his portfolio.

"The Orioles have a huge market area and a great new facility," he later said. "We felt it could make a lot of money if bought at the right price."

That price was $141 million. DeWitt and Jacobs were closing in on a deal along those lines, which received some notice in the press as well as the attention of a Baltimore attorney. His name was Peter Angelos and he'd built a whopping practice representing workers exposed to asbestos. As a moneyed man, he'd been approached by groups interested in bidding for an NFL franchise. But it was baseball that intrigued him.

"I don't understand," he told his friend Tom Clancy, the techno-thriller writer and an NFL aspirant. "Why doesn't anybody try to buy the Orioles?"

He soon found out. Jacobs and his creditors were comfortable with DeWitt and they were discouraging other overtures, as Angelos discovered when he tried some exploratory inquiries. "The attitude was 'Local people need not apply; this is a done deal,'" he recalled. "That didn't set well with me."

Existing in the shadow of Washington and on the fringes of "major city" status, Baltimore has an inferiority complex. That's what fed the drive to build Camden Yards, and that's what now drove Peter Angelos. He was only a modest baseball fan, but he was a rabid Baltimore chauvinist. "If you allow your major league club to be owned by out-of-towners, you're not really a major league city, you're a branch-office city," Angelos later explained. (As a Lord of baseball, he would also make a statement to the world *beyond* Baltimore, of course: this sixty-four-year-old son of Greek immigrants had made it.)

He put together an eclectic group of like-minded locals, determined to keep the Orioles out of carpetbaggers' hands: "Boogie" Weinglass, a ponytailed clothing-store magnate; Barry Levinson, the filmmaker who'd immortalized Boogie in the movie *Diner*; Pam Shriver, the former tennis star; Jim McKay, the sports broadcaster; and, of course, Angelos's writer friend Tom Clancy.

Angelos trumpeted the group's creation and his intent to win the Orioles. When Jacobs was forced into bankruptcy proceedings in March, Angelos finally had a shot at it. The DeWitt deal was put on hold, and the team's disposition would now be up to a bankruptcy judge.

A bankruptcy-court hearing in June revealed just how much of a prize the Orioles were. Judge Cornelius Blackshear was going over DeWitt's tentative $141 million purchase contract when Angelos's lawyer jumped up and offered $145 million. DeWitt's lawyer countered at $146.25 million. The Angelos lawyer barked out $148.1 million. In moments, the price tag on the Orioles had jumped nearly $7 million. The judge called a halt and set a date for an auction, August 2.

Besides the Angelos and DeWitt groups, there was a formidable pack of other potential bidders: Jeffrey Loria, a New York art dealer who also owned the triple-A Oklahoma City 89ers; the Jemal brothers, who owned the New Jersey-based electronics retailer Nobody Beats the Wiz; and Jean Fugett, Jr., chairman of the world's largest black-owned corporation, TLC Beatrice International, Inc.

The various interests circled around one another, exploring possible combinations. Angelos approached Fugett, a former Baltimore Colts player whom he knew and liked. But their talks about merging interests foundered over control issues. The Jemal brothers explored alliances, then dropped out. Finally, the weekend before the Monday auction, Angelos called DeWitt.

"The ownership of this team is *not* going to Ohio," he announced. "It's coming back to Maryland. We're going to bid whatever it takes."

DeWitt believed him. He also believed a contest would propel them beyond a sensible price. He was open to talks, so Angelos walked over from the Helmsley Palace, where he was staying, to the St. Regis, where DeWitt was quartered. They didn't conclude until early Monday afternoon, just before the auction's scheduled two o'clock start. The combined forces agreed to bid $151.25 million; $3 million more than Angelos offered in June, or enough to blunt any charges that the merged bid suppressed the Orioles' price.

Angelos thought they had it won as he walked into bankruptcy court, smiling and greeting well-wishers. The courtroom was stifling, for the temperature outside was approaching 100 degrees and the building's air-conditioning had given out. Soon it would get even hotter inside, and not just because the room was packed with people.

A competitor of previously little note had emerged: Jeffrey Loria, the art dealer. Angelos's lawyer started the bidding at $151.25 million, and a pattern quickly emerged. The Angelos-DeWitt group would make a bid and Loria's attorney would top it by $100,000. Angelos-DeWitt would raise to the next million-dollar increment. Then another $100,000 topper.

Eight rounds passed. In the ninth, the Angelos group bid $160 million. The Loria bid went up to $161 million. Thereafter, each side moved up $1 million a pop. The youthful Loria watched, twitching, as his lawyer bounced up and down to bid. The anxious Angelos, in turn, watched Loria. Sweat dripped down the older man's face. He occasionally gazed over at Fugett, who wasn't bidding but whom Angelos strongly suspected of being Loria's backer.

After an Angelos bid of $169 million, Loria's attorney passed and asked for a recess. The art dealer left the courtroom along with Fugett and aides. Now Angelos was sure of the alliance. He was also sure they would throw in the towel. The break signaled a loss of nerve.

But they returned and waded right back into the auction. *$170 million.*

Angelos's attorney immediately jumped up to object to the bid, maintaining that Loria had already passed. But Judge Blackshear overruled him.

Now the Angelos-DeWitt group called time-out. The investors and their lawyers huddled in the judge's chambers. There were some worried murmurs—this was getting beyond any semblance of business sense.

Then Angelos spoke. "As far as I'm concerned, I'm going to go as high as necessary to defeat it."

Bob Castellini, a Cincinnati produce dealer from the DeWitt camp, backed him. "Whatever you want to do, Peter, I'm with you."

The moment for tremulous talk had passed. They went back into the oven of a courtroom and the heat of battle. *$171 million.*

Two more rounds passed, and the ante rose to $173 million, when Jeffrey Loria finally spoke for himself. He stood up and turned to Peter Angelos. "I want to congratulate the Baltimore group," he said.

The auction was finally over; the Orioles had fetched a record price for a sports franchise—24 percent more than the Dallas Cowboys' $140 million purchase. The courtroom erupted in applause. Angelos led his group down the street to a tavern, where he celebrated with diet Cokes.

At the other end of the spectrum, the San Diego Padres were disappearing before their fans' very eyes. A National League West contender in 1992, they featured such stars as Gary Sheffield, who nearly won the batting Triple Crown; Fred McGriff, who led the league in homers; and Tony Gwynn, the four-time batting champion.

But even as they struggled to catch the Braves that August, they traded front-line pitcher Craig Lefferts and his very expensive salary to Baltimore for shortstop prospect Ricky Gutierrez and his very low salary. The players were stunned. But GM Joe McIlvaine had his orders to chop the payroll.

The Lefferts trade was just step one by a Padres ownership group grown rapidly sadder but wiser in the ways of baseball. It was led by a young TV magnate named Tom Werner, executive producer of *The Bill Cosby Show* and *Roseanne*. He loved baseball (a practicing Rotisserie player); he had money to burn; and he got his Harvard '71 roommates—Republic Pictures chairman Russell Goldsmith and L.A. lawyer Michael Monk—to give it a twirl, too. They assembled a fifteen-man syndicate and daydreamed about being presented with the World Series trophy. "Tom's attitude in the beginning was, 'Let's spend some money,' " McIlvaine recalled.

Werner didn't know, however, the kind of money baseball would require. When the purchase closed, in June 1990, only a handful of players made $3 million. That month, Jose Canseco signed his five-year contract averaging $4.7 million, and salary hyperinflation was under way.

The Padres did their part to fuel it, actually, by signing McGriff, Gwynn, and Bruce Hurst to long-term contracts totaling $40 million and giving mediocre free agents Larry Andersen and Kurt Stillwell $2 million- and $1.75 million-a-year contracts, respectively. It was typical of every new owner's we're-gonna-be-competitive phase.

But before long, Werner was reeling from shock. The Padres' payroll, $18 million in 1990, spiked up 30 percent in his first year and kept going from there. The Padres represented the worst of both worlds: good enough to be expensive, but not good enough to win and reap a revenue windfall. The club had only twice drawn 2 million: in 1985, after winning the pennant, and in 1989, when battling to the wire with the Giants. The city didn't get easily excited about baseball, and the franchise had neither a big regional draw nor a big TV contract to help carry the load.

By 1992 the payroll reached $29 million and Werner ordered McIlvaine to start unloading players. His group was en route to losing $12 million over two years, which wasn't exactly what they'd had in mind. The target, he told McIlvaine, was a $21 million payroll.

McIlvaine objected. He thought the answer was to make the team *more* competitive, not less. If they won more, he argued, they'd get blasé San Diego excited and draw more.

"Joe, you've never met a high-priced player you didn't like," Werner countered. "I don't necessarily equate success with a high-priced payroll. There are lots of examples of teams that did well without a $50 million payroll. Brains are always more important than money."

McIlvaine was unmoved. He thought Werner was being influenced as much by other owners' rhetoric as by the Padres' losses. The Lords were all talking about making deep payroll cuts, which he doubted would happen.

"Tom, I've heard this time and again and they're not going to do it," he insisted. "There may be one or two teams that do some cutting, but in general it's not going to happen."

He was right. That winter, the Angels traded a pricey star pitcher, Jim Abbott, for cheaper prospects. The Pirates bit the bullet and bid farewell to Bonds and Drabek. But overall, more teams *raised* their payrolls (sixteen) than reduced them (ten). McIlvaine was prophetic on another point, too. If the Padres started unloading players, he warned, they'd stick out like a sore thumb. Were the owners prepared to take some heat?

"If we don't reduce the payroll, one of two things is going to happen," Werner replied. "We'll either go bankrupt or another group will come in, buy the team, and move it."

McIlvaine said he understood, but he clearly wasn't happy. He turned his attention to Tony Fernandez, a gazelle at shortstop but a $2.3 million line item on the payroll. Under the terms of his contract, the Padres had forty-eight hours following the World Series to pick up his option for 1993 or cut him loose. McIlvaine spent the Series trying to deal Fernandez, so the Padres could at least get *something* in return. Finally, he had to accept fifty cents on the dollar—a marginal pitcher named Wally Whitehurst and two minor-leaguers from the Mets.

Two other prominent players, reliever Randy Myers and catcher Benito Santiago, were soon ex-Padres as well. They departed as free agents, with no compensation other than amateur draft choices. Cut loose, too, were veteran pitchers Larry Andersen, Jim Deshaies, and Mike Maddux.

When the Padres began to make other deep budget cuts— dropping a farm team, firing minor league coaches, laying off nineteen front-office employees, even eschewing a Christmas tree in the lobby—the team was publicly skewered. Werner had always thought the TV business played out publicly. Baseball, he was learning, existed in a fishbowl.

The salary-arbitration season only turned the screws tighter on the Padres. The team lost its cases against pitcher Andy Benes and outfielder Darrin Jackson, blowing a $1.1 million hole in the side of the budget (the difference between what had been offered to the two players and the arbitrator's awards). The Padres, unnerved, bagged their third arbitration case, involving Gary Sheffield. Instead of going to a hearing, they settled it for $3.11 million. That was $350,000 more than they'd proposed to pay Sheffield, in filing for arbitration, and nearly $2.4 million more than he'd made in 1992.

The stage was set for more cost cutting. Darrin Jackson was traded to the Blue Jays in April for second-year outfielder Derek Bell—a $2.1 million salary replaced by a $165,000 salary.

Now Padres fans began really tearing into the owners, who'd promised over the winter to keep the team's core intact. ("Someone should tell Tom there are two things that need cleaning up in San Diego: the Tijuana River and his act," said one outraged letter. "They're both full of the same thing.") Worse than the antipathy was apathy. Season-ticket sales were already down 28 percent, and when the Padres got off to a slow start Jack Murphy Stadium was a mausoleum.

By then, Werner and McIlvaine were at swords' points. When the GM was told to see what he could get for Gary Sheffield, he resisted. "I'm not going to do it," he said. "That's not in the best interests of the franchise."

He finally relented, but so slowly and half-heartedly, he was getting no serious offers. "If you don't want to do it, you don't do it very well," said one baseball man familiar with the process. "Joe only knows one way to approach things: 'This is competitive and I'm going to win.'"

When it came down to a clash between old-line baseball values and new-style baseball economics, it was no contest. McIlvaine resigned in June, one jump ahead of being asked to do so. (His contract was to be evaluated in July for either extension or termination.) He was replaced by Randy Smith, the Padres' former scouting director and Tal Smith's thirty-year-old son.

After Werner watched the Padres get swept by the expansion

Florida Marlins in June, he ordered the housecleaning acceler-ated. "This team *with* Sheffield, McGriff, [Bruce] Hurst, and [Greg] Harris was mired in sixth place with a 28–44 record," Werner later said. "We were taking a bath anyway, so the idea was, 'Let's do something so that maybe we can win in '94 or '95.'"

Werner was also viewing the world from a perch on the own-ers' TV committee, which he chaired. The Padres, as then con-stituted, were headed for an $8 million loss in 1993. He saw them starting out 1994 *already* down $8 million.

Randy Smith's midsummer clearance swept out every high-priced player but Tony Gwynn and Andy Benes and yielded nine decent prospects in return. The Padres' payroll was reduced to $20 million and falling. Their fans were reduced to sitting in the stands with paper bags over their heads, looking out through the slits at a club that would finish 61–101.

The fire sale made headlines across the nation and made Werner a pariah in San Diego. Also a defendant. Season-ticket holders filed a class-action suit, contending they'd been deceived by the club about its plans. The suit was dropped in exchange for a more liberal ticket refund policy, but the public wrath was unabated. "I am very upset because you had the nerve to trade Gary Sheffield for a very bad player," wrote one young fan. "You guys are stupid. I should know. I'm 11. And I'm smarter than you."

The Padres hadn't actually done anything that fellow small-market teams like the Astros, Indians, and Pirates hadn't done before. But those clubs had let the air out of their payrolls over an off-season or two. San Diego had transformed its team as the season went on: star Gary Sheffield at third one day, journeyman Archie Cianfrocco the next. Not since Charlie Finley tried to sell Rudi, Fingers, and Blue had an owner made such a dramatic midseason move.

Werner largely retreated from public view in San Diego and took comfort in the fiscal-responsibility plaudits of his fellow owners. He became one of the leading spear carriers for the small-market owners. Bud Selig called him "one of the brightest owners to have come into baseball in years."

Of course, that was akin to being called the world's tallest midget and it wasn't a unanimously held opinion. To some col-leagues, Werner was simply a naïf who'd overpaid for the Pa-dres and undergone a crash course in baseball's economics. This was supposed to be exhibit A in the case for revenue-sharing?

One agent who'd discussed it with several big-market owners kept hearing the same phrase: "Fuck San Diego."

The owners of the Orioles and Padres were clearly living on different planets. Yet in mid-August they and the rest of the disparate baseball industry would convene to try reaching a revenue-sharing agreement. The Lords held a summit at a resort forty miles north of Milwaukee.

It was in the town of Kohler, Wisconsin, a supremely ironic location. Like baseball, it had a rich history of labor strife. In 1934, a strike at a local manufacturer exploded into a riot in which two people died and during which National Guard troops massed. In 1954, a United Auto Workers local here launched the longest strike in history—eight and a half years. Kohler was also the toilet-manufacturing capital of America. Every hackneyed writer put the question in print: Could baseball save itself from going down that well-known bathroom fixture?

On Wednesday morning, Dick Ravitch welcomed the owners to the resort, called the American Club. It was a lovely spot, where middle-America vacationers could pay $100 to play a round of golf or just wander the lushly wooded 500-acre grounds. But the owners and their aides, totaling some one hundred people in all, were to be confined to an amphitheater and restricted to an all-business regimen.

Ravitch went over a packet of documents he'd loaded with financial data and posed a loaded question. Could they leave there with a revenue-sharing agreement? Don Fehr was threatening a strike on Labor Day; the National League Broadcast Agreement was set to expire; the weak clubs were getting weaker and preparing for, as he put it, "the road race to Tampa–St. Pete."

"We've got to have a deal," he said, "because the consequences of not having one are so much worse than the compromises you'll have to make."

But it didn't take long to see just how tough an agreement would be to achieve. It would take 75 percent approval—twenty-one votes—and there were so many hurdles. At one level, there were technicalities enough to make the eyes glaze over. (Was stadium income to be based on the gross, for purposes of revenue-sharing, or on the after-expenses net? That was important to teams like the Cardinals, whose Busch Stadium revenues were high but so were their costs.) At another level, there was enough emotion to make the meeting eminently combustible. "Okay," snapped Boston's John Harrington, tired of the have-nots' harping, "we'll just form another league!"

That evening, the haves did break off and form their own caucus. For the summit's duration, the big-market clubs met in a banquet room at the American Club's main hotel. The small-market owners remained down the street at the Carriage House, as the original meeting site was called. Their emissaries to the haves' caucus were received with all the respect normally accorded the underclass. Detroit's Mike Illitch and Seattle's John Ellis were forced once to wait outside for forty-five minutes before Toronto's Paul Beeston finally deigned to pop out and have a word with them.

Dick Ravitch constantly shuttled between the two groups, literally wearing a hole in his wingtip's sole from walking back and forth over the 200 yards. But he was up against a grim reality: the unspoken order of the day was pure self-interest. "You can never forget," said one participant, "these guys don't like each other and they don't trust each other."

Some of the haves were willing to modestly assist the truly needy. But, led by George Steinbrenner, they brayed in outrage against the clubs they felt had either mismanaged themselves into poverty or merely disguised themselves as paupers. The Boss particularly got after the Braves. They'd cast their lot with the have-nots, and their revenues technically were modest. But that was only because Turner Broadcasting paid the team just $15 million a year for broadcast rights, a fraction of their actual value. Ted Turner built up the super-station's profits at the Braves' expense, which didn't make the Braves disadvantaged. "Fine!" Steinbrenner exploded. "I'll buy those rights for sixteen million dollars!"

The haves did shuttle their own revenue-sharing proposal over to the Carriage House near midnight Wednesday. It was less a comprehensive proposal than a pledge card—each club declaring what it was willing to contribute. The total came to $43 million, well under what the have-nots wanted but something into which they could finally sink their teeth.

The small-market owners knocked off around 2:00 A.M.; Dick Ravitch's night went on. He and aides kept crunching numbers on portable computers, looking for a formula to merge the two sides' interests. At dawn, Ravitch finally collapsed for an hour's sleep, while aides worked frantically through to the start of Thursday's meetings, at 8:30 A.M.

The Cleveland Indians would make the best run, that day, at

a settlement. They were that rarest of creatures at Kohler—
fence-straddlers. As longtime have-nots, the Indians identified
with that group. But they were opening a new stadium in 1994.
Along with the Rangers (also moving into a new stadium), they
hoped to be the mid-nineties version of the Orioles. Their lawyers and financial people had drafted a compromise proposal reflecting that.

The Cleveland Plan, as it came to be called, proposed that
$65 million be transferred from the haves to the have-nots. That
was about 50 percent more than the big-market clubs had proposed. Yet the formula was sensitive enough to the makeup of
clubs' stadium expenses that it just might fly. (More precisely, it
might fly with those clubs for whom stadium income was a big
issue. If only three of the big-market clubs could be won over,
there would be twenty-one votes and passage.)

But the Cleveland Plan didn't even get out of the Carriage
House, at first. The smallest of the small-market clubs (San
Diego, Montreal, Pittsburgh, Milwaukee, Minnesota, and Seattle)
didn't like the formula. It would allow them to break even but,
they felt, make it impossible to turn a profit. As their revenues
grew, their revenue-sharing subsidies would decrease. It was a
zero-sum game.

Jerry Reinsdorf put forth a compromise. There would be no
immediate decreases in revenue-sharing subsidies for teams as
they increased their own gross. The Cleveland Plan was
amended with the so-called Reinsdorf Wrinkle, endorsed by all
eighteen Carriage House clubs and sent over to the haves.

They turned it down flat.

Time was running out. In an industry that had to reconcile the
extremes of the Orioles and Padres—and all the points in
between—the differences were too great. Dick Ravitch had been
too optimistic to think an intense encounter session would produce a deal. Bud Selig had been too cheap to book the American
Club hotel a third night. The owners would have to clear out regardless of where the talks stood.

The big-market owners had the last at-bat in the proposal ex-
changes. At 9:15 P.M., George Bush and Paul Beeston walked it
over to the Carriage House. There was a bounce in the two
men's steps and an optimism in the air, which had begun to
thicken with a fog coming off Lake Michigan. The street was
crowded with baseball writers, TV cameramen, and more than
one hundred apple-cheeked citizens of Kohler, there to witness
the excitement. Jerry Reinsdorf welcomed the two men in and

everyone outside waited. TV sports reporters set up outside the door, waiting to flash the news to the world.

Inside, the owners circulated the proposal, which at first blush looked promising. The haves were now proposing a revenue-sharing transfer of $54 million. It was short of the Cleveland Plan, certainly, but it was a 25 percent advance from their old $43 million offer. But then a closer look at the details: the additional $11 million was *all* to come from the Braves, Cubs, and White Sox.

It was out of the question—not only to those clubs but to the rest of the Carriage House caucus. It was true that those three were no paupers. But it was also true that they'd stuck with the have-nots through this ordeal. It wasn't fair, now, to wring a solution out of their hides.

After thirty-one hours of meetings in the past thirty-eight hours, tempers were frayed and brains fried. George Bush and Paul Beeston suffered the fate of all bearers of ill tidings: they were verbally shot between the eyes.

Bush emerged visibly agitated. Writers shouted out questions, but he just shouldered his way past. "I have nothin' to say about nothin'," he growled.

It was just before eleven o'clock when five vans pulled up in front of the Carriage House. As reporters clambered after them, the owners and their minions all jumped into the idling vans, each bound for Milwaukee, Chicago, or, for those with private jets, the Sheboygan airport. It was the flotilla at Dunkirk, the evacuation of Saigon, and the Keystone Kops all rolled into one. The minicam lights bathed the area in light and captured the owners in bold relief as they jumped back and forth among vans, trying to find the one headed the right way. Abruptly, abjectly, the Kohler summit was over.

The good citizens of Kohler were stunned. Some of them were boys on bicycles, up past their bedtimes, hoping to see famous and mighty leaders, to see history in the making. They were instead watching dozens of sallow, middle-aged men piling into getaway vehicles. They joined the press in calling out questions, the most profound one hanging out there like a towering fly ball against an evening sky: "Will there be baseball?"

There were no answers from the vans, just haunted visages peering out with "that deer-in-the-headlights look," as one witness put it. And then the Lords of baseball drove off through the gathering fog, into the night.

Epilogue

DICK RAVITCH QUICKLY moved to head off confrontation with the players. He briefed reporters that night, telling them the owners' failure to reach a revenue-sharing accord did not mean an imminent war with the players.

"No drama, fellas," he said, in a voice gone raspy. "There will be no lockout. Baseball will be played, and I hope everybody enjoys the rest of the season."

Ravitch elaborated on the one thing the owners *had* been able to agree on. They pledged no lockout for spring '94 and no off-season effort to impose unilateral changes. The rules on free agency, salary arbitration, and other parts of the system would remain the same.

That effectively averted a Labor Day strike, though it didn't signal a harmonious new turn in baseball labor relations. Even as Ravitch extended the olive branch, he chided Don Fehr for sending him a "childish, lawyer-like letter" that suggested his schedule was too crowded for them to meet anytime soon.

Fehr would later move to refute that, publicly releasing a copy of his letter. But that was just one symptom of deteriorating relations between the two men. Fehr thought that Ravitch wasn't shooting straight with either him or the owners. Ravitch thought Fehr was undermining him at every turn, trying to squeeze a few extra years out of a doomed, sick system. Not since the days of Ray Grebey and Marvin Miller had personal chemistry been so poisonous. "They both have egos the size of Rhode Island, and they genuinely don't like each other," said one person familiar with the dynamics.

As a practical matter, that didn't immediately make much difference for as of early 1994 the owners still hadn't made any bargaining proposals. For Ravitch, who felt he'd been within inches of success at Kohler, revenue-sharing remained maddeningly elusive. The harder he ran after that goal, the further it slid away from his reach. A group of owners was assigned to keep negotiations going, but it soon became reminiscent of Fay Vincent's big market–small market committee—a prescription for gridlock.

The same could be said of the industry in general, one year after Vincent's ouster. The restructuring committee still hadn't completed its work, leaving baseball not only without a commissioner but without even a job definition for one. Chairman Fred Wilpon kicked around draft reports like his hapless Mets kicked ground balls, but the balkanized owners couldn't agree on how to reshape the office. The commissioner search committee also dawdled along without making any recommendations, reflecting the owners' divisions. The labor hawks didn't *want* a new commissioner, at least not until baseball had a new labor contract.

It was widely believed there was another reason for no new commissioner, as well: Bud Selig enjoyed being the interim one too much. He occupied the ceremonial box at the World Series. He chaired the nonstop round-robin of owners' meetings. He was, more than ever, at the center of the baseball world. "Bud's got commissioneritis," grumbled one colleague.

There was growing talk, indeed, that Selig would become permanent commissioner. He protested that he didn't want the job, but his protests weren't very convincing. Dick Ravitch grew privately dismayed. Selig, once a stout ally on revenue-sharing, distanced himself from the issue. He refused to put himself on the line when it came to making the tough choices and enduring the howls of the aggrieved. It remained to be seen whether that was just good old Buddy, refusing to get out front on issues, or candidate Selig, refusing to jeopardize commissioner votes. But the relationship between the two men, once warm, rapidly cooled in the months after Kohler.

Unable to grapple with substantive matters, the Lords turned with gusto to peripheral ones. At their September 1993 ownership meeting in Boston they pushed revenue-sharing off the agenda and labored to realign the leagues into three divisions, setting the stage for an extra round of playoffs.

It was a pathetic piece of business—a diversion from the more vital issue and a grab for more revenue. It gave Ken Schanzer some new TV inventory to sell. It gave more owners some premium-priced tickets to sell and faux pennant races to push. It also held out, for the first time, the possibility of the baseball season going into November.

The Lords maintained that fans would love the new format. Their scientific surveys said so. Others were skeptical. Announcer Bob Costas called the roll of baseball's great down-to-the-wire pennant races—Giants-Dodgers, 1951; Phillies-Reds-Cardinals, 1964; Impossible Dream Red Sox, 1967—and rued that classic finishes had been sacrificed to business expediency. "If baseball were financially solid, had no financial worries, no one would stand up at an owners' meeting and say, 'You know, boys, here's something we should do just because it makes baseball better: wildcard teams in the playoffs.'"

This was one ownership move that didn't vex Don Fehr, for it set the stage for the next round of expansion. Each league would have one division with just four teams, and they were behooved to add to that. Bingo. More jobs for ballplayers. Fehr supported realignment, as long as it was done in that expansion-enhancing way.

Fehr otherwise busied himself in Washington, lobbying for a bill to repeal baseball's antitrust exemption. Among those leading the charge were some politicians who knew baseball best: Senator Connie Mack (R-Fla.), grandson of the A's longtime owner and attuned to the frustrations of his Tampa Bay constituents; Senator Howard Metzenbaum (D-Ohio), former part-owner of the Cleveland Indians; and Representative Jim Bunning, Republican from Kentucky and right-hander par excellence.

"All that exemption has done is allow a controlled monopoly to dictate for years to the fans, players, and taxpayers," said Bunning in his Capitol Hill office one day, surrounded by mementos of his pitching career. "It's allowed them to say, 'Major League Baseball knows better than anybody else how to conduct its business,' and they've proved time and time again that is not the case."

And so the man who once helped install Marvin Miller now pushed for the next step in the baseball revolution. In a Congress preoccupied with health care and fiscal reform, however, baseball reform wasn't a top priority. The bill still hadn't gotten out of committee by the end of 1993.

Marvin Miller himself was ever more the icon in his seventies, sought out even by the other side. In his early days on the TV job, Ken Schanzer set up a lunch with Miller. One finalist for commissioner (Miller wouldn't say who) sought him out to consult about whether he should pursue the job. Even some of Miller's old adversaries had mellowed enough to offer some admiring words. "You have to respect what he did for the players," said Buzzie Bavasi. "They were entitled to their freedom after a certain amount of time."

Current management operatives were less sanguine about Miller, who many felt still controlled the union. They privately used almost the same words: "Nothing will ever change as long as Marvin Miller is alive."

Miller has remained a consultant to the union, in fact, often conferring with Don Fehr. But both deny that Miller is the power behind the throne at the union, with Fehr happy to assert that the two of them sometimes "fought like cats and dogs." Nonetheless, the union of 1993 remained recognizably the same as that of 1973. It took no guff and took no prisoners.

The union revenged itself on Miller's old nemesis Jerry Kapstein by decertifying him as an agent. Kapstein had gone management for a time, marrying Ray Kroc's daughter, Linda, and becoming president of the Padres. He lost the wife; lost the job; and tried to return to agentry. But the union disqualified him for his front-office stint. (One happy note, however; Kapstein did remarry Linda.)

The union also revenged itself on Barry Rona, who decided to become an agent after being fired by Fay Vincent. Rona picked up numerous football players as clients but was denied certification in baseball, where Fehr couldn't forgive his collusion-era stint as PRC chief. Rona took the matter to an arbitration hearing, where Miller testified at length on his sins. The arbitrator found for Rona.

For the most part, however, Miller had been elevated from the trenches to the ranks of labor's distinguished senior statesmen. When the National Academy of Arbitrators held its 1992 annual meeting, it was Miller who gave the keynote address. The dais overflowed with arbitrators whose decisions had marked baseball:

- Tom Roberts, who decided the first collusion case.
- Richard Bloch, who'd reinstated Roberts when the owners tried to fire him from the case.
- George Nicolau, who decided the other two collusion cases and was still baseball's arbitrator.
- And then there was an empty chair. That, said academy pres-

ident David Feller, was for Peter Seitz, "who is smiling down on us."

Many of Miller's former acolytes wound up with jobs in baseball management, including Joe Torre, Phil Garner, Don Baylor, and Bob Boone as field managers, and Sal Bando and Ted Simmons as general managers.

Some found this gave them a whole new perspective on the union. Garner groused about all the rules that hamstrung clubs' abilities to make player moves. Ted Simmons was the defendant in a union grievance alleging he'd cut a player (reliever Bill Landrum) for budgetary, not skill, reasons. After one and a half years of trying to keep the low-budget Pirates in contention, Simmons's health gave out. He required heart surgery and resigned in May 1993.

Many of these former union leaders privately rued the current generation of players—their lack of institutional memory, and their lack of commitment, it seemed, to anything but themselves. It made them wonder how long the union could maintain the gains for which they'd once battled.

"The real problem comes in the young players today, who don't know who Marvin Miller is, what the history is, where this all came from," said Doug DeCinces, who stayed close to baseball with his licensing company. "They just know if they play and do well, they'll make a lot of money. I think the Players Association has a major task in educating them."

Charlie Finley, like Marvin Miller, remained active well into his seventies, but he changed sports. He invented an aerodynamically improved football, tried to launch a new international football league, and, from a downtown-Chicago office lined with A's memorabilia, kept his hand in the insurance business.

Finley's bushy eyebrows have turned snowy white and match his toupee beautifully, but he hasn't mellowed a whit. "Stupid," he growled, when asked to talk about baseball's owners. "Stupid, stupid, stupid. If they'd had a brain they would have been idiots."

Bill Veeck, baseball's other ranking maverick of the century, died in 1986. His name lived on in baseball, however, through son Mike. The man who gave the world Anti-Disco Night became a minor league operator, first with the Miami Miracle of the Florida State League and then, in 1993, the St. Paul Saints of the new, independent Northern League.

Mike Veeck was a chip off the old Barnum, with gimmicks like Mime-O-Vision (a mime who performed "instant replays") and a masseuse (a nun masseuse, yet) who gave rubdowns in the stands behind home plate. The Saints sold out twenty-eight of their thirty-six games and won the league championship. Mike also carried on his father's contempt for all things establishment. When Bowie Kuhn made a bid to buy a Northern League team, Veeck prepared to move on. "Bowie Kuhn is everything this league doesn't want to be," he said.

Ex-commissioner Kuhn became involved in buying and selling minor league franchises in his latter years, a difficult period for him. He kicked around the law firm of Willkie, Farr and Gallagher for a time, after leaving office, then founded a new law firm in 1988 with a fast-lane litigator named Harvey Myerson. They wanted to assemble a dream team of high-powered, high-priced lawyers, but Myerson and Kuhn collapsed in bankruptcy within two years.

Myerson was eventually convicted of bilking clients. Kuhn fled to Florida, a state with generous legal protection of property for people in bankruptcy proceedings. He bought a $1 million home near Jacksonville and dropped out of sight for a time, finally emerging to become a partner in the franchise-brokering business.

Other commissioners found post-czar life difficult, too. Peter Ueberroth made an unsuccessful run at buying Eastern Airlines. He also made a mostly unsuccessful effort to draw corporate investment to inner-city Los Angeles after the 1992 riots. He resigned as chairman of Rebuild L.A. in May 1993, little more than a year after his appointment. Ueberroth otherwise oversaw a variety of investments, most notably in struggling Hawaiian Airlines.

Fay Vincent retreated to England, where he spent the first part of 1993 residing in a country house writing a book on fifteen people he'd admired. None of them, he sometimes pointedly noted, were owners. Just as pointedly, upon his return he avoided major league baseball parks. (The exception was Opening Day at Shea Stadium, where he'd promised Don Baylor he'd catch his managerial debut.)

Vincent had entered a phase of life at age fifty-five that he called a sabbatical but others saw as involuntary early retirement. He was appointed to Time Warner's board, but otherwise found little market for his services. He turned down Fred

Wilpon's offer to be the Mets' president and settled into an office with another corporate exile, former Shearson Lehman investment banker Peter Solomon.

Some thought it a curious choice of locale—350 Park Avenue—and some wondered just when Vincent would get over his funk about baseball. On the anniversary of his ouster, he gave a series of bitter interviews, with observations on Pete Rose ("He bet [on baseball] as a player with the Phillies"), the Tribune Company ("[It's] gradually taking control of baseball"), and George Steinbrenner ("a pathetic guy").

One thing Vincent didn't say about George Steinbrenner, though: they'd switched places on the isle of Elba. The Boss returned to baseball in customary low-key fashion on March 1, 1993. He went on WFAN radio that day at 12:01 A.M. for two hours of Yankee talk; he swept into the Fort Lauderdale spring training camp amid a crush of minicams; and he appeared on the cover of *Sports Illustrated* in Napoleonic garb, atop a horse. Steinbrenner went through the season with no firings, no bluster, little public profile at all, save for the obligatory threat of the modern-day owner: to move his team. Disgruntled with Yankee Stadium's location, he talked of moving the Bronx Bombers to New Jersey.

Howard Spira was convicted of extortion and sentenced to two and a half years in prison. Dave Winfield's career rolled gloriously on, as he collected his three thousandth hit in September 1993 for the Minnesota Twins. He never reconciled with Steinbrenner, though Reggie Jackson did. The owner and number 44 didn't speak for years after falling out during Jackson's latter days in New York. But they made peace in 1993, a year when Jackson became the Yankees' "special adviser to the general partner" and a member of baseball's Hall of Fame.

Jackson has been an instrumental figure in the transformation of the baseball business. He was in the middle of the 1972 players' strike when the first shots of the revolution were fired. He was front and center in 1976, when players first reaped free-agency riches. But in his induction speech in Cooperstown, he delivered a warning to those in the mega-bucks industry of 1993. They forgot that baseball was a game at their own peril.

"Whether your name is Peter O'Malley, George Steinbrenner, or Ted Turner, or if you're Kirby, Roger, Barry, or Cal, realize you're just a part—just a link in the chain in the big scheme of things. Remember along the way that something we can all learn from these guys behind me [thirty-eight fellow Hall-of-Famers] is the need to humanize the game.

"If the game is lost to the economics that drives it, then we'll lose the humanity that is unique to the game. We all must feel it and live it in our way and be mindful of its vulnerability to abuse. From the millions to the billions that this game has come to represent, we all take from this cherished game. Stop and remember Buck O'Neil and The Scooter and all the people who played for the love of the game."

Another Hall-of-Famer on that stage reflected on the past quarter-century's baseball revolution with mixed measures of pride and regret.

"For all the players have gained, the changes took something away from baseball," said Robin Roberts. "For me, it was fun and a privilege to be a ballplayer. The union made it a job—a high-paying job but a job. Only rarely now—like when you see a Joe Carter jumping around the bases after winning the World Series—does it seem like anything else."

And yet . . . and yet baseball survived; by some measures, in 1993, even thrived. Attendance surged past 70 million, smashing the old attendance record by 24 percent. The Lords finally learned to love expansion, as the new Colorado and Florida teams accounted for 7.5 million fans between them. Even just counting the old teams, baseball's attendance rose 13 percent. Six clubs set attendance records, including San Francisco, for whom Barry Bonds proved to be worth every bit of his $43 million.

Major League Properties's licensing revenue approached $3 billion, double the level of 1990. A "Rookie League" line of kids' clothing was flying off the shelves, as was an apparel line with minor league teams' logos. (The minors' resurgence also continued in 1993, with attendance increasing 10 percent, to 30 million.)

At the All-Star Game in Baltimore, tickets were being scalped for $500. Nearly 48,000 packed Camden Yards the day before the game, just to see a workout and home run–hitting contest. There, the young stars who were proliferating and dominating baseball put on a show. David Justice hit a ball clear out of Camden, nearly becoming the first player to hit the B & O Warehouse on the fly. Then Ken Griffey, Jr., jolted one out which *did* dent the building and arouse the crowd. Finally, Juan

Gonzalez won the contest and yet more thunderous cheers, reaching the third deck in left field.

Even the next day, it was all the talk among the fans swarming the street between the warehouse and Camden Yards. People stood at the spot where Griffey's drive had met brick, pointing up at the chink. They stared through the grating at the green expanse of the ballpark, watching a groundskeeper mow the perfect outfield grass. "Awesome," murmured one gazer.

Crowds also surged into the nearby FanFest, a temporary baseball theme park which would draw 100,000 people over five days. It was sort of Walt Disney meets Cooperstown, spread over the expanse of the Baltimore Convention Center. Visitors were greeted by giant hanging pictures of baseball greats, past and present: Ted Williams and Christy Mathewson; Ryne Sandberg and George Brett. Also the video of a Deion Sanders Nike commercial.

FanFest was, like the game itself, partly an orgy of crass commercialism, partly a celebration of heritage. Ted Williams had it down perfectly. He was at FanFest both to serve as a living, breathing icon and to promote his new line of baseball cards.

A kid could step into the Burger King Bullpen to throw his best fastball, measure its speed, and hear Mel Allen say, "That's a high, hard one." He could step into the Easton video batting cages and take his cuts against pitches from a simulated Roger Clemens. He could stand in a long, snaking line to get a baseball immortal's autograph. The afternoon wait for Bob Feller was two hours. The autograph was free; a certification that it was authentic cost five dollars. (Read the sign: IF IT'S NOT AUTHENTICATED, IT'S JUST A SOUVENIR.)

People lined up a hundred deep just to get into the FanFest Store, where just about everything ever licensed by Major League Properties was on sale. People bunched up in front of the Rawlings booth to watch a craftsman turn out a bat on a lathe and mull whether they wanted to buy a PERSONALIZED ALL-STAR GAME BAT for fifty dollars.

Giant TV monitors throughout the hall presented baseball's great moments: the Miracle Mets rejoicing after their 1969 World Series win; the Bob Welch–Reggie Jackson showdown in the 1978 World Series; the last out of Orel Hershiser's record-breaking shutout streak and of Nolan Ryan's umpteenth no-hitter. Fathers stood with sons, pointing and telling them about what had happened.

Even Harry Dalton, the veteran GM of Baltimore, California,

and Milwaukee, was standing there, gawking. "There's no talking about the commissioner or money," he explained. "The focus is on the players and the great moments. It gives you chills."

People also crowded into the Hall of Fame exhibit, even though nothing was for sale. It was a collection on loan from Cooperstown: balls autographed by Honus Wagner and Cy Young; Babe Ruth's uniform hanging in an old metal locker; a montage of Reggie Jackson photos; and lists of baseball's all-time leaders, posted on the walls.

Standing there, gazing at the lists, a man in reverie was interrupted by his wife. She had been searching high and low for him and now shook her head in wonderment. "You're still here," she said.

And that about summed it up. The Lords and the agents, the lawyers and the czars, had done their best to kill baseball. There was something about the national pastime that made the people in it behave badly. They were, perhaps, blinded by the light of what it represented—a glowing distillate of America. Men fought to control it as though they could own it. They wallowed in dubious battle, locked in ugly trench warfare for dominion over the green fields. The money poured into the game and men gorged and gouged over it—made damned fools of themselves over it.

And the fans, ever forgiving, were still there.

Afterword

THE LORDS FINALLY broke the revenue-sharing logjam in January 1994. Thirteen months after re-opening the labor contract in Louisville and five months after the debacle of Kohler, they reached a revenue-sharing agreement in Fort Lauderdale.

The politics of baseball was finally swayed by the politics of beer. Anheuser-Busch remained, of course, both the producer of Budweiser and the parent of the Cardinals. The ballclub represented but a drop in the vat compared to brewery revenues.

The Cardinals were one of the eight staunch opponents of revenue-sharing.

Then, in early 1994, a delegation from the retail trade forcefully reminded August A. Busch III of his larger interests. The group consisted of David Glass, president of Anheuser-Busch's biggest customer, Wal-Mart Stores; Drayton McLane, Jr., vice chairman of Wal-Mart; and Peter Magowan, chairman of the nation's number three supermarket chain, Safeway. The three wore different hats—or caps, as it were—in the baseball business: Glass as chairman of the Kansas City Royals; McLane as the Astros' new owner; and Magowan as the Giants' new owner.

All three wanted—in some cases, desperately needed—more revenue-sharing. All three pressed to move the Cardinals off their position. Ultimately Busch agreed, instructing club president Stewart Meyer to draw up a plan they could live with. That finally broke the stalemate and enacted revenue-sharing.

The Lords exploded with cheers upon the vote; the union camp exuded gloom. It was another inexorable step toward confrontation. "The problem is they've negotiated to closure," Don Fehr explained. "They have arrived at this intricate system among themselves that allows for no disturbance by us."

Baseball's training camps opened and so did a bargaining of sorts. Dick Ravitch set up meetings in Florida and Arizona so players could attend. They did, en masse, quickly recalling for Ravitch the tone of his 1993 spring-training tour.

"Why don't we keep the system the way it is now?" asked veteran pitcher Larry Andersen, a sentiment repeated in various forms throughout the player group.

After two sessions, Ravitch halted this unproductive dialog and returned to the Lords' inner councils, where the *real* negotiating was taking place. It was again between the haves and have-nots, but with even more intensity than usual.

For the have-nots, the baseball economy was unrelievedly grim. They'd come to count on $14 million in national TV money. In 1994, the first year of the post-CBS era, that sum would be less than half. They'd long assumed they could sell out at a hefty price if they tired of the struggle. Now Oakland, San Diego, Minnesota, Kansas City, and Pittsburgh were all for sale—with not a buyer in sight.

"You could always count on the 'greater fool' to come along," said one investment banker trying to peddle a team. "But with all the attention on the economics of baseball, the 'greater fool' market has gotten educated. They don't want to look dumb."

That made small-market interests more hawkish than ever. They beat the war drums in a rising crescendo through the first half of 1994. "We've lost $40 million to $50 million in hard cash over the past six years," said Pirates managing partner Doug Danforth, whose team needed an $8 million advance from Pittsburgh just to stay afloat. "The status quo isn't acceptable."

The big-market boys snorted their usual unsympathetic line: well-managed clubs could still do quite well. Sure they'd voted for revenue-sharing with teeth clenched. But they'd be damned if they'd go to war for those whimpering have-nots. "Look at Montreal," George Steinbrenner said, as the Expos burst into the NL East lead. "The best record in baseball is the team with the second-lowest payroll. So you can shoot that argument right in the butt."

It was the same old standoff of interests, but with a crucial difference—an influx of new owners. Nine of them had entered baseball since the 1990 lockout, representing not only a near one-third turnover but a big change in thinking. This crowd ignored the old convention about new owners being seen and not heard. Their investments, upwards of $100 million, were too big for passivity. They were also highly influential, in some cases, because they were skilled union-battlers in their other businesses.

The Marlins' Wayne Huizenga had survived bruising labor wars to make his first fortune—bigtime garbage-collecting with Waste Management Inc. The Royals' David Glass was chief executive of Wal-Mart, the nation's number one retailer, and a premier union-basher. He had rebuffed all attempts to organize clerks, truckers, and other workers. The Giants' Peter Magowan had squeezed huge concessions and cutbacks from his workforce after Safeway's leveraged buyout. He'd shut down altogether one 9,000-employee division where unions were troublesome. Drayton McLane had run a huge grocery distribution business, serving 40,000 convenience stores, and he'd run off the Teamsters at every opportunity.

After selling his McLane Co. to Wal-Mart for $274 million worth of that company's stock, he had some mad money to play with. He decided to play some ball. McLane bought the Astros from John McMullen in November 1992 and quickly succumbed to new-owner syndrome. Within three months, he'd committed $68 million to free agents Doug Drabek and Greg Swindell and Astro holdovers Ken Caminiti, Craig Biggio, and Steve Finley. McLane was the toast of Houston for being what John McMullen was not: a Texan, a spender, and a purveyor of pennant hopes.

Cruel reality quickly struck. In 1993, Drabek didn't win twenty games; he lost eighteen. Swindell suffered arm troubles and won just twelve games. The Astros never contended, finishing nineteen games back and losing Drayton McLane a lot of money. By 1994, he was sadder, wiser and, above all, louder about reforming the system. At one level, it was a cry of "Stop me before I spend again." At another, it was an even more vehement, "Stop the union." He wouldn't let unions run McLane Co., and he didn't want one running baseball.

It was McLane, among these labor-savvy newcomers, who would play the most crucial early role. The Lords were to meet on June 8 in Cincinnati with a major agenda: to determine bargaining proposals and strategies. A few weeks before, McLane convened a select, secret meeting in Dallas. The invitees were primarily from "middle-market" teams like his own, neither baseball's richest nor poorest. His idea was to coalesce this centrist group's thinking. They were the swing vote; they comprised more clubs than the rich or poor extremes; and they were, as McLane put it, "getting lobbied in every direction."

The middle-marketers considered the big-market clubs' dovish stance, a kind of Wilsonian refrain of "peace in our time." They mulled the small-marketers' Curtis LeMay-style approach of "nuke 'em back to the Stone Age." And ultimately, influenced by organizer McLane, they tilted heavily toward the hardliners. The spirit of Dallas was summed up by one baseball lawyer: "The players will only see the light when they're on their backs looking up at it."

The hawks picked up even more clout in Cincinnati by pushing through a Reinsdorf-inspired procedural change. It would now take twenty-one votes—75 percent of the Lords—to approve settlement of a strike or lockout. The super-majority rule vastly changed the dynamics from the old simple-majority requirement of fifteen votes. It would take just eight votes to veto a proposed settlement. The hard liners easily commanded such numbers and could thus thwart any dove-inspired cave-ins. "The twenty-one-vote rule kept the guys who would like to cave from trying," said one owner. "From there, this thing took on a life of its own."

The Lords made their proposal the following week: a 50 percent cut of revenues to players and a guarantee that total pay wouldn't dip below 1994's $1 billion. In addition to the salary cap, they proposed to end salary arbitration in exchange for four-year free-agency eligibility. Dick Ravitch insisted that the owners didn't want givebacks, they just wanted what other industries enjoyed: a predictable labor budget. "We have to obtain cost certainty," he told reporters, following an icy union briefing. "The players have to tell us how much it's going to cost to play ball."

"What the owners are saying," fired back Don Fehr, "is that they'll do revenue-sharing as long as the players pay for it with a salary cap."

They would chant these lines like mantras in the next few months. Across the bargaining table and under the klieg lights of Larry King, they hurled their stock assertions at one another. Some insiders called their act "Fehr and Loathing." Others feared for the clearly emerging picture: no negotiating progress and, worse, no apparent *interest* in progress.

Bob Boone watched and worried. The longtime union stalwart, now a Reds coach, could see both sides' positions and pitfalls. The players, rich beyond their wildest dreams, were nonetheless determined not to countenance "givebacks." The owners, pride wounded worse than pocketbooks, were fixated on seizing back control after twenty years. "There are no dealmakers," he despaired in midsummer. "Both sides are confrontational, and there's never a ground where a deal can be made."

The players rejected a salary cap as repugnant at any price. Dick Ravitch urged them to counter the 50 percent offer, even with an outrageously high figure. Ownership lawyer Rob Manfred ran into Steve Fehr at the All-Star game and accosted Don's brother and adviser with an increasingly shrill refrain: "Give us a number! Give us a number! Give us a number!"

Steve Fehr would not. Instead he preferred to cite a joke first attributed to George Bernard Shaw: "A man asks a woman if she'd go to bed with him for a million dollars. 'Certainly,' she says. 'Well,' he says, 'how about going to bed with me for ten dollars?' She asks him indignantly just what he thinks she is. 'We've already established what you are,' he replies. 'Now we're just haggling over price.' "

The players had even more reason to reject a cap than they had in 1985 and 1990. Their keen antennae monitored developments in other sports. The NBA players union, also negotiating a new labor contract, was insisting on dropping that league's ten-year-old cap. Free-agent basketball players had found little market for their services, as most teams had little room under their payroll limits. Pro football players derisively called *their* union leader, Gene Upshaw, "Commander Cap." This was the first year of the system he'd crafted with NFL owners, and many veterans had taken big pay cuts—or had been cut altogether. Phil Simms, the Giants' longtime quarterback, was released in June when the club said his $2.5 million salary wouldn't fit under its cap. If the rallying cry for the 1898 Spanish–American War was "Remember the Maine," the slogan for baseball's looming 1994 labor war was, "Remember Phil Simms!"

In late July, the union's executive board met by teleconference to set a strike deadline. The players had to go on the offensive, if only for defensive purposes. If no contract was reached by collective bargaining, the Lords could eventually shove the salary cap down their throats. Federal labor law allowed employers to declare a bargaining impasse, after a decent interval for negotiations, and impose employment terms.

Don Fehr believed this would come right after the World Series, when baseball's off-season business cycle began. The players had to try forcing a deal while they still had some leverage—

during the season, when lost games meant lost money for the Lords.

The only question was when. Some players urged a late-September date. Why not play out nearly the entire season, collect nearly every paycheck, and strike when it hurt most: the post-season. That was baseball's showcase and cash cow—the source of at least 80 percent of network TV money. That was a brinkshmanship approach, however, leaving little time to negotiate. Some players liked Labor Day, for its delicious significance and its timing: pennant races would be coming to a full boil, and owners with contending teams would want a rapid settlement. But the weight of opinion finally tilted toward an earlier date in mid-August. That built in more time to bargain, and if it also meant more lost paychecks . . . so what? The union had a $200 million strike fund (from licensing revenue) to fall back on. The owners had no such warchest. The losses inflicted on them—and the pressure to settle—could be far worse than on the players' side.

And thus was a decision reached and a date set: August 12. No deal, no play—and virtually no chance of beating that deadline. "This is like *Speed*," said Oakland GM Sandy Alderson, referring to the summer's hit action movie about a runaway bus. "The playoffs and World Series are the hostage; the players are driving with the explosives taped to their bodies; and the owners are the cops chasing them."

One could argue about who the good guys and bad guys were in this plot. One couldn't argue they stood to detonate a magnificent season. It featured some of the most stunning performances seen in years. In early August, the Giants' Matt Williams, with forty-three home runs, and the Mariners' Ken Griffey, Jr., with forty, both stood to challenge Roger Maris's sixty-one-homer record. The Padres' Tony Gwynn was hitting .394 and threatening to become the first player to hit .400 since Ted Williams did it in 1941. The White Sox' Frank Thomas had a chance to be the first player since Carl Yastrzemski in 1967 to win batting's Triple Crown. The Braves' Greg Maddux had sixteen wins and an Earned Run Average of 1.56, compiling perhaps the greatest pitching numbers since Bob Gibson's 1.12 ERA of 1968.

Some cities shimmered with baseball excitement unknown for years. Cleveland was breaking in a magnificent new stadium and dared hope for post-season play for the first time in forty years. The Indians were nineteen games over .500 and one game back in the AL Central Division. The Yankees had the American

League's best record, headed for a playoff berth for the first time since 1981. The Expos had the National League's best record, after years in eclipse, with exciting young players like Moises Alou, led by his sage manager (and father) Felipe Alou.

It all came to a halt after the games of August 11. In Oakland, following the A's–Mariners game, fans lingered outside the clubhouse trying to squeeze a last moment out of the season. One held up a protest sign: "Quit cryin' and just play ball." In his New York office, Don Fehr stayed late with his staff to field any possible last-minute proposal. None came, and they settled for playing a few rubbers of bridge. At midnight, baseball's eighth work stoppage in twenty-two years began.

George Steinbrenner was promptly in mid-strike form, publicly renouncing the Lords' party line and their negotiator. "I'd like to see owners at the bargaining table," he blustered. "We should get people to the table who have considerable financial interest in baseball—personal financial interest in the game and not a bunch of lawyers who are the only ones going to make money out of the strike." The Orioles' Peter Angelos seconded that motion, and the baseball world reverberated with the old, familiar sounds of fast-crumbling owner unity.

But something new happened here. The loose cannons were hushed and the Lords' battle lines held firm. A new order was asserting itself. The new owners—the McLanes and Glasses—weren't terrorized but energized by the first shots of war. Some players' anti-owner rhetoric—like seven-time drug offender Steve Howe calling them "liars"—inflamed passions. And baseball's de facto commissioner feverishly dialed up owners, exhorting them from his Milwaukee office to remember and retain the spirit of Dallas and Cincinnati. They did. The Lords were now playing Buddyball.

The phenomenon of Bud Selig as czar represented a stark, humbling change for dovish big-market owners. They'd long enjoyed the cozy advantage of friends in high places. The Mets' Fred Wilpon could always make his case for moderation—and make his influence felt—with pal Fay Vincent. The O'Malleys needed only to snap their fingers and their will would be done by Bowie Kuhn. But today's czar wasn't just more sympathetic to small-market owners, he *was* a small-market owner.

And, make no mistake, Selig was the guy who counted. Dick Ravitch was the owners' out-front figure and lightning rod for union attacks. But in the Lords' inner circles he was of diminishing consequence. His political capital had been eroded by the bruising revenue-sharing fight. His inexperience in labor-relations nitty-gritty was ever more evident. (Labor lawyer Chuck O'Connor reascended in stature as Ravitch's star fell.) His strained relationship with Bud Selig further isolated him.

Selig was still only acting commissioner and still swore on a stack of Chevys he didn't want the job long-term. But he was nearing two years in office, with no departure date set. A majority of Lords had insisted earlier that year: no new commissioner until after reaching a new labor deal. This time, there wouldn't be a Ueberroth, Vincent, or Kuhn to undercut them in mid-negotiation. This time, a lodge brother would look after baseball's "best interests"—chiefly their own, of course. Selig made no pretense of being a neutral czar. He was clearly the owners' floor leader.

"It's like [former House Speaker] Tip O'Neill, who used to say he didn't know the details of the bills but he knew where the votes were," said one veteran Selig-watcher. "He keeps the votes lined up, working that god-blessed phone constantly. He's done favors for virtually every owner; and he's not above reminding them of that."

Some of the vote-wangling techniques would have impressed even the late Speaker O'Neill. Colorado owner Jerry McMorris howled at sacrificing his club's profits to take a strike. But he came around when the expansion Rockies and Marlins were given a three-year reprieve from revenue-sharing. The Braves' and Cubs' owners weren't natural-born militants. Baseball games were valuable programming to Turner Broadcasting and Tribune Co., respectively, and strikes scuttled games. But an ownership committee was mulling an important issue about these superstations. Should the "tax" on them (payments to other clubs for territorial invasion) be vastly increased? While that committee's decision was pending—and Selig-appointed committees deliberated approximately forever—those teams would toe the party line.

(The real reason for his support, maintains Braves President Stan Kasten, was his other job: president of the NBA Atlanta Hawks. There he learned the salary cap's value. A Tribune Co. spokesman wouldn't comment.)

The players sat back, waiting for the Lords to follow form—to begin wavering and bring in a scaled-down proposal. No such thing happened. In fact, nothing happened at all. For the first thirteen days of the strike, everything was still as a muggy August evening in an empty ballpark: no talks, no move-ment, and no more to be heard from George Steinbrenner.

A team of mediators entered the picture, however, led by Fed-eral Mediation and Reconciliation Service chief John Calhoun Wells. They listened to Don Fehr's complaints about Dick Ravitch and the difficulty of negotiating sans owners. They asked the Lords if they might send a delegation to some bar-gaining meetings. Selig agreed to it, and finally, on August 24, negotiations resumed in a packed New York hotel ballroom: twenty-one players and their eight union staffers; twelve owner-ship delegates and their six lawyers; and four mediators. In the lobby outside, a throng of gawkers assembled. One of them was the noted divorce lawyer Raoul Felder. "This is my specialty," he said, "greed, avarice, self-interest."

This was, it turned out, a Tower of Babel—speech-making, strutting, and absolutely no negotiating. Don Fehr lectured the owners on cartel behavior. Gene Orza held forth on their repeat-edly incorrect projections of doom. Players recited the history of ownership horrors and how it made them recoil at their talk of "partnership."

The ownership delegation listened and seethed. Who was Gene Orza to tell a world-class retailer like David Glass how to run a business? Who cared about how long-deceased owners had done Marvin Miller wrong? "They wanted to go back to what was done wrong in 1976," said Drayton McLane. "You can learn from history and all, but we need to deal with where the game is at today, in 1994."

The players bridled, in turn, when Glass began the second day's meeting with a homily on how they should help baseball better compete for the entertainment dollar. He also chided them for seeming disinterested in bargaining. "Where's your sense of urgency?" Glass asked.

The players were incredulous and resented the onus being put on them. They also believed Ravitch was the obstacle to prog-ress.

Nor did the players' mood brighten when Jerry Reinsdorf of-fered his version of "Give us a number!"

"Let's do a deal," he said. "Just tell us the percentage you want."

There was no response.

Reinsdorf persisted: "What percentage do you want?"

"How much profit do you want?" Don Fehr finally shot back. That was the end of the session and, as it turned out, the end of the meetings. John Calhoun Wells adjourned negotiations at midday on August 25 before relations could deteriorate further. It was already too late.

Just to ensure the gathering broke up on a maximally hostile note, the union immediately released a report by its economist Roger Noll. He'd been retained to review clubs' books and, as in 1985, his findings skewered any notion of distress. "Baseball is financially healthy," he concluded. "The claim of widespread disaster in the sport is pure fiction."

The combination of incendiary meeting and sneering report was a turning point, in the view of one management-side lawyer. "It galvanized and hardened the owners in a way Selig couldn't have done if he worked the phones twenty-eight hours a day," he said.

Agent Tom Reich, viewing matters from the players' standpoint, agreed. "All it stimulated was posturing. It only increased hostilities."

Reich would attempt to mend fences through much of the strike, trying through back-channels communications to find some common ground. Several other agents—loyal to players but on good terms with owners—also tried. All wound up supremely frustrated.

Randy Hendricks was exasperated with both sides' penchant for emotional, visceral responses to each other. "Come on now," he wailed, at one point, "are we dating or are we negotiating?" Tony Attanasio, another go-between, figured he heard the gut-level essence of it from one owner: "Hey, you guys have won every one of these things since 1972. Let us win one now."

It was actually an *owner* working the back channels who would prove the last best chance for peace. As chairman of the wildly popular—and highly profitable—Colorado Rockies, Jerry McMorris desperately wanted to resume the season. He was well steeped in labor matters, moreover, though different in mind-set from the militant Wal-Mart crowd. McMorris had built his NW Transport Service business from nothing into the West's biggest privately owned trucking firm. And he did it with an all-union workforce that never had gone on strike. "I'm not the most knowledgable baseball person or the most knowledgable person on the revenue-sharing plan," he would later say, "but I felt I might be able to reach some kind of compromise deal."

McMorris secured Bud Selig's permission to open communication lines with the union. Then he began talking by phone with Don Fehr, sometimes up to five times in a day. When he thought he knew the man and the issues well enough, he set up a very private dinner at his Four Seasons Hotel suite in New York. The invitees: himself, Chuck O'Connor, and Don and Steve Fehr.

The owners wanted to float an idea: instead of a salary cap, what about a graduated "luxury tax?" If a club's payroll totalled more than 20 percent of the major-league average, they would pay a tax of, say, 25 percent for one bracket, 50 percent for another bracket higher, 75 percent for the next and so on. That tax would go into a pool to be distributed to the poorer teams. It would satisfy some owner objectives, but it would enable Fehr to avert the "two dirty words," as union people sometimes called the salary cap.

"We started bouncing ideas off each other, and when Don left I would have bet ten to one we were going into a full negotiating mode the next day," McMorris said. Instead, he recalled, "Don called back the next day and said he couldn't go for it."

Something else did emerge from the meeting, however: a discovery by McMorris that the union didn't know the owners' revenue-sharing plan. Union officials had pressed for the details since early 1994, figuring it was important to know how the small-market clubs fared under this plan. If they could provide more relief for the have-nots without succumbing to a salary cap, they had the basis for a counter-proposal.

They got the plan on Friday, September 2, and were stunned at the owners' creation—"a Rube Goldberg contraption," as one of the union people put it. They feverishly crunched numbers over Labor Day weekend to try devising their own plan. They were working against a deadline now. Bud Selig had declared that without a deal by September 9 the season was dead. By midweek after Labor Day—the deadline nigh—the players had a new proposal for the Lords.

There was to be no Tower-of-Babel-style session this time. The players would meet with a core committee of just five owners in New York on September 8. The night before, four top union officials met two of the owners—McMorris and Red Sox managing partner John Harrington—for dinner. It was cordial but not giddy, neither side entertaining outsized hopes for success.

"I know what it will take to get twenty-one votes," McMorris told Don Fehr. "It has to be something that slows down the percentage of revenues going to salaries." A flat tax—one that didn't carry disincentives for big spending—wouldn't fly.

That, nonetheless, is just what the union placed before the Lords Thursday afternoon. Illustrated with charts and laden with figures, it proposed to tax the sixteen richest clubs' payrolls and revenues 1.5 percent each. That would generate $50 million for the have-nots, which obviously didn't equal the Lords' own $70 million revenue-sharing package. But, Don Fehr believed, it was a starting point for dickering. Certainly it was about the best he could do. His constituency, as surely as the owners, had grown more militant each day. Only after much discussion and dissent did the union's executive board approve the offer.

It was promptly dismissed by the owners. What might have worked as an opening gambit in mid-August was far too late now. "They played for the [owners'] fold too long," said one of the Lords. "The owners' thinking now is, 'If I've lost fifteen to twenty million dollars on this strike, what do I have to get out of a deal to make that worthwhile?' "

Bud Selig swooped into New York from Milwaukee on Friday to announce the rejection; Don Fehr took the podium to re-affirm the players' resolve; a crushed Jerry McMorris left town. Both owners and players, he thought, were prisoners of history. "I never would have believed the level of mistrust and lack of confidence in each other," he said. "It made it very difficult for people to compromise or experiment."

One desultory run at bargaining did remain. Boston's John Harrington and Braves President Stan Kasten remained in New York for Saturday meetings with the union. As usual, the two sides saw what transpired very differently. Mr. Kasten recalled trying to explore some new taxation concepts. "I went down four tracks with that," he recalled. "Everything we threw up they shot down."

Union participants mostly took note of the atmospherics at 350 Park Avenue, where they met. The lights were off, the coffee pot was off, and Kasten and Harrington's suitcases were standing in the corner, ready for departure. To call Kasten's points "ideas," they felt, was a gross exaggeration. One proposal called for payroll-tax proceeds to be put into an entity to be jointly administered by the owners and players.

"What if the extra money went to something we owned jointly, a marketing company or charitable foundation?" said Kasten. "We could put it to good use."

But if the Braves executive saw it as a good experiment and great PR, the union officials saw it as crazy. They later privately called it "the Rwanda plan."

"We made a good offer," union lawyer Lauren Rich insisted to Kasten and Harrington. "If you want something from us that gives you a substantial deterrent to signing players, you won't get it."

Kasten and Harrington insisted the union should work with the graduated luxury-tax concept. It was the best offer they were ever going to get.

The Dodgers' Orel Hershiser, a meeting participant, disagreed. "Here's what's going to happen," he said. "Once we go over the cliff, you're going to change your negotiating team, and we're going to get a deal."

And there the two sides sat, in an unlit office, looking at one another.

Four days later, baseball went dark.

Twenty-six of the twenty-eight owners faxed in signatures to Bud Selig, supporting a resolution that pulled the plug on the 1994 season. (Peter Angelos and Marge Schott refused to sign.) For the first time in ninety years, there would be no World Series.

Yet Randy Hendricks, in his shuttle-diplomacy efforts, found some owners to be positively giddy. They'd finally held together and faced down the players! They could declare an impasse and impose the system of their dreams! They'd won!

It was, thought Hendricks, a wholly unreasonable view. The owners had also invited Congress to repeal baseball's antitrust status. They faced a fierce legal battle with the union, which would claim unfair bargaining tactics. They would have to try selling 1995 season tickets and TV rights with no assurance of a season. And, if it opened, would the fans *still* be there? Baseball had sorely tested the allegiance of untold millions of them, who were left with these lingering, damning images: Lou Whitaker of the Tigers arriving at a union meeting in his stretch limo; Bud Selig announcing the end of a once-great season with great crocodile tears; and ballparks sitting empty in October, World Series heroes supplanted by business combatants. If this was indeed to be the Lords' triumph, it shaped up as one of history's great Pyrrhic victories. "To save the art, they burned down the museum," said Randy Hendricks.

Don Fehr turned to Washington, getting congressional allies behind a movement to repeal baseball's antitrust exemption. It was to be a limited version, applying just to labor relations, and it attracted strong support. The House Judiciary Committee cleared a bill in early October, while Senator Howard Metzenbaum sought a Senate-side vehicle to accompany it. (He was looking for a bill already on the floor that lent itself to being amended.) But proponents ran out of time when Congress recessed to campaign for election.

The election results would set back the repeal cause. Congressmen Mike Synar and Jack Brooks, the most influential repeal champions in the House, were ousted in the Republican landslide. Metzenbaum, the leading Senate advocate, retired. Amidst Capitol Hill's massive upheaval, baseball suddenly was well down on the legislative agenda. More than ever, baseball's strike seemed mired in stalemate.

And yet, in another corner of Washington, a possible solution suddenly emerged. It came in the form of a man named W. J. "Bill" Usery, Jr. He was a Ford-era Labor Secretary and, even at age seventy, an indefatigable freelance mediator. Usery had stepped into labor disputes from press rooms to coal fields to schoolrooms, settling many by simply making the two sides talk 'til they dropped. Now President Clinton asked him to try his hand at the bitter baseball war.

Usery plunged into work, chalking up at least one solid achievement by mid-November. He got the players and the Lords together for the first time in two months, with a series of meetings at a Westchester County (NY) conference center. Peace hadn't exactly broken out, but Dick Ravitch had been *thrown* out—of the lead negotiator's chair. He'd been Grebey-ized: replaced by the less abrasive John Harrington of the Red Sox. The Lords also seemed poised to replace their long-standing salary-cap demand with a "luxury tax" proposal, along the lines first explored by Jerry McMorris.

The Westchester session broke up after three days, with another session scheduled for the following week. The two sides were hardly out of the woods. Harrington warned that if there wasn't a newly negotiated system by December 20—the deadline for teams to offer contracts to holdover players—the owners would impose one. They had to get on with the 1995 season after all. "The real calendar that's driving everybody is the business calendar," he said.

But for the first time in the great strike of '94 there was a glimmer of optimism. "There just may be a basis for cooking up a settlement," said one well-placed aide to the Lords, "and the yeast in that bread is Bill Usery."

Atlanta
November 1994

Index

Aaron, Hank, 72, 84, 117, 125, 126, 403, 428
Aaron, Henry J., 555–56
Abbott, Jim, 574
ABC, 15, 69, 390, 393–97, 407–8, 412–13
Abdul-Jabbar, Kareem, 150
Abel, I. W., 19–20
Able, John, 127–28
Abraham, Seth, 335, 336
Adams, Franklin Pierce, 134
agents, player, 94, 216, 228, 316, 317
  in football, 310
  and free agency, 194, 195, 206–7, 225
  and holdouts, 23–24, 216
  and owner ignorance, 260–61
  owners' resistance to, 195
  players' resistance to, 215–16
  and salary arbitration, 214–15, 308–21, 325–28
  and statistics, 214–15, 319–20, 321
Agnos, Art, 437–38
Aikens, Willie, 364
Alderson, Sandy, 328, 373–75, 596
Alevezos, John, 210
Alexander, Doyle, 383
Algren, Nelson, 2
Allen, Dick, 96
Allen, Herbert, 424
Allen, Mel, 589
All-Star Game:
  broadcasts of, 69, 390

and pension fund, 12–13, 15, 27
Allyn, John, 250
Alou, Felipe, 597
Alou, Moises, 597
Alston, Walter, 51–52, 64
Ameche, Alan, 67
American Association, 2, 3
American Baseball Guild, 9
American League, 3, 66, 68, 78, 98, 195, 201, 202, 203, 234, 249–50, 250, 257, 291, 299–300, 302, 380, 384, 399, 415, 431, 450, 456, 491, 494–501, 542, 545, 557–58, 596
  see also specific teams and owners
America's Cup, 189, 225–26
Amorosa, Dom, 538–39
Andersen, Larry, 573, 574, 592
Anderson, Dave, 520
Andrews, Mike, 135, 201
Angell, Roger, 419
Angelos, Peter, 570–72, 597, 603
Anheuser-Busch, 99, 102–4, 233, 271, 289, 392–93, 591
antitampering rules, 171, 210–12
antitrust laws, 5, 98–99
  exemption from, 8, 80, 109, 112, 134, 160, 257, 268, 583, 603
arbitration, 36–39
  commissioner's role in, 37–39, 83, 109–10, 112–14, 131, 172–74

final offer, *see* salary arbitration
and free agency, 148–49, 165–66
and ignorance of game, 308–9, 327
and *Messersmith*, 170–80
as plum assignment, 327
salary, *see* salary arbitration
and statistics, 309
vs. negotiation, 164, 166, 172–74, 177–79
Argyros, George, 260, 474, 485
Arledge, Roone, 393, 396–97, 407
Armas, Tony, 322
Astrodome, 72–75, 76, 322
AstroTurf, 75
Atlanta Braves, 24, 66, 96, 98, 153, 165, 189–94, 210–11, 213, 226, 265–69, 271, 321, 329, 338, 340, 347, 355, 358, 362, 369, 375–76, 382–83, 402–3, 456, 521–23, 543, 559, 573, 578–80, 596, 598, 602
Atlanta Hawks, 369, 454, 598
Attanasio, Tony, 368–69, 370–71, 600
attendance, 8, 66, 70, 263, 588–89
and broadcasts, 42, 68–69, 388–89, 391, 475
and income, 53, 55–56, 62–63, 204, 388–89, 403–4, 573
as measure of success, 69, 82, 234, 246, 349, 256, 279, 379
and promotions, 63, 78, 248, 337, 586
and stadiums, 74, 139, 476, 477, 483
and stars, 234, 273, 318
and ticket prices, 63, 234
Autry, Gene, 24, 77, 127, 153, 222–23, 227, 250, 399, 497–98
Autry, Jackie, 499, 518

Bahnsen, Stan, 135
Baker, James, 332
Baldwin, Doug, 358

Baltimore, Md., 478–80, 569–72
Baltimore Bullets, 478
Baltimore Colts, 478
Baltimore Orioles, 66, 86, 122, 124–25, 145–46, 155, 167, 168, 194, 199, 219, 220, 224, 234, 239–41, 244, 261, 280, 325, 337, 389, 411, 445, 470, 473, 478–80, 489, 530, 531, 547, 549, 553, 569–72, 573, 579, 597
Bando, Sal, 169, 196, 199, 274, 585
Banker, Bob, 465
Banks, Ernie, 72
Barber, Red, 42, 51
Barger, Carl, 496, 497, 554
Barrow, Ed, 41
Barry, Rick, 131
Bartholomay, Bill, 101, 128, 191, 375, 471, 543
baseball cards, 16, 89–90, 379, 427, 446, 589
baseball clubs, *see* owners; *specific teams*
Basic Agreement:
  of 1968, 29, 36–37, 38–39, 83
  of 1969, 101
  of 1970, 94, 109, 113, 114–15, 131
  of 1972, 116–17
  of 1973, 120, 139
  of 1975, 208
  of 1976, 228
  of 1981, 243
  of 1985, 446
basketball:
  free agency in, 131, 171, 595
  player drafts in, 64
  salaries in, 126, 150, 276, 441, 488
  vs. baseball, 276–77, 369–70, 564, 567
Bass, Kevin, 560
Bast, Joseph, 478
Bavasi, Buzzie, 47, 115, 135–36, 292, 399–400, 454–55, 584
  and contracts, 31, 262

Bavasi, Buzzie, *(cont.)*
  and Dodgers, 10, 53–54, 62, 63–65, 93
  and Hunter, 150–54, 157–58
  and Padres, 33, 111
  paternalism of, 34–35, 124
  and salaries, 29, 32, 309
Bavasi, Evit, 399
Bavasi, Peter, 214, 246, 264–65, 341, 360, 364–65, 375, 399–400, 401, 495
Baylor, Don, 85, 194, 195, 199, 212, 215, 218, 220, 223, 252, 349, 585
Beck, David, 104
beer, 7, 46, 102–4, 392–93, 400–401, 529, 591
Beeston, Paul, 477, 547–48, 550, 578, 579–80
Begelman, David, 424
Belanger, Mark, 85, 237, 244, 277, 282, 284–85, 289, 296, 304, 345
Bell, Bert, 67
Bell, Buddy, 254
Bell, Derek, 575
Bell, Gary, 155
Bell, Jay, 552
Bench, Johnny, 138, 183, 210
Benchley, Peter, 425
Benes, Andy, 575, 576
Benswanger, William, 9
Berger, Sy, 90
Berger, Victor, 5
Bernazard, Tony, 325, 358
Berra, Yogi, 10
Berry, Chuck, 319
Biggio, Craig, 593
Billings, Dick, 135
Birmingham Barons, 77
Black, Bud, 486, 487
Blackmun, Harry, 134
blacks, discrimination against, 87–88
Blackshear, Cornelius, 570–72
"Black Sox" scandal, 6, 81, 427
Bloch, Richard, 584

Blue, Vida, 144–45, 194–99, 200, 204, 205, 238, 246
Blyleven, Bert, 372
Boddicker, Mike, 486
Bodie, Ping, 4
Bodley, Hal, 437, 509, 520
Boggs, Wade, 321
Bonda, Ted, 150, 153, 219
Bonds, Barry, 492, 552, 553, 565, 566, 574, 588
Bonds, Bobby, 155
Bonilla, Bobby, 492, 524, 544, 566
bonuses, 64, 95, 201, 218
Boone, Bob, 83, 85, 274, 300–301, 349–50, 369, 443–44, 585, 594
  and January 8 Eight, 373–74, 382
  as negotiator, 87, 182, 282–83, 298, 300–301
  and salary arbitration, 448–51
Boone, Ray, 282–83
Boras, Scott, 567
Bosley, Thad, 381
Boston Beaneaters, 3
Boston Braves, 54, 66, 403
Boston Bruins, 397
Boston Pilgrims, 3
Boston Red Sox, 35, 117, 142, 154, 169, 194, 195–97, 204, 205–6, 210, 213, 216, 239, 373–74, 383, 391, 397, 415, 417, 420, 433, 479, 490, 491, 492, 499–500, 560, 583, 601, 602, 604
Boswell, Tom, 277
Boulware, Lemuel, 230
Bouton, Jim, 24, 27, 84, 132
Bowa, Larry, 272
Bowen, Rex, 137
Braun, Steve, 175
Breadon, Sam, 46
Brennan, Arthur, 230
Brett, George, 239, 254, 355, 446
Brett, Ken, 252
Brochu, Claude, 530, 558
Brock, Lou, 104, 107, 320
Broff, Nancy, 289, 297

Bronfman, Charles, 64, 259, 279, 329, 340, 346, 401, 417
and free agents, 212, 223–24, 366–67
on leaving baseball, 487–88
Bronner, Jim, 253–54, 312–16, 326, 339, 340, 376
Brooklyn Dodgers, 10, 11, 23, 40–62, 66, 111, 389, 482, 495, 556, 557, 583
Brooklyn Trust Company, 40–44, 49
Brooks, Jack, 604
Brosnan, Jim, 109
Brotherhood of Professional Base Ball Players, 3
Brown, Bobby, 443, 498–99, 513, 546
Brown, Joe, 318
Brown, Kevin, 563
Brown, Leo, 227
Brown, Mordecai "Three Finger," 4
Browning, Tom, 486
Bruton, Billy, 505
Bry, Richie, 215, 216, 370
Buck, Ray, 514
Buckner, Bill, 301
Bunning, Jim, 16, 21, 22, 85, 86, 583
Buoniconti, Nick, 320, 328
Burke, Joe, 153, 297
Burke, Mike, 98, 155
Burks, Ellis, 560
Burleson, Rick, 216, 239
Burns, Bryan, 334, 340, 363, 410–14
Burns, David, 564
Burrell, Stanley, 246
Busch, Augustus A., III, 233, 292, 591
Busch, Augustus A., Jr., "Gussie," 102–6, 107, 136, 183, 187, 229, 249
and Anheuser-Busch, 102–5, 233, 271, 289, 392
as anti-union, 38, 105, 116–17, 133, 166, 209
clubhouse speech of, 104–6
and free agency, 211–12
paternalism of, 103, 105, 128–29
and strike, 118–19, 121, 123, 125, 127
and Susman, 233–34
Busch, Corey, 437–38
Busch Stadium, 105
Bush, George, 423, 473, 474, 485, 499, 501, 511, 517, 531, 544, 548–49, 579–80
business, vs. sport, 7, 12, 22, 23, 39, 61–62, 65, 96, 336, 340–43, 419, 426–27, 554–55, 575
Butler, Brett, 327, 360, 443

Cabell, Enos, 319
Cablevision, 404, 406, 475
California Angels, 23, 24, 64, 77, 153, 218, 220–23, 248, 252, 262, 312, 358, 371, 382, 384, 385, 386, 399–400, 491, 496, 499, 527–28, 574
Camden Yards, 479–80, 530, 569–70
Camilli, Dolf, 42, 44
Caminiti, Ken, 593
Camp, Rick, 267
Campanella, Roy, 50, 53
Campaneris, Bert, 206, 215, 218, 220, 227, 263
Campanis, Al, 65, 153, 162–64, 309
Campbell, Bill, 213, 234
Campbell, Jim, 11, 94, 124, 197–98, 233, 310, 322, 377, 390, 435
Candelaria, John, 318
Candlestick Park, 210, 436–38
Cannizzaro, Chris, 125
Cannon, Raymond J., 13
Cannon, Robert C., 13–14, 16–17, 21, 23, 26, 98
Canseco, Jose, 485, 491, 566, 573
Caples, Bill, 231
Caray, Harry, 104, 255, 402
Caray, Skip, 266, 523
Carew, Rod, 238, 362, 302, 314, 350
Carey, Max, 320

Caridi, Joseph, 459
Carling O'Keefe, 400–401
Carlton, Steve, 117, 376
Carpenter, Bob, 11, 38, 47–48, 82, 115, 124, 202
Carpenter, Ruly, 153, 149–50, 268–73, 292–93
Carrasquel, Chico, 321
Carroll, Clay, 97
Carroll, Lou, 31, 36, 99, 110, 186
Carter, Gary, 317, 367
Carter, Joe, 588
Casey, Frank, 491
Cash, Dave, 218
Cashen, Frank, 178, 274, 310, 399
Castellini, Bob, 572
Cavanaugh, Bill, 532, 536
CBC, 400–401
CBS, 67, 393, 396, 407–14, 440, 474, 529, 553, 592
  and *Game of the Week*, 69, 567
  Yankees owned by, 16, 69, 155
CBS Sports Spectacular, 394
Cedeno, Cesar, 261
Central Fund, 336, 363–64, 398
Cepeda, Orlando, 107, 175
Cerone, Rick, 324
Chance, Dean, 496
Chandler, Happy, 9, 12, 80–81, 393
Chass, Murray, 295, 428, 457, 509, 515, 520
Chavez, Cesar, 32
Chavez, Julian, 60
cheating, 419
Cherry, J. Carlton, 149–55, 157–58
Chester, Hilda, 50
Chicago Bulls, 481
Chicago Cubs, 4, 11, 58–59, 230, 231, 239, 259, 312–16, 325, 326, 355, 380–82, 389, 402, 479, 489, 521–25, 526–28, 559, 580, 598
Chicago White Sox, 6, 31–32, 77, 99, 199, 217, 248, 250–59, 325, 480–84, 495, 506, 527–28, 560, 580, 596
Chicago White Stockings (NL), 3

Chiles, Eddie, 265, 280–81, 290, 292, 403, 474
Christensen, Tom, 316
Churchill, Winston, 53
Cianfrocco, Archie, 576
Cincinnati Reds, 7, 41, 48, 70, 136, 137–39, 170, 184, 213, 216–17, 219, 232–33, 239, 246, 266, 270–71, 305, 318, 320, 322, 328, 389, 402–3, 427, 430, 521, 583, 594
Claiborne, John, 213
Clancy, Jim, 264
Clancy, Tom, 570
Clark, Bobby, 309
Clark, Jack, 63, 385–86
Clark, Will, 441, 486
Clemens, Roger, 380, 383, 440, 490–91, 589
Clendenon, Donn, 110, 112
Cleveland Indians, 10, 23, 154, 219, 248–49, 310, 311, 327, 360, 375, 385, 403, 487, 491, 499, 528, 576, 578–79, 596
clubs, baseball, *see* owners; *specific teams*
Clydesdales, 104
Cobb, Ty, 4, 321, 427
Coca-Cola, 90, 338, 425, 426
Coggins, Rich, 168
Coleman, Choo Choo, 496
Coleman, Joe, 185
Coleman, Ken, 420, 433
Collins, Dave, 324, 404
Collins, Jimmy, 3
Collins, Phyllis, 422–23
collusion, 94–95, 353, 407, 445, 474
  and free agency, 211–12, 338–39, 354–87, 440
  and Information Bank, 383–87
  rulings on, 384, 387, 421
Colorado Rockies, 527, 543, 598, 600
Columbus Clippers, 286
Comiskey, Charles, 6
Comiskey Park, 480–84

commissioner:
  arbitration role of, 38–39, 83,
     109–10, 112–14, 131, 172–74
  authority of, 37, 81, 187, 281,
     306, 332, 363, 435
  and "best interests" power, 110,
     114, 204, 207–8, 226, 363,
     504, 524, 541
  diminishing powers of, 112–13,
     207–8, 510–11, 540–43
  interventions of, 504–5, 510–13
  and Major League Agreement,
     112, 435, 510–13, 518–19,
     541–43
  owners' control of, 80, 207
  reelection of, 201–3
  selection of, 80, 97–99, 332,
     417–18, 433–35, 541, 582
  and work stoppages, 99–100,
     421–22
  see also specific commissioners
compensation, for free agents,
     233–37, 238, 242–43, 273,
     274–75, 277, 289, 290, 297,
     299–300, 304, 310
Concepcion, Dave, 270
Congress, U.S., 67, 522–23, 583
Connors, Chuck, 48
Continental League, 495
contracts, 31
  and cost-of-living escalator,
     456–57
  dummy, 93
  lifetime, 339, 355
  million-a-year, 262, 339, 485
  multiyear, 150, 157, 194, 218,
     261, 262, 268, 312–13, 323,
     325, 351–52, 354–55, 357,
     360, 361, 380, 456–57, 486
  no-trade clause in, 162–64, 167
  players educated about, 27–29
  and severance, 29, 113
  and side letters, 386
  and suiting up, 101, 130
  see also Basic Agreement; Uni-
     form Players Contract
Cook, Murray, 368

Cook, Stanton, 522, 523–25,
     527–28, 548
Cooper, Irving Ben, 109
Corbett, Brad, 199, 201–3, 219,
     227, 260, 263–65, 270
Corkins, Mike, 115
Cosell, Howard, 395
Costas, Bob, 583
Costello, Bob, 534–35, 538–39
Coveleski, Stan, 4
Cox, Bobby, 373, 375–76
Coyle, Harry, 393–94
Crawford, Wahoo Sam, 134
Cronin, Joe, 26, 28, 30, 32, 87–88,
     98, 119, 442
Crosley, Powell, 41, 397
Crosley Field, 28, 139
Crown, Lester, 257
Cruz, Jose, 129, 261, 319
Curran, Paul, 466–69

Dade, Paul, 212
Dallas Cowboys, 572
Dalton, Harry, 221, 223, 274, 277,
     326, 507, 589–90
Danforth, Doug, 421, 497, 544–45,
     548, 592
Daniel, Chris, 198
Danzansky, Joe, 112
Darling, Ron, 327, 446
Darwin, Danny, 384, 385, 490
Daulton, Darren, 486
David M. Winfield Foundation,
     455–61
Davidson, Donald, 193
Davis, Al, 68, 247
Davis, Alvin, 476
Davis, Eric, 560
Davis, Jody, 373
Davis, Mark, 440
Davis, Martin, 406
Davis, Marvin, 247
Davis, Ron, 320, 328
Davis, Tommy, 93, 175
Davis, Willie, 34
Dawson, Andre, 317, 366–67,
     380–82

Dean, Dizzy, 7

DeBartolo, Edward, 257–58

DeCinces, Doug, 293, 304, 369, 585
   and E. Williams, 277, 287, 289
   as negotiator, 282, 283, 285
   and player meetings, 298–302
   as union leader, 86, 244, 276

DeConcini, Dennis, 523

Dent, Bucky, 252

Denver Bears, 137, 138

Denver Nuggets, 273

Deshaies, Jim, 574

designated hitter, 79

Detroit Tigers, 124, 197, 205, 256,
   310–11, 322, 328, 357–58,
   359–60, 370–73, 377–79,
   385, 390, 528, 603

Detroit Wolverines, 556

Devine, Bing, 108, 117, 132–33,
   219

DeWitt, William O., Jr., 569–70

DiMaggio, Joe, 9, 240, 417, 428,
   470

Ditmar, Art, 77

Dobson, Chuck, 121

Dodger Stadium, 62–63

Doerr, Bobby, 415, 417

Dolan, Chuck, 404–6

Dolson, Frank, 520

Dombrowsky, David, 251, 255

Donahue, Dan, 190–91

Donlan, Jack, 230, 231

Donovan, Ray, 293–95, 297

Doubleday, Abner, 82, 398

Doubleday, Nelson, 398–99, 405,
   516–17, 546

Dowd, John, 428–30, 432, 462–67,
   471

Downing, Al, 130–31

Downing, Brian, 369

Drabek, Doug, 488–89, 491–92,
   552, 553, 565, 574, 593

drafts, player, 64, 259, 283
   for expansion teams, 496
   free-agent, 210–13, 236, 304
   re-entry, 212–13, 274
   Rule 5, 95

Dressen, Chuck, 51

Dressen, Ruth, 51

Driessen, Dan, 318

drugs, 364–65, 531–32, 537–38

Drysdale, Don, 23–24, 29, 65, 359,
   420

Duke, Willie, 45

Dupuy, Bob, 540–41, 547, 551

Durham, Leon, 326

Durocher, Leo, 43, 48, 115

Durso, Ed, 338, 363, 413

Early, Joe, 248

Ebbets, Charles, 40, 541–42

Ebbets Field, 42, 53, 56, 57, 62, 111

Ebersol, Dick, 529

Eckersley, Dennis, 296, 387

Eckert, William "Spike," 22, 26, 31,
   37–38, 80, 82, 91, 97, 299

Einhorn, Eddie, 258–59, 291,
   394–97, 414, 481, 567

Eisenhardt, Roy, 247, 302, 306, 374

Eisentein, Sergei, 476

Ellis, Dock, 318

Ellis, John, 509, 543, 546, 550, 551,
   568, 578

endorsements, 270, 378

Erra, Bob, 455, 457

ESPN, 427, 440, 567

Evans, Dwight, 170, 239

Evinrude, Ralph, 183

executive council, 201–2, 204–5,
   340–41, 420, 471

expansion, 53, 111, 202, 495–501,
   524
   and attendance, 66, 588
   and money, 493, 494–99
   and ownership, 77, 259
   and pension, 88–89, 92
   and realignment, 582–83
   and stadiums, 72, 389

Fairly, Ron, 29, 93

FanFest, 589–90

fans:
   in Brooklyn, 57, 61
   and fun, 70, 192, 255–56, 337

hate mail from, 187, 575, 576
importance of, 541–42
loss of, 71, 563–66
marketing of, 138–39
and player salaries, 9, 234–35, 379
and strikes, 120, 125–26, 129, 239, 286, 305, 597
and Veeck, 248, 249
and winning teams, 481
farm systems, 64–65, 137, 234, 253
opposition to, 7–8, 42, 58
and player development, 259, 269, 293, 322
Rickey as pioneer in, 7, 42–43, 45, 47, 65
Federal League, 4–6, 228, 495
Federal Mediation and Reconciliation Service, 599
Feeney, Chub, 60, 94–95, 97–98, 100, 109, 205, 207, 268, 284, 422–23
as NL president, 82, 118, 119, 164, 193, 241, 300, 306, 332, 418
Fehr, Don, 339, 344–45, 439, 505, 519, 552, 555, 584
and drug testing, 365
and lockout, 442–52
and Ravitch, 560–64, 577, 581
and reform, 583
and strikes, 239, 241–42, 297, 303, 307, 349, 350–51, 591, 594–603
as union's lawyer, 235, 262, 274, 282
Fehr, Steven, 384, 385, 443, 601
Felder, Raoul, 597
Feller, Bob, 27, 589
Feller, David, 585
Fernandez, Sam, 540
Fernandez, Tony, 574
Fernandomania, 279, 317, 318
Ferrara, Al, 90
Fetzer, John, 79, 201, 205, 251, 297, 328, 359, 390, 435
Fidrych, Mark, 215, 317–18

Fielder, Cecil, 563
Fiery, Ben, 146–47
Figure Skating Association, U.S., 567
Fingers, Rollie, 169, 194, 196–97, 199, 204, 206, 212, 215, 223
Finks, Jim, 69
Finley, Charles Oscar "Charlie," 76–79, 128, 336, 556, 585
and A's, 77–78, 161, 245–47, 283, 495
and free agents, 178, 183, 194–202, 203–4, 209, 218
and Hunter, 143–44, 169
and Kuhn, 199–200, 226, 246, 541
and salary arbitration, 161, 215
and truth, 146–49, 195–96, 224
Finley, Paul, 147, 203
Finley, Steve, 593
"fiscal responsibility," 362, 369, 374, 375–77, 576
Fisher, Ben, 19, 20, 32, 343
Fisk, Carlton, 170, 358, 394
Fitzgerald, Ed, 136, 146, 147–48, 153, 178, 179, 201, 205, 207, 208, 209, 506
and lockout, 183, 185–86
as PRC chairman, 160–61, 165–66, 229, 278, 293, 297, 306, 308
Fitzgibbon, Henry, 427
Fleisher, Larry, 276
Fletcher, Scott, 421
Flood, Curt, 106, 107–10, 180, 246, 368
Flood v. *Kuhn*, 109, 110, 134–35, 136, 176, 235, 250
Florida Marlins, 554, 559, 576, 593, 598
Fogelman, Avron, 339, 355
football:
free agency in, 231, 236, 310–12
and "league-think," 68, 70, 336
and licensing, 336
and player agents, 310
player draft in, 64

salaries in, 69, 126, 150
salary cuts, 595
vs. baseball, 25, 66–70, 311
Forster, Terry, 252
Foster, George, 318
Fox, Matty, 54, 56, 60
Foxx, Jimmie, 8, 450
free agency:
    and arbitration, 148–49, 165–66
    in basketball, 131, 171
    and collusion, 212, 338, 354–87,
        440
    compensation for, *see* compensation
    and economics, 181–85, 227,
        234, 236, 308, 338, 356, 366
    in football, 231, 236, 310–12
    ground rules for, 207–9, 221, 242,
        274, 304, 349, 358, 359
    as players' right, 295, 306
    post-*Messersmith*, 181–85, 187,
        194, 233, 270, 319
    and Rozelle Rule, 236, 310–12
    teams stripped by, 232–33, 245
    vs. loyalty, 565
free agents:
    bidding for, 149–59, 162, 194–99,
        204, 210–28, 271–73, 324,
        384–85
    and farm teams, 7–8, 42–43
    in frozen market, 360–61, 366–77
    "premium," 236, 238, 243, 304
    and protected players, 242, 243,
        277, 297, 304
    and "re-entry drafts," 212–13,
        274
    and reserve clause, 131, 135, 136,
        139, 145–49, 170–71, 176
    revenge on, 194
    and salary arbitration, 308–29,
        360–61, 371–73
    "second-look," 387
    senior, 290–91, 304
    signing of, 212, 213, 217–24
    and statistics, 236, 351–52, 355
    threshold of, 182, 183, 207, 208,
        349, 443

Fregosi, Jim, 496
Frick, Ford, 81–82
Friend, Bob, 15, 16, 21, 22
Frohman, Al, 454–60
Fuentes, Tito, 212
Fugett, Jean, Jr., 571–72
Fuller, Buckminster, 71
Fuller, Craig, 294
Fultz, David, 4
Furillo, Carl, 10

Gaedel, Eddie, 249, 569
Gaetti, Gary, 384, 385, 387
Gaherin, John, 52, 137, 181,
        185–186, 227, 503, 505
    and arbitrator, 110, 112–15
    and free agency, 146, 147–48,
        183, 207–9
    and *Messersmith*, 176–79
    as PRC negotiator, 30–31, 34–36,
        38–39, 87, 92, 97, 100–101,
        229–30
    and reserve clause, 36, 134–36,
        164–65, 168
    and salary arbitration, 160, 162
    and strike, 116–28
Galbreath, Dan, 271, 287, 297, 361
Galbreath, John, 12, 16, 48, 49–50,
        271, 361
Gamble, Oscar, 234, 252, 253, 260
Game of the Week, 15, 69, 266, 390,
        397, 398, 411, 567
Gammons, Peter, 448, 449, 499–500
Gantner, Jim, 296, 326
Garagiola, Joe, 109, 326, 391
Gardella, Danny, 12
Gardner, Billy, 328
Garland, Wayne, 219, 227
Garner, Jim, 30–31, 146, 170, 178,
        355
Garner, John Nance, 418
Garner, Phil, 182, 183, 208, 236,
        282, 283–84, 287–88, 295,
        306, 348, 585
Garvey, Ed, 311
Garvey, Steve, 216
gate splits, 68, 558, 559

Gedman, Rich, 369, 373, 374–75, 383

Gehrig, Lou, 8

Giamatti, A. Bartlett, 332, 415–34, 440, 495, 513, 557
  as commissioner, 415, 419–34, 439
  as NL president, 417–18
  writings of, 415–16, 419, 433

Gibbs, Harry, 333

Gibson, Bob, 107, 117, 129, 305, 596

Gibson, Kirk, 357–61, 387, 487

Gilbert, Dennis, 487, 554

Giles, Bill, 74, 112, 248, 292, 337, 372, 391, 394, 475, 498
  and free agents, 272–73, 376–79
  and Vincent, 545, 548, 551

Giles, Warren, 26, 30, 61, 248, 337, 376, 388

Gilhooley, Bob, 253–54, 312–16, 339, 340

Gillette, Pat, 264, 369

Gillette Company, 80–81, 335–36, 394

Gillick, Pat, 264, 369

Glass, David, 591, 593, 597, 599

Goldberg, Arthur, 18–19, 108

Goldberg, Rube, 601

Goldmark, Peter, 530

Goldsmith, Russell, 573

Gonzalez, Juan, 588–89

Gooden, Dwight, 440, 516

Gooding, Gladys, 50–51, 61

Gorman, Lou, 440, 489–92

Goslin, Goose, 134

Gossage, Goose, 199, 252, 253, 315, 338

Gould, Jack, 256, 325

Grant, M. Donald, 22, 38

Grebey, C. Raymond, Jr., 230–44, 257, 273, 274, 315, 346, 604
  and strike, 275–300, 303–5
  "trust me," 238, 244, 288, 297

Green, Dallas, 380–82

Greenberg, Hank, 10, 109, 439, 566

Greenberg, Steve, 439, 467–69, 516–17, 533–38, 551, 566

"Green Fields of the Mind, The" (Giamatti), 420, 433

Greenwald, Ed, 158

Greenwell, Mike, 362, 490

Grich, Bobby, 219–25, 252, 302

grievance arbitration, see arbitration

Grieve, Tom, 123, 215

Griffey, Ken, Jr., 318, 484, 588–89, 596

Griffith, Calvin, 22, 56, 98, 128, 138, 213, 253, 337
  financial problems of, 161, 233, 279, 328, 557
  and Messersmith, 174–76

Griffith, Clark, 41, 70, 94, 166, 179–80, 186, 233, 276, 297

Griffith family, 12, 328

Groat, Dick, 322

Gross, Kevin, 419

Grote, Jerry, 97

Guidry, Ron, 369, 372

Gullett, Don, 210, 219, 223, 227, 252

Gutierrez, Ricky, 573

Gutkowski, Bob, 406

Guzman, Jose, 553

Gwynn, Tony, 573, 576, 596

Haas, Wally, 247, 544

Haas, Walter A., Jr., 247, 444, 501, 544

Hadden, Alexander "Sandy," 110, 136, 147, 203, 211, 212, 226, 266, 507

Haganah, Bill, 59

Hahn, Kenneth, 56–57, 60

Halas, George, 68

Hallinan, Kevin, 460, 462–66

Hamilton, Steve, 26–27

Hammaker, Atlee, 385

Haney, Fred, 222

Hannon, Jim, 123

Hargan, Steve, 265

Harmon, Terry, 124

Harrah, Toby, 218

Harrington, John, 150, 491, 578, 602–4

Harris, Greg, 576
Hatcher, Billy, 419, 561
Hawkins, Andy, 421
Hayes, Bill, 23–24
Hayes, Von, 376, 378
Hebner, Richie, 225, 296
Hegan, Mike, 153
Hemond, Roland, 217, 252, 254
Henderson, Ken, 192
Henderson, Rickey, 317, 440, 502
Hendricks, Alan, 309–12, 490
Hendricks, Randy, 309–12, 488–91, 554, 600, 603
Hermanski, Gene, 46
Hershiser, Orel, 318, 440, 486, 589, 603
Herzog, Whitey, 326
Hickey, Harry, 49
Hiller, David, 540
Hillerich and Bradsby, 89
Hinton, Chuck, 95
Hisle, Larry, 175
hockey, 126, 150, 405
Hodges, Gil, 10, 50, 93
Hoffberger, Jerry, 11, 88–89, 124–25, 187, 202, 206, 211, 240
Hofheinz, Roy, 71–76, 260, 322, 336, 389
Hogan, Gerry, 189
holdouts:
  and baseball-card contracts, 89
  DiMaggio, 9
  fines of, 132
  and free agency, 175–76, 208
  Koufax-Drysdale, 23–24, 359
  and no-trade clause, 162–64, 167
  and pension, 89, 91–92, 184
  and player agents, 23–24, 216
  and reserve clause, 130–36
  and trades, 117, 200
Holland, Al, 323, 360
Holtzman, Jerome, 295, 363, 520
Holtzman, Ken, 194, 215, 282
Horner, Bob, 267, 369, 373, 374, 382

Hornsby, Rogers, 321
Houk, Ralph, 132
House Judiciary Committee, 603
Houston Astros, 72–76, 112, 260–63, 312, 322, 382, 389, 403, 418, 501, 559, 560, 576, 593
Houston Colt .45s, 71–72
Howard, Elston, 212
Howard, Mrs. Elston, 87
Howard, Frank, 117, 123
Howe, Gordie, 150
Howe, Steve, 531–32, 535, 537–38, 597
Howell, Roy, 264
Howsam, Robert L., 136–39, 178, 210, 213, 216, 232, 278, 288, 297
Hoynes, Lou, 110, 136, 231, 242, 266, 349, 557
  and Basic Agreement of 1970, 113–14
  and collusion, 355, 366, 384, 387
  and free agency, 146, 147–48, 229, 377
  and Giamatti, 421–23, 430
  and *Messersmith*, 170–72, 176, 178
  and strike of 1981, 277, 392, 306, 307
Hrabosky, Al, 193, 260, 265–67
Hrbek, Kent, 490
Hubbell, Carl, 59
Huizenga, H. Wayne, 497, 498, 544, 551, 558, 593
Hull, Bobby, 126, 150
Hunter, James Augustus "Catfish," 141–58, 162, 169, 180, 181, 227, 404
Hurst, Bruce, 421, 573, 576

Idelson, Jeff, 532–33
Iglehart, Joe, 77
Illitch, Mike, 546, 550, 568, 578
Incaviglia, Pete, 451
Indianapolis Clowns, 403
inflation, 88, 116, 456–57

of salaries, 485–93, 573
Information Bank, 384–87

Jackson, Bo, 29
Jackson, Danny, 446, 486
Jackson, Darrin, 575
Jackson, Jesse, 554
Jackson, Keith, 214
Jackson, Larry, 22
Jackson, Reggie, 169, 194, 200, 212, 252
    salaries of, 144, 145, 148, 228, 235, 309, 404
    and Steinbrenner, 223–24, 587
    as union activist, 84, 85, 86, 120–21, 275, 290–91, 304, 587–88
Jackson, Shoeless Joe, 13, 480
Jacobs, Dick, 516
Jacobs, Eli, 444, 473, 497, 499, 501, 530, 544, 569–70
Jacobs, Irwin, 328
Jacobs, Paul, 540
James, Bill, 319–20, 489
Janszen, Paul, 429
January 8 Eight, 574, 379, 382
Jemal brothers, 571
Jensen, Jackie, 126
John A. Messersmith v. *Los Angeles Dodgers*, 170–80, 182–83, 187, 207, 269, 284, 310
John Labatt Ltd., 400–401
Johnson, Arnold, 77
Johnson, Byron Bancroft, 3
Johnson, Darrell, 169, 195, 196
Johnson, Deron, 175
Johnson, Howard, 451
Johnston, Bruce, 33, 169
Jones, Randy, 217
Jones, Ruppert, 358
Jordan, Michael, 566–67
Justice, David, 588

Kalifatis, George, 310–11
Kaline, Al, 10–11, 94
Kaminsky, Arthur, 235

Kansas City Athletics, 66, 77, 143, 156, 389, 495
Kansas City Chiefs, 310
Kansas City Royals, 153, 154, 157–58, 195, 265, 271, 337, 339, 340, 354, 357–58, 364, 368, 370, 374, 385, 404, 456, 489, 532, 591, 592, 593
Kapstein, Dan, 214, 216, 218
Kapstein, Jerry, 194–95, 199, 206, 213–21, 223, 227, 267, 311, 313
    decertification of, 584
Kaseff, Gary, 477
Kasten, Stan, 369–70, 376, 492, 543, 598, 602–3
Katz, Reuven, 271–72, 430–32
Kauffman, Ewing, 79, 82, 103, 127, 271, 359, 375, 435, 501, 544
Kaufman, Steve, 467, 469
Kelley, Clarence, 428
Kelly, Mike "King," 4
Keltner, Ken, 10
Kemp, Steve, 296, 404
Kennedy, Bob, 232, 313–15
Kennedy, Walter, 169
Kenney, Jerry, 135
Kheel, Bob, 498, 524, 540
Kiner, Ralph, 8, 12, 13
King, Larry, 594
Kingdome, 476–77, 484, 508
Kirby, Gene, 195, 196, 391
Kittle, Ron, 325
Kleinman, Leonard, 471
Kluttz, Clyde, 141–42, 155–58
Knight, Ray, 369
Knowles, Darold, 215
Kohl, Herb, 497
Koufax, Sandy, 23–24, 29, 65, 359
Kroc, Ray, 151–54, 224, 227, 253, 260, 305, 365
Krukow, Mike, 301
Kuenn, Harvey, 16, 21
Kuhlmann, Fred, 445, 505, 509, 511–12, 514, 519, 548
Kuhn, Bowie Kent, 130, 145, 149,

Kuhn, Bowie Kent, *(cont.)*
      161, 235–36, 256, 257, 335,
      340, 418, 586, 597, 598
   and antitampering rules, 210, 213
   and antitrust exemption, 99
   as commissioner, 99–100,
      108–114, 207, 328–29, 421,
      439, 524
   and economics, 234, 279, 328–29
   and Finley, 199–207, 226, 246,
      541
   and lockout of 1976, 186–87
   and *Messersmith*, 170, 172–74,
      178
   and Steinbrenner, 155, 158, 197
   and strike of 1980, 241–43
   and strike of 1981, 277, 280–81,
      290, 291, 292, 297, 305–6
   and Turner, 225–26, 266, 268
   and TV, 266, 392, 394–97, 401

Lachemann, Rene, 374
Lajoie, Bill, 356, 370
Lajoie, Napoleon, 3
Landis, Kenesaw Mountain, 5–8,
      38, 58, 130, 207, 435, 512,
      540–43
   as commissioner, 6–8, 42, 80, 393
Landrum, Bill, 585
Lane, Frank, 96, 249
Langston, Mark, 439, 440, 474
Lansford, Carney, 374
LaRussa, Tony, 254, 374
Lasorda, Tommy, 420
Law, Rudy, 368, 370–71
Lawn, Jack, 532, 533–34, 536–39,
      540
Lazarus, John, 395
Leary, Tim, 513
Lee, Bill, 222
Lefferts, Craig, 573
Lemanczyk, Dave, 321
LeMay, Curtis, 594
Lemon, Chet, 256
Letterman, David, 472
Levin, Richard, 422, 509
Levinson, Barry, 570

Lewis, J. Norman, 12–13
licensing, 15, 70, 90, 336, 363, 379,
      446, 557, 588–89, 596
Lillis, Bob, 261
Lindell, Johnny, 418
Lindeman, Jim, 358
Lindemann, Carl, 395
Lloyd's of London, 277, 287
Locker, Bob, 31–32
lockouts:
   in 1976, 183–87, 208–9, 256–57,
      451
   in 1990, 422, 433, 434, 441–52
   in 1993–94, 560–64, 581
Lombardi, Vince, 94
Lopat, Eddie, 92–93
Lopes, Davey, 298, 301, 302
Lopez, Hector, 77
Loria, Jeffrey, 571–72
Los Angeles Dodgers, 29, 31, 35,
      61–65, 66, 127, 162–64,
      168, 170–76, 179, 187, 222,
      241, 263, 317–18, 336, 342,
      347, 384, 387, 389, 420,
      485, 492, 500, 521–23,
      527–28, 531, 557, 558–61,
      603
Los Angeles Olympics Organizing
      Committee, 330–33
Louisville Slugger, 89
Lucas, Bill, 267
Lucchino, Larry, 479, 517, 531,
      547, 549, 553, 555
Lupica, Mike, 509
Lurie, Bob, 210–11, 212, 213, 247,
      279, 437–38, 524, 544, 551,
      554
Luzinski, Greg, 269, 272
Lyle, Sparky, 135
Lyons, Barry, 451

McAdoo, Bob, 126
McCarver, Tim, 16, 27, 29, 33, 85,
      116, 121, 124, 185, 269
McDonald, David J., 18–20
McElwaine, Guy, 424–25
McEnaney, Will, 216–17

McGee, Willie, 486

McGraw, Tug, 192, 326

McGriff, Fred, 572–73, 576

McGuire, Ben, 72

McGuire, Skip, 345

McHale, John, 98, 109, 161, 168–70, 180, 201, 297, 367, 368, 401

McIlvaine, Joe, 489, 565, 573–75

Mack, Connie, 4, 8, 12, 200

Mack, Connie (grandson), 583

McKay, Jim, 570

McKenna, Andy, 257

Mackey, John, 310, 312

McLane, Drayton, 558, 541, 593–94, 597, 599

McLaughlin, George V., 40–44, 49, 57

McMorris, Jerry, 598, 600, 601, 602

McMullen, John J., 241, 322, 348–49, 362, 403, 451, 452, 593

and salaries, 260–63, 382, 524

and Vincent, 501, 514, 517, 546, 550

McNally, Dave, 167–69

McNamara, John, 150, 152

McNiff, Phil, 460

MacPhail, Andy, 315, 326, 351, 372, 499–501, 554

MacPhail, Lee, 22, 80, 94, 95, 98, 130, 155, 186, 207, 228, 504

as American League president, 146, 148, 158, 199, 205, 306, 399–400, 415

as negotiator, 346, 349, 350–53, 354

and strike of 1981, 280–81, 298, 299–300, 302–6

MacPhail, Leland Stanford "Larry," 7, 11, 41–44, 58, 299, 351, 389

Madden, Bill, 251

Maddox, Garry, 269

Maddux, Mike, 574, 596

Madison Square Garden Network, 406–7

Magowan, Peter, 554, 591, 593

Maisel, Bob, 126

Major League Agreement:

and commissioner, 112, 435, 510–13, 518–19, 540

drafting of, 541–43

revisions of, 510–21

Rule 3C (suiting up), 130

Rule 3G (antitampering), 171

Rule 4A (reserve list), 171

Rule 5 (draft), 95

and Rules of Procedure, 465

Major League Baseball Players Association, see Players Association

Major League Properties (formerly Major League Promotions Corporation), 336, 379, 471, 588–89

Major League Scouting Bureau, 137, 260

Malloy, Joe, 535, 536

Mann, Steve, 269, 322

Mantle, Mickey, 74, 82, 86, 93, 379

Mara, Wellington, 68

Maris, Roger, 77, 104, 428, 596

marketing:

of baseball, 69, 70, 138, 336–37, 401–2, 476

of basketball, 567

of football, 67–68, 336

Marquard, Rube, 4

Marshall, Mike, 25, 84, 85, 181–82, 267

Martin, Billy, 206, 279, 386

Martin, Herschel, 417

Martin, Jerry, 364

Martin, Ned, 391

Martinez, Dennis, 385, 486

Martinez, Tino, 476

Martzke, Rudy, 409

Mason, Jim, 264–65

Mathewson, Christy, 59, 589

Matthews, Eddie, 24–25

Matthews, Gary, 210–11, 213, 225–26

Mattingly, Don, 488, 491

Mawkler, Coleman, 335

Maxvill, Dal, 246

May, Rudy, 239

Mays, Willie, 59, 69, 107, 117, 125, 473

MC Hammer, 246

meal money, 27, 38, 83, 102, 138, 208

media:
    as anti-union, 96–97
    and earthquake, 437, 439
    and football, 67–68
    and free agents, 199, 211–13, 243–44, 381–82, 565
    and holdouts, 9, 163
    leaks to, 185, 277, 347, 377
    and lockout of 1976, 184
    and lockout of 1990, 447, 448, 451, 452–53
    and money, 4, 102, 565
    and public suspicion, 173
    and revenue sharing, 579–80, 581
    and Rose, 430, 432
    and strike of 1972, 119, 120, 121, 123, 125–26
    and strike of 1981, 275, 285–86, 294, 295, 297, 301–2, 304–5
    and strike of 1985, 351, 446
    and Vincent, 469–70, 501, 509, 513, 514, 520–21, 539–40
    see also radio broadcasts; sponsors; television

Medich, Doc, 263–64, 296

merchandising, 16, 68, 363, 427, 432

Merritt, Jim, 122

Messersmith, John Alexander "Andy," 162–64, 167–80, 183, 191–92, 247

Messersmith v. Dodgers, 170–80, 182, 183, 187, 207, 269, 284, 310

Metzenbaum, Howard, 583, 603, 604

Meyer, Dick, 99–100, 118, 161, 165, 234

Meyer, Stewart, 591

Miami Miracle, 585

Michael, Gene, 532–34, 535–40

Miller, Bob, 496

Miller, Keith, 451

Miller, Marvin Julian:
    aging of, 276, 583–85
    and arbitration, 36–39, 109, 113–14, 148–49, 166, 599
    background of, 17–22
    building-block approach of, 29, 36, 83
    and collusion, 359
    data disseminated by, 29, 92, 326
    and free agency, 145, 148–49, 181–85, 207–9, 212, 236–37, 308
    and Gaherin, 31, 35–36
    and givebacks, 349, 443
    and Grebey, 243–44, 274, 276, 282
    and grievances, 114–16, 136, 138
    and lockout of 1976, 183–86
    and lockout of 1990, 441, 448–51
    and media, 91, 285–86, 295
    owners' hatred for, 34, 118, 233
    owners' tactics against, 21–23, 26–27, 30, 33, 86, 95
    and player agents, 311, 313
    and player meetings, 23–26, 117, 125, 299, 301
    and players as oppressed workers, 137
    players' confidence in, 91, 101
    players educated by, 28–29, 83–85, 181–82, 236, 301, 344
    and reserve clause, 130–37, 158, 164, 241
    and retirement, 343
    shaky status of, 27, 34
    and strike of 1972, 117–28, 184
    and strike of 1980, 237–44
    and strike of 1981, 274–82, 285–86, 290–91, 295–306, 417
    and test case, 162–68; see also Messersmith v. Dodgers

and Ueberroth, 343–45, 348
"union" defined by, 27
Miller, Terry, 121, 122
Miller Brewing Company, 392–93
Milwaukee Braves, 52, 54–55, 66,
    98–99, 165, 389, 417,
    505
Milwaukee Brewers, 165, 194, 325,
    326, 385, 494, 506–7, 528,
    579
Mincher, Don, 123
Minnesota Twins, 70, 153, 161,
    174–76, 196, 213, 320, 328,
    336–37, 350, 372, 385, 387,
    389, 490, 500, 528, 565,
    579, 587, 592
Minnesota Vikings, 454
minority hiring, 364
minor leagues, 8, 25, 95, 286, 588
Minoso, Minnie, 255, 549–50
Mitchell, Kevin, 480, 486
Mitchell, Paul, 194
Mize, Johnny, 305
Moffett, Ken, 32, 237–38, 241–42,
    244, 277, 288–89, 294, 297,
    343–44
Molitor, Paul, 385, 441, 448–51
Molson Brewing Company,
    400–401
Monaghan, Tom, 328
Monbouquette, Bill, 94
Monday, Rick, 64, 245
money:
    Americans' fascination with, 235
    "bucks issues" of contract, 38
    and expansion, 493, 495–99
    headlines dominated by, 4, 102,
        565
    as immoral, 126, 137
    old vs. new, 201
    and rich vs. poor clubs, 205–06,
        234, 328, 389, 397–98, 401,
        403–4, 479, 492, 530, 545,
        552–80
    and sickness, 351
    and status, 90, 326
    vs. principle, 449

and winning, 205, 223, 225, 228,
    234, 270, 359, 487
Monk, Michael, 573
Montreal Canadiens, 400
Montreal Expos, 110, 128, 153,
    167–68, 180, 212, 218, 219,
    224, 259, 366–68, 373,
    380–81, 382, 385, 400–401,
    558–60, 579, 592, 597
Moore, Donnie, 358
Moreno, Omar, 319, 324, 362
Morgan, Joe, 138, 233, 318
Morris, Jack, 317, 369, 371–73,
    377, 380, 385, 565
Moses, Robert, 55, 57
Moss, Richard M. "Dick," 32–33,
    145–46, 164, 344
    as agent, 228, 262, 317–18, 326,
        366–67, 371–73, 380–82,
        456
    and Howe case, 531–32, 535–37
    and Messersmith, 167, 170–74,
        179
    in negotiations, 113–15, 207, 242,
        316, 349, 443
    and strike of 1981, 119–20, 121
Motley, Darryl, 357
Murcer, Bobby, 154
Murphy, Robert, 9
"Murphy money," 9, 38, 83, 446
Murray, Eddie, 346
Murray, Phil, 37
Musial, Stan, 16, 104, 116, 280, 305
Myers, Randy, 574
Myerson, Harvey, 586

Namath, Joe, 69, 126
Nash, Walter, 63
National Association of Professional
    Baseball Players, 1, 2
National Commission, 3, 6, 541
National Labor Relations Board, 32,
    279, 304, 540
National League, 2, 15, 60, 66, 68,
    97–98, 111, 162, 163, 191,
    201, 202, 203, 263, 269,
    272, 291–92, 305, 314, 321,

National League, *(cont.)*
    332, 338, 339, 368, 373,
    375, 382, 387, 388, 389,
    398, 402, 418, 420, 422–23,
    488, 492–93, 495–501,
    521–22, 524, 542, 544, 556,
    557–58, 565, 572, 577, 592,
    597
  *see also specific teams and own-
    ers*
National League Broadcast Agree-
    ment, 557–58, 577
NBA, *see* basketball
NBC, 67, 69, 81, 390, 393–97,
    407–13
negotiation:
  and salary arbitration, 314–15,
    319, 444–52
  vs. arbitration, 164, 165–67,
    172–74, 177–79
  vs. meetings, 238
negotiators:
  owners' need for, 31
  players as, 86–87, 281–82
  players' need for, 16–17, 21
Nelson, Isiah, 437
Newcombe, Don, 50
New England Patriots, 214
New England Sports Network, 397
Newsom, Bobo, 43
New York Giants, 4, 12, 42, 49, 54,
    59, 60, 66, 389, 495, 583
New York Islanders, 405
New York Knicks, 406
New York Mets, 64, 70, 153, 154,
    239, 323, 327, 382, 389,
    398–99, 402, 404, 405–6,
    416, 418, 456, 473, 489,
    496–97, 516, 521, 524, 530,
    547, 553, 558, 574, 589
New York Rangers, 406
New York Yankees, 7, 10–11, 12,
    16, 24, 42, 50, 54, 55, 57,
    66, 69, 77, 98, 135, 154–57,
    158, 194, 196–98, 203, 204,
    205–6, 212, 219, 220,
    221–22, 223, 227, 234, 249,

    252, 261, 270, 323–24, 328,
    336, 347, 350, 358, 362,
    371–72, 384, 386–87,
    389–90, 402–7, 417, 420,
    421, 424, 426, 440, 456–63,
    465, 468–70, 471, 479, 495,
    500, 503, 527–28, 531–40,
    556, 559, 587, 596
NFL, *see* football
Nicolau, George, 384, 387, 540, 584
Niekro, Phil, 320
night games, 7, 41, 58
  World Series, 79, 390, 567
Nintendo, 508–10, 512, 551
Nolan, Gary, 126
Noll, Roger, 347, 600
Nordbrook, Tim, 221
Norris, Mike, 322
no-trade clause, 162–64, 167
NW Transport Service, 600

Oakland Athletics, 143, 145–46,
    149, 156, 161, 169,
    194–200, 204, 205, 206,
    212, 215, 220, 224, 245–47,
    322, 347, 373–75, 384, 386,
    387, 436–37, 456, 485, 492,
    494, 592, 596, 597
Oakland Raiders, 247
O'Brien, Dan, 217, 219, 227, 264
O'Brien, Pete, 476, 485
O'Connell, Dick, 31, 35, 94, 147,
    150, 169, 195–98
O'Connor, Chuck, 384, 422,
    439–42, 443–48, 452, 502,
    510, 532, 598, 601
Odom, Johnny Lee "Blue Moon,"
    142–43
O'Donoghue, John, 92
O'Doul, Lefty, 160
Oester, Ron, 496
Ojeda, Bob, 451
Oklahoma City 89ers, 571
Oliva, Tony, 174–76
Oliver, Al, 318
Olympics, 330–43, 408–10
O'Malley, Peter, 52, 110–11, 306,

O'Malley, Peter, *(cont.)*
　　347–48, 392–93, 418, 444,
　　471
　and Messersmith, 162–64
　and Ueberroth, 333, 342, 366
　and Vincent, 436, 438–39, 501,
　　529, 548
O'Malley, Walter, 22, 23–24, 119,
　　127, 161, 318, 389, 397,
　　556–57
　and Dodger move, 55–62
　and Dodger Stadium, 62–64, 222
　as hard-hearted businessman, 51,
　　186–87
　influence of, 40–65, 82, 98,
　　110–12, 168, 186–87, 201–3,
　　205–7, 212, 232
　and Rickey, 44–45, 48–50, 65,
　　494
180 Minutes, 403
O'Neill, Tip, 598
Orosco, Jesse, 326
Orza, Gene, 321, 441, 442, 447,
　　452, 561, 599
Ostertag, Tom, 411, 535, 537
Owen, Mickey, 44
Owens, Paul, 269
owners:
　accounting systems of, 259,
　　347
　and celebrity, 153, 192, 259–62
　and control, 1–14, 30, 80, 92–94,
　　207, 219, 233, 235–37, 240,
　　306
　data withheld by, 32, 279, 347,
　　568
　ego and involvement of, 259, 473
　and executive council, 201, 204,
　　340–41, 420, 471
　franchise moves of, 16, 56–62,
　　66, 77, 98, 165, 417, 494,
　　505–6
　ignorance of, 259–60, 340,
　　345–46
　and lockout of 1976, 183–84
　and lockout of 1990, 422–23,
　　433–34, 441–52

　and meetings, 340–41, 354–56,
　　384, 420
　Miller hated by, 34, 118, 126
　as multiemployer bargaining unit,
　　38
　and profits, 11, 53, 194, 235, 440
　refusal to negotiate, 26, 30
　revenue sharing by, *see* revenue
　　sharing
　sponsorships resisted by, 45, 336
　and strike of 1972, 119–29, 165
　and strike of 1981, 277–78,
　　288–93, 300, 303
　and strike of 1985, 348–53
　and strike threat of 1980, 237–44
　syndicates of, 248–49, 250, 258,
　　265, 570, 573
　tactics against Miller, 22–23,
　　26–27, 30, 32, 86–87, 95
　as throwback capitalists, 33, 70
　tight fraternity of, 94–95, 191–92,
　　248, 257, 306
　and tradition, 30, 171, 176, 194,
　　270, 328
　see also PRC (player relations
　　committee); *specific owners*

Palmer, Jim, 97, 99, 167, 199
Pappas, Milt, 28
Parker, Dave, 262, 318, 364
Parker, Wes, 122
Parrish, Lance, 356, 369, 377–79
Pasqua, Dan, 358
paternalism, 11–12, 16, 34, 93, 102,
　　104, 124, 129, 143, 167
Paul, Gabe, 155, 156, 158–59, 196,
　　197–98, 219–21, 269, 270,
　　303, 322
Payson, Joan Whitney, 22
Pena, Tony, 373, 470
Pendleton, Terry, 326, 486
Penner, Jerry, 541–43
pension:
　and expansion, 88, 92
　funding for, 12–13, 15–16, 26,
　　88, 91–92, 101, 116, 128,
　　348

and holdouts, 89, 91–93, 184
    as players' money, 28–29
    as strike issue, 118–19, 120
    surplus funds in, 116, 119,
        127–28
Perez, Pascual, 440, 470
Perez, Tony, 138, 216–17
Perini, Lou, 52
Perry, Gaylord, 153
Perry, Jim, 125
Peters, Gary, 96
Peters, Hank, 225
Peters, Ron, 429–30
Peterson, Fritz, 310
Peterson, Pete, 287
Petrocelli, Rico, 206
Pezzolo, Francesco Stephano, 4
Philadelphia Athletics, 4, 8, 12, 66,
        77–80, 200
Philadelphia Phillies, 47, 109, 117,
        154, 184, 269, 272–73, 280,
        323, 325, 371–72, 376–79,
        380, 384, 386, 390, 475,
        486, 527, 583
Phillips, Richie, 289, 332
Pickett, John, 405
Pilson, Neal, 396, 407–14, 529
Pinson, Vada, 125
Pitcairn, Robert, Jr., 429
Pittsburgh Pirates, 9, 50, 86, 137,
        153, 154, 241, 252, 261,
        271, 318, 488–89, 492, 528,
        544, 552, 565, 574, 576,
        579, 592
player agents, see agents, player
player-management relationships, in
        age of innocence, 10–12
player reps:
    hand-picked by owners, 13–14
    owners' revenge against, 86,
        101–2, 125
    and phone-a-thons, 91, 295–96
    and union formation, 12–13,
        15–16
players:
    as activists, 15, 84–85, 96
    agents resisted by, 215–16

    black and Latino, 318–19
    comparison of, 488–89
    competitiveness of, 10, 123–24
    leverage of, 4, 24, 28, 86
    migratory, 565
    Miller's education of, 28–29, 83,
        181, 236, 301, 344
    million-dollar, 228, 239, 262, 382
    as negotiators, 86–87, 281–88
    as property, 3, 4, 8, 32, 34, 137,
        235, 274
    of "special achievement," 489
    stratification of, 239, 349, 444,
        560
    unfair treatment of, 86, 89, 92–95
    union resisted by, 9–10, 22–24
    see also Players Association; spe-
        cific players
Players Association, 13, 14, 83–106,
        585
    development of, 15–39
    grievances filed by, 114–17, 169,
        359
    and lockout of 1976, 183–87
    and lockout of 1990, 443–51
    reserve fund of, 446
    and strike of 1972, 116–29
    and strike of 1981, 275–307
    and strike of 1985, 348–50
    and strike threat of 1980,
        237–39
    see also unions
Players Fraternity, 4, 6
Players National League, 3
Podesta, Joe, 334
Pohlad, Carl, 328, 372, 499, 514,
        529, 530, 548
Polner, Murray, 49
Pope, Edwin, 126
Port, Mike, 371–73, 373
Porter, Paul, 306
Posedel, Bill, 150–52
Poulson, Norris, 61
PRC (player relations committee):
    and grievances, 115
    and Information Bank, 384–87
    and player-negotiators, 86–87

and restructuring, 551, 561, 582–83
see also owners
press, see media
Price, Frank, 425
Prime Sports Network, 475
promotions, 63, 78–79, 192, 248, 254–56, 338, 378, 476, 586
Providence Steamrollers, 214
Puckett, Kirby, 440, 490
Purdy, Mark, 239

Quinn, Bob, 386, 459–60
Quinn, John, 124
Quirk, Jamie, 239
Quisenberry, Dan, 339, 355

radio broadcasts:
and attendance, 42, 389
revenues from, 7, 12, 15, 53
sponsors of, 7, 104, 389, 391
Raines, Tim, 320, 368, 373–74, 382
Randolph, Willie, 369, 372
Ravitch, Richard, 502–6, 526, 552–55, 591–92, 594–95, 597–99, 604
and Fehr, 560–64, 577, 581
and Major League Agreement, 510–12, 516–17, 519
and revenue sharing, 568–69, 577–79, 581–82
Rawlings, 338, 589
realignment, 521–25, 582–83
Reese, Pee Wee, 50
Regan, Phil, 32, 420
Reich, Sam, 319, 320, 361, 378
Reich, Tom, 261–62, 318–19, 324, 356, 360–61, 377–78, 382, 386, 600
Reichardt, Rick, 64, 135
Reichler, Joe, 24
Reinsdorf, Jerry, 258, 302, 306, 325, 362, 377, 471, 541, 543, 579, 593, 599
and Comiskey Park, 481–82, 484
and lockouts, 421, 433
and Nintendo, 509–10

and Smulyan, 433, 484, 492
and Vincent, 433–35, 445, 470, 501, 508, 513–16, 521, 544–51
Reiser, Pete, 42–43
"rent-a-player," 252–53
reserve clause:
and Basic Agreement of 1968, 38
challenges to, 108–9
defenders of, 16
and free agency, 131, 135, 136–37, 139, 145–49, 170–71, 176
and holdouts, 130–36
and Landis, 7–8
and Miller, 158, 169, 241
origin of, 2, 171
and player agents, 215
post-Messersmith, 184–85
relaxation of, 167, 178
and Rule 4A, 171
and salary arbitration, 133, 169
as Section 10A, 35–36
and Supreme Court, 8, 12, 109, 133–34
and test case, 133, 135, 145–49, 162, 169–80, 209
wording of, 36, 171
Reuschel, Rick, 313
Reuss, Jerry, 116, 182, 296, 301
revenue sharing:
among clubs, 556–60, 568–69, 576–80, 581–82, 591, 592, 594, 598, 600, 601, 602
with players, 13, 441, 444, 445, 488, 591
Revering, Dave, 246
Reynolds, Allie, 12, 27
Rice, Grantland, 222–23
Rich, Lauren, 603
Richard, J. R., 261–62
Richards, Paul, 66, 95–96, 101–2, 118, 251, 254, 496
Richert, Pete, 97
Richman, Arthur, 434
Richman, Milton, 205

Rickey, Branch, 8, 11, 44–45, 94, 155
  and farm system, 7–8, 42–43, 45, 47–48, 65
  as "Mahatma," 46, 137
  and O'Malley, 44–45, 48–50, 52, 65, 494
Rickey, Branch, Jr., "Twig," 47, 137
Righetti, Dave, 323, 384–85
Rijo, Jose, 486
Rizzuto, Phil, 10, 588
Roberts, Robin, 10, 15–16, 21–23, 24–25, 86, 92, 126–27, 588
Roberts, Tom, 365, 384, 387, 584
Robinson, Brooks, 11, 85, 86, 94, 122, 125, 282, 284
Robinson, Eddie, 193, 264
Robinson, Frank, 117
Robinson, Jackie, 10, 46, 48, 50, 53, 65, 109, 503
Rodgers, Buck, 23
Roenicke, Gary, 358
Rogers, Roy, 77
Rogers, Steve, 282, 284, 288, 367
Rona, Barry, 170, 179, 243–44, 349, 355, 421, 431, 439, 584
  and lockouts, 185, 187, 422
  and player deals, 146, 147, 374, 377, 382
  and strikes, 277–78, 292, 303, 304, 350–51
Roosevelt, Teddy, 5
Rose, Pete, 138, 233, 262, 270–73, 280, 305, 314, 379, 413, 439
  gambling problem of, 427–32, 587
Rose, Rusty, 473, 474
Rosen, Al, 486–87, 490
Rosenstein, Jay, 410
Roush, Edd, 171
Royko, Mike, 482
Rozelle, Alvin Ray "Pete," 67–69, 80, 236, 310, 392
Rozelle Rule, 236, 310–12
Rozema, Dave, 360
Rubenstein, Joel, 337–38
Rubin, Carl, 430

Rubinstein, Aaron, 467–68
Rudd, Irving, 52, 57
Rudi, Joe, 169, 194–99, 204, 206, 212, 215, 218, 223, 252
Ruppert, Jacob, 9, 542
Russell, John, 377
Ruth, Babe, 7, 81, 364, 452, 590
Ryan, Nolan, 262, 280, 312, 317, 455, 470, 564

Sabol, Steve, 68
Sadecki, Ray, 121
Safeway, 591, 593
Saigh, Fred, 81, 103, 249
St. Louis Browns, 8, 66, 249, 556, 569
St. Louis Cardinals, 7–8, 42, 45, 46, 102, 103–10, 128, 131–34, 153, 219, 233, 249, 271, 305, 338, 339–40, 347, 354, 358, 385–86, 389, 440, 521–22, 528, 583
St. Paul Saints, 586
St. Petersburg, 482–83, 492–93, 495, 508, 544, 577
salaries:
  in basketball, 126, 150, 276, 441, 488
  and bonuses, 64, 95, 201, 218
  and disability benefits, 27
  and economics, 487–93
  and fans, 9, 234–35, 379
  in football, 69, 126, 150
  guaranteed, 301, 314, 339
  and incentives, 192, 193, 261, 325, 381
  inflation of, 485–93, 573
  lack of data on, 29, 31–32
  "luxury tax" and, 601, 604
  and media, 4, 102, 565
  in open market, 149–59, 162, 183, 194–99, 206, 213, 219, 227, 236, 253, 308–29, 357, 422
  and packages, 271–72
  paid to released players, 351, 354, 357, 361

and performance, 351, 355,
381–82, 421, 441, 445
and revenue participation (cap),
13, 441, 443, 445, 488
and second jobs, 10
of stars, 4, 235, 236, 316, 317
and statistics, 421, 441, 489
and taxes, 313
salary, average:
in 1913, 4
in 1915, 4
in 1951, 10
in 1967, 29
in 1975, 150
in 1976, 234
in 1977, 227, 252
in 1980, 234
in 1984, 328
in 1985, 349
in 1986, 361, 380
in 1989–92, 485
salary, minimum:
in 1950s, 13
bargaining for, 29, 33, 36, 445
in 1967, 29
in 1968, 38, 83
in 1970, 113
salary, top:
in 1889, 2–3
in 1951, 10
in 1953, 69
in 1971, 116–17, 126
in 1975, 150
in 1980, 262, 263
in 1985, 440
in 1989, 440–41
salary arbitration, 160–62, 182–83,
194, 214–15, 349, 564–65
benchmarks in, 308, 325, 327,
487
and club debts, 328–29, 361
and economics, 488–93
and filing number, 321, 491
and free agents, 308–29, 360–61,
372–73
and negotiation, 315, 319,
444–52

and player agents, 214–15,
309–21, 325–28
post-*Messersmith*, 308–9
and precedent, 323
and reserve clause, 133–34, 169
spreads in, 309, 325, 361, 488
salary caps, 3, 346, 347, 421, 441,
445, 555, 559–60, 594–95,
598, 601, 604
salary cuts:
maximum, 83, 113
self-imposed, 10–11
of star players, 8, 86
Saltwell, E. R. "Salty," 11, 245–46,
389
Sambito, Joe, 312, 315
Sandberg, Ryne, 524
San Diego Padres, 33, 34, 111–12,
114–15, 135–36, 150–54,
156, 157, 163, 173, 217,
218, 223, 224, 253, 305,
338, 382, 421, 454–55, 523,
528, 572–73, 576–77, 579,
592, 596
Sands, Jack, 373, 374–75, 383
San Francisco earthquake, 536–39
San Francisco Giants, 59, 61, 66,
160, 210–11, 325, 384–85,
437–38, 473, 485–87,
521–23, 554, 560, 573, 591,
593, 595, 596
Sanguillen, Manny, 318
Santiago, Benito, 574
Santo, Ron, 97
Sauer, Mark, 552, 565
Schaefer, William Donald, 478
Schaffer, Rudie, 251
Schanzer, Ken, 395–97, 411–12,
567–68, 582
scheduling, as grievance, 28, 31
Schmidt, Mike, 270, 378
Schoendienst, Red, 116
Schott, Marge, 328, 346, 522, 550,
554, 561, 603
Schuerholz, John, 217, 310, 358,
368–69, 370–71, 404
Schultz, Howie "Steeple," 47–48

Schweitzer, Bill, 540–41
scoreboards, 28, 74, 76, 78, 112, 248, 477
Scott, Frank, 16
Scott, George, 184
Scott, Mike, 420
scouting systems, 45, 47, 64, 260, 269, 322
Scully, Vin, 51, 395
Seattle Mariners, 202, 382, 472–78, 480, 484–85, 489, 492, 495, 499, 508–10, 565, 579, 596, 597
Seattle Pilots, 202, 473, 494, 506
Seattle Seahawks, 485
Seattle SuperSonics, 485
Seaver, Tom, 85, 86, 184, 350, 416
Seghi, Phil, 150, 153, 219, 310
Segui, Diego, 78
Seitz, Peter, 148–49, 169–80, 181, 187, 209, 247, 585
Selig, Allan H. "Bud," 286–87, 306, 377, 421, 440–41, 474, 497, 502–8, 579, 597–603
  as acting commissioner, 551, 582
  and Giamatti, 417–18, 419, 433–34
  and Ueberroth, 332, 362
  and Vincent, 435, 444, 447–48, 501, 510–17, 526, 546–47, 550
Sewell, Rip, 9
Shaw, George Bernard, 595
Shea, William A., 494
Sheehan, Shaun, 523
Sheffield, Gary, 572, 575–77
Sheinman, Drew, 337
Sheridan, Pat, 357
Shor, Toots, 240
Shorin, Joel, 90
Short, Bob, 114, 202–3, 263
Short, Ed, 31–32
Showalter, Buck, 532–35, 538–40
Shriver, Pam, 570
Siegle, Tony, 376
Sierra, Ruben, 492
Simm, Phil, 595

Simmons, Ted, 84, 85, 130, 131–33, 182, 275–76, 296, 321, 585
Simon, Roger, 478–79
Sinatra, Frank, 222
Singleton, Ken, 168, 296
Skiatron, 54, 56, 60, 62
SkyDome, 477–78
Slaton, Jim, 507
Slusher, Howard, 25
Smiley, John, 553
Smith, Ballard, 293
Smith, Billy, 212
Smith, Bryn, 475–76, 490
Smith, C. Arnholt, 111
Smith, Claire, 509, 520
Smith, Dave, 261, 385
Smith, John L., 44, 49
Smith, Ozzie, 235, 346, 385
Smith, Randy, 575–76
Smith, R. E. "Bob," 71, 75
Smith, Red, 50, 62
Smith, Reggie, 301
Smith, Talbot M. "Tal," 72, 75, 261–63, 309, 322–23, 325, 560, 575
Smith, Zane, 321
Smulyan, Jeffrey Howard "Jeff," 472–93, 509, 565
Snider, Duke, 50, 53
Soderholm, Eric, 225, 252, 254
Solomon, Peter, 587
Soto, Mario, 302
Spahn, Warren, 117, 470
Spalding, Albert Goodwill, 2–3
Speaker, Tris, 4
Speed, 596
Spenser, Edmund, 415
Spira, Howard, 453, 458–65, 466, 587
Spitz, Larry, 20
sponsors:
  of All-Star balloting, 335
  beer companies, 7, 46, 103–4, 392–93, 400–401, 529
  influence of, 102–3, 390
  owner resistance to, 336

of radio broadcasts, 7, 104, 389, 391
and stadiums, 477–78, 480
and Ueberroth, 331, 334–36, 337–38
sport, vs. business, 7, 12, 22, 23, 38, 61–62, 65, 66, 96, 336, 340–43, 419, 426–27, 554–55, 575
Sporting News, The, 96–97, 260
SportsChannel, 398, 404–6
SportsVision, 258
Springer, Ken, 463
spring training:
    and lockouts, 183–87, 441, 443–44, 560
    Rickey as pioneer in, 45
Stachler, Robert, 430–31
stadiums:
    artificial turf in, 75, 76
    and attendance, 74, 139, 476, 477, 483
    concessions in, 62
    design of, 72–74, 75–76
    and economics, 477–84, 579
    and expansion, 72, 389
    lights in, 7, 41, 42
    livestock in, 78
    and local communities, 4, 105, 477–78
    ownership of, 62
    and sponsors, 477, 480
    see also specific stadiums
Staley, Gerry, 505
Stanley, Fred, 220
Stargell, Willie, 184, 236
Stark, Abe, 57
stars:
    and attendance, 235, 273, 318
    as jerks, 566
    as mentors, 86
    salaries of, 4, 235, 236, 316, 317
    salary cuts of, 8, 86
    sales of, 200, 204
    and ticket sales, 234, 273
    and unions, 85–86

statistics:
    and arbitrators, 309
    database of, 323
    and free agents, 236, 351–52, 355
    and player agents, 214–15, 319–20, 321
    and salaries, 421, 441, 488–90
    and sickness, 351–52
Staub, Rusty, 110, 288, 294, 304–5
Stearns, Frederick Kimball, 556
Steinbrenner, George, 202, 203, 289, 347, 359, 362, 372, 399, 587
    deals made by, 154, 158–59, 197, 220–22, 223–24, 323–24, 386, 404–7, 456–58
    and haves/have-nots, 266, 557, 578
    as new boy, 154, 232, 260, 270
    and Spira, 453, 459–65
    and strikes, 241, 280, 281, 592, 597, 599
    suspension of, 154–55, 201, 460–70
    and Vincent, 434, 465–71, 533, 535
    and Winfield, 456–61, 465
Steinbrenner, Hank, 468
Stengel, Casey, 446
Stern, David, 276–77, 567
Stewart, Dave, 296
Stillwell, Kurt, 573
Stone, Steve, 225, 252, 296, 313
Stoneham, Horace, 59–60, 94, 98, 149, 166
Stoneham family, 12, 59
Stoneman, Bill, 327, 368
Strawberry, Darryl, 64, 323, 485
strike insurance, 277, 287, 295, 300, 306
strikes:
    in 1972, 116–29, 160, 165, 184
    in 1980, averted, 237–44, 450
    in 1981, 274–307, 343–44, 359, 416
    in 1985, 348–53, 446, 450
    in 1994, 591–604
    of umpires, 332

Sullivan, Brendan, 545
Sullivan, Haywood, 150, 233, 359, 362, 383, 544, 549, 557
Sullivan, Marc, 383
Summers, Champ, 296
Suncoast Dome, 482–83, 492–93
Sundberg, Jim, 264
Supreme Court, U.S., and reserve system, 8, 12, 109, 133–34
Susman, Lou, 212, 219, 229, 233–34, 289, 305, 339, 386, 392, 441
Sussman, David, 533, 536, 538
Sutcliffe, Rick, 340, 355
Sutter, Bruce, 313–17, 338–40, 355, 362, 488
Sutton, Don, 263, 338
Swanson, Dennis, 397, 407, 412
Swift, Bill, 480
Swindell, Greg, 491, 593
Symington, Stuart, 494
Synar, Mike, 604

Tagliabue, Paul, 529
Tanner, Chuck, 198–99, 206
Taylor, George, 20–21
Taylor, Reese, 62
Tebbetts, Birdie, 23
television, 388–414
  and Braves, 402, 578
  cable, 190, 191, 194, 394, 397–98, 402–7, 411, 475, 522–23, 529, 557–58
  and compulsory license, 522–23
  "free," 54, 63, 405, 475
  owners' resistance to, 54, 69
  pay, 54, 56, 62, 63, 258, 389, 397, 405, 557–58
  and player image, 265
  programming for, 188–91, 193, 259, 265–66, 411, 485, 522
  sports inventory for, 529
  super-stations, 265–68, 347, 375, 402–4, 522–24, 558–59
  and Turner, 188–91, 193, 259, 375, 402, 403, 404, 407, 501, 522–23, 578
television broadcasts:
  and attendance, 68–69, 388–89, 391
  and commercials, 42
  first, 42, 48
  football, 67–68
  income from, see television revenues
  pooling, 54
  rights, 49, 67, 80–81, 256, 347, 389–90, 394, 402–5, 527, 558
  technical improvements in, 393–94, 567
  of World Series, 69, 390, 396, 408
television revenues, 15, 54, 59, 69, 263, 372–73, 354, 355, 363, 440, 567
  of football, 67, 80
  and haves vs. have-nots, 557–60, 592
  and national advertising, 266, 391–92
  negotiations for, 344, 388–414
  and pension fund, 12, 15–16, 27, 88–89, 92
  and ratings, 522
  sharing of, 556–60
  see also sponsors
Tenace, Gene, 218, 227
Terrell, Walt, 440
Terry, Ralph, 77
Teufel, Tim, 451
Texas Rangers, 199, 202–3, 218–19, 253, 162–65, 361, 402, 403, 421, 473–74, 484–85, 500, 531, 579
Thau, Roland, 461–65, 471
Thigpen, Bobby, 482
Thomas, Frank, 596
Thompson, David, 273
Thompson, Fresco, 35, 65
Thompson, Jason, 327
Thompson, Jim, 481–83
Thompson, Robby, 486
Thomson, Bobby, 49

Thorpe, Jim, 67

Throneberry, Marvelous Marv, 496

Tiant, Luis, 35, 170

tickets:
  and attendance, 63, 234
  and income, 53, 263, 476, 558
  season, 63, 138, 256, 273, 576, 603

Tinker, Grant, 393

"Tinker to Evers to Chance," 134

Tisch, Laurence, 407–10, 413–14

Tolan, Bobby, 135–36, 138, 163

Toolson, George, 12, 109

Toomey, Jim, 108

Topping, Dan, 77, 81, 249

Topps Company, 89–91, 379

Toronto Blue Jays, 264, 386, 399–401, 477–78, 495, 528, 530, 565, 575

Torre, Joe, 85, 86, 88, 96, 125, 129, 132, 284, 585

Torrez, Mike, 168, 194

Tracewski, Dick, 34

Trammell, Alan, 320

travel accommodations, 28, 83, 102, 114, 138

Tribune Company, 259, 402, 403, 501, 521–24, 526–27, 587, 598

Tripartite Agreement (1883), 2, 171

Turner, Robert Edward, II "Ed," 188–89

Turner, Robert Edward, III "Ted," 187–94, 362, 544, 551
  and America's Cup, 189, 225–26
  and Braves, 189–93, 375–76, 578
  and player deals, 210–11, 213, 260, 265–68, 271, 338–40
  and TV, see television

Tyler, Harold, 467–69, 532, 535, 538

Ueberroth, Ginnie, 332

Ueberroth, Peter Victor, 307, 329, 330–53, 418, 428, 466, 495, 586, 598

  and collusion, 353, 354–69, 375–76, 379, 380, 387
  as commissioner, 332–53, 419, 421, 422, 439, 442, 459, 511
  and Olympics, 330–43
  and owner meetings, 340–42, 362–63
  and "stupidity," 342–43, 345–46, 354
  and TV, 388, 403, 407–14

Ughetta, Henry, 49

umpires, contracts of, 513

umpire strike, 332

Uniform Players Contract:
  Section 7A, 145–46
  Section 10A of, see reserve clause

Union Oil, 62

unions:
  defined by Miller, 27
  democracy in, 26, 450–51
  end of, 6
  formation of, 3, 4, 9, 13
  goals of, 24, 449–50
  owners' opposition to, 9, 13, 22, 105, 137, 593
  owners' revenge against, 86, 101, 194
  players' resistance to, 9–10, 22
  and stars, 85–86
  turnover in, 349
  and unity, 84–85, 89, 96, 184, 301, 349, 446, 448–51
  see also Players Association

Upshaw, Gene, 595

Uribe, Jose, 486

USA Today, 336

Usery, W. J. Bill, Jr., 604

Valenzuela, Fernando, 279, 317–18, 371–72

Veeck, Bill, 10, 46, 47, 202, 247–60, 328, 556
  aging of, 256–58
  and promotions, 247–56, 337, 569
  and reserve clause, 8–9, 109, 247–48, 250

Veeck, Bill, Sr., 248
Veeck, Mary Frances, 248, 251
Veeck, Mike, 251, 255, 258, 480, 585–86
Veeck as in Wreck (Veeck), 250
Versalles, Zoilo, 34–35
Villante, Tom, 49, 54, 256, 391, 398–99, 403, 405, 568
Vincent, Francis T., Jr. "Fay," 423–29, 431–35, 502, 586–87, 597, 598
  as commissioner, 436–53, 500–501, 503–5, 508–21
  and expansion, 497–501
  and media, 469–70, 501, 509, 513, 514, 520–21, 539–40
  ouster of, 508, 514, 526–51
  and Steinbrenner, 434, 465–71, 533, 535, 587
Vincent, Francis T., Sr., 423
Vincent, Valerie, 436
Viola, Frank, 440, 486
Volcker, Paul, 530

Waddell, Rube, 134
Wade, Ed, 323, 327
Wagner, Dick, 63, 137, 138, 202, 216, 266, 271, 316, 379, 427, 431
Wagner, Honus, 4, 590
Wagner, Robert, 56
Waitkus, Eddie, 11
Walker, Jerry, 370
Wal-Mart, 591, 593, 600
Walsh, Dick, 163
Waner, Lloyd, 320
Ward, Gary, 361
Ward, John Montgomery, 1
Washington, Claudell, 268, 273
Washington Bullets, 214
Washington Redskins, 240
Washington Senators, 12, 70, 77, 174, 286, 389
Waste Management, Inc., 593
Watson, Arthur, 394–97, 409, 410, 413
Watson, Bob, 319

Weaver, Earl, 234
Webb, Bill, 540
Webb, Del, 13, 81, 249
Weinglass, "Boogie," 570
Weiss, George, 70–71, 86, 92–93, 95, 249
Welch, Bob, 589
Wells, John Calhoun, 599, 600
Werker, Judge, 279
Werner, Roger, 427
Werner, Tom, 497, 547, 558, 573–75
West, Joe, 498, 513
Western League, 3
Westhoff, John, 386
Whitaker, Lou, 320, 603
White, Bill, 420–21, 433, 497, 498, 513–16, 522, 524–25, 546, 550, 558
White, Byron R. "Whizzer," 98
White, Jeff, 530, 562
Whitehurst, Wally, 574
White Rat (Herzog), 326
Whitson, Ed, 324, 404
Widdrington, Peter, 517, 530, 547
Wilhelm, Hoyt, 95
Will, George, 445
Williams, Edward Bennett "Ed," 244, 337, 366, 478
  financial concerns of, 239–40, 277–78, 289
  and Grebey, 240–41, 278, 281, 287, 291
  and strikes, 240–41, 277–78, 280, 281, 289–94, 300, 302, 305
Williams, Matt, 486–87, 596
Williams, Ted, 321, 470, 589, 596
Wills, Bump, 218
Wills, Maury, 29, 63
Wilpon, Fred, 291, 444, 514, 517, 530, 544, 549, 551, 553, 561, 597
Wilson, Earl, 94
Wilson, Hack, 364
Wilson, Willie, 355, 364
Wilson Company, 338
Winfield, Dave, 86, 257, 338, 404,

Winfield, Dave, (cont.)
451, 454–61, 465–66, 565,
587
Wirtz, Bill, 546
Witt, Mike, 372, 384, 385, 387
Woods, Jim, 391
Woodson, Dick, 175
Woolf, Bob, 94, 321
working conditions, 28, 29, 36
World Series:
and "Black Sox" scandal, 6
broadcasts of, 69, 390, 396, 408
and earthquake, 436–39
and FunFest, 589
at night, 79, 390, 567
and 1994 strike, 595–96, 603
and pension fund, 12, 15, 27
sponsorships of, 7
Woy, Bucky, 267
Wright, Elmo, 310

Wrigley, Bill, 259, 314–15
Wrigley, Phil, 11, 12, 52, 57–59, 97,
202, 521
Wrigley, William, Jr., 58
Wrigley Field, 6, 58, 61, 259
Wynegar, Butch, 336–37

Yakult Swallows, 382
Yardley, Jonathan, 480
Yastrzemski, Carl, 82, 97, 117, 491,
596
Yawkey, Jean, 383
Yawkey, Tom, 97, 117, 169, 196
Young, Cy, 3, 171, 590
Young, Matt, 490
Yount, Robin, 441

Zeckendorf, William, 50
Ziegler, John, 546
Zisk, Richie, 252, 260, 263